KṚṢṆA

The Supreme Personality of Godhead

BOOKS BY HIS DIVINE GRACE A. C. BHAKTIVEDANTA SWAMI PRABHUPĀDA

Bhagavad-gītā As It Is
Śrīmad-Bhāgavatam (multiple volumes; with disciples)
Śrī Caitanya-caritāmṛta
Kṛṣṇa, the Supreme Personality of Godhead
Teachings of Lord Caitanya
The Nectar of Devotion
The Nectar of Instruction
Śrī Īśopaniṣad
The Light of the Bhāgavata
Easy Journey to Other Planets
Teachings of Lord Kapila, the Son of Devahūti
Teachings of Queen Kuntī
Message of Godhead
The Science of Self-Realization
The Perfection of Yoga
Beyond Birth and Death
On the Way to Kṛṣṇa
Rāja-vidyā: The King of Knowledge
Elevation to Kṛṣṇa Consciousness
Kṛṣṇa Consciousness: The Matchless Gift
Kṛṣṇa Consciousness: The Topmost Yoga System
Perfect Questions, Perfect Answers
Life Comes from Life
Geetār-gan (Bengali)
Buddhi-yoga (Bengali)
Bhakti-ratna-boli (Bengali)
Back to Godhead magazine (founder)

BOOKS COMPILED AND EDITED AFTER ŚRĪLA PRABHUPĀDA'S LIFETIME

The Journey of Self-Discovery
Civilization and Transcendence
The Laws of Nature
Renunciation Through Wisdom
Beyond Illusion and Doubt
Dharma, The Way of Transcendence
The Quest for Enlightenment

AVAILABLE FROM:

ISKCON Reader Services, P. O. Box 730, Watford, WD25 8ZE, UK; www.iskcon.org.uk
The Bhaktivedanta Book Trust, P. O. Box 262, Botany, N.S.W. 1455, Australia; www.krishna.com
The Bhaktivedanta Book Trust, 3764 Watseka Ave., Los Angeles, CA 90034, USA; www.krishna.com
Karuna Bhavan, Bankhouse Rd, Lesmahagow, Lanarkshire, ML11 0ES, Scotland

KṚṢṆA

The Supreme Personality of Godhead

PART ONE

A SUMMARY STUDY OF ŚRĪLA VYĀSADEVA'S
ŚRĪMAD-BHĀGAVATAM, TENTH CANTO

BY

HIS DIVINE GRACE
A.C. BHAKTIVEDANTA SWAMI
PRABHUPĀDA

FOUNDER-ĀCĀRYA OF THE INTERNATIONAL
SOCIETY FOR KRISHNA CONSCIOUSNESS

THE BHAKTIVEDANTA BOOK TRUST

Readers interested in the subject matter of this book are invited by the International Society for Krishna Consciousness to visit an ISKCON center (see address list in the back of the book) or to correspond with the secretary.

ISKCON Reader Services
P. O. Box 730
Watford, WD25 8ZE, United Kingdom
Website: www.iskcon.org.uk

International Society for Krishna Consciousness
3764 Watseka Avenue
Los Angeles, California 90034, USA
Website: www.harekrishna.com

International Society for Krishna Consciousness
P. O. Box 459, Cammeray
NSW 2062, Australia

International Society for Krishna Consciousness
Karuna Bhavan, Bankhouse Rd, Lesmahagow,
Lanarkshire, ML11 0ES, Scotland

Websites:
www.krishna.com
www.iskcon.com
www.iskcon.org

Set in Minion

ISBN 0-89213-354-6

Printed in Germany

To My Father, Gour Mohan De (1849-1930),
a pure devotee of Kṛṣṇa, who raised me as a
Kṛṣṇa conscious child from the beginning
of my life. In my boyhood ages he instructed
me how to play the *mṛdaṅga*. He gave me
Rādhā-Kṛṣṇa *vigraha* to worship, and he gave
me Jagannātha-ratha to duly observe the
festival as my childhood play. He was kind to
me, and I imbibed from him the ideas later
on solidified by my spiritual master,
the eternal father.

FROM APPLE

Everybody is looking for KṚṢṆA.

Some don't realize that they are, but they are.

KṚṢṆA is GOD, the Source of all that exists, the Cause of all that is, was, or ever will be.

As GOD is unlimited, HE has many Names.

Allah-Buddha-Jehovah-Rāma: All are KṚṢṆA, all are ONE.

God is not abstract; He has both the impersonal and the personal aspects to His personality, which is SUPREME, ETERNAL, BLISSFUL, and full of KNOWLEDGE. As a single drop of water has the same qualities as an ocean of water, so has our consciousness the qualities of GOD'S consciousness . . . but through our identification and attachment with material energy (physical body, sense pleasures, material possessions, ego, etc.) our true TRANSCENDENTAL CONSCIOUSNESS has been polluted, and like a dirty mirror it is unable to reflect a pure image.

With many lives our association with the TEMPORARY has grown. This impermanent body, a bag of bones and flesh, is mistaken for our true self, and we have accepted this temporary condition to be final.

Through all ages, great SAINTS have remained as living proof that this nontemporary, permanent state of GOD CONSCIOUSNESS can be revived in all living Souls. Each Soul is potentially divine.

Kṛṣṇa says in *Bhagavad-gītā:* "Steady in the Self, being freed from all material contamination, the yogi achieves the highest perfectional stage of happiness in touch with the Supreme Consciousness." (VI, 28)

YOGA (a scientific method for GOD (SELF) realization) is the process by which we purify our consciousness, stop further pollution, and arrive at the state of Perfection, full KNOWLEDGE, full BLISS.

If there's a God, I want to see Him. It's pointless to believe in something without proof, and Kṛṣṇa Consciousness and meditation are methods where you can actually obtain GOD perception. You can actually see God, and hear Him, play with Him. It might sound crazy, but He is actually there, actually with you.

There are many yogic Paths—Rāja, Jñāna, Haṭha, Kriyā, Karma, Bhakti—which are *all* acclaimed by the MASTERS of each method.

SWAMI BHAKTIVEDANTA is, as his title says, a BHAKTI Yogi following the path of DEVOTION. By serving GOD through each thought, word, and DEED, and by chanting of HIS Holy Names, the devotee quickly develops God-consciousness. By chanting

Hare Kṛṣṇa, Hare Kṛṣṇa
Kṛṣṇa Kṛṣṇa, Hare Hare
Hare Rāma, Hare Rāma
Rāma Rāma, Hare Hare

one inevitably arrives at KṚṢṆA Consciousness. (The proof of the pudding is in the eating!)

I request that you take advantage of this book, *KṚṢṆA,* and enter into its understanding. I also request that you make an appointment to meet your God now, through the self-liberating process of YOGA (UNION) and GIVE PEACE A CHANCE.

ALL YOU NEED IS LOVE (KṚISHṆA) HARI BOL.
George Harrison

TABLE OF CONTENTS

Preface

nivṛtta-tarṣair upagīyamānād
bhavauṣadhāc chrotra-mano-'bhirāmāt
ka uttamaśloka-guṇānuvādāt
pumān virajyeta vinā paśu-ghnāt
(*Śrīmad-Bhāgavatam* 10.1.4)

In the Western countries, when someone sees the cover of a book like *Kṛṣṇa,* he immediately asks, "Who is Kṛṣṇa? Who is the girl with Kṛṣṇa?" etc.

The immediate answer is that Kṛṣṇa is the Supreme Personality of Godhead. How is that? Because He conforms in exact detail to descriptions of the Supreme Being, the Godhead. In other words, Kṛṣṇa is the Godhead because He is all-attractive. Outside the principle of all-attraction, there is no meaning to the word "Godhead." How is it one can be all-attractive? First of all, if one is very wealthy, if he has great riches, he becomes attractive to the people in general. Similarly, if someone is very powerful, he also becomes attractive, and if someone is very famous, he also becomes attractive, and if someone is very beautiful or wise or unattached to all kinds of possessions, he also becomes attractive. So from practical experience we can observe that one is attractive due to (1) wealth, (2) power, (3) fame, (4) beauty, (5) wisdom and (6) renunciation. One who is in possession of all six of these opulences at the same time, who possesses them to an unlimited degree, is understood to be the Supreme Personality of Godhead. These opulences of the Godhead are delineated by Parāśara Muni, a great Vedic authority.

We have seen many rich persons, many powerful persons, many famous persons, many beautiful persons, many learned and scholarly persons, and persons in the renounced order of life unattached to material possessions. But we have never seen any one person who is unlimitedly and simultaneously wealthy, powerful, famous, beautiful, wise and unattached, like Kṛṣṇa, in the history of humanity. Kṛṣṇa, the Supreme Personality of Godhead, is a historical person who appeared on this earth 5,000 years ago. He stayed on this earth for 125 years and played exactly like a human being, but His activities were unparalleled. From the very moment of His appearance to the moment of His disappearance, every one of His activities is unparalleled in the history of the world, and therefore anyone who knows what we mean by Godhead will accept Kṛṣṇa as the Supreme Personality of Godhead. No one is equal to the Godhead, and no one is greater than Him. That is the import of the familiar saying "God is great."

There are various classes of men in the world who speak of God in different ways, but according to the Vedic literatures and according to the great *ācāryas,* the authorized persons versed in the knowledge of God in all ages, like *ācāryas* Śaṅkara, Rāmānuja, Madhva, Viṣṇu Svāmī, Lord Caitanya and all their followers by disciplic succession, all unanimously agree that Kṛṣṇa is the Supreme Personality of Godhead. As far as we, the followers of Vedic civilization, are concerned, we accept the Vedic history of the whole universe, which consists of different planetary systems called Svargaloka, or the higher planetary system, Martyaloka, or the intermediary planetary system, and Pātālaloka, or the lower planetary system. The modern historians of this earth cannot supply historical evidences of events that occurred before 5,000 years ago, and the anthropologists say that 40,000 years ago *Homo sapiens* had not appeared on this planet because evolution had not reached that point. But the Vedic histories, the *Purāṇas* and *Mahābhārata,* relate human histories which extend millions and billions of years into the past.

For example, from these literatures we are given the histories of Kṛṣṇa's appearances and disappearances millions and billions of years ago. In the Fourth Chapter of the *Bhagavad-gītā* Kṛṣṇa tells Arjuna that both He and Arjuna had had many births before and that He (Kṛṣṇa) could remember all of them but Arjuna could not. This illustrates the difference between the knowledge of Kṛṣṇa and that of Arjuna. Arjuna might have been a very great warrior, a well-cultured member of the Kuru dynasty, but after all, he was an ordinary human being, whereas Kṛṣṇa, the Supreme Personality of Godhead, is the possessor of unlimited knowledge. Because He possesses unlimited knowledge, Kṛṣṇa has a memory that is boundless.

The knowledge Kṛṣṇa possesses is so perfect that He remembers all the incidents of His appearances some millions and billions of years in the past, but Arjuna's memory and knowledge are limited by time and space, for he is an ordinary human being. In the Fourth Chapter Kṛṣṇa states that He can remember instructing the lessons of the *Bhagavad-gītā* some millions of years ago to the sun-god, Vivasvān.

Nowadays it is the fashion of the atheistic class of men to try to become God by following some mystic process. Generally the atheists claim to be God by dint of their imagination or their meditational prowess. Kṛṣṇa is not that kind of God. He does not become God by manufacturing some mystic process of meditation, nor does He become God by undergoing the severe austerities of the mystic yogic exercises. Properly speaking, He never *becomes* God because He is the Godhead in all circumstances.

Within the prison of His maternal uncle Kaṁsa, where His father and mother were confined, Kṛṣṇa appeared outside His mother's body as the four-handed Viṣṇu-Nārāyaṇa. Then He turned Himself into a baby and told His father to carry Him to the house of Nanda Mahārāja and his wife Yaśodā. When Kṛṣṇa was just a small baby the gigantic demoness Pūtanā attempted to kill Him, but when He sucked her breast He pulled out her life. That is the difference between the real Godhead and a God manufactured in the mystic factory. Kṛṣṇa had no chance to practice the mystic *yoga* process, yet He manifested Himself as the Supreme Personality of Godhead at every step, from infancy to childhood, from childhood to boyhood, and from boyhood to young manhood. In this book, *Kṛṣṇa,* all of His activities as a human being are described. Although Kṛṣṇa plays like a human being, He always maintains His identity as the Supreme Personality of Godhead.

Since Kṛṣṇa is all-attractive, one should know that all his desires should be focused on Kṛṣṇa. In the *Bhagavad-gītā* it is said that the individual person is the proprietor or master of his own body but that Kṛṣṇa, who is the Supersoul present in everyone's heart, is the supreme proprietor and supreme master of each and every individual body. As such, if we concentrate our loving propensities upon Kṛṣṇa only, then immediately universal love, unity and tranquillity will be automatically realized. When one waters the root of a tree, he automatically waters the branches, twigs, leaves and flowers; when one supplies food to the stomach through the mouth, he satisfies all the various parts of the body.

The art of focusing one's attention on the Supreme and giving one's love to Him is called Kṛṣṇa consciousness. We have inaugurated the Kṛṣṇa consciousness movement so that everyone can satisfy his propensity for loving others simply by directing his love toward Kṛṣṇa. The whole world is very eager to satisfy the dormant propensity of love for others, but the various invented methods like socialism, communism, altruism, humanitarianism and nationalism, along with whatever else may be manufactured for the peace and prosperity of the world, are all useless and frustrating because of our gross ignorance of the art of loving Kṛṣṇa. Generally people think that by advancing the cause of moral principles and religious rites they will be happy. Others may think that happiness can be achieved by economic development, and yet others think that simply by sense gratification they will be happy. But the real fact is that people can be happy only by loving Kṛṣṇa.

Kṛṣṇa can perfectly reciprocate one's loving propensities in different relationships called mellows, or *rasas*. Basically there are twelve loving relationships. One can love Kṛṣṇa as the supreme unknown, as the supreme master, the supreme friend, the supreme child, the supreme lover. These are the five basic love *rasas*. One can also love Kṛṣṇa indirectly in seven different relationships, which are apparently different from the five primary relationships. All in all, however, if one simply reposes his dormant loving propensity in Kṛṣṇa, then his life becomes successful. This is not a fiction but is a fact that can be realized by practical application. One can directly perceive the effects that love for Kṛṣṇa has on his life.

In the Ninth Chapter of the *Bhagavad-gītā* this science of Kṛṣṇa consciousness is called the king of all knowledge, the king of all confidential things, and the supreme science of transcendental realization. Yet we can directly experience the results of this science of Kṛṣṇa consciousness because it is very easy to practice and is very pleasurable. Whatever percentage of Kṛṣṇa consciousness we can perform will become an eternal asset to our life, for it is imperishable in all circumstances. It has now been actually proved that today's confused and frustrated younger generation in the Western countries can directly perceive the results of channeling the loving propensity toward Kṛṣṇa alone.

It is said that although one executes severe austerities, penances and sacrifices in his life, if he fails to awaken his dormant love for Kṛṣṇa, then all his penances are to be considered useless. On the other hand, if one has awakened his dormant love for Kṛṣṇa, then what is the use in executing austerities and penances unnecessarily?

The Kṛṣṇa consciousness movement is the unique gift of Lord Caitanya to the fallen souls of this age. It is a very simple method which has actually been carried out during the last four years in the Western countries, and there is no doubt that this movement can satisfy the dormant loving propensities of humanity. This book, *Kṛṣṇa,* is another presentation to help the Kṛṣṇa consciousness movement in the Western world. This transcendental literature is published with profuse illustrations. People love to read various kinds of fiction to spend their time and energy. Now this tendency can be directed to Kṛṣṇa. The result will be the imperishable satisfaction of the soul, both individually and collectively.

It is said in the *Bhagavad-gītā* that even a little effort expended on the path of Kṛṣṇa consciousness can save one from the greatest danger. Hundreds of thousands of examples can be cited of people who have escaped the greatest dangers of life due to a slight advancement in Kṛṣṇa consciousness. We therefore request everyone to take advantage of this great transcendental literature. One will find that by reading one page after another, an immense treasure of knowledge in art, science, literature, philosophy and religion will be revealed, and ultimately, by reading this one book, *Kṛṣṇa*, love of Godhead will fructify.

My grateful acknowledgment is due to Śrīmān George Harrison, now chanting Hare Kṛṣṇa, for his liberal contribution of $19,000 to meet the entire cost of printing this volume. May Kṛṣṇa bestow upon this nice boy further advancement in Kṛṣṇa consciousness.

And at last my ever-willing blessings are bestowed upon Śrīmān Śyāmasundara dāsa Adhikārī, Śrīmān Brahmānanda dāsa Brahmacārī, Śrīmān Hayagrīva dāsa Adhikārī, Śrīmān Satsvarūpa dāsa Adhikārī, Śrīmatī Devahūti-devī dāsī, Śrīmatī Jadurāṇī-devī dāsī, Śrīmān Muralīdhara dāsa Brahmacārī, Śrīmān Bhāradvāja dāsa Adhikārī and Śrīmān Pradyumna dāsa Adhikārī, etc., for their hard labor in different ways to make this publication a great success.

Hare Kṛṣṇa.

A. C. Bhaktivedanta Swami

Advent Day of
Śrīla Bhaktisiddhānta Sarasvatī
February 26th, 1970
ISKCON Headquarters
3764 Watseka Avenue
Los Angeles, California

Introduction

kṛṣṇa! kṛṣṇa! kṛṣṇa! kṛṣṇa! kṛṣṇa! kṛṣṇa! kṛṣṇa! he
kṛṣṇa! kṛṣṇa! kṛṣṇa! kṛṣṇa! kṛṣṇa! kṛṣṇa! kṛṣṇa! he
kṛṣṇa! kṛṣṇa! kṛṣṇa! kṛṣṇa! kṛṣṇa! kṛṣṇa! rakṣa mām
kṛṣṇa! kṛṣṇa! kṛṣṇa! kṛṣṇa! kṛṣṇa! kṛṣṇa! pāhi mām
rāma! rāghava! rāma! rāghava! rāma! rāghava! rakṣa mām
kṛṣṇa! keśava! kṛṣṇa! keśava! kṛṣṇa! keśava! pāhi mām
Caitanya-caritāmṛta (*Madhya* 7.96)

While attempting to write this book, *Kṛṣṇa,* let me first offer my respectful obeisances unto my spiritual master, Oṁ Viṣṇupāda 108 Śrī Śrīmad Bhaktisiddhānta Sarasvatī Gosvāmī Mahārāja Prabhupāda. Then let me offer my respectful obeisances to the ocean of mercy, Lord Śrī Kṛṣṇa Caitanya Mahāprabhu. He is the Supreme Personality of Godhead, Kṛṣṇa Himself, appearing in the role of a devotee just to distribute the highest principles of devotional service. Lord Caitanya began His preaching from the country known as Gauḍadeśa (West Bengal). And as I belong to the Madhva-Gauḍīya-sampradāya, I must therefore offer my respectful obeisances to the disciplic succession of that name. This Madhva-Gauḍīya-sampradāya is also known as the Brahma-sampradāya because the disciplic succession originally began from Brahmā. Brahmā instructed the sage Nārada, Nārada instructed Vyāsadeva, and Vyāsadeva instructed Madhva Muni, or Madhvācārya. Śrī Mādhavendra Purī, the originator of the Madhva-Gauḍīya-sampradāya, was a *sannyāsī* (renunciant) who belonged to the Madhvācārya disciplic succession. He had many renowned disciples, such as Nityānanda Prabhu, Advaita Prabhu and Īśvara Purī. Īśvara Purī happened to be the spiritual master of Lord Caitanya Mahāprabhu. So let us offer our respectful obeisances to Īśvara Purī, Nityānanda Prabhu, Śrī Advaita Ācārya Prabhu, Śrīvāsa Paṇḍita and Śrī Gadādhara Paṇḍita. Next, let us offer our respectful obeisances to Svarūpa Dāmodara, who acted as the private secretary to Lord Caitanya Mahāprabhu; and let us offer our respectful obeisances to Śrī Vāsudeva Datta and the constant attendant of Lord Caitanya, Śrī Govinda, and the constant friend of Lord Caitanya, Mukunda, and also to Murāri Gupta. And let us offer our respectful obeisances to the six Gosvāmīs of Vṛndāvana—Śrī Rūpa Gosvāmī, Śrī Sanātana Gosvāmī, Śrī Raghunātha Bhaṭṭa Gosvāmī, Śrī Gopāla Bhaṭṭa Gosvāmī, Śrī Jīva Gosvāmī and Śrī Raghunātha dāsa Gosvāmī.

Kṛṣṇa Himself has explained in the *Bhagavad-gītā* that He is the Supreme Personality of Godhead and that whenever there are discrepancies in the regulative principles of man's religious life and a prominence of irreligious activities, He appears on this earthly planet. In other words, when Lord Śrī Kṛṣṇa appeared, there was a necessity of minimizing the load of sinful activities accumulated on this planet, or in this universe.

For affairs of the material creation, Lord Mahā-Viṣṇu, the plenary portion of Kṛṣṇa, is in charge. Thus, when the Lord descends, the incarnation emanates from Viṣṇu. Mahā-Viṣṇu is the original cause of material creation, and from Him Garbhodakaśāyī Viṣṇu expands, and then Kṣīrodakaśāyī Viṣṇu. Generally, all the incarnations appearing within this material universe are plenary expansions from Kṣīrodakaśāyī Viṣṇu. Therefore, the business of minimizing the overload of sinful activities on this earth does not belong to the Supreme Personality of Godhead, Kṛṣṇa Himself. But when Kṛṣṇa appears, all the Viṣṇu expansions join with Him. Kṛṣṇa's different expansions—namely Nārāyaṇa, the quadruple expansion of Vāsudeva, Saṅkarṣaṇa, Pradyumna and Aniruddha, as well as partial plenary expansions like Matsya, the incarnation of a fish, and the *yuga-avatāras* (incarnations for the millennium) and the *manvantara-avatāras* (incarnations who appear during the reigns of the Manus)—all combine together and appear with the body of Kṛṣṇa, the Supreme Personality of Godhead. Kṛṣṇa is the complete whole, and thus all plenary expansions and incarnations always live with Him.

Therefore when Kṛṣṇa appeared, Lord Viṣṇu was with Him. Kṛṣṇa actually appears in order to demonstrate His Vṛndāvana pastimes and in this way attract the fortunate conditioned souls and invite them back home, back to Godhead. The killing of the demons in Vṛndāvana was carried out only by the Viṣṇu portion of Kṛṣṇa.

The Lord's abode is described in the *Bhagavad-gītā,* Eighth Chapter, twentieth verse, where it is stated that there is another, eternal nature, the spiritual sky, which is transcendental to this manifested and nonmanifested matter. The manifested world can be seen in the form of many stars and planetary systems, such as the sun and moon, but beyond this there is a nonmanifested portion, which is not approachable by anyone in this body. And beyond that nonmanifested matter is the spiritual kingdom. That kingdom is described in the *Bhagavad-gītā* as supreme and eternal, never to be annihilated. This material nature is subjected to repeated creation and annihilation. But that part, the spiritual nature, remains as it is, eternally.

The supreme abode of the Personality of Godhead, Kṛṣṇa, is also described in the *Brahma-saṁhitā* as the abode of *cintāmaṇi.* That abode of Lord Kṛṣṇa, known as Goloka Vṛndāvana, is full of palaces made of touchstone. There the trees are called desire trees, and the cows are called *surabhi.* The Lord is served there by hundreds and thousands of goddesses of fortune. His name is Govinda, the Primeval Lord, and He is the cause of all causes. There the Lord plays His flute, His eyes are like lotus petals, and the color of His body is like that of a beautiful cloud. On His head is a peacock feather. He is so attractive that He excels thousands of Cupids. Lord Kṛṣṇa gives only a little hint in the *Gītā* of His personal abode, which is the supermost planet in the spiritual kingdom. But in *Śrīmad-Bhāgavatam* Kṛṣṇa actually appears with all His paraphernalia and demonstrates His activities in Vṛndāvana, then at Mathurā, and then at Dvārakā. The subject matter of this book will gradually reveal all these activities.

The family in which Kṛṣṇa appeared is called the Yadu dynasty. This Yadu dynasty belongs to the family descending from Soma, the god in the moon planet. There are two different *kṣatriya* families of the royal order, one descending from the king of the moon planet and the other descending from the king of the sun planet. When the Supreme Personality of Godhead appears, He generally appears in a *kṣatriya* family because He has to establish religious principles, or the life of righteousness. The *kṣatriya* family is the protector of the human race, according to the Vedic system. When the Supreme Personality of Godhead appeared as Lord Rāmacandra, He appeared in the family descending from the sun-god, known as the Raghu-vaṁśa; and when He appeared as Lord Kṛṣṇa, He did so in the family known as the Yadu-vaṁśa. There is a long list of the kings of the Yadu-vaṁśa in the Ninth Canto, Twenty-fourth Chapter, of *Śrīmad-Bhāgavatam.* All of them were great, powerful kings. Kṛṣṇa's father's name was Vasudeva, son of Śūrasena, descending from the Yadu dynasty. Actually, the Supreme Personality of Godhead does not belong to any dynasty of this material world, but the family in which the Supreme Personality of Godhead appears becomes famous, by His grace. For example, sandalwood is produced in the states of Malaya. Sandalwood has its own qualifications apart from Malaya, but because accidentally this wood is mainly produced in the states of Malaya, it is known as Malayan sandalwood. Similarly, Kṛṣṇa, the Supreme Personality of Godhead, belongs to everyone, but just as the sun rises from the east, although there are other directions from which it could rise, so by His own choice the Lord appears in a particular family, and that family becomes famous.

As explained above, when Kṛṣṇa appears, all His plenary expansions appear with Him. Kṛṣṇa appeared along with Balarāma (Baladeva), who is known as His elder brother. Balarāma is the origin of Saṅkarṣaṇa, of the quadruple expansion. Balarāma is also the plenary expansion of Kṛṣṇa. In this book, the attempt will be made to show how Kṛṣṇa appeared in the family of the Yadu dynasty and how He displayed His transcendental characteristics. This is very vividly described in *Śrīmad-Bhāgavatam*—specifically, the Tenth Canto—and thus the basis of this book will be the Tenth Canto of *Śrīmad-Bhāgavatam.*

The pastimes of the Lord are generally heard and relished by liberated souls. Those who are conditioned souls are interested in reading stories of the material activities of some common man. Although similar narrations describing the transcendental activities of the Lord are found in *Śrīmad-Bhāgavatam* and other *Purāṇas,* the conditioned souls still prefer to study ordinary narrations. They are not so interested in studying the narrations of the pastimes of the Lord, Kṛṣṇa. And yet the descriptions of the pastimes of Lord Kṛṣṇa are so attractive that they are relishable for all classes of men. There are three classes of men in this world. One class consists of liberated souls, another consists of those who are trying to be liberated, and the third consists of materialistic men. Whether one is liberated or is trying to be liberated, or is even grossly materialistic, the pastimes of Lord Kṛṣṇa are worth studying.

Liberated souls have no interest in materialistic activities. The impersonalist theory that after liberation one becomes inactive and need not hear anything does not prove that a liberated person is actually inactive. A living soul cannot be inactive. He is active either in the conditioned state or in the liberated state. A diseased person, for example, is also active, but his activities are all painful. The same person, when freed from the diseased condition, is still active, but in the healthy condition the activities are full of pleasure. Similarly, the impersonalists only seek to get free from the diseased, conditioned activities, but they have no information of activities in the healthy condition. Those who are actually liberated and in full knowledge take to hearing the activities of Kṛṣṇa; such engagement is pure spiritual activity.

It is essential for persons who are actually liberated to hear about the pastimes of Kṛṣṇa. That is the supreme relishable subject matter for one in the liberated state. Also, if persons who are trying to be liberated hear such narrations as the *Bhagavad-gītā* and *Śrīmad-Bhāgavatam,* then their path of liberation becomes very clear. The *Bhagavad-gītā* is the preliminary study of *Śrīmad-Bhāgavatam.* By studying the *Gītā,* one becomes fully conscious of the position of Lord Kṛṣṇa; and when he is situated at the lotus feet of Kṛṣṇa, he understands the narrations of Kṛṣṇa as described in *Śrīmad-Bhāgavatam.* Lord Caitanya has therefore advised His followers that their business is to propagate *kṛṣṇa-kathā.*

Kṛṣṇa-kathā means narrations about Kṛṣṇa. There are two *kṛṣṇa-kathās:* narrations spoken *by* Kṛṣṇa and narrations spoken *about* Kṛṣṇa. The *Bhagavad-gītā* is the narration or the philosophy on the science of God, spoken by Kṛṣṇa Himself. *Śrīmad-*

Bhāgavatam is the narration about the activities and transcendental pastimes of Kṛṣṇa. Both are *kṛṣṇa-kathā.* It is the order of Lord Caitanya that *kṛṣṇa-kathā* should be spread all over the world, because if the conditioned souls, suffering under the pangs of material existence, take to *kṛṣṇa-kathā,* then their path of liberation will be open and clear. The purpose of presenting this book is primarily to induce people to understand Kṛṣṇa or *kṛṣṇa-kathā,* because thereby they can become freed from material bondage.

This *kṛṣṇa-kathā* will also be very much appealing to the most materialistic persons because Kṛṣṇa's pastimes with the *gopīs* (cowherd girls) are exactly like the loving affairs between young girls and boys within this material world. Actually, the sex feeling found in human society is not unnatural because this same sex feeling is there in the original Personality of Godhead. The pleasure potency is called Śrīmatī Rādhārāṇī. The attraction of loving affairs on the basis of sex feeling is the original feature of the Supreme Personality of Godhead, and we, the conditioned souls, being part and parcel of the Supreme, have such feelings also, but they are experienced within a perverted, minute condition. Therefore, when those who are after sex life in this material world hear about Kṛṣṇa's pastimes with the *gopīs,* they will relish transcendental pleasure, although it appears to be materialistic. The advantage will be that they will gradually be elevated to the spiritual platform. In the *Bhāgavatam* it is stated that if one hears the pastimes of Lord Kṛṣṇa with the *gopīs, from authorities with submission,* then he will be promoted to the platform of transcendental loving service to the Lord, and the material disease of lust within his heart will be completely vanquished. In other words, such hearing will counteract material sex life.

This book, *Kṛṣṇa,* which is filled with *kṛṣṇa-kathā,* will thus appeal equally to the liberated souls and to persons who are trying to be liberated, as well as to the gross, conditioned materialist. According to the statement of Mahārāja Parīkṣit, who heard about Kṛṣṇa from Śukadeva Gosvāmī, *kṛṣṇa-kathā* is equally applicable to every human being, whatever condition of life he is in. Surely everyone will appreciate it to the highest magnitude. But Mahārāja Parīkṣit also warned that persons who are simply engaged in killing animals and in killing themselves may not be very much attracted to *kṛṣṇa-kathā.* In other words, ordinary persons who are following the regulative moral principles of scriptures, no matter in what condition they are found, will certainly be attracted, but not persons who are killing themselves. The exact word used in *Śrīmad-Bhāgavatam* is *paśu-ghna,* which means killing animals or killing oneself. Persons who are not self-realized and who are not interested in spiritual realization are killing themselves; they are committing suicide. Because this human form of life is especially meant for self-realization, by neglecting this important part of his activities one simply wastes his time like the animals. So he is *paśu-ghna.* The other meaning of the word refers to those who are actually killing animals. This means persons who are animal-eaters (even dog-eaters), for they are all engaged in killing animals in so many ways, such as hunting and opening slaughterhouses. Such persons cannot be interested in *kṛṣṇa-kathā.*

King Parīkṣit was especially interested in hearing *kṛṣṇa-kathā* because he knew that his forefathers, particularly his grandfather, Arjuna, were victorious in the great Battle of Kurukṣetra only because of Kṛṣṇa. We may also take this material world as a Battlefield of Kurukṣetra. Everyone is struggling hard for existence on this battlefield, and at every step there is danger. According to Mahārāja Parīkṣit, the Battlefield of Kurukṣetra was just like a vast ocean full of dangerous animals. His grandfather Arjuna had to fight with such great heroes as Bhīṣma, Droṇa, Karṇa and many others who were not ordinary fighters. Such warriors have been compared to the *timiṅgila* fish in the ocean. The *timiṅgila* fish can very easily swallow up big whales. The great fighters on the Battlefield of Kurukṣetra could swallow many, many Arjunas very easily, but simply due to Kṛṣṇa's mercy, Arjuna was able to kill all of them. Just as one can cross with no exertion over the little bit of water contained in the hoofprint of a calf, so Arjuna, by the grace of Kṛṣṇa, was able to very easily jump over the ocean of the Battle of Kurukṣetra.

Mahārāja Parīkṣit very much appreciated Kṛṣṇa's activities for many other reasons. Not only was his grandfather saved by Kṛṣṇa, but he himself also was saved by Kṛṣṇa. By the end of the Battle of Kurukṣetra, all the members of the Kuru dynasty, both the sons and grandsons on the side of Dhṛtarāṣṭra and those on the side of the Pāṇḍavas, had died in the fighting. Except for the five Pāṇḍava brothers, everyone died on the Battlefield of Kurukṣetra. Mahārāja Parīkṣit was at that time within the womb of his mother. His father, Abhimanyu, the son of Arjuna, also died on the Battlefield of Kurukṣetra, and so Mahārāja Parīkṣit was a posthumous child. When he was in the womb of his mother, a *brahmāstra* weapon was released by Aśvatthāmā to kill the child. When Parīkṣit Mahārāja's mother, Uttarā, approached Kṛṣṇa, Kṛṣṇa, seeing the danger of abortion, entered her womb as the Supersoul and saved Mahārāja Parīkṣit. Mahārāja Parīkṣit's other name is Viṣṇurāta because he was saved by Lord Viṣṇu Himself while still within the womb.

Thus everyone, in any condition of life, should be interested in hearing about Kṛṣṇa and His activities because He is the Supreme Absolute Truth, the Personality of Godhead. He is all-pervading: inside He is living within everyone's heart, and outside He is living as His universal form. And yet, as described in the *Bhagavad-gītā,* He appears as He is in the human society just to invite everyone to His transcendental abode, back home, back to Godhead. Everyone should be interested in knowing about Kṛṣṇa, and this book is presented with this purpose: that people may know about Kṛṣṇa and be perfectly benefited in this human form of life.

In the Ninth Canto of *Śrīmad-Bhāgavatam,* Śrī Baladeva is described as the son of Rohiṇī, a wife of Vasudeva. Vasudeva, the father of Kṛṣṇa, had sixteen wives, and one of them was Rohiṇī, the mother of Baladeva. But Baladeva is also described as the son of Devakī, so how could He be the son of both Devakī and Rohiṇī? This was one of the questions put by Mahārāja Parīkṣit to Śukadeva Gosvāmī, and it will be answered in due course. Mahārāja Parīkṣit also asked Śukadeva Gosvāmī why Śrī Kṛṣṇa, just after His appearance as the son of Vasudeva, was immediately carried to the house of Nanda Mahārāja in Vṛndāvana, Gokula. He also wanted to know what the activities of Lord Kṛṣṇa were while He was in Vṛndāvana and while He was in Mathurā. Besides that, he was especially inquisitive to know why Kṛṣṇa killed His maternal uncle, Kaṁsa. Kaṁsa, being the brother of His mother, was a very intimate superior to Kṛṣṇa, so how was it that He killed Kaṁsa? Also, Mahārāja Parīkṣit asked how many years Lord Kṛṣṇa remained in human society, how many years He reigned over the kingdom of Dvārakā, and how many wives He accepted there. A *kṣatriya* king is generally accustomed to accept more than one wife; therefore Mahārāja Parīkṣit also inquired about His number of wives. The subject matter of this book is Śukadeva Gosvāmī's answering of these and other questions asked by Mahārāja Parīkṣit.

The position of Mahārāja Parīkṣit and Śukadeva Gosvāmī is unique. Mahārāja Parīkṣit is the right person to hear about the transcendental pastimes of Kṛṣṇa, and Śukadeva Gosvāmī is the right person to describe them. If such a fortunate combination is made possible, then *kṛṣṇa-kathā* immediately becomes revealed, and people may benefit to the highest possible degree from such a conversation.

This narration was presented by Śukadeva Gosvāmī when Mahārāja Parīkṣit was prepared to give up his body, fasting on the bank of the Ganges. In order to assure Śukadeva Gosvāmī that by hearing *kṛṣṇa-kathā* he would not feel tired, Mahārāja Parīkṣit expressed himself very frankly: "Hunger and thirst may give trouble to ordinary persons or to me, but the topics of Kṛṣṇa are so nice that one can continue to hear them without feeling tired because such hearing situates one in the transcendental position." It is understood that one must be very fortunate to hear *kṛṣṇa-kathā* as seriously as Mahārāja Parīkṣit did. He was especially intent on the subject matter because he was expecting death at any moment. Every one of us should be conscious of death at every moment. This life is not at all assured; at any time one can die. It does not matter whether one is a young man or an old man. So before death takes place, we must be *fully* Kṛṣṇa conscious.

At the point of his death, King Parīkṣit was hearing *Śrīmad-Bhāgavatam* from Śukadeva Gosvāmī. When King Parīkṣit expressed his untiring desire to hear about Kṛṣṇa, Śukadeva Gosvāmī was very pleased. Śukadeva was the greatest of all *Bhāgavata* reciters, and thus he began to speak about Kṛṣṇa's pastimes, which destroy all inauspiciousness in this Age of Kali. Śukadeva Gosvāmī thanked the King for his eagerness to hear about Kṛṣṇa, and he encouraged him by saying, "My dear King, your intelligence is very keen because you are so eager to hear about the pastimes of Kṛṣṇa." He informed Mahārāja Parīkṣit that hearing and chanting the pastimes of Kṛṣṇa are so auspicious that the processes purify the three varieties of men involved: he who recites the transcendental topics of Kṛṣṇa, he who hears such topics, and he who inquires about Him. These pastimes are just like the Ganges water, which flows from the toe of Lord Viṣṇu: they purify the three worlds, the upper, middle and lower planetary systems.

CHAPTER 1

The Advent of Lord Kṛṣṇa

ONCE THE WORLD WAS OVERBURDENED by the unnecessary defense force of different kings, who were actually demons but were posing themselves as the royal order. At that time, the whole world became perturbed, and the predominating deity of this earth, known as Bhūmi, went to see Lord Brahmā to tell of her calamities due to the demoniac kings. Bhūmi assumed the shape of a cow and presented herself before Lord Brahmā with tears in her eyes. She was bereaved and was weeping just to invoke the lord's compassion. She related the calamitous position of the earth, and after hearing this, Lord Brahmā became much aggrieved, and he at once started for the ocean of milk, where Lord Viṣṇu resides. Lord Brahmā was accompanied by all the demigods, headed by Lord Śiva, and Bhūmi also followed. Arriving on the shore of the milk ocean, Lord Brahmā began to pacify Lord Viṣṇu, who had formerly saved the earthly planet by assuming the transcendental form of a boar.

In the Vedic *mantras,* there is a particular type of prayer called *Puruṣa-sūkta.* Generally, the demigods offer their obeisances unto Viṣṇu, the Supreme Personality of Godhead, by chanting the *Puruṣa-sūkta.* It is understood herein that the predominating deity of every planet can see the supreme lord of this universe, Brahmā, whenever there is some disturbance on his planet. And Brahmā can approach the Supreme Lord

Viṣṇu, not by seeing Him directly but by standing on the shore of the ocean of milk. There is a planet within this universe called Śvetadvīpa, and on that planet there is an ocean of milk. It is understood from various Vedic literatures that just as there is the ocean of salt water on this planet, there are various kinds of oceans on other planets. Somewhere there is an ocean of milk, somewhere there is an ocean of oil, and somewhere there are oceans of liquor and of many other types of liquids. The *Puruṣa-sūkta* is the standard prayer which the demigods recite to appease the Supreme Personality of Godhead, Kṣīrodakaśāyī Viṣṇu. Because He is lying on the ocean of milk, He is called Kṣīrodakaśāyī Viṣṇu. He is the form of the Supreme Personality of Godhead through whom all the incarnations within this universe appear.

After all the demigods offered the *Puruṣa-sūkta* prayer to the Supreme Personality of Godhead, they apparently heard no response. Then Lord Brahmā personally sat in meditation, and there was a message-transmission from Lord Viṣṇu to Brahmā. Brahmā then broadcast the message to the demigods. That is the system of receiving Vedic knowledge. The Vedic knowledge is received first by Brahmā from the Supreme Personality of Godhead, through the medium of the heart. As stated in the beginning of *Śrīmad-Bhāgavatam, tene brahma hṛdā ya ādi-kavaye:* the transcendental knowledge of the *Vedas* was transmitted to Lord Brahmā through the heart. Here also, in the same way, only Brahmā could understand the message transmitted by Lord Viṣṇu, and he broadcast it to the demigods for their immediate action. The message was this: The Supreme Personality of Godhead would appear on the earth very soon along with His supreme powerful potencies, and as long as He remained on the earth planet to execute His mission of annihilating the demons and establishing the devotees, the demigods should also remain there to assist Him. They should all immediately take birth in the family of the Yadu dynasty, wherein the Lord would also appear in due course of time. The Supreme Personality of Godhead Himself, Kṛṣṇa, would personally appear as the son of Vasudeva. Before His appearance, all the demigods, along with their wives, should appear in different pious families in the world just to assist the Lord in executing His mission. The exact word used here is *tat-priyārtham,* which means the demigods should appear on the earth in order to please the Lord. In other words, any living entity who lives only to satisfy the Lord is a demigod. The demigods were further informed that Ananta, the plenary portion of Lord Kṛṣṇa who is maintaining the universal planets by extending His millions of hoods, would also appear on earth before Lord Kṛṣṇa's appearance. They were also informed that the external potency of Viṣṇu (Māyā), with whom all the conditioned souls are enamored, would also appear by the order of the Supreme Lord, just to execute His purpose.

After instructing and pacifying all the demigods, as well as Bhūmi, with sweet words, Lord Brahmā, the father of all *prajāpatis,* or progenitors of universal population, departed for his abode, the highest material planet, called Brahmaloka.

The leader of the Yadu dynasty, King Śūrasena, was ruling over the country known as Māthura, wherein lies the city of Mathurā, as well as the district known as Śūrasena, which was named after him. On account of the rule of King Śūrasena, Mathurā became the capital city of all the kings of the Yadus. Mathurā was also made the capital of the kings of the Yadu dynasty because the Yadus were a very pious family and knew that Mathurā is the place where Lord Śrī Kṛṣṇa lives eternally, just as He also lives in Dvārakā.

Once upon a time, Vasudeva, the son of Śūrasena, just after marrying Devakī, was going home on his chariot with his newly wedded wife. The father of Devakī, known as Devaka, had contributed a sufficient dowry because he was very affectionate toward his daughter. He had contributed hundreds of chariots completely decorated with gold equipment. At that time, Kaṁsa, the son of Ugrasena, in order to please his sister, Devakī, had voluntarily taken the reins of the horses of Vasudeva's chariot and was driving. According to the custom of the Vedic civilization, when a girl is married, the brother takes the sister and brother-in-law to their home. Because the newly married girl may feel too much separation from her father's family, the brother goes with her until she reaches her father-in-law's house.

The full dowry contributed by Devaka was as follows: 400 elephants fully decorated with golden garlands, 15,000 decorated horses and 1,800 chariots. He also arranged for 200 beautiful girls to follow his daughter. The *kṣatriya* system of marriage, still current in India, dictates that when a *kṣatriya* is married, a few dozen of the bride's young girlfriends (in addition to the bride) go to the house of the king. The followers of the queen are called maidservants, but actually they act as friends of the queen. This practice is prevalent from time immemorial, traceable at least to the time before the advent of Lord Kṛṣṇa 5,000 years ago. So Vasudeva brought home another 200 beautiful girls along with his wife Devakī.

While the bride and bridegroom were passing along on the chariot, there were different kinds of musical instruments playing to indicate the auspicious moment. There were conchshells, bugles, drums and kettledrums; combined together, they were vibrating a nice concert. The procession was passing very pleasingly, and Kaṁsa was driving the chariot, when suddenly there was a miraculous sound vibrated from the sky which especially announced to Kaṁsa: "Kaṁsa, you are such a fool! You are driving the chariot of your sister and your brother-in-law, but you do not know that the eighth child of this sister will kill you."

Kaṁsa was the son of Ugrasena, of the Bhoja dynasty. It is said that Kaṁsa was the most demoniac of all the Bhoja dynasty kings. Immediately after hearing the prophecy from the sky, he caught hold of Devakī's hair and was just about to kill her with his sword. Vasudeva was astonished at Kaṁsa's behavior, and in order to pacify the cruel, shameless brother-in-law, he began to speak as follows, with great reason and evidence. He said, "My dear brother-in-law Kaṁsa, you are the most famous king of the Bhoja dynasty, and people know that you are the greatest warrior and a valiant king. How is it that you are so infuriated that you are prepared to kill a woman who is your own sister at this auspicious time of her marriage? Why should you be so much afraid of death? Death is already born along with your birth. From the very day you took your birth, you began to die. Suppose you are twenty-five years old; that means you have already died twenty-five years. Every moment, every second, you are dying. Why then should you be so much afraid of death? Final death is inevitable. You may die either today or in a hundred years; you cannot avoid death. Why should you be so much afraid? Actually, death means annihilation of the present body. As soon as the present body stops functioning and mixes with the five elements of material nature, the living entity within the body accepts another body, according to his present actions and reactions. It is just like when a man walks on the street: he puts forward his foot, and when he is confident that his foot is situated on sound ground, he lifts the other foot. In this way, one after another, the bodies change and the soul transmigrates. See how the plantworms change from one twig to another so carefully! Similarly, the living entity changes his body as soon as the higher authorities decide on his next body. As long as a living entity is conditioned within this material world, he must take material bodies one after another. His next particular body is offered by the laws of nature, according to the actions and reactions of this life.

"This body is exactly like one of the bodies which we always see in dreams. During our dream of sleep, we create so many bodies according to mental creation. We have seen gold, and we have also seen a mountain, so in a dream we can see a golden mountain by combining the two ideas. Sometimes in dreams we see that we have a body which is flying in the sky, and at that time we completely forget our present body. Similarly, these bodies are changing. When you have one body, you forget the past body. During a dream, we may make contact with so many new kinds of bodies, but when we are awake we forget them all. And actually these material bodies are the creations of our mental activities. But at the present moment we do not recollect our past bodies.

"The nature of the mind is flickering. Sometimes it accepts something, and immediately it rejects the same thing. Accepting and rejecting is the process of the mind in contact with the five objects of sense gratification—form, taste, smell, sound and touch. In its speculative way, the mind comes in touch with the objects of sense gratification, and when the living entity desires a particular type of body, he gets it. Therefore, the body is an offering by the laws of material nature. The living entity accepts a body and comes out again into the material world to enjoy or suffer according to the construction of the body. Unless we have a particular type of body, we cannot enjoy or suffer according to our mental proclivities inherited from the previous life. The particular type of body is actually offered to us according to our mental condition at the time of death.

"The luminous planets like the sun, moon or stars reflect themselves in different types of reservoirs, like water, oil or ghee. The reflection moves according to the movement of the reservoir. The reflection of the moon is on the water, and the moving water makes the moon also appear to be moving, but actually the moon is not moving. Similarly, by mental concoction the living entity attains different kinds of bodies, although actually he has no connection with such bodies. But on account of illusion, being enchanted by the influence of *māyā,* the living entity thinks that he belongs to a particular type of body. That is the way of conditioned life. Suppose a living entity is now in a human form of body. He thinks that he belongs to the human community, or a particular country or particular place. He identifies himself in that way and unnecessarily prepares for another body, which is not required by him. Such desires and mental concoctions are the cause of different types of bodies. The covering influence of material nature is so strong that the living entity is satisfied in whatever body he gets, and he identifies with that body with great pleasure. Therefore, I beg to request you not to be overwhelmed by the dictation of your mind and body."

Vasudeva thus requested Kaṁsa not to be envious of his newly married sister. One should not be envious of anyone, because envy is the cause of fear both in this world and in the next, when one is before Yamarāja (the lord of punishment after death). Vasudeva appealed to Kaṁsa on behalf of Devakī, stating that she was his younger sister. He also appealed at an auspicious moment, at the time of marriage. A younger sister or brother is supposed to be protected as one's child. "The position is overall so delicate," Vasudeva reasoned, "that if you kill her, it will go against your high reputation."

In this way Vasudeva tried to pacify Kaṁsa by good instruction as well as by philosophical discrimination, but Kaṁsa was not to be pacified because his association was demoniac. Because of his demoniac association, he was a demon, although born in a very high royal family. A demon never cares for any good instruction. He is just like a determined thief: one can give him moral instruction, but it will not be effective. Similarly, those who are demoniac or atheistic by nature can hardly assimilate any good instruction, however authorized it may be. That is the difference between demigods and demons. Those who can accept good instruction and try to live their lives in that way are called demigods, and those who are unable to take such good instruction are called demons.

Failing in his attempt to pacify Kaṁsa, Vasudeva wondered how he would protect his wife, Devakī. When there is imminent danger, an intelligent person should try to avoid the dangerous position as far as possible. But if, in spite of endeavoring by all intelligence, one fails to avoid the dangerous position, there is no fault on his part. One should try his best to execute his duties, but if the attempt fails, he is not at fault.

Vasudeva thought of his wife as follows: "For the present let me save the life of Devakī; then later on, if there are children, I shall see how to save them." He further thought, "If in the future I get a child who can kill Kaṁsa—just as Kaṁsa is thinking—then both Devakī and the child will be saved because the law of providence is inconceivable. But now, some way or other, let me save the life of Devakī."

There is no certainty how a living entity contacts a certain type of body, just as there is no certainty how a blazing fire comes in contact with a certain type of wood in the forest. When there is a forest fire, it is experienced that the blazing fire sometimes leaps over one tree and catches another by the influence of the wind. Similarly, a living entity may be very careful in the matter of executing his duties, but it is still very difficult for him to know what type of body he is going to get in the next life. Mahārāja Bharata was very faithfully executing the duties of self-realization, but by chance he developed temporary affection for a deer, and in his next life he had to accept the body of a deer.

Vasudeva, after deliberating on how to save his wife, began to speak to Kaṁsa with great respect, although Kaṁsa was the most sinful man. Sometimes it happens that a most virtuous person like Vasudeva has to flatter a person like Kaṁsa, a most vicious person. That is the way of all diplomatic transactions. Although Vasudeva was deeply aggrieved, he smiled outwardly. He addressed the shameless Kaṁsa in that way because he was so atrocious. Vasudeva said to Kaṁsa, "My dear brother-in-law, please consider that you have no danger from your sister. You are awaiting some danger because you have heard a prophetic voice in the sky. But the danger is to come from the sons of your sister, who are not present now. And who knows? There may or may not be sons in the future. Considering all this, you are safe for the present. Nor is there cause of fear from your sister. If there are any sons born of her, I promise that I shall present all of them to you for necessary action."

Kaṁsa knew the value of Vasudeva's word of honor, and he was convinced by his argument. For the time being, he desisted from the heinous killing of his sister. Thus Vasudeva was pleased and praised the decision of Kaṁsa. In this way, he returned to his home.

Each year thereafter, in due course of time, Devakī gave birth to a child. Thus she gave birth to eight male children, as well as one daughter. When the first son was born, Vasudeva kept his word of honor and immediately brought the child before Kaṁsa. It is said that Vasudeva was very much elevated and famous for his word of honor, and he wanted to maintain this fame. Although it was very painful for Vasudeva to hand over the newly born child, Kaṁsa was very glad to receive him. But he became a little compassionate with the behavior of Vasudeva. This event is very exemplary. For a great soul like Vasudeva, there is nothing considered to be painful in the course of discharging one's duty. A learned person like Vasudeva carries out his duties without hesitation. On the other hand, a demon like Kaṁsa never hesitates in committing any abominable action. It is said, therefore, that a saintly person can tolerate all kinds of miserable conditions of life, a learned man can discharge his duties without awaiting favorable circumstances, a heinous person like Kaṁsa can act in any sinful way, and a devotee can sacrifice everything to satisfy the Supreme Personality of Godhead.

Kaṁsa became satisfied by the action of Vasudeva. He was surprised to see Vasudeva keeping his promise, and being compassionate upon him and pleased, he began to speak as follows: "My dear Vasudeva, you need not present this child to me. I am not in danger from this child. I have heard that the eighth child born of you and Devakī will kill me. Why should I accept this child unnecessarily? You can take him back."

When Vasudeva was returning home with his firstborn child, although he was pleased by the behavior of Kaṁsa, he could not believe in him because he knew that Kaṁsa was uncontrolled. An atheistic person cannot be firm in his word of honor. One who cannot control the senses cannot be steady in his determination. The great politician Cāṇakya Paṇḍita said, "Never put your trust in a diplomat or a woman." Those who are addicted to unrestricted sense gratification can never be truthful, nor can they be trusted with any faith.

At that time the great sage Nārada came to Kaṁsa. He was informed of Kaṁsa's becoming compassionate to Vasudeva and returning his firstborn child. Nārada was very eager to accelerate the descent of Lord Kṛṣṇa as soon as possible. He therefore informed Kaṁsa that in Vṛndāvana personalities like Nanda Mahārāja and all the other cowherd men and their wives, and on the other side Vasudeva, his father Śūrasena and all his relatives born in the family of Vṛṣṇi of the Yadu dynasty, along with all their friends and well-wishers, were actually demigods. Nārada warned Kaṁsa to be careful of them, since Kaṁsa and his friends and advisors were all demons. Demons are always afraid of demigods. After being thus informed by Nārada about the appearance of the demigods in different families, Kaṁsa at once became very much alarmed. He understood that since the demigods had already appeared, Lord Viṣṇu must be coming soon. He at once arrested both his brother-in-law Vasudeva and Devakī and put them behind prison bars.

Within the prison, shackled in iron chains, Vasudeva and Devakī gave birth to a male child year after year, and Kaṁsa, thinking each of the babies to be the incarnation of Viṣṇu, killed them one after another. He was particularly afraid of the eighth child, but after the visit of Nārada, he came to the conclusion that any child might be Kṛṣṇa. Therefore it was better to kill all the babies who took birth from Devakī and Vasudeva.

This action of Kaṁsa is not very difficult to understand. There are many instances in the history of the world of persons in the royal order who have killed their father, brother or whole family and friends for the satisfaction of their ambitions. There is nothing astonishing about this, for members of the demoniac, greedy royal order can kill anyone for their nefarious ambitions.

Kaṁsa was made aware of his previous birth by the grace of Nārada. He learned that in his previous birth he had been a demon of the name Kālanemi and that he had been killed by Viṣṇu. Having now taken his birth in the Bhoja family, he decided to become the deadly enemy of the Yadu dynasty; Kṛṣṇa was going to take birth in that family, and Kaṁsa was very much afraid that he would be killed by Kṛṣṇa, just as he had been killed in his last birth.

He first of all imprisoned his father, Ugrasena, because he was the chief king among the Yadu, Bhoja and Andhaka dynasties, and he also occupied the kingdom of Śūrasena, Vasudeva's father. He declared himself the king of all such places.

Thus ends the Bhaktivedanta purport of the First Chapter of Kṛṣṇa, *"The Advent of Lord Kṛṣṇa."*

CHAPTER 2

Prayers by the Demigods for Lord Kṛṣṇa in the Womb

KING KAṀSA NOT ONLY OCCUPIED the kingdoms of the Yadu, Bhoja and Andhaka dynasties and the kingdom of Śūrasena, but he also made alliances with all the other demoniac kings, as follows: the demon Pralamba, demon Baka, demon Cāṇūra, demon Tṛṇāvarta, demon Aghāsura, demon Muṣṭika, demon Ariṣṭa, demon Dvivida, demon Pūtanā, demon Keśī and demon Dhenuka. At that time, Jarāsandha was the king of Magadha Province (known at present as Bihar State). Thus by his diplomatic policy, Kaṁsa consolidated the most powerful kingdom of his time, under the protection of Jarāsandha. He made further alliances with such kings as Bāṇāsura and Bhaumāsura, until he was the strongest. Then he began to behave most inimically toward the Yadu dynasty, into which Kṛṣṇa was to take His birth.

Being harassed by Kaṁsa, the kings of the Yadu, Bhoja and Andhaka dynasties began to take shelter in different states, such as the state of the Kurus, the state of the Pañcālas and the states known as Kekaya, Śālva, Vidarbha, Niṣadha, Videha and Kośala. Kaṁsa broke the solidarity of the Yadu kingdom, as well as the Bhoja and Andhaka. He made his position the most solid within the vast tract of land known at that time as Bhārata-varṣa.

When Kaṁsa was killing the six babies of Devakī and Vasudeva one after another, many friends and relatives of Kaṁsa approached him and requested him to discontinue these heinous activities. But all of them became worshipers of Kaṁsa.

When Devakī became pregnant for the seventh time, a plenary expansion of Kṛṣṇa known as Ananta appeared within her womb. Devakī was overwhelmed with both jubilation and lamentation. She was joyful, for she could understand that Lord Viṣṇu had taken shelter within her womb, but at the same time she was sorry that as soon as her child would come out, Kaṁsa would kill Him. At that time the Supreme Personality of Godhead, Kṛṣṇa, being compassionate upon the Yadus, who were fearful due to the atrocities committed by Kaṁsa, ordered the appearance of Yogamāyā, His internal potency. Kṛṣṇa is the Lord of the universe, but He is especially the Lord of the Yadu dynasty.

Yogamāyā is the principal potency of the Personality of Godhead. In the *Vedas* it is stated that the Lord, the Supreme Personality of Godhead, has multipotencies: *parāsya śaktir vividhaiva śrūyate.* All the different potencies are acting externally and internally, and Yogamāyā is the chief of all potencies. The Lord ordered the appearance of Yogamāyā in the land of Vrajabhūmi, in Vṛndāvana, which is always decorated and full with beautiful cows. In Vṛndāvana, Rohiṇī, one of the wives of Vasudeva, was residing at the house of King Nanda and Queen Yaśodā. Not only Rohiṇī but many others in the Yadu dynasty were scattered all over the country due to their fear of the atrocities of Kaṁsa. Some of them were even living in the caves of the mountains.

The Lord thus informed Yogamāyā, "Under the imprisonment of Kaṁsa are Devakī and Vasudeva, and at the present moment My plenary expansion Śeṣa is within the womb of Devakī. You can arrange the transfer of Śeṣa from the womb of Devakī to the womb of Rohiṇī. After this arrangement, I am personally going to appear in the womb of Devakī with My full potencies. Then I shall appear as the son of Devakī and Vasudeva. And you shall appear as the daughter of Nanda and Yaśodā in Vṛndāvana.

"Since you will appear as My contemporary sister, and since you will quickly satisfy desires for sense gratification, people within the world will worship you with all kinds of valuable presentations—incense, candles, flowers and offerings of sacrifice. People who are after materialistic perfection will worship you under the different forms of your expansions, which will be named Durgā, Bhadrakālī, Vijayā, Vaiṣṇavī, Kumudā, Caṇḍikā, Kṛṣṇā, Mādhavī, Kanyakā, Māyā, Nārāyaṇī, Īśānī, Śāradā and Ambikā."

Kṛṣṇa and Yogamāyā appeared as brother and sister—the Supreme Powerful and the supreme power. Although there is no clear distinction between the Powerful and the power, power is always subordinate to the Powerful. Those who are materialistic are worshipers of the power, but those who are transcendentalists are worshipers of the Powerful. Kṛṣṇa is the Supreme Powerful, and Durgā is the supreme power within the material world. Actually people in the Vedic culture worship both the Powerful and the power. There are many hundreds and thousands of temples of Viṣṇu and Devī, and sometimes they are worshiped simultaneously. The worshiper of the power, Durgā, or the external energy of Kṛṣṇa, may achieve all kinds of material success very easily, but anyone who wants to be elevated transcendentally must engage in worshiping the Powerful in Kṛṣṇa consciousness.

The Lord also declared to Yogamāyā, "My plenary expansion Ananta Śeṣa is within the womb of Devakī. On account of being forcibly attracted to the womb of Rohiṇī, He will be known as Saṅkarṣaṇa and will be the source of all spiritual power, or *bala*, by which one can attain the highest bliss of life, which is called *ramaṇa*. Therefore the plenary portion Ananta will be known after His appearance either as Saṅkarṣaṇa or as Balarāma."

In the *Upaniṣads* it is stated, *nāyam ātmā bala-hīnena labhyaḥ.* The purport is that one cannot attain the supreme platform of self-realization without being sufficiently favored by Balarāma. *Bala* does not mean physical strength. No one can attain spiritual perfection by physical strength. One must have the spiritual strength which is infused by Balarāma, or Saṅkarṣaṇa. Ananta, or Śeṣa, is the source of the power which sustains all the planets in their different positions. Materially this sustaining power is known as the law of gravitation, but actually it is a display of the potency of Saṅkarṣaṇa. Balarāma, or Saṅkarṣaṇa, is the source of spiritual power, or the original spiritual master. Therefore Lord Nityānanda Prabhu, who is also the incarnation of Balarāma, is the original spiritual master. And the spiritual master is the representative of Balarāma, the form of the Supreme Personality of Godhead who supplies spiritual strength. In the *Caitanya-caritāmṛta* it is confirmed that the spiritual master is the manifestation of the mercy of Kṛṣṇa.

Thus ordered by the Supreme Personality of Godhead, Yogamāyā circumambulated the Lord and then appeared within this material world according to His order. When Yogamāyā, the supreme power of the supremely powerful Personality of Godhead, transferred Lord Śeṣa from the womb of Devakī to the womb of Rohiṇī, both Devakī and Rohiṇī were under Yogamāyā's spell, which is called *yoga-nidrā.* When this was done, people thought that Devakī's seventh pregnancy had been a miscarriage. Thus although Balarāma appeared as the son of Devakī, He was transferred to the womb of Rohiṇī to appear as her son. After this arrangement, the Supreme Personality of Godhead, Kṛṣṇa, who is always ready to protect His unalloyed devotees, entered within the mind of Vasudeva as the Lord of the whole creation, with full inconceivable potencies. It is understood in this connection that Lord Kṛṣṇa first of all situated Himself in the unalloyed heart of Vasudeva and was then transferred to the heart of Devakī. He was not put into the womb of Devakī by seminal discharge. The Supreme Personality of Godhead, by His inconceivable potency, can appear in any way. It is not necessary for Him to appear in the ordinary way, by seminal injection within the womb of a woman.

When Vasudeva was sustaining the form of the Supreme Personality of Godhead within his heart, he appeared just like the glowing sun, whose shining rays are always unbearable and scorching to the common man. The form of the Lord situated in the pure unalloyed heart of Vasudeva is not different from the original form of Kṛṣṇa. The appearance of the form of Kṛṣṇa anywhere, and specifically within the heart, is called *dhāma. Dhāma* refers not only to Kṛṣṇa's form but also to His name, His qualities and His paraphernalia. Everything becomes manifest simultaneously.

Thus the eternal form of the Supreme Personality of Godhead with full potencies was transferred from the mind of Vasudeva to the mind of Devakī, exactly as the setting sun's rays are transferred to the full moon rising in the east.

Kṛṣṇa, the Supreme Personality of Godhead, thus entered the body of Devakī from the body of Vasudeva without being subject to any of the conditions of an ordinary living entity. Since Kṛṣṇa was there, it is to be understood that all His plenary expansions, such as Nārāyaṇa, and incarnations like Lord Nṛsiṁha and Varāha, were with Him, and They also were not subject to the conditions of material existence. In this way, Devakī became the residence of the Supreme Personality of Godhead, who is one without a second and the cause of all creation. Devakī became the residence of the Absolute Truth, but because she was confined within the house of Kaṁsa, she looked just like a suppressed fire, or like misused education. When fire is kept in a jug, the illuminating rays of the fire cannot be very much appreciated. Similarly, misused knowledge, which does not benefit the people in general, is not very much appreciated. So Devakī was kept within the prison walls of Kaṁsa's palace, and no one could see her transcendental beauty, which resulted from her conceiving the Supreme Personality of Godhead.

Kaṁsa, however, saw the transcendental beauty of his sister Devakī, and he at once concluded that the Supreme Personality of Godhead had taken shelter in her womb. She had never before looked so wonderfully beautiful. He could distinctly understand that there was something wonderful within the womb of Devakī. In this way, Kaṁsa became perturbed because he was sure that the Supreme Personality of Godhead, who would kill him in the future, had now come. Kaṁsa began to think, "What is to be done with Devakī? Surely she has Viṣṇu or Kṛṣṇa within her womb, so it is certain that Kṛṣṇa has come to execute the mission of the demigods. And even if I immediately kill Devakī, His mission cannot be frustrated." Kaṁsa knew very well that no one can frustrate the purpose of Viṣṇu. Any intelligent man can understand that the laws of God cannot be violated. His purpose will be served in spite of all impediments offered by the demons. Kaṁsa thought, "If I kill Devakī at the present moment, Viṣṇu will enforce His supreme will more vehemently. To kill Devakī just now would be a most abominable act. No one desires to kill his reputation, even in an awkward situation; if I kill Devakī now, my reputation will be spoiled. Devakī is a woman, and she is under my shelter; she is pregnant, and if I kill her, immediately my reputation, the results of my pious activities and my duration of life will all be finished."

He further deliberated, "A person who is too cruel is as good as dead, even in this lifetime. No one likes a cruel person during his lifetime, and after his death, people curse him. On account of his self-identification with the body, he must be degraded and pushed into the darkest region of hell." Kaṁsa thus meditated on all the pros and cons of killing Devakī at that time.

Kaṁsa finally decided not to kill Devakī right away but to wait for the inevitable future. But his mind became absorbed in animosity against the Personality of Godhead. He patiently waited for the delivery of the child, expecting to kill Him, as he had done previously with the other babies of Devakī. Thus being merged in the ocean of animosity against the Personality of Godhead, he began to think of Kṛṣṇa or Viṣṇu while sitting, while sleeping, while walking, while eating, while working—in all the situations of his life. His mind became so much absorbed with the thought of the Supreme Personality of Godhead that indirectly he could see only Kṛṣṇa or Viṣṇu around him. Unfortunately, although his mind was so absorbed in the thought of Viṣṇu, he is not recognized as a devotee because he was thinking of Kṛṣṇa as an enemy. The state of mind of a great devotee is also to be always absorbed in Kṛṣṇa, but a devotee thinks of Him favorably, not unfavorably. To think of Kṛṣṇa favorably is Kṛṣṇa consciousness, but to think of Kṛṣṇa unfavorably is not Kṛṣṇa consciousness.

At this time Lord Brahmā and Lord Śiva, accompanied by great sages like Nārada and followed by many other demigods, invisibly appeared in the house of Kaṁsa. They began to pray to the Supreme Personality of Godhead in select verses, which are very pleasing to the devotees and which award fulfillment of their desires. The first words they spoke acclaimed that the Lord is true to His vow. As stated in the *Bhagavad-gītā,* Kṛṣṇa descends to this material world just to protect the pious and destroy the impious. That is His vow. The demigods could understand that the Lord had taken His residence within the womb of Devakī to fulfill His vow, and they were very glad that the Lord was appearing in order to fulfill His mission.

Then the demigods addressed the Lord as *satyaṁ param,* or the Supreme Absolute Truth. Everyone is searching after the truth. That is the philosophical way of life. The demigods give information that the Supreme Absolute Truth is Kṛṣṇa. One who becomes fully Kṛṣṇa conscious can attain the Absolute Truth. Kṛṣṇa is the Absolute Truth because, unlike relative truth, He is Truth in all the three phases of eternal time. Time is divided into past, present and future. Kṛṣṇa is Truth always—past, present and future. In the material world everything is being controlled by supreme time, in the course of past, present and future. But before the creation, Kṛṣṇa was existing, and when there is creation, everything is resting in Kṛṣṇa, and when this creation is finished, Kṛṣṇa will remain. Therefore, He is the Absolute Truth in all circumstances. If there is any truth within this material world, it emanates from the Supreme Truth, Kṛṣṇa. If there is any opulence within this material world, the cause of the opulence is Kṛṣṇa. If there is any reputation within this material world, the cause of the reputation is Kṛṣṇa. If there is any strength within this material world, the cause of such strength is Kṛṣṇa. If there is any wisdom and education within this material world, the cause of such wisdom and education is Kṛṣṇa. Therefore Kṛṣṇa is the source of all relative truths.

This material world is composed of five principal elements—earth, water, fire, air and ether—and all such elements are emanations from Kṛṣṇa. The material scientists accept these five primary elements as the cause of the material manifestation, but the elements in their gross and subtle states are produced by Kṛṣṇa. The living entities who are working within this material world are products of His marginal potency. In the Seventh Chapter of the *Bhagavad-gītā*, it is clearly stated that the whole manifestation is a combination of two kinds of energies of Kṛṣṇa, the superior energy and the inferior energy. The living entities are the superior energy, and the dead material elements are His inferior energy. In its dormant stage, everything remains in Kṛṣṇa.

The demigods continued to offer their respectful prayers unto the supreme form of the Personality of Godhead, Kṛṣṇa, by analytical study of the material manifestation. What is this material manifestation? It is just like a tree. A tree stands on the ground. Similarly, the tree of the material manifestation is standing on the ground of material nature. This material manifestation is compared to a tree because a tree is ultimately cut off in due course of time. A tree is called *vṛkṣa. Vṛkṣa* means that thing which will be ultimately cut off. Therefore, this tree of the material manifestation cannot be accepted as the Ultimate Truth, because it is influenced by time. But Kṛṣṇa's body is eternal: He existed before the material manifestation, He is existing while the material manifestation is continuing, and when it will be dissolved, He will continue to exist. Therefore only Kṛṣṇa can be accepted as the Absolute Truth.

The *Kaṭha Upaniṣad* also cites this example of the tree of the material manifestation standing on the ground of material nature. This tree has two kinds of fruits, distress and happiness. Those who are living in the tree of the body are just like two birds. One bird is the localized aspect of Kṛṣṇa known as the Paramātmā, and the other bird is the living entity. The living entity is eating the fruits of this material manifestation. Sometimes he eats the fruit of happiness, and sometimes he eats the fruit of distress. But the other bird is not interested in eating the fruit of distress or happiness because he is self-satisfied. The *Kaṭha Upaniṣad* states that one bird on the tree of the body is eating the fruits, and the other bird is simply witnessing. The roots of this tree extend in three directions. This means that the root of the tree is the three modes of material nature: goodness, passion and ignorance. Just as the tree's root expands, so, by association of the modes of material nature (goodness, passion and ignorance), one expands his duration of material existence. The tastes of the fruits are of four kinds: religiosity, economic development, sense gratification and, ultimately, liberation. According to the different associations in the three modes of material nature, the living entities are tasting different kinds of religiosity, different kinds of economic development, different kinds of sense gratification and different kinds of liberation. Practically all material work is performed in ignorance, but because there are three qualities, sometimes the quality of ignorance is covered with goodness or passion. The taste of these material fruits is accepted through five senses. The five sense organs through which knowledge is acquired are subjected to six kinds of whips: lamentation, illusion, infirmity, death, hunger and thirst. This material body, or the material manifestation, is covered by seven layers: skin, flesh, blood, marrow, bone, fat and semen. The branches of the tree are eight: earth, water, fire, air, ether, mind, intelligence and ego. There are nine gates in this body: the two eyes, two nostrils, two ears, one mouth, one genital, one rectum. And there are ten kinds of internal air passing within the body: *prāṇa, apāna, udāna, vyāna, samāna,* etc. The two birds seated in this tree, as explained above, are the living entity and the localized Supreme Personality of Godhead, Paramātmā.

The root cause of the material manifestation described here is the Supreme Personality of Godhead. The Supreme Personality of Godhead expands Himself to take charge of the three qualities of the material world. Viṣṇu takes charge of the mode of goodness, Brahmā takes charge of the mode of passion, and Lord Śiva takes charge of the mode of ignorance. Brahmā, by the mode of passion, creates this manifestation, Lord Viṣṇu maintains this manifestation by the mode of goodness, and Lord Śiva annihilates it by the mode of ignorance. The whole creation ultimately rests in the Supreme Lord. He is the cause of creation, maintenance and dissolution, and when the whole manifestation is dissolved, in its subtle form as the Supreme Lord's energy it rests within His body.

"At present," the demigods prayed, "the Supreme Lord Kṛṣṇa is appearing just for the maintenance of this manifestation. Actually the Supreme Cause is one, but less intelligent persons, being deluded by the three modes of material nature, see that the material world is manifested through different causes. Those who are intelligent can see that the cause is one, Kṛṣṇa." As it is stated in the *Brahma-saṁhitā, īśvaraḥ paramaḥ kṛṣṇaḥ ... sarva-kāraṇa-kāraṇam:* "Kṛṣṇa, the Supreme Personality of Godhead, is the cause of all causes." Brahmā is the deputed agent for creation, Viṣṇu is the expansion of Kṛṣṇa for maintenance, and Lord Śiva is the expansion of Kṛṣṇa for dissolution.

"Our dear Lord," the demigods prayed, "it is very difficult to understand Your eternal form or personality. People in general are unable to understand Your actual form; therefore You are personally descending to exhibit Your original eternal form.

Somehow people can understand the different incarnations of Your Lordship, but they are puzzled to understand the eternal form of Kṛṣṇa with two hands, moving among human beings exactly like one of them. This eternal form of Your Lordship gives ever-increasing transcendental pleasure to the devotees, but for the nondevotees this form is very dangerous." As stated in the *Bhagavad-gītā,* Kṛṣṇa is very pleasing to the *sādhus* (*paritrāṇāya sādhūnām*). But this form is very dangerous for the demons because Kṛṣṇa also descends to kill the demons. He is, therefore, simultaneously pleasing to the devotees and dangerous to the demons.

"Our dear lotus-eyed Lord, You are the source of pure goodness. There are many great sages who simply by *samādhi,* or transcendentally meditating upon Your lotus feet and thus being absorbed in Your thought, have easily transformed the great ocean of nescience created by the material nature into no more than the water in a calf's hoofprint." The purpose of meditation is to focus the mind upon the Personality of Godhead, beginning from His lotus feet. Simply by meditation on the lotus feet of the Lord, great sages cross over this vast ocean of material existence without difficulty.

"O self-illuminated one, the great saintly persons who have crossed over the ocean of nescience by the help of the transcendental boat of Your lotus feet have not taken away that boat. It is still lying on this side." If one takes a boat to cross over a river, the boat also goes with one to the other side of the river. And so when one reaches the destination, how can the same boat be available to those who are still on this side? To answer this difficulty, the demigods say in their prayer that the boat of the Lord's lotus feet is not taken away. The devotees still remaining on this side are able to pass over the ocean of material nature because the pure devotees do not take the boat with them when they cross over. When one simply approaches the boat, the whole ocean of material nescience is reduced to the size of the water in a calf's hoofprint. Therefore, the devotees do not need to take the boat to the other side: they simply cross the ocean immediately. Because the great saintly persons are compassionate toward all conditioned souls, the boat is still lying on this side. In other words, one can meditate upon the lotus feet of the Lord at any time, and by so doing one can cross over the great ocean of material existence.

Meditation means concentration upon the lotus feet of the Lord. Lotus feet indicate the Supreme Personality of Godhead. But those who are impersonalists do not recognize the lotus feet of the Lord, and therefore their object of meditation is something impersonal. The demigods express their mature verdict that persons who are interested in meditating on something void or impersonal cannot cross over the ocean of nescience. Such persons are simply imagining that they have become liberated. "O lotus-eyed Lord! Their intelligence is contaminated because they fail to meditate upon the lotus feet of Your Lordship. As a result of this neglectful activity, the impersonalists fall down again into the material way of conditioned life, although they may temporarily rise to the point of impersonal realization." Impersonalists undergo severe austerities and penances to merge themselves into the Brahman effulgence, or impersonal Brahman existence. But their minds are not free from material contamination; they have simply tried to negate the material ways of thinking. That does not mean that they have become liberated. Thus they fall down.

In the *Bhagavad-gītā* it is stated that the impersonalist has to undergo great tribulation in realizing his ultimate goal. At the beginning of *Śrīmad-Bhāgavatam* it is also stated that without devotional service to the Supreme Personality of Godhead, one cannot achieve liberation from the bondage of fruitive activities. The statement of Lord Kṛṣṇa is there in the *Bhagavad-gītā,* and in *Śrīmad-Bhāgavatam* the statement of the great sage Nārada is there, and here also the demigods confirm it. "Persons who have not taken to devotional service are understood to have come short of the ultimate purpose of knowledge and are not favored by Your grace." The impersonalists simply *think* that they are liberated, but actually they have no feeling for the Personality of Godhead. They think that when Kṛṣṇa comes into the material world He accepts a material body. They therefore overlook the transcendental body of Kṛṣṇa. This is confirmed in the *Bhagavad-gītā: avajānanti māṁ mūḍhāḥ.* In spite of conquering material lust and rising to the point of liberation, the impersonalists fall down. If they are engaged just in knowing things for the sake of knowledge and do not take to the devotional service of the Lord, they cannot achieve the desired result. Their achievement is the trouble they take, and that is all.

It is clearly stated in the *Bhagavad-gītā* that to realize Brahman identification is not all. Brahman identification may help one become joyful without material attachment or detachment and to achieve the platform of equanimity, but after this stage one has to take to devotional service. When one takes to devotional service after being elevated to the platform of Brahman realization, he is then admitted into the spiritual kingdom for permanent residence in association with the Supreme Personality of Godhead. That is the result of devotional service. Those who are devotees of the Supreme Personality of Godhead never fall down like the impersonalists. Even if the devotees fall down, they remain affectionately attached to their Lord. They can meet all kinds of obstacles on the path of devotional service, and freely, without any fear, they can surmount such obstacles. Because of their surrender, they are certain that Kṛṣṇa will always protect them. As it is promised by Kṛṣṇa in the *Bhagavad-gītā,* "My devotees are never vanquished."

"Our dear Lord," the demigods continued, "You have appeared in Your original unalloyed form, the eternal form of goodness, for the welfare of all living entities within this material world. Taking advantage of Your appearance, all of them can now very easily understand the nature and form of the Supreme Personality of Godhead.

Persons who belong to the four divisions of the social order (the *brahmacārīs, gṛhasthas, vānaprasthas* and *sannyāsīs*) can all take advantage of Your appearance.

"Dear Lord, husband of the goddess of fortune, devotees who are dovetailed in Your service do not fall down from their high position like the impersonalists. Being protected by You, the devotees are able to traverse over the heads of many of Māyā's commanders in chief, who can always put stumbling blocks on the path of liberation. Dear Lord, You appear in Your eternal transcendental form for the benefit of the living entities so that they can see You face to face and offer their worshipful sacrifices by ritualistic performance of the *Vedas,* mystic meditation and devotional service as recommended in the scriptures. Dear Lord, if You did not appear in Your eternal transcendental form, full of bliss and knowledge—a form which can eradicate all kinds of speculative ignorance about Your position—then all people would simply speculate about You according to their respective modes of material nature."

The appearance of Kṛṣṇa is the answer to all imaginative iconography of the Supreme Personality of Godhead. Everyone imagines the form of the Supreme Personality of Godhead according to his mode of material nature. In the *Brahma-saṁhitā* it is said that the Lord is the oldest person. Therefore a section of religionists imagine that God must be very old, and therefore they depict a form of the Lord like a very old man. But in the same *Brahma-saṁhitā,* that is contradicted: although He is the oldest of all living entities, He has His eternal form as a fresh youth. The exact words used in this connection in *Śrīmad-Bhāgavatam* are *vijñānam ajñāna-bhidāpamārjanam. Vijñānam* means transcendental knowledge of the Supreme Personality of Godhead. *Vijñānam* is also experienced knowledge. Transcendental knowledge has to be accepted by the descending process of disciplic succession, as Brahmā presents the knowledge of Kṛṣṇa in the *Brahma-saṁhitā.* The *Brahma-saṁhitā* is *vijñānam* as realized by Brahmā's transcendental experience, and in that way he presented the form and the pastimes of Kṛṣṇa in the transcendental abode. This knowledge is *ajñāna-bhidāpamārjanam,* that which can smash all kinds of speculation in ignorance. People are imagining the form of the Lord: sometimes He has no form and sometimes He has form, according to their different imaginations. But the presentation of Kṛṣṇa in the *Brahma-saṁhitā* is *vijñānam*—scientific, experienced knowledge given by Lord Brahmā and accepted by Lord Caitanya. There is no doubt about it. Kṛṣṇa's form, Kṛṣṇa's flute, Kṛṣṇa's color—everything is reality. Here it is said that this *vijñānam* is always defeating all kinds of speculative knowledge. "Therefore, without Your appearing as Kṛṣṇa, as You are, neither *ajñāna-bhidāpamārjanam* (destruction of the nescience of speculative knowledge) nor *vijñānam* would be realized. In other words, Your appearance will vanquish the ignorance of speculative knowledge and establish the real experienced knowledge of authorities like Lord Brahmā. Men influenced by the three modes of material nature imagine their own God according to the modes of material nature. In this way

God is presented in various ways, but Your appearance will establish what the real form of God is."

The highest blunder committed by the impersonalists is to think that when the incarnation of God comes He accepts the form of matter in the mode of goodness. Actually, the form of Kṛṣṇa or Nārāyaṇa is transcendental to any material idea. Even the greatest impersonalist, Śaṅkarācārya, has admitted, *nārāyaṇaḥ paro 'vyaktāt:* the material creation is caused by the *avyakta* (impersonal) manifestation of matter, or the nonphenomenal total reservoir of matter, but Kṛṣṇa is transcendental to that material conception. That is expressed in *Śrīmad-Bhāgavatam* as *śuddha-sattva,* or transcendental goodness. He does not belong to the material mode of goodness, and He is above the position of material goodness. He belongs to the transcendental, eternal status of bliss and knowledge.

"Dear Lord, when You appear in Your different incarnations, You take different names and forms according to different situations. Lord Kṛṣṇa is Your name because You are all-attractive; You are called Śyāmasundara because of Your transcendental beauty. *Śyāma* means 'blackish,' yet it is said that You are more beautiful than thousands of Cupids (*kandarpa-koṭi-kamanīya*). Although You appear in a color which is compared to the blackish cloud, because You are the Transcendental Absolute, Your beauty is many, many times more attractive than the delicate body of Cupid. Sometimes You are called Giridhārī because You lifted the hill known as Govardhana. You are sometimes called Nandanandana or Vāsudeva or Devakīnandana because You appear as the son of Mahārāja Nanda or Vasudeva or Devakī. Impersonalists think that Your many names or forms are given according to a particular type of work and quality because they accept You from the position of a material observer.

"Our dear Lord, the way of understanding is not to study Your absolute nature, form and activities by mental speculation. One must engage himself in devotional service; then one can understand Your absolute nature and Your transcendental form, name and qualities. Actually, only a person who has a little taste for the service of Your lotus feet can understand Your transcendental nature or form and qualities. Others may go on speculating for millions of years, but it is not possible for them to understand even a single part of Your actual position." In other words, the Supreme Personality of Godhead, Kṛṣṇa, cannot be understood by the nondevotees because there is a curtain of Yogamāyā which covers Kṛṣṇa's actual features. As confirmed in the *Bhagavad-gītā, nāhaṁ prakāśaḥ sarvasya.* The Lord says, "I am not exposed to anyone and everyone." When Kṛṣṇa came, He was actually present on the Battlefield of Kurukṣetra, and everyone saw Him. But not everyone could understand that He was the Supreme Personality of Godhead. Still, everyone who died in His presence attained complete liberation from material bondage and was transferred to the spiritual world.

"O Lord, the impersonalists or nondevotees cannot understand that Your name is identical with Your form." Since the Lord is absolute, there is no difference between His name and His actual form. In the material world there is a difference between form and name. The mango fruit is different from the name of the mango. One cannot taste the mango fruit simply by chanting "mango, mango, mango." But the devotee who knows that there is no difference between the name and the form of the Lord chants Hare Kṛṣṇa, Hare Kṛṣṇa, Kṛṣṇa Kṛṣṇa, Hare Hare/ Hare Rāma, Hare Rāma, Rāma Rāma, Hare Hare and realizes that he is always in Kṛṣṇa's company.

For persons who are not very advanced in absolute knowledge of the Supreme, Lord Kṛṣṇa exhibits His transcendental pastimes. Such persons can simply think of the pastimes of the Lord and get full benefit. Since there is no difference between the transcendental name and form of the Lord, there is no difference between the transcendental pastimes and the form of the Lord. For those who are less intelligent (like women, laborers or the mercantile class), the great sage Vyāsadeva wrote the *Mahābhārata.* In the *Mahābhārata* Kṛṣṇa is present in His different activities. The *Mahābhārata* is history, and simply by studying, hearing and memorizing the transcen- dental activities of Kṛṣṇa, the less intelligent can also gradually rise to the standard of pure devotees.

The pure devotees, who are always absorbed in the thought of the transcendental lotus feet of Kṛṣṇa and who are always engaged in devotional service in full Kṛṣṇa consciousness, are never to be considered to be in the material world. Śrīla Rūpa Gosvāmī has explained that those who are always engaged in Kṛṣṇa consciousness with body, mind and activities are to be considered liberated even within this body. This is confirmed in the *Bhagavad-gītā:* those who are engaged in the devotional service of the Lord have already transcended the material position.

Kṛṣṇa appears in order to give a chance to both the devotees and the nondevotees for realization of the ultimate goal of life. The devotees get the direct chance to see Him and worship Him. Those who are not on that platform get the chance to become acquainted with His activities and thus become elevated to the same position.

"Our dear Lord, O supreme controller, when You appear on earth, all the demons like Kaṁsa and Jarāsandha will be vanquished, and all good fortune will be ushered into the world. When You walk on the globe, Your lotus feet will impress on the ground the marks of Your soles, such as the flag, the trident and the thunderbolt. Thus You will grace both the earth and us on the heavenly planets who shall see those marks.

"O dear Lord," the demigods continued, "You are unborn; therefore we do not find any reason for Your appearance other than for Your pleasurable pastimes." Although the reason for the appearance of the Lord is stated in the *Bhagavad-gītā* (He descends just to give protection to the devotees and vanquish the nondevotees), actually He descends for His pleasure-meeting with the devotees, not really to vanquish the nondevotees. The nondevotees can be vanquished simply by one kick of material nature. "The actions and reactions of material nature (creation, maintenance and annihilation) are being carried out automatically. But simply by taking shelter of Your holy name the devotees are sufficiently protected, because Your holy name and Your personality are nondifferent." The protection of the devotees and the annihilation of the nondevotees are actually not the business of the Supreme Personality of Godhead. When He descends, it is just for His transcendental pleasure. There cannot be any other reason for His appearance.

"Our dear Lord, You are appearing as the best of the Yadu dynasty, and we are offering our respectful humble obeisances unto Your lotus feet. Before this appearance, You also appeared as the fish incarnation, as the horse incarnation, as the tortoise incarnation, as the half-man, half-lion incarnation, as the boar incarnation, as the swan incarnation, as King Rāmacandra, as Paraśurāma and as many other incarnations. You appeared just to protect the devotees, and we request You in Your present appearance as the Supreme Personality of Godhead Himself to give us similar protection all over the three worlds and remove all obstacles for the peaceful execution of our lives.

"Dear mother Devakī, within your womb is the Supreme Personality of Godhead, appearing along with all His plenary extensions. He is the original Personality of Godhead, appearing for our welfare. Therefore you should not be afraid of your brother, the King of Bhoja. Your son Lord Kṛṣṇa, who is the original Personality of Godhead, will appear for the protection of the pious Yadu dynasty. The Lord is appearing not alone but accompanied by His immediate plenary portion, Baladeva."

Devakī was very much afraid of her brother Kaṁsa because he had already killed so many of her children. So she was very anxious about Kṛṣṇa. In the *Viṣṇu Purāṇa* it is stated that in order to pacify Devakī, all the demigods, along with their wives, used to visit her to encourage her not to be afraid that her son would be killed by Kaṁsa. Kṛṣṇa, who was within her womb, was to appear not only to diminish the burden of the world but specifically to protect the interests of the Yadu dynasty, and certainly to protect Devakī and Vasudeva. It is understood that Kṛṣṇa had been transferred from the mind of Vasudeva to the mind of Devakī, and from there to her womb. Thus all the demigods worshiped Devakī, the mother of Kṛṣṇa.

After thus worshiping the transcendental form of the Lord, all the demigods, with Lord Brahmā and Lord Śiva placed in front, departed for their heavenly abodes.

Thus ends the Bhaktivedanta purport of the Second Chapter of Kṛṣṇa, *"Prayers by the Demigods for Lord Kṛṣṇa in the Womb."*

CHAPTER 3

The Birth of Lord Kṛṣṇa

IN THE *BHAGAVAD-GĪTĀ* THE LORD says that His appearance, birth and activities are all transcendental and that one who understands them factually becomes immediately eligible to be transferred to the spiritual world. The Lord's appearance or birth is not like that of an ordinary man, who is forced to accept a material body according to his past deeds. The Lord's appearance is explained in the Second Chapter: He appears out of His own sweet pleasure. When the time was mature for the appearance of the Lord, the constellations became very auspicious. The astrological influence of the star known as Rohiṇī was predominant. This star is considered to be very auspicious and is under the direct supervision of Brahmā. According to the astrological conclusion, besides the proper situation of the stars, there are auspicious and inauspicious moments due to the different situations of the different planetary systems. At the time of Kṛṣṇa's birth, the planetary systems were automatically adjusted so that everything became auspicious.

At that time, in all directions—east, west, south, north, everywhere—there was an atmosphere of peace and prosperity. There were auspicious stars visible in the sky, and on the surface in all towns and villages and pasturing grounds and within the minds of everyone there were signs of good fortune. The rivers were flowing full of waters, and lakes were beautifully decorated with lotus flowers. The forests were full with beautiful birds and peacocks. All the birds within the forests began to sing with sweet voices, and the peacocks began to dance along with their consorts. The wind blew very pleasantly, carrying the aroma of different flowers, and the sensation of bodily touch was very pleasing. At home, the *brāhmaṇas,* who were accustomed to offering sacrifices in the fire, found their homes very pleasant for offerings. Due to disturbances created by the demoniac kings, the sacrificial fire had been almost stopped in the houses of *brāhmaṇas,* but now they could find the opportunity to start the fire peacefully. Being forbidden to offer sacrifices, the *brāhmaṇas* had been very much distressed in mind, intelligence and activities, but just on the point of Kṛṣṇa's appearance, automatically their minds became full of joy because they could hear transcendental vibrations in the sky proclaiming the appearance of the Supreme Personality of Godhead.

The denizens of the Gandharva and Kinnara planets began to sing, and the denizens of Siddhaloka and the planets of the Cāraṇas began to offer prayers in the service of the Personality of Godhead. In the heavenly planets, the angels and their wives, along with the Vidyādharas and their wives, began to dance.

The great sages and the demigods, being pleased, began to shower flowers. At the seashore there was the sound of mild waves, and above the sea there were clouds in the sky which began to thunder very pleasingly.

When things were adjusted like this, Lord Viṣṇu, who is residing within the heart of every living entity, appeared in the darkness of night as the Supreme Personality of Godhead before Devakī, who appeared as one of the demigoddesses. The appearance of Lord Viṣṇu at that time could be compared to the rising of the full moon over the eastern horizon. The objection may be raised that since Lord Kṛṣṇa appeared on the eighth day of the waning moon, there could be no rising of the full moon. In answer to this it may be said that Lord Kṛṣṇa appeared in the dynasty which is in the hierarchy of the moon; therefore, although the moon was incomplete on that night, because of the Lord's appearance in the dynasty wherein the moon is himself the original person, the moon was in an overjoyous condition, so by the grace of Kṛṣṇa he could appear just like a full moon.

In an astronomical treatise by the name *Khamaṇikya,* the constellations at the time of the appearance of Lord Kṛṣṇa are very nicely described. It is confirmed that the child born at that auspicious moment was the Supreme Brahman, or the Absolute Truth.

Vasudeva saw that wonderful child born as a baby with four hands, holding conchshell, club, disc and lotus flower, decorated with the mark of Śrīvatsa, wearing the jeweled necklace of *kaustubha* stone, dressed in yellow silk, appearing dazzling like a bright blackish cloud, wearing a helmet bedecked with the *vaidūrya* stone, valuable bracelets, earrings and similar other ornaments all over His body, and beautified by an abundance of hair on His head. Due to the extraordinary features of the child, Vasudeva was struck with wonder. How could a newly born child be so decorated? He could therefore understand that Lord Kṛṣṇa had now appeared, and he became overpowered by the occasion. Vasudeva very humbly wondered that although he was an ordinary living entity conditioned by material nature and was externally imprisoned by Kaṁsa, the all-pervading Personality of Godhead, Viṣṇu, or Kṛṣṇa, had appeared as a child in his home, exactly in His original position. No earthly child is born with four hands, decorated with ornaments and nice clothing, fully equipped with all the signs of the Supreme Personality of Godhead. Over and over again Vasudeva glanced at his child, and he considered how to celebrate this auspicious moment, "Generally, when a male child is born," he thought, "people observe the occasion with jubilant celebrations, and in my home, although I am imprisoned, the Supreme Personality of Godhead has taken birth. How many millions and millions of times should I be prepared to observe this auspicious ceremony!"

When Vasudeva, who is also called Ānakadundubhi, was looking at his newborn baby, he was so happy that he wanted to give many thousands of cows in charity to the *brāhmaṇas.* According to the Vedic system, whenever there is an auspicious ceremony in the *kṣatriya* king's palace, out of joy the king gives many things in charity. Cows decorated with golden ornaments are delivered to the *brāhmaṇas* and sages. Vasudeva wanted to perform a charitable ceremony to celebrate Kṛṣṇa's appearance, but because he was shackled within the walls of Kaṁsa's prison, this was not possible. Instead, within his mind he gave thousands of cows to the *brāhmaṇas.*

When Vasudeva was convinced that the newborn child was the Supreme Personality of Godhead Himself, he bowed down with folded hands and began to offer Him prayers. At that time Vasudeva was in the transcendental position, and he became completely free from all fear of Kaṁsa. The newborn baby was also flashing His effulgence within the room in which He appeared.

Vasudeva then began to offer his prayers. "My dear Lord, I can understand who You are. You are the Supreme Personality of Godhead, the Supersoul of all living entities and the Absolute Truth. You have appeared in Your own eternal form, which is directly perceived by us. I understand that because I am afraid of Kaṁsa You have appeared just to deliver me from that fear. You do not belong to this material world; You are the same person who brings about the cosmic manifestation simply by glancing over material nature."

One may argue that the Supreme Personality of Godhead, who creates the whole cosmic manifestation simply by His glance, cannot come within the womb of Devakī, the wife of Vasudeva. To eradicate this argument, Vasudeva said, "My dear Lord, it is not a very wonderful thing that You have appeared within the womb of Devakī, because the creation was also made in that way. You were lying in the Causal Ocean as Mahā-Viṣṇu, and by Your breathing process, innumerable universes came into existence. Then You entered into each of the universes as Garbhodakaśāyī Viṣṇu. Then again You expanded Yourself as Kṣīrodakaśāyī Viṣṇu and entered into the hearts of all living entities and even within the atoms. Therefore Your entrance into the womb of Devakī is understandable in the same way. You appear to have entered, but You are simultaneously all-pervading. We can understand Your entrance and nonentrance from material examples. The total material energy remains intact even after being divided into sixteen elements. The material body is nothing but the combination of the five gross elements—namely earth, water, fire, air and ether. Whenever there is a material body, it appears that such elements are newly created, but actually the elements are always existing outside of the body. Similarly, although You have appeared as a child in the womb of Devakī, You are also existing outside. You are always in Your abode, but still You can simultaneously expand Yourself into millions of forms.

"One has to understand Your appearance with great intelligence because the material energy is also emanating from You. You are the original source of the material energy, just as the sun is the source of the sunshine. The sunshine cannot cover the sun globe, nor can the material energy—being an emanation from You—cover You. You appear to be in the three modes of material energy, but actually the three modes of material energy cannot cover You. This is understood by the highly intellectual philosophers. In other words, although You appear to be within the material energy, You are never covered by it."

We hear from the Vedic version that the Supreme Brahman exhibits His effulgence and therefore everything becomes illuminated. We can understand from the *Brahma-saṁhitā* that the *brahmajyoti,* or the Brahman effulgence, emanates from the body of the Supreme Lord. And from the Brahman effulgence, all creation takes place. It is also stated in the *Bhagavad-gītā* that the Lord is the support of the Brahman effulgence. Therefore, originally He is the root cause of everything. But persons who are less intelligent think that when the Supreme Personality of Godhead comes within this material world, He accepts the material qualities. Such conclusions are not very mature, but are made by the less intelligent.

The Supreme Personality of Godhead is directly and indirectly existing everywhere; He is outside this material creation, and He is also within it. He is within this material creation not only as Garbhodakaśāyī Viṣṇu; He is also within the atom. The existence of the atom is due to His presence. Nothing can be separated from His existence. In the Vedic injunctions we find that the Supreme Soul, or the root cause of everything, has to be searched out because nothing exists independently of the Supreme Soul. Therefore the material manifestation is also a transformation of His potency. Both inert matter and the living force—the soul—are emanations from Him. Only the foolish conclude that when the Supreme Lord appears He accepts the conditions of matter. Even if He appears to have accepted a material body, He is still not subjected to any material condition. Kṛṣṇa has therefore appeared and defeated all imperfect conclusions about the appearance and disappearance of the Supreme Personality of Godhead.

"My Lord, Your appearance, existence and disappearance are beyond the influence of the material qualities. Because Your Lordship is the Supreme Brahman and the controller of everything, there is nothing inconceivable or contradictory in You. As You have said, material nature works under Your superintendence, just like a government officer working under the orders of the chief executive. The influence of subordinate activities cannot affect You. Since You are the Supreme Brahman, everything is existing within You, and since all the activities of material nature are controlled by Your Lordship, none of these activities affect You.

"You are called *śuklam. Śuklam,* or 'whiteness,' is the symbolic representation of the Absolute Truth because it is unaffected by the material qualities. Lord Brahmā is called *rakta,* or red, because Brahmā represents the quality of passion for creation. Darkness is entrusted to Lord Śiva because he annihilates the cosmos. The creation, annihilation and maintenance of this cosmic manifestation are conducted by Your potencies, yet You are always unaffected by those qualities. As confirmed in the *Vedas, harir hi nirguṇaḥ sākṣāt:* 'The Supreme Personality of Godhead is always free from all material qualities.' It is also said that the qualities of passion and ignorance are nonexistent in the person of the Supreme Lord.

"My Lord, You are the supreme controller, the Personality of Godhead, the supreme great, maintaining the order of this cosmic manifestation. Yet in spite of Your being the supreme controller, You have so kindly appeared in my home. The purpose of Your appearance is to kill the followers of the demoniac rulers of the world, who are in the dress of royal princes but are actually demons. I am sure that You will kill all of them and their followers and soldiers.

"I understand that You have appeared in order to kill the uncivilized Kaṁsa and his followers. But knowing that You were to appear in order to kill him and his followers, he has already killed so many of Your predecessors, Your elder brothers. Now he is simply awaiting the news of Your birth. As soon as he hears about it, he will immediately appear with all kinds of weapons to kill You."

After this prayer of Vasudeva, Devakī, the mother of Kṛṣṇa, offered her prayers. She was very frightened because of her brother's atrocities. Devakī said, "My dear Lord, Your eternal forms, like Nārāyaṇa, Lord Rāma, Hayaśīrṣa, Varāha, Nṛsiṁha, Vāmana, Baladeva and millions of similar incarnations emanating from Viṣṇu, are described in the Vedic literature as original. You are original because all Your forms as incarnations are outside of this material creation. Your form was existing before this cosmic manifestation was created. Your forms are eternal and all-pervading. They are also self-effulgent, changeless and uncontaminated by the material qualities. Such eternal forms are ever cognizant and full of bliss; they are situated in transcendental goodness and are always engaged in different pastimes. You are not limited to a particular form only; all such transcendental, eternal forms are self-sufficient. I can understand that You are the Supreme Lord Viṣṇu.

"After many millions of years, when Lord Brahmā comes to the end of his life, the annihilation of the cosmic manifestation takes place. At that time the five elements—namely earth, water, fire, air and ether—enter into the *mahat-tattva*. The *mahat-tattva* then enters, by the force of time, into the nonmanifested total material energy, the total material energy enters into the energetic *pradhāna*, and the *pradhāna* enters into You. Therefore after the annihilation of the whole cosmic manifestation, You alone remain with Your transcendental name, form, qualities and paraphernalia.

"My Lord, I offer my respectful obeisances unto You because You are the director of the unmanifested total energy and the ultimate reservoir of the material nature. My Lord, the whole cosmic manifestation is under the influence of time, beginning from the moment up to the duration of the year. All act under Your direction. You are the original director of everything and the reservoir of all potent energies.

"All the conditioned souls are continually fleeing from one body to another and one planet to another, yet they do not get free from the onslaught of birth and death. But when one of these fearful living entities comes under the shelter of Your lotus feet, he can lie down without anxiety of being attacked by formidable death." This statement by Devakī is confirmed in the *Bhagavad-gītā* by the Lord Himself. There the Lord says that even after traveling all over the universe, from Brahmaloka to Pātālaloka, one cannot escape the attack of birth, death, disease and old age. But one who enters the kingdom of God, the Lord says, is never again obliged to come to the material world.

"Therefore, my Lord, I request You to save me from the cruel hands of Kaṁsa, the son of Ugrasena. I am praying to Your Lordship to please rescue me from this fearful condition because You are always ready to give protection to Your servitors." The Lord has confirmed this statement in the *Bhagavad-gītā* by assuring Arjuna, "You may declare to the world, My devotee shall never be vanquished."

While thus praying to the Lord for rescue, mother Devakī nonetheless expressed her motherly affection: "I understand that this transcendental form is generally perceived in meditation by the great sages, but I am still afraid because as soon as Kaṁsa understands that You have appeared, he might harm You. So I request that for the time being You become invisible to our material eyes." In other words, she requested the Lord to assume the form of an ordinary child. "My only cause of fear from my brother Kaṁsa is due to Your appearance. My Lord Madhusūdana, Kaṁsa may not know that You are already born. Therefore I request You to conceal this four-armed form of Your

Lordship, which holds the four symbols of Viṣṇu— namely the conchshell, the disc, the club and the lotus flower. My dear Lord, at the end of the annihilation of the cosmic manifestation, You put the whole universe within Your abdomen; still, by Your unalloyed mercy You have appeared in my womb. I am surprised that You imitate the activities of ordinary human beings just to please Your devotee."

On hearing the prayers of Devakī, the Lord replied, "My dear mother, in the millennium of Svāyambhuva Manu, My father Vasudeva was living as one of the Prajāpatis. His name at that time was Sutapā, and you were his wife named Pṛśni. At that time, when Lord Brahmā was desiring to increase the population, he requested you to generate offspring. You controlled your senses and performed severe austerities. By practicing the breathing exercises of the *yoga* system, both you and your husband could tolerate all the influences of the material laws: the rainy season, the onslaught of the wind, and the scorching heat of the sunshine. You also executed all religious principles. In this way you were able to cleanse your heart and control the influences of the material laws. In executing your austerity, you used to eat only the leaves of the trees which fell to the ground. Then with a steady mind and controlled sex drive, you worshiped Me, desiring some wonderful benediction from Me. Both of you practiced severe austerities for twelve thousand years by the calculation of the demigods. During that time, your mind was always absorbed in Me. When you were executing devotional service and always thinking of Me within your heart, I was very pleased with you. O sinless mother, your heart is therefore always pure. At that time also I appeared before you in this form just to fulfill your desire, and I asked you to ask whatever you desired. At that time you wished to have Me born as your son. Although you saw Me personally, instead of asking for your complete liberation from material bondage, under the influence of My energy you asked Me to become your son."

In other words, to appear in the material world the Lord selected His mother and father—namely Pṛśni and Sutapā, respectively. Whenever the Lord comes as a human being, He must have a mother and a father, so He selected Pṛśni and Sutapā perpetually as His mother and father. And on account of this, neither Pṛśni nor Sutapā could ask the Lord for liberation. Liberation is not so important as the transcendental loving service of the Lord. The Lord could have awarded Pṛśni and Sutapā immediate liberation, but He preferred to keep them within this material world for His different appearances, as will be explained in the following verses. On receiving the benediction from the Lord to become His father and mother, Sutapā and Pṛśni retired from the activities of austerity and lived as husband and wife in order to beget a child who was the Supreme Lord Himself.

In due course of time Pṛśni became pregnant and gave birth to the child. The Lord spoke to Devakī and Vasudeva: "At that time My name was Pṛśnigarbha. In the next millennium you took birth as Aditi and Kaśyapa, and I became your child of the name

Upendra. At that time My form was just like a dwarf, and for this reason I was known as Vāmanadeva. I gave you the benediction that I would take birth as your son three times. The first time I was known as Pṛśnigarbha, born of Pṛśni and Sutapā, in the next birth I was Upendra, born of Aditi and Kaśyapa, and now for the third time I am born as Kṛṣṇa from you, Devakī and Vasudeva. I have appeared in this Viṣṇu form just to convince you that I am the same Supreme Personality of Godhead again taken birth. I could have appeared just like an ordinary child, but in that way you would not have believed that the Supreme Personality of Godhead had taken birth in your womb. My dear father and mother, you have therefore raised Me many times as your child, with great affection and love, and I am therefore very much pleased and obliged to you. And I assure you that this time you shall go back home, back to Godhead, on account of your perfection in your mission. I know you are very concerned about Me and afraid of Kaṁsa. Therefore I order you to take Me immediately to Gokula and exchange Me for the daughter who has just been born to Yaśodā."

Having spoken thus to His father and mother, the Lord turned Himself into an ordinary child in their presence and remained silent.

Being ordered by the Supreme Personality of Godhead, Vasudeva prepared to take his son from the delivery room, and exactly at that time, a daughter was born to Nanda and Yaśodā. She was Yogamāyā, the internal potency of the Lord. By the influence of this internal potency, Yogamāyā, all the residents of Kaṁsa's palace, especially the doorkeepers, were overwhelmed with deep sleep, and all the palace doors opened, although they were barred and shackled with iron chains. The night was very dark, but as soon as Vasudeva took Kṛṣṇa on his lap and went out, he could see everything just as in the sunlight.

In the *Caitanya-caritāmṛta* it is said that Kṛṣṇa is just like sunlight and that wherever there is Kṛṣṇa the illusory energy, which is compared to darkness, cannot remain. When Vasudeva was carrying Kṛṣṇa, the darkness of the night disappeared. All the prison doors automatically opened. At the same time there was thunder in the sky and severe rainfall. While Vasudeva was carrying his son Kṛṣṇa in the falling rain, Lord Śeṣa in the shape of a serpent spread His hood over the head of Vasudeva so that he would not be hampered by the rainfall. Vasudeva came onto the bank of the Yamunā and saw that the water of the Yamunā was roaring with waves and that the whole span was full of foam. Still, in that furious feature, the river gave passage to Vasudeva to cross, just as the great Indian Ocean gave a path to Lord Rāma when He was bridging over the gulf. In this way Vasudeva crossed the river Yamunā. On the other side, he went to the place of Nanda Mahārāja, situated in Gokula, where he saw that all the cowherd men were fast asleep. He took the opportunity to silently enter the house of Yaśodā, and without difficulty he exchanged his son for the baby girl newly born there. Then, after entering the house very silently and exchanging the boy for the girl, he returned to the prison of Kaṁsa and silently put the girl on the lap of Devakī. He again clamped the shackles on himself so that Kaṁsa could not recognize that so many things had happened.

Mother Yaśodā understood that a child had been born to her, but because she was very tired from the labor of childbirth, she fell fast asleep. When she awoke, she could not remember whether she had given birth to a male or a female child.

Thus ends the Bhaktivedanta purport of the Third Chapter of Kṛṣṇa, *"The Birth of Lord Kṛṣṇa."*

CHAPTER 4

Kaṁsa Begins His Persecutions

AFTER VASUDEVA ADJUSTED THINGS as they had been before he carried Kṛṣṇa to Gokula, and all the doors and gates became similarly closed, the gatekeepers awoke and heard the newborn child crying. Kaṁsa was waiting to hear the news of the child's birth, and the gatekeepers immediately approached him and informed him that the child was born. At that time, Kaṁsa got up from his bed very quickly and exclaimed, "Now the cruel death of my life is born!" Kaṁsa became perplexed now that his death was approaching, and his hair scattered. Immediately he proceeded toward the place where the child was born. Devakī, on seeing her brother approaching, prayed in a very meek attitude to Kaṁsa: "My dear brother, please do not kill this female child. I promise that this child will be the wife of your son; therefore don't kill her. You are not to be killed by any female child. That was the prophecy. You are to be killed by a male child, so please do not kill her. My dear brother, you have killed so many of my children who were just born, shining like the sun. That is not your fault. You have been advised by demoniac friends to kill my children. But now I beg you to excuse this girl at least. Let her live as my daughter."

Kaṁsa was so cruel that he did not listen to the pitiful prayers of his sister Devakī. He forcibly grabbed the newborn child to rebuke his sister and attempted to dash her on the stone mercilessly. This is a graphic example of a cruel demon who could sacrifice all relationships for the sake of personal gratification. But the child immediately slipped out of his hands, went up into the sky and appeared with eight arms as the younger sister of Viṣṇu. She was decorated with nice garments and flower garlands and ornaments; in her eight hands she held a bow, lance, arrows, sword, conchshell, disc, club and shield.

Seeing the appearance of the child (who was actually the goddess Durgā), all the demigods from different planets like Siddhaloka, Cāraṇaloka, Gandharvaloka, Apsaroloka, Kinnaraloka and Uragaloka presented her with various articles and began to offer their respective prayers. From above, the goddess addressed Kaṁsa: "You rascal, how can you kill me? The child who will kill you is already born before me somewhere within this world. Don't be so cruel to your poor sister." After this appearance, goddess Durgā became known by various names in various parts of the world.

After hearing these words, Kaṁsa became very much overwhelmed with fear. Out of pity, he immediately released Vasudeva and Devakī from the bondage of their shackles and very politely began to address them. He said, "My dear sister and brother-in-law, I have acted just like a demon in killing my own nephews—your children—and thereby I have given up all consideration of our intimate relationship. I do not know what will be the result of these envious acts of mine. Probably I shall be sent to the hell where killers of *brāhmaṇas* go. I am surprised, however, that the celestial prophecy has not come true. It is not only in human society that false propaganda is found. Now it appears that even the celestial denizens speak lies. Because I believed in the words of the celestial denizens, I have committed so many sins by killing the children of my sister. My dear Vasudeva and Devakī, you are both very great souls. I have no instructions to give you, but still I request that you not be sorry for the death of your children. Every one of us is under the control of superior power, and that superior power does not allow us to remain together. We are bound to be separated from our friends and relatives in due course of time. But we must know for certain that even after the disappearance of the different material bodies, the soul remains intact eternally. For example, there are many pots made of earthly clay, and they are prepared and also broken. But in spite of this, the earth remains as it is perpetually. Similarly, the bodies of the soul under different conditions are made and destroyed, but the spirit soul remains eternally. So there is nothing to lament over. Everyone should understand that this material body is different from the spirit soul, and so long as one does not come to that understanding, he is sure to accept the processes of transmigration from one body to another."

"My dear sister Devakī, you are so gentle and kind. Please excuse me—don't be aggrieved by the death of your children, which I have caused. Actually this was not done by me, because all these are predestined activities. One has to act according to the predestined plan, even unwillingly. People misunderstand that with the end of the body the self dies, or they think that one can kill another living entity. All these misconceptions oblige one to accept the conditions of material existence. In other words, as long as one is not firmly convinced of the eternality of the soul, one is subjected to the tribulation of being killer and killed. My dear sister Devakī and brother-in-law Vasudeva, kindly excuse the atrocities I have committed against you. I am very poor-hearted, and you are so great-hearted, so take compassion upon me and excuse me."

While Kaṁsa was speaking to his brother-in-law and sister, tears flowed from his eyes, and he fell down at their feet. Believing the words of Durgādevī, whom he had tried to kill, Kaṁsa immediately released his brother-in-law and sister. He personally unlocked the iron shackles and very sympathetically showed his friendship for his family members.

When Devakī saw her brother so repentant, she also became pacified and forgot all his atrocious activities against her children. Vasudeva also, forgetting all past incidents, spoke smilingly with his brother-in-law. Vasudeva told Kaṁsa, "My dear fortunate brother-in-law, what you are saying about the material body and the soul is correct. Every living entity is born ignorant, misunderstanding this material body to be his self. This conception of life is due to ignorance, and on the basis of this ignorance we create enmity or friendship. Lamentation, jubilation, fearfulness, envy, greed, illusion and madness are different features of our material concept of life. A person influenced like this engages in enmity only due to the material body. Being engaged in such activities, we forget our eternal relationship with the Supreme Personality of Godhead."

Vasudeva took the opportunity of Kaṁsa's benevolence and informed him that his atheistic activities were also due to this misconception of life—namely taking the material body to be the self. When Vasudeva talked with Kaṁsa in such an illuminating way, Kaṁsa became very pleased, and his guilt for killing his nephews subsided. With the permission of his sister Devakī and brother-in-law Vasudeva, he returned to his home with a relieved mind.

But the next day Kaṁsa called all his counselors together and narrated to them all the incidents that had happened the night before. All the counselors of Kaṁsa were demons and eternal enemies of the demigods, so they became depressed upon hearing their master speak of the night's events. And although they were not very much experienced or learned, they began to give instructions to Kaṁsa as follows: "Dear sir, let us now make arrangements to kill all children who were born within the last ten days in all towns, counties, villages and pasturing grounds. Let us execute this plan indiscriminately. We think that the demigods cannot do anything against us if we perform these atrocities. They are always afraid of fighting with us, and even if they wish to check our activities, they will not dare to do so. Because of your immeasurable strength, they fear your bow. Indeed, we have practical experience that whenever you stood to fight with them and began to shower your arrows on them, they immediately fled in all directions just to save their lives. Many of the demigods were unable to fight with you, and they immediately surrendered themselves unto you by loosening their turbans and the tufts of hair on their heads. With folded hands they begged you to spare them and said, 'My lord, we are all afraid of your strength. Please release us from this dangerous fight.' We have also seen many times that you would never kill such surrendered fighters when they were all fearful, their bows, arrows and chariots broken, forgetful of their military activities and unable to fight with you. So actually we have nothing to fear from these demigods. They are very proud of being great fighters in peacetime outside the war field, but actually they cannot show any talent or military power on the war field. Although Lord Viṣṇu, Lord Śiva and Lord Brahmā are always ready to help the demigods, headed by Indra, we have no reason to be afraid of them. As far as Lord Viṣṇu is concerned, He has already hidden Himself within the hearts of all living entities, and He cannot come out. As far as Lord Śiva is concerned, he has renounced all activities; he has already entered into the forest. And Lord Brahmā is always engaged in different types of austerities and meditation. And what to speak of Indra—he is a straw in comparison to your strength. Therefore we have nothing to fear from any of these demigods. But we must not neglect them, for the demigods are our determined enemies. We must be careful to protect ourselves. To root them out from their very existence, we should just engage ourselves in your service and be always ready for your command."

The demons continued to say, "If there is some disease in the body which is neglected, it worsens and becomes incurable. Similarly, when one is not careful about restraining the senses and lets them loose, it is then very difficult to control them. Therefore, we must now be very careful of the demigods before they get too strong to be subdued. The foundation of the strength of the demigods is Lord Viṣṇu, because the ultimate goal of all religious principles is to satisfy Him. The Vedic injunctions, the *brāhmaṇas,* the cows, austerities, sacrifices, performances of charity and distribution of wealth are all for the satisfaction of Lord Viṣṇu. So let us immediately begin by killing all the *brāhmaṇas* who are in charge of the Vedic knowledge, along with the great sages who are in charge of sacrificial ritualistic performances. Let us kill all the cows, which are the source of butter, which is so necessary for performing sacrifices. Please give us your permission to kill all these creatures.

"Actually the limbs of the transcendental body of Lord Viṣṇu are the *brāhmaṇas,* the cows, Vedic knowledge, austerity, truthfulness, sense and mind control, faithfulness, charity, tolerance and performance of sacrifices. Lord Viṣṇu is situated in everyone's heart and is the leader of all demigods, including Lord Śiva and Lord Brahmā. Therefore we think that to persecute the great sages and *brāhmaṇas* is to kill Lord Viṣṇu."

Thus being advised by his demoniac ministers, Kaṁsa, who was from the very beginning the greatest rascal, decided to persecute the *brāhmaṇas* and Vaiṣṇavas, being entrapped by the shackles of all-devouring, eternal time. He ordered the demons to harass all kinds of saintly persons, and then he entered his house. The adherents of Kaṁsa were all influenced by the mode of passion as well as illusioned by the mode of ignorance, and their only business was to create enmity with saintly persons. Such activities can only reduce one's duration of life. The demons accelerated the process and invited their deaths as soon as possible. The result of persecuting saintly persons is not only untimely death. The act is so offensive that the perpetrator also gradually loses his beauty, his fame and his religious principles, and thus his promotion to higher planets is checked. Driven by various kinds of mental concoctions, the demons diminish all kinds of auspiciousness. An offense at the lotus feet of the devotees and *brāhmaṇas* is a greater offense than that committed at the lotus feet of the Supreme Personality of Godhead. A civilization that commits such sinful activities generally loses all faith in the Supreme Lord, and such a godless civilization becomes the source of all calamities in human society.

Thus ends the Bhaktivedanta purport of the Fourth Chapter of Kṛṣṇa, *"Kaṁsa Begins His Persecutions."*

CHAPTER 5

The Meeting of Nanda and Vasudeva

ALTHOUGH KṚṢṆA WAS THE REAL SON of Vasudeva and Devakī, because of Kaṁsa's atrocious activities Vasudeva could not enjoy the birth ceremony of his son. But Nanda Mahārāja, the foster father, celebrated the birth ceremony of Kṛṣṇa very joyfully. The next day, it was declared that a male child had been born to Yaśodā. According to Vedic custom, Nanda Mahārāja called for learned astrologers and *brāhmaṇas* to perform the birth ceremony. After the birth of a child, the astrologers calculate the moment of the birth and make a horoscope of the child's future life.

Another ceremony takes place after the birth of the child: the family members take baths, cleanse themselves and decorate themselves with ornaments and nice garments; then they come before the child and the astrologer to hear of the future life of the child. Nanda Mahārāja and other members of the family dressed and sat down in front of the birthplace. All the *brāhmaṇas* who were assembled there on this occasion chanted auspicious *mantras,* according to the rituals, while the astrologers performed the birth ceremony. All the demigods are also worshiped on this occasion, as well as the forefathers of the family. Nanda Mahārāja distributed to the *brāhmaṇas* 200,000 cows, which were well decorated with cloth and ornaments. He gave the *brāhmaṇas* not only cows in charity but also hills of grain decorated with ornaments and golden-bordered cloth.

In the material world we possess riches and wealth in many ways, but sometimes not in very honest and pious ways, because that is the nature of accumulating wealth. According to Vedic injunction, therefore, one should purify such wealth by giving cows and gold in charity to the *brāhmaṇas.* A newborn child is also purified by gifts of grains in charity to the *brāhmaṇas.* In this material world it is to be understood that we are always living in a contaminated state. We therefore have to purify the duration of our lives, our possession of wealth and our self. We can purify our duration of life by taking a daily bath and cleansing the body inside and outside and accepting the ten kinds of purificatory processes. By austerities, by worship of the Lord, and by distribution of charity, we can purify the possession of wealth. We can purify our self by studying the *Vedas* in order to understand the Absolute Truth and achieve self-realization. It is therefore stated in the Vedic literature that by birth everyone is born a *śūdra,* that by accepting the purificatory process one becomes twice-born, that by studying the *Vedas* one becomes a *vipra,* which is the preliminary qualification for becoming a *brāhmaṇa,* and that when one perfectly understands the Absolute Truth he is called a *brāhmaṇa.* And when the *brāhmaṇa* reaches further perfection, he becomes a Vaiṣṇava, or a devotee.

In Kṛṣṇa's birth ceremony, all the assembled *brāhmaṇas* began to chant different kinds of Vedic *mantras* to invoke all good fortune for the child. There are different kinds of chanting, known as *sūta, māgadha, vandī* and *virudāvalī.* Along with this chanting of *mantras* and songs, bugles and kettledrums sounded outside the house. On this occasion, the joyous vibrations could be heard in all the pasturing grounds and all the houses. Within and outside of the houses there were varieties of artistic paintings, done with rice pulp, and scented water was sprinkled everywhere, even on the roads and streets. Ceilings and roofs were decorated with different kinds of flags, festoons and green leaves. The gates were made of green leaves and flowers. All the cows, bulls and calves were smeared with a mixture of oil and turmeric and painted with minerals like red oxide, yellow clay and manganese. They wore garlands of peacock feathers and were covered with nice colored cloths and gold necklaces.

When all the ecstatic cowherd men heard that Nanda Mahārāja, the father of Kṛṣṇa, was celebrating the birth ceremony of his son, they became spontaneously joyful. They dressed themselves with very costly garments and ornamented their bodies with different kinds of earrings and necklaces and wore great turbans on their heads. After dressing themselves in this gorgeous way, they took various kinds of presentations and thus approached the house of Nanda Mahārāja.

As soon as they heard that mother Yaśodā had given birth to a child, all the cowherd women became overwhelmed with joy, and they also dressed themselves with various kinds of costly garments and ornaments and smeared scented cosmetics on their bodies.

As the dust on the lotus flower exhibits the exquisite beauty of the flower, all the *gopīs* (cowherd women) applied the dust of *kuṅkuma* on their lotuslike faces. These beautiful *gopīs* took their different presentations and very soon reached the house of Mahārāja Nanda. Overburdened with their heavy hips and swollen breasts, the *gopīs* could not proceed very quickly toward the house of Nanda Mahārāja, but out of ecstatic love for Kṛṣṇa they proceeded as quickly as possible. Their ears were decorated with pearl rings, their necks were decorated with jeweled lockets, their lips and eyes were decorated with different kinds of lipstick and ointment, and their hands were decorated with nice golden bangles. As they were very hastily passing over the stone road, the flower garlands which were decorating their bodies fell to the ground, and it appeared that a shower of flowers was falling from the sky. From the movement of the different kinds of ornaments on their bodies, they were looking still more beautiful. In this way, they all reached the house of Nanda-Yaśodā and blessed the child: "Dear child, You live long just to protect us." While they were blessing child Kṛṣṇa in this way, they offered a mixture of turmeric powder, oil, yogurt, milk and water. They sprinkled this mixture not only on the body of child Kṛṣṇa but on all other persons who were present there. Also on that auspicious occasion, there were different bands of expert musicians playing.

When the cowherd men saw the pastimes of the cowherd women, they became very joyful, and in response they also began to throw yogurt, milk, clarified butter and water upon the bodies of the *gopīs.* Then both parties began to throw butter on each other's bodies. Nanda Mahārāja was also very happy to see the pastimes of the cowherd men and women, and he became very liberal in giving charity to the different singers who were assembled there. Some singers were reciting great verses from the *Upaniṣads* and *Purāṇas,* some were glorifying the family ancestors, and some were singing very sweet songs. There were also many learned *brāhmaṇas* present, and Nanda Mahārāja, being very satisfied on this occasion, gave them different kinds of garments, ornaments and cows in charity.

It is very important to note in this connection how wealthy the inhabitants of Vṛndāvana were simply by raising cows. All the cowherd men belonged to the *vaiśya* community, and their business was to protect the cows and cultivate crops. By their dress and ornaments, and by their behavior, it appears that although they were in a small village, they still were rich in material possessions. They possessed such an abundance of various kinds of milk products that they were throwing butter lavishly on each other's bodies without restriction. Their wealth was in milk, yogurt, clarified butter and many other milk products, and by trading their agricultural products, they were rich in various kinds of jewelry, ornaments and costly garments. Not only did they possess all these things, but they could give them away in charity lavishly, as did Nanda Mahārāja.

Thus Nanda Mahārāja, the foster father of Lord Kṛṣṇa, began to satisfy the desires of all the men assembled there. He respectfully received them and gave them in charity whatever they desired. The learned *brāhmaṇas,* who had no other source of income, were completely dependent on the *vaiśya* community for their maintenance, and they received gifts on such festive occasions as birthdays and marriages. While Nanda Mahārāja was worshiping Lord Viṣṇu on this occasion and was trying to satisfy all the people there, his only desire was that the newborn child Kṛṣṇa would be happy. Nanda Mahārāja had no knowledge that this child was the origin of Viṣṇu; he was praying to Lord Viṣṇu to protect Him.

Rohiṇīdevī, the mother of Balarāma, was the most fortunate wife of Vasudeva. She was away from her husband, yet just to congratulate Mahārāja Nanda on the occasion of the birth ceremony of his son, Kṛṣṇa, she dressed herself very nicely. Wearing a garland, a necklace and other bodily ornaments, she appeared on the scene and moved hither and thither. According to the Vedic system, a woman whose husband is not at home does not dress herself very nicely. But although Rohiṇī's husband was away, she still dressed herself very nicely on this occasion.

From the opulence of the birth ceremony of Kṛṣṇa, it is very clear that at that time Vṛndāvana was rich in every respect. Because Lord Kṛṣṇa took birth in the house of King Nanda and mother Yaśodā, the goddess of fortune was obliged to manifest her opulences in Vṛndāvana. It appeared that Vṛndāvana had already become a site for the pastimes of the goddess of fortune.

After the birth ceremony, Nanda Mahārāja decided to go to Mathurā to pay the annual tax to the government of Kaṁsa. Before leaving, he called for the able cowherd men of the village and asked them to take care of Vṛndāvana in his absence. When Nanda Mahārāja arrived in Mathurā, Vasudeva got the news and was very eager to congratulate his friend. He immediately went to the place where Nanda Mahārāja was staying. When Nanda saw Vasudeva, he felt that he had regained his life. Nanda, overwhelmed with joy, immediately stood up and embraced Vasudeva. Vasudeva was received very warmly and offered a nice place to sit. Anxious about his two sons, who had been put under the protection of Nanda without Nanda's knowledge, Vasudeva inquired about Them with great anxiety. Both Balarāma and Kṛṣṇa were the sons of Vasudeva. Balarāma was transferred to the womb of Rohiṇī, Vasudeva's own wife, but Rohiṇī was kept under the protection of Nanda Mahārāja. Kṛṣṇa was personally delivered to Yaśodā and exchanged for her daughter. Nanda Mahārāja knew that Balarāma was the son of Vasudeva, but he did not know that Kṛṣṇa was also Vasudeva's son. Vasudeva, of course, was aware of this fact and inquired very eagerly about both Kṛṣṇa and Balarāma.

Vasudeva then addressed Nanda, "My dear brother, you were old and very anxious to beget a son, and yet you had none. Now by the grace of the Lord you are fortunate to have a very nice son. I think that this incident is very auspicious for you. Dear friend, I was imprisoned by Kaṁsa, and now I am released; therefore this is another birth for me. I had no hope of seeing you again, but by God's grace I can see you." In this way, Vasudeva indirectly expressed his anxiety about Kṛṣṇa. Kṛṣṇa was sent incognito to the bed of mother Yaśodā, and after Nanda very pompously celebrated Kṛṣṇa's birth ceremony, he went to Mathurā. So Vasudeva was very pleased and said, "This is a new birth for me." He never expected that Kṛṣṇa would live, because all his other sons had been killed by Kaṁsa.

Vasudeva continued, "My dear friend, it is very difficult for us to live together. Although we have our family and relatives, sons and daughters, by nature's way we are generally separated from one another. The reason for this is that every living entity appears on this earth under different pressures of fruitive activities; although they assemble together, there is no certainty of their remaining together for a long time. According to one's fruitive activities, one has to act differently and thereby be separated. For example, many plants and creepers are floating on the waves of the ocean. Sometimes they come together, and sometimes they separate forever: one plant goes one way, and another plant goes another. Similarly, our family assembly may be very nice while we are living together, but after some time, in the course of the waves of time, we are separated."

The purport of this expression by Vasudeva is this: although he had eight sons born in the womb of Devakī, unfortunately they were all gone. He could not even keep his one son Kṛṣṇa with him. Vasudeva was feeling His separation, but he could not express the real fact. "Please tell me about the welfare of Vṛndāvana," he said. "You have many animals—are they happy? Are they getting sufficient grass and water? Please also let me know whether the place where you are now living is undisturbed and peaceful." This inquiry was made by Vasudeva because he was very anxious about Kṛṣṇa's safety. He knew that Kaṁsa and his followers were trying to kill Kṛṣṇa by sending various kinds of demons. They had already resolved that all children born within ten days of the birthday of Kṛṣṇa should be killed. Because Vasudeva was so anxious about Kṛṣṇa, he inquired about the safety of His residence. He also inquired about Balarāma and His mother, Rohiṇī, who were entrusted to the care of Nanda Mahārāja. Vasudeva also reminded Nanda Mahārāja that Balarāma did not know His real father. "He knows you as His father. And now you have another child, Kṛṣṇa, and I think you are taking very nice care of both of Them." It is also significant that Vasudeva inquired about the welfare of Nanda Mahārāja's animals. The animals, and especially the cows, were protected exactly in the manner of one's children. Vasudeva was a *kṣatriya,* and Nanda Mahārāja was a *vaiśya.* It is the duty of the *kṣatriyas* to give protection to the citizens, and it is the duty of the *vaiśyas* to give protection to the cows. The cows are as important as the citizens. Just as the human citizens should be given all kinds of protection, so the cows also should be given full protection.

Vasudeva continued to say that the maintenance of religious principles, economic development and the satisfactory execution of meeting the demands of the senses depend on cooperation among relatives, nations and all humanity. Therefore, it is everyone's duty to see that his fellow citizens and the cows are not put into difficulty. One should see to the peace and comfort of his fellow man and the animals. The development of religious principles, economic development and sense gratification can then be achieved without difficulty. Vasudeva expressed his sorrow due to not being able to give protection to his own sons born of Devakī. He was thinking that religious principles, economic development and the satisfaction of his senses were therefore all lost.

Upon hearing this, Nanda Mahārāja replied, "My dear Vasudeva, I know that you are very much aggrieved because the cruel king Kaṁsa has killed all your sons born of Devakī. Although the last child was a daughter, Kaṁsa could not kill her, and she has entered into the celestial planets. My dear friend, do not be aggrieved; we are all being controlled by our past unseen activities. Everyone is subjected to his past deeds, and one who is conversant with the philosophy of *karma* and its reactions is a man in knowledge. Such a person will not be aggrieved at any incident, happy or miserable."

Vasudeva then replied, "My dear Nanda, if you have already paid the government taxes, then return soon to your place, because I think that there may be some disturbances in Gokula."

After the friendly conversation between Nanda Mahārāja and Vasudeva, Vasudeva returned to his home. Nanda Mahārāja and the other cowherd men, who had come to Mathurā to pay their taxes, also returned home.

Thus ends the Bhaktivedanta purport of the Fifth Chapter of Kṛṣṇa, *"The Meeting of Nanda and Vasudeva."*

CHAPTER 6

Pūtanā Killed

WHILE NANDA MAHĀRĀJA was returning home, he considered Vasudeva's warning that there might be some disturbance in Gokula. Certainly the advice was friendly and not false. So Nanda thought, "There is some truth in it." Therefore, out of fear, he began to take shelter of the Supreme Personality of Godhead. It is quite natural for a devotee in danger to think of Kṛṣṇa, because he has no other shelter. When a child is in danger, he takes shelter of his mother or father. Similarly, a devotee is always under the shelter of the Supreme Personality of Godhead, but when he specifically sees some danger, he remembers the Lord very rapidly.

After consulting with his demoniac ministers, Kaṁsa instructed a witch named Pūtanā, who knew the black art of killing small children by ghastly sinful methods, to kill all kinds of children in the cities, villages and pasturing grounds. Such witches can play their black art only where there is no chanting or hearing of the holy name of Kṛṣṇa. It is said that wherever the chanting of the holy name of Kṛṣṇa is done, even negligently, all bad elements—witches, ghosts and dangerous calamities—immediately disappear. And this is certainly true of the place where the chanting of the holy name of Kṛṣṇa is done seriously—especially in Vṛndāvana when the Supreme Lord was personally present. Therefore, the doubts of Nanda Mahārāja were certainly based on affection for Kṛṣṇa. Actually there was no danger from the activities of Pūtanā, despite her powers. Such witches are called *khecarī*, which means they can fly in the sky. This black art of witchcraft is still practiced by some women in the remote northwestern side of India. They can transfer themselves from one place to another on the branch of an uprooted tree. Pūtanā knew this witchcraft, and therefore she is described in the *Bhāgavatam* as *khecarī*.

Pūtanā entered the county of Gokula, the residential quarter of Nanda Mahārāja, without permission. Dressing herself just like a beautiful woman, she entered the house of mother Yaśodā. She appeared very beautiful, with raised hips, nicely swollen breasts, earrings, and flowers in her hair. She looked especially beautiful on account of her thin waist. She was glancing at everyone with very attractive looks and smiling face, and all the residents of Vṛndāvana were captivated. The innocent cowherd women thought that she was the goddess of fortune appearing in Vṛndāvana with a lotus flower in her hand. It seemed to them that she had personally come to see Kṛṣṇa, who is her husband. Because of her exquisite beauty, no one checked her movement, and therefore she freely entered the house of Nanda Mahārāja. Pūtanā, the killer of many, many children, found baby Kṛṣṇa lying on a small bed, and she could at once perceive that the baby was hiding His unparalleled potencies, which resembled fire covered by ashes. Pūtanā thought, "This child is so powerful that He can destroy the whole universe immediately."

Pūtanā's understanding is very significant. The Supreme Personality of Godhead, Kṛṣṇa, is situated in everyone's heart. It is stated in the *Bhagavad-gītā* that He gives one necessary intelligence, and He also causes one to forget. Pūtanā was immediately aware that the child whom she was observing in the house of Nanda Mahārāja was the Supreme Personality of Godhead Himself. He was lying there as a small baby, but that does not mean He was less powerful. The materialistic theory that God-worship is anthropomorphic is not correct. No living being can become God by undergoing meditation or austerities. God is always God. Kṛṣṇa as a baby is as complete as He is as a full-fledged youth. The Māyāvāda theory holds that the living entity was formerly God but has now become overwhelmed by the influence of *māyā*. Therefore the Māyāvādīs say that presently he is not God but when the influence of *māyā* is taken away then he again becomes God. This theory cannot be applied to the minute living entities. The living entities are minute parts and parcels of the Supreme Personality of Godhead; they are minute particles or sparks of the original fire. So these sparks can be covered by the influence of *māyā*, but the original fire, Kṛṣṇa, cannot. Kṛṣṇa is the Supreme Personality of Godhead, even from the beginning of His appearance in the house of Vasudeva and Devakī.

Kṛṣṇa showed the nature of a small baby and closed His eyes, as if to avoid the face of Pūtanā. This closing of the eyes is interpreted and studied in different ways by the devotees. Some say that Kṛṣṇa closed His eyes because He did not like to see the face of

Pūtanā, who had killed so many children and who had now come to kill Him. Others say that Pūtanā hesitated to take the baby on her lap because something extraordinary was being dictated to her from within, and in order to give her assurance, Kṛṣṇa closed His eyes so that she would not be frightened. And yet others interpret in this way: Kṛṣṇa appeared in order to kill the demons and give protection to the devotees, as stated in the *Bhagavad-gītā: paritrāṇāya sādhūnāṁ vināśāya ca duṣkṛtām.* The first demon to be killed was a woman. According to Vedic rules, the killing of a woman, a *brāhmaṇa,* cows or a child is strictly forbidden. Kṛṣṇa was obliged to kill the demon Pūtanā, and because the killing of a woman is forbidden according to Vedic *śāstra,* He could not help but close His eyes. Another interpretation is that Kṛṣṇa closed His eyes because He simply took Pūtanā to be His nurse. Pūtanā came to Kṛṣṇa just to offer her breast for the Lord to suck. Kṛṣṇa is so merciful that even though He knew Pūtanā was there to kill Him, He took her as His nurse or mother.

There are seven kinds of mothers according to Vedic injunction: the real mother, the wife of a teacher or spiritual master, the wife of a king, the wife of a *brāhmaṇa,* the cow, the nurse and mother earth. Because Pūtanā came to take Kṛṣṇa on her lap and offer her breast milk to be sucked by Him, she was accepted by Kṛṣṇa as one of His mothers. That is considered to be another reason He closed His eyes: He had to kill a nurse or mother. But His killing of His mother or nurse was no different from His love for His real mother or His foster mother, Yaśodā. We further understand from Vedic information that Pūtanā was also treated as a mother and given the same facility as Yaśodā. As Yaśodā was given liberation from the material world, Pūtanā was also given liberation. When the baby Kṛṣṇa closed His eyes, Pūtanā took Him on her lap. She did not know that she was holding death personified. If a person mistakes a snake for a rope, he dies. Similarly, Pūtanā had killed so many babies before meeting Kṛṣṇa, and she mistook Him to be like them, but now she was accepting the snake that would kill her immediately.

When Pūtanā was taking baby Kṛṣṇa on her lap, both Yaśodā and Rohiṇī were present, but because she was so beautifully dressed and showed motherly affection toward Kṛṣṇa, they did not forbid her. They could not understand that she was a sword within a decorated case. Pūtanā had smeared a very powerful poison on her breasts, and immediately after taking the baby on her lap, she pushed her breastly nipple within His mouth. She was hoping that as soon as He would suck her breast, He would die. But baby Kṛṣṇa very quickly took the nipple in anger. He sucked the milk-poison along with the life air of the demon. In other words, Kṛṣṇa simultaneously sucked the milk from her breast and killed her by sucking out her life. Kṛṣṇa is so merciful that because the demon Pūtanā came to offer her breast milk to Him, He fulfilled her desire and accepted her activity as motherly. But to stop her from further nefarious activities, He immediately killed her. And because the demon was killed by Kṛṣṇa, she got liberation. As Kṛṣṇa pressed her breast extremely hard and sucked out her very breath, Pūtanā fell down on the ground, spread her arms and legs and began to cry, "Oh, child, leave me, leave me!" She was crying loudly and perspiring, and her whole body became wet.

As she died screaming, there was a tremendous vibration on the earth and in the sky, on the upper and lower planets and in all directions, and people thought that thunderbolts were falling. Thus the nightmare of the Pūtanā witch was over, and she assumed her real feature as a great demon. She opened her fierce mouth and spread her arms and legs all over. She fell exactly as Vṛtrāsura did when struck by the thunderbolt of Indra. The long hair on her head was scattered all over her body. Her fallen body extended up to twelve miles and smashed all the trees to pieces, and everyone was struck with wonder upon seeing this gigantic body. Her teeth appeared just like plows, and her nostrils appeared just like mountain caves. Her breasts appeared like small hills, and her hair was a vast reddish bush. Her eye sockets appeared like blind wells, and her two thighs appeared like two banks of a river. Her two hands appeared like two strongly constructed bridges, and her abdomen seemed like a dried-up lake. All the cowherd men and women became struck with awe and wonder upon seeing this. And the tumultuous sound of her falling shocked their brains and ears and made their hearts beat strongly.

When the *gopīs* saw little Kṛṣṇa fearlessly playing on Pūtanā's lap, they very quickly came and picked Him up. Mother Yaśodā, Rohiṇī and other elder *gopīs* immediately performed the auspicious rituals by taking the tail of a cow and circumambulating His body. The child was completely washed with the urine of a cow, and the dust created by the hooves of the cows was thrown all over His body. This was all just to save little Kṛṣṇa from future inauspicious accidents. This incident gives us a clear indication of how important the cow is to the family, society and to living beings in general. The transcendental body of Kṛṣṇa did not require any protection, but to instruct us on the importance of the cow, the Lord was smeared over with cow dung, washed with the urine of a cow, and sprinkled with the dust upraised by the walking of the cows.

After this purificatory process, the *gopīs,* headed by mother Yaśodā and Rohiṇī, chanted the names of Viṣṇu to give Kṛṣṇa's body full protection from all evil influences. They washed their hands and feet and sipped water three times, as is the custom before chanting *mantra.* They chanted as follows: "My dear Kṛṣṇa, may the Lord who is known as Aja protect Your legs; may Lord Maṇimān protect Your knees; may Lord Yajña protect Your thighs; may Lord Acyuta protect Your upper waist; may Lord Hayagrīva protect Your abdomen; may Lord Keśava protect Your heart; may Lord Īśa protect Your chest; may Lord Sūrya protect Your neck; may Lord Viṣṇu protect Your arms; may Lord Urukrama protect Your face; may Lord Īśvara protect Your head; may Lord Cakradhara protect Your front; may Lord Gadādhara protect Your back; may

Lord Madhusūdana, who carries a bow in His hand, protect Your right side; may Lord Ajana protect Your left side; may Lord Urugāya with His conchshell protect You on all sides; may the Personality of Godhead Upendra protect You from above; may Lord Tārkṣya protect You on the ground; may Lord Haladhara protect You from all sides; may the Personality of Godhead known as Hṛṣīkeśa protect all Your senses; may Lord Nārāyaṇa protect Your life airs; may the Lord of Śvetadvīpa, Nārāyaṇa, protect the core of Your heart; may Lord Yogeśvara protect Your mind; may Lord Pṛśnigarbha protect Your intelligence; and may the Supreme Personality of Godhead protect Your soul. While You are playing, may Lord Govinda protect You from all sides, and when You are sleeping, may Lord Mādhava protect You from all danger; when You are walking, may the Lord of Vaikuṇṭha protect You from falling down; when You are sitting, may Lord Nārāyaṇa give You all protection; and while You are eating, may the Lord of all sacrifices give You all protection."

Thus mother Yaśodā chanted different names of Viṣṇu to protect child Kṛṣṇa's different bodily parts. Mother Yaśodā was firmly convinced that she should protect her child from different kinds of evil spirits and ghosts—namely Ḍākinīs, Yātudhānīs, Kuṣmāṇḍas, Yakṣas, Rākṣasas, Vināyakas, Koṭarās, Revatīs, Jyeṣṭhās, Pūtanās, Mātṛkās, Unmādas and similar other evil spirits, who cause persons to forget their own existence and give trouble to the life airs and the senses. Sometimes they appear in dreams and cause much perturbation; sometimes they appear as old women and suck the blood of small children. But no such ghosts and evil spirits can remain where there is chanting of the holy name of God. Mother Yaśodā was firmly convinced of the Vedic injunctions about the importance of cows and the holy name of Viṣṇu; therefore she took all shelter in the cows and the name of Viṣṇu just to protect her child Kṛṣṇa. She recited all the holy names of Viṣṇu so that He might save the child. Vedic culture has taken advantage of keeping cows and chanting the holy name of Viṣṇu since the beginning of history, and persons who are still following the Vedic ways, especially the householders, keep at least one dozen cows and worship the Deity of Lord Viṣṇu, who is installed in their house. Persons who are advancing in Kṛṣṇa consciousness should take instruction from this pastime and also be very interested in cows and the holy name of Viṣṇu.

The elder *gopīs* of Vṛndāvana were so absorbed in affection for Kṛṣṇa that they wanted to save Him, although there was no need to, for He had already protected Himself. They could not understand that Kṛṣṇa was the Supreme Personality of Godhead playing as a child. After performing the formalities to protect the child, mother Yaśodā took Kṛṣṇa and let Him suck her breast. When the child was protected by *viṣṇu-mantra*, mother Yaśodā felt that He was safe. In the meantime, all the cowherd men who had gone to Mathurā to pay tax returned home and were struck with wonder at seeing the gigantic dead body of Pūtanā.

Nanda Mahārāja recalled the prophecy of Vasudeva and considered him a great sage and mystic *yogī;* otherwise, how could he have foretold an incident that happened during his absence from Vṛndāvana? After this, all the residents of Vraja cut the gigantic body of Pūtanā into pieces and piled it up with wood for burning. When all the limbs of Pūtanā's body were burning, the smoke emanating from the fire created a good aroma of *aguru.* This aroma was due to her being killed by Kṛṣṇa. This means that the demon Pūtanā was washed of all her sinful activities and attained a celestial body. Here is an example of how the Supreme Personality of Godhead is all-good: Pūtanā came to kill Kṛṣṇa, but because He sucked her milk, she was immediately purified, and her dead body attained a transcendental quality. Her only business was to kill small children; she was only fond of blood. But in spite of being envious of Kṛṣṇa, she attained salvation because she gave her milk to Him to drink. So what can be said of those who are affectionate to Kṛṣṇa in the relationship of mother, who with great love and affection always serve Him, the Supreme Personality of Godhead and the Supersoul of every living entity?

It is concluded, therefore, that even a little energy expended in the service of the Lord gives one immense transcendental profit. This is explained in the *Bhagavad-gītā: sv-alpam apy asya dharmasya trāyate mahato bhayāt.* Devotional service in Kṛṣṇa consciousness is so sublime that even a little service rendered to Kṛṣṇa, knowingly or unknowingly, gives one the greatest transcendental benefit. The system of worshiping Kṛṣṇa by offering flowers from a tree is also beneficial for the living entity who is confined to the bodily existence of that tree. When flowers and fruits are offered to Kṛṣṇa, the tree that bore them also receives much benefit, indirectly. The *arcana* process, or worshiping procedure, is therefore beneficial for everyone. Kṛṣṇa is worshipable by great demigods like Brahmā and Lord Śiva, and Pūtanā was so fortunate that the same Kṛṣṇa played in her lap as a little child. The lotus feet of Kṛṣṇa, which are worshiped by great sages and devotees, were placed on the body of Pūtanā. People worship Kṛṣṇa and offer food with great reverence and devotion, but automatically He sucked the milk from the body of Pūtanā. Devotees therefore pray that if simply by offering something as an enemy Pūtanā got so much benefit, then who can measure the benefit of worshiping Kṛṣṇa in love and affection? Therefore only Kṛṣṇa should be worshiped, for so much benefit awaits the worshiper.

Although Pūtanā was an evil spirit, she gained elevation just like the mother of the Supreme Personality of Godhead. It is clear that the cows and the elder *gopīs* who offered milk to Kṛṣṇa were also elevated to the transcendental position. Kṛṣṇa can offer anyone anything, from liberation to anything materially conceivable. Therefore, there cannot be any doubt of the salvation of Pūtanā, whose bodily milk was sucked by Kṛṣṇa for such a long time. And how can there be any doubt about the salvation of the *gopīs,* who were so fond of Kṛṣṇa? Undoubtedly all the *gopīs*, cowherd boys, cows and everyone else who served Kṛṣṇa in Vṛndāvana with love and affection were liberated from the miserable condition of material existence.

When all the inhabitants of Vṛndāvana smelled the good aroma from the smoke of the burning Pūtanā, they inquired from each other, "Where is this good fragrance coming from?" And while conversing, they came to understand that it was the fumes of the burning Pūtanā. They were very fond of Kṛṣṇa, and as soon as they heard that the demon Pūtanā had been killed by Kṛṣṇa, they offered blessings to the little child out of affection. After the burning of Pūtanā, Nanda Mahārāja came home and immediately took up the child on his lap and began to smell His head. In this way, he was quite satisfied that his little child was saved from this great calamity. Śrīla Śukadeva Gosvāmī has given a blessing to all persons who hear the narration of the killing of Pūtanā by Kṛṣṇa: they will surely attain the favor of Govinda.

Thus ends the Bhaktivedanta purport of the Sixth Chapter of Kṛṣṇa, *"Pūtanā Killed."*

CHAPTER 7

The Salvation of Tṛṇāvarta

THE SUPREME PERSONALITY OF GODHEAD, Lord Kṛṣṇa, is always full with six opulences—namely complete wealth, complete strength, complete fame, complete knowledge, complete beauty and complete renunciation. The Lord appears in different complete, eternal forms of incarnation. The conditioned soul has immense opportunity to hear about the transcendental activities of the Lord in these different incarnations. In the *Bhagavad-gītā* it is said, *janma karma ca me divyam.* The pastimes and activities of the Lord are not material—they are beyond the material conception—and the conditioned soul can benefit by hearing such uncommon activities. Hearing is an opportunity to associate with the Lord; to hear His activities is to evolve to the transcendental nature—simply by hearing. The conditioned soul has a natural aptitude to hear something about other conditioned souls in the form of fiction, drama and novel. That inclination to hear something about others may be utilized in hearing the pastimes of the Lord. Then one can immediately evolve to the transcendental nature. Kṛṣṇa's pastimes are not only beautiful; they are also very pleasing to the mind.

If someone takes advantage of hearing the pastimes of the Lord, the material contamination of dust, accumulated in the heart due to long association with material nature, can be immediately cleansed. Lord Caitanya also instructed that simply by hearing the transcendental name of Lord Kṛṣṇa one can cleanse the heart of all material contamination. There are different processes for self-realization, but this process of devotional service—of which hearing is the most important function—when adopted by any conditioned soul, will automatically cleanse him of the material contamination and enable him to realize his real constitutional position. Conditional life is due to this contamination only, and as soon as it is cleared off, then naturally the dormant function of the living entity—rendering service to the Lord—awakens. By developing his eternal relationship with the Supreme Lord, one becomes eligible to create friendship with the devotees. Mahārāja Parīkṣit recommended, from practical experience, that everyone try to hear about the transcendental pastimes of the Lord. This *Kṛṣṇa* treatise is meant for that purpose, and the reader may take advantage of it to attain the ultimate goal of human life.

The Lord, out of His causeless mercy, descends to this material world and displays His activities just like an ordinary man. Unfortunately the impersonalists or the atheistic class of men consider Kṛṣṇa to be an ordinary man like themselves, and so they deride Him. This is condemned in the *Bhagavad-gītā* by the Lord Himself when He says *avajānanti māṁ mūḍhāḥ.* The *mūḍhas,* or rascals, take Kṛṣṇa to be an ordinary man or a slightly more powerful man; out of their great misfortune, they cannot accept Him as the Supreme Personality of Godhead. Sometimes such unfortunate persons misrepresent themselves as incarnations of Kṛṣṇa without referring to the authorized scriptures.

When Kṛṣṇa grew up a little more, He began to turn Himself backside up; He did not merely lie down on His back. And another function was observed by Yaśodā and Nanda Mahārāja: Kṛṣṇa's first birthday. They arranged for Kṛṣṇa's birthday ceremony, which is still observed by all followers of the Vedic principles. (Kṛṣṇa's birthday ceremony is observed in India by all Hindus, irrespective of different sectarian views.) All the cowherd men and women were invited to participate in the jubilant celebration. A nice band played, and the assembled people enjoyed it. All the learned *brāhmaṇas* were invited, and they chanted Vedic hymns for the good fortune of Kṛṣṇa. During the chanting of the Vedic hymns and playing of the bands, Kṛṣṇa was bathed by mother Yaśodā. This bathing ceremony is technically called *abhiṣeka,* and even today this is observed in all the temples of Vṛndāvana on Janmāṣṭamī Day, or the birthday anniversary of Lord Kṛṣṇa.

On this occasion, mother Yaśodā arranged to distribute a large quantity of grain, and first-class cows decorated with golden ornaments were made ready to be given in charity to the learned, respectable *brāhmaṇas.* Yaśodā took her bath and dressed herself nicely, and taking child Kṛṣṇa, duly dressed and bathed, on her lap, she sat down to hear the Vedic hymns chanted by the *brāhmaṇas.* While mother Yaśodā was listening to the chanting of the Vedic hymns, the child appeared to be falling asleep, and therefore she very silently laid Him down on the bed. Being engaged in receiving all the friends, relatives and residents of Vṛndāvana on that holy occasion, she forgot to feed the child milk. He was crying, being hungry, but mother Yaśodā could not hear Him cry because of the various noises. The child, however, became angry because He was hungry and His mother was not paying attention to Him. So He lifted His legs and began to kick His lotus feet just like an ordinary child. Baby Kṛṣṇa had been placed underneath a hand-driven cart, and while He was kicking His legs, He accidentally touched the wheel of the cart, and it collapsed. Various kinds of utensils and dishes made of brass and other metals had been piled up in the handcart, and they all fell down with a great noise. The wheel of the cart separated from the axle, and the spokes of the wheel were all broken and scattered hither and thither. Mother Yaśodā and all the *gopīs,* as well as Mahārāja Nanda and the cowherd men, were astonished as to how the cart could have collapsed by itself. All the men and women who were assembled for the holy function crowded around and began to suggest how the cart might have collapsed. No one could ascertain the cause, but some small children who were entrusted to play with baby Kṛṣṇa informed the crowd that it was due to Kṛṣṇa's striking His feet against the wheel. They assured the crowd that they had seen how it happened with their own eyes, and they strongly asserted the point. Some were listening to the statement of the small children, but others said, "How can you believe the statements of these children?" The cowherd men and women could not understand that the all-powerful Personality of Godhead was lying there as a baby and that He could do anything. Both the possible and impossible were in His power.

While the discussion was going on, baby Kṛṣṇa cried. Without remonstration, mother Yaśodā picked the child up on her lap and called the learned *brāhmaṇas* to chant holy Vedic hymns to counteract the evil spirits. At the same time she allowed the baby to suck her breast. If a child sucks the mother's breast nicely, it is to be understood that he is out of all danger. After this, all the stronger cowherd men put the broken cart in order, and all the scattered things were set up nicely as before. The *brāhmaṇas* thereafter began to offer oblations to the sacrificial fire with yogurt, butter, *kuśa* grass and water. They worshiped the Supreme Personality of Godhead for the good fortune of the child.

The *brāhmaṇas* who were present at that time were all qualified because they were not envious, they never indulged in untruthfulness, they were never proud, they were nonviolent, and they never claimed any false prestige. They were all bona fide *brāhmaṇas,* and there was no reason to think that their blessings would be useless. With firm faith in the qualified *brāhmaṇas,* Nanda Mahārāja took his child on his lap and bathed Him with water mixed with various herbs while the *brāhmaṇas* chanted hymns from the *Ṛg, Yajur* and *Sāma Vedas.*

It is said that without being a qualified *brāhmaṇa* one should not read the *mantras* of the *Vedas.* Here is the proof that the *brāhmaṇas* were qualified with all the brahminical symptoms. Mahārāja Nanda also had full faith in them. Therefore they were allowed to perform the ritualistic ceremonies by chanting the Vedic *mantras.* There are many different varieties of sacrifices recommended for different purposes, but the *mantras* are all to be chanted by qualified *brāhmaṇas.* And because in this Age of Kali such qualified *brāhmaṇas* are not available, all Vedic ritualistic sacrifices are forbidden. Śrī Caitanya Mahāprabhu has therefore recommended only one kind of sacrifice in this age—namely the *saṅkīrtana-yajña,* or chanting the *mahā-mantra,* Hare Kṛṣṇa, Hare Kṛṣṇa, Kṛṣṇa Kṛṣṇa, Hare Hare/ Hare Rāma, Hare Rāma, Rāma Rāma, Hare Hare. As the *brāhmaṇas* chanted the Vedic hymns and performed the ritualistic ceremonies for the second time, Nanda Mahārāja again gave them huge quantities of grain and many cows. All the cows which were given in charity were covered with nice gold-embroidered garments, and their horns were bedecked with golden rings; their hooves were covered with silver plate, and they wore garlands of flowers. He gave so many cows just for the welfare of his wonderful child, and the *brāhmaṇas* in return bestowed their heartfelt blessings. And the blessings offered by the able *brāhmaṇas* were never to be baffled.

One day, shortly after the ceremony, when mother Yaśodā was patting her baby on her lap, the baby felt too heavy, and being unable to carry Him, she unwillingly placed Him on the ground. After a while, she became engaged in household affairs. At that time, a servant of Kaṁsa's known as Tṛṇāvarta, as instructed by Kaṁsa, appeared there in the shape of a whirlwind. He picked the child up on his shoulders and raised a great dust storm all over Vṛndāvana, covering everyone's eyes. Within a few moments the whole area of Vṛndāvana became so densely dark that no one could see himself or anyone else. During this great catastrophe, mother Yaśodā could not see her baby, who had been taken away by the whirlwind, and she began to cry very piteously. She fell down on the ground exactly like a cow who has just lost her calf. When mother Yaśodā was so piteously crying, all the cowherd women immediately came and began to look for the baby, but they were disappointed and could not find Him.

The Tṛṇāvarta demon went high into the sky with baby Kṛṣṇa on his shoulder, but the baby assumed such a weight that suddenly he could not go any further, and he had to stop his whirlwind activities. Baby Kṛṣṇa made Himself heavy and began to weigh down the demon, catching hold of his neck. Tṛṇāvarta felt the baby to be as heavy as a big mountain, and he tried to get out of His clutches, but he was unable to do so, and his eyes popped out from their sockets. Crying very fiercely, he fell down to the ground of Vṛndāvana and died. The demon fell exactly like Tripurāsura, who was pierced by the arrow of Lord Śiva. Tṛṇāvarta hit a stone slab, and his limbs were smashed. His body became visible to all the inhabitants of Vṛndāvana.

When the *gopīs* saw the demon killed and child Kṛṣṇa very happily playing on his body, they immediately picked Kṛṣṇa up with great affection. The cowherd men and women became very happy to get back their beloved child Kṛṣṇa. At that time they began to talk about how wonderful it was that the demon had taken away the child to devour Him but could not do so; instead he fell down dead. Some of them supported the situation: "This is proper because those who are too sinful die from their sinful reactions, and child Kṛṣṇa is pious; therefore He is safe from all kinds of fearful situations. And we too must have performed great sacrifices in our previous lives, worshiping the Supreme Personality of Godhead, giving great wealth in charity and acting philanthropically for the general welfare of men. Because of such pious activities, the child is safe from all danger."

The *gopīs* assembled there spoke among themselves: "What sort of austerities and penances we must have undergone in our previous lives! We must have worshiped the Supreme Personality of Godhead, offered different kinds of sacrifices, made charities and performed many welfare activities for the public, such as growing banyan trees and excavating wells. As a result of these pious activities, we have gotten back our child, even though He was supposed to be dead. Now He has come back to enliven His relatives." After observing such wonderful happenings, Nanda Mahārāja began to think of the words of Vasudeva again and again.

After this incident, when Yaśodā once was nursing her child and patting Him with great affection, there streamed a profuse supply of milk from her breast, and when she opened the mouth of the child with her fingers, she suddenly saw the universal manifestation within His mouth. She saw within the mouth of Kṛṣṇa the whole sky, including the luminaries, stars in all directions, the sun, moon, fire, air, seas, islands, mountains, rivers, forests and all other movable and immovable entities. When mother Yaśodā saw this, her heart began to throb, and she murmured within herself, "How wonderful this is!" She could not express anything, but simply closed her eyes. She was absorbed in wonderful thoughts. Kṛṣṇa's showing the universal form of the Supreme Personality of Godhead, even when lying down on the lap of His mother, proves that the Supreme Personality of Godhead is always the Supreme Personality of Godhead, whether He is manifested as a child on the lap of His mother or as a charioteer on the Battlefield of Kurukṣetra. The concoction of the impersonalists, that one can become God by meditation or by some artificial material activities, is herewith declared false. God is always God in any condition or status, and the living entities are always the parts and parcels of the Supreme Lord. They can never be equal to the inconceivable, supernatural power of the Supreme Personality of Godhead.

Thus ends the Bhaktivedanta purport of the Seventh Chapter of Kṛṣṇa, *"The Salvation of Tṛṇāvarta."*

CHAPTER 8

Vision of the Universal Form

AFTER THIS INCIDENT, Vasudeva asked his family priest, Garga Muni, to visit the place of Nanda Mahārāja in order to astrologically calculate the future life of Kṛṣṇa. Garga Muni was a great saintly sage who had undergone many austerities and penances and been appointed priest of the Yadu dynasty. When Garga Muni arrived at the home of Nanda Mahārāja, Nanda Mahārāja was very pleased to see him and immediately stood up with folded hands and offered his respectful obeisances. He received Garga Muni with the feeling of one who is worshiping the Supreme Personality of Godhead. He offered him a nice sitting place, and when he sat down, Nanda Mahārāja offered him a warm reception. Addressing him very politely, he said, "My dear *brāhmaṇa,* your appearance in a householder's place is only to enlighten. We are always engaged in household duties and are forgetting our real duty of self-realization. Your coming to our house is to give us some enlightenment about spiritual life. You have no other purpose in visiting householders." Actually, a saintly person or a *brāhmaṇa* has no business visiting householders, who are always busy in the matter of dollars and cents. The only reason saintly persons and *brāhmaṇas* go to the place of a householder is to enlighten him. If it is asked, "Why don't the householders go to a saintly person or a *brāhmaṇa* for enlightenment?" the answer is that householders are very poor-hearted. Generally householders think that engaging in family affairs is their prime duty and that self-realization or enlightenment in spiritual knowledge is secondary. Out of compassion only, saintly persons and *brāhmaṇas* go to householders' homes. Nanda Mahārāja addressed Garga Muni as one of the great authorities in astrological science. The foretellings of astrological science, such as the occurrence of solar or lunar eclipses, are wonderful calculations, and by this particular science a person can understand the future very clearly. Garga Muni was proficient in this knowledge. By this knowledge one can understand what his previous activities were that are causing him to enjoy or suffer in this life.

Nanda Mahārāja also addressed Garga Muni as "the best of the *brāhmaṇas.*" A *brāhmaṇa* is one who is expert in the knowledge of the Supreme. Without knowledge of the Supreme Absolute, one cannot be recognized as a *brāhmaṇa.* The exact word used in this connection is *brahma-vidām,* which means those who know the Supreme very well. An expert *brāhmaṇa* is able to give reformatory facilities to the subcastes—namely the *kṣatriyas* and *vaiśyas.* The *śūdras* observe no reformatory performances. The *brāhmaṇa* is considered to be the spiritual master or priest for the *kṣatriya* and *vaiśya.* Nanda Mahārāja happened to be a *vaiśya,* and he accepted Garga Muni as a first-class *brāhmaṇa.* He therefore offered his two foster sons—namely Kṛṣṇa and Balarāma—to him to purify. Nanda stated that not only these boys but all human beings just after birth should accept a qualified *brāhmaṇa* as spiritual master.

Upon this request, Garga Muni replied, "Vasudeva has sent me to see to the reformatory performances of these boys, especially Kṛṣṇa's, but if I do so it may incidentally appear that Kṛṣṇa is the son of Devakī, since I am Vasudeva's family priest." By his astrological calculation, Garga Muni could understand that Kṛṣṇa was the son of Devakī, which Nanda did not know. Indirectly Garga Muni said that Kṛṣṇa and Balarāma were both sons of Vasudeva. Balarāma was known as the son of Vasudeva because His mother, Rohiṇī, was present there, but Nanda Mahārāja did not know about Kṛṣṇa. Garga Muni indirectly disclosed the fact that Kṛṣṇa was the son of Devakī. Garga Muni also warned Nanda Mahārāja that if he would perform the reformatory ceremony, then Kaṁsa, who was naturally very sinful, would understand that Kṛṣṇa was the son of Devakī and Vasudeva. According to astrological calculation, Devakī could not have a female child, although everyone thought that the eighth child of Devakī was female. In this way Garga Muni intimated to Nanda Mahārāja that the female child was born of Yaśodā and that Kṛṣṇa was born of Devakī and they were exchanged. Also, the female child, or Durgā, had informed Kaṁsa that the child who would kill him was already born somewhere else. Garga Muni stated, "If I give your child a name and if He fulfills the prophecy of the female child to Kaṁsa, then it may be that the sinful demon will come and kill this child also after the name-giving ceremony. But I do not want to become responsible for all these future calamities."

On hearing the words of Garga Muni, Nanda Mahārāja said, "If there is such danger, then it is better not to plan any gorgeous name-giving ceremony. It would be better for you to simply chant the Vedic hymns and perform the purificatory process. We belong to the twice-born caste, and I am taking this opportunity of your presence. So please perform the name-giving ceremony without external pomp." Nanda Mahārāja wanted to keep the name-giving ceremony a secret and yet take advantage of Garga Muni's performing the ceremony.

When Garga Muni was so eagerly requested by Nanda Mahārāja, he performed the name-giving ceremony as secretly as possible in the cowshed of Nanda Mahārāja. He informed Nanda Mahārāja that the son of Rohiṇī would be very pleasing to His family members and relatives and therefore would be called Rāma. In the future He would be extraordinarily strong and therefore would be called Baladeva. Garga Muni said further, "Because your family and the family of the Yadus are so intimately connected and attracted, His name will also be Saṅkarṣaṇa." This means that Garga Muni awarded three names to the son of Rohiṇī—namely Balarāma, Saṅkarṣaṇa and Baladeva. But he carefully did not disclose the fact that Balarāma had also appeared in the womb of Devakī and was subsequently transferred to the womb of Rohiṇī. Kṛṣṇa and Balarāma are real brothers, being originally sons of Devakī.

Garga Muni then informed Nanda Mahārāja, "As far as your son is concerned, this child has taken different bodily complexions in different *yugas* [millennia]. First of all He assumed the color white, then the color red, and then the color yellow, and now He has assumed the color black. Besides that, He was formerly the son of Vasudeva; therefore His name should be Vāsudeva as well as Kṛṣṇa. Some people will call Him Kṛṣṇa, and some will call Him Vāsudeva. But one thing you must know: this son has had many, many other names and activities due to His different pastimes."

Garga Muni further hinted to Nanda Mahārāja that his son would also be called Giridhārī because of His uncommon pastime of lifting Govardhana Hill. Since Garga Muni was an astrologer, he could understand everything past and future, and thus he said, "I know everything about His activities and names, but others do not know. This child will be very pleasing to all the cowherd men and cows. Being very popular in Vṛndāvana, He will be the cause of all good fortune for you. Because of His presence, you will overcome all kinds of material calamities, despite opposing elements."

Garga Muni continued to say, "My dear King of Vraja, in His previous births this child many times protected righteous persons from the hands of rogues and thieves whenever there was political disruption. Your child is so powerful that anyone who will become a devotee of your boy will never be troubled by enemies. Just as demigods are always protected by Lord Viṣṇu, the devotees of your child will always be protected by Nārāyaṇa, the Supreme Personality of Godhead. This child will grow in power, beauty, opulence—in everything—on the level of Nārāyaṇa, the Supreme Personality of Godhead. Therefore I would advise that you protect Him very carefully so that He may grow without disturbance." In other words, Garga Muni informed Nanda Mahārāja that because he was a great devotee of Nārāyaṇa, Lord Nārāyaṇa had given Nanda a son equal to Him. At the same time, Garga Muni indicated that this son would be disturbed by so many demons and that Nanda should therefore be careful and protect Him. In this way, Garga Muni convinced Nanda Mahārāja that Nārāyaṇa Himself had become his son. In various ways he described the transcendental qualities of his son. After giving this information, Garga Muni returned to his home. Nanda Mahārāja began to think of himself as the most fortunate person, and he was very satisfied to receive such a benediction in this way.

A short time after this incident, both Balarāma and Kṛṣṇa began to crawl on Their hands and knees. When They were crawling like that, They pleased Their mothers. The bells tied to Their waist and ankles sounded fascinating, and They would move around very pleasingly. Sometimes, just like ordinary children, They would be frightened by others and would immediately hurry to Their mothers for protection. Sometimes They would fall into the clay and mud of Vṛndāvana and would approach Their mothers smeared with clay and saffron. They were actually smeared with saffron and sandalwood pulp by Their mothers, but due to crawling over muddy clay, They would simultaneously smear Their bodies with clay. As soon as They would come crawling to Their mothers, Yaśodā and Rohiṇī would take Them on their laps and, covering Them with the lower portion of their saris, allow Them to suck their breasts. When the babies were sucking their breasts, the mothers would see small teeth coming in. Thus their joy would be intensified to see their children grow. Sometimes the naughty babies would crawl up to the cowshed, catch the tail of a calf and stand up. The calves, being disturbed, would immediately begin running here and there, and the children would be dragged over clay and cow dung. To see this fun, Yaśodā and Rohiṇī would call all their neighborhood friends, the *gopīs*. Upon seeing these childhood pastimes of Lord Kṛṣṇa, the *gopīs* would be merged in transcendental bliss. In their enjoyment they would laugh very loudly.

Kṛṣṇa and Balarāma were so restless that Their mothers Yaśodā and Rohiṇī would try to protect Them from cows, bulls, monkeys, water, fire and birds while they were executing their household duties. Always being anxious to protect the children and to execute their duties, they were not very tranquil. In a very short time, Kṛṣṇa and Balarāma began to stand up and slightly move on Their legs. When Kṛṣṇa and Balarāma began to walk, other friends of the same age joined Them, and together They gave the highest transcendental pleasure to the *gopīs*, specifically to mother Yaśodā and Rohiṇī.

All the *gopī* friends of Yaśodā and Rohiṇī enjoyed the naughty childish activities of Kṛṣṇa and Balarāma in Vṛndāvana. In order to enjoy further transcendental bliss, they all assembled and went to mother Yaśodā to lodge complaints against the restless boys. When Kṛṣṇa was sitting before mother Yaśodā, all the elder *gopīs* began to lodge complaints against Him so that Kṛṣṇa could hear. They said, "Dear Yaśodā, why don't you restrict your naughty Kṛṣṇa? He comes to our houses along with Balarāma every morning and evening, and before the milking of the cows They let loose the calves, and the calves drink all the milk of the cows. So when we go to milk the cows, we find no milk, and we have to return with empty pots. If we warn Kṛṣṇa and Balarāma about doing this, They simply smile so charmingly that we cannot do anything. Also, your Kṛṣṇa and Balarāma find great pleasure in stealing our stock of yogurt and butter from wherever we keep it. When Kṛṣṇa and Balarāma are caught stealing the yogurt and butter, They say, 'Why do you charge Us with stealing? Do you think that butter and yogurt are in scarcity in Our house?' Sometimes They steal butter, yogurt and milk and distribute them to the monkeys. When the monkeys are well fed and do not take any more, then your boys chide, 'This milk and butter and yogurt are useless—even the monkeys won't take it.' And They break the pots and throw them hither and thither. If we keep our stock of yogurt, butter and milk in a solitary dark place, your Kṛṣṇa and Balarāma find it in the darkness by the glaring effulgence of the ornaments and jewels on Their bodies. If by chance They cannot find the hidden butter and yogurt, They go to our little babies and pinch their bodies so that they cry, and then They go away. If out of fear of these naughty boys we keep our stock of butter and yogurt high on the ceiling, hanging on a swing, although it is beyond Their reach They arrange to reach it by piling all kinds of wooden planks over the grinding machine. And if They cannot reach, They make a hole in the pot. We think therefore that you'd better take all the jeweled ornaments from the bodies of your children."

On hearing this, Yaśodā would say, "All right, I will take all the jewels from Kṛṣṇa so that He cannot see the butter hidden in the darkness." Then the *gopīs* would say, "No, no, don't do this. What good will you do by taking away the jewels? We do not know what kind of boys these are, but even without ornaments They spread some kind of effulgence so that even in darkness They can see everything." Then mother Yaśodā would inform them, "All right, keep your butter and yogurt carefully so that They may not reach it." In reply to this, the *gopīs* said, "Yes, actually we do so, but because we are sometimes engaged in our household duties, these naughty boys enter our house somehow or other and spoil everything. Sometimes, being unable to steal our butter and yogurt, out of anger They pass urine on the clean floor and sometimes spit on it. Now just see how your boy is hearing these complaints. All day He simply makes arrangements to steal our butter and yogurt, and now He is sitting just like a very silent good boy. Just see His face." When mother Yaśodā thought to chastise her boy after hearing all the complaints, she saw His pitiable face, and smiling, she did not chastise Him.

Another day, when Kṛṣṇa and Balarāma were playing with Their friends, all the boys joined Balarāma and complained to mother Yaśodā that Kṛṣṇa had eaten clay. On hearing this, mother Yaśodā caught hold of Kṛṣṇa's hand and said, "My dear Kṛṣṇa, why have You eaten earth in a solitary place? Just see, all Your friends, including Balarāma, are complaining about You." Being afraid of His mother, Kṛṣṇa replied, "My dear mother, all these boys, including My elder brother, Balarāma, are speaking lies against Me. I have never eaten any clay. My elder brother, Balarāma, while playing with Me today, became angry, and therefore He has joined with the other boys to complain against Me. They have all combined together to complain so you will be angry and chastise Me. If you think they are truthful, then you can look within My mouth to see whether I have eaten clay or not." His mother replied, "All right, if You have actually not eaten any clay, then just open Your mouth. I shall see."

When the Supreme Personality of Godhead Kṛṣṇa was so ordered by His mother, He immediately opened His mouth just like an ordinary boy. Then mother Yaśodā saw within that mouth the complete opulence of creation. She saw the entire outer space in all directions, mountains, islands, oceans, seas, planets, air, fire, moon and stars. Along with the moon and the stars she also saw all the elements—water, sky, the extensive ethereal existence along with the total ego and its products, namely the senses, the controllers of the senses, all the demigods and the objects of the senses like sound and smell. Within His mouth she also saw the three qualities of material nature, all living entities, eternal time, material nature, spiritual nature, activity, consciousness and different forms of the whole creation. Yaśodā could find within the mouth of her child everything necessary for cosmic manifestation. She also saw, within His mouth, herself taking Kṛṣṇa on her lap and having Him suck her breast. Upon seeing all this, she became struck with awe and began to wonder whether she were dreaming or actually seeing something extraordinary. She concluded that she was either dreaming or seeing the play of the illusory energy of the Supreme Personality of Godhead. She thought that she had become mad, mentally deranged, to see all those wonderful things. Then she thought, "It may be cosmic mystic power attained by my child, and therefore I am perplexed by such visions within His mouth. Let me offer my respectful obeisances unto the Supreme Personality of Godhead, who is beyond the expression of consciousness, mind, work and philosophical speculation, and whose different energies produce everything manifested and unmanifested. Under His energy, bodily self and bodily possessions are conceived." She then said, "Let me offer my respectful obeisances unto Him under whose illusory energy I am thinking that Nanda Mahārāja is my husband and Kṛṣṇa is my son, that all the properties of Nanda Mahārāja belong to me and that all the cowherd men and women are my subjects. All this misconception is due to the illusory energy of the Supreme Lord. So let me pray to Him that He may protect me always."

While mother Yaśodā was thinking in this high philosophical way, Lord Kṛṣṇa again expanded His internal energy just to bewilder her with maternal affection. Immediately mother Yaśodā forgot all philosophical speculation and accepted Kṛṣṇa as her own child. She took Him on her lap and became overwhelmed with maternal affection. She thus began to think of the Supreme Personality of Godhead, who is understood through the processes of cultivating knowledge derived from the *Upaniṣads* and the *Vedānta-sūtra*, practicing mystic *yoga* and studying Sāṅkhya philosophy, as her own begotten child.

Certainly mother Yaśodā had executed many, many pious activities, as a result of which she got the Absolute Truth, the Supreme Personality of Godhead, as her son who sucked milk from her breast. Similarly, Nanda Mahārāja also must have performed many great sacrifices and pious activities for Lord Kṛṣṇa to become his son and address him as "father." But it is surprising that Vasudeva and Devakī did not enjoy the transcendental bliss of Kṛṣṇa's childhood pastimes, although Kṛṣṇa was their real son. The childhood pastimes of Kṛṣṇa are glorified even today by many sages and saintly persons, but Vasudeva and Devakī could not enjoy such childhood pastimes personally. The reason for this was explained by Śukadeva Gosvāmī to Mahārāja Parīkṣit as follows.

When the best of the Vasus, named Droṇa, and his wife Dharā were ordered to increase progeny by Lord Brahmā, they said unto him, "Dear father, we are seeking your benediction. When we take birth again within the universe, may the Supreme Lord Kṛṣṇa in His most attractive feature of childhood absorb our whole attention. May our dealings with Him be so powerful that simply by hearing of these childhood activities of His, anyone will very easily cross over the nescience of birth and death." Lord Brahmā agreed to give them the benediction, and as a result the same Droṇa appeared as Nanda Mahārāja in Vṛndāvana, and the same Dharā appeared as mother Yaśodā, the wife of Nanda Mahārāja.

In this way, Nanda Mahārāja and his wife, mother Yaśodā, developed their unalloyed devotion for the Supreme Personality of Godhead, having gotten Him as their son. And all the *gopīs* and cowherd men who were associates of Kṛṣṇa naturally developed their own different feelings of love for Kṛṣṇa.

Therefore, just to fulfill the benediction of Lord Brahmā, Lord Kṛṣṇa appeared along with His plenary expansion, Balarāma, and performed all kinds of childhood pastimes in order to increase the transcendental pleasure of all the residents of Vṛndāvana.

Thus ends the Bhaktivedanta purport of the Eighth Chapter of Kṛṣṇa, *"Vision of the Universal Form."*

CHAPTER 9

Mother Yaśodā Binds Lord Kṛṣṇa

ONCE UPON A TIME, seeing that her maidservant was engaged in different household duties, mother Yaśodā personally took charge of churning butter. And while she churned butter, she sang the childhood pastimes of Kṛṣṇa and enjoyed thinking of her son.

The end of her sari was tightly wrapped while she churned, and on account of her intense love for her son, milk automatically dripped from her breasts, which moved as she labored very hard, churning with two hands. The bangles and bracelets on her hands tinkled as they touched each other, and her earrings and breasts shook. There were drops of perspiration on her face, and the flower garland which was on her head scattered here and there. Before this picturesque sight, Lord Kṛṣṇa appeared as a child. He felt hungry, and to increase His mother's love, He wanted her to stop churning. He indicated that her first business was to let Him suck her breast, and then she could churn butter later.

Mother Yaśodā took her son on her lap and pushed the nipple of her breast into His mouth, and while Kṛṣṇa was sucking the milk, she was smiling, enjoying the beauty of her child's face. Suddenly, the milk which was on the stove began to boil over. Just to stop the milk from spilling, mother Yaśodā at once put Kṛṣṇa aside and went to the stove. Left in that state by His mother, Kṛṣṇa became very angry, and His lips and eyes became red in rage. He pressed His teeth and lips, and taking up a piece of stone, He immediately broke the butter pot. He took butter out of it, and with false tears in His eyes, He began to eat the butter in a secluded place.

In the meantime, mother Yaśodā returned to the churning place after setting the overflowing milk pan in order. She saw the broken pot, in which the churning yogurt had been kept. Since she could not find her boy, she concluded that the broken pot was His work. She smiled as she thought, "The child is very clever. After breaking the pot He has left this place, fearing punishment." After she sought all over, she found her son sitting on a big wooden grinding mortar, which was kept upside down. He was taking butter from a pot which was hanging from the ceiling on a swing, and He was feeding it to the monkeys. She saw Kṛṣṇa looking this way and that way in fear of her because He was conscious of His naughty behavior. After seeing her son so engaged, she very silently approached Him from behind. Kṛṣṇa, however, saw her coming toward Him with a stick in her hand, and He immediately got down from the grinding mortar and began to flee in fear. Mother Yaśodā chased Him to all corners, trying to capture the Supreme Personality of Godhead, who is never approached even by the meditations of great *yogīs*. In other words, the Supreme Personality of Godhead, Kṛṣṇa, who is never caught by the *yogīs* and speculators, was playing just like a little child for such a great devotee as mother Yaśodā. Mother Yaśodā, however, could not easily catch the fast-running child because of her thin waist and heavy body. Still she tried to follow Him as fast as possible. Her hair loosened, and the flowers in her hair fell to the ground. Although she was tired, she somehow reached her naughty child and captured Him. When He was caught, Kṛṣṇa was almost on the point of crying. He smeared His hands over His eyes, which were anointed with black eye cosmetics. The child saw His mother's face while she stood over Him, and His eyes became restless from fear.

Mother Yaśodā could understand that Kṛṣṇa was unnecessarily afraid, and for His benefit she wanted to allay His fears. Being the topmost well-wisher of her child, mother Yaśodā thought, "If the child is too fearful of me, I don't know what will happen to Him." Mother Yaśodā then threw away her stick. In order to punish Him, she thought to bind His hands with some ropes. She did not know it, but it was actually impossible for her to bind the Supreme Personality of Godhead. Mother Yaśodā was thinking that Kṛṣṇa was her tiny child; she did not know that the child had no limitation. There is no inside or outside of Him, nor beginning or end. He is unlimited and all-pervading. Indeed, He is Himself the whole cosmic manifestation. Still, mother Yaśodā was thinking of Kṛṣṇa as her child. Although He is beyond the reach of all senses, she endeavored to bind Him to a wooden grinding mortar. But when she tried to bind Him, she found that the rope she was using was too short—by two inches. She gathered more ropes from the house and added to it, but still she found the same shortage. In this way, she connected all the ropes available at home, but when the final knot was added, she saw that the rope was still two inches too short. Mother Yaśodā was smiling, but she was astonished. How was it happening?

In attempting to bind her son, she became tired. She was perspiring, and the garland on her head fell down. Then Lord Kṛṣṇa appreciated the hard labor of His mother, and being compassionate upon her, He agreed to be bound up by the ropes. Kṛṣṇa, playing as a human child in the house of mother Yaśodā, was performing His own selected pastimes. Of course, no one can control the Supreme Personality of Godhead. The pure devotee surrenders himself unto the lotus feet of the Lord, who may either protect or vanquish the devotee. But for his part, the devotee never forgets his own position of surrender. Similarly, the Lord also feels transcendental pleasure by submitting Himself to the protection of the devotee. This was exemplified by Kṛṣṇa's surrender unto His mother, Yaśodā.

Kṛṣṇa is the supreme bestower of all kinds of liberation to His devotees, but the benediction which was bestowed upon mother Yaśodā was never experienced even by Lord Brahmā or Lord Śiva or the goddess of fortune.

The Supreme Personality of Godhead, who is known as the son of Yaśodā and Nanda Mahārāja, is never so completely known to the *yogīs* and speculators. But He is easily available to His devotees. Nor is He appreciated as the supreme reservoir of all pleasure by the *yogīs* and speculators.

After binding her son, mother Yaśodā engaged herself in household affairs. At that time, bound up to the wooden mortar, Kṛṣṇa could see a pair of trees before Him which were known as *arjuna* trees. The great reservoir of pleasure, Lord Śrī Kṛṣṇa, thus thought to Himself, "Mother Yaśodā first of all left without feeding Me sufficient milk, and therefore I broke the pot of yogurt and distributed the stock butter in charity to the monkeys. Now she has bound Me up to a wooden mortar. So I shall do something more mischievous than before." And thus He thought of pulling down the two very tall *arjuna* trees.

There is a history behind the pair of *arjuna* trees. In their previous lives, the trees were born as the human sons of Kuvera, and their names were Nalakūvara and Maṇigrīva. Fortunately, they came within the vision of the Lord. In their previous lives they were cursed by the great sage Nārada in order to receive the highest benediction of seeing Lord Kṛṣṇa. This benediction-curse was bestowed upon them because of their forgetfulness due to intoxication. This story will be narrated in the next chapter.

Thus ends the Bhaktivedanta purport of the Ninth Chapter of Kṛṣṇa, *"Mother Yaśodā Binds Lord Kṛṣṇa."*

CHAPTER 10

The Deliverance of Nalakūvara and Maṇigrīva

THE STORY OF THE CURSING of Nalakūvara and Maṇigrīva and their deliverance by Kṛṣṇa, under the all-blissful desire of the great sage Nārada, is here described.

The two great demigods Nalakūvara and Maṇigrīva were sons of the treasurer of the demigods, Kuvera, who was a great devotee of Lord Śiva. By the grace of Lord Śiva, Kuvera's material opulences had no limit. As a rich man's sons often become addicted to wine and women, so these two sons of Kuvera were also addicted to wine and sex. Once, these two demigods, desiring to enjoy, entered the garden of Lord Śiva in the province of Kailāsa, on the bank of the Mandākinī Ganges. There they drank much and engaged in hearing the sweet singing of the beautiful women who accompanied them in that garden of fragrant flowers. In an intoxicated condition, they entered the water of the Ganges, which was filled with lotus flowers, and there they began to enjoy the company of the young girls exactly as a male elephant enjoys female elephants within the water.

While they were thus enjoying themselves in the water, all of a sudden Nārada, the great sage, happened to pass that way. He could understand that the demigods Nalakūvara and Maṇigrīva were too much intoxicated and could not even see that he was passing. The young girls, however, were not so much intoxicated as the demigods, and they at once became ashamed at being naked before the great sage Nārada. They began to cover themselves with all haste. The two demigod sons of Kuvera were so much intoxicated that they could not appreciate the presence of the sage Nārada and therefore did not cover their bodies. On seeing the two demigods so degraded by intoxication, Nārada desired their welfare, and therefore he exhibited his causeless mercy upon them by cursing them.

Because the great sage was compassionate upon them, he wanted to finish their false enjoyment of intoxication and association with young girls and wanted them to see Lord Kṛṣṇa face to face. He conceived of cursing them as follows. He said that the attraction for material enjoyment is due to an increase of the mode of passion. A person in the material world, when favored by the material opulence of riches, generally becomes addicted to three things—intoxication, sex and gambling. Materially opulent men, being puffed up with the accumulation of wealth, also become so merciless that they indulge in killing animals by opening slaughterhouses. And they think that they themselves will never die. Such foolish persons, forgetting the laws of nature, become overly infatuated with the body. They forget that the material body, even though very much advanced in civilization, up to the position of the demigods, will finally turn into ashes or stool. And while one is living, whatever the external condition of the body may be, within there is only stool, urine and various kinds of worms. Thus being engaged in jealousy and violence to other bodies, materialists cannot understand the ultimate goal of life, and without knowing this goal of life, they generally glide down to a hellish condition in their next life. Such foolish persons commit all kinds of sinful activities on account of the temporary body, and they are even unable to consider whether the body actually belongs to them. Generally it is said that the body belongs to the persons who feed it. One might therefore consider whether the body belongs to one personally or to the master to whom one renders service. The master of slaves claims full right to the bodies of the slaves because the master feeds the slaves. It may also be questioned whether the body belongs to the father, who is the seed-giving master of the body, or to the mother, who develops the child's body in her womb.

Foolish persons are engaged in committing all sorts of sins due to the misconception of identifying the material body with the self. But one should be intelligent enough to understand to whom the body belongs. A foolish person indulges in killing animals to maintain the body, but he does not consider whether the body belongs to him or to his father or mother or maternal grandfather. Sometimes a father gives his daughter in charity to a person with a view of getting back the daughter's child as a son. The body may also belong to a stronger man who forces it to work for him. Sometimes a slave's body is sold to a master, and from that day on the body belongs to the master. And at the end of life the body belongs to the fire, because the body is given to the fire and burned to ashes. Or the body is thrown into the street to be eaten by the dogs and vultures.

Before committing all kinds of sins to maintain the body, one should understand to whom the body belongs. Ultimately it is concluded that the body is a product of material nature, and at the end it merges into material nature; therefore, the conclusion should be that the body belongs to material nature. One should not wrongly think that the body belongs to him. To maintain a false possession, why should one indulge in killing? Why should one kill innocent animals to maintain the body?

When a man is infatuated with the false prestige of opulence, he does not care for any moral instruction but indulges in wine, women and animal-killing. In such circumstances, a poverty-stricken man is often better situated because a poor man thinks of himself in relation to other bodies. A poor man often does not wish to inflict injuries upon other bodies because he can understand more readily that when he himself is injured he feels pain. As such, the great sage Nārada considered that because the demigods Nalakūvara and Maṇigrīva were so infatuated by false prestige, they should be put into a condition of life devoid of opulence.

A person who has a pinprick in his body does not wish others to be pricked by pins; a considerate man in the life of poverty does not wish others to be also put into that condition. Generally it is seen that one who has risen from a poverty-stricken life and becomes wealthy creates some charitable institution at the end of his life so that other poverty-stricken men might be benefited. In short, a compassionate poor man may consider others' pains and pleasures with empathy. A poor man is seldom puffed up with false pride, and he may be freed from all kinds of infatuation. He may remain satisfied by whatever he gets for his maintenance by the grace of the Lord.

To remain in the poverty-stricken condition is a kind of austerity. According to Vedic culture, therefore, the *brāhmaṇas,* as a matter of routine, keep themselves in a poverty-stricken condition to save themselves from the false prestige of material opulence. False prestige due to advancement of material prosperity is a great impediment for spiritual emancipation. A poverty-stricken man cannot become unnaturally fat by eating more and more. And on account of not being able to eat more than he requires, his senses are not very turbulent. When the senses are not very turbulent, he cannot become violent.

Another advantage of poverty is that a saintly person can easily enter a poor man's house, and thus the poor man can take advantage of the saintly person's association. A very opulent man does not allow anyone to enter his house; therefore, the saintly person cannot enter. According to the Vedic system, a saintly person takes the position of a mendicant so that on the plea of begging something from the householder, he can enter any house. The householder, who has usually forgotten everything about spiritual advancement because he is busy maintaining family affairs, can be benefited by the association of a saintly person. There is a great chance for the poor man to become liberated through association with a saint. Of what use are persons who are puffed up with material opulence and prestige if they are bereft of the association of saintly persons and devotees of the Supreme Personality of Godhead?

The great sage Nārada thereafter thought that it was his duty to put those demigods into a condition where they could not be falsely proud of their material opulence and prestige. Nārada was compassionate and wanted to save them from their fallen life. They were in the mode of darkness, and being therefore unable to control their senses, they were addicted to sex life. It was the duty of a saintly person like Nārada to save them from their abominable condition. In animal life, the animal has no sense to understand that he is naked. But Kuvera was the treasurer of the demigods, a very responsible man, and Nalakūvara and Maṇigrīva were two of his sons. And yet they became so animalistic and irresponsible that they could not understand, due to intoxication, that they were naked. To cover the lower part of the body is a principle of human civilization, and when men or women forget this principle, they become no better than animals. Nārada therefore thought that the best punishment for them was to make them immovable living entities, or trees. Trees are, by nature's laws, immovable. Although trees are covered by the mode of ignorance, they cannot do harm. The great sage Nārada thought it fitting that, although the brothers would be punished to become trees, by his mercy they would continue to keep their memory and be able to know why they were being punished. After changing the body, a living entity generally forgets his previous life, but in special cases, by the grace of the Lord, as with Nalakūvara and Maṇigrīva, one can remember.

Sage Nārada therefore contemplated that the two demigods should remain for one hundred years, in the time of the demigods, in the form of trees, and after that they would be fortunate enough to see the Supreme Personality of Godhead face to face, by His causeless mercy. And thus they would be again promoted to the life of the demigods and become great devotees of the Lord.

After this, the great sage Nārada returned to his abode, known as Nārāyaṇāśrama, and the two demigods turned into trees, known as twin *arjuna* trees. The two demigods were favored by the causeless mercy of Nārada and given a chance to grow in Nanda's courtyard and see Lord Kṛṣṇa face to face.

Although child Kṛṣṇa was bound up to the wooden mortar, He began to proceed toward the twin trees in order to fulfill the prophecy of His great devotee Nārada. Lord Kṛṣṇa knew that Nārada was His great devotee and that the trees standing before Him as twin *arjuna* trees were actually the sons of Kuvera. "I must now fulfill the words of My great devotee Nārada," He thought. Then He proceeded through the passage between the two trees. Although He was able to pass through the passage, the large wooden mortar stuck horizontally between the trees. Taking advantage of this, with great strength Lord Kṛṣṇa began to pull the rope, which was tied to the mortar. As soon as He pulled, the two trees, with all their branches and limbs, fell down with a great sound. Out of the broken, fallen trees came two great personalities, shining like blazing fire. All sides became illuminated and beautiful by their presence. The two purified personalities immediately came before child Kṛṣṇa and bowed down to offer their respects and prayers in the following words.

"Dear Lord Kṛṣṇa, You are the original Personality of Godhead, master of all mystic powers. Learned *brāhmaṇas* know very well that this cosmic manifestation is an expansion of Your potencies, which are sometimes manifest and sometimes unmanifest. You are the original provider of the life, body and senses of all living entities. You are the eternal God, Lord Viṣṇu, who is all-pervading, the imperishable controller of everything, and You are eternal time. You are the original source of the cosmic manifestation, which is acting under the spell of the three modes of material nature—goodness, passion and ignorance. You are living as the Supersoul in all the multiforms of living entities, and You know very well what is going on within their bodies and minds. Therefore You are the supreme director of all activities of all living entities. But although You are in the midst of everything which is under the spell of the material modes of nature, You are not affected by such contaminated qualities. No one under the jurisdiction of the material modes can understand Your transcendental qualities, which existed before the creation; therefore You are called the Supreme Transcendence. Let us offer our respectful obeisances unto the lotus feet of You, Lord Vāsudeva, the Supreme Brahman, who are always glorified by Your personal internal potencies.

"In this material world You make Yourself known only by Your different incarnations. Although You assume different types of bodies, these bodies are not part of the material creation. They are always full of the transcendental potencies of unlimited opulence, strength, beauty, fame, wisdom and renunciation. In the material existence there is a difference between the body and the owner of the body, but because You appear in Your original spiritual body, there is no such difference for You. When You appear, Your uncommon activities indicate that You are the Supreme Personality of Godhead. Such uncommon activities are not possible for anyone in material existence. You, the Supreme Personality of Godhead, cause the birth and death as well as the liberation of the living entities, and You are full with all Your plenary expansions. You can bestow on everyone all kinds of benedictions. O Lord! O source of all auspiciousness and goodness, we offer our respectful obeisances unto You. You are the all-pervading Supreme Personality of Godhead, the supreme source of peace and the supreme personality in the dynasty of King Yadu. O Lord, our father, known as Kuvera, the demigod, is Your servant. Similarly, the great sage Nārada is also Your servitor, and only by their grace have we been able to see You personally. We therefore pray that we may always be engaged in Your transcendental loving service by speaking only about Your glories and hearing about Your transcendental activities. May our hands and other limbs be engaged in Your service and our minds always be concentrated at Your lotus feet and our heads always bowed down before the all-pervading universal form of Your Lordship."

When the demigods Nalakūvara and Maṇigrīva finished their prayers, the child, Lord Kṛṣṇa, the master and proprietor of Gokula, bound to the wooden grinding mortar by the ropes of Yaśodā, smiled and said, "It was already known to Me that My great devotee Nārada Muni had shown his causeless mercy by saving you from the abominable condition of pride due to possessing extraordinary beauty and opulence in a family of demigods. He has saved you from gliding down into the lowest condition of hellish life. All these facts are already known to Me. You are very fortunate because not only were you cursed by him, but you had the great opportunity to see him. If someone is able, by chance, to see face to face a great saintly person like Nārada, who is always serene and merciful to everyone, then immediately that conditioned soul becomes liberated. This is exactly like being situated in the full light of the sun: there cannot be any visionary impediment. Therefore, O Nalakūvara and Maṇigrīva, your lives have now become successful because you have developed ecstatic love for Me. This is your last birth within material existence. Now you can go back to your father's residence in the heavenly planets, and by remaining in the attitude of devotional service, you will be liberated in this very life."

After this, the demigods circumambulated the Lord many times and bowed down before Him again and again, and thus they left. The Lord remained bound up with ropes to the grinding mortar.

Thus ends the Bhaktivedanta purport of the Tenth Chapter of Kṛṣṇa, *"The Deliverance of Nalakūvara and Maṇigrīva."*

CHAPTER 11

Killing the Demons Vatsāsura and Bakāsura

WHEN THE TWIN *ARJUNA* TREES fell to the ground, making a sound like the falling of thunderbolts, all the inhabitants of Gokula, including Nanda Mahārāja, immediately came to the spot. They were very much astonished to see how the two great trees had suddenly fallen. Because they could find no reason for their falling down, they were puzzled. When they saw child Kṛṣṇa bound up to the wooden mortar by the ropes of mother Yaśodā, they thought that it must have been caused by some demon. Otherwise, how was it possible? At the same time, they were very much perturbed because such uncommon incidents were always happening to child Kṛṣṇa. While the cowherd men were thus contemplating, the small children who were playing there informed the men that the trees had fallen because Kṛṣṇa had pulled the wooden mortar with the rope binding Him. "Kṛṣṇa came in between the two trees," they explained, "and the wooden mortar was topsy-turvied and stuck in between the trees. Kṛṣṇa pulled the rope, and the trees fell down. When the trees fell down, two very dazzling men came out of the trees, and they said something to Kṛṣṇa."

Most of the cowherd men did not believe the statement of the children. They could not believe that such things were at all possible. Some of the men, however, believed them and told Nanda Mahārāja, "Your child is different from all other children. He just might have done it." Nanda Mahārāja smiled to hear about the extraordinary abilities of his son. He came forward and untied the knot just to free his wonderful child. After being freed by Nanda Mahārāja, Kṛṣṇa was taken onto the laps of the elder *gopīs.* They took Him away to the courtyard of the house and began to clap, praising His wonderful activities. Kṛṣṇa danced along with their clapping, just like an ordinary child. The Supreme Lord Kṛṣṇa, being completely controlled by the *gopīs,* sang and danced just like a puppet in their hands.

Sometimes mother Yaśodā used to ask Kṛṣṇa to bring her a wooden plank for sitting. Although the wooden plank was too heavy to be carried by a child, still somehow or other Kṛṣṇa would bring it to His mother. Sometimes His father, while worshiping Nārāyaṇa, would ask Him to bring his wooden slippers, and Kṛṣṇa, with great difficulty, would put the slippers on His head and bring them to His father. When He was asked to lift some heavy article and was unable to lift it, He would simply move His arms. In this way, daily, at every moment, He was the reservoir of all pleasure for His parents. The Lord was exhibiting such childish dealings with the inhabitants of Vṛndāvana because He wanted to show the great philosophers and sages searching after the Absolute Truth how the Supreme Absolute Truth Personality of Godhead is controlled by and subject to the desires of His pure devotees.

One day, a fruit vendor came before the house of Nanda Mahārāja. Upon hearing the vendor call, "If anyone wants fruits, please come and take them from me!" child Kṛṣṇa immediately took some grains in His palm and went to get fruits in exchange. In those days exchange was by barter; therefore Kṛṣṇa might have seen His parents acquire fruits and other things by bartering grain, and so He imitated. But His palms were very small, and He was not very careful to hold the grains tight, so He was dropping them. The vendor who came to sell fruits saw this and was very much captivated by the beauty of the Lord, so she immediately accepted whatever few grains were left in His palm and filled His hands with fruits. In the meantime, the vendor saw that her whole basket of fruit had become filled with jewels. The Lord is the bestower of all benedictions. If someone gives something to the Lord, he is not the loser; he is the gainer by a million times.

One day Lord Kṛṣṇa, the liberator of the twin *arjuna* trees, was playing with Balarāma and the other children on the bank of the Yamunā, and because it was already late in the morning, Rohiṇī, the mother of Balarāma, went to call them back home. But Balarāma and Kṛṣṇa were so engrossed in playing with Their friends that They did not wish to go back; They just engaged Themselves in playing more and more. When Rohiṇī was unable to take Them back home, she went home and sent mother Yaśodā to call Them again. Mother Yaśodā was so affectionate toward her son that as soon as she came out to call Him back home, her breasts filled up with milk.

She loudly cried, "My dear child, please come back home. Your time for lunch is already past." She then said, "My dear Kṛṣṇa, O my dear lotus-eyed child, please come and suck my breast. You have played enough. You must be very hungry, my dear little child. You must be tired from playing for so long." She also addressed Balarāma thus: "My dear Rāma, the glory of Your family, my dear child, please come back with Your younger brother Kṛṣṇa immediately. You have been engaged in playing since early morning, and You must be very tired. Please come back and take Your lunch at home. Your father Nandarāja is waiting for You. He has to eat, so You must come back so that he can eat."

As soon as Kṛṣṇa and Balarāma heard that Nanda Mahārāja was waiting for Them and could not take his food in Their absence, They started to return. Their playmates complained, "Kṛṣṇa is leaving us just at the point when our playing is at the summit. Next time we shall not allow Him to leave."

His playmates then threatened not to allow Him to play with them again. Kṛṣṇa became afraid, and instead of going back home, He went back again to play with the boys.

At that time, mother Yaśodā scolded the children and told Kṛṣṇa, "My dear Kṛṣṇa, do You think that You are a street boy? You have no home? Please come back to Your home! I see that Your body has become very dirty from playing since early morning. Now come home and take Your bath. Besides, today is Your birthday ceremony; therefore You should come back home and give cows in charity to the *brāhmaṇas.* Don't You see how Your playmates are decorated with ornaments by their mothers? You should also be cleansed and decorated with nice dress and ornaments. Please, therefore, come back, take Your bath, dress Yourself nicely, and then again You may go on playing."

In this way mother Yaśodā called back Lord Kṛṣṇa and Balarāma, who are worshipable by great demigods like Lord Brahmā and Lord Śiva. She was thinking of Them as her children.

When mother Yaśodā's children, Kṛṣṇa and Balarāma, came home, she bathed Them very nicely and dressed Them with ornaments. She then called for the *brāhmaṇas,* and through her children she gave many cows in charity for the occasion of Kṛṣṇa's birthday. In this way she performed the birthday ceremony of Kṛṣṇa at home.

After this incident, all the elder cowherd men assembled together, and Nanda Mahārāja presided. They began to consult amongst themselves how to stop the great disturbances in Mahāvana on account of the demons. In this meeting, Upananda, the brother of Nanda Mahārāja, was present. He was considered to be learned and experienced, and he was a well-wisher of Kṛṣṇa and Balarāma. He was a leader, and he addressed the meeting as follows: "My dear friends! Now we should leave here for another place because we are continually finding that great demons are coming here to disturb the peaceful situation, and they are especially attempting to kill the small children. Just consider Pūtanā and Kṛṣṇa. It was simply by the grace of Lord Hari that Kṛṣṇa was saved from the hands of such a great demon. Next the whirlwind demon took Kṛṣṇa away into the sky, but by the grace of Lord Hari He was saved, and the demon fell down on a stone slab and died. Very recently, this child was playing between two trees, and the trees fell down violently, and yet there was no injury to the child. So Lord Hari saved Him again. Just imagine the calamity if this child or any other child playing with Him were crushed by the falling trees! Considering all these incidents, we must conclude that this place is no longer safe. Let us leave. We have all been saved from different calamities by the grace of Lord Hari. Now we should be cautious and leave this place and reside somewhere where we can live peacefully. I think that we should all go to the forest known as Vṛndāvana, where just now there are newly grown plants and herbs. It is very suitable for pasturing ground for our cows, and we and our families, the *gopīs* with their children, can very peacefully live there. Near Vṛndāvana is Govardhana Hill, which is very beautiful, and there are newly grown grass and fodder for the animals, so there will be no difficulty in living there. I therefore suggest that we start immediately for that beautiful place, as there is no need to waste any more time. Let us prepare all our carts immediately, and, if you like, let us go, keeping all the cows in front."

On hearing the statement of Upananda, all the cowherd men immediately agreed. "Let us immediately go there." Everyone then loaded all their household furniture and utensils onto the carts and prepared to go to Vṛndāvana. All the children, women and old men of the village were arranged on seats, and the cowherd men equipped themselves with bows and arrows to follow the carts. All the cows and bulls were placed in the front along with their calves, and the men, with their bows and arrows, surrounded the herds and carts and began to blow on their horns and bugles. In this way, with tumultuous sound, they started for Vṛndāvana.

And who can describe the damsels of Vraja? They were all seated on the carts and were very beautifully dressed with ornaments and costly saris. They chanted the pastimes of child Kṛṣṇa as usual. Mother Yaśodā and mother Rohiṇī were seated on a separate cart, and Kṛṣṇa and Balarāma were seated on their laps. While mother Rohiṇī and Yaśodā were riding on the cart, they talked to Kṛṣṇa and Balarāma, and feeling the pleasure of such talks, they looked very, very beautiful.

In this way, after reaching Vṛndāvana, where everyone lives eternally, very peacefully and happily, they encircled Vṛndāvana, drew all the carts together in a half circle, and in this way constructed a temporary residence. When Kṛṣṇa and Balarāma saw the beautiful appearance of Vṛndāvana, Govardhana Hill and the banks of the river Yamunā, They felt very happy. As They grew up They began talking with Their parents and others in childish language, and thus They gave great pleasure to all the inhabitants of Vṛndāvana.

Soon Kṛṣṇa and Balarāma had grown sufficiently to be given charge of the calves. From the very beginning of their childhood, cowherd boys are trained to take care of the cows, and their first responsibility is to take care of the little calves. So along with the other little cowherd boys, Kṛṣṇa and Balarāma went into the pasturing ground and took charge of the calves, and there They played with Their playmates. While taking charge of the calves, sometimes the two brothers played on Their flutes. And sometimes They played with *āmalaka* fruits and bael fruits, just as small children play with balls. Sometimes They danced and made tinkling sounds with Their ankle bells. Sometimes They made Themselves into bulls and cows by covering Themselves with blankets. Thus Kṛṣṇa and Balarāma played. The two brothers also used to imitate the sounds of bulls and cows and play at bullfighting. Sometimes They used to imitate the sounds of various animals and birds. In this way, They enjoyed Their childhood pastimes apparently like ordinary, mundane children.

Once, when Kṛṣṇa and Balarāma were playing on the bank of the Yamunā, a demon of the name Vatsāsura assumed the shape of a calf and came there intending to kill the brothers. By taking the shape of a calf, the demon could mingle with the other calves. Kṛṣṇa, however, specifically noticed this, and He immediately alerted Balarāma about the entrance of the demon. Both brothers then silently approached him. Kṛṣṇa caught hold of the demon-calf by the two hind legs and tail, whipped him around very forcibly and threw him up into a tree. The demon lost his life and fell down from the top of the tree to the ground. When the demon lay dead on the ground, all the playmates of Kṛṣṇa congratulated Him, "Well done, well done!" and the demigods in the sky showered flowers with great satisfaction. In this way, the maintainers of the complete creation, Kṛṣṇa and Balarāma, used to take care of the calves every day, beginning in the morning, and thus They enjoyed Their childhood pastimes as cowherd boys in Vṛndāvana.

One day, all the cowherd boys went to the bank of the river Yamunā to water their calves. When the calves drank water from the Yamunā, the boys also drank. After drinking, when they were sitting on the bank of the river, they saw a huge animal which looked something like a heron and was as big as a hill. Its top was as strong as a thunderbolt. When they saw that unusual animal, they became afraid of it. The name of this beast was Bakāsura, and he was a friend of Kaṁsa's. He appeared on the scene suddenly and immediately attacked Kṛṣṇa with his pointed, sharp beak and quickly swallowed Him up. When Kṛṣṇa was thus swallowed, all the boys, headed by Balarāma, became almost breathless, as if they had died. But when the Bakāsura demon was swallowing up Kṛṣṇa, he felt a burning, fiery sensation in his throat. This was due to the glowing effulgence of Kṛṣṇa. The demon quickly threw Kṛṣṇa up and tried to kill Him by pinching Him with his beak. Bakāsura did not know that although Kṛṣṇa was playing the part of a child of Nanda Mahārāja, He was still the original father of Lord Brahmā, the creator of the universe. Mother Yaśodā's child, who is the reservoir of pleasure for the demigods and who is the maintainer of saintly persons, caught hold of the great gigantic heron by the two halves of his beak and, before His cowherd boyfriends, bifurcated his mouth, just as a child very easily splits a blade of grass. From the sky, the denizens of the heavenly planets showered flowers like the *mallikā*, the most fragrant of all flowers, as a token of their congratulations. Accompanying the showers of flowers was a vibration of bugles, drums and conchshells.

When the boys saw the showering of flowers and heard the celestial sounds, they were struck with wonder. And when they saw Kṛṣṇa freed from the mouth of the great demon Bakāsura, all of them, including Balarāma, were so pleased that it seemed as if they had regained their very source of life. As soon as they saw Kṛṣṇa coming toward them, they one after another embraced the son of Nanda and held Him to their chests. After this, they assembled all the calves under their charge and began to return home.

When they arrived home, they spoke of the wonderful activities of the son of Nanda. When the *gopīs* and cowherd men all heard the story from the boys, they felt great happiness because naturally they loved Kṛṣṇa, and by hearing about His glories and victorious activities they became still more affectionate toward Him. Thinking that child Kṛṣṇa had been saved from the mouth of death, they looked upon His face with great love and affection. They were full of anxiety and could not turn their faces from the vision of Kṛṣṇa. The *gopīs* and the men began to converse amongst themselves about how wonderful it was that child Kṛṣṇa had been attacked in so many ways and so many times by so many demons, and yet the demons themselves had been killed and Kṛṣṇa had remained uninjured. They continued to converse amongst themselves about how so many great demons in such fierce bodies had attacked Kṛṣṇa to kill Him but, by the grace of Hari, had not been able to cause even a slight injury. Rather, they had died like small flies in a fire. Thus they remembered the words of Garga Muni, who had foretold, by dint of his vast knowledge of the *Vedas* and astrology, that this boy would be attacked by many demons. Now they were actually seeing that this was coming true, word for word.

All the cowherd men, including Nanda Mahārāja, used to talk of the wonderful activities of Lord Kṛṣṇa and Balarāma, and they were always so much absorbed in those talks that they forgot the threefold miseries of this material existence. This is the effect of Kṛṣṇa consciousness. What was enjoyed five thousand years ago by Nanda Mahārāja can still be enjoyed by Kṛṣṇa conscious persons simply by talking about the transcendental pastimes of Kṛṣṇa and His associates.

In this way Balarāma and Kṛṣṇa enjoyed Their childhood pastimes, imitating Lord Rāmacandra's monkeys, who constructed the bridge over the ocean, and Hanumān, who jumped over the water to Ceylon. They used to imitate such pastimes among Their friends and so happily passed Their childhood life.

Thus ends the Bhaktivedanta purport of the Eleventh Chapter of Kṛṣṇa, *"Killing the Demons Vatsāsura and Bakāsura."*

CHAPTER 12

The Killing of the Aghāsura Demon

ONCE THE LORD DESIRED to go early in the morning with all His cowherd boyfriends to the forest, where they were to assemble together and take lunch. As soon as He got up from bed, He blew His buffalo-horn bugle and called all His friends together. Keeping the calves before them, they started for the forest in a great procession. In this way, Lord Kṛṣṇa assembled thousands of His boyfriends. They were each equipped with a stick, flute and horn, as well as a lunch bag, and each of them was taking care of thousands of calves. All the boys appeared very jolly and happy in that excursion. Each and every one of them, including Kṛṣṇa, was attentive to his personal calves as he herded them in the different places in the forest. The boys were fully decorated with various kinds of golden ornaments, yet out of sporting propensities they began to pick up flowers, leaves, twigs, peacock feathers and red clay from different places in the forest and further decorate themselves in different ways. While passing through the forest, one boy stole another boy's lunch package and passed it to a third. And when the boy whose lunch package was stolen came to know of it, he tried to take it back. But the boy who had it threw it to another boy. This sportive playing went on amongst the boys as childhood pastimes.

When Lord Kṛṣṇa went ahead to a distant place in order to see some specific scenery, the boys behind Him ran to try to catch up and be the first to touch Him. So there was a great competition. One would say, "I will go there and touch Kṛṣṇa," and another would say, "Oh, you cannot go. I'll touch Kṛṣṇa first." Some of them played on their flutes or vibrated bugles made of buffalo horn. Some of them gladly followed the peacocks and imitated the onomatopoetic sounds of the cuckoo. While the birds were flying in the sky, the boys ran after the birds' shadows along the ground and tried to follow their exact courses. Some of them went to the monkeys and silently sat down by them, and some of them imitated the dancing of the peacocks. Some of them caught monkeys by the tail and played with them, and when the monkeys jumped into a tree, the boys followed. When a monkey showed its face and teeth, a boy imitated and showed his teeth to the monkey. Some of the boys played with the frogs on the bank of the Yamunā, and when, out of fear, the frogs jumped into the water, the boys immediately dove in after them, and they would come out of the water when they saw their own shadows and stand imitating, making caricatures and laughing. They would also go to an empty well and make loud sounds, and when the echo came back, they would call it ill names and laugh.

As stated personally by the Supreme Personality of Godhead in the *Bhagavad-gītā,* He is realized proportionately by transcendentalists as Brahman, Paramātmā and the Supreme Personality of Godhead. Here, in confirmation of the same statement, Lord Kṛṣṇa, who awards the impersonalist the pleasure of Brahman realization by His bodily effulgence, also gives pleasure to the devotees as the Supreme Personality of Godhead. Those who are under the spell of the external energy, *māyā,* take Him only as a beautiful child. Yet He gave full transcendental pleasure to the cowherd boys who played with Him. Only after accumulating heaps of pious activities were those boys promoted to personally associate with the Supreme Personality of Godhead. Who can estimate the transcendental fortune of the residents of Vṛndāvana? They were personally seeing the Supreme Personality of Godhead face to face, He whom many *yogīs* cannot find even after undergoing severe austerities, although He is sitting within their hearts. This is confirmed in the *Brahma-saṁhitā:* One may search for Kṛṣṇa, the Supreme Personality of Godhead, through the pages of the *Vedas* and *Upaniṣads,* but it is difficult to find Him there. However, one who is fortunate enough to associate with a devotee can see the Supreme Personality of Godhead face to face. After accumulating pious activities in many, many previous lives, the cowherd boys were seeing Kṛṣṇa face to face and playing with Him as friends. They could not understand that Kṛṣṇa is the Supreme Personality of Godhead, but they were playing as intimate friends with intense love for Him.

When Lord Kṛṣṇa was enjoying His childhood pastimes with His boyfriends, one Aghāsura demon became very impatient. He was unable to tolerate seeing Kṛṣṇa play so happily, and therefore he appeared before the boys intending to kill them all. This Aghāsura was so dangerous that even the denizens of heaven were afraid of him. Although the denizens of heaven drank nectar daily to prolong their lives, they were afraid of this Aghāsura and were wondering, "When will the demon be killed?" The denizens used to drink nectar to become immortal, but actually they were not confident of their immortality. On the other hand, the boys who were playing with Kṛṣṇa had no fear of the demons. They were free of fear. Any material arrangement for protecting oneself from death is always unsure, but if one is in Kṛṣṇa consciousness, then immortality is confidently assured.

The demon Aghāsura appeared before Kṛṣṇa and His friends. Aghāsura happened to be the younger brother of Pūtanā and Bakāsura, and he thought, "Kṛṣṇa has killed my brother and sister. Now I shall kill Him along with all His friends and calves." Aghāsura was instigated by Kaṁsa, so he had come with determination. Aghāsura also thought that when he would offer grains and water in memory of his brother and sister and kill Kṛṣṇa and all the cowherd boys, then automatically all the inhabitants of Vṛndāvana would die. Generally, for the householders, the children are the life and breath force. When all the children die, then naturally the parents also die on account of strong affection for them.

Aghāsura, thus deciding to kill all the inhabitants of Vṛndāvana, expanded himself by the yogic *siddhi* called *mahimā*. The demons are generally expert in achieving almost all kinds of mystic powers. In the *yoga* system, by the perfection called *mahimā-siddhi,* one can expand himself as he desires. The demon Aghāsura expanded himself up to eight miles and assumed the shape of a very fat serpent. Having attained this wonderful body, he stretched his mouth open just like a mountain cave. Desiring to swallow all the boys at once, including Kṛṣṇa and Balarāma, he sat on the path.

The demon in the shape of a big fat serpent expanded his lips from land to sky; his lower lip was touching the ground, and his upper lip was touching the clouds. His jaws appeared like a big mountain cave, without limitation, and his teeth appeared just like mountain summits. His tongue appeared to be a broad traffic way, and he was breathing just like a hurricane. His eyes were blazing like fire. At first the boys thought that the demon was a statue, but after examining it they saw that it was a big serpent lying down on the road and widening his mouth. The boys began to talk among themselves: "Dear friends, this figure appears to be a great animal, and he is sitting in such a posture just to swallow us all. Just see—is it not a big snake that has widened his mouth to eat all of us?"

One of them said, "Yes, what you say is true. This animal's upper lip appears to be just like the sunshine, and its lower lip is just like the reflection of red sunshine on the ground. Dear friends, just look to the right- and left-hand side of the mouth of the animal. Its mouth appears to be like a big mountain cave, and its height cannot be estimated. The chin is also raised just like a mountain summit. That long highway appears to be its tongue, and inside the mouth it is as dark as in a mountain cave. The hot wind that is blowing like a hurricane is his breathing, and the fishy bad smell coming out from his mouth is the smell of his intestines."

Then they further consulted among themselves: "If we all at one time entered into the mouth of this great serpent, how could it possibly swallow all of us? And even if it were to swallow all of us at once, it could not swallow Kṛṣṇa. Kṛṣṇa will immediately kill him, as He did Bakāsura." Talking in this way, all the boys looked at the beautiful lotuslike face of Kṛṣṇa, and they began to clap and smile. And so they marched forward and entered the mouth of the gigantic serpent.

Meanwhile, Kṛṣṇa, who is the Supersoul within everyone's heart, could understand that the big statuesque figure was a demon. The boys did not know this, however, and thus while Kṛṣṇa was planning how to stop the destruction of His intimate friends, all the boys along with their calves entered the mouth of the serpent. But Kṛṣṇa did not enter. The demon was awaiting Kṛṣṇa's entrance, and he was thinking, "Everyone has entered except Kṛṣṇa, who has killed my brother and sister."

Kṛṣṇa is the assurance of safety to everyone. But when He saw that His friends were already out of His hands and were lying within the belly of a great serpent, He became momentarily aggrieved. He was also struck with wonder at how the external energy works so wonderfully. He then began to consider how He could kill the demon and at the same time save the boys and calves. Although there was no factual concern on Kṛṣṇa's part, He was thinking like that. Finally, after some deliberation, He also entered the mouth of the demon. When Kṛṣṇa entered, all the demigods, who had gathered to see the fun and who were hiding within the clouds, expressed their feelings with the words "Alas! Alas!" At the same time, all the friends of Aghāsura, especially Kaṁsa, who were all accustomed to eating flesh and blood, expressed their jubilation, understanding that Kṛṣṇa had also entered the mouth of the demon.

While the demon was trying to smash Kṛṣṇa and His companions, Kṛṣṇa heard the demigods crying "Alas! Alas!" and He immediately began to expand Himself within the throat of the demon. Although he had a gigantic body, the demon choked by the expanding of Kṛṣṇa. His big eyes moved violently, and he quickly suffocated. His life air could not come out from any source, and ultimately it burst out of a hole in the upper part of his skull. Thus his life air passed off. After the demon was dead, Kṛṣṇa, with His transcendental glance alone, brought all the boys and calves back to consciousness and came with them out of the mouth of the demon. While Kṛṣṇa was within the mouth of Aghāsura, the demon's spirit soul came out like a dazzling light, illuminating all directions, and waited in the sky. As soon as Kṛṣṇa came out of the mouth of the demon with His calves and friends, that glittering effulgent light immediately merged into the body of Kṛṣṇa within the vision of all the demigods.

The demigods became overwhelmed with joy and showered flowers on the Supreme Personality of Godhead, Kṛṣṇa, and thus they worshiped Him. The denizens of heaven danced in jubilation, and the denizens in Gandharvaloka offered various kinds of prayers. Drummers beat drums in jubilation, the *brāhmaṇas* recited Vedic hymns, and all the devotees of the Lord chanted the words "*Jaya! Jaya!* All glories to the Supreme Personality of Godhead!"

When Lord Brahmā heard those auspicious vibrations, which sounded throughout the higher planetary system, he immediately came down to see what had happened. He saw that the demon was killed, and he was struck with wonder at the uncommon, glorious pastimes of the Personality of Godhead.

The gigantic mouth of the demon remained in an open position for many days and gradually dried up; it remained a spot of pleasure pastimes for all the cowherd boys.

The killing of Aghāsura took place when Kṛṣṇa and all His boyfriends were under five years old. Children under five years old are called *kaumāra,* from five years up to the tenth year they are called *paugaṇḍa,* and from the tenth year up to the fifteenth year they are called *kaiśora.* After the fifteenth year, boys are called youths. For one year there was no discussion of the incident of the Aghāsura demon in the village of Vraja. But when the boys attained their sixth year, they informed their parents of the incident with great wonder.

For Śrī Kṛṣṇa, the Supreme Personality of Godhead, who is far greater than such demigods as Lord Brahmā, it is not at all difficult to award one the opportunity of merging with His eternal body. This He awarded to Aghāsura. Aghāsura was certainly the most sinful living entity, and it is not possible for the sinful to merge into the existence of the Absolute Truth. But in this particular case, because Kṛṣṇa entered into Aghāsura's body, the demon became fully cleansed of all sinful reactions. Persons constantly thinking of the eternal form of the Lord in the shape of the Deity or in the shape of a mental form are awarded the transcendental benediction of entering into the kingdom of God and associating with the Supreme Personality of Godhead. So we can just imagine the elevated position of someone like Aghāsura, into whose body the Supreme Personality of Godhead, Kṛṣṇa, personally entered. Great sages, meditators and devotees constantly keep the form of the Lord within their hearts, or they see the Deity form of the Lord in the temples; in that way they become liberated from all material contamination and at the end of the body enter into the kingdom of God. This perfection is possible simply by keeping the form of the Lord within the mind. But in the case of Aghāsura, the Supreme Personality of Godhead personally entered. Aghāsura's position was therefore greater than the ordinary devotee's or the greatest *yogī's.*

Mahārāja Parīkṣit, who was engaged in hearing the transcendental pastimes of Lord Kṛṣṇa (who saved the life of Mahārāja Parīkṣit while he was in the womb of his mother), became more and more interested to hear about Him. And thus he questioned the sage Śukadeva Gosvāmī, who was reciting *Śrīmad-Bhāgavatam* before the King.

King Parīkṣit was a bit astonished to understand that the killing of the Aghāsura demon was not discussed for one year, until after the boys attained the *paugaṇḍa* age. Mahārāja Parīkṣit was very inquisitive to learn about this, for he was sure that such an incident was due to the working of Kṛṣṇa's different energies.

Generally, the *kṣatriyas* or the administrative class are always busy with their political affairs, and they have very little chance to hear about the transcendental pastimes of Lord Kṛṣṇa. But while Parīkṣit Mahārāja was hearing these transcendental pastimes, he considered himself to be very fortunate because not only was he hearing Kṛṣṇa's pastimes but he was doing so from Śukadeva Gosvāmī, the greatest authority on *Śrīmad-Bhāgavatam.* Thus being requested by Mahārāja Parīkṣit, Śukadeva Gosvāmī continued to speak about the transcendental pastimes of Lord Kṛṣṇa in the matter of His form, quality, fame and paraphernalia.

Thus ends the Bhaktivedanta purport of the Twelfth Chapter of Kṛṣṇa, *"The Killing of the Aghāsura Demon."*

CHAPTER 13

The Stealing of the Boys and Calves by Brahmā

ŚUKADEVA GOSVĀMĪ was very much encouraged when Mahārāja Parīkṣit asked him why the cowherd boys did not discuss the death of Aghāsura until after one year had passed. He explained thus: "My dear King, you are making the subject matter of the transcendental pastimes of Kṛṣṇa fresher by your inquisitiveness."

It is said that it is the nature of a devotee to constantly apply his mind, energy, words, ears, etc., in hearing and chanting about Kṛṣṇa. This is called Kṛṣṇa consciousness, and for one who is rapt in hearing and chanting about Kṛṣṇa, the subject matter never becomes hackneyed or old. That is the significance of transcendental subject matter in contrast to material subject matter. Material subject matter becomes stale, and one cannot hear a certain subject for a long time; he wants change. But as far as transcendental subject matter is concerned, it is called *nitya-nava-navāyamāna.* This means that one can go on chanting and hearing about the Lord and never feel tired but remain fresh and eager to hear more and more. It is the duty of the spiritual master to disclose all confidential subject matter to the inquisitive and sincere disciple. Thus Śukadeva Gosvāmī began to explain why the killing of Aghāsura was not discussed until one year had passed. Śukadeva Gosvāmī told the King, "Now hear of this secret with attention. After saving His friends from the mouth of Aghāsura and killing the demon, Lord Kṛṣṇa brought His friends to the bank of the Yamunā and addressed them as follows: 'My dear friends, just see how this spot is very nice for taking lunch and playing on the soft, sandy Yamunā bank. You can see how the lotus flowers in the water are beautifully blown and how they distribute their fragrance all around. The chirping of the birds along with cooing of the peacocks, surrounded by the whispering of the leaves in the trees, combine and present sound vibrations that echo one another. And this just enriches the beautiful scenery created by the trees here. Let us have our lunch in this spot because it is already late and we are feeling hungry. Let the calves remain near us, and let them drink water from the Yamunā. While we engage in our lunch-taking, the calves may engage in eating the soft grasses that are in this spot.' "

On hearing this proposal from Kṛṣṇa, all the boys became very glad and said, "Certainly, let us all sit down here to take our lunch." They then let loose the calves to eat the soft grass. Sitting down on the ground and keeping Kṛṣṇa in the center, they began to open their lunch boxes brought from home. Lord Śrī Kṛṣṇa was seated in the center of the circle, and all the boys kept their faces toward Him. They ate and constantly enjoyed seeing the Lord face to face. Kṛṣṇa appeared to be the whorl of a lotus flower, and the boys surrounding Him appeared to be its different petals. The boys collected flowers, leaves of flowers and the bark of trees and placed their lunch on them, as well as in their lunch boxes, and thus they began to eat their lunch, keeping company with Kṛṣṇa. While taking lunch, each boy began to manifest different kinds of relations with Kṛṣṇa, and they enjoyed each other's company with joking words. While Lord Kṛṣṇa was thus enjoying lunch with His friends, His flute was pushed within the belt of His cloth on His right side, and His bugle and cane were pushed in on the left-hand side of His cloth. In his left palm He was holding a lump of food prepared with yogurt, butter, rice and pieces of fruit salad, which could be seen through His petallike fingerjoints. The Supreme Personality of Godhead, who accepts the results of all great sacrifices, was laughing and joking, enjoying lunch with His friends in Vṛndāvana. And thus the scene was being observed by the demigods from heaven. As for the boys, they were simply enjoying transcendental bliss in the company of the Supreme Personality of Godhead.

At that time, the calves that were pasturing nearby entered into the deep forest, allured by new grasses, and gradually went out of sight. When the boys saw that the calves were not nearby, they became afraid for their safety, and they immediately cried out, "Kṛṣṇa!" Kṛṣṇa is the killer of fear personified. Everyone is afraid of fear personified, but fear personified is afraid of Kṛṣṇa. By crying out the word "Kṛṣṇa," the boys at once transcended the fearful situation. Out of His great affection, Kṛṣṇa did not want His friends to give up their pleasing lunch engagement and go searching for the calves. He therefore said, "My dear friends, you need not interrupt your lunch. Go on enjoying. I am going personally to find the calves." Thus Lord Kṛṣṇa, still carrying the lump of yogurt-and-rice preparation in His left hand, immediately started to search out the calves in the caves and bushes. He searched in the mountain holes and in the forests, but nowhere could He find them.

At the time when Aghāsura was killed and the demigods were looking on the incident with great surprise, Brahmā, who was born of the lotus flower growing out of the navel of Viṣṇu, also came to see. He was surprised how a little boy like Kṛṣṇa could act so wonderfully. Although he was informed that the little cowherd boy was the Supreme Personality of Godhead, he wanted to see more of the Lord's glorious pastimes, and thus he stole all the calves and cowherd boys and took them to a different place. Lord Kṛṣṇa, therefore, in spite of searching for the calves, could not find them, and He even lost His boyfriends on the bank of the Yamunā, where they had been taking their lunch. In the form of a cowherd boy, Lord Kṛṣṇa was very little in comparison to Brahmā, but because He is the Supreme Personality of Godhead, He could immediately understand that all the calves and boys had been stolen by Brahmā. Kṛṣṇa thought, "Brahmā has taken away all the boys and calves. How can I alone return to Vṛndāvana? The mothers will be aggrieved!"

Therefore in order to satisfy the mothers of His friends, as well as to convince Brahmā of the supremacy of the Personality of Godhead, He immediately expanded Himself as the cowherd boys and calves. In the *Vedas* it is said that the Supreme Personality of Godhead has already expanded Himself into so many living entities by His energy. Therefore it was not very difficult for Him to expand Himself again into so many boys and calves. He expanded Himself to become exactly like the boys, who were of all different features and facial and bodily constructions, and who were different in their clothing and ornaments and in their behavior and personal activities. In other words, although each boy, being an individual soul, had entirely different tastes, activities and behavior, Kṛṣṇa exactly expanded Himself into all the different positions of the individual boys. He also became the calves, who were also of different sizes, colors, activities, etc. This was possible because everything is an expansion of Kṛṣṇa's energy. In the *Viṣṇu Purāṇa* it is said, *parasya brahmaṇaḥ śaktiḥ.* Whatever we actually see in the cosmic manifestation—be it matter or the activities of the living entities—is simply an expansion of the energies of the Lord, as heat and light are the different expansions of fire.

Thus expanding Himself as the boys and calves in their individual capacities, and surrounded by such expansions of Himself, Kṛṣṇa entered the village of Vṛndāvana. The residents had no knowledge of what had happened. After entering the village of Vṛndāvana, all the calves entered their respective cowsheds, and the boys went to their respective mothers and homes.

The mothers of the boys heard the vibration of their flutes before their entrance, and to receive them, they came out of their homes and embraced them. And out of maternal affection, milk was flowing from their breasts, and they allowed the boys to drink it. However, their offering was not exactly to their boys but to the Supreme Personality of Godhead, who had expanded Himself into such boys. This was a chance for all the mothers of Vṛndāvana to feed the Supreme Personality of Godhead with their own milk. Therefore not only did Lord Kṛṣṇa give Yaśodā the chance to feed Him, but this time He gave the chance to all the other elder *gopīs*.

All the boys dealt with their mothers as usual, and the mothers also, on the approach of evening, bathed their respective children, decorated them with *tilaka* and ornaments and gave them necessary food after the day's labor. The cows also, who were away in the pasturing ground, returned in the evening and called their respective calves. The calves immediately came to their mothers, and the mothers began to lick the bodies of the calves. These relations between the cows and the *gopīs* with their calves and boys remained unchanged, although actually the original calves and boys were not there. Actually the cows' affection for their calves and the elder *gopīs'* affection for the boys causelessly increased. Their affection increased naturally, even though the calves and boys were not their offspring. Although the cows and elder *gopīs* of Vṛndāvana had greater affection for Kṛṣṇa than for their own offspring, after this incident their affection for their offspring increased unlimitedly, exactly as it did for Kṛṣṇa. For one year continuously, Kṛṣṇa Himself expanded as the calves and cowherd boys and was present in the pasturing ground.

As it is stated in the *Bhagavad-gītā*, Kṛṣṇa's expansion is situated in everyone's heart as the Supersoul. Similarly, instead of expanding Himself as the Supersoul, He expanded Himself as a portion of calves and cowherd boys for one continuous year.

One day, a few days before a year had passed, Kṛṣṇa and Balarāma were maintaining the calves in the forest when They saw some cows grazing on the top of Govardhana Hill. The cows could see down into the valley where the calves were being taken care of by the boys. Suddenly, on sighting the calves, the cows began to run toward them. They leaped downhill with joined front and rear legs. The cows were so melted with affection for the calves that they did not care about the rough path from the top of Govardhana Hill down to the pasturing ground. They approached the calves with their milk bags full of milk, and they raised their tails upwards. When they were coming down the hill, their milk bags were pouring milk on the ground out of intense maternal affection for the calves, although they were not their own calves. These cows had their own calves, and the calves that were grazing beneath Govardhana Hill were larger; they were not expected to drink milk directly from the milk bag but were satisfied with the grass. Yet all the cows came immediately and began to lick their bodies, and the calves also began to suck milk from the milk bags. There appeared to be a great bond of affection between the cows and calves.

When the cows were running down from the top of Govardhana Hill, the men who were taking care of them tried to stop them. Older cows are taken care of by the men, and the calves are taken care of by the boys; and as far as possible, the calves are kept separate from the cows, so that the calves do not drink all the available milk. Therefore the men who were taking care of the cows on the top of Govardhana Hill tried to stop them, but they failed. Baffled by their failure, they were feeling ashamed and angry. They were very unhappy, but when they came down and saw their children taking care of the calves, they all of a sudden became very affectionate toward the children. It was very astonishing. Although the men came down disappointed, baffled and angry, as soon as they saw their own children, their hearts melted with great affection. At once their anger, dissatisfaction and unhappiness disappeared. They began to show paternal love for the children, and with great affection they lifted them in their arms and embraced them. They began to smell their children's heads and enjoy their company with great happiness. After embracing their children, the men took the cows back to the top of Govardhana Hill. Along the way they began to think of their children, and affectionate tears fell from their eyes.

When Balarāma saw this extraordinary exchange of affection between the cows and their calves and between the fathers and their children—when neither the calves nor the children needed so much care—He began to wonder why this extraordinary thing had happened. He was astonished to see all the residents of Vṛndāvana so affectionate to their own children, exactly as they had been to Kṛṣṇa. Similarly, the cows had grown affectionate to their calves—as much as to Kṛṣṇa. Balarāma therefore concluded that the extraordinary show of affection was something mystical, either performed by the demigods or by some powerful man. Otherwise, how could this wonderful change take place? He concluded that this mystical change must have been caused by Kṛṣṇa, whom Balarāma considered His worshipable Personality of Godhead. He thought, "It was arranged by Kṛṣṇa, and even I could not check its mystic power." Thus Balarāma understood that all those boys and calves were only expansions of Kṛṣṇa.

Balarāma inquired from Kṛṣṇa about the actual situation. He said, "My dear Kṛṣṇa, in the beginning I thought that all these calves and cowherd boys were either great sages and saintly persons or demigods, but at present it appears that they are actually Your expansions. They are all You; You Yourself are playing as the calves and boys. What is the mystery of this situation? Where have those other calves and boys gone? And why are You expanding Yourself as the calves and boys? Will You kindly tell Me what is the cause?" At the request of Balarāma, Kṛṣṇa briefly explained the whole situation: how the calves and boys had been stolen by Brahmā and how Kṛṣṇa was concealing the incident by expanding Himself so people would not know that the original calves and boys were missing.

While Kṛṣṇa and Balarāma were talking, Brahmā returned after a moment's interval (according to the duration of his life). We have information of Lord Brahmā's duration of life from the *Bhagavad-gītā:* 1,000 times the duration of the four ages, or 1,000 x 4,320,000 years, constitute Brahmā's twelve hours. Similarly, one moment of Brahmā's time is equal to one year of our solar calculation. After one moment of Brahmā's calculation, Brahmā came back to see the fun caused by his stealing the boys and calves. But he was also afraid that he was playing with fire. Kṛṣṇa was his master, and he had played mischief for fun by taking away His calves and boys. He was really anxious, so he did not stay away very long; he came back after a moment (of his calculation). He saw that all the boys and calves were playing with Kṛṣṇa in the same way as when he had come upon them, although he was confident that he had taken them and made them lie down asleep under the spell of his mystic power. Brahmā began to think, "All the boys and calves were taken away by me, and I know they are still sleeping. How is it that a similar batch of boys and calves is playing with Kṛṣṇa? Is it that they are not influenced by my mystic power? Have they been playing continually for one year with Kṛṣṇa?" Brahmā tried to understand who they were and how they were uninfluenced by his mystic power, but he could not ascertain it. In other words, he himself came under the spell of his own mystic power. The influence of his mystic power appeared like snow in darkness or a glowworm in the daytime. During the night's darkness, the glowworm can show some glittering power, and the snow piled up on the top of a hill or on the ground can shine during the daytime. But at night the snow has no silver glitter, nor does the glowworm have any illuminating power during the daytime. Similarly, when the small mystic power exhibited by Brahmā was before the mystic power of Kṛṣṇa, it was just like snow at night or a glowworm during the day. When a man of small mystic power wants to show potency in the presence of greater mystic power, he diminishes his own influence; he does not increase it. Even such a great personality as Brahmā, when he wanted to show his mystic power before Kṛṣṇa, became ludicrous. Brahmā was thus confused about his own mystic power.

In order to convince Brahmā that all those calves and boys were not the original ones, the calves and boys who were playing with Kṛṣṇa transformed into Viṣṇu forms. Actually, the original ones were sleeping under the spell of Brahmā's mystic power, but the present ones, seen by Brahmā, were all immediate expansions of Kṛṣṇa, or Viṣṇu. Viṣṇu is the expansion of Kṛṣṇa, so the Viṣṇu forms appeared before Brahmā. All the Viṣṇu forms were of bluish color and dressed in yellow garments; all of Them had four hands decorated with club, disc, lotus flower and conchshell. On Their heads were glittering golden helmets inlaid with jewels; They were bedecked with pearls and earrings and garlanded with beautiful flowers. On Their chests was the mark of Śrīvatsa, Their arms were decorated with armlets and other jewelry, and Their necks were just like conchshells. Their legs were decorated with bells, Their waists with golden belts, and Their fingers with jeweled rings. Brahmā also saw that upon the whole body of each Lord Viṣṇu, from the lotus feet up to the top of the head, fresh *tulasī* leaves and buds had been thrown. Another significant feature of the Viṣṇu forms was that all of Them were looking transcendentally beautiful. Their smiling resembled the moonshine, and Their glancing resembled the early rising of the sun. Just by Their glancing They showed Themselves to be the creators and maintainers of the modes of ignorance and passion. Viṣṇu represents the mode of goodness, Brahmā the mode of passion, and Lord Śiva the mode of ignorance. Therefore as the maintainer of everything in the cosmic manifestation, Viṣṇu is also the creator and maintainer of Brahmā and Lord Śiva.

After this manifestation of Lord Viṣṇu, Brahmā saw that many other Brahmās and Śivas and demigods and even insignificant living entities down to the ants and very small straws—all moving and nonmoving living entities—were dancing, surrounding Lord Viṣṇu. Their dancing was accompanied by various kinds of music, and all of Them were worshiping Lord Viṣṇu. Brahmā realized that all those Viṣṇu forms were complete in mystic power, from the *aṇimā* perfection of becoming small like an atom up to becoming infinite like the cosmic manifestation. All the mystic powers of Brahmā, Śiva, all the demigods and the twenty-four elements of cosmic manifestation were fully represented in the person of Viṣṇu. By the influence of Lord Viṣṇu, all subordinate mystic powers were engaged in His worship. He was being worshiped by time, space, the cosmic manifestation, reformation, desire, activity and the three qualities of material nature. Lord Viṣṇu, Brahmā also realized, is the reservoir of all truth, knowledge and bliss. He is the combination of three transcendental features, namely eternity, knowledge and bliss, and He is the object of worship by the followers of the *Upaniṣads.*

Brahmā realized that all the different forms of boys and calves transformed into Viṣṇu forms were not transformed by a mysticism of the type that a *yogī* or a demigod can display by specific powers invested in him. The calves and boys transformed into *viṣṇu-mūrtis,* or Viṣṇu forms, were not displays of *viṣṇu-māyā,* or Viṣṇu's energy, but were Viṣṇu Himself. The respective qualifications of Viṣṇu and *viṣṇu-māyā* are just like fire and heat. In the heat there is the qualification of fire, namely warmth; and yet heat is not fire. The manifestation of the Viṣṇu forms of the boys and calves was not like the heat but rather the fire—they were all actually Viṣṇu. Factually, the qualification of Viṣṇu is full truth, full knowledge and full bliss. Another example can be given with material objects, which are reflected in many, many forms. For example, the sun is reflected in many waterpots, but the reflections of the sun in the many pots are not actually the sun. There is no actual heat or light from the suns in the pots, although they appear like the sun. But the forms which Kṛṣṇa assumed were each and every one full Viṣṇu. The specific word used in this connection is *satya-jñānānantānanda: satya* means truth; *jñāna,* full knowledge; *ananta,* unlimited; and *ānanda,* full bliss.

The glories of the Supreme Personality of Godhead are so great that the impersonalistic followers of the *Upaniṣads* cannot reach the platform of knowledge to understand them. Especially the transcendental forms of the Lord are beyond the reach of the impersonalists, who can only understand, through studying the *Upaniṣads*, that the Absolute Truth is not matter, or is not materially restricted. From Kṛṣṇa's expansion into Viṣṇu forms, Lord Brahmā could understand by his limited potency that everything movable and immovable within the cosmic manifestation is existing due to the expansion of the energy of the Supreme Lord.

When Brahmā was thus standing baffled in his limited power and conscious of his limited activities within the eleven senses, he could realize that he was also a creation of the material energy, just like a puppet. As a puppet has no independent power to dance but dances according to the direction of the puppet master, so the demigods and living entities are all subordinate to the Supreme Personality of Godhead. As it is stated in the *Caitanya-caritāmṛta,* the only master is Kṛṣṇa, and all others are His servants. The whole world is under the waves of the material spell, and beings are floating like straws in water. So their struggle for existence is continuing. But as soon as one becomes conscious that he is the eternal servant of the Supreme Personality of Godhead, this *māyā,* or illusory struggle for existence, is immediately stopped.

Lord Brahmā, who has full control over the goddess of learning and who is considered to be the best authority in Vedic knowledge, was thus perplexed, being unable to understand the extraordinary power manifested by the Supreme Personality of Godhead. In the mundane world, even a personality like Brahmā is unable to understand the mystic power of the Supreme Lord. Not only did Brahmā fail to understand, but he was perplexed even to see the display which was being manifested by Kṛṣṇa before him.

Kṛṣṇa took compassion upon Brahmā because of his inability to see how Kṛṣṇa was displaying the forms of Viṣṇu and transforming Himself into calves and cowherd boys, and thus, while fully manifesting the Viṣṇu expansions, He suddenly pulled His curtain of *yogamāyā* over the scene. In the *Bhagavad-gītā* it is said that the Supreme Personality of Godhead is not visible due to the curtain spread by *yogamāyā.* That which covers the reality is *mahāmāyā,* or the external energy, which does not allow a conditioned soul to understand the Supreme Personality of Godhead beyond the cosmic manifestation. But the energy which partially manifests the Supreme Personality of Godhead and partially does not allow one to see is called *yogamāyā.* Brahmā is not an ordinary conditioned soul. He is far, far superior to all the other demigods, and yet he could not comprehend the display of the Supreme Personality of Godhead; therefore Kṛṣṇa willingly stopped manifesting any further potency. The conditioned soul not only becomes bewildered but is completely unable to understand. The curtain of *yogamāyā* was drawn so that Brahmā would not become more and more perplexed.

When Brahmā was relieved from his perplexity, he appeared to awaken from an almost dead state, and he began to open his eyes with great difficulty. Thus he could see the external cosmic manifestation with common eyes. He saw all around him the superexcellent view of Vṛndāvana—full with trees—which is the source of life for all living entities. He could appreciate the transcendental land of Vṛndāvana, where all the living entities are transcendental to ordinary nature. In the forest of Vṛndāvana, even ferocious animals like tigers live peacefully along with the deer and human beings. He could understand that because of the presence of the Supreme Personality of Godhead, Vṛndāvana is transcendental to all other places and is free of lust and greed.

Brahmā thus found Śrī Kṛṣṇa, the Supreme Personality of Godhead, playing the part of a small cowherd boy; he saw that little child with a lump of food in His left hand, searching out His friends and calves, just as He had actually been doing one year before, after their disappearance.

Immediately Brahmā descended from his great swan carrier and fell down before the Lord just like a golden stick. The word used among the Vaiṣṇavas for offering respect is *daṇḍavat.* This word means "falling down like a stick"; one should offer respect to the superior Vaiṣṇava by falling down straight, with his body just like a stick. So Brahmā fell down before the Lord just like a stick to offer respect; and because the complexion of Brahmā is golden, he appeared to be like a golden stick lying down before Lord Kṛṣṇa. All the four helmets on the heads of Brahmā touched the lotus feet of Kṛṣṇa. Brahmā, being very joyful, began to shed tears, and he washed the lotus feet of Kṛṣṇa with his tears. Repeatedly he fell and rose as he recalled the wonderful activities of the Lord. After repeating obeisances for a long time, Brahmā stood up and smeared his hands over his eyes. Seeing the Lord before him, he, trembling, began to offer prayers with great respect, humility and attention.

Thus ends the Bhaktivedanta purport of the Thirteenth Chapter of Kṛṣṇa, *"The Stealing of the Boys and Calves by Brahmā."*

CHAPTER 14

Prayers Offered by Lord Brahmā to Lord Kṛṣṇa

BRAHMĀ SAID, "MY DEAR LORD, You are the only worshipful Supreme Lord, the Personality of Godhead; therefore I am offering my humble obeisances and prayers just to please You. Your bodily features are the color of clouds filled with water. You are glittering with a silver electric aura emanating from Your yellow garments. Let me offer my respectful repeated obeisances unto the son of Mahārāja Nanda, who is standing before me with conchshell earrings and a peacock feather on His head. His face is beautiful; He is wearing a helmet and is garlanded by forest flowers, and He stands with a morsel of food in His hand. He is decorated with a cane, a buffalo-horn bugle and a flute. He stands before me with small lotus feet.

"My dear Lord, people may say that I am the master of all Vedic knowledge, and I am supposed to be the creator of this universe, but it has been proved now that I cannot understand You, who are present before me just like a child. You are playing with Your boyfriends and calves, which might imply that You do not even have sufficient education. You are appearing just like a village boy, carrying Your food in Your hand and searching for Your calves. And yet there is so much difference between Your body and mine that I cannot estimate the potency of Your body. As I have already stated in the *Brahma-saṁhitā*, Your body is not material."

In the *Brahma-saṁhitā* it is stated that the body of the Lord is all-spiritual; there is no difference between the Lord's body and His self. Each limb of His body can perform the actions of all the others. The Lord can see with His hands, He can hear with His eyes, He can accept offerings with His legs, and He can create with His mouth.

Brahmā continued, "Your appearance as a cowherd child is for the benefit of the devotees, and although I have committed an offense at Your lotus feet by stealing away Your boys and calves, I can understand that You have bestowed Your mercy upon me. That is Your transcendental quality: You are very affectionate toward Your devotees. But in spite of Your great affection for me, I cannot estimate the potency of Your bodily activities. It is to be understood that when I, Lord Brahmā, the supreme personality of this universe, cannot estimate the childlike body of the Supreme Personality of Godhead, then what to speak of others? And if I cannot estimate the spiritual potency of Your childlike body, then what can I understand about Your transcendental pastimes? Therefore, as it is said in the *Bhagavad-gītā,* anyone who can understand a little of the transcendental pastimes, appearance and disappearance of the Lord becomes immediately eligible to enter into the kingdom of God after quitting the material body. This statement is also confirmed in the *Vedas,* where it is stated: Simply by understanding the Supreme Personality of Godhead, one can overcome the chain of repeated birth and death. I therefore recommend that people should not try to understand You by their speculative knowledge.

"The best process for understanding You is to submissively give up the speculative process and try to hear about You, either from Yourself as You have given statements in the *Bhagavad-gītā* and many similar Vedic literatures, or from a realized devotee who has taken shelter at Your lotus feet. One has to hear from a devotee without speculation. One does not even need to change his worldly position; he simply has to hear Your message. Although You are not understandable by the material senses, simply by hearing about You one can gradually conquer the nescience of misunderstanding. By Your own grace only, You become revealed to a devotee. You are unconquerable by any other means. Speculative knowledge without any trace of devotional service is simply a useless waste of time in the search for You. Devotional service is so important that even a little attempt can raise one to the highest perfectional platform. One should not, therefore, neglect this auspicious process of devotional service and take to the speculative method.

By the speculative method one may gain partial knowledge of Your cosmic manifestation, but it is not possible to understand You, the origin of everything. The attempt of persons who are interested only in speculative knowledge is simply wasted labor, like the labor of a person who attempts to gain something by beating an empty husk of rice paddy. A little quantity of paddy can be husked by the grinding wheel, and one can gain some grains of rice, but if the skin of the paddy has already been beaten by the grinding wheel, there is no further gain in beating even a huge quantity of the husk. It is simply useless labor.

"My dear Lord, there are many instances in the history of human society where a person, after failing to achieve the transcendental platform, engaged himself in devotional service with his body, mind and words and thus attained the highest perfectional state of entering into Your abode. The processes of understanding You by speculation or mystic meditation are all useless without devotional service. One should therefore engage himself in Your devotional service even in his worldly activities, and one should always keep himself near You by the process of hearing and chanting Your transcendental glories. Simply by being attached to hearing and chanting Your glories, one can attain the highest perfectional stage of entering into Your kingdom. If a person, therefore, always keeps in touch with You by hearing and chanting Your glories and offers the results of his work for Your satisfaction only, he very easily and happily attains entrance into Your supreme abode. You are realizable by persons who have cleansed their hearts of all contamination. This cleansing of the heart is made possible by chanting and hearing the glories of Your Lordship."

The Lord is all-pervading. As it is stated by Lord Kṛṣṇa in the *Bhagavad-gītā*, "Everything is sustained by Me, but at the same time I am not in everything." Since the Lord is all-pervading, there is nothing existing without His knowledge. The all-pervasive nature of the Supreme Personality of Godhead can never be within the limited knowledge of a living entity; therefore, a person who has attained steadiness of the mind by fixing the mind on the lotus feet of the Lord is able to understand the Supreme Lord to some extent. It is the business of the mind to wander over varied subject matter for sense gratification. Therefore only a person who always engages the senses in the service of the Lord can control the mind and be fixed at the lotus feet of the Lord. This concentration of the mind upon the lotus feet of the Lord is called *samādhi.* Until one reaches the stage of *samādhi,* or trance, he cannot understand the nature of the Supreme Personality of Godhead. There may be some philosophers or scientists who can study the cosmic nature from atom to atom; they may be so advanced that they can count the atomic composition of the cosmic atmosphere or all the planets and stars in the sky, or even the shining molecular parts of the sun or of the stars and other luminaries in the sky. But it is not possible to count the qualities of the Supreme Personality of Godhead.

As described in the beginning of the *Vedānta-sūtra,* the Supreme Person is the origin of all qualities. He is generally called *nirguṇa. Nirguṇa* means "whose qualities are beyond estimation." *Guṇa* means "quality," and *nir* means "beyond estimation." But impersonalists interpret this word *nirguṇa* as "having no quality." Because they are unable to estimate the qualities of the Lord in transcendental realization, they conclude that the Supreme Lord has no qualities. But that is actually not the position. The real position is that He is the original source of all qualities. All qualities are emanating constantly from Him. How, therefore, can a limited person count the qualities of the Lord? One may estimate the qualities of the Lord at one moment, but the next moment the qualities have increased; so it is not possible to make an estimation of the transcendental qualities of the Lord. He is therefore called *nirguṇa,* one whose qualities cannot be estimated.

One should not uselessly labor in mental speculation to estimate the Lord's qualities. There is no need of adopting the speculative method or exercising the body to attain mystic *yoga* perfection. One should simply understand that the distress and happiness of this body are predestined; there is no need to try to avoid the distress of this bodily existence or to attempt to achieve happiness by different types of exercises. The best course is to surrender unto the Supreme Personality of Godhead with body, mind and words and always be engaged in His service. This transcendental labor is fruitful, but other attempts to understand the Absolute Truth are never successful. Therefore an intelligent man does not try to understand the Absolute Truth by speculative or mystic power. Rather, he engages in devotional service and depends on the Supreme Personality of Godhead. He knows that whatever may happen to the body is due to his past fruitive activities. If one lives such a simple life in devotional service, then automatically he inherits the transcendental abode of the Lord. Actually, every living entity is part and parcel of the Supreme Lord and a son of the Godhead. Each has the natural right to inherit and share the transcendental pleasures of the Lord, but due to the contact of matter, conditioned living entities have been practically disinherited. If one adopts the simple method of engaging himself in devotional service, automatically he becomes eligible to be freed from material contamination and elevated to the transcendental position of associating with the Supreme Lord.

Lord Brahmā presented himself to Lord Kṛṣṇa as the most presumptuous living creature because he wanted to examine the wonder of His personal power. He stole the boys and calves of the Lord in order to see how the Lord would recover them. Now Lord Brahmā admitted that his attempt was most presumptuous, for he was attempting to test his energy before the person of original energy. Coming to his senses, Lord Brahmā saw that although he was a very powerful living creature in the estimation of all other living creatures within this material world, his power was nothing in comparison with the power and energy of the Supreme Personality of Godhead. The scientists of the material world have invented wonders such as atomic weapons, and when tested in a city or some insignificant place on this planet, such powerful weapons create so-called havoc, but if the atomic weapons are tested on the sun, what is their significance? They are insignificant there. Similarly, Brahmā's stealing of the calves and boys from Śrī Kṛṣṇa may be a wonderful display of mystic power, but when Śrī Kṛṣṇa exhibited His expansive power in so many calves and boys and maintained them without effort, Brahmā could understand that his own power was insignificant.

Brahmā addressed Lord Kṛṣṇa as Acyuta because the Lord is never forgetful of a little service rendered by His devotee. He is so kind and affectionate toward His devotees that a little service by them is accepted by Him as a great deal. Brahmā has certainly rendered much service to the Lord. As the supreme personality in charge of this particular universe, he is, without a doubt, a faithful servant of Kṛṣṇa; therefore he could appease Kṛṣṇa. He asked that the Lord understand him as a subordinate servant whose little mistake and impudence might be excused. He admitted that he was puffed up by his powerful position as Lord Brahmā. Because he is the qualitative incarnation of the mode of passion within this material world, this was natural for him, and therefore he committed the mistake. But Lord Brahmā hoped that since he was, after all, Lord Kṛṣṇa's subordinate, the Lord would kindly take compassion upon him and excuse him for his gross mistake.

Lord Brahmā realized his actual position. He is certainly the supreme teacher of this universe, in charge of the production of material nature, consisting of the complete material energy, false ego, sky, air, fire, water and earth. Such a universe may be gigantic, but it can be measured, just as we measure our body as seven spans. Generally everyone's personal bodily measurement is calculated to be seven spans of his hand. This particular universe may appear as a very gigantic body, but it is nothing but the measurement of seven spans for Lord Brahmā. Aside from this universe, there are unlimited other universes which are outside the jurisdiction of this particular Lord Brahmā. Just as innumerable atomic infinitesimal fragments pass through the holes of a screened window, so millions and trillions of universes in their seedling form are coming out from the bodily pores of Mahā-Viṣṇu, and that Mahā-Viṣṇu is but a part of a part of the plenary expansion of Kṛṣṇa. Under these circumstances, although Lord Brahmā is the supreme creature within this universe, what is his importance in the presence of Lord Kṛṣṇa?

Lord Brahmā therefore compared himself to a little child within the womb of his mother. If the child within the womb plays with his hands and legs, and while playing touches the body of the mother, is the mother offended with the child? Of course she isn't. Similarly, Lord Brahmā may be a very great personality, and yet not only Brahmā but everything that be is existing within the womb of the Supreme Personality of Godhead. The Lord's energy is all-pervading: there is no place in the creation where it is not acting. Since everything is existing within the energy of the Lord, the Brahmā of this universe and the Brahmās of the many other millions and trillions of universes are existing within the energy of the Lord; therefore the Lord is considered to be the mother, and everything existing within the womb of the mother is considered to be the child. And the good mother is never offended with the child, even if he touches the body of the mother by kicking his legs.

Lord Brahmā then said that his birth was from the lotus flower which blossomed from the navel of Nārāyaṇa after the dissolution of the three worlds, or three planetary systems, known as Bhūrloka, Bhuvarloka and Svarloka. The universe is divided into three divisions, namely Svarga, Martya and Pātāla. These three planetary systems are merged into water at the time of dissolution. At that time Nārāyaṇa, a plenary portion of Kṛṣṇa, lies down on the water, and gradually a lotus stem grows from His navel, and from that lotus flower, Brahmā is born. It is naturally concluded that the mother of Brahmā is Nārāyaṇa. Because the Lord is the resting place of all the living entities after the dissolution of the universe, He is called Nārāyaṇa. The word *nāra* means the aggregate total of all living entities, and *ayana* means the resting place. The form of Garbhodakaśāyī Viṣṇu is called Nārāyaṇa because He rests Himself on that water. In addition, He is the resting place of all living creatures. Besides that, Nārāyaṇa is also present in everyone's heart, as confirmed in the *Bhagavad-gītā.* In that sense, also, the Lord is Nārāyaṇa, as *ayana* means the source of knowledge as well as the resting place. It is also confirmed in the *Bhagavad-gītā* that the remembrance of the living entity is due to the presence of the Supersoul within the heart. After changing the body, a living creature forgets everything of his past life, but because Nārāyaṇa, the Supersoul, is present within his heart, he is reminded by Him to act according to his past desire. Lord Brahmā wanted to prove that Kṛṣṇa is the original Nārāyaṇa, that He is the source of Nārāyaṇa, and that Nārāyaṇa is not an exhibition of the external energy, *māyā,* but is an expansion of spiritual energy. The activities of the external energy, or *māyā,* are exhibited after the creation of this cosmic world, and the original spiritual energy of Nārāyaṇa was acting before the creation. So the expansions of Nārāyaṇa—from Nārāyaṇa to Kāraṇodakaśāyī Viṣṇu, from Kāraṇodakaśāyī Viṣṇu to Garbhodakaśāyī Viṣṇu, from Garbhodakaśāyī Viṣṇu to Kṣīrodakaśāyī Viṣṇu, and from Kṣīrodakaśāyī Viṣṇu to everyone's heart—are actually Kṛṣṇa's expansions, manifestations of His spiritual energy. They are not conducted by the material energy; therefore they are not temporary. Anything conducted by the material energy is temporary, but everything executed by the spiritual energy is eternal.

Lord Brahmā reconfirmed his statement establishing Lord Kṛṣṇa as the original Nārāyaṇa. He said that the Lord's gigantic universal form is resting on the water known as Garbhodaka. He spoke as follows: "This gigantic universal form is another manifestation of Your energy. On account of His resting on the water, this universal form is also Nārāyaṇa, and we are all within the womb of this Nārāyaṇa form. I see Your different Nārāyaṇa forms everywhere. I can see You on the water, I can feel You within my heart, and I can also see You before me now. You are the original Nārāyaṇa.

"My dear Lord, in this incarnation You have proved that You are the supreme controller of *māyā.* You remain within the cosmic manifestation, and yet the whole creation is within You. This fact has already been proved by You when You exhibited the whole universal creation within Your mouth before Your mother, Yaśodā. By Your inconceivable potency of *yogamāyā*, You can effect such things without external help.

"My dear Lord Kṛṣṇa, the whole cosmic manifestation that we are visualizing at present is all within Your body. Yet I am seeing You outside, and You are also seeing me outside. How can such things happen without being influenced by Your inconceivable energy?"

Lord Brahmā stressed herein that without accepting the inconceivable energy of the Supreme Personality of Godhead, one cannot explain things as they are. He continued, "My dear Lord, leaving aside all other things and just considering today's happenings—what I have seen—are they not all due to Your inconceivable energies? First of all I saw You alone; thereafter You expanded Yourself as Your cowherd boyfriends, the calves and all the existence of Vṛndāvana; then I saw You and all the boys and calves as four-handed Viṣṇus, and They were being worshiped by all elements and all demigods, including myself. Again They were all wound up, and You remained alone, as You were before. Does this not mean that You are the Supreme Lord Nārāyaṇa, the origin of everything, that everything emanates from You and again enters into You, leaving You the same as before?

"Persons who are unaware of Your inconceivable energy cannot understand that You alone expand Yourself as the creator (Brahmā), the maintainer (Viṣṇu) and the annihilator (Śiva). Persons who are not in awareness of things as they are contemplate that I, Brahmā, am the creator, Viṣṇu is the maintainer, and Lord Śiva is the annihilator. Actually, You alone are everything—creator, maintainer and annihilator. Similarly, You expand Yourself in different incarnations: among the demigods You incarnate as Vāmanadeva, among the great sages You incarnate as Paraśurāma, among the human beings You appear as Yourself, Lord Kṛṣṇa, or as Lord Rāma; among the animals You appear as the boar incarnation, and among the aquatics You appear as the fish incarnation. And yet You have no appearance or disappearance: You are always eternal. Your appearance and disappearance are made possible by Your inconceivable energy just to give protection to the faithful devotees and to annihilate the faithless demons. O my Lord, O all-pervading Supreme Personality of Godhead, O Supersoul, controller of all mystic powers, no one can appreciate Your transcendental pastimes as they are exhibited within these three worlds. No one can estimate how You have expanded Your *yogamāyā* and Your incarnations and how You act by Your transcendental energy. My dear Lord, this whole cosmic manifestation is just like a flashing dream, and its temporary existence simply disturbs the mind. As a result, we are full of anxiety in this existence; to live within this material world means simply to suffer and to be full of all miseries. And yet this temporary existence of the material world appears to be pleasing and dear on account of its having evolved from Your body, which is eternal and full of bliss and knowledge.

"My conclusion is, therefore, that You are the Supreme Soul, the Absolute Truth, and the supreme original person; and although by Your inconceivable transcendental potencies You have expanded Yourself in so many Viṣṇu forms, and also in the living entities and other energies, You are the supreme one without a second, the supreme Supersoul. The innumerable living entities are simply like sparks of the original fire, Your Lordship. The conception of the Supersoul as impersonal is wrong because I see that You are the original person. Persons with a poor fund of knowledge may think that because You are the son of Mahārāja Nanda You are not the original person, that You are born just like a human being. They are mistaken. You are the actual original person; that is my conclusion. In spite of Your being the son of Nanda, You are the original person, and there is no doubt about it. You are the Absolute Truth, and You are not of this material darkness. You are the source of the original *brahmajyoti* as well as the material luminaries—the sun, moon and stars. Your transcendental effulgence is identical with the *brahmajyoti.* As it is described in the *Brahma-saṁhitā,* the *brahmajyoti* is nothing but Your personal bodily effulgence. There are many Viṣṇu incarnations and incarnations of Your different qualities, but all those incarnations are not on the same level. You are the original lamp. Other incarnations may possess the same candlepower as the original lamp, but the original lamp is the beginning of all light. And because You are not one of the creations of this material world, even after the annihilation of this world, Your existence as You are will continue.

"Because You are the original person, You are described in the *Gopāla-tāpanī Upaniṣad,* as well as in the *Brahma-saṁhitā,* as *govindam ādi-puruṣam.* Govinda is the original person, the cause of all causes. In the *Bhagavad-gītā* also it is stated that You are the source of the Brahman effulgence. No one should conclude that Your body is like an ordinary material body. Your body is *akṣara,* or indestructible. The material body is always full of threefold miseries, but Your body is *sac-cid-ānanda-vigraha:* full of bliss, knowledge and eternality. You are also *nirañjana* because Your pastimes, as the little son of mother Yaśodā or the lover of the *gopīs,* are never contaminated by the material qualities. And although You exhibited Yourself as so many cowherd boys and calves, Your transcendental potency was not reduced. You are always complete. As it is described in the Vedic literature, even if the complete is taken away from the complete—the Supreme Absolute Truth—it remains the complete Supreme Absolute Truth. And although many expansions from the complete are visible, the complete is one without a second. Since all Your pastimes are spiritual, there is no possibility of their being contaminated by the material modes of nature. When You place Yourself as subordinate to Your father and mother, Nanda and Yaśodā, You are not reduced in Your potency; this is an expression of Your loving attitude toward Your devotees. There is no second identity to compete with You. A person with a poor fund of knowledge concludes that Your appearance and pastimes are simply material designations.

You are transcendental to both nescience and knowledge, as it is confirmed in the *Gopāla-tāpanī Upaniṣad.* You are the original *amṛta,* indestructible nectar of immortality. As confirmed in the *Vedas, amṛtaṁ śāśvataṁ brahma.* Brahman is the eternal, the supreme origin of everything, who has no birth or death.

"In the *Upaniṣads* it is stated that the Supreme Brahman is as effulgent as the sun and is the origin of everything, and anyone who can understand that original person becomes liberated from the material, conditioned life. Anyone who can simply be attached to You by devotional service can know Your actual position, birth, appearance, disappearance and activities. As confirmed in the *Bhagavad-gītā,* simply by understanding Your constitutional position, appearance and disappearance, one can be immediately elevated to the spiritual kingdom after quitting this present body. Therefore to cross over the ocean of material nescience, an intelligent person takes shelter of Your lotus feet and is easily transferred to the spiritual world.

"There are many so-called meditators who do not know that You are the Supreme Soul. As stated in the *Bhagavad-gītā,* You are the Supreme Soul present in everyone's heart. Therefore there is no necessity of one's meditating on something beyond You. One who is always absorbed in meditation on Your original form of Kṛṣṇa easily crosses over the ocean of material nescience. But persons who do not know that You are the Supreme Soul remain within this material world in spite of their so-called meditation. If, by the association of Your devotees, a person comes to the knowledge that Lord Kṛṣṇa is the original Supersoul, then it is possible for him to cross over the ocean of material ignorance. For instance, when a person mistakes a rope for a snake he is filled with fear, but as soon as he understands that the rope is not a snake, he is liberated from fear. If one understands You, therefore, through Your personal teachings, as stated in the *Bhagavad-gītā,* or through the teachings of Your pure devotees, as stated in *Śrīmad-Bhāgavatam* and all other Vedic literatures—if one realizes that You are the ultimate goal of understanding— he need no more fear this material existence.

"So-called liberation and bondage have no meaning for a person who is already engaged in Your devotional service, just as a rope is not fearful to a person who knows that it is not a snake. A devotee knows that this material world belongs to You, and he therefore engages everything in Your transcendental loving service. Thus there is no bondage for him. For a person who is already situated in the sun planet, there is no question of the appearance or disappearance of the sun in the name of day or night. It is also said that You, Kṛṣṇa, are just like the sun, and that *māyā* is like darkness. When the sun is present, there is no question of darkness; so, for those who always remain in Your presence by engaging in Your service, there is no question of bondage or liberation. They are already liberated. On the other hand, persons who falsely think themselves to be liberated without taking shelter of Your lotus feet fall down because their intelligence is not pure.

"If one therefore thinks that the Supersoul is something different from Your personality and thus searches out the Supersoul or the Supreme Brahman somewhere else, in the forest or in the caves of the Himālayas, his condition is very lamentable. Your teachings in the *Bhagavad-gītā* are that one should give up all other processes of self-realization and simply surrender unto You, for that is complete. Because You are the Supreme in every respect, those who are searching after the Brahman effulgence are also searching after You. And those who are searching after Supersoul realization are also searching after You. You state in the *Bhagavad-gītā* that You Yourself, by Your partial representation as the Supersoul, have entered into this material cosmic manifestation. You are present in everyone's heart, and there is no need to search out the Supersoul anywhere else. If someone does so, he is simply in ignorance. One who is transcendental to such a position understands that You are unlimited; You are both within and without. Therefore Your presence is everywhere. Instead of searching for the Supersoul anywhere else, a devotee only concentrates his mind on You within. Actually, one who is liberated from the material concept of life can search for You; others cannot. The example of thinking the rope to be a snake is applicable only to those who are still in ignorance of You. Actually, when one mistakes a rope for a snake, the existence of the snake is only within the mind. The existence of *māyā,* similarly, is only within the mind. *Māyā* is nothing but ignorance of Your personality. When one forgets Your personality, that is the conditioned state of *māyā*. Therefore one who is fixed upon You both internally and externally is not illusioned.

"One who has attained a little result of devotional service can understand Your glories. Even one striving for Brahman realization or Paramātmā realization cannot understand these features of Your personality unless You bestow on him the result of at least a slight bit of devotional service. One may be the spiritual master of many impersonalists, or he may go to the forest or to a mountain cave and meditate as a hermit for many, many years, but he cannot understand Your glories without being favored by a slight degree of devotional service. Brahman realization or Paramātmā realization are also not possible even after one searches for many, many years unless one is touched by the wonderful effect of devotional service.

"Therefore, my dear Lord, I pray that I may be so fortunate that in this life or in another life, wherever I may take my birth, I may be counted as one of Your devotees. Wherever I may be, I pray that I may be engaged in Your devotional service. I do not even care what form of life I get in the future, because I can see that even in the form of cows and calves or cowherd boys, the devotees are so fortunate to be always engaged in Your transcendental loving service and association. Therefore I wish to be one of them instead of such an exalted person as I am now, for I am full of ignorance. The *gopīs* and cows of Vṛndāvana are so fortunate that they have been able to supply their breast milk to You. Persons who are engaged in performing great sacrifices and offering many valuable goats in sacrifice cannot attain the perfection of understanding You, but simply by devotional service these innocent village women and cows are all able to satisfy You with their milk. You have drunk their milk to satisfaction, yet You are never satisfied as much by those engaged in performing sacrifices. I am simply surprised, therefore, with the fortunate position of Mahārāja Nanda, mother Yaśodā and the cowherd men and *gopīs,* because You, the Supreme Personality of Godhead, the Absolute Truth, are existing here as their most intimate lovable object. My dear Lord, no one can actually appreciate the good fortune of these residents of Vṛndāvana. We are all demigods, controlling deities of the various senses of the living entities, and we are proud of enjoying such privileges, but actually there is no comparison between our position and the position of these fortunate residents of Vṛndāvana because they are actually relishing Your presence and enjoying Your association by dint of their sensory activities. We may be proud of being controllers of the senses, but here the residents of Vṛndāvana are so transcendental that they are not under our control. Actually they are enjoying their senses through service to You. I shall therefore consider myself fortunate to be given a chance to take birth in this land of Vṛndāvana in any of my future lives.

"My dear Lord, I am therefore not interested in either material opulences or liberation. I am most humbly praying at Your lotus feet for You to please give me any sort of birth within this Vṛndāvana forest so that I may be able to be favored by the dust of the feet of some of the devotees of Vṛndāvana. If I am given the chance to grow as a humble blade of grass in this land, that would be a glorious birth for me. But if I am not so fortunate to take birth within the forest of Vṛndāvana, I beg to be allowed to take birth outside the immediate area of Vṛndāvana so that when the devotees go out they will walk over me. Even that would be a great fortune for me. I am just aspiring for a birth in which I will be smeared by the dust of the devotees' feet, because I can see that everyone here is simply full of Kṛṣṇa consciousness. No one here knows anything but the lotus feet of Kṛṣṇa, or Mukunda, for which the *Vedas* themselves are searching."

It is confirmed in the *Bhagavad-gītā* that the purpose of Vedic knowledge is to find Kṛṣṇa. And it is said in the *Brahma-saṁhitā* that it is very difficult to find Kṛṣṇa, the Supreme Personality of Godhead, by systematic reading of the Vedic literature. But He is very easily available through the mercy of a pure devotee. The pure devotees of Vṛndāvana are fortunate because they can see Mukunda (Lord Kṛṣṇa) all the time. This word *mukunda* can be understood in two ways. *Muk* means liberation. Lord Kṛṣṇa can give liberation and therefore transcendental bliss. The word also refers to His smiling face, which is just like the *kunda* flower. *Mukha* means "face." The *kunda* flower is very beautiful, and it appears to be smiling. Thus the comparison is made.

The difference between the pure devotees of Vṛndāvana and devotees in other places is that the residents of Vṛndāvana have no other desire but to be associated with Kṛṣṇa.

Kṛṣṇa, being very kind to His devotees, fulfills their desire; because they always want Kṛṣṇa's association, the Lord is always prepared to give it to them. The devotees of Vṛndāvana are also spontaneous lovers. They are not required to strictly follow regulative principles because they are already naturally developed in transcendental love for Kṛṣṇa. Regulative principles are required for persons who have not achieved such a position of spontaneous love. Brahmā is also a devotee of the Lord, but he is an ordinary devotee subject to following regulative principles. He prays to Kṛṣṇa to give him the chance to take birth in Vṛndāvana so that he might be elevated to the platform of spontaneous love.

Lord Brahmā continued, "My Lord, sometimes I am puzzled as to how Your Lordship will be able to repay, in gratitude, the devotional service of these residents of Vṛndāvana. Although I know that You are the supreme source of all benedictions, I am puzzled to know how You will be able to repay all the service that You are receiving from these residents of Vṛndāvana. I think of how You are so kind, so magnanimous, that even Pūtanā, who came to cheat You by dressing herself as a very affectionate mother, was awarded liberation and the actual post of a mother. And other demons belonging to the same family, such as Aghāsura and Bakāsura, were also favored with liberation and achieved You. Under the circumstances, I am puzzled. These residents of Vṛndāvana have given You everything—their bodies, their minds, their love, their homes, their possessions. Everything is being utilized for Your purpose. So how will You be able to repay Your debt to them? You have already given Yourself to Pūtanā! I surmise that You shall ever remain a debtor to the residents of Vṛndāvana, being unable to repay their loving service.

"My Lord, I can understand that the superexcellent quality of the service rendered by the residents of Vṛndāvana is due to their spontaneously engaging all natural instincts in Your loving service. It is said that attachment for material objects and home is due to illusion, which makes a living entity conditioned in the material world. But this is only the case for persons who are not Kṛṣṇa conscious. In the case of the residents of Vṛndāvana, such obstructions as attachment to hearth and home are nonexistent. Because their attachment has been directed unto You and their homes have been converted into temples by Your constant presence there, and because they have forgotten everything for Your sake, there is no impediment. For a Kṛṣṇa conscious person, there is no such thing as impediments due to attachment for hearth and home. Nor is there illusion.

"I can also understand that Your appearance as a small cowherd boy, a child of the cowherd men, is not at all a material activity. You are so much obliged by their affection that You are here to inspire them with more loving service by Your transcendental presence. In Vṛndāvana there is no distinction between material and spiritual because everything is dedicated to Your loving service. My dear Lord, Your Vṛndāvana pastimes are simply to inspire Your devotees. If someone takes Your Vṛndāvana pastimes to be material, he will be misled.

"My dear Lord Kṛṣṇa, those who deride You, claiming that You have a material body like an ordinary man, are described in the *Bhagavad-gītā* as demoniac and less intelligent. You are always transcendental. The nondevotees are cheated because they consider You to be a material creation. Actually, You have assumed this body, which exactly resembles that of an ordinary cowherd boy, simply to increase the devotion and transcendental bliss of Your devotees.

"My dear Lord, I have nothing to say about people who advertise that they have already realized God or that by their realization they have themselves become God. But as far as I am concerned, I admit frankly that for me it is not possible to realize You by my body, mind or speech. What can I say about You, or how can I realize You by my senses? I cannot even think of You perfectly with my mind, which is the master of the senses. Your qualities, Your activities and Your body cannot be conceived of by any person within this material world. Only by Your mercy can one understand, to some extent, what You are. My dear Lord, You are the Supreme Lord of all creation, although I sometimes falsely think that I am the master of this universe. I may be the master of this universe, but there are innumerable universes, and there are innumerable Brahmās also who preside over these universes. But actually You are the master of them all. As the Supersoul in everyone's heart, You know everything. Please, therefore, accept me as Your surrendered servant. I hope that You will excuse me for committing the great offense of disturbing You in Your pastimes with Your friends and calves. Now if You will kindly allow me, I will immediately leave so You can enjoy Your friends and calves without my presence.

"My dear Lord Kṛṣṇa, Your very name suggests that You are all-attractive. The attraction of the sun and the moon are all due to You. By the attraction of the sun, You are beautifying the very existence of the Yadu dynasty. With the attraction of the moon, You are enhancing the potency of the land, the demigods, the *brāhmaṇas,* the cows and the oceans. Because of Your supreme attraction, demons like Kaṁsa and others are annihilated. Therefore it is my deliberate conclusion that You are the only worshipable Deity within the creation. Accept my humble obeisances until the annihilation of this material world. As long as there is sunshine within this material world, kindly accept my humble obeisances."

In this way, Brahmā, the master of this universe, after offering humble and respectful obeisances unto the Supreme Personality of Godhead and circumambulating Him three times, was ready to return to his abode, known as Brahmaloka. By His gesture, the Supreme Personality of Godhead gave him permission to return.

As soon as Brahmā left, Lord Śrī Kṛṣṇa immediately returned to the bank of the Yamunā and rejoined His calves and cowherd boyfriends, who were situated just as they had been on the very day they had vanished. Kṛṣṇa had left His friends on the bank of the Yamunā while they were engaged in lunch, and although He returned exactly one year later, the cowherd boys thought that He had returned within a second. That is the way Kṛṣṇa's different energies act. It is stated in the *Bhagavad-gītā* that Kṛṣṇa Himself is residing in everyone's heart, and He causes both remembrance and forgetfulness. All living entities are controlled by the supreme energy of the Lord, and sometimes they remember and sometimes they forget their constitutional position. His friends, being controlled in such a way, could not understand that for one whole year they were absent from the Yamunā's bank and were under the spell of Brahmā's illusion. When Kṛṣṇa appeared before the boys, they thought, "Kṛṣṇa has returned within a minute." They began to laugh, thinking that Kṛṣṇa was not willing to leave their lunchtime company. They were very jubilant and invited Him, "Dear friend Kṛṣṇa, You have come back so quickly! All right, we have not as yet begun our lunch, not even taken one morsel of food. So please come and join us, and let us eat together." Kṛṣṇa smiled and accepted their invitation, and He began to enjoy the lunchtime company of His friends. While eating, Kṛṣṇa was thinking, "These boys believe that I have come back within a second, but they do not know that for the last year I have been involved with the mystic activities of Lord Brahmā."

After finishing their lunch, Kṛṣṇa and His friends and calves began to return to their Vrajabhūmi homes. While passing, they enjoyed seeing the dead carcass of Aghāsura in the shape of a gigantic serpent. When Kṛṣṇa returned home to Vrajabhūmi, He was seen by all the inhabitants of Vṛndāvana. He was wearing a peacock feather in His helmet, which was also decorated with forest flowers. Kṛṣṇa was also garlanded with flowers and painted with different colored minerals collected from the caves of Govardhana Hill. Govardhana Hill is always famous for supplying natural red oxides, and Kṛṣṇa and His friends painted their bodies with them. Each of them had a bugle made of buffalo horn and a stick and a flute, and each called his respective calves by their particular names. The cowherd boys were so proud of Kṛṣṇa's wonderful activities that, while entering the village, they all sang His glories. All the *gopīs* in Vṛndāvana saw beautiful Kṛṣṇa entering the village. The boys composed nice songs describing how they were saved from being swallowed by the great serpent and how the serpent was killed. Some described Kṛṣṇa as the son of Yaśodā, and others as the son of Nanda Mahārāja. "He is so wonderful that He saved us from the clutches of the great serpent and killed him," they said. But little did they know that one year had passed since the killing of Aghāsura.

In this regard, Mahārāja Parīkṣit asked Śukadeva Gosvāmī how the inhabitants of Vṛndāvana suddenly developed so much love for Kṛṣṇa although He was not a member of any of their families. Mahārāja Parīkṣit inquired, "During the absence of the original cowherd boys, when Kṛṣṇa expanded Himself, why is it that the boys' parents became more loving toward Him than toward their own sons? Also, why did the cows become so loving toward the calves, more than toward their own calves?"

Śukadeva Gosvāmī told Mahārāja Parīkṣit that every living entity is actually most attached to his own self. Outward paraphernalia such as home, family, friends, country, society, wealth, opulence and reputation are all only secondary in pleasing the living entity. They please only because they bring pleasure to the self. For this reason, one is self-centered and is attached to his body and self more than he is to relatives like wife, children and friends. If there is some immediate danger to one's own person, he first of all takes care of himself, then others. That is natural. That means he loves his own self more than anything else. The next important object of affection, after his own self, is his material body. A person who has no information of the spirit soul is very much attached to his material body, so much so that even in old age he wants to preserve the body in so many artificial ways, thinking that his old and broken body can be saved. Everyone is working hard day and night just to give pleasure to his own self, under either the bodily or spiritual concept of life. We are attached to material possessions because they give pleasure to the senses or to the body. The attachment to the body is there only because the "I," the spirit soul, is within the body. Similarly, when one is further advanced, he knows that the spirit soul is pleasing because it is part and parcel of Kṛṣṇa. Ultimately, it is Kṛṣṇa who is pleasing and all-attractive. He is the Supersoul of everything. And in order to give us this information, Kṛṣṇa descends and tells us that the all-attractive center is He Himself. Without being an expansion of Kṛṣṇa, nothing can be attractive.

Whatever is attractive within the cosmic manifestation is due to Kṛṣṇa. Kṛṣṇa is therefore the reservoir of all pleasure. The active principle of everything is Kṛṣṇa, and highly elevated transcendentalists see everything in connection with Him. In the *Caitanya-caritāmṛta* it is stated that a *mahā-bhāgavata,* or highly advanced devotee, sees Kṛṣṇa as the active principle in all moving and nonmoving living entities. Therefore he sees everything within this cosmic manifestation in relation to Kṛṣṇa. For the fortunate person who has taken shelter of Kṛṣṇa as everything, liberation is already there. He is no longer in the material world. This is confirmed in the *Bhagavad-gītā:* Whoever is engaged in the devotional service of Kṛṣṇa is already on the *brahma-bhūta,* or spiritual, platform. The very name Kṛṣṇa suggests piety and liberation. Anyone who takes shelter of the lotus feet of Kṛṣṇa enters the boat for crossing over the ocean of nescience. For him, this vast expanse of the material manifestation becomes as insignificant as the water in a calf's hoofprint. Kṛṣṇa is the shelter of all great souls, and He is also the shelter of the material worlds. For one who is on the platform of Kṛṣṇa consciousness, Vaikuṇṭha, or the spiritual world, is not far away. He does not live within the material world, where there is danger at every step.

In this way, Kṛṣṇa consciousness was fully explained to Mahārāja Parīkṣit by Śukadeva Gosvāmī as he recited to the King the statements and prayers of Lord Brahmā. These descriptions of Lord Kṛṣṇa's pastimes with His cowherd boys, His eating with them on the bank of the Yamunā and Lord Brahma's prayers unto Him, are all transcendental subject matters. Anyone who hears, recites or chants them surely gets all his spiritual desires fulfilled. Thus Kṛṣṇa's childhood pastimes, His sporting with Balarāma and the cowherd boys in Vṛndāvana, were described.

Thus ends the Bhaktivedanta purport of the Fourteenth Chapter of Kṛṣṇa , *"Prayers Offered by Lord Brahmā to Lord Kṛṣṇa."*

CHAPTER 15

The Killing of Dhenukāsura

IN THIS WAY ŚRĪ KṚṢṆA, along with His elder brother Balarāma, passed the childhood age known as *kaumāra* and stepped into the age of *paugaṇḍa*, from the sixth year up to the tenth. At that time, all the cowherd men conferred and agreed to give those boys who had passed their fifth year charge of the cows in the pasturing ground. Given charge of the cows, Kṛṣṇa and Balarāma traversed Vṛndāvana, purifying the land with Their lotus footprints.

Accompanied by the cowherd boys and Balarāma, Kṛṣṇa brought forward the cows and played on His flute as He entered the forest of Vṛndāvana, which was full of flowers, vegetables and pasturing grass. The Vṛndāvana forest was as sanctified as the clear mind of a devotee and was full of bees, flowers and fruits. There were chirping birds and clear-water lakes, with waters that could relieve one of all fatigue. Sweet-smelling breezes blew always, refreshing the mind and body. Kṛṣṇa, with His friends and Balarāma, entered the forest and, seeing the favorable situation, desired to enjoy the atmosphere to the fullest extent. Kṛṣṇa saw all the trees, overloaded with fruits and fresh twigs, bending down to touch the ground as if welcoming Him by touching His lotus feet. He was very pleased by the behavior of the trees, fruits and flowers, and He began to smile, realizing their desires.

Kṛṣṇa then spoke to His elder brother Balarāma as follows: "My dear brother, You are superior to all of us, and Your lotus feet are worshiped by the demigods. Just see how these trees, full with fruits and flowers, have bent down to worship Your lotus feet. It appears that they are trying to get out of the darkness that has obliged them to accept the form of trees. Actually, the trees born in the land of Vṛndāvana are not ordinary living entities. Having held the impersonal point of view in their past lives, they have been put into this stationary condition of life, but now they have the opportunity of seeing You in Vṛndāvana, and they are praying for further advancement in spiritual life through Your personal association.

"Generally, living entities in the mode of darkness obtain the bodies of trees. The impersonalist philosophers are in that darkness, but they eradicate it by taking full advantage of Your presence. I think the drones that are buzzing all around You must have been Your devotees in their past lives. They cannot leave Your company because no one can be a better, more affectionate master than You. You are the supreme and original Personality of Godhead, and the drones are just trying to spread Your glories by chanting at every moment. I think some of them must be great sages, devotees of Your Lordship, and they are disguising themselves in the form of drones because they are unable to give up Your company even for a moment. My dear brother, You are the supreme worshipable Godhead. Just see how the peacocks are dancing before You in great ecstasy. The deer, whose behavior is just like that of the *gopīs,* are welcoming You with the same affection. And the cuckoos who are residing in this forest are welcoming You with their joyful, sweet cries because they consider that Your appearance in their home is so auspicious. Even though they are trees and animals, these residents of Vṛndāvana are glorifying You. They are prepared to welcome You to the best of their ability, as is the practice of great souls in receiving another great soul at home. As for the land, it is so pious and fortunate because the footprints of Your lotus feet are marking its body.

"It is quite natural for these Vṛndāvana inhabitants to thus receive a great personality like You. The herbs, creepers and plants are also so fortunate to touch Your lotus feet. And by Your touching the twigs with Your fingernails, these small plants are also made glorious. As for the hills and the rivers, they too are now glorious because You are glancing at them. Above all, the damsels of Vraja, the *gopīs,* are the most glorious because You embrace them with Your strong arms, being attracted by their beauty."

In this way, Lord Kṛṣṇa and Balarāma began to enjoy the residents of Vṛndāvana to Their full satisfaction as They herded the calves and cows on the bank of the Yamunā. In some places Kṛṣṇa and Balarāma were accompanied by Their friends. The boys were singing, imitating the humming sound of the drones and accompanying Kṛṣṇa and Balarāma, who were garlanded with forest flowers. While walking, the boys sometimes imitated the quacking sound of the swans in the lakes, or when they saw the peacocks dancing, they imitated them before Kṛṣṇa. Kṛṣṇa also moved His neck, imitating the dancing and making His friends laugh.

The cows taken care of by Kṛṣṇa had different names, and Kṛṣṇa would call them with love. After hearing Kṛṣṇa calling, the cows would immediately respond by mooing, and the boys would enjoy this exchange to their hearts' content. They would all imitate the sound vibrations made by the different kinds of birds, especially the *cakoras,* peacocks, cuckoos and *bhāradvājas.* Sometimes, when they would see the weaker animals fleeing out of fear of the sounds of tigers and lions, the boys, along with Kṛṣṇa and Balarāma, would imitate the animals and run away with them. When they felt some fatigue, they would sit down, and Balarāma would put His head on the lap of one of the boys just to take rest, and Kṛṣṇa would immediately come and begin massaging the legs of Balarāma. And sometimes He would take a palm fan and fan the body of Balarāma, causing a pleasing breeze to relieve Him of His fatigue. Other boys would sometimes dance or sing while Balarāma took rest, and sometimes they would wrestle amongst themselves or jump. When the boys were thus engaged, Kṛṣṇa would immediately join them, and catching their hands, He would enjoy their company and laugh and praise their activities. When Kṛṣṇa would feel tired and fatigued, He would sometimes take shelter of the root of a big tree or the lap of a cowherd boy and lie down. When He would lie down with a boy or a root as His pillow, some of the boys would come and massage His legs, and some would fan His body with a fan made from leaves. Some of the more talented boys would sing in very sweet voices to please Him. Thus very soon His fatigue would go away. The Supreme Personality of Godhead, Kṛṣṇa, whose legs are tended by the goddess of fortune, shared Himself with the cowherd boys as one of them, expanding His internal potency to appear exactly like a village boy. But despite His appearing just like a village boy, there were occasions when He proved Himself to be the Supreme Personality of Godhead. Sometimes men pose themselves as the Supreme Personality of Godhead and cheat innocent people, but they can only cheat; they cannot exhibit the potency of God.

While Kṛṣṇa was thus engaged in His transcendental pastimes, exhibiting His internal potency in the company of the supermost fortunate cowherd boys, there occurred another chance for Him to exhibit the superhuman powers of Godhead. His most intimate friends Śrīdāmā, Subala and Stoka Kṛṣṇa addressed Kṛṣṇa and Balarāma with great love and affection thus: "Dear Balarāma, You are very powerful; Your arms are very strong. Dear Kṛṣṇa, You are very expert in killing all kinds of disturbing demons. Will You kindly note that just near this place there is a big forest of the name Tālavana? This forest is full of palm trees, and all the trees are filled with fruits. Some have fallen down, and some of them are very ripe even in the trees. It is a very nice place, but because of a great demon, Dhenukāsura, it is very difficult to go there. No one can reach the trees to collect the fruits. Dear Kṛṣṇa and Balarāma, this demon is present there in the form of an ass, and he is surrounded by similar demon friends who have assumed the same shape. All of them are very strong, so it is very difficult to approach this place. Dear brothers, You are the only persons who can kill such demons. Other than You, no one can go there for fear of being killed. Not even animals go there, and no birds are living there; they have all left. One can only appreciate the sweet aroma that is coming from that place. It appears that up until now, no one has tasted the sweet fruits there, either on the tree or on the ground. Dear Kṛṣṇa, to tell You frankly, we are very attracted by this sweet aroma. Dear Balarāma, if You like, let us all go there and enjoy these fruits. The aroma of the fruits is now spread everywhere. Don't You smell it from here?"

When Balarāma and Kṛṣṇa were thus petitioned by Their intimate friends, They were inclined to please them, and with smiling faces They proceeded toward the forest, surrounded by all Their friends. Immediately upon entering the Tālavana, Balarāma began to yank the trees with His arms, exhibiting the strength of an elephant. Because of this jerking, all the ripe fruits fell down on the ground. Upon hearing the sound of the falling fruits, the demon Dhenukāsura, who was living there in the form of an ass, approached with great force, shaking the whole field so that all the trees moved as if there were an earthquake. The demon appeared before Balarāma and kicked His chest with his hind legs. At first Balarāma did not say anything, but with great anger the demon kicked Him again more vehemently. This time Balarāma immediately caught hold of the legs of the ass with one hand and, wheeling him around, threw him into the treetops. While he was being wheeled around by Balarāma, the demon lost his life. Balarāma threw the demon into the biggest palm tree about, and the demon's body was so heavy that the palm tree fell upon other trees, and several fell down. It appeared as if a great hurricane had passed through the forest, and all the trees were falling down, one after another. This exhibition of extraordinary strength is not astonishing because Balarāma is the Personality of Godhead known as Ananta Śeṣa Nāga, who is holding all the planets on the hoods of His millions of heads. He maintains the whole cosmic manifestation exactly as horizontal and vertical threads hold the weaving of a cloth.

After the demon had been thrown into the trees, all the friends and associates of Dhenukāsura immediately assembled and attacked Balarāma and Kṛṣṇa with great force. They were determined to retaliate and avenge the death of their friend. But Kṛṣṇa and Balarāma caught each of the asses by the hind legs and, exactly in the same way, wheeled them around. Thus They killed all of them and threw them into the palm trees. Because of the dead bodies of the asses, there was a panoramic scene. It appeared as if clouds of various colors were assembled in the trees. Hearing of this great incident, the demigods from the higher planets showered flowers on Kṛṣṇa and Balarāma and beat their drums and offered devotional prayers.

A few days after the killing of Dhenukāsura, people began to come into the Tālavana forest to collect the fruits, and animals began to return without fear to feed on the nice grasses growing there. Just by chanting or hearing these transcendental activities and pastimes of the brothers Kṛṣṇa and Balarāma, one can amass pious activities.

When Kṛṣṇa and Balarāma entered the village of Vṛndāvana along with Their friends, They played Their flutes, and the boys praised Their uncommon activities in the forest. Their faces were decorated with *tilaka* and smeared with the dust raised by the cows, and Kṛṣṇa's head was decorated with a peacock feather. Both He and Balarāma played Their flutes, and the young *gopīs* were joyous to see Kṛṣṇa returning home. All the *gopīs* in Vṛndāvana remained very morose on account of Kṛṣṇa's absence. All day they were thinking of Kṛṣṇa in the forest or of Him herding cows in the pasture. When they saw Kṛṣṇa returning, all their anxieties were immediately relieved, and they began to look at His face the way drones hover over the honey of the lotus flower. When Kṛṣṇa entered the village, the young *gopīs* smiled and laughed. Kṛṣṇa, while playing the flute, enjoyed the beautiful smiling faces of the *gopīs*.

Then Kṛṣṇa and Balarāma were immediately received by Their affectionate mothers, Yaśodā and Rohiṇī, who, according to the time's demands, began to fulfill the desires of their affectionate sons. Simultaneously, the mothers rendered service and bestowed benediction upon their transcendental sons. They took care of their children by bathing Them and dressing Them very nicely. Kṛṣṇa was dressed in yellowish garments, and Balarāma was dressed in bluish garments, and They were given all sorts of ornaments and flower garlands. Being relieved of the fatigue of Their day's work in the pasturing ground, They looked refreshed and very beautiful.

They were given palatable dishes by Their mothers, and They pleasantly ate everything. After eating, They were seated nicely on clean bedding, and the mothers began to sing various songs of Their activities. As soon as They lay down on the bedding, They very quickly fell fast asleep. In this way, Kṛṣṇa and Balarāma used to enjoy Vṛndāvana life as cowherd boys.

Sometimes Kṛṣṇa used to go with His boyfriends and Balarāma, and sometimes He used to go alone with His friends to the bank of the Yamunā and tend the cows. Gradually, the summer season arrived, and one day, while in the field, the boys and cows became very thirsty and began to drink the water of the Yamunā. The river, however, had been made poisonous by the venom of the great serpent known as Kāliya.

Because the water was so poisonous, the boys and cows became visibly affected immediately after drinking. They suddenly fell down on the ground, apparently dead. Then Kṛṣṇa, who is the life of all that lives, simply cast His merciful glance over them, and all the boys and cows regained consciousness and began to look at one another with great astonishment. They could understand that by drinking the water of the Yamunā they had died and that the merciful glance of Kṛṣṇa had restored their lives.

Thus they appreciated the mystic power of Kṛṣṇa, who is known as Yogeśvara, the master of all mystic *yogīs.*

Thus ends the Bhaktivedanta purport of the Fifteenth Chapter of Kṛṣṇa, *"The Killing of Dhenukāsura."*

CHAPTER 16

Subduing Kāliya

WHEN HE UNDERSTOOD that the water of the Yamunā was being polluted by the black serpent Kāliya, Lord Kṛṣṇa took action against him and made him leave the Yamunā and go elsewhere, and thus the water became purified.

When this story was being narrated by Śukadeva Gosvāmī, Mahārāja Parīkṣit became eager to hear more about Kṛṣṇa's childhood pastimes. He inquired from Śukadeva Gosvāmī how Kṛṣṇa chastised Kāliya, who had been living in the water for many years. Actually, Mahārāja Parīkṣit was becoming more and more enthusiastic to hear the transcendental pastimes of Kṛṣṇa, and his inquiry was made with great interest. Śukadeva Gosvāmī narrated the story as follows. Within the river Yamunā there was a great lake, and in that lake the black serpent Kāliya used to live. Because of his poison, the whole area was so contaminated that it emanated a poisonous vapor twenty-four hours a day. If a bird happened to even pass over the spot, it would immediately die and fall down into the water. Due to the poisonous effect of the Yamunā's vapors, the trees and grass near the bank of the Yamunā had all dried up. Lord Kṛṣṇa saw the effect of the great serpent's poison: the whole river that ran before Vṛndāvana was now deadly.

Kṛṣṇa, who advented Himself just to kill all undesirable elements in the world, immediately climbed up into a big *kadamba* tree on the bank of the Yamunā. The *kadamba* is a tree bearing round yellow flowers that is generally seen only in the Vṛndāvana area. After climbing to the top of the tree, He tightened His belt cloth and, flapping His arms just like a wrestler, jumped into the midst of the poisonous lake. The *kadamba* tree from which Kṛṣṇa jumped was the only tree there which was not dead. Some commentators say that due to being touched by the lotus feet of Kṛṣṇa, the tree immediately became alive. In some other *Purāṇas* it is stated that Garuḍa, the eternal carrier of Viṣṇu, knew that Kṛṣṇa would take this action in the future, and so he put some nectar on this tree to preserve it. When Lord Kṛṣṇa jumped into the water, the river overflooded its banks to a distance of one hundred yards, as if something very large had fallen into it. This exhibition of Kṛṣṇa's strength is not at all uncommon, because Kṛṣṇa is the reservoir of all strength.

When Kṛṣṇa was swimming about just like a great strong elephant, He made a tumultuous sound, which the great black serpent Kāliya could hear. The tumult was intolerable for him, and he could understand that this was an attempt to attack his home. Therefore he immediately came before Kṛṣṇa. Kāliya saw that Kṛṣṇa was indeed worth seeing because His body was so beautiful and delicate; its color resembled that of a cloud, and His feet resembled a lotus flower. He was decorated with Śrīvatsa, jewels and yellow garments. He was smiling with a beautiful face and was playing in the river Yamunā with great strength. But in spite of Kṛṣṇa's beautiful features, Kāliya felt great anger within his heart, and thus he grabbed Kṛṣṇa with his mighty coils.

Seeing the incredible way in which Kṛṣṇa was enveloped in the coils of the serpent, the affectionate cowherd boys and other inhabitants of Vṛndāvana immediately became stunned out of fear. They had dedicated everything to Kṛṣṇa: their lives, property, affection, activities—everything was for Kṛṣṇa—and when they saw Him in that condition, they became overwhelmed with fear and fell down on the ground. All the cows, bulls and small calves became overwhelmed with grief, and they began to look at Him with great anxiety. Out of fear they could only cry in agony and stand erect on the bank, unable to help their beloved Kṛṣṇa.

While this scene was taking place on the bank of the Yamunā, there were ill omens manifest. The earth trembled, meteors fell from the sky, and the left side of men's bodies shivered. All these are indications of great immediate danger. Observing the inauspicious signs, the cowherd men, including Mahārāja Nanda, became very anxious out of fear. At the same time they were informed that Kṛṣṇa had gone to the pasturing ground without His elder brother, Balarāma. As soon as Nanda and Yaśodā and the cowherd men heard this news, they became even more anxious. Out of their great affection for Kṛṣṇa, and being unaware of the extent of His potencies, they became overwhelmed with grief and anxiety because they had nothing dearer than Kṛṣṇa and because they had dedicated their everything—life, property, affection, mind and activities—to Kṛṣṇa. Because of their great attachment for Kṛṣṇa, they thought, "Today Kṛṣṇa is surely going to be vanquished!"

All the inhabitants of Vṛndāvana came out of the village to see Kṛṣṇa. The assembly consisted of children, old men, women, animals and all living entities; they knew that Kṛṣṇa was their only means of sustenance. While this was happening, Balarāma, who is the master of all knowledge, stood there simply smiling. He knew how powerful His younger brother was and that there was no cause for anxiety when Kṛṣṇa was fighting with an ordinary serpent of the material world. He did not, therefore, personally take any part in their sorrow. On the other hand, all the inhabitants of Vṛndāvana, being disturbed, began to search out Kṛṣṇa by following the impression of His footprints on the ground, and thus they moved hastily toward the bank of the Yamunā. Finally, by following the footprints marked with flag, bow and conchshell, the inhabitants of Vṛndāvana arrived at the riverbank and saw that all the cows and boys were weeping to behold Kṛṣṇa enwrapped in the coils of the black serpent. Then they became still more overwhelmed with grief.

While Balarāma was smiling to see their lamentation, all the inhabitants of Vrajabhūmi merged into the ocean of grief because they thought that Kṛṣṇa was finished. Although the residents of Vṛndāvana did not know much about Kṛṣṇa, their love for Him was beyond comparison. As soon as they saw that Kṛṣṇa was in the river Yamunā enveloped by the serpent Kāliya and that all the boys and cows were lamenting, they simply began to think of Kṛṣṇa's friendship, His smiling face, His sweet words and His dealings with them. Thinking of all these and seeing that their Kṛṣṇa was now within the clutches of Kāliya, they at once felt that the three worlds had become vacant. Lord Caitanya also said that He was seeing the three worlds as vacant for want of Kṛṣṇa. This is the highest stage of Kṛṣṇa consciousness. Almost all of the inhabitants of Vṛndāvana had the highest ecstatic love for Kṛṣṇa.

When mother Yaśodā arrived, she wanted to enter the river Yamunā, and being checked, she fainted. Her friends, who were equally aggrieved, were shedding tears like torrents of rain or waves of the river, but in order to bring mother Yaśodā to consciousness, they began to speak loudly about the transcendental pastimes of Kṛṣṇa. Mother Yaśodā remained still, as if dead, because her consciousness was concentrated on the face of Kṛṣṇa. Nanda and all the other cowherd men, who had dedicated everything, including their lives, to Kṛṣṇa, were ready to enter the waters of the Yamunā, but Lord Balarāma checked them because He was in perfect knowledge that there was no danger.

For two hours Kṛṣṇa remained like an ordinary child gripped in the coils of Kāliya, but when He saw that all the inhabitants of Gokula—including His mother and father, the *gopīs,* the boys and the cows—were just on the point of death and that they had no shelter for salvation from imminent death, Kṛṣṇa immediately freed Himself.

He began to expand His body, and when the serpent tried to hold Him, he felt a great strain. On account of the strain, his coils slackened, and he had no alternative but to let loose the Personality of Godhead, Kṛṣṇa, from his grasp. Kāliya then became very angry, and his great hoods expanded. He exhaled poisonous fumes from his nostrils, his eyes blazed like fire, and flames issued from his mouth. The great serpent remained still for some time, looking at Kṛṣṇa. Licking his lips with bifurcated tongues, the serpent looked at Kṛṣṇa with double hoods, and his eyesight was full of poison. Kṛṣṇa immediately pounced upon him, just as Garuḍa swoops upon a snake. Thus attacked, Kāliya looked for an opportunity to bite Him, but Kṛṣṇa moved around him. As Kṛṣṇa and Kāliya moved in a circle, the serpent gradually became fatigued, and his strength seemed to diminish considerably. Kṛṣṇa immediately pressed down the serpent's hoods and jumped up on them. The Lord's lotus feet became tinged with red from the rays of the jewels on the snake's hoods. Then He who is the original artist of all fine arts, such as dancing, began to dance upon the hoods of the serpent, although they were moving to and fro. Upon seeing this, the denizens of the upper planets showered flowers, beat drums, played different types of flutes and sang various prayers and songs. In this way, all the denizens of heaven, such as the Gandharvas, Siddhas and demigods, became very pleased.

While Kṛṣṇa was dancing on his hoods, Kāliya tried to push Him down with some of his other hoods. Kāliya had about a hundred hoods, but Kṛṣṇa took control of them. He began to dash Kāliya with His lotus feet, and this was more than the serpent could bear. Gradually, Kāliya was reduced to struggling for his very life. He vomited all kinds of refuse and exhaled fire. While throwing up poisonous material from within, Kāliya became reduced in his sinful situation. Out of great anger, he began to struggle for existence and tried to raise one of his hoods to kill the Lord. The Lord immediately captured that hood and subdued it by kicking it and dancing on it. It actually appeared as if the Supreme Personality of Godhead Viṣṇu was being worshiped; the poisons emanating from the mouth of the serpent appeared to be like flower offerings. Kāliya then began to vomit blood instead of poison; he was completely fatigued. His whole body appeared to be broken by the kicks of the Lord. Within his mind, however, he finally began to understand that Kṛṣṇa is the Supreme Personality of Godhead, and he surrendered unto Him. He realized that Kṛṣṇa is the Supreme Lord, the master of everything.

The wives of the serpent, known as the Nāgapatnīs, saw that their husband had been subdued by the Lord's kicking and that he was almost at the point of death due to bearing the heavy burden of the Lord, within whose abdomen the whole universe remains. Kāliya's wives prepared to worship the Lord, and in their haste their clothes, hair and ornaments became disarrayed. They also surrendered unto the Supreme Lord and began to pray. They appeared before Him, put forward their offspring and anxiously offered respectful obeisances, falling down on the bank of the Yamunā. The Nāgapatnīs knew that Kṛṣṇa is the shelter of all surrendered souls, and they desired to release their husband from the impending danger by pleasing the Lord with their prayers.

The Nāgapatnīs began to offer their prayers as follows: "O dear Lord, You are equal to everyone. For You there is no distinction between Your sons, friends or enemies. Therefore the punishment which You have so kindly offered to Kāliya is exactly befitting. O Lord, You have descended especially for the purpose of annihilating all kinds of disturbing elements within the world, and because You are the Absolute Truth, there is no difference between Your mercy and Your punishment. We think, therefore, that this apparent punishment of Kāliya is actually some benediction. We consider that Your punishment is Your great mercy upon us because when You punish someone it is to be understood that the reactions of his sinful activities are eradicated. It is already clear that this creature appearing in the body of a serpent must have been overburdened with all kinds of sin; otherwise, how could he have the body of a serpent? Your dancing on his hoods has reduced all the sinful results of actions caused by his having this body of a serpent. It is therefore very auspicious that You have become angry and have punished him in this way. We are very much astonished to see how You have become so pleased with this serpent, who evidently performed various religious activities in his past lives that pleased everyone. He must have undergone all kinds of penances and austerities, humbly honored others and executed universal welfare activities for all living creatures."

The Nāgapatnīs confirm that one cannot come in contact with Kṛṣṇa without having executed pious activities in devotional service in his previous lives. As Lord Caitanya advised in His *Śikṣāṣṭaka,* one has to execute devotional service by humbly chanting the Hare Kṛṣṇa *mantra,* thinking oneself lower than the straw in the street and not expecting honor for himself but offering all kinds of honor to others. The Nāgapatnīs were astonished that, although Kāliya had the body of a serpent as the result of grievous sinful activities, at the same time he was in contact with the Lord to the extent that the Lord's lotus feet were touching his hoods. Certainly this was not the ordinary result of pious activities. These two contradictory facts astonished them. Thus they continued to pray: "O dear Lord, we are simply astonished to see that he is so fortunate as to have the dust of Your lotus feet on his head. This is a fortune sought after by great saintly persons. Even the goddess of fortune underwent severe austerities just to have the blessing of the dust of Your lotus feet, so how is it that Kāliya is so easily getting this dust on his head? We have heard from authoritative sources that those who are blessed with the dust of Your lotus feet do not care even for the highest post within the universe, namely the post of Lord Brahmā, or the kingship of the heavenly planets, or the sovereignty of this planet. Nor do such persons desire to rule the planets above this earth, such as Siddhaloka; nor do they aspire for the mystic powers achieved by the *yoga* process. Nor do the pure devotees aspire for liberation by becoming one with You. My Lord, although he is born in a species of life which is fostered by the most abominable mode of material nature, accompanied with the quality of anger, this king of the serpents has achieved something very, very rare. Living entities who are wandering within this universe in different species of life can very easily achieve the greatest benediction only by Your mercy."

It is confirmed in the *Caitanya-caritāmṛta* that the living entities are wandering within the universe in various species of life but by the mercy of Kṛṣṇa and the spiritual master they can get the seed of devotional service, and thus their path of liberation can be cleared.

The Nāgapatnīs continued, "We therefore offer our respectful obeisances unto You, our dear Lord, because You are the Supreme Person, who are living as the Supersoul within every living entity; although You are transcendental to the cosmic manifestation, everything is resting in You. You are the personified indefatigable eternal time. The entire time force is existing in You, and You are therefore the seer and the embodiment of total time in the shape of past, present and future, month, day, hour, moment—everything. In other words, O Lord, You can see perfectly all the activities happening in every moment, in every hour, in every day, in every month, in every year, past, present and future. You are Yourself the universal form, and yet You are different from this universe. You are simultaneously one with and different from the universe. We therefore offer our respectful obeisances unto You.

"You are Yourself the whole universe, and yet You are the creator of the whole universe. You are the superintendent and maintainer of this whole universe, and You are its original cause. Although You are present within this universe by Your three qualitative incarnations, Brahmā, Viṣṇu and Maheśvara, You are transcendental to the material creation. Although You are the cause of the appearance of all kinds of living entities—their senses, their lives, their minds, their intelligence—You are to be realized by Your internal energy. Let us therefore offer our respectful obeisances unto You, who are unlimited, finer than the finest, the center of all creation and knower of everything.

"Different varieties of philosophical speculators try to reach You. You are the ultimate goal of all philosophical efforts, and it is actually only You who are described by all philosophies and by different kinds of doctrines. Let us offer our respectful obeisances unto You, because You are the origin of all scripture and the source of knowledge. You are the root of all evidences, and You are the Supreme Person who can bestow upon us the supreme knowledge. You are the cause of all kinds of desires, and You are the cause of all kinds of satisfaction. You are the *Vedas* personified. Therefore we offer You our respectful obeisances.

"Our dear Lord, You are the Supreme Personality of Godhead, Kṛṣṇa, and You are also the supreme enjoyer. You have now appeared as the son of Vasudeva, a manifestation of the pure state of goodness. You are the predominating Deities of mind and intelligence, Aniruddha and Pradyumna, and You are the Lord of all Vaiṣṇavas. By Your expansion as the *catur-vyūha*—namely Vāsudeva, Saṅkarṣaṇa, Aniruddha and Pradyumna—You are the cause of the development of mind and intelligence. By Your activities only, the living entities become covered by forgetfulness or discover their real identity. This is confirmed in the *Bhagavad-gītā* (Fifteenth Chapter): the Lord is sitting as the Supersoul in everyone's heart, and due to His presence the living entity either forgets himself or revives his original identity. We can partially understand that You are within our hearts as the witness of all our activities, but it is very difficult to appreciate Your presence, although every one of us can do so to some extent. You are the supreme controller of both the material and spiritual energies; therefore You are the supreme leader, although You are different from this cosmic manifestation. You are the witness and creator and the very ingredient of this cosmic manifestation. We therefore offer our respectful obeisances unto You.

"Our dear Lord, in the matter of creating this cosmic manifestation, personally You have nothing to exert; by expanding Your different kinds of energy—namely the mode of passion, the mode of goodness and the mode of ignorance—You create, maintain and annihilate this cosmic manifestation. As the controller of the entire time force, You simply glance over the material energy, thereby creating this universe and energizing the different modes of material nature, which act differently in different creatures. No one can estimate, therefore, how Your activities are going on within this world.

"Our dear Lord, although You have expanded into the three principal deities of this universe—namely Lord Brahmā, Lord Viṣṇu and Lord Śiva—for creation, maintenance and destruction, Your appearance as Lord Viṣṇu is actually for the benediction of living creatures. Therefore, for those who are actually peaceful and who are aspiring after the supreme peace, worship of Your peaceful appearance as Lord Viṣṇu is recommended.

"O Lord, we are submitting our prayers unto You. You can appreciate that this poor serpent is going to give up his life. You know that for us women our husband is our life and everything; therefore, we are praying unto You that You kindly excuse Kāliya, our husband, because if this serpent dies, then we shall be in great difficulty. Looking upon us only, please excuse this great offender. Our dear Lord, every living creature is Your offspring, and You maintain everyone. This serpent is also Your offspring, and You can excuse him once although he has offended You, undoubtedly without knowing Your supremacy. We are praying that he may be excused this time. Our dear Lord, we are offering our loving service unto You because we are all eternal servitors of Your

Lordship. You can order us to do whatever You please. Every living being can be relieved from all kinds of despair if he agrees to abide by Your orders."

After the Nāgapatnīs submitted their prayers, Lord Kṛṣṇa released Kāliya from his punishment. Kāliya was already unconscious from being struck by the Lord. Upon regaining consciousness and being released from the punishment, Kāliya got back his life force and the working power of his senses. With folded hands, he humbly began to pray to the Supreme Lord Kṛṣṇa: "My dear Lord, I have been born in such a species that by nature I am angry and envious, being in the darkest region of the mode of ignorance. Your Lordship knows well that it is very difficult to give up one's natural instincts, although by such instincts the living creature transmigrates from one body to another." It is also confirmed in the *Bhagavad-gītā* that it is very difficult to get out of the clutches of material nature, but if anyone surrenders unto the Supreme Personality of Godhead, Kṛṣṇa, the modes of material nature can no longer act on him. "My dear Lord," Kāliya continued, "You are the original creator of the modes of material nature, by which the universe is created. You are the cause of the different kinds of mentality possessed by living creatures, by which they have obtained different varieties of bodies. My dear Lord, I am born as a serpent; therefore, by natural instinct I am very angry. How is it then possible to give up my acquired nature without Your mercy? It is very difficult to get out of the clutches of Your *māyā*. By Your *māyā* we remain enslaved. My dear Lord, kindly excuse me for my inevitable material tendencies. I surrender unto You. Now You can punish me or save me, as You desire."

After hearing this, the Supreme Personality of Godhead, who was acting as a small human child, ordered the serpent thus: "You must immediately leave this place and go to the ocean. Leave without delay. You can take with you all your offspring, wives and everything that you possess. Don't pollute the waters of the Yamunā. Let it be drunk by My cows and cowherd boys without hindrance." The Lord then declared that the order given to the Kāliya snake be recited and heard by everyone so that no one need fear Kāliya any longer.

Anyone who hears the narration of the Kāliya serpent and his punishment will need fear no more the envious activities of snakes. The Lord also declared, "If one takes a bath in the Kāliya lake, where My cowherd boyfriends and I have bathed, or if one fasts for a day and offers oblations to the forefathers from the water of this lake, he will be relieved from all kinds of sinful reactions." The Lord also assured Kāliya, "You came here out of fear of Garuḍa, who wanted to eat you in the beautiful land by the ocean. Now, after seeing the marks where I have touched your head with My lotus feet, Garuḍa will not disturb you."

The Lord was pleased with Kāliya and his wives. Immediately after hearing His order, the snake and his wives began to worship Him with great offerings of nice garments, flowers, garlands, jewels, ornaments, sandal pulp, lotus flowers and nice eatable fruits. In this way they pleased the master of Garuḍa, of whom they were very much afraid. Then, obeying the orders of Lord Kṛṣṇa, all of them left the lake within the Yamunā.

Thus ends the Bhaktivedanta purport of the Sixteenth Chapter of Kṛṣṇa, *"Subduing Kāliya."*

CHAPTER 17

Extinguishing the Forest Fire

KING PARĪKṢIT, after hearing of the chastisement of Kāliya, inquired from Śukadeva Gosvāmī as to why Kāliya left his beautiful land and why Garuḍa was so antagonistic to him. Śukadeva Gosvāmī informed the King that the island known as Nāgālaya was inhabited by serpents and that Kāliya was one of the chief serpents there. Being accustomed to eating snakes, Garuḍa used to come to this island and kill many serpents at will. Some of them he actually ate, but some were unnecessarily killed. The reptile society became so disturbed that their leader, Vāsuki, appealed to Lord Brahmā for protection. Lord Brahmā made an arrangement by which Garuḍa would not create a disturbance: on each half-moon day, the reptile community would offer a serpent to Garuḍa. The serpent was to be kept underneath a tree as a sacrificial offering to Garuḍa. Garuḍa was satisfied with this offering, and therefore he did not disturb any other serpents.

But gradually, Kāliya took advantage of this situation. He was unnecessarily puffed up by the volume of his accumulated poison, as well as by his material power, and he thought, "Why should Garuḍa be offered this sacrifice?" He then ceased offering any sacrifice; instead, he himself ate the offering intended for Garuḍa. When Garuḍa, the great devotee-carrier of Viṣṇu, understood that Kāliya was eating the offered sacrifices, he became very angry and rushed to the island to kill the offensive serpent. Kāliya tried to fight Garuḍa and faced him with his many hoods and poisonous sharp teeth. Kāliya attempted to bite him, and Garuḍa, the son of Tārkṣya, in great anger and with the great force befitting the carrier of Lord Viṣṇu, struck the body of Kāliya with his effulgent golden wings. Kāliya, who is also known as Kadrusuta, son of Kadru, immediately fled to the lake known as Kāliya-hrada, which lay within the Yamunā River and which Garuḍa could not approach.

Kāliya took shelter within the water of the Yamunā for the following reason. Just as Garuḍa went to the island of the Kāliya snake, he also used to go to the Yamunā to catch fish to eat. There was, however, a great *yogī* known as Saubhari Muni who used to meditate within the water there and who was sympathetic with the fish. He asked Garuḍa not to come there and disturb the fish. Although Garuḍa was not under anyone's order, being the carrier of Lord Viṣṇu, he did not disobey the order of the great *yogī.* Instead of staying and eating many fish, he carried off one big fish, who was their leader. Saubhari Muni was sorry that one of the leaders of the fish was taken away by Garuḍa, and thinking of their protection, he cursed Garuḍa with the following words: "Henceforward, from this day, if Garuḍa comes here to catch fish, then—I say this with all my strength—he will be immediately killed."

This curse was known only to Kāliya. Kāliya was therefore confident that Garuḍa would not be able to come there, and so he thought it wise to take shelter of the lake within the Yamunā. But Kāliya's taking shelter of Saubhari Muni was not successful; he was driven away from the Yamunā by Kṛṣṇa, the master of Garuḍa. It may be noted that Garuḍa is directly related to the Supreme Personality of Godhead and is so powerful that he is never subject to anyone's order or curse. Actually the cursing of Garuḍa—who is stated in *Śrīmad-Bhāgavatam* to be of the stature of the Supreme Personality of Godhead, Bhagavān—was an offense on the part of Saubhari Muni. Although Garuḍa did not try to retaliate, the Muni was not saved from his offensive act against a great Vaiṣṇava personality. Due to this offense, Saubhari fell down from his yogic position and afterwards became a householder, a sense enjoyer in the material world. The falldown of Saubhari Muni, who was supposed to be absorbed in spiritual bliss by meditation, is an instruction to the offender of Vaiṣṇavas.

When Kṛṣṇa finally came out of Kāliya's lake, He was seen by all His friends and relatives on the bank of the Yamunā. He appeared before them nicely decorated, smeared all over with *candana* pulp, bedecked with valuable jewels and stones, and almost completely covered with gold. The inhabitants of Vṛndāvana, including the cowherd boys and men, the *gopīs,* mother Yaśodā, Mahārāja Nanda and all the cows and calves, saw Kṛṣṇa coming from the Yamunā, and it was as though they had recovered their very life. When a person regains his life, naturally he becomes absorbed in pleasure and joyfulness. They each in turn pressed Kṛṣṇa to their chests, and thus they felt a great relief. Mother Yaśodā, Rohiṇī, Mahārāja Nanda and the cowherd men became so happy that as they embraced Kṛṣṇa they thought they had achieved their ultimate goal of life.

Balarāma also embraced Kṛṣṇa, but He was laughing because when everyone else had been so overwhelmed with anxiety, He had known what would happen to Kṛṣṇa. All the trees on the bank of the Yamunā, along with all the cows, bulls and calves, were full of pleasure because of Kṛṣṇa's appearance there. The *brāhmaṇa* inhabitants of Vṛndāvana immediately came with their wives to congratulate Kṛṣṇa and His family members. And because *brāhmaṇas* are considered to be the spiritual masters of society, they offered their blessings to Kṛṣṇa and His family on account of Kṛṣṇa's release. They also asked Mahārāja Nanda to give them some charity on that occasion. Being so pleased by Kṛṣṇa's return, Mahārāja Nanda gave many cows and much gold in charity to the *brāhmaṇas.* While Nanda Mahārāja was thus engaged, mother Yaśodā simply embraced Kṛṣṇa and made Him sit on her lap while she shed tears continuously.

Since it was almost night and all the inhabitants of Vṛndāvana, including the cows and calves, were very tired, they decided to take their rest on the riverbank. In the middle of the night, while they were taking rest, there was suddenly a great forest fire, and it quickly appeared that the fire would soon devour all the inhabitants of Vṛndāvana. As soon as they felt the warmth of the fire, they immediately took shelter of Kṛṣṇa, the Supreme Personality of Godhead, although He was playing just like their child. They began to say, "Our dear Kṛṣṇa! O Supreme Personality of Godhead! Our dear Balarāma, the reservoir of all strength! Please try to save us from this all-devouring and devastating fire. We have no shelter other than You. This devastating fire will swallow us all!" Thus they prayed to Kṛṣṇa, saying that they could not take any shelter other than His lotus feet. Lord Kṛṣṇa, being compassionate upon His own townspeople, immediately swallowed up the whole forest fire and saved them. This was not impossible for Kṛṣṇa, because He is unlimited. He has unlimited power to do anything He desires.

Thus ends the Bhaktivedanta purport of the Seventeenth Chapter of Kṛṣṇa, *"Extinguishing the Forest Fire."*

CHAPTER 18

Killing the Demon Pralambāsura

AFTER EXTINGUISHING THE DEVASTATING FIRE, Kṛṣṇa, surrounded by His relatives, friends, cows, calves and bulls and glorified by His friends' singing, again entered Vṛndāvana, which is always full of cows. While Kṛṣṇa and Balarāma were enjoying life in Vṛndāvana in the midst of the cowherd boys and girls, the season gradually changed to summer. The summer season in India is not very much welcomed because of the excessive heat, but in Vṛndāvana everyone was pleased because summer there appeared just like spring. This was possible only because Lord Kṛṣṇa and Balarāma, who are the controllers even of Lord Brahmā and Lord Śiva, were residing there. In Vṛndāvana there are many falls which are always pouring water, and the sound is so sweet that it covers the sound of the crickets. And because water flows all over, the forest always looks very green and beautiful.

The inhabitants of Vṛndāvana were never disturbed by the scorching heat of the sun or the high summer temperatures. The lakes of Vṛndāvana are surrounded by green grasses, and various kinds of lotus flowers bloom there, such as the *kahlāra, kañja* and *utpala,* and the air blowing in Vṛndāvana carries the aromatic pollen of those lotus flowers. When the particles of water from the waves of the Yamunā, the lakes and the waterfalls touched the bodies of the inhabitants of Vṛndāvana, they automatically felt a cooling effect. Therefore they were practically undisturbed by the summer season.

Vṛndāvana is such a nice place. Flowers are always blooming, and there are even various kinds of decorated deer. Birds are chirping, peacocks are crowing and dancing, and bees are humming. The cuckoos there sing nicely in five kinds of tunes.

Kṛṣṇa, the reservoir of pleasure, blowing His flute, accompanied by His elder brother Balarāma and the other cowherd boys and the cows, entered the beautiful forest of Vṛndāvana to enjoy the atmosphere. They walked into the midst of newly grown leaves of trees whose flowers resembled peacock feathers. They were garlanded by those flowers and decorated with saffron chalk. Sometimes they were dancing and singing and sometimes wrestling with one another. While Kṛṣṇa danced, some of the cowherd boys sang, and others played on flutes; some bugled on buffalo horns or clapped their hands, praising Kṛṣṇa, "Dear brother, You are dancing very nicely." Actually, all these boys were demigods descended from higher planets to assist Kṛṣṇa in His pastimes. The demigods garbed in the dress of the cowherd boys were encouraging Kṛṣṇa in His dancing, just as one artist encourages another with praise. Up to that time, neither Balarāma nor Kṛṣṇa had undergone the haircutting ceremony; therefore Their hair was clustered like crows' feathers. They were always playing hide-and-seek with Their boyfriends or jumping or fighting with them. Sometimes, while His friends were chanting and dancing, Kṛṣṇa would praise them, "My dear friends, you are dancing and singing very nicely." The boys played at catching ball with fruits such as bael and *āmalaka*. They played blindman's buff, challenging and touching one another. Sometimes they imitated the forest deer and various kinds of birds. They joked with one another by imitating croaking frogs, and they enjoyed swinging underneath the trees. Sometimes they would play like a king and his subjects amongst themselves. In this way, Balarāma and Kṛṣṇa, along with all Their friends, played all kinds of sports and enjoyed the soothing atmosphere of Vṛndāvana, full of rivers, lakes, rivulets, fine trees and excellent gardens filled with fruits and flowers.

Once while the boys were engaged in their transcendental pastimes, a great demon of the name Pralambāsura entered their company, desiring to kidnap both Balarāma and Kṛṣṇa. Although Kṛṣṇa was playing the part of a cowherd boy, as the Supreme Personality of Godhead He could understand everything—past, present and future. So when Pralambāsura entered their company, Kṛṣṇa began to think how to kill the demon, but externally He received him as a friend. "O My dear friend," He said, "it is very good that you have come to take part in our pastimes." Kṛṣṇa then called all His friends and ordered them, "Now we shall play in pairs. We shall challenge one another in pairs." With this proposal, all the boys assembled together. Some of them took the side of Kṛṣṇa, and some of them took the side of Balarāma, and they arranged to play in duel. The defeated members in duel fighting had to carry the victorious members on their backs, as a horse carries its master. They began playing, and at the same time tended the cows as they proceeded through the Bhāṇḍīravana forest.

The party of Balarāma, accompanied by Śrīdāmā and Vṛṣabha, came out victorious, and Kṛṣṇa's party had to carry them on their backs through the Bhāṇḍīravana forest. The Supreme Personality of Godhead, Kṛṣṇa, being defeated, had to carry Śrīdāmā on His back, and Bhadrasena carried Vṛṣabha. Imitating their play, Pralambāsura, who appeared there as a cowherd boy, carried Balarāma on his back. Pralambāsura was the greatest of the demons, and he had calculated that Kṛṣṇa was the most powerful of the cowherd boys.

In order to avoid the company of Kṛṣṇa, Pralambāsura carried Balarāma far away. The demon was undoubtedly very strong and powerful, but he was carrying Balarāma, who is compared to a mountain; therefore he began to feel the burden, and thus he assumed his real form. When he appeared in his real feature, he was decorated with a golden helmet and earrings and looked just like a cloud with lightning carrying the moon. Balarāma observed the demon's body expanding up to the limits of the clouds, his eyes dazzling like blazing fire and his mouth flashing with sharpened teeth. At first, Balarāma was surprised by the demon's appearance, and He began to wonder, "How is it that all of a sudden this carrier has changed in every way?" But with a clear mind He could quickly understand that He was being carried away from His friends by a demon who intended to kill Him. Immediately He struck the head of the demon with His strong fist, just as the King of the heavenly planets strikes a mountain with his thunderbolt. Stricken by the fist of Balarāma, the demon fell down dead, just like a snake with a smashed head, and blood poured from his mouth. When the demon fell, he made a tremendous sound, and it sounded as if a great hill were falling upon being struck by the thunderbolt of King Indra. All the boys then rushed to the spot. Astonished by the ghastly scene, they began to praise Balarāma with the words "Well done! Well done!" All of them then embraced Balarāma with great affection, thinking that He had returned from death, and they offered their blessings and congratulations. All the demigods in the heavenly planets became very satisfied and showered flowers on the transcendental body of Balarāma, and they also offered their blessings and congratulations for His having killed the great demon Pralambāsura.

Thus ends the Bhaktivedanta purport of the Eighteenth Chapter of Kṛṣṇa, *"Killing the Demon Pralambāsura."*

CHAPTER 19

Devouring the Forest Fire

WHILE KṚṢṆA AND BALARĀMA and Their friends were engaged in the pastimes described above, the cows, being unobserved, began to wander off on their own, entering farther and farther into the deepest part of the forest, allured by fresh grasses. The goats, cows and buffalo traveled from one forest to another and entered the forest known as Īṣīkāṭavī. This forest was full of green grass, and therefore they were allured; but when they entered, they saw that there was a forest fire, and they began to cry. On the other side Balarāma and Kṛṣṇa, along with Their friends, could not find their animals, and they became very aggrieved. They began to trace the cows by following their footprints, as well as the path of eaten grass. All of the boys were fearing that their very means of livelihood, the cows, were now lost. When searching out the cows in the forest, they themselves became very tired and thirsty. Soon, however, they heard the crying of their cows. Kṛṣṇa began to call the cows by their respective names, with great noise. Upon hearing Kṛṣṇa calling, the cows immediately replied with joy. But by this time the forest fire had surrounded all of them, and the situation appeared to be very fearful. The flames increased as the wind blew very quickly, and it appeared that everything movable and immovable would be devoured. All the cows and the boys became very frightened, and they looked toward Balarāma and Kṛṣṇa the way a dying man looks at the picture of the Supreme Personality of Godhead. They said, "My dear Kṛṣṇa! My dear Kṛṣṇa! You and Balarāma are very powerful. We are now burning from the heat of this blazing fire. Let us take shelter of Your lotus feet. We know You can protect us from this great danger. Our dear friend Kṛṣṇa, we are Your intimate friends. It is not right that we should suffer in this way. We are all completely dependent on You, and You are the knower of all religious life. We do not know anyone except You."

The Personality of Godhead heard the appealing voices of His friends, and casting a pleasing glance over them, He began to answer. By speaking through His eyes, He impressed upon His friends that there was no cause for fear, and He assured them, "Don't worry." Then Kṛṣṇa, the supreme mystic, the powerful Personality of Godhead, immediately swallowed up all the flames of the fire. The cows and boys were thus saved from imminent danger. Out of fear, the boys were almost unconscious, but when they regained their consciousness and opened their eyes, they saw that they were again in the Bhāṇḍīra forest with Kṛṣṇa, Balarāma and the cows. They were astonished to see that they were completely free from the attack of the blazing fire and that the cows were saved. They secretly thought that Kṛṣṇa must not be an ordinary boy but must be some demigod.

In the evening, Kṛṣṇa and Balarāma, along with the boys and cows, returned to Vṛndāvana, playing Their flutes. As they approached the village, all the *gopīs* became very joyous. Throughout the day the *gopīs* used to think of Kṛṣṇa while He was in the forest, and in His absence they were considering one moment to be like twelve years.

Thus ends the Bhaktivedanta purport of the Nineteenth Chapter of Kṛṣṇa, *"Devouring the Forest Fire."*

CHAPTER 20

Description of Autumn

THE KILLING OF PRALAMBĀSURA and the devouring of the devastating forest fire by Kṛṣṇa and Balarāma became household topics in Vṛndāvana. The cowherd men described these wonderful activities to their wives and to everyone else, and all were struck with wonder. They concluded that Kṛṣṇa and Balarāma were demigods who had kindly come to Vṛndāvana to become their children. In this way, the rainy season ensued. In India, after the scorching heat of the summer, the rainy season is very welcome. The clouds accumulating in the sky, covering the sun and the moon, become very pleasing to the people, and they expect rainfall at every moment. After summer, the advent of the rainy season is considered to be a life-giving source for everyone. The thunder and occasional lightning are also pleasurable to the people.

The symptoms of the rainy season may be compared to the symptoms of the living entities who are covered by the three modes of material nature. The unlimited sky is like the Supreme Brahman, and the tiny living entities are like the covered sky, or Brahman covered by the three modes of material nature. Originally, everyone is part and parcel of Brahman. The Supreme Brahman, or the unlimited sky, can never be covered by a cloud, but a portion of it can be covered. As stated in the *Bhagavad-gītā*, the living entities are part and parcel of the Supreme Personality of Godhead. But they are only an insignificant portion of the Supreme Lord. This portion is covered by the modes of material nature, and therefore the living entities are residing within this material world. The *brahmajyoti*—spiritual effulgence—is just like the sunshine; as the sunshine is full of molecular shining particles, so the *brahmajyoti* is full of minute portions of the Supreme Personality of Godhead. Out of that unlimited expansion of minute portions of the Supreme Lord, some are covered by the influence of material nature, whereas others are free.

Clouds are accumulated water drawn from the land by the sunshine. Continually for eight months the sun evaporates all kinds of water from the surface of the globe, and this water is accumulated in the shape of clouds, which are distributed as water when there is need. Similarly, a government exacts various taxes from the citizens, such as income tax and sales tax, which the citizens are able to pay by their different material activities: agriculture, trade, industry and so on. This taxation is compared to the sun's drawing water from the earth. When there is again need of water on the surface of the globe, the same sunshine converts the water into clouds and distributes it all over the globe. Similarly, the taxes collected by the government must be distributed to the people again, as educational work, public work, sanitation work, etc. This is very essential for a good government. The government should not simply exact taxes for useless squandering; the tax collection should be utilized for the public welfare of the state.

During the rainy season, there are strong winds blustering all over the country and carrying clouds from one place to another to distribute life-giving water to the needy living entities. Water is urgently needed after the summer season, and thus the clouds are just like a rich man who, in times of need, distributes his money even to the point of exhausting his whole treasury. So the clouds exhaust themselves by distributing water all over the surface of the globe.

When Mahārāja Daśaratha, the father of Lord Rāmacandra, used to fight with his enemies, it was said that he approached them just like a farmer uprooting unnecessary plants and trees. And when there was need of giving charity, he used to distribute money exactly as the cloud distributes rain. The distribution of rain by clouds is so sumptuous that it is compared to the distribution of wealth by a great, munificent person. The clouds' downpour is so profuse that the rains even fall on rocks and hills and on the oceans and seas, where there is no need for water. The clouds resemble a charitable person who opens his treasury for distribution and who does not discriminate whether the charity is needed or not. He gives in charity openhandedly.

Before the rainfall, the whole surface of the globe becomes almost depleted of all kinds of energies and appears very lean. After the rainfall, the whole surface of the earth becomes green with vegetation and appears to be very healthy and strong. Here, a comparison is made to the person undergoing austerities for fulfillment of a material desire. The flourishing condition of the earth after the rainy season is compared to the fulfillment of material desires. Sometimes, when a country is subjugated by an undesirable government, persons and parties undergo severe penances and austerities to get control of the government, and when they attain control, they flourish by giving themselves generous salaries. This temporary profit is like the flourishing of the earth in the rainy season. Actually, one should undergo severe austerities and penances only to achieve spiritual happiness. In *Śrīmad-Bhāgavatam* it is recommended that *tapasya,* or austerity, should be accepted for realizing the Supreme Lord. By accepting austerity in devotional service, one regains his spiritual life, and as soon as one regains his spiritual life, he enjoys unlimited spiritual bliss. But if someone undertakes austerities and penances for some material gain, it is stated in the *Bhagavad-gītā* that the results are temporary and that they are desired by persons of less intelligence.

During the rainy season, in the evening, there are many glowworms visible about the tops of trees, hither and thither, and they glitter just like lights. But the luminaries of the sky, the stars and the moon, are not visible. Similarly, in the Age of Kali, persons who are atheists or miscreants become very prominently visible, whereas persons who are actually following the Vedic principles for spiritual emancipation are practically obscured. This age, Kali-yuga, is compared to the cloudy season of the living entities. In this age, real knowledge is covered by the influence of the material advancement of civilization. The cheap mental speculators, atheists and manufacturers of so-called religious principles become prominent like the glowworms, whereas persons strictly following the Vedic principles or scriptural injunctions become covered by the clouds of this age. People should learn to take advantage of the actual luminaries of the sky—the sun, moon and stars—instead of the glowworms' light. Actually, the glowworms cannot give any light in the darkness of night. As clouds sometimes clear, even in the rainy season, and sometimes the moon, stars and sun become visible, so even in this Kali-yuga there are sometimes advantages. For example, sometimes Lord Caitanya's Vedic movement of distributing the chanting of the Hare Kṛṣṇa *mantra* is heard. People seriously eager to find real light should take advantage of this movement instead of looking toward the light of mental speculators and atheists.

After the first rainfall, when there is a thundering sound in the clouds, all the frogs begin to croak, like students suddenly engaged in reading their studies. Students are generally supposed to rise early in the morning. They do not usually arise of their own accord, however, but only when there is a bell sounded in the temple or other spiritual institution. By the order of the spiritual master they immediately rise, and after finishing their morning duties they sit down to study the *Vedas* or chant Vedic *mantras.* Everyone is sleeping in the darkness of Kali-yuga, but when there is a great *ācārya,* by his calling only, everyone takes to the study of the *Vedas* to acquire actual knowledge.

During the rainy season, many small ponds, lakes and rivulets become filled with water; otherwise, the rest of the year they remain dry. Similarly, materialistic persons are dry, but sometimes, when they are in a so-called opulent position, with a home or children or a little bank balance, they appear to be flourishing, but immediately afterwards they become dry again, like the small rivulets and ponds. The poet Vidyāpati said that in the society of friends, family, children, wife, etc., there is certainly some pleasure, but that pleasure is compared to a drop of water in the desert. Everyone is hankering after happiness, just as in the desert everyone is hankering after water. If in the desert there is a drop of water, it may of course be said that water is there, but the benefit from that drop of water is very insignificant. In our materialistic way of life, which is just like a desert, we are hankering after an ocean of happiness, but in the form of society, friends and mundane love we are getting no more than a drop of water. Our satisfaction is never achieved, as the small rivulets, lakes and ponds are never filled with water in the dry season.

Due to rainfall, the grass, trees and other vegetation look very green. Sometimes the grass is covered by a certain kind of red insect, and when the green and red combine with the umbrellalike mushrooms, the entire scene changes, just like a person who has suddenly become rich. The farmer then becomes very happy to see his field full of grains, but the capitalists—who are always unaware of the activities of a supernatural power—become unhappy because they are afraid of a competitive price due to abundant production. In some places certain capitalists in government restrict the farmers' production of grain, not knowing the actual fact that all food grains are supplied by the Supreme Personality of Godhead. According to the Vedic injunction, *eko bahūnāṁ yo vidadhāti kāmān:* the Supreme Personality of Godhead maintains this creation; therefore, He arranges for a supply of whatever is required for all living entities. When there is a population increase, it is the business of the Supreme Lord to feed the people. But atheists or miscreants do not like abundant production of food grains, especially if their business might be hampered.

During the rainy season, all living entities in the land, sky and water become very much refreshed, exactly like one who engages in the transcendental loving service of the Lord. We have practical experience of this with our students in the International Society for Krishna Consciousness. Before becoming students, they were dirty-looking, although they had naturally beautiful personal features; due to having no information of Kṛṣṇa consciousness they appeared very dirty and wretched. Since they have taken to Kṛṣṇa consciousness, their health has improved, and by their following the rules and regulations, their bodily luster has increased. When they are dressed with saffron-colored cloth, with *tilaka* on their foreheads and beads in their hands and on their necks, they look exactly as if they have come directly from Vaikuṇṭha.

In the rainy season, when the rivers swell and rush to the oceans and seas, they appear to agitate the ocean. Similarly, if a person who is engaged in the mystic *yoga* process is not very much advanced in spiritual life, he can become agitated by the sex impulse. Although during the rainy season the high mountains are splashed by torrents of rain, they do not change; similarly, a person who is advanced in Kṛṣṇa consciousness, even if put into difficulties, is not embarrassed. A person who is spiritually advanced accepts any adverse condition of life as the mercy of the Lord, and thus he is completely eligible to enter into the spiritual kingdom.

In the rainy season some of the roads are not frequently used, and they become covered with long grasses. These roads are exactly like a *brāhmaṇa* who is not accustomed to studying and practicing the reformatory methods of the Vedic injunctions—he becomes covered with the long grasses of *māyā*. In that condition, forgetful of his constitutional nature, he forgets his position of eternal servitorship to the Supreme Personality of Godhead. By being deviated by the seasonal overgrowth of long grasses created by *māyā*, a person identifies himself with the māyic production and succumbs to illusion, forgetting his spiritual life.

During the rainy season, lightning appears in one group of clouds and then immediately in another group of clouds. This phenomenon is compared to a lusty woman who does not fix her mind on one man. A cloud is compared to a qualified person because it pours rain and gives sustenance to many people; a man who is qualified similarly gives sustenance to many living creatures, such as family members or many workers in business. Unfortunately, his whole life can be disturbed by a wife who divorces him; when the husband is disturbed, the whole family is ruined, the children are dispersed or the business is closed, and everything is affected. It is therefore recommended that a woman desiring to advance in Kṛṣṇa consciousness live peacefully with a husband and that the couple not separate under any condition. The husband and wife should control sex indulgence and concentrate their minds on Kṛṣṇa consciousness so their life may be successful. After all, in the material world a man requires a woman and a woman requires a man. When they are combined, they should live peacefully in Kṛṣṇa consciousness and should not be restless like the lightning, flashing from one group of clouds to another.

Sometimes, in addition to the roaring thunder of the clouds, there is an appearance of a rainbow, which stands as a bow without a string. Actually, a bow is in the curved position because it is tied at its two ends by the bowstring; but in the rainbow there is no such string, and yet it rests in the sky so beautifully. Similarly, when the Supreme Personality of Godhead descends to this material world, He appears just like an ordinary human being, but He is not resting on any material condition. In the *Bhagavad-gītā,* the Lord says that He appears by His internal potency, which is free from the bondage of the external potency. What is bondage for the ordinary creature is freedom for the Personality of Godhead. In the rainy season, the moonlight is covered by clouds but is visible at intervals. It sometimes appears that the moon is moving with the movement of the clouds, but actually the moon is still; due to the clouds it also appears to move. Similarly, for one who has identified himself with the moving material world, his actual spiritual luster is covered by illusion, and with the movement of material activities he thinks that he is moving through different spheres of life. This is due to false ego, which is the demarcation between spiritual and material existence, just as the moving cloud is the demarcation between moonlight and darkness. In the rainy season, when the clouds appear for the first time, the peacocks dance with joy upon seeing them. The peacocks can be compared to persons who are very much harassed in the materialistic way of life. If they can find the association of a person engaged in the loving devotional service of the Lord, they become enlightened and dance just like peacocks. We have practical experience of this: many of our students were dry and morose previous to their coming to Kṛṣṇa consciousness, but having come into contact with devotees, they are now dancing like jubilant peacocks.

Plants and creepers grow by drinking water from the ground. Similarly, a person practicing austerities becomes dry, but after the austere performances are completed and he gets the result, he begins to enjoy life in sense gratification with family, society, love, home and other paraphernalia. He becomes jolly, like newly grown plants and grass. Sometimes it is seen that cranes and ducks meander continually on the banks of the lakes and rivers, although the banks are filled with muddy garbage and thorny creepers. Similarly, persons who are householders without Kṛṣṇa consciousness are constantly tarrying in material life, in spite of all kinds of inconveniences. In family life, or any life, one cannot be perfectly happy without being Kṛṣṇa conscious. Śrīla Narottama dāsa Ṭhākura prays that he will have the association of a person—either a householder or a man in the renounced order of life—who is engaged in the transcendental loving service of the Lord and is always crying the holy name of Lord Caitanya. For the materialistic person, worldly affairs become too aggressive, whereas to a person who is in Kṛṣṇa consciousness, everything appears to be happily situated.

The barriers around the agricultural field sometimes break due to heavy torrents of rain. Similarly, the unauthorized atheistic propaganda in the Age of Kali breaks the boundary of the Vedic injunctions. Thus people gradually degenerate to godlessness. In the rainy season, the clouds, tossed by the wind, deliver water which is welcomed like nectar. When the Vedic followers, the *brāhmaṇas,* inspire rich men like kings and members of the wealthy mercantile community to give charity in the performance of great sacrifices, the distribution of such wealth is also nectarean. The four sections of human society, namely the *brāhmaṇas,* the *kṣatriyas,* the *vaiśyas* and the *śūdras,* are meant to live peacefully in a cooperative mood; this is possible when they are guided by expert Vedic *brāhmaṇas* who perform sacrifices and distribute wealth equally.

Vṛndāvana forest improved from the rains and was replete with ripened dates, mangoes, blackberries and other fruits. Lord Kṛṣṇa, the Supreme Personality of Godhead, along with His boyfriends and Lord Balarāma, entered the forest to enjoy the new seasonal atmosphere. The cows, being fed by new grasses, became very healthy, and their milk bags were all very full. When Lord Kṛṣṇa called them by name, they immediately came to Him out of affection, and in their joyful condition the milk flowed from their bags. Lord Kṛṣṇa was very pleased when passing through the Vṛndāvana forest by the site of Govardhana Hill. On the bank of the Yamunā He saw all the trees decorated with beehives pouring honey. There were many waterfalls on Govardhana Hill, and their flowing made a nice sound. Kṛṣṇa heard them as He looked into the caves of the hill. When the rainy season was not ended completely but was gradually turning to autumn, sometimes, especially when there was rainfall within the forest, Kṛṣṇa and His companions would sit under a tree or within the caves of Govardhana Hill and enjoy eating the ripened fruits and talking with great pleasure. When Kṛṣṇa and Balarāma were in the forest, mother Yaśodā used to send Them some fruits, sweetmeats and rice mixed with yogurt. Kṛṣṇa would take them, sit down on a slab of stone on the bank of the Yamunā, and call His friends to join Him. While Kṛṣṇa and Balarāma and Their friends were eating, they watched the cows, calves and bulls. The cows appeared to be a little tired from standing with their heavy milk bags. By sitting and chewing grass, they became happy, and Kṛṣṇa was pleased to see them. He was proud to see the beauty of the forest due to the rainy season, which was nothing but the manifestation of His own energy. At such times Kṛṣṇa would praise nature's special activities during the rainy season. It is stated in the *Bhagavad-gītā* that the material energy, or nature, is not independent in its actions. Nature is acting under the superintendence of Kṛṣṇa. This is confirmed in the *Brahma-saṁhitā,* which states that material nature, known as Durgā, is acting as the shadow of Kṛṣṇa. Whatever order is sent from Kṛṣṇa, material nature obeys. Therefore the natural beauty created by the rainy season was acted out according to the indications of Kṛṣṇa, who thus felt very proud of material nature's beautiful activities.

While Kṛṣṇa and Balarāma were enjoying the gifts of the rainy season in this way, the autumn season gradually arrived, when all the water reservoirs become very clean, and when pleasing and refreshing air blows everywhere. With the appearance of autumn, the sky was completely cleared of all clouds, and it recovered its natural blue color. The blooming lotus flowers in the clear water in the forest appeared like persons who have fallen down from *yoga* practice but again have become beautiful by resuming their spiritual life. Everything becomes naturally beautiful with the appearance of the autumn season. Similarly, when a materialistic person takes to Kṛṣṇa consciousness and spiritual life, he also becomes as clear as the sky and water in autumn.

The autumn season takes away the rolling of dark clouds in the sky as well as the polluted water. Filthy conditions on the ground also become cleansed. Similarly, a person who takes to Kṛṣṇa consciousness immediately becomes cleansed of all dirty things within and without. Kṛṣṇa is therefore known as Hari. *Hari* means "he who takes away." Kṛṣṇa immediately takes away all unclean habits from anyone who takes to Kṛṣṇa consciousness. The clouds of autumn are white, for they do not carry any water. Similarly, a retired man, being freed from all responsibility of family affairs (namely, maintaining the home, wife and children) and taking completely to Kṛṣṇa consciousness, becomes freed from all anxieties and looks as white as clouds in autumn. Sometimes in autumn the falls come down from the top of the hill to supply clean water, and sometimes they stop. Similarly, sometimes great saintly persons distribute clear knowledge, and sometimes they are silent. The small ponds, which were filled with water because of the rainy season, gradually dry up in autumn. As for the small aquatics living in the reservoirs, they cannot understand that their ponds are diminishing day by day, as the materially engrossed persons cannot understand that their duration of life is being reduced day by day. Such persons are engaged in maintaining cows, property, children, wife, society and friendship. Due to the reduced water and scorching heat from the sun in the autumn season, the small creatures living in small reservoirs of water are very much disturbed; they are exactly like uncontrolled persons who are always unhappy from being unable to enjoy life or maintain their family members. The muddy earth gradually dries up, and newly grown fresh vegetation begins to wither. Similarly, for one who has taken to Kṛṣṇa consciousness, desire for family enjoyment gradually dries up.

Because of the appearance of the autumn season, the water of the ocean becomes calm and quiet, just as a person developed in self-realization becomes free from disturbance by the three modes of material nature. In autumn, farmers save the water within the fields by building strong walls so that the water contained within the field cannot run out. There is hardly any hope for new rainfall; therefore they want to save whatever is in the field. Similarly, a person who is actually advanced in self-realization protects his energy by controlling the senses. It is advised that after the age of fifty one should retire from family life and should conserve the energy of the body for utilization in the advancement of Kṛṣṇa consciousness. Unless one is able to control the senses and engage them in the transcendental loving service of Mukunda, there is no possibility of salvation.

During the daytime in autumn, the sun is very scorching, but at night, due to the clear moonshine, people get relief from the day's fatigue. Similarly, a person who takes shelter of Mukunda, or Kṛṣṇa, can be saved from the fatigue of misidentifying the body with the self. Mukunda, or Kṛṣṇa, is also the source of solace for the damsels of Vṛndāvana. The damsels of Vrajabhūmi are always suffering because of separation from Kṛṣṇa, but when they meet Kṛṣṇa during the moonlit autumn night, their fatigue of separation is relieved. When the sky is clear of all clouds, the stars at night shine very beautifully; similarly, when a person is actually situated in Kṛṣṇa consciousness, he is cleared of all dirty things, and he becomes as beautiful as the stars in the autumn sky. Although the *Vedas* contain instructions for pursuing knowledge (*jñāna*), for practicing mystic *yoga* and for engaging in karmic activities in the form of sacrifices, the ultimate purpose of the *Vedas* is stated in the *Bhagavad-gītā:* one has to accept Kṛṣṇa consciousness after thoroughly studying the *Vedas.* Therefore the clean heart of a devotee in Kṛṣṇa consciousness can be compared to the clean sky of the autumn season. During autumn, the moon looks very bright along with the stars in the clear sky. Lord Kṛṣṇa Himself appeared in the sky of the Yadu dynasty, and He was exactly like the moon surrounded by the stars, or the members of the Yadu dynasty. When there are ample blooming flowers in the gardens in the forest, the fresh, aromatic breeze gives a great relief to the person who has suffered during the summer and rainy seasons. Unfortunately, such breezes could not give any relief to the *gopīs* because of their hearts' dedication to Kṛṣṇa. People in general might have taken pleasure in that nice autumn breeze, but the *gopīs,* not being embraced by Kṛṣṇa, were not very much satisfied.

On the arrival of the autumn season, all the cows, deer, birds and females in general become pregnant, because in that season all the husbands generally become impelled by sex desire. Such pregnant females are exactly like the transcendentalists who, by the grace of the Supreme Lord, are bestowed with the benediction of their destinations in life. Śrīla Rūpa Gosvāmī has instructed in his *Upadeśāmṛta* that one should execute devotional service with great enthusiasm, patience and conviction and should follow the rules and regulations, keep oneself clean from material contamination and stay in the association of devotees. By following these six principles, one is sure to achieve the desired result of devotional service. For him who patiently follows the regulative principles of devotional service, the time will undoubtedly come when he will achieve the desired result, as the females reap results by becoming pregnant.

During the autumn, the lotus flowers in the lakes grow in large numbers because of the absence of lilies; both the lilies and the lotus flowers grow by sunshine, but during the autumn season the scorching sunshine helps only the lotus. This is compared to a country where the king or the government is strong: the unwanted elements like thieves and robbers cannot prosper. When the citizens become confident that they will not be attacked by robbers, they develop with great satisfaction. A strong government is compared to the scorching sunshine in the autumn season, the lilies are compared to unwanted persons like robbers, and the lotus flowers are compared to the satisfied citizens. During autumn, the fields become filled with ripened grain. At that time, the people become happy over the harvest and observe various ceremonies, such as Navānna, the offering of new grain to the Supreme Personality of Godhead. The new grain is first offered to the Deities in various temples, and all are invited to take sweet rice made with this new grain. There are other religious ceremonies and methods of worship, particularly in Bengal, where the greatest of all such ceremonies is held, called Durgā-pūjā.

In Vṛndāvana the autumn season was very beautiful then because of the presence of the Supreme Personality of Godhead, Kṛṣṇa and Balarāma. The mercantile community, the royal order and great sages were free to move about in order to achieve their desired benedictions. Similarly, the transcendentalists, when freed from the encagement of the material body, also achieve their desired goal. During the rainy season, the mercantile community cannot move from one place to another and so do not get their desired profit. Nor can the royal order go from one place to another to collect taxes from the people. As for saintly persons, who must travel to preach transcendental knowledge, they also are restrained by the rainy season. But during the autumn, all of them leave their confines. In the case of the transcendentalist, be he a *jñānī*, a *yogī* or a devotee, because of the material body he cannot actually enjoy spiritual achievement. But as soon as he gives up the body, or after death, the *jñānī* merges into the spiritual effulgence of the Supreme Lord, the *yogī* transfers himself to the various higher planets, and the devotee goes to the planet of the Supreme Lord, Goloka Vṛndāvana or one of the Vaikuṇṭhas, and thus enjoys his eternal spiritual life.

Thus ends the Bhaktivedanta purport of the Twentieth Chapter of Kṛṣṇa, *"Description of Autumn."*

CHAPTER 21

The Gopīs Attracted by the Flute

WITH THE ARRIVAL of the beautiful autumn season, the waters in the lakes and rivers became as clear as crystal and filled with fragrant lotus flowers, and breezes blew very pleasantly. At that time Kṛṣṇa entered the forest of Vṛndāvana with the cows and cowherd boys. Kṛṣṇa was very pleased with the atmosphere of the forest, where flowers bloomed and bees and drones hummed very jubilantly. While the birds, trees and plants were all looking very happy, Kṛṣṇa, tending the cows and accompanied by Śrī Balarāma and the cowherd boys, began to vibrate His transcendental flute. After hearing the vibration of the flute of Kṛṣṇa, the *gopīs* in Vṛndāvana remembered Him and began to talk amongst themselves about how nicely Kṛṣṇa was playing His flute. When the *gopīs* were describing the sweet vibration of Kṛṣṇa's flute, they also remembered their pastimes with Him; thus their minds became disturbed, and they were unable to describe completely the beautiful vibrations. While discussing the transcendental vibration, they remembered also how Kṛṣṇa dressed, decorated with a peacock feather on His head, just like a dancing actor, and with blue flowers pushed over His ear. His garment glowed yellow-gold, and He was garlanded with a Vaijayantī necklace. Dressed in such an attractive way, Kṛṣṇa filled up the holes of His flute with the nectar emanating from His lips. So they remembered

Him, entering the forest of Vṛndāvana, which is always glorified by the footprints of Kṛṣṇa and His companions.

Kṛṣṇa was very expert in playing the flute, and the *gopīs* were captivated by the sound vibration, which was attractive not only to them but to all living creatures who heard it. One of the *gopīs* told her friends, "The highest perfection of the eyes is to see Kṛṣṇa and Balarāma entering the forest and playing Their flutes and tending the cows with Their friends."

Persons who are constantly engaged in the transcendental meditation of seeing Kṛṣṇa, internally and externally, by thinking of Him playing the flute, entering the Vṛndāvana forest and tending the cows with the cowherd boys, have really attained the perfection of *samādhi. Samādhi* (trance) means absorption of all the activities of the senses in a particular object, and the *gopīs* indicate that the pastimes of Kṛṣṇa are the perfection of all meditation and *samādhi.* It is confirmed in the *Bhagavad-gītā* that anyone who is always absorbed in the thought of Kṛṣṇa is the topmost of all *yogīs.*

Another *gopī* expressed her opinion that Kṛṣṇa and Balarāma, while tending the cows, appeared just like actors going to play on a dramatic stage. Kṛṣṇa was dressed in glowing garments of yellow, Balarāma in blue, and They held new twigs of mango tree, peacock feathers and bunches of flowers in Their hands. Dressed with garlands of lotus flowers, They were sometimes singing very sweetly among Their friends.

One *gopī* told her friends, "How is it Kṛṣṇa and Balarāma are looking so beautiful?" Another *gopī* said, "My dear friends, we cannot even think of His bamboo flute—what sort of pious activities did it execute so that it is now enjoying the nectar of the lips of Kṛṣṇa, which is actually the property of us *gopīs*?" Kṛṣṇa sometimes kisses the *gopīs;* therefore the transcendental nectar of His lips is available only to them. So the *gopīs* asked, "How is it possible that the flute, which is nothing but a bamboo rod, is always engaged in enjoying the nectar from Kṛṣṇa's lips? Because the flute is engaged in the service of the Supreme Lord, the mother and the father of the flute must be happy."

The lakes and the rivers are considered to be the mothers of the trees because the trees live simply by drinking water. So the waters of the lakes and rivers of Vṛndāvana were in a happy mood, full of blooming lotus flowers, because the waters were thinking, "How is it that our son, the bamboo rod, is enjoying the nectar of Kṛṣṇa's lips?" The bamboo trees standing by the banks of the rivers and the lakes were also happy to see their descendant so engaged in the service of the Lord, just as persons who are advanced in transcendental knowledge take pleasure in seeing their descendants engage in the service of the Lord. The trees were overwhelmed with joy and were incessantly yielding honey, which flowed from the beehives hanging on their branches.

Another *gopī* spoke thus to her friends about Kṛṣṇa: "Dear friends, our Vṛndāvana is proclaiming the glories of this entire earth because this planet is glorified by the lotus footprints of the son of Devakī. Besides that, when Govinda plays His flute, the peacocks immediately become mad, as if they had heard the rumbling of a new cloud. When all the animals and trees and plants, either on the top of Govardhana Hill or in the valley, see the dancing of the peacocks, they all stand still and listen to the transcendental sound of the flute with great attention. We think that this boon is not possible or available on any other planet." Although the *gopīs* were village cowherd women and girls, they had extensive Vedic knowledge. Such is the effect of Vedic civilization. People in general would learn the highest truths of the *Vedas* simply by hearing from authoritative sources.

Another *gopī* said, "My dear friends, just see the deer! Although they are dumb animals, they have approached the son of Mahārāja Nanda, Kṛṣṇa. Not only are they attracted by the dress of Kṛṣṇa and Balarāma, but as soon as they hear the playing of the flute, the deer, along with their husbands, offer respectful obeisances unto the Lord by looking at Him with great affection." The *gopīs* were envious of the deer because the deer were able to offer their service to Kṛṣṇa along with their husbands. The *gopīs* thought themselves not so fortunate because whenever they wanted to go to Kṛṣṇa, their husbands were not very happy.

Another *gopī* said, "My dear friends, Kṛṣṇa is so nicely dressed that He appears to be the impetus to various kinds of ceremonies held by the womenfolk. Even the wives of the denizens of heaven become attracted after hearing the transcendental sound of His flute. Although they are traveling in the air in their airplanes, enjoying the company of their husbands, on hearing the sound of Kṛṣṇa's flute, they immediately become perturbed. Their hair is loosened, and their tight belts are slackened." This means that the transcendental sound of the flute of Kṛṣṇa extended to all corners of the universe. Also, it is significant that the *gopīs* knew about the different kinds of airplanes flying in the sky.

Another *gopī* said to her friends, "My dear friends, the cows are also charmed as soon as they hear the transcendental sound of the flute of Kṛṣṇa. It sounds to them like the pouring of nectar, and they immediately spread their long ears just to catch the liquid nectar of the flute. As for the calves, they are seen with the nipples of their mothers pressed in their mouths, but they cannot suck the milk. They remain struck with devotion, and tears glide down from their eyes, illustrating vividly how they are embracing Kṛṣṇa heart to heart." These phenomena indicate that even the cows and calves in Vṛndāvana knew how to cry for Kṛṣṇa and embrace Him heart to heart. Actually, the perfection of Kṛṣṇa consciousness can be culminated in the shedding of tears from the eyes.

Another young *gopī* told her mother, "My dear mother, the birds, who are all looking at Kṛṣṇa playing on His flute, are sitting very attentively on the branches and twigs of different trees. From their features it appears that they have forgotten everything and are engaged only in hearing Kṛṣṇa's flute. This proves that they are not ordinary birds; they are great sages and devotees, and just to hear Kṛṣṇa's flute they have appeared in Vṛndāvana forest as birds." Great sages and scholars are interested in Vedic knowledge, but the essence of Vedic knowledge is stated in the *Bhagavad-gītā: vedaiś ca sarvair aham eva vedyaḥ*. Through the knowledge of the *Vedas*, Kṛṣṇa has to be understood. From the behavior of these birds, it appeared that they were great scholars in Vedic knowledge and that they took to Kṛṣṇa's transcendental vibration and rejected all branches of Vedic knowledge. Even the river Yamunā, being desirous of embracing the lotus feet of Kṛṣṇa after hearing the transcendental vibration of His flute, broke her fierce waves to flow very nicely with lotus flowers in her hands, just to present flowers to Mukunda with deep feeling.

The scorching heat of the autumn sunshine was sometimes intolerable, and therefore the clouds in the sky appeared in sympathy above Kṛṣṇa and Balarāma and Their boyfriends while They engaged in blowing Their flutes. The clouds served as a soothing umbrella over Their heads just to make friendship with Kṛṣṇa.

The aborigine girls became fully satisfied when they smeared their faces and breasts with the dust of Vṛndāvana, which was reddish from the touch of Kṛṣṇa's lotus feet. The aborigine girls had very full breasts, and they were also very lusty, but when their lovers touched their breasts, the girls were not very much satisfied. When they came out into the midst of the forest, they saw that while Kṛṣṇa was walking some of the leaves and creepers of Vṛndāvana had turned reddish from the *kuṅkuma* powder which fell from His lotus feet. His lotus feet are held by the *gopīs* on their breasts, which are smeared with *kuṅkuma* powder, but when Kṛṣṇa travels in the Vṛndāvana forest with Balarāma and His boyfriends, the reddish powder falls on the ground of the Vṛndāvana forest. So the lusty aborigine girls, while looking toward Kṛṣṇa playing His flute, saw the reddish *kuṅkuma* on the ground and immediately took it and smeared it over their faces and breasts. In this way they became fully satisfied, although they were not satisfied when their lovers touched their breasts. All material lusty desires can be immediately satisfied if one comes in contact with Kṛṣṇa consciousness.

Another *gopī* began to praise the unique position of Govardhana Hill in this way: "How fortunate is this Govardhana Hill, for it is enjoying the association of Lord Kṛṣṇa and Balarāma, who are accustomed to walk on it. Thus Govardhana is always in touch with the lotus feet of the Lord. And because Govardhana Hill is so obliged to Lord Kṛṣṇa and Balarāma, it is supplying different kinds of fruits, roots and herbs, as well as very pleasing crystal water from its lakes, in presentation to the Lord. The best presentation offered by Govardhana Hill, however, is newly grown grass for the cows and calves. Govardhana Hill knows how to please the Lord by pleasing His most beloved associates, the cows and the cowherd boys."

Another *gopī* said, "Everything appears wonderful when Kṛṣṇa and Balarāma travel in the forest of Vṛndāvana playing Their flutes and making intimate friendship with all kinds of moving and nonmoving living creatures. When Kṛṣṇa and Balarāma play on Their transcendental flutes, the moving creatures become stunned and stop their activities, and the nonmoving living creatures, like trees and plants, begin to shiver with ecstasy. These are the wonderful reactions to the vibration of the transcendental flutes of Kṛṣṇa and Balarāma."

Kṛṣṇa and Balarāma carried binding ropes on Their shoulders and in Their hands, just like ordinary cowherd boys. While milking the cows, the boys bound their hind legs with a small rope. This rope almost always hung from the shoulders of the boys, and it was not absent from the shoulders of Kṛṣṇa and Balarāma. In spite of Their being the Supreme Personality of Godhead, They played exactly like cowherd boys, and therefore everything became wonderful and attractive.

While Kṛṣṇa was engaged in tending the cows in the forest of Vṛndāvana or on Govardhana Hill, the *gopīs* in the village were always absorbed in thinking of Him and discussing His different pastimes. This is the perfect example of Kṛṣṇa consciousness: to somehow or other remain always engrossed in thoughts of Kṛṣṇa. The vivid example is always present in the behavior of the *gopīs;* therefore Lord Caitanya declared that no one can worship the Supreme Lord by any method which is better than the method of the *gopīs.* The *gopīs* were not born in very high *brāhmaṇa* or *kṣatriya* families; they were born in the families of *vaiśyas,* and not in big mercantile communities but in the families of cowherd men. They were not very well educated, although they heard all sorts of knowledge from the *brāhmaṇas,* the authorities of Vedic knowledge. The *gopīs'* only purpose was to remain always absorbed in thoughts of Kṛṣṇa.

Thus ends the Bhaktivedanta purport of the Twenty-first Chapter of Kṛṣṇa, *"The* Gopīs *Attracted by the Flute."*

CHAPTER 22

Stealing the Garments of the Unmarried Gopī Girls

ACCORDING TO VEDIC CIVILIZATION, unmarried girls from ten to fourteen years of age are supposed to worship either Lord Śiva or goddess Durgā in order to get a nice husband. But the unmarried girls of Vṛndāvana were already attracted by the beauty of Kṛṣṇa. They were, however, engaged in the worship of goddess Durgā in the beginning of the Hemanta season (just prior to the winter season). The first month of Hemanta is Agrahāyana (October–November), and at that time all the unmarried *gopīs* of Vṛndāvana began to worship goddess Durgā with a vow. They first ate *haviṣyānna,* a kind of food prepared by boiling together mung dhal and rice without any spices or turmeric. According to Vedic injunction, this kind of food is recommended to purify the body before one enacts a ritualistic ceremony. All the unmarried *gopīs* in Vṛndāvana used to daily worship goddess Kātyāyanī early in the morning after taking a bath in the river Yamunā. Kātyāyanī is another name for goddess Durgā. The goddess is worshiped by preparing a doll made of sand from the bank of the Yamunā. It is recommended in the Vedic scriptures that a deity may be made from different kinds of material elements: it can be painted, made of metal, made of jewels, made of wood, earth or stone or can be conceived within the heart of the worshiper. The Māyāvādī philosopher takes all these forms of the deity to be imaginary, but actually they are accepted in the Vedic literatures to be identical with either the Supreme Lord or a respective demigod.

The unmarried *gopīs* used to prepare the deity of goddess Durgā and worship it with *candana* pulp, garlands, incense, lamps and all kinds of presentations—fruits, grain and twigs of plants. After worshiping, it is the custom to pray for some benediction. The unmarried girls used to pray with great devotion to goddess Kātyāyanī, addressing her as follows: "O supreme external energy of the Personality of Godhead, O supreme mystic power, O supreme controller of this material world, O goddess, please be kind to us and arrange for our marriage with the son of Nanda Mahārāja, Kṛṣṇa." The Vaiṣṇavas generally do not worship any demigods. Śrīla Narottama dāsa Ṭhākura has strictly forbidden all worship of the demigods for anyone who wants to advance in pure devotional service. Yet the *gopīs,* who are beyond compare in their affection for Kṛṣṇa, were seen to worship Durgā. The worshipers of demigods sometimes mention that the *gopīs* worshiped goddess Durgā, but we must understand the purpose of the *gopīs.* Generally, people worship goddess Durgā for some material benediction. Here, the *gopīs* prayed to the goddess to become wives of Lord Kṛṣṇa. The purport is that if Kṛṣṇa is the center of activity, a devotee can adopt any means to achieve that goal. The *gopīs* could adopt any means to satisfy or serve Kṛṣṇa. That was the superexcellent characteristic of the *gopīs.* They worshiped goddess Durgā completely for one month in order to have Kṛṣṇa as their husband. Every day they prayed for Kṛṣṇa, the son of Nanda Mahārāja, to become their husband.

Early in the morning, the *gopīs* used to go to the bank of the Yamunā to take a bath. They would assemble together and, holding one another's hands, loudly sing of the wonderful pastimes of Kṛṣṇa. It is an old system among Indian girls and women that when they take a bath in the river they place their garments on the bank and dip into the water completely naked. The portion of the river where the girls and women bathe was strictly prohibited to any male, and this is still the system. The Supreme Personality of Godhead, knowing the minds of the unmarried young *gopīs,* blessed them with their desired objective. They had prayed for Kṛṣṇa to become their husband, and Kṛṣṇa wanted to fulfill their desires.

At the end of the month, Kṛṣṇa, along with His friends, appeared on the scene. Another name of Kṛṣṇa is Yogeśvara, or master of all mystic powers. By practicing meditation, the *yogī* can study the psychic movement of other men, and certainly Kṛṣṇa could understand the desire of the *gopīs.* Appearing on the scene, Kṛṣṇa immediately collected all the garments of the *gopīs,* climbed up into a nearby tree, and with a smiling face began to speak to them.

"My dear girls," He said, "please come here one after another and pray for your garments and then take them away. I'm not joking with you. I'm just telling the truth. I have no desire to play any joke with you, for you are tired from observing the regulative principles for one month by worshiping goddess Kātyāyanī. Please do not come here all at once. Come alone; I want to see each of you in your complete beauty, for you all have thin waists. I have requested you to come alone. Now please comply."

When the girls in the water heard such joking words from Kṛṣṇa, they began to look at one another and smile. They were very joyous to hear such a request from Kṛṣṇa because they were already in love with Him. Out of shyness, they looked at one another, but they could not come out of the water because they were naked. Due to remaining in the water for a long time, they felt cold and were shivering, yet upon hearing the pleasing, joking words of Govinda, their minds were perturbed with great joy. They told Kṛṣṇa, "Dear son of Nanda Mahārāja, please do not joke with us in that way. It is completely unjust to us. You are a very respectable boy because You are the son of Nanda Mahārāja, and You are very dear to us, but You should not play this joke on us, because now we are all shivering from the cold water. Kindly deliver our garments immediately; otherwise we shall suffer." They then began to appeal to Kṛṣṇa with great submission. "Dear Śyāmasundara," they said, "we are all Your eternal servitors. Whatever You order us to do, we are obliged to perform without hesitation because we consider it our religious duty. But if You insist on putting this proposal to us, which is impossible to perform, then certainly we will have to go to Nanda Mahārāja and lodge a complaint against You. If Nanda Mahārāja does not take action, then we shall tell King Kaṁsa about Your misbehavior."

Upon hearing this appeal by the unmarried *gopīs,* Kṛṣṇa answered, "My dear girls, if you think that you are My eternal servitors and you are always ready to execute My order, then My request is that, with your smiling faces, you please come here alone, one after another, and take away your garments. If you do not come here, however, and if you lodge complaints with My father, I shall not care anyway, for I know My father is old and cannot take any action against Me."

When the *gopīs* saw that Kṛṣṇa was strong and determined, they had no alternative but to abide by His order. One after another they came out of the water, but because they were completely naked, they tried to cover their nakedness by placing their left hand over their pubic area. In that posture they were all shivering. Their simple presentation was so pure that Lord Kṛṣṇa immediately became pleased with them. All the unmarried *gopīs* who prayed to Kātyāyanī to have Kṛṣṇa as their husband were thus satisfied. A woman cannot be naked before any male except her husband. The unmarried *gopīs* desired Kṛṣṇa as their husband, and He fulfilled their desire in this way. Being pleased with them, He took their garments on His shoulder and began to speak as follows: "My dear girls, you have committed a great offense by going naked in the river Yamunā. Because of this, the predominating deity of the Yamunā, Varuṇadeva, has become displeased with you. Please, therefore, just touch your foreheads with folded palms and bow down before the demigod Varuṇa in order to be excused from this offensive act." The *gopīs* were all simple souls, and whatever Kṛṣṇa said they took to be true. In order to be freed from the wrath of Varuṇadeva, as well as to fulfill the desired end of their vows and ultimately to please their worshipable Lord, Kṛṣṇa, they immediately abided by His order. Thus they became the greatest lovers of Kṛṣṇa, and His most obedient servitors.

Nothing can compare to the Kṛṣṇa consciousness of the *gopīs*. Actually, the *gopīs* did not care for Varuṇa or any other demigod; they only wanted to satisfy Kṛṣṇa. Kṛṣṇa became very ingratiated and satisfied by the simple dealings of the *gopīs*, and He immediately delivered their respective garments, one after another. Although Kṛṣṇa cheated the young unmarried *gopīs* and made them stand naked before Him and enjoyed joking words with them, and although He treated them just like dolls and stole their garments, they were still pleased with Him and never lodged complaints against Him. This attitude of the *gopīs* is described by Lord Caitanya Mahāprabhu when He prays, "My dear Lord Kṛṣṇa, You may embrace Me or trample Me under Your feet, or You may make Me brokenhearted by never being present before Me. Whatever You like, You can do, because You have complete freedom to act. But in spite of all Your dealings, You are My Lord eternally, and I have no other worshipable object." This is the attitude of the *gopīs* toward Kṛṣṇa.

Lord Kṛṣṇa was pleased with them, and since they all desired to have Him as their husband, He told them, "My dear well-behaved girls, I know of your desire for Me and why you worshiped goddess Kātyāyanī, and I completely approve of your action. Anyone whose full consciousness is always absorbed in Me, even if in lust, is elevated. As a fried seed cannot fructify, so any desire in connection with My loving service cannot produce any fruitive result, as in ordinary *karma*."

There is a statement in the *Brahma-saṁhitā: karmāṇi nirdahati kintu ca bhakti-bhājām.* Everyone is bound by his fruitive activities, but the devotees, because they work completely for the satisfaction of the Lord, suffer no reactions. Similarly, the *gopīs'* attitude toward Kṛṣṇa, although seemingly lusty, should not be considered to be like the lusty desires of ordinary women. The reason is explained by Kṛṣṇa Himself. Activities in devotional service to Kṛṣṇa are transcendental to any fruitive result.

"My dear *gopīs*," Kṛṣṇa continued, "your desire to have Me as your husband will be fulfilled because it is with this desire that you worshiped goddess Kātyāyanī. I promise you that during the next autumn season you shall be able to meet with Me, and you shall enjoy Me as your husband."

Later Kṛṣṇa, in the company of His cowherd boyfriends, took shelter of the shade of some trees and became very happy. Thus He addressed the inhabitants of Vṛndāvana: "My dear Stoka Kṛṣṇa, My dear Varūthapa, My dear Bhadrasena, My dear Sudāmā, My dear Subala, My dear Arjuna, My dear Viśāla, My dear Ṛṣabha—just look at these most fortunate trees of Vṛndāvana. They have dedicated their lives to the welfare of others. Individually they are tolerating all kinds of natural disturbances, such as hurricanes, torrents of rain, scorching heat and piercing cold, but they are very careful to relieve our fatigue and give us shelter. My dear friends, I think they are glorified in this birth as trees. They are so careful to give shelter to others that they are like noble, highly elevated charitable men who never deny charity to one who approaches them. No one is denied shelter by these trees. They supply various kinds of facilities to human society, such as leaves, flowers, fruit, shade, roots, bark, flavor extracts and fuel. They are the perfect example of noble life. They are like a noble person who has sacrificed everything possible—his body, mind, activities, intelligence and words—for the welfare of all living entities."

Thus the Supreme Personality of Godhead walked on the bank of the Yamunā, touching the leaves of the trees and their fruits, flowers and twigs and praising their glorious welfare activities. Different people may accept certain welfare activities to be beneficial for human society, according to their own views, but the welfare activity that can be rendered to people in general, for eternal benefit, is the spreading of the Kṛṣṇa consciousness movement. Everyone should be prepared to propagate this movement. As instructed by Lord Caitanya, one should be humbler than the grass on the ground and more tolerant than the tree. The toleration of the tree is explained by Lord Kṛṣṇa Himself, and those who are engaged in the preaching of Kṛṣṇa consciousness should learn lessons from the teachings of Lord Kṛṣṇa and Lord Caitanya through Their direct disciplic succession.

While passing through the forest of Vṛndāvana on the bank of the Yamunā, Kṛṣṇa sat down at a beautiful spot and allowed the cows to drink the cold and transparent water of the Yamunā. Being fatigued, the cowherd boys, Kṛṣṇa and Balarāma also drank. After seeing the young *gopīs* bathe in the Yamunā, Kṛṣṇa passed the rest of the morning with the boys.

Thus ends the Bhaktivedanta purport of the Twenty-second Chapter of Kṛṣṇa, *"Stealing the Garments of the Unmarried* Gopī *Girls."*

CHAPTER 23

Delivering the Wives of the Brāhmaṇas Who Performed Sacrifices

THE MORNING PASSED, and the cowherd boys were very hungry because they had not eaten breakfast. They immediately approached Kṛṣṇa and Balarāma and said, "Dear Kṛṣṇa and Balarāma, You are both all-powerful; You can kill many, many demons, but today we are much afflicted with hunger, and this is disturbing us. Please arrange for something that will mitigate our hunger."

Requested in this way by Their friends, Lord Kṛṣṇa and Balarāma arranged to show compassion to certain wives of *brāhmaṇas* who were performing sacrifices. These wives were great devotees of the Lord, and Kṛṣṇa took this opportunity to bless them. He said, "My dear friends, please go to the house of the *brāhmaṇas* nearby. They are now engaged in performing Vedic sacrifices known as Āṅgirasa, for they desire elevation to the heavenly planets. All of you please go to them."

Then Lord Kṛṣṇa warned His friends, "These *brāhmaṇas* are not Vaiṣṇavas. They cannot even chant Our names, Kṛṣṇa and Balarāma. They are very busy in chanting the Vedic hymns, although the purpose of Vedic knowledge is to find Me. But because they are not attracted by the names of Kṛṣṇa and Balarāma, you had better not ask them for anything in My name. Better ask for some charity in the name of Balarāma."

Charity is generally given to high-class *brāhmaṇas,* but Kṛṣṇa and Balarāma did not appear in a *brāhmaṇa* family. Balarāma was known as the son of Vasudeva, a *kṣatriya,* and Kṛṣṇa was known in Vṛndāvana as the son of Nanda Mahārāja, who was a *vaiśya.* Neither belonged to the *brāhmaṇa* community. Therefore, Kṛṣṇa considered that the *brāhmaṇas* engaged in performing sacrifices might not be induced to give charity to a *kṣatriya* and *vaiśya.* "But at least if you utter the name of Balarāma, they may prefer to give in charity to a *kṣatriya* rather than to Me, because I am only a *vaiśya.*"

Being thus ordered by the Supreme Personality of Godhead, all the boys went to the *brāhmaṇas* and began to ask for some charity. They approached them with folded hands and fell down on the ground to offer respect. "O earthly gods, kindly hear us, who are ordered by Lord Kṛṣṇa and Balarāma. We hope you know Them both very well, and we wish you all good fortune. Kṛṣṇa and Balarāma are tending cows nearby, and we have accompanied Them. We have come to ask for some food from you. You are all *brāhmaṇas* and knowers of religious principles, and if you think that you should give us charity, then give us some food, and we shall all eat along with Kṛṣṇa and Balarāma. You are the most respectable *brāhmaṇas* within the human society, and you are expected to know all the principles of religious procedure."

Although the boys were village boys and were not expected to be learned in all the Vedic principles of religious ritual, they hinted that because of their association with Kṛṣṇa and Balarāma, they knew all those principles. By addressing the *brāhmaṇas* as "knowers of all religious principles," the boys expressed the point of view that when the Supreme Personality of Godhead, Kṛṣṇa and Balarāma, were asking for food, the *brāhmaṇas* should immediately deliver some without hesitation because, as statedin the *Bhagavad-gītā,* one should perform *yajña* (sacrifices) only for the satisfaction of Viṣṇu.

The boys continued, "Lord Viṣṇu as Kṛṣṇa and Balarāma is standing waiting, and you should immediately deliver whatever food you have in your stock." They also explained to the *brāhmaṇas* when food is to be accepted and when it is not to be accepted. Generally, the Vaiṣṇavas, or pure devotees of the Lord, do not take part in ordinary sacrificial performances. But they know very well the ceremonials called *dīkṣā, paśu-saṁsthā* and *sautrāmaṇi.* One is permitted to take food after the procedure of *dīkṣā* and before the animal sacrificial ceremony and the *sautrāmaṇi,* or ceremony in which liquors are also offered. The boys said, "We can take your food at the present stage of your ceremony, for now it will not be prohibited. So you can deliver us the food."

Although the companions of Lord Kṛṣṇa and Balarāma were simple cowherd boys, they were in a position to dictate even to the high-class *brāhmaṇas* engaged in the Vedic rituals of sacrifice. But the *smārta-brāhmaṇas,* who were simply sacrificial-minded, could not understand the dictation of the transcendental devotees of the

Lord. They could not even appreciate the begging of the Supreme Lord, Kṛṣṇa and Balarāma. Although they heard all the arguments on behalf of Kṛṣṇa and Balarāma, they did not care for them, and they refused to speak to the boys. Despite being highly elevated in the knowledge of Vedic sacrificial rites, all such nondevotee *brāhmaṇas,* although they think of themselves as very highly elevated, are ignorant, foolish persons. All their activities are childish because they do not know the purpose of the *Vedas,* as it is explained in the *Bhagavad-gītā:* to understand Kṛṣṇa. In spite of their advancement in Vedic knowledge and rituals, they do not understand Kṛṣṇa; therefore their knowledge of the *Vedas* is useless. Lord Caitanya, therefore, gave His valuable opinion that although a person may not be born in a *brāhmaṇa* family, if he knows Kṛṣṇa or the science of Kṛṣṇa consciousness he is more than a *brāhmaṇa,* and he is quite fit to become a spiritual master.

There are various details to be observed in the performance of sacrifices. They are known as *deśa,* place; *kāla,* time; *pṛthag-dravya,* the different detailed paraphernalia; *mantra,* hymns; *tantra,* scriptural evidences; *agni,* fire; *ṛtvik,* learned performers of sacrifices; *devatā,* the demigods; *yajamāna,* the performer of the sacrifices; *kratu,* the sacrifice itself; and *dharma,* the procedures. All these are for satisfying Kṛṣṇa. It is confirmed in the *Bhagavad-gītā* that He is the actual enjoyer of all sacrifices because He is directly the Supreme Personality of Godhead and the Supreme Absolute Truth, beyond the conception or speculation of material senses. He is present just like an ordinary human boy, but for persons who identify themselves with the body, it is very difficult to understand Him. The *brāhmaṇas* were very interested in the comforts of this material body and in elevation to the higher planetary residences called *svarga-vāsa.* They were therefore completely unable to understand the position of Kṛṣṇa.

When the boys saw that the *brāhmaṇas* would not reply to them even with a simple yes or no, they became very much disappointed. They then returned to Lord Kṛṣṇa and Balarāma and explained everything that had happened. After hearing their statements, the Supreme Personality of Godhead smiled. He told them that they should not be sorry for being refused by the *brāhmaṇas,* because that is the way of begging. He convinced them that one who is engaged in collecting or begging should not think that he will be successful everywhere. He may be unsuccessful in some places, but that should not be cause for disappointment. Lord Kṛṣṇa then asked all the boys to go again, but this time to the wives of those *brāhmaṇas* engaged in sacrifices. He also informed them that these wives were great devotees. "They are always absorbed in thinking of Us. Go there and ask for some food in My name and the name of Balarāma, and I am sure that they will deliver you as much food as you desire."

Carrying out Kṛṣṇa's order, the boys immediately went to the wives of the *brāhmaṇas.* They found the wives sitting inside the *brāhmaṇas'* house. They were very beautifully decorated with ornaments. After offering them all respectful obeisances, the boys said, "Dear mothers, please accept our humble obeisances and hear our statement. May we inform you that Lord Kṛṣṇa and Balarāma are nearby. They have come here with the cows, and you may know also that we have come here under Their instructions. All of us are very hungry; therefore, we have come to you for some food. Please give us something to eat for Kṛṣṇa, Balarāma and ourselves."

Immediately upon hearing this, the wives of the *brāhmaṇas* became anxious for Kṛṣṇa and Balarāma. These reactions were spontaneous. They did not have to be convinced of the importance of Kṛṣṇa and Balarāma; immediately upon hearing Their names, they became very eager to see Them. Being advanced by thinking of Kṛṣṇa constantly, they were performing the greatest form of mystic meditation. All the wives then became very busily engaged in filling up different pots with nice food. Due to the performance of the sacrifice, the various foods were all very palatable. After collecting a feast, they prepared to go to Kṛṣṇa, their most beloved object, exactly in the way rivers flow to the sea.

For a long time the wives had been eager to see Kṛṣṇa. However, when they were preparing to leave home to go see Him, their husbands, fathers, sons and relatives asked them not to go. But the wives did not comply. When a devotee is called by the attraction of Kṛṣṇa, he does not care for bodily ties. The women entered the forest of Vṛndāvana on the bank of the Yamunā, which was verdant with vegetation and newly grown vines and flowers. Within that forest they saw Kṛṣṇa and Balarāma engaged in tending the cows along with Their very affectionate boyfriends.

The *brāhmaṇas'* wives saw Kṛṣṇa with a blackish complexion, wearing a garment that glittered like gold. He wore a nice garland of forest flowers and a peacock feather on His head. He was also painted with the minerals found in Vṛndāvana, and He looked exactly like a dancing actor on a theatrical stage. They saw Him resting one hand on the shoulder of His friend, and in His other hand He was holding a lotus flower. His ears were decorated with lilies, He wore marks of *tilaka,* and He was smiling charmingly. With their very eyes the wives of the *brāhmaṇas* saw the Supreme Personality of Godhead, of whom they had heard so much, who was so dear to them, and in whom their minds were always absorbed. Now they saw Him eye to eye and face to face, and Kṛṣṇa entered within their hearts through their eyes.

Within themselves they began to embrace Kṛṣṇa to their hearts' content, and the distress of separation was mitigated immediately. They were just like great sages who, by their advancement of knowledge, merge into the existence of the Supreme. As the Supersoul living in everyone's heart, Lord Kṛṣṇa could understand their minds; they had come to Him despite all the protests of their relatives, fathers, husbands and brothers, and despite all the duties of household affairs. They came just to see Him, who was their life and soul. They were exactly following Kṛṣṇa's instruction in the *Bhagavad-gītā:* one should surrender to Him, giving up all varieties of occupational and religious duties. He therefore began to speak to them, smiling very magnificently. It should be noted in this connection that when Kṛṣṇa entered into the wives' hearts and when they embraced Him and felt the transcendental bliss of being merged with Him, the Supreme Lord Kṛṣṇa did not lose His identity, nor did the individual wives lose theirs. The individuality of both the Lord and the wives remained, yet they felt oneness in existence. When a lover submits to his lover without any pinch of personal consideration, that is called oneness. Lord Caitanya has taught us this feeling of oneness in His *Śikṣāṣṭaka:* Kṛṣṇa may act freely, doing whatever He likes, but the devotee should always be in oneness or in agreement with His desires. That oneness was exhibited by the wives of the *brāhmaṇas* in their love for Kṛṣṇa.

Kṛṣṇa welcomed them with the following words: "My dear wives of the *brāhmaṇas*, you are all very fortunate and are welcome here. Please let Me know what can I do for you. Your coming here to see Me, neglecting all the restrictions and hindrances of relatives, fathers, brothers and husbands, is completely befitting. One who does this actually knows his self-interest, because rendering transcendental loving service unto Me, without motive or restriction, is actually auspicious for the living entities."

Lord Kṛṣṇa here confirms that the conditioned soul can reach the highest perfectional stage by surrendering to Him. One must give up all other responsibilities. This complete surrender unto the Supreme Personality of Godhead is the most auspicious path for the conditioned soul because the Supreme Lord is the supreme objective of love. Everyone is loving his self according to the advancement of his knowledge. Ultimately, when a person comes to understand that his self is the spirit soul and that the spirit soul is nothing but a part and parcel of the Supreme Lord, he recognizes the Supreme Lord as the ultimate goal of love and then surrenders unto Him. This surrender is considered auspicious for the conditioned soul. Our life, property, home, wife, children, house, country, society and all paraphernalia which are very dear to us are expansions of the Supreme Personality of Godhead. He is the central object of love because He gives us all bliss, expanding Himself in so many ways according to our different situations, namely bodily, mental or spiritual.

"My dear wives of the *brāhmaṇas*," Kṛṣṇa said, "you can now return to your homes. Engage yourselves in sacrificial activities and in the service of your husbands and household affairs so that your husbands will be pleased with you and the sacrifice which they have begun will be properly executed. After all, your husbands are householders, and without your help how can they execute their prescribed duties?"

The wives of the *brāhmaṇas* replied, "Dear Lord, this sort of instruction does not befit You. Your eternal promise is that You will always protect Your devotees, and now You must fulfill this promise. Anyone who comes and surrenders unto You never goes back to the conditioned life of material existence. We expect that You will now fulfill Your promise. We have surrendered unto Your lotus feet, which are covered by *tulasī* leaves, so we have no desire to give up the shelter of Your lotus feet and return to the company of our so-called relatives, friends and society. And what shall we do if we return home? Our husbands, brothers, fathers, sons, mothers and friends will no longer accept us at home, because we have already left them all. Therefore we have no shelter to return to. Please, therefore, do not ask us to return home, but arrange for our stay under Your lotus feet so that we can eternally live under Your protection."

The Supreme Personality of Godhead replied, "My dear wives of the *brāhmaṇas*, rest assured that your husbands will not neglect you on your return, nor will your brothers, sons, or fathers refuse to accept you. Because you are My pure devotees, not only your relatives but also people in general, as well as the demigods, will be satisfied with you." Kṛṣṇa is situated as the Supersoul in everyone's heart. So someone who becomes a pure devotee of Lord Kṛṣṇa immediately becomes pleasing to everyone. The pure devotee of Lord Kṛṣṇa is never inimical to anyone, nor can any sane person be an enemy of a pure devotee. "Transcendental love for Me does not depend upon bodily connection," Kṛṣṇa said further, "but anyone whose mind is always absorbed in Me will surely, very soon, come to Me for My eternal association."

After being instructed by the Supreme Personality of Godhead, all the wives returned home to their respective husbands. Pleased to see their wives back home, the *brāhmaṇas* sat together with them and executed the performances of sacrifices, as enjoined in the *śāstras*. According to Vedic principle, religious rituals must be executed by the husband and wife together. When the *brāhmaṇas'* wives returned, the sacrifice was duly and nicely executed. One of the *brāhmaṇas'* wives, however, who had been forcibly checked from going to see Kṛṣṇa, began to remember Him as she heard of His bodily features. Being completely absorbed in His thought, she gave up her material body, conditioned by the laws of nature.

After the departure of the *brāhmaṇas'* wives, Śrī Govinda and His cowherd boyfriends enjoyed the food they had offered. In this way the ever-joyful Personality of Godhead exhibited His transcendental pastimes in the guise of an ordinary human being in order to attract the common people to Kṛṣṇa consciousness. With His words and beauty He attracted all the cows, cowherd boys and damsels in Vṛndāvana. All of them together enjoyed the pastimes of the Lord.

After the return of their wives from Kṛṣṇa, the *brāhmaṇas* engaged in the performance of sacrifices began to regret their sinful activities in refusing food to the Supreme Personality of Godhead. They could finally understand their mistake; engaged in the performance of Vedic rituals, they had neglected the Supreme Personality of Godhead, who had appeared just like an ordinary human being and asked for some food. They began to condemn themselves after seeing the faith and devotion of their wives. They regretted very much that, although their wives were elevated to the platform of pure devotional service, they themselves could not understand even a little bit of how to love and offer transcendental loving service to the Supreme Soul. They began to talk among themselves: "To hell with our being born *brāhmaṇas*! To hell with our learning all the Vedic literatures! To hell with our performing great sacrifices and observing all the rules and regulations! To hell with our family! To hell with our expert service in performing the rituals exactly according to the description of the scriptures! To hell with it all, for we have not developed transcendental loving service to the Supreme Personality of Godhead, who is beyond the speculation of the mind, body and senses."

The learned *brāhmaṇas,* expert in Vedic ritualistic performances, were properly regretful, because if one does not develop Kṛṣṇa consciousness, all discharge of religious duties is simply a waste of time and energy. They continued to talk among themselves: "The external energy of Kṛṣṇa is so strong that it can create illusion to overcome even the greatest mystic *yogī.* Although we expert *brāhmaṇas* are considered to be the teachers of all other sections of human society, we also have been illusioned by the external energy. Just see how fortunate these women are! They have so devotedly dedicated their lives to the Supreme Personality of Godhead, Kṛṣṇa, that they easily did what is ordinarily so difficult: they gave up their family connections, which are just like a dark well for the continuation of material miseries." Women in general, being very simple at heart, can very easily take to Kṛṣṇa consciousness, and when they develop love of Kṛṣṇa they can easily get liberation from the clutches of *māyā,* which are very difficult for even so-called intelligent and learned men to surpass.

The *brāhmaṇas* continued, "According to Vedic injunction, women are not allowed to undergo the purificatory process of initiation by the sacred thread, nor are they allowed to live as *brahmacāriṇīs* in the *āśrama* of the spiritual master, nor are they advised to undergo the strict disciplinary procedures, nor are they very expert in discussing the philosophy of self-realization. And by nature they are not very pure, nor are they very much attached to auspicious activities. Therefore, how wonderful it is that these women have developed transcendental love for Kṛṣṇa, the Lord of all mystic *yogīs*! They have surpassed all of us in firm faith and devotion unto Kṛṣṇa. Although we are considered to be masters in all purificatory processes, we did not actually know what their goal is because we are too much attached to the materialistic way of life. Even though we were reminded of Kṛṣṇa and Balarāma by the cowherd boys, we disregarded Them. We now think that the Supreme Personality of Godhead simply played a trick of mercy on us by sending His friends to beg food from us. Otherwise, He had no need to send them. He could have satisfied their hunger then and there just by willing to do so."

If someone denies the self-sufficiency of Kṛṣṇa on hearing that He was tending the cows for His livelihood, or if someone doubts His not being in need of the food, thinking that He was actually hungry, then such a person should understand that the goddess of fortune is always engaged in His service. In this way the goddess can break her faulty habit of restlessness. In Vedic literatures like the *Brahma-saṁhitā* it is stated that Kṛṣṇa is served in His abode with great respect by not only one goddess of fortune but many thousands. Therefore it is simply illusion for one to think that Kṛṣṇa begged food from the *brāhmaṇas.* It was actually a trick to show them mercy by teaching them that they should accept Him in pure devotional service instead of engaging in ritualistic ceremonies. The Vedic ceremonial paraphernalia, the suitable place, the suitable time, the different grades of articles for performing the ritualistic ceremonies, the Vedic hymns, the process of sacrifice, the priest who is able to perform the sacrifice, the fire, the demigods, the performer of the sacrifice and the religious principles are all meant for understanding Kṛṣṇa, for Kṛṣṇa is the Supreme Personality of Godhead. He is the Supreme Lord Viṣṇu and the Lord of all mystic *yogīs.*

"Because He has appeared as a child in the dynasty of the Yadus, we were so foolish that we could not understand that He is the Supreme Personality of Godhead," the *brāhmaṇas* said. "But on the other hand, we are very proud because we have such exalted wives who have developed pure transcendental service of the Lord without being shackled by our rigid opposition. Let us therefore offer our respectful obeisances unto the lotus feet of Lord Kṛṣṇa, under whose illusory energy, called *māyā,* we are absorbed in fruitive activities. We therefore pray to the Lord to be kind enough to excuse us because we are simply captivated by His external energy. We transgressed His order without knowing His transcendental glories."

The *brāhmaṇas* repented their sinful activities. They wanted to go personally to offer their obeisances unto Him, but being afraid of Kaṁsa, they could not go to Kṛṣṇa and surrender unto Him. In other words, it is very difficult for one to surrender fully unto the Personality of Godhead without being purified by devotional service. The example of the learned *brāhmaṇas* and their wives is vivid. The wives of the *brāhmaṇas,* because they were inspired by pure devotional service, did not care for any kind of opposition. They immediately went to Kṛṣṇa. But the *brāhmaṇas,* although they had come to know the supremacy of the Lord and were repenting, were still afraid of King Kaṁsa because they were too much addicted to fruitive activities.

Thus ends the Bhaktivedanta purport of the Twenty-third Chapter of Kṛṣṇa, *"Delivering the Wives of the* Brāhmaṇas *Who Performed Sacrifices."*

CHAPTER 24

Worshiping Govardhana Hill

WHILE ENGAGED WITH THE *BRĀHMAṆAS* who were too much involved in the performance of Vedic sacrifices, Kṛṣṇa and Balarāma also saw that the cowherd men were preparing a similar sacrifice in order to pacify Indra, the King of heaven, who is responsible for supplying water. As stated in the *Caitanya-caritāmṛta,* a devotee of Kṛṣṇa has strong and firm faith in the understanding that if he is simply engaged in Kṛṣṇa consciousness and Kṛṣṇa's transcendental loving service, then he is freed from all other obligations. A pure devotee of Lord Kṛṣṇa doesn't have to perform any of the ritualistic functions enjoined in the *Vedas;* nor is he required to worship any demigods. Being a devotee of Lord Kṛṣṇa, one is understood to have performed all kinds of Vedic rituals and all kinds of worship to the demigods. One does not develop devotional service for Kṛṣṇa by performing the Vedic ritualistic ceremonies or worshiping the demigods, but it should be understood that one who is engaged fully in the service of the Lord has already fulfilled all Vedic injunctions.

In order to stop all such activities by His devotees, Kṛṣṇa wanted to firmly establish exclusive devotional service during His presence in Vṛndāvana. Because He is the omniscient Personality of Godhead, Kṛṣṇa knew that the cowherd men were preparing for the Indra sacrifice, but as a matter of etiquette He began to inquire with great honor and submission from elder personalities like Mahārāja Nanda.

Kṛṣṇa asked His father, "My dear father, what is this arrangement going on for a great sacrifice? What is the result of such a sacrifice, and for whom is it meant? How is it performed? Will you kindly let Me know? I am very eager to know this procedure, so please explain to Me the purpose of this sacrifice." Upon this inquiry, His father, Nanda Mahārāja, remained silent, thinking that his young boy would not be able to understand the intricacies of performing the *yajña.* Kṛṣṇa, however, persisted: "My dear father, for those who are liberal and saintly, there is no secrecy. They do not think anyone to be a friend, an enemy or a neutral party, because they are always open to everyone. And even for those who are not so liberal, nothing should be kept secret from the family members and friends, although secrecy may be maintained for persons who are inimical. Therefore you cannot keep any secrets from Me. All persons are engaged in fruitive activities. Some know what these activities are, and they know the result, and some execute activities without knowing the purpose or the result. A person who acts with full knowledge gets the full result; one who acts without knowledge does not get such a perfect result. Therefore, please let Me know the purpose of the sacrifice you are going to perform. Is it according to Vedic injunction? Or is it simply a popular ceremony? Kindly let Me know in detail about the sacrifice."

On hearing this inquiry from Kṛṣṇa, Mahārāja Nanda replied, "My dear boy, this ceremonial performance is more or less traditional. Because rainfall is due to the mercy of King Indra and the clouds are his representatives, and because water is so important for our living, we must show some gratitude to the controller of this rainfall, Mahārāja Indra. We are arranging, therefore, to pacify King Indra, because he has very kindly sent us clouds to pour down a sufficient quantity of rain for successful agricultural activities. Water is very important: without rainfall we cannot farm or produce grain, and without grain we cannot live. Therefore rain is necessary for successful religious ceremonies, economic development and, ultimately, liberation. So we should not give up this traditional ceremonial function; if one gives it up, being influenced by lust, greed or fear, then it does not look very good for him."

After hearing this, Kṛṣṇa, the Supreme Personality of Godhead, in the presence of His father and all the elder cowherd men of Vṛndāvana, spoke in such a way as to make the heavenly King, Indra, very angry. He suggested that they forgo the sacrifice. His reasons for discouraging the sacrifice performed to please Indra were twofold. First, as stated in the *Bhagavad-gītā,* there is no need to worship the demigods for any material advancement; all results derived from worshiping the demigods are simply temporary, and only those who are less intelligent are interested in temporary results. Second, whatever temporary result one derives from worshiping the demigods is actually granted by the permission of the Supreme Personality of Godhead. It is clearly stated in the *Bhagavad-gītā: mayaiva vihitān hi tān.* Whatever benefit is supposed to be derived from the demigods is actually bestowed by the Supreme Personality of Godhead. Without the permission of the Supreme Personality of Godhead, one cannot bestow any benefit upon others. But sometimes the demigods become puffed up by the influence of material nature; thinking themselves all in all, they forget the supremacy of the Personality of Godhead. In *Śrīmad-Bhāgavatam* it is clearly stated that in this instance Kṛṣṇa wanted to make King Indra angry. Kṛṣṇa's advent was especially meant for the annihilation of the demons and protection of the devotees. King Indra was certainly a devotee, not a demon, but because he was puffed up, Kṛṣṇa wanted to teach him a lesson. He first made Indra angry by stopping the Indra-pūjā, which had been arranged by the cowherd men in Vṛndāvana.

With this purpose in mind, Kṛṣṇa began to talk as if He were an atheist supporting the philosophy of Karma-mīmāṁsā. Advocates of this philosophy do not accept the supreme authority of the Personality of Godhead. They put forward the argument that if anyone works nicely, the result is sure to come. Their opinion is that even if there is a God who gives man the result of his fruitive activities, there is no need to worship Him because unless man works He cannot bestow any good result. They say that instead of worshiping a demigod or God, people should give attention to their own duties, and thus the good result will surely come. Lord Kṛṣṇa began to speak to His father according to these principles of the Karma-mīmāṁsā philosophy. "My dear father," He said, "I don't think you need to worship any demigod for the successful performance of your agricultural activities. Every living being is born according to his past *karma* and leaves this life simply taking the result of his present *karma.* Everyone is born in different types or species of life according to his past activities, and he gets his next birth according to the activities of this life. Different grades of material happiness and distress, comforts and disadvantages of life, are different results of different kinds of activities, from either the past or present life."

Mahārāja Nanda and other elder members argued that without satisfying the predominating god one cannot derive any good result simply by material activities. This is actually the fact. For example, it is sometimes found that in spite of first-class medical help and treatment by a first-class physician, a diseased person dies. It is concluded, therefore, that first-class medical treatment or the attempts of a first-class physician are not in themselves the cause for curing a patient; there must be the hand of the Supreme Personality of Godhead. Similarly, a father's and mother's taking care of their children is not the cause of the children's comfort. Sometimes it is found that in spite of all care by the parents, the children go bad or succumb to death. Therefore material causes are not sufficient for results. There must be the sanction of the Supreme Personality of Godhead. Nanda Mahārāja therefore advocated that in order to get good results for agricultural activities, they must satisfy Indra, the superintending deity of the rain supply. Lord Kṛṣṇa nullified this argument, saying that the demigods give results only to persons who have executed their prescribed duties. The demigods cannot give any good results to the person who has not executed the prescribed duties; therefore demigods are dependent on the execution of duties and are not absolute in awarding good results to anyone. So why should one care about them?

"My dear father," Lord Kṛṣṇa said, "there is no need to worship the demigod Indra. Everyone has to achieve the result of his own work. We can actually see that one becomes busy according to the natural tendency of his work; and according to that natural tendency, all living entities—whether human beings or demigods—achieve their respective results. All living entities achieve higher or lower bodies and create enemies, friends or neutral parties only because of their different kinds of work. One should be careful to discharge duties according to his natural instinct and not divert attention to the worship of various demigods. The demigods will be satisfied by proper execution of all duties, so there is no need to worship them. Let us, rather, perform our prescribed duties very nicely. Actually one cannot be happy without executing his proper prescribed duty. One who does not, therefore, properly discharge his prescribed duties is compared to an unchaste wife. The proper prescribed duty of the *brāhmaṇas* is the study of the *Vedas;* the proper duty of the royal order, the *kṣatriyas,* is engagement in protecting the citizens; the proper duty of the *vaiśya* community is agriculture, trade and protection of the cows; and the proper duty of the *śūdras* is service to the higher classes, namely the *brāhmaṇas, kṣatriyas* and *vaiśyas.* We belong to the *vaiśya* community, and our proper duty is to farm, to trade with the agricultural produce, to protect cows or to take to banking."

Kṛṣṇa identified Himself with the *vaiśya* community because Nanda Mahārāja was protecting many cows and Kṛṣṇa was taking care of them. He enumerated four kinds of business engagements for the *vaiśya* community, namely agriculture, trade, protection of cows and banking. Although the *vaiśyas* can take to any of these occupations, the men of Vṛndāvana were engaged primarily in the protection of cows.

Kṛṣṇa further explained to His father, "This cosmic manifestation is going on under the influence of three modes of material nature—goodness, passion and ignorance. These three modes are the causes of creation, maintenance and destruction. The cloud is caused by the action of the mode of passion; therefore it is the mode of passion which causes the rainfall. And after the rainfall, the living entities derive the result—success in agricultural work. What, then, has Indra to do with this affair? Even if you do not please Indra, what can he do? We do not derive any special benefit from Indra. Even if he is there, he pours water on the ocean also, where there is no need of water. So he is pouring water on the ocean or on the land; it does not depend on our worshiping him. As far as we are concerned, we do not need to go to another city or village or foreign country. There are palatial buildings in the cities, but we are satisfied living in this forest of Vṛndāvana. Our specific relationship is with Govardhana Hill and Vṛndāvana forest and nothing more. I therefore request you, My dear father, to begin a sacrifice which will satisfy the local *brāhmaṇas* and Govardhana Hill, and let us have nothing to do with Indra."

After hearing this statement by Kṛṣṇa, Nanda Mahārāja replied, "My dear boy, since You are asking, I shall arrange for a separate sacrifice for the local *brāhmaṇas* and Govardhana Hill. But for the present let me execute this sacrifice known as Indra-yajña."

But Kṛṣṇa replied, "My dear father, don't delay. The sacrifice you propose for Govardhana and the local *brāhmaṇas* will take much time. Better take the arrangement and paraphernalia you have already made for the Indra-yajña and immediately engage them to satisfy Govardhana Hill and the local *brāhmaṇas*."

Mahārāja Nanda finally relented. The cowherd men then inquired from Kṛṣṇa how He wanted the *yajña* performed, and Kṛṣṇa gave them the following directions. "Prepare very nice foods of all descriptions from the grain and ghee collected for the *yajña*. Prepare rice, dhal, then *halavā, pakorā, purī* and all kinds of milk preparations, such as sweet rice, *rabrī,* sweetballs, *sandeśa, rasagullā* and *laḍḍu*, and invite the learned *brāhmaṇas* who can chant the Vedic hymns and offer oblations to the fire. The *brāhmaṇas* should be given all kinds of grain in charity. Then decorate all the cows and feed them well. After performing this, give money in charity to the *brāhmaṇas*. As far as the lower animals are concerned, such as the dogs, and the lower grades of people, such as the *caṇḍālas,* or the fifth class of men, who are considered untouchable, they also may be given sumptuous *prasādam*. After nice grasses have been given to the cows, the sacrifice known as Govardhana-pūjā may immediately begin. This sacrifice will very much satisfy Me."

In this statement, Lord Kṛṣṇa practically described the whole economy of the *vaiśya* community. In all communities in human society—including the *brāhmaṇas, kṣatriyas, vaiśyas, śūdras, caṇḍālas,* etc.—and in the animal kingdom—including the cows, dogs, goats, etc.—everyone has his part to play. Each is to work in cooperation for the total benefit of all society, which includes not only animate objects but also inanimate objects like hills and land. The *vaiśya* community is specifically responsible for the economic improvement of the society by producing grain, by giving protection to the cows, by transporting food when needed, and by banking and finance.

From this statement we learn also that although the cats and dogs, which have now become so important, are not to be neglected, cow protection is actually more important than protection of cats and dogs. Another hint we get from this statement is that the *caṇḍālas,* or the untouchables, are also not to be neglected by the higher classes and should be given necessary protection. Everyone is important, but some are directly responsible for the advancement of human society, and some are only indirectly responsible. However, when Kṛṣṇa consciousness is there, then everyone's total benefit is taken care of.

The sacrifice known as Govardhana-pūjā is observed in the Kṛṣṇa consciousness movement. Lord Caitanya has recommended that since Kṛṣṇa is worshipable, so His land—Vṛndāvana and Govardhana Hill—is also worshipable. To confirm this statement, Lord Kṛṣṇa said that Govardhana-pūjā is as good as worship of Him. From that day, Govardhana-pūjā has been going on and is known as Annakūṭa. In all the temples of Vṛndāvana or outside of Vṛndāvana, huge quantities of food are prepared in this ceremony and are very sumptuously distributed to the general population. Sometimes the food is thrown to the crowds, and they enjoy collecting it off the ground. From this we can understand that *prasādam* offered to Kṛṣṇa never becomes polluted or contaminated, even if it is thrown on the ground. The people therefore collect and eat it with great satisfaction.

The Supreme Personality of Godhead, Kṛṣṇa, therefore advised the cowherd men to stop the Indra-yajña and begin the Govardhana-pūjā in order to chastise Indra, who was very much puffed up at being the supreme controller of the heavenly planets. The honest and simple cowherd men, headed by Nanda Mahārāja, accepted Kṛṣṇa's proposal and executed in detail everything He advised. They performed Govardhana worship and circumambulation of the hill. (Following the inauguration of Govardhana-pūjā, people in Vṛndāvana still dress nicely and assemble near Govardhana Hill to offer worship and circumambulate the hill, leading their cows all around.) According to the instruction of Lord Kṛṣṇa, Nanda Mahārāja and the cowherd men called in learned *brāhmaṇas* and began to worship Govardhana Hill by chanting Vedic hymns and offering *prasādam.* The inhabitants of Vṛndāvana assembled together, decorated their cows and gave them grass. Keeping the cows in front, they began to circumambulate Govardhana Hill. The *gopīs* dressed themselves very luxuriantly and sat in bull-driven carts, chanting the glories of Kṛṣṇa's pastimes. The *brāhmaṇas,* assembled there to act as priests for Govardhana-pūjā, offered their blessings to the cowherd men and their wives, the *gopīs.*

When everything was complete, Kṛṣṇa assumed a great transcendental form and declared to the inhabitants of Vṛndāvana that He was Himself Govardhana Hill in order to convince the devotees that Govardhana Hill and Kṛṣṇa Himself are identical. Then Kṛṣṇa began to eat all the food offered there. The identity of Kṛṣṇa and Govardhana Hill is still honored, and great devotees take rocks from Govardhana Hill and worship them exactly as they worship the Deity of Kṛṣṇa in the temples. The followers of the Kṛṣṇa consciousness movement may therefore collect small rocks or pebbles from Govardhana Hill and worship them at home, because this worship is as good as Deity worship. The form of Kṛṣṇa who began to eat the offerings was separately constituted, and Kṛṣṇa Himself, along with the other inhabitants of Vṛndāvana, offered obeisances to the Deity as well as Govardhana Hill. In offering obeisances to the huge form of Kṛṣṇa and Govardhana Hill, Kṛṣṇa declared, "Just see how Govardhana Hill has assumed this huge form and is favoring us by accepting all the offerings!" Kṛṣṇa also declared at that meeting, "One who neglects the worship of Govardhana-pūjā, as I am personally conducting it, will not be happy. There are many snakes on Govardhana Hill, and persons neglecting the prescribed duty of Govardhana-pūjā will be bitten by these snakes and killed. In order to assure the good fortune of the cows and themselves, all people of Vṛndāvana near Govardhana must worship the hill, as prescribed by Me."

Thus performing the Govardhana-pūjā sacrifice, all the inhabitants of Vṛndāvana followed the instructions of Kṛṣṇa, the son of Vasudeva, and afterwards they returned to their respective homes.

Thus ends the Bhaktivedanta purport of the Twenty-fourth Chapter of Kṛṣṇa, *"Worshiping Govardhana Hill."*

CHAPTER 25

Devastating Rainfall in Vṛndāvana

WHEN INDRA UNDERSTOOD that the sacrifice that was to be offered by the cowherd men in Vṛndāvana had been stopped by Kṛṣṇa, he became angry, and he vented his anger upon the inhabitants of Vṛndāvana, who were headed by Nanda Mahārāja, although Indra knew perfectly well that Kṛṣṇa was personally protecting them. As the director of different kinds of clouds, Indra called for the Sāṁvartaka. This cloud is invited when there is a need to devastate the whole cosmic manifestation. The Sāṁvartaka was ordered by Indra to go over Vṛndāvana and inundate the whole area with an extensive flood. Demonically, Indra thought himself to be the all-powerful supreme personality. When demons become very powerful, they defy the supreme controller, the Personality of Godhead. Indra, though not a demon, was puffed up by his material position, and he wanted to challenge the supreme controller. He thought himself, at least for the time being, as powerful as Kṛṣṇa. Indra said, "Just see the impudence of the inhabitants of Vṛndāvana! They are simply inhabitants of the forest, but being infatuated with their friend Kṛṣṇa, who is nothing but an ordinary human being, they have dared to defy the demigods."

Kṛṣṇa has declared in the *Bhagavad-gītā* that the worshipers of the demigods are not very intelligent. He has also declared that one has to give up all kinds of worship and simply concentrate on Kṛṣṇa consciousness. Kṛṣṇa's invoking the anger of Indra and later on chastising him is a clear indication to His devotees that those who are engaged in Kṛṣṇa consciousness have no need to worship any demigod, even if it is found that the demigod has become angry. Kṛṣṇa gives His devotees all protection, and they should completely depend on His mercy.

Indra cursed the action of the inhabitants of Vṛndāvana and said, "By defying the authority of the demigods, the inhabitants of Vṛndāvana will suffer in material existence. Having neglected the sacrifice to the demigods, they cannot cross over the impediments of the ocean of material existence." Indra further declared, "These cowherd men in Vṛndāvana have neglected my authority on the advice of this talkative boy who is known as Kṛṣṇa. He is nothing but a child, and by believing this child, they have enraged me." Thus he ordered the Sāṁvartaka cloud to go and destroy the prosperity of Vṛndāvana. "The men of Vṛndāvana," said Indra, "have become too puffed up over their material opulence and are overconfident due to the presence of their tiny friend, Kṛṣṇa. He is simply talkative, childish and unaware of the complete cosmic situation, although He is thinking Himself very advanced in knowledge. Because they have taken Kṛṣṇa so seriously, they must be punished. They should be destroyed with their cows." In this way Indra ordered the Sāṁvartaka cloud to go to Vṛndāvana and inundate the place.

It is indicated here that in the villages or outside the towns, the inhabitants must depend on the cows for their prosperity. When the cows are destroyed, the people are destitute of all kinds of opulences. When King Indra ordered the Sāṁvartaka and companion clouds to go to Vṛndāvana, the clouds were afraid of doing this mischief. But King Indra assured them, "You go ahead, and I will also go, riding on my elephant, accompanied by great storms. And I shall apply all my strength to punishing the inhabitants of Vṛndāvana."

Ordered by King Indra, all the dangerous clouds appeared above Vṛndāvana and began to pour water incessantly, with all their strength and power. There was constant lightning and thunder, blowing of severe wind and incessant falling of rain. The rainfall seemed to fall like piercing sharp arrows. By pouring water as thick as pillars, without cessation, the clouds gradually filled all the lands in Vṛndāvana with water, and there was no visible distinction between higher and lower land. The situation was very dangerous, especially for the animals. The rainfall was accompanied by great winds, and every living creature in Vṛndāvana began to tremble from the severe cold. Unable to find any other source of deliverance, they all approached Govinda to take shelter at His lotus feet. The cows especially, being much aggrieved from the heavy rain, bowed down their heads, and taking their calves underneath their bodies, they approached the Supreme Personality of Godhead to take shelter of His lotus feet. At that time all the inhabitants of Vṛndāvana began to pray to Lord Kṛṣṇa. "Dear Kṛṣṇa," they prayed,

"You are all-powerful, and You are very affectionate to Your devotees. Now please protect us, who have been much harassed by angry Indra."

Upon hearing their prayer, Kṛṣṇa could understand that Indra, being bereft of his sacrificial honor, was pouring down rain that was accompanied by heavy pieces of ice and strong winds, although all this was out of season. Kṛṣṇa understood that this was a deliberate exhibition of anger by Indra. He therefore concluded, "This demigod who thinks himself supreme has shown his great power, but I shall answer him according to My position, and I shall teach him that he is not autonomous in managing universal affairs. I am the Supreme Lord over all, and I shall thus take away his false prestige, which has risen from his power. The demigods are My devotees, and therefore it is not possible for them to forget My supremacy, but somehow or other he has become puffed up with material power and thus is now maddened. I shall act in such a way as to relieve him of this false prestige. I shall give protection to My pure devotees in Vṛndāvana, who are at present completely dependent on My mercy and whom I have taken completely under My protection. I must save them by My mystic power."

Thinking in this way, Lord Kṛṣṇa immediately picked up Govardhana Hill with one hand, exactly as a child picks up a mushroom from the ground. Thus He exhibited His transcendental pastime of lifting Govardhana Hill. Lord Kṛṣṇa then addressed His devotees, "My dear brothers, My dear father, My dear inhabitants of Vṛndāvana, you can now safely enter under the umbrella of Govardhana Hill, which I have just lifted. Do not be afraid of the hill and think that it will fall from My hand. You have been too much afflicted from the heavy rain and strong wind; therefore I have lifted this hill, which will protect you exactly like a huge umbrella. I think this is a proper arrangement to relieve you of your immediate distress. Be happy along with your animals underneath this great umbrella." Being assured by Lord Kṛṣṇa, all the inhabitants of Vṛndāvana entered beneath the great hill along with their property and animals, and they all appeared to be safe.

The inhabitants of Vṛndāvana and their animals remained there for one week without being disturbed by hunger, thirst or any other discomforts. They were simply astonished to see how Kṛṣṇa was holding up the mountain with the little finger of His left hand. Seeing the extraordinary mystic power of Kṛṣṇa, Indra, the King of heaven, was thunderstruck and baffled in his determination. He immediately called for all the clouds and asked them to desist. When the sky became completely cleared of all clouds and there was sunrise again, the strong wind stopped. At that time Kṛṣṇa, the Supreme Personality of Godhead, known now as the lifter of Govardhana Hill, said, "My dear cowherd men, now you can leave and take your wives, children, cows and valuables, because everything is ended. The inundation has gone down, along with the swelling waters of the river."

His Divine Grace A. C. Bhaktivedanta Swami Prabhupāda
Founder-Ācārya of the International Society for Krishna Consciousness

While riding with his sister Devakī during the wedding procession, Kaṁsa heard a voice from the sky proclaim that her eighth child would kill him. The demon instantly grabbed Devakī's hair and raised his sword to kill her—but the bride's husband, Vasudeva, dissuaded him. (*p.* 11)

While carrying child Kṛṣṇa across the storm-tossed river Yamunā, Vasudeva was sheltered by the hoods of Lord Śeṣa, an expansion of the Supreme Personality of Godhead. The effulgence from Kṛṣṇa's body dissipated the darkness so Vasudeva could find his way. (*p.* 37)

Nanda Mahārāja, Kṛṣṇa's foster father, celebrated the birth ceremony of his newborn son with great opulence. Everyone was overwhelmed with joy. (*p.* 44)

Once Tṛṇāvarta, a demon with mystic powers, appeared in Vṛndāvana in the form of a great whirlwind and carried baby Kṛṣṇa aloft to kill Him. But to the amazement of all, Kṛṣṇa easily killed the demon and was totally unharmed. (*p.* 60)

The cowherd women of Vṛndāvana complained to Mother Yaśodā that Kṛṣṇa and His brother Balarāma would secretly enter their homes to steal the yogurt and butter they stored in pots hanging from the ceiling. (*p.* 66)

Once Mother Yaśodā instructed Kṛṣṇa to open His mouth so she could see whether He had eaten dirt. She was astonished to see everything within the entire universe, including her very self. (*p.* 67)

The cowherd boys entered the mouth of the serpent Aghāsura in a playful mood, supremely confident that Kṛṣṇa would protect them. (*p.* 88)

In the forest of Vṛndāvana, Kṛṣṇa and His friends ate their lunch with great transcendental pleasure. Kṛṣṇa appeared like the whorl of a lotus flower, and His friends like its petals. (*p.* 92)

When the demigod Indra poured massive torrents of rain upon Vṛndāvana because Kṛṣṇa had prevented a sacrifice meant to please him, the Lord protected the inhabitants by lifting Govardhana Hill with one hand. (*p.* 176)

Kṛṣṇa expanded Himself into many identical forms to enjoy His rāsa dance with the gopīs. In the company of those supremely beautiful cowherd girls, who worshiped Him with pure devotion, Lord Kṛṣṇa appeared like a greenish sapphire locket in the midst of a golden necklace decorated with valuable stones. (*p.* 216)

Lord Kṛṣṇa danced with great force upon the heads of the serpent Kāliya, who had poisoned the waters of the river Yamunā. When near death from this battering, Kāliya realized Kṛṣṇa was the Supreme Personality of Godhead and surrendered to Him. (*p.* 125)

Lord Kṛṣṇa dragged the demoniac King Kaṁsa from his high seat and threw him down. Straddling Kaṁsa's chest, Kṛṣṇa punched the demon again and again until he lost his life. (*p.* 278)

Uddhava went to Vṛndāvana with Kṛṣṇa's message to the *gopīs*. Rādhārāṇī, however, was so much absorbed in thoughts of Kṛṣṇa that She began to talk with a bumblebee flying here and there, taking him to be Kṛṣṇa's messenger. (*p.* 299)

All the men loaded their valuables on carts and slowly left with their cows and other paraphernalia. After they had cleared out everything, Lord Kṛṣṇa very slowly replaced Govardhana Hill exactly in the same position as it had been before. When everything was done, all the inhabitants of Vṛndāvana approached Kṛṣṇa with feelings of love and embraced Him with great ecstasy. The *gopīs,* being naturally very affectionate to Kṛṣṇa, began to offer Him yogurt mixed with their tears, and they poured incessant blessings upon Him. Mother Yaśodā, mother Rohiṇī, Nanda and Balarāma, who is the strongest of the strong, embraced Kṛṣṇa one after another and, from spontaneous feelings of affection, blessed Him over and over again. In the heavens, different demigods from different planetary systems, such as Siddhaloka, Gandharvaloka and Cāraṇaloka, also began to show their complete satisfaction. They poured showers of flowers on the surface of the earth and sounded different conchshells. There was beating of drums, and being inspired by godly feelings, residents of Gandharvaloka began to play on their tambouras to please the Lord. After this incident, the Supreme Personality of Godhead, surrounded by His dear friends and the animals, returned to His home. As usual, the *gopīs* began to chant the glorious pastimes of Lord Kṛṣṇa with great feeling, for they were chanting from the heart.

Thus ends the Bhaktivedanta purport of the Twenty-fifth Chapter of Kṛṣṇa, *"Devastating Rainfall in Vṛndāvana."*

CHAPTER 26

Wonderful Kṛṣṇa

WITHOUT UNDERSTANDING the intricacies of Kṛṣṇa, the Supreme Personality of Godhead, and without knowing His uncommon spiritual opulences, the innocent cowherd boys and men of Vṛndāvana began to discuss the wonderful activities of Kṛṣṇa, which surpass the activities of all men.

One of them said, "My dear friends, considering His wonderful activities, how is it possible that such an uncommon boy would come and live with us in Vṛndāvana? It is really not possible. Just imagine! He is now only seven years old! How is it possible for Him to lift Govardhana Hill in one hand and hold it up just as the king of elephants holds a lotus flower? To lift a lotus flower is a most insignificant thing for an elephant, and similarly Kṛṣṇa lifted Govardhana Hill without exertion. When He was simply a small baby and could not even see properly, He killed a great demon, Pūtanā. While sucking her breast, He also sucked out her life air. Kṛṣṇa killed the Pūtanā demon exactly as eternal time kills a living creature in due course. When He was only three months old, He was sleeping underneath a hand-driven cart. Being hungry for His mother's breast, He began to cry and throw His legs upwards. And from the kicking of His small feet the cart immediately broke apart and fell to pieces. When He was only one year old, He was carried away by the Tṛṇāvarta demon disguised as a whirlwind, and although He was taken very high in the sky, He simply hung on the neck of the demon and forced him to fall from the sky and immediately die. Once His mother, being disturbed by His stealing butter, tied Him to a wooden mortar, and the child pulled it toward a pair of trees known as *yamala-arjuna* and caused them to fall. Once, when He was engaged in tending the calves in the forest along with His elder brother, Balarāma, a demon named Bakāsura appeared, and Kṛṣṇa at once bifurcated the demon's beak. When the demon known as Vatsāsura entered among the calves tended by Kṛṣṇa with a desire to kill Him, He immediately detected the demon, killed him and threw him into a tree. When Kṛṣṇa, along with His brother, Balarāma, entered the Tālavana forest, the demon known as Dhenukāsura, in the shape of an ass, attacked Them and was immediately killed by Balarāma, who caught his hind legs and threw him into a palm tree. Although the Dhenukāsura demon was assisted by his cohorts, also in the shape of asses, all were killed, and the Tālavana forest was then open for the use of the animals and inhabitants of Vṛndāvana. When Pralambāsura entered amongst Kṛṣṇa's cowherd boyfriends, Kṛṣṇa caused him to be killed by Balarāma. Thereafter, Kṛṣṇa saved His friends and cows from a severe forest fire, and He chastised the Kāliya serpent in the lake of the Yamunā River and forced him to leave the vicinity of the Yamunā; He thereby made the water of the Yamunā poisonless."

Another one of the friends of Nanda Mahārāja said, "My dear Nanda, we do not know why we are so attracted by your son Kṛṣṇa. We want to forget Him, but this is impossible. Why are we so naturally affectionate toward Him? Just imagine how wonderful it is! On one hand He is only a boy of seven years, and on the other hand there is a huge hill like Govardhana Hill, and He lifted it so easily! O Nanda Mahārāja, we are now in great doubt—your son Kṛṣṇa must be one of the demigods. He is not at all an ordinary boy. Maybe He is the Supreme Personality of Godhead."

On hearing the praises of the cowherd men in Vṛndāvana, King Nanda said, "My dear friends, in reply to you I can simply present the statement of Garga Muni so that your doubts may be cleared. When he came to perform the name-giving ceremony, he said that this boy descends in different periods of time in different colors and that this time He has appeared in Vṛndāvana in a blackish color, known as *kṛṣṇa*. Previously He had a white color, then a red color, then a yellow color. He also said that this boy was once the son of Vasudeva, and everyone who knows of His previous birth calls Him Vāsudeva. Actually he said that my son has many varieties of names, according to His different qualities and activities. Gargācārya assured me that this boy would be all-auspicious for my family and that He would be able to give transcendental blissful pleasure to all the cowherd men and cows in Vṛndāvana. Even though we would be put into various kinds of difficulties, by the grace of this boy we would be very easily freed from them. He also said that formerly this boy saved the world from an unregulated condition, and He saved all honest men from the hands of the dishonest thieves. He also said that any fortunate man who becomes attached to this boy, Kṛṣṇa, is never vanquished or defeated by his enemy. On the whole, He is exactly like Lord Viṣṇu, who always takes the side of the demigods, who are consequently never defeated by the demons. Gargācārya thus concluded that my child would grow to be exactly like Viṣṇu in transcendental beauty, qualification, activities, influence and opulence, and so we should not be very astonished by His wonderful activities. After telling me this, Gargācārya returned home, and since then we have been continually seeing the wonderful activities of this child. According to the version of Gargācārya, I consider that He must be Nārāyaṇa Himself, or maybe a plenary portion of Nārāyaṇa."

When all the cowherd men had very attentively heard the statements of Gargācārya through Nanda Mahārāja, they better appreciated the wonderful activities of Kṛṣṇa and became very jubilant and satisfied. They began to praise Nanda Mahārāja, because by consulting him their doubts about Kṛṣṇa were cleared. They said, "Let Kṛṣṇa, who is so kind, beautiful and merciful, protect us. When angry Indra sent torrents of rain, accompanied by showers of ice blocks and high wind, He immediately took compassion upon us and saved us and our families, cows and valuable possessions by picking up Govardhana Hill, just as a child picks up a mushroom. He saved us so wonderfully. May He continue to glance mercifully over us and our cows. May we live peacefully under the protection of wonderful Kṛṣṇa."

Thus ends the Bhaktivedanta purport of the Twenty-sixth Chapter of Kṛṣṇa, *"Wonderful Kṛṣṇa."*

CHAPTER 27

Prayers by Indra, the King of Heaven

WHEN KṚṢṆA SAVED THE INHABITANTS of Vṛndāvana from the wrath of Indra by lifting Govardhana Hill, a *surabhi* cow from Goloka Vṛndāvana, as well as King Indra from the heavenly planets, appeared before Him. Indra, the King of heaven, was conscious of his offense before Kṛṣṇa; therefore he stealthily appeared before Him in a secluded place. He immediately fell down at the lotus feet of Kṛṣṇa, although his own crown was dazzling like sunshine. Indra knew about the exalted position of Kṛṣṇa because Kṛṣṇa is the master of Indra, but he could not believe that Kṛṣṇa could come down and live in Vṛndāvana among the cowherd men. When Kṛṣṇa defied the authority of Indra, Indra became angry because he thought that he was all in all within this universe and that no one was as powerful as he. But after this incident, his false, puffed-up prestige was destroyed. Being conscious of his subordinate position, he appeared before Kṛṣṇa with folded hands and began to offer the following prayers.

"My dear Lord," Indra said, "being puffed up by my false prestige, I thought that You had offended me by not allowing the cowherd men to perform the Indra-yajña, and I thought that You wanted to enjoy the offerings that were arranged for the sacrifice. I thought that in the name of a Govardhana sacrifice You were taking my share of profit, and therefore I mistook Your position. Now by Your grace I can understand that You are the Supreme Lord, the Personality of Godhead, and that You are transcendental to all material qualities. Your transcendental position is *viśuddha-sattva,* which is above the platform of the material mode of goodness, and Your transcendental abode is beyond the disturbance of the material qualities. Your name, fame, form, qualities, paraphernalia and pastimes are all beyond this material nature, and they are never disturbed by the three material modes. Your abode is accessible only for one who undergoes severe austerities and penances and becomes completely freed from the onslaught of material qualities like passion and ignorance. If someone thinks that when You enter within this material world You accept the modes of material nature, he is mistaken. The waves of the material qualities are never able to touch You, and You certainly do not accept them when You are present within this world. Your Lordship is never conditioned by the laws of material nature.

"My dear Lord, You are the original father of this cosmic manifestation. You are the supreme spiritual master of this cosmic world, and You are the original proprietor of everything. As eternal time, You are competent to chastise offenders. Within this material world there are many fools like me who consider themselves to be the Supreme Lord or the all in all within the universe. You are so merciful that without accepting their offenses You devise means so that their false prestige is subdued and they can know that You, and no one else, are the Supreme Personality of Godhead.

"My dear Lord, You are the supreme father, the supreme spiritual master and the supreme king. Therefore, You have the right to chastise all living entities whenever there is any discrepancy in their behavior. The father, the spiritual master and the supreme executive officer of the state are always well-wishers of their sons, their students and their citizens respectively. As such, the well-wishers have the right to chastise their dependents. By Your own desire You appear auspiciously on the earth in Your eternal varieties of forms; You come to glorify the earthly planet and specifically to chastise persons who are falsely claiming to be God. In the material world there is regular competition between different types of living entities to become supreme leaders of society, and after being frustrated in achieving the supreme positions of leadership, foolish persons claim to be God, the Supreme Personality. There are many such foolish personalities in this world, like me, but in due course of time, when they come to their senses, they surrender unto You and again engage themselves properly by rendering service unto You. And that is the purpose of Your chastising persons envious of You.

"My dear Lord, I committed a great offense unto Your lotus feet, being falsely proud of my material opulences, not knowing Your unlimited power. Therefore, my Lord, kindly excuse me, because I am fool number one. Kindly give me Your blessings so that I may not act so foolishly again. If You think, my Lord, that the offense is very great and cannot be excused, then I appeal to You that I am Your eternal servant; You appear in this world to give protection to Your eternal servants and to destroy the demons who maintain great military strength just to burden the very existence of the earth. As I am Your eternal servant, kindly excuse me.

"My dear Lord, You are the Supreme Personality of Godhead. I offer my respectful obeisances unto You because You are the Supreme Person and the Supreme Soul. You are the son of Vasudeva, and You are the Supreme Lord, Kṛṣṇa, the master of all pure devotees. Please accept my prostrated obeisances. You are the personification of supreme knowledge. You can appear anywhere, according to Your desire, in any one of Your eternal forms. You are the root of all creation and the Supreme Soul of all living entities. Due to my gross ignorance, I created a great disturbance in Vṛndāvana by sending torrents of rain and a heavy hailstorm. I acted out of severe anger caused by Your stopping the sacrifice which was to be held to satisfy me. But, my dear Lord, You are so kind to me that You have bestowed Your mercy upon me by destroying all my false pride. I therefore take shelter of Your lotus feet. My dear Lord, You are not only the supreme controller but also the spiritual master of all living entities."

Thus praised by Indra, Lord Kṛṣṇa, the Supreme Personality of Godhead, smiled beautifully and then replied in a grave voice like a rumbling cloud: "My dear Indra, I stopped your sacrifice just to show you My causeless mercy and to remind you that I am your eternal master. I am the master not only of you but of all the other demigods as well. You should always remember that all your material opulences are due to My mercy. No living entity can independently become opulent: one must be favored by My mercy. Everyone should always remember that I am the Supreme Lord. I can show anyone My favor, and I can chastise anyone, because no one is superior to Me. If I find someone overpowered by false pride, in order to show him My causeless mercy I withdraw all his opulences."

It is noteworthy that Kṛṣṇa sometimes removes all of a rich man's opulences in order to facilitate his becoming a soul surrendered to Him. This is a special favor of the Lord's. Sometimes it is seen that a person is very opulent materially, but due to his devotional service to the Lord he may be reduced to poverty. One should not think, however, that because he worshiped the Supreme Lord he became poverty-stricken. The real purport is that when a person is a pure devotee but at the same time, by miscalculation, wants to lord it over material nature, the Lord shows His special mercy by taking away all material opulences until at last he surrenders unto the Supreme Lord.

After instructing Indra, Lord Kṛṣṇa asked him to return to his kingdom in the heavenly planets and to remember always that he is never the supreme but is always subordinate to the Supreme Personality of Godhead. He also advised him to remain as King of heaven but to be careful of false pride.

After this, the transcendental *surabhi* cow who had come with Indra to see Kṛṣṇa offered her respectful obeisances unto Him and worshiped Him. The *surabhi* offered her prayer as follows: "My dear Lord Kṛṣṇa, You are the most powerful of all mystic *yogīs* because You are the soul of the complete universe, and only from You has all this cosmic manifestation taken place. Therefore, although Indra tried his best to kill my descendant cows in Vṛndāvana, they remained under Your shelter, and You have protected them all so well. We do not know anyone else as the Supreme, nor do we go to any other god or demigods for protection. Therefore, You are our Indra, You are the supreme father of the whole cosmic manifestation, and You are the protector and elevator of all the cows, *brāhmaṇas,* demigods and others who are pure devotees of Your Lordship. O Supersoul of the universe, let us bathe You with our milk, for You are our Indra. O Lord, You appear just to diminish the burden of impure activities on the earth."

Then the *surabhi* cow bathed Kṛṣṇa with her milk, and Indra bathed Him with the water of the celestial Ganges through the trunk of his carrier elephant. After this, the *surabhi* cows and all the demigods and their mothers joined the heavenly King, Indra, in worshiping Lord Kṛṣṇa by bathing Him with Ganges water and the milk of the *surabhis.* Thus Govinda, Lord Kṛṣṇa, was pleased with all of them. The residents of all higher planetary systems, such as Gandharvaloka, Vidyādharaloka, Siddhaloka and Cāraṇaloka, all combined and glorified the Lord by chanting His holy name as their wives and damsels danced with great joy. They very much satisfied the Lord by incessantly pouring flowers from the sky. When everything was very nicely and joyfully settled, the cows overflooded the surface of the earth with their milk. The water of the rivers began to flow with various tasty liquids and give nourishment to the trees, producing fruits and flowers of different colors and tastes. The trees began to pour drops of honey. The hills and mountains began to produce potent medicinal plants and valuable stones. Because of Kṛṣṇa's presence, all these things happened very nicely, and the lower animals, who were generally envious of one another, were envious no longer.

After satisfying Kṛṣṇa, who is the Lord of all the cows in Vṛndāvana and who is known as Govinda, King Indra took His permission to return to his heavenly kingdom. As he passed through cosmic space, he was surrounded by all kinds of demigods. This great incident is a powerful example of how Kṛṣṇa consciousness can benefit the world. Even the lower animals forget their envious nature and become elevated to the qualities of the demigods.

Thus ends the Bhaktivedanta purport of the Twenty-seventh Chapter of Kṛṣṇa, *"Prayers by Indra, the King of Heaven."*

CHAPTER 28

Releasing Nanda Mahārāja from the Clutches of Varuṇa

THE GOVARDHANA-PŪJĀ CEREMONY took place on the new-moon day. After this, there were torrents of rain and hailstorms imposed by King Indra for seven days. Nine days of the waxing moon having passed, on the tenth day King Indra worshiped Lord Kṛṣṇa, and thus the matter was satisfactorily settled. After this, on the eleventh day of the full moon, Ekādaśī, Mahārāja Nanda observed fasting for the whole day, and early in the morning of the next day, Dvādaśī, he went to take a bath in the river Yamunā. He entered deep into the water of the river, but he was arrested immediately by one of the servants of Varuṇadeva. This servant brought Nanda Mahārāja before the demigod Varuṇa and accused him of taking a bath in the river at the wrong time. According to astronomical calculations, the time in which he took a bath was considered demoniac. The fact was that Nanda Mahārāja wanted to take a bath in the river Yamunā early in the morning before the sunrise, but somehow or other he was a little too early, and he bathed at an inauspicious time. Consequently he was arrested.

When Nanda Mahārāja was taken away by one of Varuṇa's servants, Nanda's companions began to call loudly for Kṛṣṇa and Balarāma. Immediately Kṛṣṇa and Balarāma could understand that Nanda Mahārāja had been taken by a servant of

Varuṇa. Thus They went to the abode of Varuṇa, for They were pledged to give protection to the inhabitants of Vṛndāvana, who were all unalloyed devotees of the Lord. Devotees, having no shelter other than the Supreme Personality of Godhead, naturally cry to Him for help, exactly like children who do not know anything but the protection of their parents.

The demigod Varuṇa received Lord Kṛṣṇa and Balarāma with great respect and said, "My dear Lord, actually at this very moment, because of Your presence, my life as the demigod Varuṇa has become successful. Although I am the proprietor of all the treasures in the water, I know that such possessions do not make for a successful life. But at this moment, as I look at You, my life is made completely successful because by seeing You I no longer have to accept a material body. Therefore, O Lord, Supreme Personality of Godhead, Supreme Brahman and Supersoul of everything, let me offer my respectful obeisances unto You. You are the supreme transcendental personality; there is no possibility of imposing the influence of material nature upon You. I am very sorry that my foolish man, by not knowing what to do or what not to do, has mistakenly arrested Your father, Nanda Mahārāja. So I beg Your pardon for the offense of my servant. I think that it was Your plan to show me Your mercy by Your personal presence here. My dear Lord Kṛṣṇa, Govinda, be merciful upon me—here is Your father. You can take him back immediately."

In this way Lord Kṛṣṇa, the Supreme Personality of Godhead, rescued His father and presented him before his friends, bringing them great jubilation. Nanda Mahārāja was surprised that although the demigod was so opulent, he had offered such respect to Kṛṣṇa. That was very astonishing to Nanda, and he began to describe the incident to his friends and relatives with great wonder.

Actually, although Kṛṣṇa was acting so wonderfully, Mahārāja Nanda and mother Yaśodā could not think of Him as the Supreme Personality of Godhead. Instead, they always accepted Him as their beloved child. Thus Nanda Mahārāja did not accept the fact that Varuṇa had worshiped Kṛṣṇa because He is the Supreme Personality of Godhead; rather he took it that because Kṛṣṇa was such a wonderful child He had been respected even by Varuṇa. The friends of Nanda Mahārāja, all the cowherd men, became eager to know if Kṛṣṇa was actually the Supreme Personality and if He was going to give them all salvation. When they were all thus consulting among themselves, Kṛṣṇa understood their minds, and in order to assure them of their destiny in the spiritual kingdom, He showed them the spiritual sky. Generally, ordinary persons are engaged simply in working hard in the material world, and they have no information that there is another kingdom or another sky, which is known as the spiritual sky, where life is eternal, blissful and full of knowledge. As it is stated in the *Bhagavad-gītā*, a person returning to that spiritual sky never returns to this material world of death and suffering.

Kṛṣṇa, the Supreme Personality of Godhead, is always eager to give information to the conditioned soul that there is a spiritual sky far, far beyond this material sky, transcendental to the innumerable universes created within the total material energy. Kṛṣṇa is, of course, always very kind to every conditioned soul, but, as stated in the *Bhagavad-gītā,* He is especially inclined to the pure devotees. Hearing their inquiries, Kṛṣṇa immediately thought that His devotees in Vṛndāvana should be informed of the spiritual sky and the Vaikuṇṭha planets therein.

Within the material world, every conditioned soul is in the darkness of ignorance. This means that all conditioned souls are under the concept of bodily existence. Everyone is under the impression that he is of this material world, and with this concept of life everyone is working in ignorance in different forms of life. The activities of the particular type of body are called *karma,* or fruitive action. All conditioned souls, being under the impression of the bodily concept, are working according to their particular type of body. These activities are creating their future conditioned life. Because they have very little information of the spiritual world, they do not generally take to spiritual activities, which are called *bhakti-yoga.* Those who successfully practice *bhakti-yoga* go directly to the spiritual world after giving up this present body, and there they become situated in one of the Vaikuṇṭha planets. The inhabitants of Vṛndāvana are all pure devotees. Their destination after quitting the body is Kṛṣṇaloka. They even surpass the Vaikuṇṭhalokas. The fact is that those who are always engaged in Kṛṣṇa consciousness and mature, pure devotional service are given the chance, after death, to gain Kṛṣṇa's association in one of the universes within the material world. Kṛṣṇa's pastimes are continuously going on, either in this universe or in another universe. Just as the sun globe is passing over many places across this earthly planet, so *kṛṣṇa-līlā,* or the transcendental advent and pastimes of Kṛṣṇa, are also going on continuously, either in this or another universe. The mature devotees, who have completely executed Kṛṣṇa consciousness, are immediately transferred to the universe where Kṛṣṇa is appearing. In that universe the devotees get their first opportunity to associate with Kṛṣṇa personally and directly. The training goes on, as we see in the *vṛndāvana-līlā* of Kṛṣṇa within this planet. Kṛṣṇa therefore revealed the actual features of the Vaikuṇṭha planets so that the inhabitants of Vṛndāvana could know their destination.

Thus Kṛṣṇa showed them the eternal, ever-existing spiritual sky, which is unlimited and full of knowledge. Within this material world there are different grades of forms, and according to the grade, knowledge is proportionately manifested. For example, the knowledge in the body of a child is not as perfect as the knowledge in the body of an adult man. Everywhere there are different grades of living entities—in aquatic animals, in the plants and trees, in the reptiles and insects, in birds and beasts and in the civilized and uncivilized human forms of life. Above the human form of life there are demigods, Cāraṇas and Siddhas on up to Brahmaloka, where Lord Brahmā lives, and among these demigods there are always different grades of knowledge. But beyond this material world, in the spiritual sky, everyone is in full knowledge, and therefore all the living entities there are engaged in devotional service to the Lord, either in the Vaikuṇṭha planets or in Kṛṣṇaloka.

As it is confirmed in the *Bhagavad-gītā,* full knowledge means knowing Kṛṣṇa to be the Supreme Personality of Godhead. In the *Vedas* and the *Bhagavad-gītā* it is also stated that in the *brahmajyoti,* or spiritual sky, there is no need of sunlight, moonlight or electricity. All the planets there are self-illuminating, and all of them are eternally situated. There is no question of creation and annihilation in the *brahmajyoti,* or spiritual sky. The *Bhagavad-gītā* also confirms that beyond the material sky there is another, eternal, spiritual sky, where everything is eternally existing. Direct knowledge of the spiritual sky can be had only by great sages and saintly persons who have already surpassed the influence of the three material modes of nature by engaging in devotional service, or Kṛṣṇa consciousness. Unless one is constantly situated on that transcendental platform, it is not possible to understand the spiritual nature.

Therefore it is recommended that one should take to *bhakti-yoga* and keep himself engaged twenty-four hours a day in Kṛṣṇa consciousness, which places one beyond the reach of the modes of material nature. One in Kṛṣṇa consciousness can easily understand the nature of the spiritual sky and Vaikuṇṭhaloka. The inhabitants of Vṛndāvana, being always engaged in Kṛṣṇa consciousness, could therefore very easily understand the transcendental nature of the Vaikuṇṭhalokas.

Thus Kṛṣṇa led all the cowherd men, headed by Nanda Mahārāja, to the lake where Akrūra would later be shown the Vaikuṇṭha planetary system. They took their bath immediately and saw the real nature of the Vaikuṇṭhalokas. After seeing the spiritual sky and the Vaikuṇṭhalokas, all the men, headed by Nanda Mahārāja, felt wonderfully blissful, and upon coming out of the lake they saw Kṛṣṇa, who was being worshiped with excellent prayers.

Thus ends the Bhaktivedanta purport of the Twenty-eighth Chapter of Kṛṣṇa, *"Releasing Nanda Mahārāja from the Clutches of Varuṇa."*

CHAPTER 29

The Rāsa Dance: Introduction

IN *ŚRĪMAD-BHĀGAVATAM* it is stated that the *rāsa* dance took place on the full-moon night of the *śarat* season. From the statements of previous chapters, it appears that the festival of Govardhana-pūjā was performed just after the dark-moon night of the month of Kārttika, and thereafter the ceremony of Bhrātṛ-dvitīyā was performed; then the wrath of Indra was exhibited in the shape of torrents of rain and hailstones, and Lord Kṛṣṇa held up Govardhana Hill for seven days, until the ninth day of the moon. Thereafter, on the tenth day, the inhabitants of Vṛndāvana were talking amongst themselves about the wonderful activities of Kṛṣṇa, and the next day Ekādaśī was observed by Nanda Mahārāja. On the next day, Dvādaśī, Nanda Mahārāja went to take a bath in the Ganges and was arrested by one of the men of Varuṇa; then he was released by Lord Kṛṣṇa. Then Nanda Mahārāja, along with the cowherd men, was shown the spiritual sky.

In this way, the full-moon night of the *śarat* season came to an end. The full-moon night of Āśvina is called *śarat-pūrṇimā.* It appears from the statements of *Śrīmad-Bhāgavatam* that Kṛṣṇa had to wait another year for such a moon before enjoying the *rāsa* dance with the *gopīs.* At the age of seven years He lifted Govardhana Hill. Therefore the *rāsa* dance took place during His eighth year.

From the Vedic literature it appears that when a theatrical actor dances among many dancing girls, the group dance is called a *rāsa* dance. When Kṛṣṇa saw the full-moon night of the *śarat* season, decorated with various seasonal flowers—especially the *mallikā* flowers, which are very fragrant—He remembered the *gopīs'* prayers to goddess Kātyāyanī, wherein they prayed for Kṛṣṇa to be their husband. He thought that the full-moon night of the *śarat* season was just suitable for a nice dance. So their desire to have Kṛṣṇa as their husband would then be fulfilled.

The words used in this connection in *Śrīmad-Bhāgavatam* are *bhagavān api.* This means that although Kṛṣṇa is the Supreme Personality of Godhead and thus has no desire that needs to be fulfilled (because He is always full with six opulences), He still wanted to enjoy the company of the *gopīs* in the *rāsa* dance. *Bhagavān api* signifies that this dance is not like the ordinary dancing of young boys and young girls. The specific words used in *Śrīmad-Bhāgavatam* are *yogamāyām upāśritaḥ,* which mean that this dancing with the *gopīs* is on the platform of *yogamāyā,* not *mahāmāyā.* The dancing of young boys and girls within the material world is in the kingdom of *mahāmāyā,* or the external energy. The *rāsa* dance of Kṛṣṇa with the *gopīs* is on the platform of *yogamāyā.* The difference between the platforms of *yogamāyā* and *mahāmāyā* is compared in the *Caitanya-caritāmṛta* to the difference between gold and iron. From the viewpoint of metallurgy, gold and iron are both metals, but the quality is completely different. Similarly, although the *rāsa* dance and Lord Kṛṣṇa's association with the *gopīs* appear like the ordinary mixing of young boys and girls, the quality is completely different. The difference is appreciated by great Vaiṣṇavas because they can understand the difference between love of Kṛṣṇa and lust.

On the *mahāmāyā* platform, dances take place on the basis of sense gratification. But when Kṛṣṇa called the *gopīs* by sounding His flute, the *gopīs* very hurriedly rushed toward the spot of the *rāsa* dance with the transcendental desire to satisfy Kṛṣṇa. The author of the *Caitanya-caritāmṛta,* Kṛṣṇadāsa Kavirāja Gosvāmī, has explained that lust means sense gratification, and love also means sense gratification—but for Kṛṣṇa. In other words, when activities are enacted on the platform of personal sense gratification, they are called material activities, but when they are enacted for the satisfaction of Kṛṣṇa, then they are spiritual activities.

On any platform of activities, the principle of sense gratification is there. But on the spiritual platform, sense gratification is for the Supreme Personality of Godhead, Kṛṣṇa, whereas on the material platform it is for the performer. For example, on the material platform, when a servant serves a master, he is trying to satisfy not the senses of his master but rather his own senses. The servant would not serve the master if the payment stopped. That means that the servant engages himself in the service of the master just to satisfy his own senses. On the spiritual platform, however, the servitor of the Supreme Personality of Godhead serves Kṛṣṇa without payment, and he continues his service in all conditions. That is the difference between Kṛṣṇa consciousness and material consciousness.

As mentioned above, it appears that Kṛṣṇa enjoyed the *rāsa* dance with the *gopīs* when He was eight years old. At that time, many of the *gopīs* were married, because in India, especially in those days, girls were married at a very early age. There are even many instances of a girl's giving birth to a child at the age of twelve. Under the circumstances, all the *gopīs* who wanted to have Kṛṣṇa as their husband were already married. At the same time, they continued to hope that Kṛṣṇa would be their husband. Their attitude toward Kṛṣṇa was that of paramour love. Therefore, the loving affairs of Kṛṣṇa with the *gopīs* are called *parakīya-rasa.* The attitude of a married man who desires another wife or a wife who desires another husband is called *parakīya-rasa.*

Actually, Kṛṣṇa is the husband of everyone because He is the supreme enjoyer. The *gopīs* wanted Kṛṣṇa to be their husband, but factually there was no possibility of His marrying all the *gopīs.* But because they had that natural tendency to accept Kṛṣṇa as their supreme husband, the relationship between the *gopīs* and Kṛṣṇa is called *parakīya-rasa.* This *parakīya-rasa* is ever-existent in Goloka Vṛndāvana, in the spiritual sky, where there is no possibility of the inebriety which characterizes *parakīya-rasa* in the material world. In the material world, *parakīya-rasa* is abominable, whereas in the spiritual world it is present in the superexcellent relationship of Kṛṣṇa and the *gopīs.* There are many relationships with Kṛṣṇa—master and servant, friend and friend, parent and son, and lover and beloved. Out of all these *rasas,* the *parakīya-rasa* is considered to be the topmost.

This material world is the perverted reflection of the spiritual world; it is just like the reflection of a tree on the bank of a reservoir of water: the topmost part of the tree is seen as the lowest part. Similarly, *parakīya-rasa,* when pervertedly reflected in this material world, is most abominable. Therefore when people imitate the *rāsa* dance of Kṛṣṇa with the *gopīs,* they simply enjoy the perverted, abominable reflection of the transcendental *parakīya-rasa.* There is no possibility of enjoying this transcendental *parakīya-rasa* within the material world. It is stated in *Śrīmad-Bhāgavatam* that one should not imitate this *parakīya-rasa* even in dream or imagination. Those who do so drink the most deadly poison.

When Kṛṣṇa, the supreme enjoyer, desired to enjoy the company of the *gopīs* on that full-moon night of the *śarat* season, exactly at that very moment the moon, the lord of the stars, appeared in the sky, displaying its most beautiful features. The full-moon night of the *śarat* season is the most beautiful night in the year. In the Indian city of Agra, in Uttar Pradesh Province, there is a great monument called the Taj Mahal, which is a tomb made of first-class marble stone. During the night of the full moon of the *śarat* season, many foreigners go to see the beautiful reflections of the moon on the tomb. Thus this full-moon night is celebrated even today for its beauty.

When the full moon rose in the east, it tinged everything with a reddish color. With the rising of the moon, the whole sky appeared smeared by red *kuṅkuma*. When a husband long separated from his wife returns home, he decorates the face of his wife with red *kuṅkuma*. This long-expected moonrise of the *śarat* season was thus smearing the eastern sky.

The appearance of the moon increased Kṛṣṇa's desire to dance with the *gopīs*. The forests were filled with fragrant flowers. The atmosphere was cooling and festive. When Lord Kṛṣṇa began to blow His flute, the *gopīs* all over Vṛndāvana became enchanted. Their attraction to the vibration of the flute increased a thousand times due to the rising full moon, the red horizon, the calm and cool atmosphere and the blossoming flowers. All the *gopīs* were by nature very much attracted to Kṛṣṇa's beauty, and when they heard the vibration of His flute, they became apparently lustful to satisfy the senses of Kṛṣṇa.

Immediately upon hearing the vibration of the flute, they all left their respective engagements and proceeded to the spot where Kṛṣṇa was standing. While they ran very swiftly, their earrings swung back and forth. They all rushed toward the place known as Vaṁśīvaṭa. Some of them were engaged in milking cows, but they left their milking business half finished and immediately went to Kṛṣṇa. One of them had just collected milk and put it in a milk pan on the stove to boil, but she did not care whether the milk overboiled and spilled—she immediately left to go see Kṛṣṇa. Some of them were breast-feeding their small babies, and some were engaged in distributing food to the members of their families, but they left all such engagements and immediately rushed toward the spot where Kṛṣṇa was playing His flute. Some were engaged in serving their husbands, and some were themselves engaged in eating, but caring neither to serve their husbands nor eat, they immediately left. Some of them wanted to decorate their faces with cosmetic ointments and to dress themselves very nicely before going to Kṛṣṇa, but unfortunately they could not finish their cosmetic decorations or put on their clothes in the right way because of their anxiety to meet Kṛṣṇa immediately. Their faces were decorated hurriedly and were haphazardly finished; some even put the lower part of their clothes on the upper part of their bodies and the upper part on the lower part.

While all the *gopīs* were hurriedly leaving their respective places, their husbands, brothers and fathers were all struck with wonder to know where they were going. Being young girls, they were protected either by husbands, elder brothers or fathers. All their guardians forbade them to go to Kṛṣṇa, but they disregarded them. When a person becomes attracted by Kṛṣṇa and is in full Kṛṣṇa consciousness, he does not care for any worldly duties, even though very urgent. Kṛṣṇa consciousness is so powerful that it gives everyone relief from all material activities. Śrīla Rūpa Gosvāmī has written a very nice verse wherein one *gopī* advises another, "My dear friend, if you desire to enjoy the company of material society, friendship and love, then please do not go to see this smiling boy Govinda, who is standing on the bank of the Yamunā and playing His flute, His lips brightened by the beams of the full moonlight." Śrīla Rūpa Gosvāmī indirectly instructs that one who has been captivated by the beautiful smiling face of Kṛṣṇa has lost all attraction for material enjoyments. This is the test of advancement in Kṛṣṇa consciousness: a person advancing in Kṛṣṇa consciousness must lose interest in material activities and personal sense gratification.

Some of the *gopīs* were factually detained from going to Kṛṣṇa by their husbands and were locked up by force within their rooms. Being unable to go to Kṛṣṇa, they began to meditate upon His transcendental form by closing their eyes. They already had the form of Kṛṣṇa within their minds. They proved to be the greatest *yogīs;* as is stated in the *Bhagavad-gītā,* a person who is constantly thinking of Kṛṣṇa within his heart with faith and love is considered to be the topmost of all *yogīs.* Actually, a *yogī* concentrates his mind on the form of Lord Viṣṇu. That is real *yoga.* Kṛṣṇa is the original form of all *viṣṇu-tattvas.* The *gopīs* could not go to Kṛṣṇa personally, so they began to meditate on Him as perfect *yogīs.*

In the conditioned stage of the living entities, there are two kinds of results of fruitive activities: the conditioned living entity who is constantly engaged in sinful activities has suffering as his result, and he who is engaged in pious activities has material enjoyment as a result. In either case—material suffering or material enjoyment—the enjoyer or sufferer is conditioned by material nature.

The *gopī* associates of Kṛṣṇa who assembled in the place where Kṛṣṇa was appearing were from different groups. Most of the *gopīs* were eternal companions of Kṛṣṇa. As stated in the *Brahma-saṁhitā, ānanda-cin-maya-rasa-pratibhāvitābhiḥ:* in the spiritual world the associates of Kṛṣṇa, especially the *gopīs,* are manifestations of the pleasure potency of Lord Kṛṣṇa. They are expansions of Śrīmatī Rādhārāṇī. But when Kṛṣṇa exhibits His transcendental pastimes within the material world in some of the universes, not only the eternal associates of Kṛṣṇa come but also those who are being promoted to that status from this material world. The *gopīs* who joined Kṛṣṇa's pastimes within this material world were coming from the status of ordinary human beings. If they had been bound by fruitive action, they were fully freed from the reaction of *karma* by constant meditation on Kṛṣṇa. Their severely painful yearnings caused by their not being able to see Kṛṣṇa freed them from all sinful reactions, and their ecstasy of transcendental love for Kṛṣṇa in His absence ended all their reactions to material pious activities. The conditioned soul is subjected to birth and death, either by pious or sinful activities, but the *gopīs* who began to meditate on Kṛṣṇa transcended both positions and became purified and thus elevated to the status of the *gopīs* already expanded by His pleasure potency. All the *gopīs* who concentrated their minds on Kṛṣṇa in the spirit of paramour love became fully purified of all the fruitive reactions of material nature, and some of them immediately gave up their material bodies developed under the three modes of material nature.

Mahārāja Parīkṣit heard Śukadeva Gosvāmī explain the situation of the *gopīs* who assembled with Kṛṣṇa in the *rāsa* dance. When he heard that some of the *gopīs*, simply by concentrating on Kṛṣṇa as their paramour, became freed from all contamination of material birth and death, he said, "The *gopīs* did not know that Kṛṣṇa is the Supreme Personality of Godhead. They accepted Him as a beautiful boy and considered Him to be their paramour. So how was it possible for them to get freed from the material condition just by thinking of a paramour?" One should consider here that Kṛṣṇa and ordinary living beings are qualitatively one. The ordinary living beings, being part and parcel of Kṛṣṇa, are also Brahman, but Kṛṣṇa is the Supreme—Parabrahman. The question is, If it is possible for a devotee to get free from the material, contaminated stage simply by thinking of Kṛṣṇa, then why should this not be possible for others who are also thinking of someone? If one is thinking of a husband or son, or if anyone at all is thinking of another living entity, then, since all living entities are also Brahman, why are all those who thus think of others not freed from the contaminated stage of material nature? This is a very intelligent question, because there are always atheists imitating Kṛṣṇa. In these days of Kali-yuga, there are many rascals who think themselves to be as good as Kṛṣṇa and who cheat people into believing that thinking of them is as good as thinking of Lord Kṛṣṇa. Parīkṣit Mahārāja, apprehending the future dangerous condition of blind followers of demoniac imitators, therefore asked this question, and fortunately it is recorded in *Śrīmad-Bhāgavatam* to warn innocent people that thinking of an ordinary man and thinking of Kṛṣṇa are not the same.

Actually, even thinking of the demigods cannot compare to thinking of Kṛṣṇa. It is warned in the *vaiṣṇava-tantra* that one who puts Viṣṇu, Nārāyaṇa or Kṛṣṇa on the same level as the demigods is called a *pāṣaṇḍī*, or rascal. On hearing this question from Mahārāja Parīkṣit, Śukadeva Gosvāmī replied, "My dear King, your question is already answered, even before this incident." Because Parīkṣit Mahārāja wanted to clear up the situation, his spiritual master answered him very intelligently, "Why are you again asking about the same subject matter which has already been explained to you? Why are you so forgetful?" A spiritual master is always in the superior position, so he has the right to chastise his disciple in this way. Śukadeva Gosvāmī knew that Mahārāja Parīkṣit asked the question not for his own understanding but as a warning to the future innocent people who might think others to be equal to Kṛṣṇa.

Śukadeva Gosvāmī then reminded Parīkṣit Mahārāja about the salvation of Śiśupāla. Śiśupāla was always envious of Kṛṣṇa, and because of his envy Kṛṣṇa killed him. But since Kṛṣṇa is the Supreme Personality of Godhead, Śiśupāla gained salvation simply by seeing Him. If an envious person can get salvation simply by concentrating his mind on Kṛṣṇa, then what to speak of the *gopīs*, who are so dear to Kṛṣṇa and always think of Him in love? There must be some difference between the enemies and the friends. If Kṛṣṇa's enemies could get freed from material contamination and become one with the Supreme, then certainly His dear friends like the *gopīs* can achieve such freedom and much more.

Besides that, in the *Bhagavad-gītā* Kṛṣṇa is called Hṛṣīkeśa. Śukadeva Gosvāmī also said that Kṛṣṇa is Hṛṣīkeśa, the Supersoul. Whereas an ordinary man is a conditioned soul covered by the material body, Kṛṣṇa and Kṛṣṇa's body are the same because He is Hṛṣīkeśa. Any person making a distinction between Kṛṣṇa and Kṛṣṇa's body is fool number one. Kṛṣṇa is Hṛṣīkeśa and Adhokṣaja. These two particular words have been used by Śukadeva Gosvāmī in this instance. Hṛṣīkeśa is the Supersoul, and Adhokṣaja is the Supreme Personality of Godhead, transcendental to the material nature. Just to show favor to the ordinary living entities, out of His causeless mercy He appears as He is. Unfortunately, foolish persons mistake Him to be an ordinary person, and so they become eligible to go to hell.

Śukadeva Gosvāmī continued to inform Mahārāja Parīkṣit that Kṛṣṇa is not an ordinary person but rather the Supreme Personality of Godhead—imperishable, immeasurable and without any material qualities but full of all spiritual qualities. He appears in this material world out of His causeless mercy, and whenever He appears, He appears as He is, without change. This is confirmed in the *Bhagavad-gītā,* where the Lord says that He appears by His spiritual potency. He does not appear under the control of the material potency. The material potency is under His control. In the *Bhagavad-gītā* it is stated that the material potency is working under His superintendence. It is also confirmed in the *Brahma-saṁhitā* that the material potency, known as Durgā, is acting just as a shadow which moves with the movement of the substance. The conclusion is that if one somehow or other becomes attached to Kṛṣṇa or attracted to Him, either because of His qualities of beauty, opulence, fame, strength, renunciation or knowledge, through affection or friendship, or even through lust, anger or fear, then one's salvation and freedom from material contamination are assured.

In the *Bhagavad-gītā,* Eighteenth Chapter, the Lord states that one who is engaged in preaching Kṛṣṇa consciousness is very dear to Him. A preacher has to face many difficulties in his struggle to preach pure Kṛṣṇa consciousness. Sometimes he has to suffer bodily injuries, and sometimes he has to meet death also. All this is taken as a great austerity on behalf of Kṛṣṇa. Kṛṣṇa therefore has said that such a preacher is very, very dear to Him. If Kṛṣṇa's enemies can expect salvation simply by concentrating their minds on Him, then what to speak of persons who are so dear to Kṛṣṇa? The conclusion should be that the salvation of those who are engaged in preaching Kṛṣṇa consciousness in the world is guaranteed in all circumstances. But such preachers never care for salvation, because factually one who is engaged in Kṛṣṇa consciousness, devotional service, has already achieved salvation. Śukadeva Gosvāmī therefore assured

King Parīkṣit that he should always rest assured that one who is attracted by Kṛṣṇa attains liberation from material bondage because Kṛṣṇa is the transcendental master of all mystic power.

When all the *gopīs* assembled, as described, before Kṛṣṇa, He began to speak to them, welcoming them as well as discouraging them by word jugglery. Kṛṣṇa is the supreme speaker; He is the speaker of the *Bhagavad-gītā*. He can speak on the highest elevated subjects of philosophy, politics, economics—everything. And He also spoke before the *gopīs,* who were so dear to Him. He wanted to enchant them by word jugglery, and thus He began to speak as follows.

"O ladies of Vṛndāvana," Kṛṣṇa said, "you are very fortunate, and you are very dear to Me. I am very pleased that you have come here, and I hope everything is well in Vṛndāvana. Now please order Me. What can I do for you? What is the purpose of your coming here in the dead of night? Kindly take your seats and let Me know what I can do for you."

The *gopīs* had come to Kṛṣṇa to enjoy His company, to dance with Him, embrace Him and kiss Him, and when Kṛṣṇa began to receive them very officially, showing all kinds of etiquette, they were surprised. He was treating them as ordinary society women. Therefore they began to smile among themselves, and though they very eagerly listened to Kṛṣṇa talk in that way, they were surprised. Then Kṛṣṇa began to instruct them: "My dear friends, you must know that it is now the dead of night and the forest is very dangerous. At this time all the ferocious jungle animals—the tigers, bears, jackals and wolves—are prowling in the forest. Therefore it is very dangerous for you. You cannot select a secure place now. Everywhere you go you will find that all these animals are loitering to find their prey. I think, therefore, that you are taking a great risk in coming here in the dead of night. Please turn back immediately, without delay."

When He saw that they continued to smile, He said, "I very much appreciate your bodily features. All of you have nice, very thin waists." All of the *gopīs* there were exquisitely beautiful. They are described by the word *sumadhyamā;* the standard of beauty of a woman is said to be *sumadhyamā* when the middle portion of the body is slender.

Kṛṣṇa wanted to impress on them that they were not old enough to take care of themselves. Actually, they required protection. It was not very wise for them to come in the dead of night to Kṛṣṇa. Kṛṣṇa also indicated that He was young and that they were young girls. "It does not look very well for young girls and boys to remain together in the dead of night." After hearing this advice, the *gopīs* did not seem very happy; therefore Kṛṣṇa began to stress the point in a different way.

"My dear friends, I can understand that you have left your homes without the permission of your guardians; therefore I think your mothers, your fathers, your elder brothers and even your sons, and what to speak of your husbands, must be very anxious to find you. As long as you are here, they must be searching in different places, and their minds must be very agitated. So don't tarry. Please go back and make them peaceful."

When the *gopīs* appeared to be a little bit disturbed and angry from hearing the free advice of Kṛṣṇa, they diverted their attention to looking at the beauty of the forest. At that time the whole forest was illuminated by the bright shining of the moon, and the air was blowing very silently over the blooming flowers, and the green leaves of the trees were moving in the breeze. Kṛṣṇa took the opportunity of their looking at the forest to advise them. "I think you have come out to see the beautiful Vṛndāvana forest on this night," He said, "but you must now be satisfied. So return to your homes without delay. I understand that you are all very chaste women, so now that you have seen the beautiful atmosphere of the Vṛndāvana forest, please return home and engage in the faithful service of your respective husbands. Some of you must have babies by this time, although you are very young. You must have left your small babies at home, and they must be crying. Please immediately go back home and just feed them with your breast milk. I can also understand that you have very great affection for Me, and out of that transcendental affection you have come here, hearing My playing on the flute. Your feelings of love and affection for Me are very appropriate because I am the Supreme Personality of Godhead. All living creatures are My parts and parcels, and naturally they are affectionate to Me. So this affection for Me is very welcome, and I congratulate you for this. Now you can go back to your homes. Another thing I must explain to you is that for a chaste woman, service to the husband without duplicity is the best religious principle. Not only should a woman be faithful and chaste to her husband but she should also be affectionate to the friends of her husband, obedient to the father and mother of her husband, and affectionate to the younger brothers of her husband. And most importantly, a woman must take care of her children."

In this way, Kṛṣṇa explained the duty of a woman. He also stressed the point of serving the husband: "Even if he is not of very good character, or even if he is not very rich or fortunate, or even if he is old or invalid on account of continued diseases, whatever her husband's condition, a woman should not divorce her husband if she actually desires to be elevated to the higher planetary systems after leaving this body. Besides that, it is considered abominable in society if a woman is unfaithful and goes searching for another man. Such habits will deter a woman from being elevated to the heavenly planets, and the results of such habits are very degrading. A married woman should not search for a paramour, for this is not sanctioned by the Vedic principles of life. If you think that you are very much attached to Me and you want My association, I advise you not to personally try to enjoy Me. It is better for you to go home, simply talk about Me and think of Me, and by this process of constantly remembering Me and chanting My names you will surely be elevated to the spiritual platform. There is no need to stand near Me. Please go back home."

The instruction given herein by the Supreme Personality of Godhead to the *gopīs* was not at all sarcastic. Such instructions should be taken very seriously by all honest women. The chastity of women is specifically stressed herein by the Supreme Personality of Godhead. Therefore this principle should be followed by any serious woman who wants to be elevated to a higher status of life. Kṛṣṇa is the center of all affection for all living creatures. When this affection is developed for Kṛṣṇa, one surpasses and transcends all Vedic injunctions. This was possible for the *gopīs* because they saw Kṛṣṇa face to face. This is not possible for any women in the conditioned state. Unfortunately, sometimes a rascal, following the philosophy of monism, or oneness, very irresponsibly takes advantage of this *rāsa-līlā* to imitate the behavior of Kṛṣṇa with the *gopīs,* entice many innocent women and mislead them in the name of spiritual realization. As a warning, Lord Kṛṣṇa has herein hinted that what was possible for the *gopīs* is not possible for ordinary women. Although a woman can actually be elevated by advanced Kṛṣṇa consciousness, she should not be enticed by an imposter who says that he is Kṛṣṇa. She should concentrate her devotional activities in chanting and meditating upon Kṛṣṇa, as is advised herein. One should not follow the men called *sahajiyās,* the so-called devotees who take everything very lightly.

When Kṛṣṇa spoke in such a discouraging way to the *gopīs,* they became very sad, for they thought that their desire to enjoy the *rāsa* dance with Kṛṣṇa would be frustrated. Thus they became full of anxiety. Out of great sadness, the *gopīs* began to breathe very heavily. Instead of looking at Kṛṣṇa face to face, they bowed their heads and looked at the ground, and they began to draw various types of curved lines on the ground with their toes. They were shedding heavy tears, and their cosmetic decorations were being washed from their faces. The water from their eyes mixed with the *kuṅkuma* on their breasts and fell to the ground. They could not say anything to Kṛṣṇa but simply stood there silently. By their silence they expressed that their hearts were grievously wounded.

The *gopīs* were not ordinary women. In essence they were on an equal level with Kṛṣṇa. They are His eternal associates. As it is confirmed in the *Brahma-saṁhitā,* they are expansions of the pleasure potency of Kṛṣṇa, and as His potency they are nondifferent from Him. Although they were depressed by the words of Kṛṣṇa, they did not like to use harsh words against Him. Yet they wanted to rebuke Kṛṣṇa for His unkind words, and therefore they began to speak in faltering voices. They did not like to use harsh words against Kṛṣṇa because He was their dearmost, their heart and soul. The *gopīs* had only Kṛṣṇa within their hearts. They were completely surrendered and dedicated souls. Naturally, when they heard such unkind words, they tried to reply, but in the attempt torrents of tears fell from their eyes. Finally they managed to speak.

"Kṛṣṇa," they said, "You are very cruel! You should not talk like that. We are full-fledged surrendered souls. Please accept us, and don't talk in that cruel way. Of course, You are the Supreme Personality of Godhead and can do whatever You like, but it is not worthy of Your position to treat us in such a cruel way. We have come to You, leaving everything behind, just to take shelter of Your lotus feet. We know that You are completely independent and can do whatever You like, but we request You, don't reject us. We are Your devotees. You should accept us as Lord Nārāyaṇa accepts His devotees. There are many devotees of Lord Nārāyaṇa who worship Him for salvation, and He awards them salvation. Similarly, how can You reject us when we have no shelter other than Your lotus feet?

"O dear Kṛṣṇa," they continued, "You are the supreme instructor. There is no doubt about it. Your instructions to women to be faithful to their husbands and merciful to their children, to take care of household affairs and to be obedient to the elderly members of the family, are surely just according to the tenets of the *śāstras.* But we know that one may perfectly observe all these instructions of the *śāstras* by keeping oneself under the protection of Your lotus feet. Our husbands, friends, family members and children are all dear and pleasing to us only because of Your presence, for You are the Supersoul of all living creatures. Without Your presence, one is worthless. When You leave the body, the body immediately dies, and according to the injunction of the *śāstras,* a dead body must immediately be thrown into a river or burned. Therefore, ultimately You are the dearmost personality in this world. By placing our faith and love in Your personality, we are assured of never being bereft of husband, friends, sons or daughters. If a woman accepts You as the supreme husband, then she will never be bereft of her husband, as in the bodily concept of life. If we accept You as our ultimate husband, then there is no question of being separated, divorced or widowed. You are the eternal husband, eternal son, eternal friend and eternal master, and one who enters into a relationship with You is eternally happy. Since You are the teacher of all religious principles, Your lotus feet have to be worshiped first. Accordingly, the *śāstras* state, *ācārya-upāsanā:* the worship of Your lotus feet is the first principle. Besides that, as stated in the *Bhagavad-gītā,* You are the only enjoyer, You are the only proprietor, and You are the only friend. As such, we have come to You, leaving aside all so-called friends, society and love, and now You have become our enjoyer. Let us be everlastingly enjoyed by You. Be our proprietor, for that is Your natural claim, and be our supreme friend, for You are naturally so. Let us thus embrace You as the supreme beloved."

Then the *gopīs* told lotus-eyed Kṛṣṇa, "Please do not discourage our long-cherished desires to have You as our husband. Any intelligent man who cares for his own self-interest reposes all his loving spirit in You. Persons who are simply misled by the external energy, who want to be satisfied by false concepts, try to enjoy themselves apart from You. The so-called husband, friend, son, daughter, father and mother are all simply sources of material misery. No one is made happy in this material world by having a so-called father, mother, husband, son, daughter and friend. Although the father and mother are expected to protect the children, there are many children who are suffering for want of food and shelter. There are many good physicians, but when a patient dies, no physician can revive him. There are many means of protection, but when one is doomed, none of the protective measures can help, and without Your protection the so-called sources of protection simply become sources of continued distress. We therefore appeal to You, dear Lord of all lords: please do not kill our long-cherished desires to have You as our supreme husband.

"Dear Kṛṣṇa, as women, we are certainly satisfied when our hearts are engaged in the activities of family affairs, but our hearts have already been stolen by You. We can no longer engage them in family affairs. Besides that, although You have repeatedly asked us to return home, and that is a very appropriate instruction, unfortunately we have been stunned here. Our legs have no power to move a step from Your lotus feet. Therefore, if even at Your request we return home, what shall we do there? We have lost all our ability to act without You. Instead of engaging our hearts in family affairs as women, we have now developed a different type of lust which is continually blazing in our hearts. Now we request You, dear Kṛṣṇa, to extinguish that fire with Your beautiful smile and the transcendental vibration emanating from Your lips. If You do not agree to do us this favor, we shall certainly be burned in the fire of separation. In that condition, we shall simply think of You and Your beautiful features and give up our bodies immediately. In that way we think it will be possible for us to reside at Your lotus feet in the next life. Dear Kṛṣṇa, if You say that if we go home our respective husbands will satisfy the lusty flame of our desire, we can only say that that is no longer possible. You have given us a chance to be enjoyed by You in the forest and have touched our breasts once in the past, which we accepted as a blessing, as do the goddesses of fortune, who are enjoyed in the Vaikuṇṭhalokas by You. Since we have tasted this transcendental enjoyment, we are no longer interested in going to anyone but You for the satisfaction of our lust. Dear Kṛṣṇa, the lotus feet of the goddess of fortune are always worshiped by the demigods. Although she is always resting on Your chest in the Vaikuṇṭha planets, she underwent great austerity and penance to have some shelter at Your lotus feet, which are always covered by *tulasī* leaves. Your lotus feet are the proper shelter of Your servitors, and the goddess of fortune, instead of abiding on Your chest, comes down and worships Your lotus feet. We have now placed ourselves under the dust of Your feet. Please do not reject us, for we are fully surrendered souls.

"Dear Kṛṣṇa, You are known as Hari. You destroy all the miseries of all living entities, specifically of those who have left their homes and family attachment and have completely taken to You. We have left our homes with the hope that we shall completely devote and dedicate our lives to Your service. We are simply begging to be engaged as Your servants. We do not wish to ask You to accept us as Your wives. Simply accept us as Your maidservants. Since You are the Supreme Personality of Godhead and like to enjoy the *parakīya-rasa* and are famous as a transcendental woman hunter, we have come to satisfy Your transcendental desires. We are also after our own satisfaction, for simply by looking at Your smiling face we have become very lusty. We have come before You decorated with all ornaments and dress, but until You embrace us, all our garments and beautiful features remain incomplete. You are the Supreme Person, and if You complete our dressing attempt as the *puruṣa-bhūṣaṇa,* or the male ornament, then all our desires and bodily decorations are complete.

"Dear Kṛṣṇa, we have simply been captivated by seeing You with *tilaka* and with earrings and by seeing Your beautiful face covered with scattered hair and bearing Your extraordinary smile. Not only that, but we are also attracted by Your arms, which always give assurance to the surrendered souls. And although we are also attracted by Your chest, which is always embraced by the goddess of fortune, we do not wish to take her position. We shall simply be satisfied by being Your maidservants. If You accuse us, however, of encouraging prostitution, then we can only ask, Where is that woman within these three worlds who is not captivated by Your beauty and the rhythmic songs vibrated by Your transcendental flute? Within these three worlds there is no distinction between men and women in relation to You because both men and women belong to the marginal potency, or *prakṛti.* No one is actually the enjoyer, or the male; everyone is meant to be enjoyed by You. There is no woman within these three worlds who cannot but deviate from her path of chastity once she is attracted to You, because Your beauty is so sublime that not only men and women but also cows, birds, beasts and even trees, fruits and flowers—everyone and everything—become enchanted, and what to speak of ourselves? It is, however, definitely decided that as Lord Viṣṇu is always protecting the demigods from the onslaught of demons, so You have also advented in Vṛndāvana just to give the residents protection from all kinds of distress. O dear friend of the distressed, kindly place Your hand on our burning breasts as well as on our heads, because we have surrendered unto You as Your eternal maidservants. If You think, however, that Your lotuslike palms might be burned to ashes if placed on our burning breasts, let us assure You that Your palms will feel pleasure instead of pain, as the lotus flower, although very delicate and soft, enjoys the scorching heat of the sun."

Upon hearing the anxious plea of the *gopīs,* the Supreme Personality of Godhead smiled, and being very kind to the *gopīs,* the Lord, although self-sufficient, began to embrace them and kiss them as they desired. When Kṛṣṇa, smiling, looked at the faces of the *gopīs,* the beauty of their faces became a hundred times enhanced. When He was enjoying them in their midst, He appeared just like the full moon surrounded by millions of shining stars. Thus the Supreme Personality of Godhead, surrounded by hundreds of *gopīs* and decorated with a flower garland of many colors, began to wander within the Vṛndāvana forest, sometimes singing to Himself and sometimes singing with the *gopīs*. In this way the Lord and the *gopīs* reached the cool, sandy bank of the Yamunā, where there were lilies and lotus flowers. In such a transcendental atmosphere, the *gopīs* and Kṛṣṇa began to enjoy one another. While they were walking on the bank of the Yamunā, Kṛṣṇa would sometimes put His arms around a *gopī's* head, breast or waist. Pinching one another and joking and looking at one another, they enjoyed. When Kṛṣṇa touched the bodies of the *gopīs,* their lust to embrace Him increased. They all enjoyed these pastimes. Thus the *gopīs* were blessed with all mercy by the Supreme Personality of Godhead, for they enjoyed His company without a tinge of mundane sex life.

The *gopīs,* however, soon began to feel very proud, thinking themselves to be the most fortunate women in the universe due to being favored by the company of Kṛṣṇa. Lord Kṛṣṇa, who is known as Keśava, could immediately understand their pride caused by their great fortune of enjoying Him personally, and in order to show them His causeless mercy and to curb their false pride, He immediately disappeared from the scene, exhibiting His opulence of renunciation. The Supreme Personality of Godhead is always full with six kinds of opulences, and this is an instance of the opulence of renunciation. This renunciation confirms Kṛṣṇa's total nonattachment. He is always self-sufficient and is not dependent on anything. This is the platform on which His transcendental pastimes are enacted.

Thus ends the Bhaktivedanta purport of the Twenty-ninth Chapter of Kṛṣṇa, *"The* Rāsa *Dance: Introduction."*

CHAPTER 30

Kṛṣṇa's Hiding from the Gopīs

When Kṛṣṇa suddently disappeared from the company of the *gopīs,* they began to search for Him everywhere. After not finding Him anywhere, they became afraid and almost mad after Him. They were simply thinking of the pastimes of Kṛṣṇa in great love and affection. Being absorbed in thought of Him, they experienced loss of memory, and with dampened eyes they began to see the very pastimes of Kṛṣṇa—His beautiful talks with them, His embracing, kissing and other activities. Being so attracted to Kṛṣṇa, they imitated His dancing, His walking and His smiling, as if they themselves were Kṛṣṇa. Due to Kṛṣṇa's absence, they all became crazy; each one of them told the others that she was Kṛṣṇa Himself. Soon they all assembled together and chanted Kṛṣṇa's name very loudly as they moved from one part of the forest to another, searching for Him.

Actually, Kṛṣṇa is all-pervasive: He is in the sky, and He is in the forest; He is within the heart, and He is always everywhere. The *gopīs* therefore began to question the trees and plants about Kṛṣṇa. There were various types of big trees and small plants in the forest, and the *gopīs* addressed them: "Dear banyan tree, have you seen the son of Mahārāja Nanda passing this way, laughing and playing on His flute? He has stolen our hearts and gone away. If you have seen Him, kindly inform us which way He has gone. Dear *aśoka* tree, dear *nāga* flower tree and *campaka* flower tree, have you seen the younger brother of Balarāma pass this way? He has disappeared because of our pride." The *gopīs* were aware of the reason for Kṛṣṇa's sudden disappearance. They could understand that when they had been enjoying Kṛṣṇa they thought themselves to be the most fortunate women within the universe, and since they were feeling proud, Kṛṣṇa had disappeared immediately just to curb their pride. Kṛṣṇa does not like His devotees to be proud of their service to Him. He accepts everyone's service, but He does not like one devotee to proudly consider himself better than others. If sometimes there are such feelings, Kṛṣṇa ends them by changing His attitude toward the devotee.

The *gopīs* then addressed the *tulasī* plants: "Dear *tulasī,* you are much beloved by Lord Kṛṣṇa because your leaves are always at His lotus feet. Dear *mālatī* flower, dear *mallikā* flower, dear jasmine flower, all of you must have been touched by Kṛṣṇa while He was passing this way after giving us transcendental enjoyment. Have you seen Mādhava passing this way? O mango trees, O trees of jackfruit, O pear trees and *āsana* trees! O blackberries and bael trees and trees of the *kadamba* flower—you are all very pious trees to be living on the bank of the Yamunā. Kṛṣṇa must have passed through this way. Will you kindly let us know which way He has gone?"

The *gopīs* then looked upon the ground they were traversing and began to address the earth, "Dear earthly planet, we do not know how many penances and austerities you have undergone to be now living with the footprints of Lord Kṛṣṇa upon you. You are very jolly; the hairs on your body are these jubilant trees and plants. Lord Kṛṣṇa must have been very pleased with you; otherwise how could He have embraced you in the form of Varāha the boar? When you were submerged in water, He delivered you, taking the whole weight of your existence on His tusks."

After addressing the innumerable trees and plants and the earth, they turned their faces toward the beautiful deer, who were looking at them very pleasingly. "It appears," they addressed the deer, "that Kṛṣṇa, who is the Supreme Nārāyaṇa Himself, must have passed through this way along with His companion, Lakṣmī, the goddess of fortune. Otherwise, how is it possible that the aroma of His garland, which is smeared with the red *kuṅkuma* from the breasts of the goddess of fortune, can be perceived in the breeze blowing here? It appears that they must have passed through here and touched your bodies, and thus you are feeling so pleasant and are looking toward us with sympathy. Will you kindly, therefore, inform us which way Kṛṣṇa has gone? Kṛṣṇa is the well-wisher of Vṛndāvana. He is as kind to you as to us; therefore after leaving us, He must have been present in your company. O fortunate trees, we are thinking of Kṛṣṇa, the younger brother of Balarāma. While passing through here, with one hand resting on the shoulder of the goddess of fortune and the other hand twirling a lotus flower, He must have been very pleased to accept your obeisances, and He must have glanced at you with great pleasure."

Some of the *gopīs* then addressed their *gopī* friends: "Dear friends, why don't you question these creepers, who are so jubilantly embracing the big trees as if the trees were their husbands? It appears that the flowers of the creepers must have been touched by the nails of Kṛṣṇa. Otherwise, how could they feel so jubilant?"

After searching for Kṛṣṇa here and there, the *gopīs* became fatigued, and then they began to talk like madwomen. They could satisfy themselves only by imitating the different pastimes of Kṛṣṇa. One of them imitated the demon Pūtanā, and one of them imitated Kṛṣṇa and sucked her breast. One *gopī* imitated a hand-driven cart, and another *gopī* lay down beneath the cart and threw up her legs, touching the wheels of the cart, as Kṛṣṇa did to kill the demon Śakaṭāsura. One *gopī* imitated child Kṛṣṇa and lay down on the ground, and one *gopī* became the demon Tṛṇāvarta and carried the small child Kṛṣṇa by force into the sky; and one of the *gopīs* began to imitate Kṛṣṇa while He was attempting to walk, ringing His ankle bells. Two *gopīs* imitated Kṛṣṇa and Balarāma, and many others imitated Their cowherd boyfriends. One *gopī* assumed the form of Bakāsura, and another forced her to fall down as the demon Bakāsura did when he was killed; similarly, another *gopī* defeated Vatsāsura. Just as Kṛṣṇa used to call His cows by their different names, so the *gopīs* imitated Him, calling the cows by their respective names. One of the *gopīs* began to play on a flute, and another praised her the way Kṛṣṇa's boyfriends praised Him while He played on His flute. One of the *gopīs* took another *gopī* on her shoulders, just as Kṛṣṇa used to take His boyfriends. Absorbed in thoughts of Kṛṣṇa, the *gopī* who was carrying her friend began to boast that she was Kṛṣṇa herself: "All of you just see my movement!" One of the *gopīs* raised her hand with her covering garments and said, "Now don't be afraid of the torrents of rain and severe hurricanes. I'll save you!" In this way she imitated the lifting of Govardhana Hill. One *gopī* forcibly put her feet on the head of another *gopī* and said, "You rascal Kāliya! I shall punish you severely. You must leave this place. I have descended on this earth to punish all kinds of miscreants!" Another *gopī* told her friends, "Just see! The flames of the forest fire are coming to devour us. Please close your eyes and I shall immediately save you from this imminent danger."

In this way all the *gopīs* were madly feeling the absence of Kṛṣṇa. They inquired about Him from the trees and plants. In some places they found the imprints of the marks on the soles of His feet—namely the flag, the lotus flower, the trident, the thunderbolt, etc. After seeing those footprints, they exclaimed, "Oh, here is the impression of the marks on the soles of Kṛṣṇa's feet! All the marks, such as the flag, the lotus flower, the trident and the thunderbolt, are distinctly visible here." They began to follow the footprints, and shortly they saw another set of footprints beside them, and immediately they became very sorry. "Dear friends, just see! Whose are these other footprints? They are beside the footprints of the son of Mahārāja Nanda. It is certainly Kṛṣṇa passing through, resting His hand on some other *gopī*, exactly as an elephant goes side by side with his beloved mate. We must, therefore, understand that this particular *gopī* served Kṛṣṇa with greater affectionate love than ourselves. Because of this, although He has left us, He could not leave Her company. He has taken Her along with Him. Dear friends, just imagine how the dust of this place is transcendentally glorious. The dust of the lotus feet of Kṛṣṇa is worshiped even by Lord Brahmā and Lord Śiva and the goddess of fortune, Lakṣmī. But at the same time, we are very sorry that this particular *gopī* has gone along with Kṛṣṇa, for She is sharing the nectar of Kṛṣṇa's kisses and leaving us aside to lament. O friends, just see! At this particular spot we do not see the footprints of that *gopī*. It appears that because there were some pinpricks from the dried grass, Kṛṣṇa took Rādhārāṇī on His shoulder. Oh, She is so dear to Him! Kṛṣṇa must have picked some flowers in this spot to satisfy Rādhārāṇī, because here, where He stood erect to get the flowers from the high branches of the tree, we find only half the impression of His feet. Dear friends, just see how Kṛṣṇa must have sat down here with Rādhārāṇī and tried to set flowers in Her hair. You can be certain that both of Them sat together here." Kṛṣṇa is self-sufficient: He has nothing to enjoy from any other source. Yet just to satisfy His devotee, He treated Rādhārāṇī exactly as a lusty boy treats his girlfriend. Kṛṣṇa is so kind that He always tolerates the disturbances created by His girlfriends.

In this way, all the *gopīs* pointed out the faults of the particular *gopī* who had been taken alone by Kṛṣṇa. They said that this chief *gopī*, Rādhārāṇī, must be very proud of Her position, thinking Herself the greatest of the *gopīs*. "Yet how could Kṛṣṇa take Her away alone, leaving all of us aside, unless She is extraordinarily qualified and beautiful? She must have taken Kṛṣṇa into the deep forest and told Him, 'My dear Kṛṣṇa, I am now very tired. I cannot go any further. Please carry Me wherever You like.' When Kṛṣṇa was spoken to in this way, He might have told Rādhārāṇī, 'All right, better get on My shoulder.' But immediately Kṛṣṇa must have disappeared, and now Rādhārāṇī must be lamenting for Him, 'My dear lover, My dearest, You are so fine and so powerful. Where have You gone? I am nothing but Your most obedient maidservant. I am very much aggrieved. Please come and be with Me again.' Kṛṣṇa, however, is not coming to Her. He must be watching Her from a distant place and enjoying Her sorrow."

All the *gopīs* then went further and further into the forest, searching out Kṛṣṇa, but when they learned that actually Rādhārāṇī was left alone by Kṛṣṇa, they became very sorry. This is the test of Kṛṣṇa consciousness. In the beginning they were a little envious that Kṛṣṇa had taken Rādhārāṇī alone, leaving aside all the other *gopīs*, but as soon as they knew that Kṛṣṇa had also left Rādhārāṇī and that She was alone lamenting for Him, they became more sympathetic to Her. The *gopīs* found Rādhārāṇī and heard everything from Her—about how She had misbehaved with Kṛṣṇa and how She was proud and was insulted for Her pride. After hearing all this, they became actually very sympathetic. Then all the *gopīs*, including Rādhārāṇī, proceeded further into the forest, until they could no longer see the moonlight. When they saw that it was getting gradually darker, they stopped. Their mind and intelligence became absorbed in thoughts of Kṛṣṇa; they all imitated the activities of Kṛṣṇa and His speeches. Due to their heart and soul being completely given to Kṛṣṇa, they began to chant His glories, completely forgetting their family interests. In this way, all the *gopīs* returned to the bank of the Yamunā and assembled there, and expecting that Kṛṣṇa must return to them, they simply engaged in chanting the glories of Śrī Kṛṣṇa—Hare Kṛṣṇa, Hare Kṛṣṇa, Kṛṣṇa Kṛṣṇa, Hare Hare/ Hare Rāma, Hare Rāma, Rāma Rāma, Hare Hare.

Thus ends the Bhaktivedanta purport of the Thirtieth Chapter of Kṛṣṇa, *"Kṛṣṇa's Hiding from the* Gopīs."

CHAPTER 31

Songs by the Gopīs

ONE *GOPĪ* SAID, "My dear Kṛṣṇa, ever since You took Your birth in this land of Vrajabhūmi, everything appears to be glorious. The land of Vṛndāvana has become glorious, and it is as if the goddess of fortune is personally always existing here. But it is only we who are very unhappy, because we are searching for You but cannot see You with our greatest effort. Our life is completely dependent upon You; therefore we request that You again come to us."

Another *gopī* said, "My dear Kṛṣṇa, You are the life and soul even of the lotus flower that grows on the water of lakes made transparent by the clear rains of autumn. Although the lotus flowers are so beautiful, without Your glance they fade away. Similarly, without You, we are also dying. Actually, we are not Your wives but are Your slaves. You never spent any money for us, yet we are simply attracted by Your glance. Now, if we die without receiving Your glance, You'll be responsible for our deaths. Certainly the killing of women is a great sin, and if You do not come to see us and we die, You will suffer the reactions of sin. So please come see us. Do not think that one can be killed only by certain weapons. We are being killed by Your absence. You should consider how You are responsible for killing women. We are always grateful to You because You have protected us many times: from the poisonous water of the Yamunā, from the serpent Kāliya, from Bakāsura, from the anger of Indra and his torrents of rain, from the forest fire and so many other incidents. You are the greatest and most powerful of all. It is wonderful for You to protect us from so many dangers, but we are surprised that You are neglecting us at this moment.

"Dear Kṛṣṇa, dear friend, we know very well that You are not actually the son of mother Yaśodā or the cowherd man Nanda Mahārāja. You are the Supreme Personality of Godhead and the Supersoul of all living entities. You have, out of Your own causeless mercy, appeared in this world, requested by Lord Brahmā for the protection of the world. It is by Your kindness only that You have appeared in the dynasty of Yadu. O best in the dynasty of Yadu, if anyone afraid of this materialistic way of life takes shelter at Your lotus feet, You never deny him protection. Your movements are sweet, and You are independent, touching the goddess of fortune with one hand and in the other bearing a lotus flower. That is Your extraordinary feature. Please, therefore, come before us and bless us with the lotus flower in Your hand.

"Dear Kṛṣṇa, You are the killer of all the fears of the inhabitants of Vṛndāvana. You are the supremely powerful hero, and we know that You can kill the unnecessary pride of Your devotees, as well as the pride of women like us, simply by Your beautiful smile. We are simply Your maidservants and slaves; please, therefore, accept us by showing us Your beautiful lotuslike face.

"Dear Kṛṣṇa, actually we have become very lusty, having been touched by Your lotus feet. Your lotus feet certainly kill all kinds of sinful activities of devotees who have taken shelter there. You are so kind that even the ordinary animals take shelter under Your lotus feet. Your lotus feet are also the residence of the goddess of fortune, yet You danced on the heads of the Kāliya serpent with them. Now we are requesting You to kindly place Your lotus feet on our breasts and pacify our lusty desires to touch You.

"O Lord, Your attractive eyes, like the lotus, are so nice and pleasing. Your sweet words are so fascinating that they please even the greatest scholars, who also become attracted to You. We are also attracted by Your speaking and by the beauty of Your face and eyes. Please, therefore, satisfy us by Your nectarean kisses. Dear Lord, words spoken by You or words describing Your activities are full of nectar, and simply by speaking or hearing Your words one can be saved from the blazing fire of material existence. Great demigods like Lord Brahmā and Lord Śiva are always engaged in chanting the glories of Your words. They do so to eradicate the sinful activities of all living entities in the material world. If one simply tries to hear Your transcendental words, he can very quickly be elevated to the platform of pious activities. For the Vaiṣṇavas, Your words give transcendental pleasure, and saintly persons who are engaged in distributing Your transcendental message all over the world are first-class charitable persons." (This was confirmed by Rūpa Gosvāmī when he addressed Lord Caitanya as the most munificent incarnation because He distributed the words of Kṛṣṇa and love of Kṛṣṇa free of charge all over the world.)

"Dear Kṛṣṇa," the *gopīs* continued, "You are very cunning. You can imagine how much we are distressed simply by remembering Your cunning smile, Your pleasing glance, Your walking with us in the forest of Vṛndāvana and Your auspicious meditations. Your talks with us in lonely places were heartwarming. Now we are all aggrieved to remember Your behavior. Please save us. Dear Kṛṣṇa, certainly You know how much we are saddened when You go out of Vṛndāvana village to tend the cows in the forest. How we are afflicted simply to think that Your soft lotus feet are being pricked by the dry grass and the tiny stones in the forest! We are so attached to You that we always think simply of Your lotus feet.

"O Kṛṣṇa, when You return from the pasturing ground with the animals, we see Your face covered by Your curly hair and dusted by the hoof dust of the cows. We see Your mildly smiling face, and our desire to enjoy You increases. O dear Kṛṣṇa, You are the supreme lover, and You always give shelter to surrendered souls. You fulfill everyone's desire; Your lotus feet are worshiped even by Lord Brahmā, the creator of the universe. To whoever worships Your lotus feet, You without a doubt always bestow Your benedictions. So kindly be pleased with us and keep Your lotus feet on our breasts and thus relieve our present distresses. Dear Kṛṣṇa, we are seeking Your kisses, which You offer even to Your flute. The vibration of Your flute enchants the whole world and our hearts also. Kindly, therefore, return and kiss us with Your mouth of nectar."

Thus ends the Bhaktivedanta purport of the Thirty-first Chapter of Kṛṣṇa, *"Songs by the* Gopīs."

CHAPTER 32

Kṛṣṇa Returns to the Gopīs

WHEN LORD KṚṢṆA FINALLY REAPPEARED among the assembled *gopīs,* He looked very beautiful, just befitting a person with all kinds of opulences. In the *Brahma-saṁhitā* it is stated, *ānanda-cin-maya-rasa-pratibhāvitābhiḥ:* Kṛṣṇa alone is not particularly beautiful, but when His energy—especially His pleasure energy, represented by Rādhārāṇī—expands, He looks very magnificent. The Māyāvāda conception of perfection—an Absolute Truth without potency—is due to insufficient knowledge. Actually, outside the exhibition of His different potencies, the Absolute Truth is not complete. *Ānanda-cin-maya-rasa* means that His body is a transcendental form of eternal bliss and knowledge. Kṛṣṇa is always surrounded by different potencies, and therefore He is perfect and beautiful. We understand from the *Brahma-saṁhitā* and *Skanda Purāṇa* that Kṛṣṇa is always surrounded by many thousands of goddesses of fortune. The *gopīs* are all goddesses of fortune, and Kṛṣṇa took them hand in hand on the bank of the Yamunā.

It is said in the *Skanda Purāṇa* that out of many thousands of *gopīs,* 16,000 are prominent, out of those 16,000, 108 are especially prominent, out of these 108 *gopīs,* eight *gopīs* are still more prominent, out of those eight *gopīs,* Rādhārāṇī and Candrāvalī are even more prominent, and out of these two *gopīs,* Rādhārāṇī is the most prominent.

When Kṛṣṇa entered the forest on the bank of the river Yamunā, the moonlight dissipated the surrounding darkness. Due to the season, flowers like the *kunda* and *kadamba* were blooming, and a gentle breeze was carrying their aroma. Due to the aroma, the bees were also flying in the breeze, thinking that the aroma was honey. The *gopīs* made a seat for Kṛṣṇa by leveling the soft sand and placing cloths over it.

The *gopīs* who were gathered there had almost all been followers of the *Vedas.* In their previous births, during Lord Rāmacandra's advent, they had been Vedic scholars who desired the association of Lord Rāmacandra in conjugal love. Rāmacandra had given them the benediction that they would be present for the advent of Lord Kṛṣṇa and He would fulfill their desires. During Kṛṣṇa's advent, the Vedic scholars took birth in the shape of the *gopīs* in Vṛndāvana; as young *gopīs,* they got the association of Kṛṣṇa in fulfillment of their previous birth's desire. The ultimate goal of their perfect desire was attained, and they were so joyous that they had nothing further to desire. This is confirmed in the *Bhagavad-gītā:* if one attains the Supreme Personality of Godhead, then he has no desire for anything. When the *gopīs* had Kṛṣṇa in their company, not only all their grief but their lamenting in the absence of Kṛṣṇa was relieved. They felt they had no desire to be fulfilled. Fully satisfied in the company of Kṛṣṇa, they spread their cloths on the ground. These garments were made of fine linen and smeared with the red *kuṅkuma* which decorated their breasts. With great care they spread a sitting place for Kṛṣṇa. Kṛṣṇa was their life and soul, and they created a very comfortable seat for Him.

Sitting on the seat amongst the *gopīs,* Kṛṣṇa became more beautiful. Great *yogīs* like Lord Śiva, Lord Brahmā or even Lord Śeṣa and others always try to fix their attention upon Kṛṣṇa in their hearts, but here the *gopīs* actually saw Kṛṣṇa seated before them on their cloths. In the society of the *gopīs,* Kṛṣṇa looked very beautiful. They were the most beautiful damsels within the three worlds, and they assembled together around Kṛṣṇa.

Kṛṣṇa seated Himself beside each of the many *gopīs,* and it may be asked herein how He did this. There is a significant word in this verse: *īśvara.* As it is stated in the *Bhagavad-gītā, īśvaraḥ sarva-bhūtānām. Īśvara* refers to the Supreme Lord as the Supersoul seated in everyone's heart. Kṛṣṇa also manifested this potency of expansion as Paramātmā in this gathering with the *gopīs.* Kṛṣṇa was sitting by the side of each *gopī,* unseen by the others. Kṛṣṇa was so kind to the *gopīs* that instead of sitting in their hearts to be appreciated in yogic meditation, He seated Himself by their sides. By seating Himself outside, He showed special favor to the *gopīs,* who were the selected beauties of all creation. Having gotten their most beloved Lord, the *gopīs* began to please Him by moving their eyebrows and smiling and also by suppressing their anger. Some of them took His lotus feet in their laps and massaged them. And while smiling, they confidentially expressed their suppressed anger and said, "Dear Kṛṣṇa, we are ordinary women of Vṛndāvana, and we do not know much about Vedic knowledge—what is right and what is wrong. We therefore put a question to You, and, since You are very learned, You can answer it properly. In dealings between lovers, we find that there are three classes of men. One class simply receives, another class reciprocates favorably, even if the lover is very contrary, and the third class neither acts contrary nor answers favorably in dealings of love. So out of these three classes, which do You prefer, or which do You call honest?"

In answer, Kṛṣṇa said, "My dear friends, persons who simply reciprocate the loving dealings of the other party are just like merchants. They give in loving affairs as much as they get from the other party. Practically there is no question of love. It is simply self-interested or self-centered business dealing. Even those without a tinge of loving affairs are better than these merchants. Better than the first class is the second class of men, who love in spite of the opposite party's contrariness. Such sincere love can be seen when the father and mother love their children in spite of their children's neglect. The third class neither reciprocates nor neglects. They can be further divided into two classes. One comprises the self-satisfied, who do not require anyone's love. They are called *ātmārāma,* which means they are absorbed in the thought of the Supreme Personality of Godhead and so do not care whether one loves them or not. But another class comprises ungrateful men. They are called callous. The men in this group revolt against superior persons. For instance, a son, in spite of receiving all kinds of things from loving parents, may be callous and not reciprocate. Those in this class are generally known as *guru-druhaḥ,* which means they receive favors from the parents or the spiritual master and yet neglect them."

Kṛṣṇa indirectly answered the questions of the *gopīs,* even those questions which implied that Kṛṣṇa did not properly reciprocate their dealings. In answer, Kṛṣṇa said that He, as the Supreme Personality of Godhead, is self-satisfied. He does not require anyone's love, but at the same time He said that He is not ungrateful.

"My dear friends," Kṛṣṇa continued, "you might be aggrieved by My words and acts, but you must know that sometimes I do not reciprocate My devotees' dealings with Me. My devotees are very much attached to Me, but sometimes I do not reciprocate their feelings properly in order to increase their love for Me more and more. If I can very easily be approached by them, they might think, 'Kṛṣṇa is so easily available.' So sometimes I do not respond. If a person has no money but after some time accumulates some wealth and then loses it, he will think of the lost property twenty-four hours a day. Similarly, in order to increase the love of My devotees, sometimes I appear to be lost to them, and instead of forgetting Me, they feel their loving sentiments for Me increase. My dear friends, do not think for a moment that I have been dealing with you as I do with ordinary devotees. I know what you are. You have forsaken all kinds of social and religious obligations; you have given up all connection with your parents.

Without caring for social convention and religious obligations, you have come to Me and loved Me, and I am so much obliged to you that I cannot treat you as ordinary devotees. Do not think that I was away from you. I was near to you. I was simply seeing how much you were anxious for Me in My absence. So please do not try to find fault with Me. Because you consider Me so dear to you, kindly excuse Me if I have done anything wrong. I cannot repay your continuous love for Me, even throughout the lifetimes of the demigods in the heavenly planets. It is impossible to repay you or show enough gratitude for your love; therefore please be satisfied by your own pious activities. You have displayed exemplary attraction for Me, overcoming the greatest difficulties arising from family connections. Please be satisfied with your highly exemplary character, for it is not possible for Me to repay My debt to you."

The exemplary character of devotional service manifested by the devotees of Vṛndāvana is the purest type of devotion. It is enjoined in authoritative *śāstras* that devotional service must be *ahaitukī* and *apratihatā*. This means that devotional service to Kṛṣṇa cannot be checked by political or religious convention. The stage of devotional service is always transcendental. The *gopīs* particularly showed pure devotional service toward Kṛṣṇa, so much so that Kṛṣṇa Himself remained indebted to them. Lord Caitanya thus said that the devotional service manifested by the *gopīs* in Vṛndāvana excelled all other methods of approaching the Supreme Personality of Godhead.

Thus ends the Bhaktivedanta purport of the Thirty-second Chapter of Kṛṣṇa, *"Kṛṣṇa Returns to the* Gopīs."

CHAPTER 33

Description of the Rāsa Dance

THUS HEARING the Supreme Personality of Godhead, Kṛṣṇa, speaking to pacify them, the *gopīs* became very pleased. They became completely relieved of the great suffering of separation, not only by hearing the words of the Supreme Personality of Godhead but also by touching His hands and legs. After this, the Supreme Personality of Godhead began His *rāsa* dance. A dance in the midst of many girls is called a *rāsa* dance. So Kṛṣṇa began to dance among the most beautiful and fortunate girls within the three worlds. The *gopīs* of Vṛndāvana, who were so attracted to Him, danced with Kṛṣṇa, hand in hand.

Kṛṣṇa's *rāsa* dance should never be compared to any kind of material dance, such as a ball dance or a society dance. The *rāsa* dance is a completely spiritual performance. In order to establish this fact, Kṛṣṇa, the supreme mystic, expanded Himself into many forms and stood beside each *gopī*. Placing His hands on the shoulders of the *gopīs* on both sides of Him, He began to dance in their midst. The mystic expansions of Kṛṣṇa were not perceived by the *gopīs* because Kṛṣṇa appeared alone to each of them. Each *gopī* thought that Kṛṣṇa was dancing with her alone. Above that wonderful dance flew many airplanes carrying the denizens of the heavenly planets, who were very eager to see the wonderful dance of Kṛṣṇa with the *gopīs*. The Gandharvas and Kinnaras began to sing, and, accompanied by their respective wives, all the Gandharvas began to shower flowers on the dancers.

As the *gopīs* and Kṛṣṇa danced together, a very blissful musical sound was produced from the tinkling of their bells, ornaments and bangles. It appeared that Kṛṣṇa was a greenish sapphire locket in the midst of a golden necklace decorated with valuable stones. While Kṛṣṇa and the *gopīs* danced, they displayed extraordinary bodily features. The movements of their legs, their placing their hands on one another, the movements of their eyebrows, their smiling, the movements of the breasts of the *gopīs* and their clothes, their earrings, their cheeks, their hair with flowers—as they sang and danced these combined to appear like clouds, thunder, snow and lightning. Kṛṣṇa's bodily features appeared just like a group of clouds, the *gopīs'* songs were like thunder, their beauty appeared to be just like lightning in the sky, and the drops of perspiration visible on their faces appeared like falling snow. In this way, the *gopīs* and Kṛṣṇa fully engaged in dancing.

The necks of the *gopīs* became tinted with red due to their desire to enjoy Kṛṣṇa more and more. To satisfy them, Kṛṣṇa began to clap His hands in time with their singing. Actually the whole world is full of Kṛṣṇa's singing, but it is appreciated in different ways by different kinds of living entities. This is confirmed in the *Bhagavad-gītā: ye yathā māṁ prapadyante tāṁs tathaiva bhajāmy aham.* Kṛṣṇa is dancing, and every living entity is also dancing, but there is a difference between the dancing in the spiritual world and that in the material world. This is expressed by the author of the *Caitanya-caritāmṛta,* who says that the master dancer is Kṛṣṇa and everyone else is His servant. Everyone is trying to imitate Kṛṣṇa's dancing. Those who are actually in Kṛṣṇa consciousness respond rightly to the dancing of Kṛṣṇa: they do not try to dance independently. But those in the material world try to imitate Kṛṣṇa as the Supreme Personality of Godhead. The living entities are dancing under the direction of Kṛṣṇa's *māyā* and are thinking that they are equal to Kṛṣṇa. But this is not a fact. In Kṛṣṇa consciousness, this misconception is absent, for a person in Kṛṣṇa consciousness knows that Kṛṣṇa is the supreme master and everyone else is His servant. One has to dance to please Kṛṣṇa, not to imitate or attempt to become equal to the Supreme Personality of Godhead. The *gopīs* wanted to please Kṛṣṇa, and therefore as Kṛṣṇa sang, they responded and encouraged Him by saying, "Well done! Well done!" Sometimes they presented beautiful music for His pleasure, and He responded by praising their singing.

When some of the *gopīs* became very tired from dancing and moving their bodies, they placed their hands on the shoulders of Śrī Kṛṣṇa. Then their hair loosened and flowers fell to the ground. When they placed their hands on Kṛṣṇa's shoulder, they became overwhelmed by the fragrance of His body, which emanated from the lotus, other aromatic flowers and the pulp of sandalwood. They became filled with attraction for Him, and they began to kiss Him. Some *gopīs* touched Kṛṣṇa cheek to cheek, and Kṛṣṇa began to offer them chewed betel nuts from His mouth, which they accepted with great pleasure by kissing. And by accepting those betel nuts, the *gopīs* spiritually advanced.

The *gopīs* became tired after long singing and dancing. Kṛṣṇa was dancing beside them, and to alleviate their fatigue they took Śrī Kṛṣṇa's hand and placed it on their raised breasts. Kṛṣṇa's hand, as well as the breasts of the *gopīs,* are eternally auspicious; therefore when they combined, both of them became spiritually enhanced. The *gopīs* so enjoyed the company of Kṛṣṇa, the husband of the goddess of fortune, that they forgot that they had any other husbands in the world, and upon being embraced by the arms of Kṛṣṇa and dancing and singing with Him, they forgot everything. *Śrīmad-Bhāgavatam* thus describes the beauty of the *gopīs* while they were *rāsa* dancing with Kṛṣṇa. There were lotus flowers over both their ears, and their faces were decorated with sandalwood pulp. They wore *tilaka,* and there were drops of perspiration on their smiling mouths. From their feet came the tinkling sound of ankle bells and bangles. The flowers within their hair were falling to the lotus feet of Kṛṣṇa, and He was very satisfied.

As stated in the *Brahma-saṁhitā,* all these *gopīs* are expansions of Kṛṣṇa's pleasure potency. Touching their bodies with His hands and looking at their pleasing eyes, Kṛṣṇa enjoyed the *gopīs* exactly as a child enjoys playing with the reflection of his body in a mirror. When Kṛṣṇa touched the different parts of their bodies, the *gopīs* felt surcharged with spiritual energy. They could not adjust their loosened clothes, although they tried to keep them adjusted properly. Their hair and garments became scattered, and their ornaments loosened as they forgot themselves in the company of Kṛṣṇa.

While Kṛṣṇa was enjoying the company of the *gopīs* in the *rāsa* dance, the astonished demigods and their wives gathered in the sky. The moon, being afflicted with a sort of lust, began to watch the dance and became stunned with wonder. The *gopīs* had prayed to the goddess Kātyāyanī to have Kṛṣṇa as their husband. Now Kṛṣṇa was fulfilling their desire by expanding Himself in as many forms as there were *gopīs* and enjoying them exactly like a husband.

Śrīla Śukadeva Gosvāmī has remarked that Kṛṣṇa is self-sufficient—He is *ātmārāma.* He doesn't need anyone else for His satisfaction. Because the *gopīs* wanted Kṛṣṇa as their husband, He fulfilled their desire. When Kṛṣṇa saw that the *gopīs* were tired from dancing with Him, He immediately began to wipe His hands over their faces so that their fatigue would be relieved. In order to reciprocate the kind hospitality of Kṛṣṇa, the *gopīs* began to look at Him lovingly. They were overjoyed by the auspicious touch of the hand of Kṛṣṇa. Their smiling cheeks shone with beauty, and they began to sing the glories of Kṛṣṇa with transcendental pleasure. As pure devotees, the more the *gopīs* enjoyed Kṛṣṇa's company, the more they became enlightened with His glories, and thus they reciprocated with Him. They wanted to satisfy Kṛṣṇa by glorifying His transcendental pastimes. Kṛṣṇa is the Supreme Personality of Godhead, the master of all masters, and the *gopīs* wanted to worship Him for His unusual exhibition of mercy upon them.

The *gopīs* and Kṛṣṇa entered the water of the Yamunā just to relieve their fatigue from the *rāsa* dance. The lily-flower garlands around the necks of the *gopīs* were strewn to pieces due to the *gopis'* embracing the body of Kṛṣṇa, and the flowers were reddish from being smeared with the *kuṅkuma* on their breasts. The bumblebees were humming about in order to get honey from the flowers. Kṛṣṇa and the *gopīs* entered the water of the Yamunā just as an elephant enters a water tank with his many female companions. Both the *gopīs* and Kṛṣṇa forgot their real identities, playing in the water, enjoying each other's company and relieving the fatigue of *rāsa* dancing. The *gopīs* began to splash water on the body of Kṛṣṇa, all the while smiling, and Kṛṣṇa enjoyed this. As Kṛṣṇa was taking pleasure in the joking words and splashing water, the demigods in the heavenly planets showered flowers. The demigods thus praised the superexcellent *rāsa* dance of Kṛṣṇa, the supreme enjoyer, and His pastimes with the *gopīs* in the water of the Yamunā.

After this, Lord Kṛṣṇa and the *gopīs* came out of the water and began to stroll along the bank of the Yamunā, where a nice breeze was blowing, carrying the aroma of different kinds of flowers over the water and land. While strolling on the bank of the Yamunā, Kṛṣṇa recited various kinds of poetry. He thus enjoyed the company of the *gopīs* in the soothing moonlight of autumn.

Sex desire is especially excited in the autumn season, but the wonderful thing about Kṛṣṇa's association with the *gopīs* is that there was no question of sex desire. It was, as clearly stated in the *Bhāgavata* description by Śukadeva Gosvāmī, *avaruddha-saurata*—the sex impulse was completely controlled. There is a distinction between Lord Kṛṣṇa's dancing with the *gopīs* and the ordinary dancing of living entities within the material world. In order to clear up further misconceptions about the *rāsa* dance and the affairs of Kṛṣṇa and the *gopīs,* Mahārāja Parīkṣit, the hearer of *Śrīmad-Bhāgavatam,* told Śukadeva Gosvāmī, "Kṛṣṇa appeared on the earth to establish the regulative principles of religion and to curb the predominance of irreligion. But the behavior of Kṛṣṇa and the *gopīs* might encourage irreligious principles in the material world. I am simply surprised that He would act in such a way, enjoying the company of others' wives in the dead of night." This statement of Mahārāja Parīkṣit's was very much appreciated by Śukadeva Gosvāmī. The answer anticipates the abominable acts of the Māyāvādī impersonalists who place themselves in the position of Kṛṣṇa and enjoy the company of young girls and women.

The basic Vedic injunctions never allow a person to enjoy sex with any woman except his own wife. Kṛṣṇa's appreciation of the *gopīs* appeared to be distinctly in violation of these rules. Mahārāja Parīkṣit understood the total situation from Śukadeva

Gosvāmī, yet to further clarify the transcendental nature of Kṛṣṇa and the *gopīs* in the *rāsa* dance, he expressed his surprise. This is very important in order to check the unrestricted association with women by the *prākṛta-sahajiyās.*

In his statement, Mahārāja Parīkṣit has used several important words which require clarification. The first word, *jugupsitam,* means "abominable." The first doubt of Mahārāja Parīkṣit was as follows: Lord Kṛṣṇa is the Supreme Personality of Godhead, who had advented Himself to establish religious principles. Why then did He mix with others' wives in the dead of night and enjoy dancing, embracing and kissing? According to the Vedic injunctions, this is not allowed. Also, when the *gopīs* first came to Him, He gave instructions to them to return to their homes. To call the wives of other persons or young girls and enjoy dancing with them is certainly abominable according to the *Vedas.* Why should Kṛṣṇa have done this?

Another word used here is *āpta-kāma.* Some may take it for granted that Kṛṣṇa was very lusty among young girls, but Parīkṣit Mahārāja said that this was not possible. He could not be lusty. First of all, from the material calculation He was only eight years old. At that age a boy cannot be lusty. *Āpta-kāma* means that the Supreme Personality of Godhead is self-satisfied. Even if He were lusty, He doesn't need to take help from others to satisfy His lusty desires. The next point is that, although not lusty Himself, He might have been seduced by the lusty desires of the *gopīs.* But Mahārāja Parīkṣit then used another word, *yadu-pati,* which indicates that Kṛṣṇa is the most exalted personality in the dynasty of the Yadus. The kings in the dynasty of Yadu were considered to be the most pious, and their descendants were also like that. Having taken birth in that family, how could Kṛṣṇa have been seduced, even by the *gopīs*? It is concluded, therefore, that it was not possible for Kṛṣṇa to do anything abominable. But Mahārāja Parīkṣit was in doubt as to why Kṛṣṇa acted in that way. What was the real purpose?

Another word Mahārāja Parīkṣit used when he addressed Śukadeva Gosvāmī is *suvrata,* which means to take a vow to enact pious activities. Śukadeva Gosvāmī was an educated *brahmacārī,* and under the circumstances it was not possible for him to indulge in sex. This is strictly prohibited for *brahmacārīs,* and what to speak of a *brahmacārī* like Śukadeva Gosvāmī. But because the circumstances of the *rāsa* dance were very suspect, Mahārāja Parīkṣit inquired for clarification from Śukadeva Gosvāmī. Śukadeva Gosvāmī immediately replied that transgressions of religious principles by the supreme controller testify to His great power. For example, fire can consume any abominable thing; that is the manifestation of the supremacy of fire. Similarly, the sun can absorb water from a urinal or from stool, and the sun is not polluted; rather, due to the influence of the sunshine, the polluted, contaminated place becomes disinfected and sterilized.

One may also argue that since Kṛṣṇa is the supreme authority, His activities should be followed. In answer to this argument, Śukadeva Gosvāmī has very clearly said that the *īśvara,* or supreme controller, may sometimes violate His own instructions, but this is possible only for the controller Himself, not for the followers. Unusual and uncommon activities by the controller can never be imitated. Śukadeva Gosvāmī warned that the conditioned followers, who are not actually in control, should never even imagine imitating the uncommon activities of the controller. A Māyāvādī philosopher may falsely claim to be God or Kṛṣṇa, but he cannot actually act like Kṛṣṇa. He can persuade his followers to falsely imitate the *rāsa* dance, but he is unable to lift Govardhana Hill. We have many experiences in the past of Māyāvādī rascals who delude their followers by posing themselves as Kṛṣṇa in order to enjoy *rāsa-līlā.* In many instances they were checked by the government, arrested and punished. In Orissa, Ṭhākura Bhaktivinoda punished a so-called incarnation of Viṣṇu who was imitating the *rāsa-līlā* with young girls. There were many complaints against the so-called incarnation. At that time Bhaktivinoda Ṭhākura was a magistrate, and the government deputed him to deal with that rascal, and he punished him very severely. The *rāsa-līlā* dance cannot be imitated by anyone. Śukadeva Gosvāmī warns that one should not even think of imitating it. He specifically mentions that if, out of foolishness, one tries to imitate Kṛṣṇa's *rāsa* dance, he will be killed, just like a person who wants to imitate Lord Śiva's drinking of an ocean of poison. Lord Śiva drank an ocean of poison and kept it within his throat. The poison made his throat turn blue, and therefore Lord Śiva is called Nīlakaṇṭha. But if any ordinary person tries to imitate Lord Śiva by drinking poison or smoking *gañjā,* he is sure to be vanquished and will die within a very short time. Lord Śrī Kṛṣṇa's dealings with the *gopīs* occurred under special circumstances.

Most of the *gopīs* in their previous lives were great sages, expert in the study of the *Vedas,* and when Lord Kṛṣṇa appeared as Lord Rāmacandra they wanted to enjoy with Him. Lord Rāmacandra gave them the benediction that their desires would be fulfilled when He would appear as Kṛṣṇa. Therefore the desire of the *gopīs* to enjoy the appearance of Lord Kṛṣṇa was long cherished. So they approached goddess Kātyāyanī to have Kṛṣṇa as their husband. There are many other circumstances which also testify to the supreme authority of Kṛṣṇa and show that He is not bound by the rules and regulations of the material world. In special cases, He acts as He likes to favor His devotees. This is possible only for Him, because He is the supreme controller. People in general should follow the instructions of Lord Kṛṣṇa as given in the *Bhagavad-gītā* and should not even imagine imitating Lord Kṛṣṇa in the *rāsa* dance.

Kṛṣṇa's lifting of Govardhana Hill and His killing of great demons like Pūtanā are all obviously extraordinary activities. Similarly, the *rāsa* dance is also an uncommon activity and cannot be imitated by any ordinary man. An ordinary person engaged in his occupational duty, like Arjuna, should execute his duty for the satisfaction of Kṛṣṇa; that is within his power. Arjuna was a fighter, and Kṛṣṇa wanted him to fight for His satisfaction. Arjuna agreed, although at first he was not willing to fight. Duties are required for ordinary persons. They should not jump up and try to imitate Kṛṣṇa and indulge in *rāsa-līlā* and thus bring about their ruin. One should know with certainty that Kṛṣṇa had no personal interest in whatever He did for the benediction of the *gopīs*. As stated in the *Bhagavad-gītā, na māṁ karmāṇi limpanti:* Kṛṣṇa never enjoys or suffers the results of His activities. Therefore it is not possible for Him to act irreligiously. He is transcendental to all religious duties and principles. He is untouched by the modes of material nature. He is the supreme controller of all living entities, whether in human society, in demigod society in the heavenly planets, or in lower forms of life, and He is also the supreme controller of material nature; therefore, He has nothing to do with religious or irreligious principles.

Śukadeva Gosvāmī further concludes that the great sages and devotees, who are washed clean of all conditioned life, can move freely even within the contamination of material nature by keeping Kṛṣṇa, the Supreme Personality of Godhead, within their hearts. In this way they also do not become subject to the laws of pleasure and pain in the modes of material nature. How, then, is it possible for Kṛṣṇa, who appears by His own internal potency, to be subjected to the laws of *karma*?

In the *Bhagavad-gītā* the Lord clearly says that whenever He appears He does so by His internal potency; He is not forced to accept a body by the laws of *karma*, like an ordinary living entity. Every other living entity is forced to accept a certain type of body by his previous actions. But when Kṛṣṇa appears, He always appears in a body that is not forced upon Him by the action of His past deeds. His body is a vehicle for His transcendental pleasure pastimes, which are enacted by His internal potency. He has no obligation to the laws of *karma*. The Māyāvādī monist must accept a certain type of body, being forced by the laws of nature; therefore, his claim to being one with Kṛṣṇa, or God, is only theoretical. Such persons who claim to be equal with Kṛṣṇa and indulge in *rāsa-līlā* create a dangerous situation for the people in general. Kṛṣṇa, the Supreme Personality of Godhead, was already present as the Supersoul within the bodies of the *gopīs* and their husbands. He is the guide of all living entities, as is confirmed in the *Kaṭha Upaniṣad: nityo nityānāṁ cetanaś cetanānām.* The Supersoul directs the individual soul to act, and the Supersoul is the actor and witness of all action.

It is confirmed in the *Bhagavad-gītā* that Kṛṣṇa is present in everyone's heart and from Him come all knowledge, remembrance and forgetfulness. He is the original person to be known by Vedic knowledge. He is the author of the Vedānta philosophy, and He knows the Vedānta philosophy perfectly well. The so-called Vedāntists and Māyāvādīs cannot understand Kṛṣṇa as He is; they simply mislead their followers by imitating the actions of Kṛṣṇa in an unauthorized way. Kṛṣṇa, the Supersoul of everyone, is already within the body of everyone; therefore if He sees someone or embraces someone there is no question of impropriety.

Some ask that if Kṛṣṇa is self-sufficient, why did He at all manifest the pastimes with the *gopīs,* which are disturbing to the so-called moralists of the world? The answer is that such activities show special mercy to the fallen, conditioned souls. The *gopīs* are expansions of His internal energy, but because Kṛṣṇa wanted to exhibit the *rāsa-līlā,* they appeared as ordinary human beings. In the material world, pleasure is ultimately manifested in the sex attraction between man and woman. The man lives simply to be attracted by women, and the woman lives simply to be attracted by men. That is the basic principle of material life. As soon as these attractions are combined, people become more and more implicated in material existence. In order to show them special favor, Kṛṣṇa exhibited this *rāsa-līlā* dance. It is just to captivate the conditioned soul. Since they are very much attracted by sex, they can enjoy the same life with Kṛṣṇa and thus become liberated from the material condition. In the Second Canto of *Śrīmad-Bhāgavatam,* Mahārāja Parīkṣit also explains that the pastimes and activities of Lord Kṛṣṇa are medicine for the conditioned souls. If they simply hear about Kṛṣṇa, they become relieved of the material disease. They are addicted to material enjoyment and are accustomed to reading sex literature, but by hearing these transcendental pastimes of Kṛṣṇa with the *gopīs,* they will be relieved of material contamination.

How they should hear and from whom is also explained by Śukadeva Gosvāmī. The difficulty is that the whole world is full of Māyāvādīs, and when they become professional reciters of *Śrīmad-Bhāgavatam,* and when people, without knowing the effect of the Māyāvāda philosophy, hear from such persons, they become confused. Discussion of the *rāsa-līlā* among people in general is discouraged because they are affected by the Māyāvāda philosophy, but if one who is advanced explains and people hear from him, certainly the hearers will be gradually elevated to the position of Kṛṣṇa consciousness and liberated from materially contaminated life.

Another important point is that none of the *gopīs* who danced with Kṛṣṇa were in their material bodies. They danced with Kṛṣṇa in their spiritual bodies. All their husbands thought that their wives were sleeping by their sides. The so-called husbands of the *gopīs* were already enamored with the influence of the external energy of Kṛṣṇa; so by dint of this very energy they could not understand that their wives had gone to dance with Kṛṣṇa. What then is the basis of accusing Kṛṣṇa of dancing with others' wives? The bodies of the *gopīs,* which were their husbands', were lying in bed, but the spiritual parts and parcels of Kṛṣṇa were dancing with Him. Kṛṣṇa is the supreme person, the whole spirit, and He danced with the spiritual bodies of the *gopīs.* There is therefore no reason to accuse Kṛṣṇa in any way.

After the *rāsa* dance was over, the night (the night of Brahmā, a very, very long period, as mentioned in the *Bhagavad-gītā*) turned into the *brāhma-muhūrta.* The *brāhma-muhūrta* takes place about one and a half hours before sunrise. It is recommended that one should rise from bed at that time and, after finishing daily ablutions, take to spiritual activities by performing *maṅgala-ārati* and chanting the Hare Kṛṣṇa *mantra.* This period is very convenient for the execution of spiritual activities. When that auspicious moment arrived, Kṛṣṇa asked the *gopīs* to leave. Although His beloveds were not willing to quit His company, they were very obedient to Him. As soon as Kṛṣṇa asked them to go home, they immediately left and returned home. Śukadeva Gosvāmī concludes this episode of the *rāsa-līlā* by pointing out that if a person hears from the right source about the pastimes of Kṛṣṇa, who is Viṣṇu Himself, and the *gopīs,* who are expansions of His energy, then he will be relieved of the most dangerous type of disease, namely lust. In other words, one who actually hears the *rāsa-līlā* will become completely freed from the lusty desire of sex life and elevated to the highest level of spiritual understanding. Generally, because they hear the *rāsa-līlā* from Māyāvādīs and they themselves are Māyāvādīs, people become more and more implicated in sex life. The conditioned soul should hear the *rāsa-līlā* dance from an authorized spiritual master and be trained by him so that he can understand the whole situation; thus one can be elevated to the highest standard of spiritual life; otherwise one will be implicated. Material lust is a kind of heart disease, and to cure the material heart disease of the conditioned soul, it is recommended that one should hear, but not from the impersonalist rascals. If one hears from the right sources with right understanding, then his situation will be different.

Śukadeva Gosvāmī has used the word *śraddhānvita* for one who is trained in spiritual life. *Śraddhā,* or faith, is the beginning. One who has developed his faith in Kṛṣṇa as the Supreme Personality of Godhead, the Supreme Spirit Soul, can both describe and hear the *rāsa-līlā.* Śukadeva also uses the word *anuśṛṇuyāt.* One must hear from the disciplic succession. *Anu* means "following," and *anu* also means "always." So one must always follow the disciplic succession and not hear from any stray professional reciter, whether a Māyāvādī or an ordinary man. *Anuśṛṇuyāt* means that one must hear from an authorized person who is in the disciplic succession and is always engaged in Kṛṣṇa consciousness. When a person hears the *rāsa-līlā* in this way, the effect will be sure: he will be elevated to the highest position of spiritual life.

Śukadeva Gosvāmī uses two specific words, *bhaktim* and *parām. Bhaktiṁ parām* means execution of devotional service above the neophyte stage. Those who are simply attracted to temple worship but do not know the philosophy of *bhakti* are in the neophyte stage. That sort of *bhakti* is not the perfectional stage. The perfectional stage of *bhakti,* or devotional service, is completely free from material contamination. The most dangerous aspect of contamination is lust, or sex life. *Bhaktiṁ parām* devotional service is so potent that the more one advances in this line, the more he loses his attraction for material life. One who is actually deriving benefit from hearing the *rāsa-līlā* dance surely achieves the transcendental position. He surely loses all traces of lust in his heart.

Śrīla Viśvanātha Cakravartī Ṭhākura points out that according to the *Bhagavad-gītā,* Brahmā's day and Brahmā's night are periods of solar years expanding to 4,300,000 multiplied by 1,000. According to Viśvanātha Cakravartī Ṭhākura, the *rāsa* dance was performed during the long period of Brahmā's night, but the *gopīs* could not understand that. In order to fulfill their desire, Kṛṣṇa extended the night to cover such a great period of time. One may ask how this was possible, and Viśvanātha Cakravartī Ṭhākura reminds us that Kṛṣṇa, although bound by a small rope, could show His mother the whole universe within His mouth. How was this possible? The answer is that He can do anything for the pleasure of His devotees. Similarly, because the *gopīs* wanted to enjoy Kṛṣṇa, they were given the opportunity to associate with Him for a long period. This was done according to His promise. When Kṛṣṇa stole the garments of the *gopīs* while they were taking a bath at Cīraghāṭa on the Yamunā, He promised to fulfill their desire in some future night. In one night, therefore, they enjoyed the company of Kṛṣṇa as their beloved husband, but that night was not an ordinary night. It was a night of Brahmā, and lasted millions and millions of years. Everything is possible for Kṛṣṇa, for He is the supreme controller.

Thus ends the Bhaktivedanta purport of the Thirty-third Chapter of Kṛṣṇa, *"Description of the* Rāsa *Dance."*

CHAPTER 34

Vidyādhara Liberated and the Demon Śaṅkhacūḍa Killed

ONCE UPON A TIME, the cowherd men of Vṛndāvana, headed by Nanda Mahārāja, desired to go to Ambikāvana to observe the Śiva-rātri ceremony. The *rāsa-līlā* was performed during the autumn, and after that the next big ceremony is Holi, or the Dolāyātrā ceremony. Between the Dolāyātrā ceremony and the *rāsa-līlā* ceremony there is one important ceremony called Śiva-rātri, which is especially observed by the Śaivites, or devotees of Lord Śiva. Sometimes the Vaiṣṇavas also observe this ceremony because they accept Lord Śiva as the foremost Vaiṣṇava. But the function of Śiva-rātri is not observed very regularly by the *bhaktas,* or devotees of Kṛṣṇa. Under the circumstances, *Śrīmad-Bhāgavatam* states that Nanda Mahārāja and the other cowherd men "once upon a time desired." This means that they were not regularly observing the Śiva-rātri function but that once upon a time they wanted to go to Ambikāvana out of curiosity. Ambikāvana is somewhere in Gujarat Province, and it is said to be situated on the river Sarasvatī. Yet we do not find any Sarasvatī River in Gujarat Province, although there is a river named Savarmatī. In India, all the big places of pilgrimage are situated on nice rivers like the Ganges, Yamunā, Sarasvatī, Narmadā, Godāvarī and Kāverī. Ambikāvana was situated on the bank of the Sarasvatī, and Nanda Mahārāja and all the other cowherd men went there.

They very devotedly began to worship the deity of Lord Śiva and Ambikā. It is the general practice that wherever there is a temple of Lord Śiva, there must be another temple, of Ambikā (or Durgā), because Ambikā is the wife of Lord Śiva and is the most exalted of chaste women. She doesn't live outside the association of her husband. After reaching Ambikāvana, the cowherd men of Vṛndāvana first bathed themselves in the river Sarasvatī. If one goes to any place of pilgrimage, his first duty is to take a bath and sometimes to shave his head. That is the first business. After taking a bath, they worshiped the deities and then distributed charity in the holy places.

According to the Vedic system, charity is given to the *brāhmaṇas.* It is stated in the Vedic *śāstras* that only the *brāhmaṇas* and the *sannyāsīs* can accept charity. The cowherd men from Vṛndāvana gave the *brāhmaṇas* cows decorated with golden ornaments and beautiful garlands. The *brāhmaṇas* are given charity because they are not engaged in any business profession. They are supposed to be engaged in brahminical occupations, as described in the *Bhagavad-gītā*—namely, they must be very learned and must perform austerity and penances. Not only must they themselves be learned, but they must also teach others. *Brāhmaṇas* are not meant to be *brāhmaṇas* alone: they should create other *brāhmaṇas* also. If a man is found who agrees to become a *brāhmaṇa's* disciple, he is also given the chance to become a *brāhmaṇa.* The *brāhmaṇa* is always engaged in the worship of Lord Viṣṇu. Therefore the *brāhmaṇas* are eligible to accept all kinds of charity. But if the *brāhmaṇas* receive excess charity, they are to distribute it for the service of Viṣṇu. In the Vedic scriptures, therefore, one is recommended to give charity to the *brāhmaṇas,* and by so doing one pleases Lord Viṣṇu and all the demigods.

The pilgrims take a bath, worship the deity and give charity; they are also recommended to fast one day. They should go to a place of pilgrimage and stay there at least for three days. The first day is spent fasting, and at night they can drink a little water because water does not break the fast.

The cowherd men, headed by Nanda Mahārāja, spent that night on the bank of the Sarasvatī. They fasted all day and drank a little water at night. But while they were taking rest, a great serpent from the nearby forest appeared before them and hungrily began to swallow up Nanda Mahārāja. Nanda cried out helplessly, "My dear son, Kṛṣṇa, please come and save me from this danger! This serpent is swallowing me!" When Nanda Mahārāja cried for help, all the cowherd men got up and saw what was happening. They immediately took up burning logs and began to beat the snake to kill it. But in spite of being beaten with burning logs, the serpent was not about to give up swallowing Nanda Mahārāja.

At that time Kṛṣṇa appeared on the scene and touched the serpent with His lotus feet. Immediately upon being touched by the lotus feet of Kṛṣṇa, the serpent shed its reptilian body and appeared as a very beautiful demigod named Vidyādhara. His bodily features were so beautiful that he appeared to be worshipable. There was a luster and effulgence emanating from his body, and he was garlanded with a gold necklace. He offered obeisances to Lord Kṛṣṇa and stood before Him with great humility. Kṛṣṇa then asked the demigod, "You appear to be a very nice demigod and to be favored by the goddess of fortune. How is it that you performed such abominable activities that you got the body of a serpent?" The demigod then began to narrate the story of his previous life.

"My dear Lord," he said, "in my previous life I was named Vidyādhara and was known all over the world for my beauty. Because I was a celebrated personality, I used to travel all over in my airplane. While traveling, I saw a great sage named Aṅgirā. He was very ugly, and because I was very proud of my beauty, I laughed at him. Due to this sinful act, I was condemned by the great sage to assume the form of a serpent."

One should note here that before being favored by Kṛṣṇa a person is always under the modes of material nature, however elevated he may be materially. Vidyādhara was a materially elevated demigod, and he was very beautiful. He also held a great material position and was able to travel all over by airplane. Yet he was condemned to become a serpent in his next life. Any materially elevated person can be condemned to an abominable species of life if he is not careful. It is a misconception that after reaching the human body one is never degraded. Vidyādhara himself stated that even though he was a demigod he was condemned to become a serpent. But because he was touched by the lotus feet of Kṛṣṇa, he immediately came to Kṛṣṇa consciousness. He admitted, however, that in his previous life he was actually sinful. A Kṛṣṇa conscious person knows that he is always the servant of the servant of Kṛṣṇa; he is most insignificant, and whatever good he does is by the grace of Kṛṣṇa and the spiritual master.

The demigod Vidyādhara continued to speak to Śrī Kṛṣṇa. "Because I was very proud of the exquisite beauty of my body," he said, "I derided the ugly features of the great sage Aṅgirā. He cursed me for my sin, and I became a snake. Now I consider that this curse by the sage was not at all a curse; it was a great benediction for me. Had he not cursed me, I would not have assumed the body of a serpent and would not have been kicked by Your lotus feet and thus freed from all material contamination."

In material existence, four things are very valuable: to be born in a decent family, to be very rich, to be very learned and to be very beautiful. These are considered to be material assets. Unfortunately, without Kṛṣṇa consciousness, these material assets sometimes become sources of sin and degradation. Despite Vidyādhara's being a demigod and having a beautiful body, he was condemned to the body of a snake due to pride. Therefore from this incident we can learn that those who are too proud of their material assets or who are inimical toward others are degraded to the bodies of snakes. A snake is considered to be the most cruel and envious living entity, but those who are human beings and are envious of others are considered to be even more vicious than snakes. The snake can be charmed or controlled by *mantras* and herbs, but a person who is envious cannot be controlled by anyone.

"My dear Lord," Vidyādhara continued, "now, since I think I have become freed from all kinds of sinful activities, I am asking Your permission to return to my abode, the heavenly planets." This request indicates that persons who are attached to fruitive activities, desiring promotion to the comforts of higher planetary systems, cannot achieve their ultimate goal of life without the sanction of the Supreme Personality of Godhead. It is also stated in the *Bhagavad-gītā* that the less intelligent want to achieve material benefits and therefore worship different kinds of demigods, but that they actually get the benedictions from the demigods through the permission of Lord Viṣṇu, or Kṛṣṇa. Demigods have no power to bestow material profit. Even if one is attached to material benedictions, he can worship Kṛṣṇa, the Supreme Personality of Godhead, and ask Him. Kṛṣṇa is completely able to give even material benedictions. There is a difference, however, between asking material benedictions from the demigods and asking them from Kṛṣṇa. Dhruva Mahārāja worshiped the Supreme Personality of Godhead for a material benediction, but when he actually achieved the favor of the Supreme Lord and saw Him, he was so satisfied that he refused to accept any material benediction. The intelligent person does not worship the demigods or ask favors from them; he directly becomes Kṛṣṇa conscious, and if he has any desire for material benefit, he asks Kṛṣṇa, not the demigods.

Vidyādhara, awaiting Kṛṣṇa's permission to return to the heavenly planets, said, "Now, because I have been touched by Your lotus feet, I am relieved of all kinds of material pangs. You are the most powerful of all mystics. You are the original Supreme Personality of Godhead. You are the master of all devotees. You are the proprietor of all planetary systems, and therefore I am asking Your permission. You may accept me as fully surrendered unto You. I know very well that persons who are constantly engaged in chanting Your holy name attain release from all sinful reactions, and certainly persons who are fortunate enough to be personally touched by Your lotus feet are freed. Therefore I am sure that I am now relieved of the curse of the *brāhmaṇa* simply by seeing You and being touched by Your lotus feet."

In this way, Vidyādhara got permission from Lord Kṛṣṇa to return to his home in the higher planetary system. After receiving this permission, he circumambulated the Lord and offered his respectful obeisances unto Him, and then he returned to his heavenly planet. Thus Nanda Mahārāja was relieved of the imminent danger of being devoured by the snake.

The cowherd men, who had come to execute the ritualistic function of worshiping Lord Śiva and Ambikā, finished their business and prepared to return to Vṛndāvana. While returning, they recalled the wonderful activities of Kṛṣṇa. By relating the incident of Vidyādhara's deliverance, they became more attached to Kṛṣṇa. They had come to worship Lord Śiva and Ambikā, but the result was that they became more and more attached to Kṛṣṇa. Similarly, the *gopīs* worshiped goddess Kātyāyanī to become more and more attached to Kṛṣṇa. It is stated in the *Bhagavad-gītā* that persons who are attached to worshiping demigods like Lord Brahmā, Śiva, Indra and Candra for some personal benefit are less intelligent and have forgotten the real purpose of life. But the cowherd men, inhabitants of Vṛndāvana, were no ordinary men. Whatever they did, they did for Kṛṣṇa. If one worships demigods like Lord Śiva and Lord Brahmā to become more attached to Kṛṣṇa, that is approved. But if one goes to the demigods for some personal benefit, that is condemned.

After this incident, on a very pleasant night Kṛṣṇa and His elder brother, Balarāma, who are inconceivably powerful, went into the forest of Vṛndāvana. They were accompanied by the damsels of Vrajabhūmi, and They began to enjoy their company. The young damsels of Vraja were very nicely dressed and anointed with pulp of sandalwood and decorated with flowers. The moon was shining in the sky, surrounded by glittering stars. The breeze was blowing, bearing the aroma of *mallikā* flowers, and the bumblebees were mad after the aroma. Taking advantage of the pleasing atmosphere, Kṛṣṇa and Balarāma began to sing very melodiously. The damsels became so absorbed in Their rhythmical song that they almost forgot themselves; their hair loosened, their clothes slackened, and their garlands began to fall to the ground.

At that time, while Kṛṣṇa, Balarāma and the damsels were so much absorbed, almost in madness, a demoniac associate of Kuvera (the treasurer of the heavenly planets) appeared on the scene. The demon's name was Śaṅkhacūḍa because on his head there was a valuable jewel resembling a conchshell. Just as the two sons of Kuvera had been puffed up over their wealth and opulence and did not care for Nārada Muni's presence, this Śaṅkhacūḍa was also puffed up over material opulence. He thought that Kṛṣṇa and Balarāma were two ordinary cowherd boys enjoying the company of many beautiful girls. Generally, in the material world, a person with riches thinks that all beautiful women should be enjoyed by him. Śaṅkhacūḍa also thought that since he belonged to the rich community of Kuvera, he, not Kṛṣṇa and Balarāma, should enjoy the company of so many beautiful girls. He therefore decided to take charge of them. He appeared before Kṛṣṇa, Balarāma and the damsels of Vraja and began to lead the girls away to the north. He commanded them as if he were their proprietor and husband, despite the presence of Kṛṣṇa and Balarāma. Being forcibly taken away by Śaṅkhacūḍa, the damsels of Vraja called out the names of Kṛṣṇa and Balarāma for protection. The two brothers immediately began to follow them, taking up big logs of *śāla* wood in Their hands. "Don't be afraid, don't be afraid," They called to the *gopīs*. "We are coming at once to chastise this demon." Very quickly They reached Śaṅkhacūḍa. Thinking the brothers too powerful, Śaṅkhacūḍa left the company of the *gopīs* and ran in fear of his life. But Kṛṣṇa would not let him go. He entrusted the *gopīs* to the care of

Balarāma and followed Śaṅkhacūḍa wherever he fled. Kṛṣṇa wanted to take the valuable jewel resembling a conchshell from the head of the demon. After following him a very short distance, Kṛṣṇa caught him, struck his head with His fist and killed him. He then took the valuable jewel and returned. In the presence of all the damsels of Vraja, He presented the valuable jewel to His elder brother, Balarāma.

Thus ends the Bhaktivedanta purport of the Thirty-fourth Chapter of Kṛṣṇa, *"Vidyādhara Liberated and the Demon Śaṅkhacūḍa Killed."*

CHAPTER 35

The Gopīs' Feelings of Separation

THE *GOPĪS* OF VṚNDĀVANA were so attached to Kṛṣṇa that they were not satisfied simply with the *rāsa* dance at night. They wanted to associate with Him and enjoy His company during the daytime also. When Kṛṣṇa went to the forest with His cowherd boyfriends and cows, the *gopīs* did not physically take part, but their hearts went with Him. And because their hearts went, they were able to enjoy His company through strong feelings of separation. To acquire this strong feeling of separation is the teaching of Lord Caitanya and His direct disciplic succession of Gosvāmīs. When we are not in physical contact with Kṛṣṇa, we can associate with Him like the *gopīs,* through feelings of separation. Kṛṣṇa's transcendental form, qualities, pastimes and entourage are all identical with Him. There are nine different kinds of devotional service. Devotional service to Kṛṣṇa in feelings of separation elevates the devotee to the highest perfectional level, to the level of the *gopīs.*

It is stated in Śrīnivāsācārya's prayer to the six Gosvāmīs that they left the material opulences of government service and the princely status of life and went to Vṛndāvana, where they lived just like ordinary mendicants, begging from door to door. But they were so much enriched with the *gopīs'* feelings of separation that they enjoyed transcendental pleasure at every moment. Similarly, when Lord Caitanya was at

Jagannātha Purī, He was in the role of Rādhārāṇī, feeling separation from Kṛṣṇa. Those who are in the disciplic succession of the Mādhva-Gauḍīya-sampradāya should always feel separation from Kṛṣṇa, worship His transcendental form and discuss His transcendental teachings, His pastimes, His qualities and His entourage. That will enrich the devotees to the highest devotional perfection. Feeling constant separation while engaged in the service of the Lord is the perfection of Kṛṣṇa consciousness.

The *gopīs* used to discuss Kṛṣṇa amongst themselves, and their talks were as follows. "My dear friends," one *gopī* said, "do you know that when Kṛṣṇa lies on the ground He rests on His left elbow, and His head rests on His left hand? He moves His attractive eyebrows while playing His flute with His delicate fingers, and the sound He produces creates such a nice atmosphere that the denizens of the heavenly planets, who travel in space with their wives and beloveds, stop their airplanes, for they are stunned by the vibration of the flute. The wives of the demigods who are seated in the planes then become very much ashamed of their singing and musical qualifications. Not only that, but they become afflicted with conjugal love, and their hair and tight clothes immediately loosen."

Another *gopī* said, "My dear friends, Kṛṣṇa is so beautiful that the goddess of fortune always remains on His chest, and He is always adorned with a golden necklace. Beautiful Kṛṣṇa plays His flute in order to enliven the hearts of many devotees. He is the only friend of the suffering living entities. When He plays His flute, all the cows and other animals of Vṛndāvana, although engaged in eating, simply take a morsel of food in their mouths and stop chewing. Their ears raise up and they become stunned. They do not appear alive but like painted animals. Kṛṣṇa's flute-playing is so attractive that even the animals become enchanted, and what to speak of ourselves."

Another *gopī* said, "My dear friends, not only living animals but even inanimate objects like the rivers and lakes of Vṛndāvana also become stunned when Kṛṣṇa passes with peacock feathers on His head and His body smeared with the minerals of Vṛndāvana. With leaves and flowers decorating His body, He looks like some hero. When He plays on His flute and calls the cows with Balarāma, the river Yamunā stops flowing and waits for the air to carry dust from His lotus feet. The river Yamunā is unfortunate like us; it does not get Kṛṣṇa's mercy. The river simply remains stunned, stopping its waves, just as we also stop crying for Kṛṣṇa in expectation."

In the absence of Kṛṣṇa the *gopīs* were constantly shedding tears, but sometimes, when they expected that Kṛṣṇa was coming, they would stop crying. But when they saw that Kṛṣṇa was not coming, then again they would become frustrated and begin to cry. Kṛṣṇa is the original Personality of Godhead, the origin of all Viṣṇu forms, and the cowherd boys are all demigods. Lord Viṣṇu is always worshiped and surrounded by different demigods like Lord Śiva, Lord Brahmā, Indra, Candra and others. When Kṛṣṇa traveled through the Vṛndāvana forest or walked on Govardhana Hill, He was accompanied by the cowherd boys. While walking, He played His flute just to call His cows. Just by His association, the trees, plants and other vegetation in the forest immediately became Kṛṣṇa conscious. A Kṛṣṇa conscious person sacrifices everything for Kṛṣṇa. Although the trees and plants were not very advanced in consciousness, by the association of Kṛṣṇa and His friends they also became Kṛṣṇa conscious. They then wanted to deliver everything— whatever they had—namely their fruits, flowers and the honey incessantly falling from their branches.

When Kṛṣṇa walked on the bank of the Yamunā, He was seen nicely decorated with *tilaka* on His face. He was garlanded with different kinds of forest flowers, and His body was smeared with the pulp of sandalwood and *tulasī* leaves. The bumblebees became mad after the fragrance and sweetness of the atmosphere. Being pleased by the humming sound of the bees, Kṛṣṇa would play His flute, and together the sounds became so sweet to hear that aquatic birds like cranes, swans and ducks were charmed. Instead of swimming or flying, they became stunned. They closed their eyes and entered a trance of meditation in worship of Kṛṣṇa.

One *gopī* said, "My dear friends, Kṛṣṇa and Balarāma are nicely dressed with earrings and pearl necklaces. They enjoy Themselves on the top of Govardhana Hill, and everything becomes absorbed in transcendental pleasure when Kṛṣṇa plays on His flute, charming the whole created manifestation. When He plays, the clouds stop their loud thundering out of fear of Him. Rather than disturb the vibration of His flute, they respond with mild thunder and so congratulate Kṛṣṇa, their friend."

Kṛṣṇa is accepted as the friend of the cloud because both the cloud and Kṛṣṇa satisfy the people when they are disturbed. When the people are burning due to excessive heat, the cloud satisfies them with rain. Similarly, when people in materialistic life become disturbed by the blazing fire of material pangs, Kṛṣṇa consciousness gives them relief like a cloud. The cloud and Kṛṣṇa, having the same bodily color also, are considered to be friends. Desiring to congratulate its superior friend, the cloud poured not water but small flowers and covered the head of Kṛṣṇa just like an umbrella to protect Him from the scorching sunshine.

One of the *gopīs* told mother Yaśodā, "My dear mother, your son is very expert among the cowherd boys. He knows all the different arts of how to tend the cows and how to play the flute. He composes His own songs, and to play them He puts His flute to His mouth. When He plays, either in the morning or in the evening, all the demigods, including Lord Śiva, Brahmā, Indra and Candra, bow their heads and listen with great attention. Although they are very learned and expert, they cannot understand the musical arrangements of Kṛṣṇa's flute. They simply listen attentively and try to understand, but they become bewildered and nothing more."

Another *gopī* said, "My dear friends, when Kṛṣṇa returns home with His cows, the footprints of the soles of His feet—with flag, thunderbolt, trident and lotus flower—

relieve the pain the earth feels when the cows traverse it. He walks in a stride which is so attractive, and He carries His flute. Just by looking at Him we become lusty to enjoy His company. At that time, our movements cease. We become just like trees and stand perfectly still, unaware that our hair and clothes are loosening."

Kṛṣṇa had many thousands of cows, and they were divided into groups according to their colors. They were also differently named according to color. When He would prepare to return from the pasturing ground, He would gather all the cows. As Vaiṣṇavas count 108 beads, which represent the 108 individual *gopīs,* so Kṛṣṇa would also count on 108 beads to count the different groups of cows.

"When Kṛṣṇa returns, He is garlanded with *tulasī* leaves," a *gopī* described Him to a friend. "He puts His hand on the shoulder of a cowherd boyfriend and begins to blow His transcendental flute. The wives of the black deer become enchanted upon hearing the vibration of His flute, which resembles the vibration of the *vīṇā.* The deer come to Kṛṣṇa and become so charmed that they stand still, forgetting their homes and husbands. Like us, who are enchanted by the ocean of the transcendental qualities of Kṛṣṇa, the she-deer become enchanted by the vibration of His flute."

Another *gopī* told mother Yaśodā, "My dear mother, when your son returns home, He decorates Himself with the buds of the *kunda* flower, and just to enlighten and gladden His friends, He blows His flute. The breeze blowing from the south creates a pleasing atmosphere because it is fragrant and very cool. Minor demigods like the Gandharvas and Siddhas take advantage of this atmosphere and offer prayers to your son by sounding their bugles and drums. Kṛṣṇa is very kind to the inhabitants of Vrajabhūmi, Vṛndāvana, and when He returns with His cows and friends, He is remembered as the lifter of Govardhana Hill. Taking advantage of this opportunity, the most exalted demigods like Lord Brahmā and Lord Śiva come down to offer their evening prayers, and they accompany the cowherd boys in glorifying the qualities of Kṛṣṇa.

"Kṛṣṇa is compared to the moon, born in the ocean of the womb of Devakī. When He returns in the evening, it appears that He is fatigued, but He still tries to gladden the inhabitants of Vṛndāvana by His auspicious presence. When Kṛṣṇa returns, garlanded with flowers, His face looks beautiful, adorned with golden earrings. He walks into Vṛndāvana with a stride just like the elephant's and slowly enters His home. Upon His return, the men, women and cows of Vṛndāvana immediately forget the scorching heat of the day."

Such descriptions of Kṛṣṇa's transcendental pastimes and activities were remembered by the *gopīs* during His absence from Vṛndāvana. They give us some idea of how attractive Kṛṣṇa is, not only to human beings but to all animate and inanimate objects. In Vṛndāvana, everyone and everything is attracted to Kṛṣṇa, including the trees, the plants, the water, and animals like the deer and cows. That is the perfect description of

Kṛṣṇa's all-attractiveness. The example of the *gopīs* is very instructive to persons who are trying to be absorbed in Kṛṣṇa consciousness. One can very easily associate with Kṛṣṇa simply by remembering His transcendental pastimes. Everyone has a tendency to love someone. That Kṛṣṇa should be the object of love is the central point of Kṛṣṇa consciousness. By constantly chanting the Hare Kṛṣṇa *mantra* and remembering the transcendental pastimes of Kṛṣṇa, one can be fully in Kṛṣṇa consciousness and thus make his life sublime and fruitful.

Thus ends the Bhaktivedanta purport of the Thirty-fifth Chapter of Kṛṣṇa, *"The* Gopīs' *Feelings of Separation."*

CHAPTER 36

Kaṁsa Sends Akrūra for Kṛṣṇa

VṚNDĀVANA WAS ALWAYS ABSORBED in the thought of Kṛṣṇa. Everyone remembered His pastimes and was constantly merged in the ocean of transcendental bliss. But the material world is so contaminated that even in Vṛndāvana the *asuras,* or demons, tried to disturb the peaceful situation.

Once a demon named Ariṣṭāsura entered the village in the form of a great bull with a gigantic body and huge horns, digging up the earth with his hooves. When the demon entered Vṛndāvana, the whole land appeared to tremble, as if there were an earthquake. He roared fiercely, and after digging up the earth on the riverside, he entered the village proper. The fearful roaring of the bull was so piercing that some of the pregnant cows and women had miscarriages. Its body was so big, stout and strong that a cloud hovered over its body just as clouds hover over mountains. Ariṣṭāsura entered Vṛndāvana with such a fearful appearance that just on seeing this great demon all the men and women were afflicted with great fear, and the cows and other animals fled the village.

The situation became very terrible, and all the inhabitants of Vṛndāvana began to cry, "Kṛṣṇa! Kṛṣṇa, please save us!" Kṛṣṇa saw that the cows were running away, and He immediately replied, "Don't be afraid. Don't be afraid." He then appeared before

Ariṣṭāsura and said, "You lowest of living entities! Why are you frightening the inhabitants of Gokula? What will you gain by this action? If you have come to challenge My authority, then I am prepared to fight you." In this way, Kṛṣṇa challenged the demon, and the demon became very angry by the words of Kṛṣṇa. Kṛṣṇa stood before the bull, resting His hand on the shoulder of a friend. The bull proceeded toward Kṛṣṇa in anger. Digging the earth with his hooves, Ariṣṭāsura lifted his tail, and it appeared that clouds were hovering about the tail. His eyes were reddish and moving in anger. Pointing his horns at Kṛṣṇa, he charged Him just like the thunderbolt of Indra. But Kṛṣṇa immediately caught his horns and tossed him away, just as a gigantic elephant repels a small inimical elephant. Although the demon was perspiring and appeared very tired, he took courage and got up. Again he charged Kṛṣṇa with great force and anger. While rushing toward Kṛṣṇa, he breathed very heavily. Kṛṣṇa again caught his horns and immediately threw him to the ground, breaking his horns. Kṛṣṇa then began to kick his body, just as one squeezes a wet cloth on the ground. Being thus kicked by Kṛṣṇa, Ariṣṭāsura rolled over and began to move his legs violently. Bleeding from the mouth and passing stool and urine, his eyes starting from their sockets, he passed to the kingdom of death.

The demigods in the celestial planets showered flowers on Kṛṣṇa for His wonderful achievement. Kṛṣṇa was already the life and soul of the inhabitants of Vṛndāvana, and after killing this demon in the shape of a bull, He became the cynosure of all eyes. With Balarāma, He triumphantly entered Vṛndāvana village, and the inhabitants glorified Him and Balarāma with great jubilation. When a person performs some wonderful feat, his kinsmen and relatives and friends naturally become jubilant.

It was after this incident that the great sage Nārada disclosed to Kaṁsa the secret of Kṛṣṇa. Nārada Muni is generally known as *deva-darśana,* which means that he can be seen only by demigods or persons on the same level with the demigods. But Nārada visited Kaṁsa, who was not at all on the level of the demigods, and allowed Kaṁsa to see him. Of course Kaṁsa also saw Kṛṣṇa, what to speak of Nārada Muni. But unless one sees the Lord or His devotees with purified eyes, one cannot derive the actual benefit. Of course, anyone who associates with a pure devotee derives imperceptible benefit, which is called *ajñāta-sukṛti.* One cannot understand how he is making progress, yet he makes progress by seeing the devotee of the Lord. Nārada Muni's mission was to finish things quickly. Kṛṣṇa appeared in order to kill the demons, and Kaṁsa was the chief among them. Nārada wanted to expedite things; therefore, he immediately approached Kaṁsa with all the real information. "You are to be killed by the eighth son of Vasudeva," Nārada told Kaṁsa. "That eighth son is Kṛṣṇa. You were misled by Vasudeva into believing that the eighth issue of Vasudeva was a daughter. Actually, the daughter was born to Yaśodā, the wife of Nanda Mahārāja, and Vasudeva exchanged his son for the daughter, so you were misled. Kṛṣṇa is the son of Vasudeva, as is

Balarāma. Being afraid of your atrocious nature, Vasudeva has tactfully hidden Them in Vṛndāvana, out of your sight." Nārada further informed Kaṁsa, "Kṛṣṇa and Balarāma have been living incognito in the care of Nanda Mahārāja. All the *asuras,* your companions who were sent to Vṛndāvana to kill different children, were killed by Kṛṣṇa and Balarāma."

As soon as Kaṁsa got this information from Nārada Muni, he took out his sharp sword and prepared to kill Vasudeva for his duplicity. But Nārada pacified him. "You are not to be killed by Vasudeva," he said. "Why are you so anxious to kill him? Better try to kill Kṛṣṇa and Balarāma." But in order to satisfy his wrath, Kaṁsa arrested Vasudeva and his wife and shackled them in iron chains. Acting on the new information, Kaṁsa immediately called for the Keśī demon and asked him to go to Vṛndāvana immediately to kill Balarāma and Kṛṣṇa. In actuality, Kaṁsa asked Keśī to go to Vṛndāvana to be killed by Kṛṣṇa and Balarāma and thus get salvation.

Then Kaṁsa called for his expert elephant trainers, as well as for the wrestlers Cāṇūra, Muṣṭika, Śala, Tośala, etc., and he told them, "My dear friends, try to hear me attentively. At Nanda Mahārāja's place in Vṛndāvana there are two brothers, Kṛṣṇa and Balarāma. They are actually two sons of Vasudeva. As you know, I have been destined to be killed by Kṛṣṇa; there is a prophecy to this effect. Now I am requesting you to arrange for a wrestling match. People from different parts of the country will come to see the festival. I will arrange to get those two boys here, and you will try to kill Them in the wrestling arena."

Wrestling matches are still enjoyed by people in northern India, and it appears from the statements of *Śrīmad-Bhāgavatam* that five thousand years ago wrestling was also popular. Kaṁsa planned to arrange such a wrestling competition and to invite people to visit. He also told the trainers of the elephants, "Be sure to bring the elephant named Kuvalayāpīḍa and keep him at the gate of the wrestling arena. Try to capture Kṛṣṇa and Balarāma on Their arrival and have the elephant kill Them."

Kaṁsa also advised his friends to arrange to worship Lord Śiva by offering animal sacrifices and performing the sacrifice called Dhanur-yajña and the sacrifice performed on the fourteenth day of the moon, known as Caturdaśī. This date falls three days after Ekādaśī, and it is set aside for the worship of Lord Śiva. One of the plenary portions of Lord Śiva is called Kālabhairava. This form of Lord Śiva is worshiped by demons who offer animals killed before him. The process is still current in India in a place called Vaidyanātha-dhāma, where demons offer animal sacrifices to the deity of Kālabhairava. Kaṁsa belonged to this demoniac group. He was also an expert diplomat, and so he quickly arranged for his demon friends to kill Kṛṣṇa and Balarāma.

He then called for Akrūra, one of the descendants in the family of Yadu, in which Kṛṣṇa was born as the son of Vasudeva. When Akrūra came to see Kaṁsa, Kaṁsa very politely shook hands with him and said, "My dear Akrūra, actually I have no better friend than you in the Bhoja and Yadu dynasties. You are the most munificent person, so as a friend I am begging charity from you. Actually I have taken shelter of you exactly as King Indra takes shelter of Lord Viṣṇu. I request you to go immediately to Vṛndāvana and find the two boys named Kṛṣṇa and Balarāma. They are the sons of Nanda Mahārāja. Take this nice chariot, especially prepared for the boys, and bring Them here immediately. That is my request to you. Now, my plan is to kill these two boys. As soon as They come in the gate, there will be a giant elephant named Kuvalayāpīḍa waiting, and possibly he will be able to kill Them. But if somehow or other They escape, They will next meet the wrestlers and will be killed by them. That is my plan. And after killing these two boys, I shall kill Vasudeva and Nanda, who are supporters of the Vṛṣṇi and Bhoja dynasties. I shall also kill my father, Ugrasena, and his brother Devaka, because they are actually my enemies and are hindrances to my diplomacy and politics. Thus I shall get rid of all my enemies. Jarāsandha is my father-in-law, and I have a great monkey friend named Dvivida. With their help it will be easy to kill all the kings on the surface of the earth who support the demigods. This is my plan. In this way I shall be free from all opposition, and it will be very pleasant to rule the world without obstruction. You may know also that Śambara, Narakāsura and Bāṇāsura are my intimate friends, and when I begin this war against the kings who support the demigods, they will help me considerably. Surely I shall be rid of all my enemies. Please go immediately to Vṛndāvana and encourage the boys to come here to see the beauty of Mathurā and take pleasure in the wrestling competition."

After hearing this plan of Kaṁsa's, Akrūra replied, "My dear King, your plan is very excellently made to counteract the hindrances to your diplomatic activities. But you should maintain equilibrium, for the result of your activities may be fruitful or may not be fruitful. After all, man proposes, God disposes. We may make very great plans, but unless they are sanctioned by the supreme authority, they will fail. Everyone in this material world knows that the supernatural power is the ultimate disposer of everything. One may make a very great plan with his fertile brain, but he must know that he will become subjected to the fruits, misery and happiness. But I have nothing to say against your proposal. As a friend, I shall carry out your order and bring Kṛṣṇa and Balarāma here, as you desire."

After instructing his friends in various ways, Kaṁsa retired, and Akrūra went back to his home.

Thus ends the Bhaktivedanta purport of the Thirty-sixth Chapter of Kṛṣṇa, *"Kaṁsa Sends Akrūra for Kṛṣṇa."*

CHAPTER 37

Killing the Keśī Demon and Vyomāsura

AFTER BEING INSTRUCTED BY KAṀSA, the demon Keśī assumed the form of a terrible horse. He entered the area of Vṛndāvana with the speed of the mind, his great mane flying and his hooves digging up the earth. He began to whinny and terrify the whole forest. Kṛṣṇa saw that the demon was terrifying all the residents of Vṛndāvana with his whinnying and his tail wheeling in the sky like a big cloud. Kṛṣṇa could understand that the horse was challenging Him to fight. The Lord accepted his challenge and stood before the Keśī demon, calling him to fight. The horse then ran toward Kṛṣṇa, making a horrible sound like a roaring lion, his jaws spread wide open as if to swallow the whole sky. Keśī rushed toward the Lord with great speed and tried to trample Him with his legs, which were strong, forceful and as hard as stone. Kṛṣṇa, however, immediately caught hold of his legs and thus baffled him. Being somewhat angry, Kṛṣṇa began to whirl the horse around. After a few rounds, He contemptuously threw him a hundred yards away, just as Garuḍa throws a big snake. Thrown by Kṛṣṇa, the horse immediately passed out, but after a little while he regained consciousness and with great anger and force again rushed toward Kṛṣṇa with his mouth open. As soon as Keśī reached Him, Kṛṣṇa pushed His left arm within the horse's mouth, and it looked as though a big snake had entered a hole in a field. The horse felt great pain because the arm of Kṛṣṇa felt to him like a hot iron rod. Immediately his teeth fell out. Kṛṣṇa's arm within the mouth of the horse at once began to expand, and Keśī's throat choked up. As the great horse suffocated, perspiration appeared on his body, and he threw his legs hither and thither. As his last breath came, his eyeballs bulged in their sockets and he passed stool and urine simultaneously. Thus the vital force of his life expired. When the horse was dead, his mouth became loose, and Kṛṣṇa could extract His hand without difficulty. He did not feel any surprise that the Keśī demon was killed so easily, but the demigods in the sky were amazed, and out of their great appreciation they offered Kṛṣṇa greetings by showering flowers.

After this incident, Nārada Muni, the greatest of all devotees, came to see Kṛṣṇa in a solitary place and began to talk with Him. "My dear Lord Kṛṣṇa," he said, "You are the unlimited Supersoul, the supreme controller of all mystic powers, the Lord of the whole universe, the all-pervading Personality of Godhead. You are the resting place of the cosmic manifestation, the master of all the devotees and the Lord of everyone. My dear Lord, as the Supersoul of all living entities, You remain concealed within their hearts exactly as fire remains concealed in every piece of fuel. You are the witness of all the activities of the living entities, and You are the supreme controller within their hearts. You are self-sufficient; before the creation, You existed, and by Your energy You have created all the material elements. According to Your perfect plan, this material world is created by the interaction of the modes of nature, and by You it is maintained and annihilated. Although You are unaffected by all these activities, You are the supreme controller eternally. My dear Lord, You have advented Yourself on the surface of this earth just to kill all the so-called kings who are actually demons. These hobgoblins are cheating people in the dress of the princely order. You have advented Yourself to fulfill Your own statement that You come within this material world just to protect the principles of religion and annihilate unwanted miscreants. My dear Lord, I am therefore sure that the day after tomorrow I shall see demons like Cāṇūra, Muṣṭika and the other wrestlers and elephants, as well as Kaṁsa himself, killed by You. I shall see this with my own eyes. After this I shall be able to see the killing of other demons, like Śaṅkha, Yavana, Mura and Narakāsura. I shall also see how You take away the *pārijāta* flower from the kingdom of heaven and how You defeat the King of heaven himself.

"My dear Lord," Nārada Muni continued, "I shall then be able to see how You marry princesses, the daughters of chivalrous kings, by paying the price of *kṣatriya* strength." (Whenever a *kṣatriya* wants to marry a very beautiful and qualified daughter of a great king, he must fight his competitors and emerge victorious. Then he is given the hand of the princess in charity.)

"I shall also see how You save King Nṛga from a hellish condition," said Nārada Muni. "This You shall enact in Dvārakā. I shall also be able to see how You get Your wife and the Syamantaka jewel and how You save the son of a *brāhmaṇa* from death after he has already been transferred to another planet. After this, I will be able to see You kill the Pauṇḍraka demon and burn to ashes the kingdom of Kāśī. I will see how You kill the King of Cedi and Dantavakra during the great sacrifice of Mahārāja Yudhiṣṭhira. Besides all this, it will be possible for me to see many other chivalrous activities while You remain in Dvārakā. And all these activities performed by Your Grace will be sung by great poets throughout the world. At the Battle of Kurukṣetra You will take part as the chariot driver of Your friend Arjuna, and as the invincible death incarnation, eternal time, You will vanquish all belligerents assembled there. I shall see a large number of military forces killed in that battlefield. My Lord, let me offer my respectful obeisances unto Your lotus feet. You are situated completely in the transcendental position, in perfect knowledge and bliss. You are complete in fulfilling all Your desires. By exhibiting Your internal potency, You have set up the influence of *māyā.* Your unlimited potency cannot even be measured by anyone. My dear Lord, You are the supreme controller. You are under Your own internal potency, and it is simply vain to think that You are dependent on any of Your creations.

"You have taken birth in the Yadu dynasty, or the Vṛṣṇi dynasty. Your advent on the surface of the earth in Your original form of eternal blissful knowledge is Your own pastime. You are not dependent on anything but Yourself; therefore I offer my respectful obeisances unto Your lotus feet." After offering his respectful obeisances to Lord Kṛṣṇa, Nārada Muni took permission and left.

Nārada Muni wanted to impress upon people in general that Kṛṣṇa is fully independent. His activities, such as His appearance in the family of Yadu or His friendship with Arjuna, do not necessarily oblige Him to act to enjoy their results. They are all pastimes, and for Him they are all play. But for us they are actual, tangible facts.

After He had killed the Keśī demon, Kṛṣṇa returned to tending the cows with His friends in the forest as though nothing had happened. Thus Kṛṣṇa is eternally engaged in His transcendental activities in Vṛndāvana with His friends, the cowherd boys and *gopīs,* but sometimes He exhibits the extraordinary prowess of the Supreme Personality of Godhead by killing different types of demons.

Later that morning, Kṛṣṇa went to play with His cowherd boyfriends on the top of Govardhana Hill. They were imitating the play of thieves and police. Some of the boys became police constables, and some became thieves, and some took the role of lambs. While they were thus enjoying their childhood pastimes, a demon known by the name of Vyomāsura, "the demon who flies in the sky," appeared on the scene. He was the son of another great demon, named Maya. These demons can perform wonderful magic. Vyomāsura took the part of a cowherd boy playing as a thief and stole many boys who were playing the parts of lambs. One after another he took away almost all the boys and put them in the caves of the mountain and sealed the mouths of the caves with stones. Kṛṣṇa could understand the trick the demon was playing; therefore He caught hold of him exactly as a lion catches hold of a lamb. The demon tried to expand himself like a hill to escape arrest, but Kṛṣṇa did not allow him to get out of His clutches. He was immediately thrown to the ground with great force and killed, just as an animal is killed in the slaughterhouse. After killing the Vyoma demon, Lord Kṛṣṇa released all His friends from the caves of the mountain. He was then praised by His friends and by the demigods for these wonderful acts. He again returned to Vṛndāvana with His cows and friends.

Thus ends the Bhaktivedanta purport of the Thirty-seventh Chapter of Kṛṣṇa, *"Killing the Keśī Demon and Vyomāsura."*

CHAPTER 38

Akrūra's Arrival in Vṛndāvana

NĀRADA MUNI DID NOT MENTION Kṛṣṇa's killing Vyomāsura, which means that he was killed on the same day as the Keśī demon. The Keśī demon was killed in the early morning, and after that the boys went to tend the cows on Govardhana Hill, and it was there that Vyomāsura was killed. Both demons were killed in the morning. Akrūra was requested by Kaṁsa to arrive in Vṛndāvana by evening. After receiving instruction from Kaṁsa, Akrūra started the next morning via chariot for Vṛndāvana. Because Akrūra himself was a great devotee of the Lord, while going to Vṛndāvana he began to pray to the Lord. Devotees are always absorbed in thoughts of Kṛṣṇa, and Akrūra was constantly thinking of Lord Kṛṣṇa's lotus eyes.

He did not know what sort of pious activities he must have performed to gain an opportunity to go see Lord Kṛṣṇa and Lord Balarāma in Vṛndāvana on that day. A pure Vaiṣṇava always thinks himself unfit to serve Kṛṣṇa. So Akrūra began to think within himself that he was unfit for gaining the transcendental opportunity of seeing the Supreme Personality of Godhead. He considered himself as unfit for seeing Kṛṣṇa as a materialistic person is for understanding the science of God or as a fourth-class person (a *śūdra*) is for studying the *Vedas*. But then Akrūra began to think, "By the grace of

Kṛṣṇa everything is possible, and thus if He likes, I will be able to see Him. Just as a blade of grass floating on the waves of a river may by chance come near the shore and gain shelter, a conditioned soul carried away by the waves of material existence may sometimes be saved by the grace of Kṛṣṇa." Akrūra thus thought that if Kṛṣṇa willed, he would be able to see Him. Akrūra considered himself most fortunate that he was going to see Kṛṣṇa, whom great mystic *yogīs* desire to see. He was confident that on that day all the sinful reactions of his past life would be finished and his fortunate human form of life would be successful. Akrūra also considered that he was very much favored by Kaṁsa, who was sending him to bring back Kṛṣṇa and Balarāma and thus enabling him to see the Lord. Akrūra continued to consider that formerly great sages and saintly persons were liberated from the material world simply by seeing the shining nails of the lotus feet of Kṛṣṇa.

"That Supreme Personality of Godhead has now come just like an ordinary human being, and it is my great fortune to be able to see Him face to face," Akrūra thought. He was thrilled with expectations of seeing the very lotus feet which are worshiped by great demigods like Brahmā, Nārada and Lord Śiva, which traverse the ground of Vṛndāvana, and which touch the breasts of the *gopīs*, covered with tinges of *kuṅkuma*. He thought, "I am so fortunate that I will be able to see those very lotus feet on this day, and certainly I shall be able to see the beautiful face of Kṛṣṇa, which is marked on the forehead and the nose with *tilaka*. And I shall also see His smile and His curling black hair. I can be sure of this opportunity because I see that today the deer are passing on my right side. Today it will be possible for me to actually see the beauty of the spiritual kingdom of Viṣṇuloka because Kṛṣṇa is the Supreme Viṣṇu and He has advented Himself out of His own good will. He is the reservoir of all beauty; therefore today my eyes will achieve perfection."

Akrūra knew beyond a doubt that Lord Kṛṣṇa is the Supreme Viṣṇu. Lord Viṣṇu glances over the material energy, and thus the cosmic manifestation comes into being. And although Lord Viṣṇu is the creator of this material world, He is free, by His own energy, from the influence of the material energy. By His internal potency He can pierce the darkness of the material energy. Similarly, Kṛṣṇa, the original Viṣṇu, by expanding His internal potency, created the inhabitants of Vṛndāvana. In the *Brahma-saṁhitā* it is confirmed that the paraphernalia and the abode of Kṛṣṇa are expansions of His internal potency. The same internal potency Kṛṣṇa exhibits in Goloka Vṛndāvana is exhibited in the earthly Vṛndāvana, where He enjoys Himself with His parents and in the company of His friends, the cowherd boys and *gopīs*. By the statement of Akrūra it is clear that, since Kṛṣṇa is transcendental to the modes of material nature, the inhabitants of Vṛndāvana, who are always engaged in loving service to the Lord, are also transcendental.

Akrūra also considered the necessity of the transcendental pastimes of the Lord. He thought that the transcendental activities, instructions, qualities and pastimes of

Kṛṣṇa are all for the good fortune of people in general. The people can remain constantly in Kṛṣṇa consciousness by discussing the Lord's transcendental form, qualities, pastimes and paraphernalia. By doing so, the whole universe can actually live auspiciously and advance peacefully. But without Kṛṣṇa consciousness, civilization is but a decorated dead body. A dead body may be decorated very nicely, but without consciousness such decorations are useless. Human society without Kṛṣṇa consciousness is useless and lifeless.

Akrūra thought, "That Supreme Personality of Godhead, Kṛṣṇa, has now appeared as one of the descendants of the Yadu dynasty. The principles of religion are His enacted laws. Those who are abiding by such laws are demigods, and those who are not abiding are demons. He has advented Himself to give protection to the demigods, who are very obedient to the laws of the Supreme Lord. The demigods and the devotees of the Lord take pleasure in abiding by the laws of Kṛṣṇa, and Kṛṣṇa takes pleasure in giving them all sorts of protection. As confirmed in the *Bhagavad-gītā,* these activities of Kṛṣṇa—His protecting the devotees and killing the demons—are always good for men to hear and narrate. The glorious activities of the Lord will ever increasingly be chanted by the devotees and demigods.

"Kṛṣṇa, the Supreme Personality of Godhead, is the spiritual master of all spiritual masters; He is the deliverer of all fallen souls and the proprietor of the three worlds. Anyone who is able to see Him with eyes smeared with love of Godhead enjoys a festival of seeing. Today I shall be able to see the Supreme Personality of Godhead, who by His transcendental beauty has attracted the goddess of fortune to live with Him perpetually. As soon as I arrive in Vṛndāvana, I will get down from this chariot and fall prostrate to offer my obeisances to the Supreme Lord, the master of material nature and all living entities. The lotus feet of Kṛṣṇa are always worshiped by great mystic *yogīs,* so I shall also worship His lotus feet and become one of His friends in Vṛndāvana like the cowherd boys. When I bow down before Lord Kṛṣṇa in that way, certainly He will place His fearless lotus hand on my head. His hand is offered to all conditioned souls who take shelter under His lotus feet. Kṛṣṇa is the ultimate goal of life for all people who fear material existence, and certainly when I see Him He will give me the shelter of His lotus feet. I am aspiring for the touch of His lotuslike hand on my head. When that hand touched the presentations of King Indra and King Bali, these two became qualified to be lords of the universe, and when that hand touched the *gopīs* as they danced with Kṛṣṇa in the *rāsa-līlā,* it relieved all their fatigue."

In this way Akrūra expected blessings from the hand of Kṛṣṇa. He knew that Indra, who is the King of heaven and the master of the three worlds—the upper, middle and lower planetary systems—was blessed by the Lord simply for his offering a little water which Kṛṣṇa accepted. Similarly, Bali Mahārāja gave only three paces of land in charity to Vāmanadeva, and he also offered a little water which Lord Vāmanadeva accepted, and thereby Bali Mahārāja attained the position of Indra. When the *gopīs* were dancing with Kṛṣṇa in the *rāsa* dance, they became fatigued, and Kṛṣṇa wiped His hand, which is as fragrant as a lotus flower growing in Mānasa-sarovara Lake, over the pearllike drops of perspiration on the faces of the *gopīs,* and immediately the *gopīs* became refreshed. Thus Akrūra was expecting benediction from that supreme hand of Kṛṣṇa. Kṛṣṇa's hand is capable of bestowing benediction upon all kinds of men if they take to Kṛṣṇa consciousness. If one wants material happiness like the King of heaven, he can derive that benediction from the hand of Kṛṣṇa; if one wants liberation from the pangs of material existence, he can also get that benediction from the hand of Kṛṣṇa; and if one in pure transcendental love for Kṛṣṇa wants personal association and the touch of His transcendental body, he can also gain that benediction from His hand.

Akrūra was afraid, however, because he had been deputed by Kaṁsa, the enemy of Kṛṣṇa. He thought, "I am going to see Kṛṣṇa as a messenger of the enemy." At the same time, he thought, "Kṛṣṇa is in everyone's heart as the Supersoul, so He must know my heart." Although Akrūra was trusted by the enemy of Kṛṣṇa, his heart was clear. He was a pure devotee of Kṛṣṇa. He risked becoming Kaṁsa's deputy just to meet Kṛṣṇa. He was certain that although he was going as a representative of Kaṁsa, Kṛṣṇa would not accept him as an enemy. "Even though I am on a sinful mission, being deputed by Kaṁsa, when I approach the Supreme Personality of Godhead, I shall stand before Him with all humility and folded hands. Surely He will be pleased with my devotional attitude, and maybe He will smile lovingly and look upon me and thereby free me from all kinds of sinful reactions. I shall then be on the platform of transcendental bliss and knowledge. Since Kṛṣṇa knows my heart, certainly when I approach Him, He will embrace me. Not only am I a member of the Yadu dynasty, but I am His relative and an unalloyed, pure devotee. By His merciful embrace, surely my body, heart and soul will be completely cleansed of the actions and reactions of my past life. When our bodies touch, I will immediately stand up with folded hands, with all humility. Certainly Kṛṣṇa and Balarāma will call me 'Akrūra, Uncle,' and at that time my whole life will be glorious. Unless one is recognized by the Supreme Personality of Godhead, his life cannot be successful."

It is clearly stated here that one should try to be recognized by the Supreme Personality of Godhead by one's service and devotion, without which the human form of life is condemned. As stated in the *Bhagavad-gītā,* the Supreme Lord, the Personality of Godhead, is equal to everyone. He has no friends and no enemies. But He is inclined to a devotee who renders Him service with devotional love. The *Bhagavad-gītā* also declares that the Supreme Lord is responsive in proportion to the devotional service rendered by the devotee. Akrūra thought that Kṛṣṇa was like the desire tree in the heavenly planets, which gives fruit according to the desire of the worshiper. The Supreme Personality of Godhead is also the source of everything. A devotee must know how to render service unto Him and thus be recognized by Him. In the *Caitanya-caritāmṛta* it is therefore explained that one should serve both the spiritual master and Kṛṣṇa simultaneously and in that way make progress in Kṛṣṇa consciousness. Service rendered to Kṛṣṇa under the direction of the spiritual master is bona fide service because the spiritual master is the manifested representative of Kṛṣṇa. Śrī Viśvanātha Cakravartī Ṭhākura says that when one satisfies the spiritual master, he satisfies the Supreme Lord. It is exactly like service in a government office. One has to work under the supervision of the departmental head. If the supervisor of the department is satisfied with the service of a particular person, a promotion and increase in pay will automatically come.

Akrūra then thought, "When Kṛṣṇa and Balarāma are pleased with my behavior, certainly They will take my hand, receive me within Their home and offer me all kinds of respectable hospitalities, and They will surely ask me about the activities of Kaṁsa and his friends."

In this way, Akrūra, the son of Śvaphalka, meditated on Śrī Kṛṣṇa on his journey from Mathurā. He reached Vṛndāvana by the end of the day. Akrūra passed the whole journey without knowing how long it took. When he reached Vṛndāvana, the sun was setting. As soon as he entered the boundary of Vṛndāvana, he saw the hoofprints of the cows and Lord Kṛṣṇa's footprints, impressed with the signs of His soles—the flag, trident, thunderbolt and lotus flower. These symbols on the soles of the Lord's transcendental lotus feet are worshiped by all the demigods and other great personalities throughout the three worlds. Upon seeing the footprints of Kṛṣṇa, Akrūra immediately jumped down from the chariot out of respect. He became overwhelmed with all the symptoms of ecstasy; he wept, and his body trembled. Out of extreme jubilation upon seeing the dust touched by the lotus feet of Kṛṣṇa, Akrūra fell flat on his face and began to roll on the ground.

Akrūra's journey to Vṛndāvana is exemplary. One who intends to visit Vṛndāvana should follow the ideal footsteps of Akrūra and always think of the pastimes and activities of the Lord. As soon as one reaches the boundary of Vṛndāvana, he should immediately smear the dust of Vṛndāvana over his body without thinking of his material position and prestige. Śrīla Narottama dāsa Ṭhākura has sung in a celebrated song, *viṣaya chāḍiyā kabe śuddha habe mana:* "When my mind will be purified after leaving the contamination of material sense enjoyment, I shall be able to visit Vṛndāvana." Actually, one cannot go to Vṛndāvana by purchasing a ticket. The process of going to Vṛndāvana is shown by Akrūra.

When Akrūra entered Vṛndāvana, he saw Kṛṣṇa and Balarāma engaged in supervising the milking of the cows. Kṛṣṇa was dressed in yellow garments and Balarāma in bluish. Akrūra also saw that Their eyes were exactly like the beautiful lotus flower that grows during the autumn season. He saw Kṛṣṇa and Balarāma in the spring of Their youth. Although They had the same bodily features, Kṛṣṇa was blackish in complexion, whereas Balarāma was whitish. Both were the shelter of the goddess of fortune. They had well-constructed bodies, beautiful hands and pleasing faces, and They were as strong as elephants. Now, after seeing Their footprints, marked with flag, trident, thunderbolt and lotus, Akrūra actually saw Kṛṣṇa and Balarāma face to face. Although They were the most influential personalities, They were glancing at him with smiling faces. Akrūra could understand that both Kṛṣṇa and Balarāma had returned from tending cows in the forest; They had taken Their baths and were dressed with fresh clothing and garlanded with flowers and with necklaces made of valuable jewels. Their bodies were smeared with the pulp of sandalwood. Akrūra greatly appreciated the aroma of the flowers and sandalwood and Their bodily presence. He considered himself very fortunate to see Kṛṣṇa, the Supreme Personality of Godhead, and His plenary expansion, Balarāma, face to face, for he knew that They were the original personalities of the creation.

As stated in the *Brahma-saṁhitā*, Kṛṣṇa is the original Personality of Godhead and the cause of all causes. Akrūra could understand that the Supreme Personality of Godhead had appeared personally for the welfare of His creation, to reestablish the principles of religion and to annihilate the demons. With Their bodily effulgence the brothers were dissipating all the darkness of the world, as if They were mountains of sapphire and silver. Without hesitating, Akrūra immediately got down from his chariot and fell flat, just like a rod, before Kṛṣṇa and Balarāma. Upon touching the lotus feet of the Supreme Personality of Godhead, he became overwhelmed with transcendental bliss; his voice choked up, and he could not speak. Due to his transcendental pleasure, incessant torrents of tears fell from his eyes. He remained stunned in ecstasy, as if devoid of all powers to see and speak. Lord Kṛṣṇa, who is very kind to His devotees, raised Akrūra with His hand and embraced him. It appeared that Lord Kṛṣṇa was very pleased with Akrūra. Balarāma also embraced Akrūra. Taking him by the hand, Kṛṣṇa and Balarāma brought him to Their sitting room, where They offered him a very nice sitting place and water for washing his feet. They also worshiped him with a suitable presentation of honey mixed with other ingredients. When Akrūra was thus comfortably seated, Kṛṣṇa and Balarāma offered Him a cow in charity and then brought very palatable dishes, and Akrūra accepted them. When Akrūra finished eating, Balarāma gave him betel nut and spices, as well as pulp of sandalwood, just to make him more pleased and comfortable. The Vedic system of receiving a guest was completely observed by Lord Kṛṣṇa Himself to teach all others how to receive a guest at home. It is a Vedic injunction that even if a guest is an enemy he should be received so well that he does not apprehend any danger from the host. If the host is a poor man, he should at least offer a straw mat as a sitting place and a glass of water to drink. Kṛṣṇa and Balarāma welcomed Akrūra in a way just befitting his exalted position.

After Akrūra was thus properly received and seated, Nanda Mahārāja, the foster father of Kṛṣṇa, said, "My dear Akrūra, what shall I inquire from you? I know that you are being protected by Kaṁsa, who is most cruel and demoniac. His protection is just like the slaughterhouse keeper's protection of animals he will kill in the future. Kaṁsa is so selfish that he has killed the sons of his own sister, so how can I honestly believe that he is protecting the citizens of Mathurā?" This statement is most significant. If the political or executive heads of the state are simply interested in themselves, they can never look after the welfare of the citizens.

As Nanda Mahārāja spoke to Akrūra with pleasing words, Akrūra forgot all the fatigue of his day's journey from Mathurā to Vṛndāvana.

Thus ends the Bhaktivedanta purport of the Thirty-eighth Chapter of Kṛṣṇa, *"Akrūra's Arrival in Vṛndāvana."*

CHAPTER 39

Akrūra's Return Journey and His Vision of Viṣṇuloka Within the Yamunā River

AKRŪRA WAS WARMLY RECEIVED by Lord Kṛṣṇa and Nanda Mahārāja and offered a resting place for the night. In the meantime, the two brothers Balarāma and Kṛṣṇa went to take Their supper. Akrūra sat on his bed and began to reflect that all the desires he had contemplated while coming from Mathurā to Vṛndāvana had been fulfilled. Lord Kṛṣṇa is the husband of the goddess of fortune; being pleased with His pure devotee, He can offer whatever the devotee desires. But the pure devotee does not ask anything from the Lord for his personal benefit.

After taking Their supper, Kṛṣṇa and Balarāma came to bid goodnight to Akrūra and asked him how Kaṁsa was dealing with Their friends and relatives. Kṛṣṇa then inquired into Kaṁsa's plans. The Supreme Personality of Godhead then informed Akrūra that his presence was very welcome. He inquired from him whether all his relatives and friends were well and free from all kinds of ailments. Kṛṣṇa stated that He was very sorry that His maternal uncle Kaṁsa was the head of the kingdom; He said that Kaṁsa was the greatest anomaly in the whole system of government and that they could not expect any welfare for the citizens while he ruled. Then Kṛṣṇa said, "My father has undergone much tribulation simply from My being his son. For this reason also he has lost many other sons. I think Myself so fortunate that you have come as My friend and relative. My dear uncle Akrūra, please tell Me the purpose of your coming to Vṛndāvana."

After this inquiry, Akrūra, who belonged to the dynasty of Yadu, explained the recent events in Mathurā, including Kaṁsa's attempt to kill Vasudeva, the father of Kṛṣṇa. He related the things which had happened after the disclosure by Nārada that Kṛṣṇa was the son of Vasudeva, hidden by Vasudeva in the house of Nanda Mahārāja. Akrūra narrated all the stories regarding Kaṁsa. He told how Nārada had met Kaṁsa and how he himself was deputed by Kaṁsa to come to Vṛndāvana. Akrūra explained to Kṛṣṇa that Nārada had told Kaṁsa all about Kṛṣṇa's being transferred from Mathurā to Vṛndāvana just after His birth and about His killing all the demons sent by Kaṁsa. Akrūra then explained to Kṛṣṇa the purpose of his coming to Vṛndāvana: to take Him back to Mathurā. After hearing of these arrangements, Balarāma and Kṛṣṇa, who are very expert in killing opponents, mildly laughed at the plans of Kaṁsa.

They immediately informed Nanda Mahārāja that Kaṁsa had invited all the cowherd men and boys to go to Mathurā to participate in the ceremony known as Dhanur-yajña. Kaṁsa wanted them all to go there to participate in the function. On Kṛṣṇa's word, Nanda Mahārāja at once called for the cowherd men and asked them to collect milk and all kinds of milk products to present to the King in the ceremony. He also sent instructions to the police chief of Vṛndāvana to tell all the inhabitants about Kaṁsa's great Dhanur-yajña function and invite them to join. Nanda Mahārāja informed the cowherd men that they would start the next morning. They therefore arranged for the cows and bulls to carry them all to Mathurā.

When the *gopīs* heard that Akrūra had come to take Kṛṣṇa and Balarāma away to Mathurā, they became overwhelmed with anxiety. Some of them became so aggrieved that their faces turned black and they began to breathe warmly and had palpitations of the heart. They discovered that their hair and clothes immediately loosened. Hearing the news that Kṛṣṇa and Balarāma were leaving for Mathurā, others, who were engaged in household duties, stopped working, as if they had forgotten everything, like a person who is called forth to die and leave this world at once. Others immediately fainted due to separation from Kṛṣṇa. Remembering His attractive smile and His talks with them, the *gopīs* became overwhelmed with grief. They all remembered the characteristics of the Personality of Godhead, how He moved within the area of Vṛndāvana and how, with joking words, He attracted all their hearts. Thinking of Kṛṣṇa and of their imminent separation from Him, the *gopīs* assembled together with heavily beating hearts. They were completely absorbed in thought of Kṛṣṇa, and with tears falling from their eyes, they spoke as follows.

"O Providence, you are so cruel! It appears that you do not know how to show mercy to others. By your arrangement, friends contact one another, but without fulfilling their desires you separate them. This is exactly like a child's game that has no meaning. It is very abominable that you arrange to show us beautiful Kṛṣṇa, whose bluish curling hair beautifies His broad forehead and sharp nose, and who is always smiling to minimize all grief in this material world, and then arrange to separate Him from us. O Providence, you are so cruel! But most astonishingly you appear now as Akrūra, which means 'not cruel.' In the beginning we appreciated your workmanship in giving us these eyes to see the beautiful face of Kṛṣṇa, but now, just like a foolish creature, you are taking away our eyes by not letting us see Kṛṣṇa here anymore. Kṛṣṇa, the son of Nanda Mahārāja, is also very cruel! He must always have new friends; He does not like to keep friendship for a long time with anyone. We *gopīs* of Vṛndāvana, having left our homes, friends and relatives, have become Kṛṣṇa's maidservants, but He is neglecting us and going away. He does not even look upon us, although we are completely surrendered unto Him. Now all the young girls in Mathurā will have the opportunity. They are expecting Kṛṣṇa's arrival, and they will enjoy His sweet smiling face and will drink its honey. Although we know that Kṛṣṇa is very steady and determined, we are afraid that as soon as He sees the beautiful faces of the young girls in Mathurā, He will forget Himself. We fear He will become controlled by them and will forget us, for we are simple village girls. He will no longer be kind to us. We therefore do not expect Kṛṣṇa to return to Vṛndāvana. He will not leave the company of the girls in Mathurā."

The *gopīs* began to imagine the great functions in the city of Mathurā. Kṛṣṇa would pass through the streets, and the ladies and young girls of the city would see Him from the balconies of their respective houses. Mathurā City contained different communities, known then as Daśārha, Bhoja, Andhaka and Sātvata. All these communities were different branches of the same family in which Kṛṣṇa appeared, namely the Yadu dynasty. They were all expecting the arrival of Kṛṣṇa. It had already been ascertained that Kṛṣṇa, who is the resting place of the goddess of fortune and the reservoir of all pleasure and transcendental qualities, was going to visit Mathurā City.

The *gopīs* then began to condemn the activities of Akrūra. They stated that he was taking Kṛṣṇa, who was more dear than the dearest to them and who was the pleasure of their eyes. He was being taken from their sight without their being informed or solaced by Akrūra. Akrūra should not have been so merciless but should have taken compassion on them.

The *gopīs* went on to say, "The most astonishing feature is that Kṛṣṇa, the son of Nanda, without consideration, has already seated Himself on the chariot. From this it appears that Kṛṣṇa is not very intelligent. Yet He may be very intelligent—but He is not very merciful. Not only Kṛṣṇa but all the cowherd men are so callous that they are already yoking the bulls and calves for the journey to Mathurā. The elderly persons in

Vṛndāvana are also merciless; they do not take our plight into consideration and stop Kṛṣṇa's journey to Mathurā. Even the demigods are very unkind to us; they are also not impeding His going to Mathurā."

The *gopīs* prayed to the demigods to create some natural disturbance, such as a hurricane, storm or heavy rainfall, so that Kṛṣṇa could not go to Mathurā. They then began to consider, "Despite our parents and guardians, we shall personally stop Kṛṣṇa from going to Mathurā. We have no alternative but to take this direct action. Everyone has gone against us to take away Kṛṣṇa from our sight. Without Him we cannot live for a moment." The *gopīs* thus decided to obstruct the passage through which the chariot of Kṛṣṇa was supposed to pass. They began to talk among themselves: "We have passed a very long night—which seemed only a moment—engaged in the *rāsa* dance with Kṛṣṇa. We looked at His sweet smile and embraced Him and talked with Him. Now, how shall we live even for a moment if He goes away from us? At the end of the day, in the evening, along with His elder brother Balarāma, Kṛṣṇa would return home with His friends. His face would be smeared with the dust raised by the hooves of the cows, and He would smile and play on His flute and look upon us so kindly. How shall we be able to forget Him? How shall we be able to forget Kṛṣṇa, who is our life and soul? He has already taken away our hearts in so many ways throughout our days and nights, and if He goes away, there is no possibility of our continuing to live." Thinking like this, the *gopīs* became more and more grief-stricken at Kṛṣṇa's leaving Vṛndāvana. They could not check their minds, and they began to cry loudly, calling the different names of Kṛṣṇa, "O dear Dāmodara! Dear Mādhava!"

The *gopīs* cried all night before the departure of Kṛṣṇa. As soon as the sun rose, Akrūra finished his morning bath, got on the chariot and started for Mathurā with Kṛṣṇa and Balarāma. Nanda Mahārāja and the cowherd men got up on bullock carts after loading them with big earthen pots filled with yogurt, milk, ghee and other milk products, and then they began to follow the chariot of Kṛṣṇa and Balarāma. In spite of Kṛṣṇa's asking the *gopīs* not to obstruct Their way, they all surrounded the chariot and stood up to see Kṛṣṇa with pitiable eyes. Kṛṣṇa was very much affected upon seeing the plight of the *gopīs*, but His duty was to start for Mathurā, for this was foretold by Nārada. Kṛṣṇa therefore consoled the *gopīs*. He told them that they should not be aggrieved: He was coming back very soon after finishing His business. But they could not be persuaded to disperse. The chariot, however, began to head west, and as it proceeded, the minds of the *gopīs* followed it as far as possible. They watched the flag on the chariot as long as it was visible; finally they could see only the dust of the chariot in the distance. The *gopīs* did not move from their places but stood until the chariot could not be seen at all. They remained standing still, as if they were painted pictures. All the *gopīs* decided that Kṛṣṇa was not returning immediately, and with greatly disappointed hearts they returned to their respective homes. Being greatly disturbed by the absence of Kṛṣṇa, they simply thought all day and night about His pastimes and thus derived some consolation.

The Lord, accompanied by Akrūra and Balarāma, traveled in the chariot with great speed toward the bank of the Yamunā. Simply by taking a bath in the Yamunā, anyone can diminish the reactions of his sinful activities. Kṛṣṇa and Balarāma took Their baths in the river and washed Their faces. After drinking the transparent, crystal-clear water of the Yamunā, They took Their seats again on the chariot. The chariot was standing underneath the shade of big trees, and the two brothers sat down there. Akrūra then took Their permission to also take a bath in the Yamunā. According to Vedic ritual, after taking a bath in a river, one should stand at least half submerged and murmur the Gāyatrī *mantra.* While he was standing in the river, Akrūra suddenly saw Balarāma and Kṛṣṇa within the water. He was surprised to see Them there because he was confident that They were sitting on the chariot. Confused, he immediately came out of the water and went to see where the boys were, and he was very much surprised to see that They were sitting on the chariot as before. When he saw Them on the chariot, he began to wonder whether he had mistakenly seen Them in the water. He therefore went back to the river. This time he saw not only Balarāma and Kṛṣṇa there but many of the demigods and all the Siddhas, Cāraṇas and Gandharvas. They were all bowing down before the Lord. He also saw Lord Śeṣa Nāga, with thousands of hoods. Lord Śeṣa Nāga was covered with bluish garments, and His necks were all white. The white necks of Śeṣa Nāga appeared exactly like snowcapped mountains. On the coiled lap of Śeṣa Nāga, Kṛṣṇa was sitting very soberly, with four hands. His eyes were like the reddish petals of the lotus flower.

In other words, after returning to the Yamunā, Akrūra saw Balarāma turned into Śeṣa Nāga and Kṛṣṇa turned into Mahā-Viṣṇu. He saw the four-handed Supreme Personality of Godhead, smiling very beautifully. He was very pleasing to all and was looking toward everyone with a merciful glance. He appeared beautiful with His raised nose, broad forehead, attractive ears and reddish lips. His arms, reaching to the knees, were very strongly built. His shoulders were high, His chest was very broad, and His neck was shaped like a conchshell. His navel was very deep, and His abdomen was marked with three lines. His hips were broad and big, resembling those of a woman, and His thighs resembled the trunks of elephants. The other parts of His legs, the joints and lower extremities, were all very beautiful; the nails of His feet were dazzling, and His toes were as beautiful as the petals of the lotus flower. His helmet was decorated with very valuable jewels. There was a nice belt around His waist, and He wore a sacred thread across His broad chest. Bangles were on His hands, and armlets on the upper portion of His arms. He wore bells on His ankles. He possessed dazzling beauty, and His palms were like lotus flowers. He was still more beautified by the different emblems of the *viṣṇu-mūrti*—the conchshell, club, disc and lotus flower—which He held in His four hands. His chest was marked with the particular signs of Viṣṇu, and He wore fresh flower garlands. All in all, He was very beautiful to look at. Akrūra also saw His Lordship surrounded by intimate associates like the four Kumāras—Sanaka, Sanātana, Sananda and Sanat-kumāra—and other associates like Sunanda and Nanda, as well as demigods like Brahmā and Lord Śiva. The nine great learned sages were there, and also devotees like Prahlāda and Nārada and the eight Vasus. All were engaged in offering prayers to the Lord with clean hearts and pure words. After seeing the transcendental Personality of Godhead, Akrūra immediately became overwhelmed with joy and great devotion, and all over his body there was transcendental shivering. Although for the moment he was bewildered, he retained his clear consciousness and bowed down his head before the Lord. With folded hands and faltering voice, he began to offer prayers to the Lord.

Thus ends the Bhaktivedanta purport of the Thirty-ninth Chapter of Kṛṣṇa, *"Akrūra's Return Journey and His Vision of Viṣṇuloka Within the Yamunā River."*

CHAPTER 40

Prayers by Akrūra

AKRŪRA OFFERED HIS PRAYERS as follows: "My dear Lord, I offer my respectful obeisances unto You because You are the supreme cause of all causes and the original inexhaustible personality, Nārāyaṇa. From Your navel a lotus flower grows, and from that lotus Brahmā, the creator of this universe, is born. Since Brahmā is the cause of this universe, You are the cause of all causes. The elements of this cosmic manifestation—earth, water, fire, air, ether, ego and the total material energy, as well as nature, the marginal energy, the living entities, the mind, the senses, the sense objects and the demigods who control the affairs of the cosmos—are all produced from Your body.

"You are the Supersoul of everything, but no one knows Your transcendental form. Everyone within this material world is influenced by the modes of material nature. Even demigods like Lord Brahmā, being covered by the influence of material nature, do not exactly know Your transcendental existence beyond the cosmic manifestation of the three modes of material nature. Great sages and mystics worship You as the Supreme Personality of Godhead, the original cause of all living entities, all cosmic manifestation and all demigods. They worship You as all-inclusive. Some of the learned *brāhmaṇas* also worship You by observing Vedic ritualistic ceremonies. They offer different kinds of sacrifices in the names of different gods. And there are others also, who are fond of worshiping transcendental knowledge. They are very peaceful, and after giving up all kinds of material activities, they engage in the sacrifice known as *jñāna-yajña,* the philosophical search for You.

"There are also devotees, known as *bhāgavatas,* who worship You as the Supreme Personality of Godhead. After being properly initiated in the method of *Pañcarātra,* they decorate their bodies with *tilaka* and engage in worshiping Your different forms of *viṣṇu-mūrti.* There are others also, known as Śaivites, followers of different *ācāryas,* who worship You in the form of Lord Śiva."

It is stated in the *Bhagavad-gītā* that worship of demigods is also indirectly worship of the Supreme Lord. But such worship is not orthodox, because the worshipable Lord is the Supreme Personality of Godhead, Nārāyaṇa. Demigods such as Brahmā and Śiva are incarnations of the material qualities, which are also emanations from the body of Nārāyaṇa. Actually, there was no one existing before the creation except Nārāyaṇa, the Supreme Personality of Godhead. The worship of a demigod is not on the same level as worship of Nārāyaṇa.

Akrūra said, "Although the minds of those who are devotees of the demigods are fixed on a particular demigod, because You are the Supersoul of all living entities, including the demigods, worship of the demigods indirectly goes to You. Sometimes, after flowing down from the mountains during the rainy season, small rivers fail to reach the sea; some reach the sea and some do not. Similarly, the worshipers of the demigods may or may not reach You. There is no guarantee. Their success depends on the strength of their worship."

According to the Vedic principles, when a worshiper worships a particular demigod, he also conducts some ritual for Nārāyaṇa, Yajñeśvara, for, as it is mentioned in the *Bhagavad-gītā,* the demigods cannot fulfill the desires of their worshipers without the sanction of Nārāyaṇa, or Kṛṣṇa. The exact words used in the *Bhagavad-gītā* are *mayaiva vihitān hi tān,* which mean that the demigods can award some benediction after being authorized by the Supreme Lord. When a demigod worshiper comes to his senses, he can reason as follows: "The demigods can offer benedictions only after being empowered by the Supreme Lord, so why not worship the Supreme Lord directly?" Such a worshiper of the demigods may come to the Supreme Personality of Godhead, but others, who take the demigods as all in all, cannot reach the ultimate goal.

Akrūra continued to pray, "My dear Lord, the whole world is filled with the three material modes of nature, namely goodness, passion and ignorance. Everyone within this material world is covered by these modes, from Lord Brahmā down to the nonmoving plants and trees. My dear Lord, I offer my respectful obeisances unto You because You are beyond the influence of the three modes. Except for You, everyone is being carried away by the waves of these modes. My dear Lord, fire is Your mouth, the earth is Your feet, the sun is Your eye, the sky is Your navel, and the directions are Your ears. Space is Your head, the demigods are Your arms, the oceans and seas are Your abdomen, and the winds and air are Your strength and vitality. All the plants and herbs are the hairs on Your body, the clouds are the hair on Your head, the mountains are Your bones and nails, the days and nights are the blinking of Your eyelids, Prajāpati (the progenitor) is Your genitals, and the rains are Your semen.

"My dear Lord, all living entities, including different grades of demigods and different grades of overlords, kings and other living entities, are resting in You as parts and parcels of the big unit. One cannot know You by experimental knowledge. One can simply understand Your transcendental existence to be like the great ocean, in which different grades of living entities are included, or like the *udumbara* fruit, out of which small mosquitoes come. My dear Lord, whatever eternal forms and incarnations You accept when You appear in this world are meant for relieving the living entities of their ignorance, illusion and lamentation. All people, therefore, can appreciate the incarnations and pastimes of Your Lordship and eternally glorify Your activities. No one can estimate how many forms and incarnations You have, nor can anyone estimate the number of universes that are existing within You.

"Let me therefore offer my respectful obeisances unto the fish incarnation, who appeared in the devastation although Your Lordship is the cause of all causes. Let me offer my respectful obeisances unto the Hayagrīva incarnation, who killed the two demons Madhu and Kaiṭabha; let me offer my respectful obeisances unto You, who appeared as the gigantic tortoise that held up the great mountain Mandara and who appeared as the boar that rescued the earth planet, which had fallen into the water of the Garbhodaka. Let me offer my respectful obeisances unto Your Lordship, who appeared as Nṛsiṁhadeva to deliver all kinds of devotees from the fearful condition of atheistic atrocities. Let me offer my respectful obeisances unto You, who appeared as Vāmanadeva and covered the three worlds simply by extending Your lotus feet. Let me offer my respectful obeisances unto You, who appeared as the Lord of the Bhṛgus in order to kill all the infidel administrators of the world. And let me offer my respectful obeisances unto You, who appeared as Lord Rāma to kill demons like Rāvaṇa. You are worshiped by all devotees as the chief of the Raghu dynasty, Lord Rāmacandra. Let me offer my respectful obeisances unto You, who appear as Lord Vāsudeva, Lord Saṅkarṣaṇa, Lord Pradyumna and Lord Aniruddha. Let me offer my respectful obeisances unto You, who appear as Lord Buddha to bewilder the atheistic and demoniac. And let me offer my respectful obeisances unto You, who appear as Kalki to chastise the so-called royal order degraded to the abominable condition of the *mlecchas,* who are below the jurisdiction of Vedic regulative principles.

"My dear Lord, everyone within this material world is conditioned by Your illusory energy. Under the impression of false identification and false possession, everyone is transmigrating from one body to another on the path of fruitive activities and their reactions. My dear Lord, I am no exception among these conditioned souls. I am falsely thinking myself happy in possessing my home, wife, children, state, property and friends. In this way I am acting as if in a dreamland, because none of these are permanent. I am a fool to be always absorbed in thoughts of such things, accepting them as permanent truths. My dear Lord, due to my false identification, I have accepted as permanent everything which is nonpermanent, such as this material body, which is not spiritual and is the source of all kinds of miserable conditions. Being bewildered by such concepts of life, I am always absorbed in thoughts of duality, and I have forgotten You, who are the reservoir of all transcendental pleasure. I am bereft of Your transcendental association, being just like a foolish creature who leaves a water spot covered by water-nourished vegetation and goes in search of water in the desert. The conditioned souls want to quench their thirst, but they do not know where to find water. They give up the spot where there is actually a reservoir of water and run into the desert, where there is no water. My dear Lord, I am completely incapable of controlling my mind, which is now driven by the unbridled senses and is attracted by fruitive activities and their results. Therefore, my intelligence is very miserly. My dear Lord, Your lotus feet cannot be appreciated by any person in the conditioned stage of material existence, but somehow or other I have come near Your lotus feet, and I consider this to be Your causeless mercy upon me. You can act in any way because You are the supreme controller. I can thus understand that when a person becomes eligible to be delivered from the path of repeated birth and death, it is only by Your causeless mercy that he comes nearer to Your lotus feet and becomes attached to Your devotional service."

Akrūra fell down before the Lord and said, "My dear Lord, Your transcendental, eternal form is full of knowledge. Simply by concentrating one's mind upon Your form, one can understand in full knowledge everything that be, because You are the original source of all knowledge. You are the supreme powerful, possessing all kinds of energies. You are the Supreme Brahman and the Supreme Person, supreme controller and master of the material energies. I offer my respectful obeisances unto You because You are Vāsudeva, the resting place of all creation. You are the all-pervading Supreme Personality of Godhead, and You are also the Supreme Soul residing in everyone's heart and giving direction to act. Now, my Lord, I am completely surrendered unto You. Please give me Your protection."

Thus ends the Bhaktivedanta purport of the Fortieth Chapter of Kṛṣṇa, *"Prayers by Akrūra."*

CHAPTER 41

Kṛṣṇa Enters Mathurā

WHILE AKRŪRA WAS OFFERING his prayers to the Supreme Personality of Godhead, the Lord disappeared from the water, exactly as an expert dramatic actor changes his dress and assumes his original feature. After the *viṣṇu-mūrti* disappeared, Akrūra got out of the water. Finishing the rest of his ritualistic performance, he went near the chariot of Balarāma and Kṛṣṇa and was struck with wonder. Kṛṣṇa asked whether he had seen something wonderful within the water or in space. Akrūra said, "My dear Lord, all wonderful things that are happening within this world, either in the sky or in the water or on the land, are factually appearing in Your universal form. So when I have seen You, what wonderful things have I not seen?" This statement confirms the Vedic version that one who knows Kṛṣṇa knows everything and that one who has seen Kṛṣṇa has seen everything, regardless of how wonderful a thing may be. "My dear Lord," Akrūra continued, "there cannot be anything more wonderful than Your transcendental form. When I have seen Your transcendental form, what is there left to see?"

After saying this, Akrūra immediately started driving the chariot, and by the end of the day they reached the precincts of Mathurā. As they rode from Vṛndāvana to Mathurā, all the passersby along the way who saw Kṛṣṇa and Balarāma could not help but look at Them again and again. In the meantime, the other inhabitants of Vṛndāvana, headed by Nanda and Upananda, had already reached Mathurā by going through the forests, and they were awaiting the arrival of Kṛṣṇa and Balarāma in a garden. Upon reaching the entrance to Mathurā, Kṛṣṇa and Balarāma got down from the chariot and shook hands with Akrūra. Kṛṣṇa informed him, "You may go home now because We shall enter Mathurā later, along with Our associates." Akrūra replied, "My dear Lord, I cannot go to Mathurā alone, leaving You aside. I am Your surrendered servant. Please do not try to avoid me. Please, come along with me, with Your elder brother and cowherd boyfriends, and sanctify my house. My dear Lord, if You come, my home will be sanctified by the dust of Your lotus feet. The water emanating from the perspiration of Your lotus feet, namely the Ganges, purifies everyone, including the forefathers, the fire-god and all other demigods. Bali Mahārāja has become famous simply by washing Your lotus feet, and he enjoyed all material opulences and later on was elevated to the highest position of liberation. The Ganges water not only sanctifies the three worlds but is carried on the head of Lord Śiva. The ancestors of Bhagīratha, sanctified by this water, achieved the heavenly planets. O Supreme Lord of lords! O master of the universe! One can achieve piety simply by hearing about Your transcendental pastimes. O Supreme Nārāyaṇa, who are praised by select verses, I offer my respectful obeisances unto You."

On hearing this, the Supreme Personality of Godhead, Kṛṣṇa, replied, "Akrūra, I shall surely come to your home with My elder brother, Balarāma, but only after killing all the demons who are envious of the Yadu dynasty. In this way I shall please all My relatives." Akrūra became a little disappointed by these words of the Supreme Personality of Godhead, but he could not disregard the order. He therefore entered Mathurā and informed Kaṁsa about the arrival of Kṛṣṇa, and then he entered his own home.

After Akrūra's departure, Lord Kṛṣṇa, Balarāma and the cowherd boys entered Mathurā to see the city. They observed that the gate of Mathurā was made of first-class marble, very well constructed, and that the doors were made of pure gold. There were gorgeous orchards and gardens all around, and the whole city was encircled by canals so that no enemy could enter very easily. They saw that all the crossroads were decorated with gold and that there were copper and brass storehouses for stocking grain. And there were many rich men's houses, all appearing symmetrical, as if constructed by one engineer. The houses were decorated with costly jewels, and each and every house had nice compounds of trees bearing fruits and flowers. The corridors and verandas of the houses were decorated with silk cloth and embroidery work in jewels and pearls. In front of the balcony windows were pigeons and peacocks walking and cooing. All the grain dealers' shops within the city were decorated with different kinds of flowers and garlands, newly grown grass and pleasing flowers like narcissus and roses. The entrance doors of the houses were decorated with waterpots filled with water. Water mixed with yogurt, sandalwood pulp and flowers was sprinkled all around the doors, which were also decorated with burning lamps of different sizes. Over all the doors were decorations of fresh mango leaves and silk festoons.

When the news spread that Kṛṣṇa, Balarāma and the cowherd boys were within Mathurā City, all the inhabitants gathered, and the ladies and girls immediately went up to the roofs of the houses to see Them. They had been awaiting the arrival of Kṛṣṇa and Balarāma with great anxiety, and in their extreme eagerness to see Kṛṣṇa and Balarāma, the ladies did not dress themselves very properly. Some of them placed their clothes in the wrong place. Some anointed their eyes on one side only, and some wore ankle bells only on one leg or wore only one earring. Thus in great haste, not even decorated properly, they went to see Kṛṣṇa from the roofs. Some of them had been taking their lunch, but as soon as they heard that Kṛṣṇa and Balarāma were in the city, they left their eating and ran to the roofs. Some of them were in the bathroom taking their baths, but without properly finishing their baths, they went to see Kṛṣṇa and Balarāma. Some were engaged in feeding their children breast milk, but they put their babies aside and went to see Kṛṣṇa and Balarāma. Passing by very slowly and smiling, Lord Kṛṣṇa immediately stole their hearts. He who is the husband of the goddess of fortune passed through the street like an elephant. For a very long time the women of Mathurā had heard about Kṛṣṇa and Balarāma and Their uncommon characteristics, and they were very much attracted and eager to see Them. Now when they actually saw Kṛṣṇa and Balarāma passing on the street and saw Them sweetly smiling, the ladies' joy reached the point of ecstasy. When they actually saw Them with their eyes, they took Kṛṣṇa and Balarāma within their hearts and began to embrace Them to their fullest desire. Their bodily hairs stood up in ecstasy. They had heard of Kṛṣṇa, but they had never seen Him, and now their longing was relieved. After going up on the roofs of the palaces of Mathurā, the ladies, their faces joyful, began to shower flowers upon Kṛṣṇa and Balarāma. When the brothers were passing through the streets, all the *brāhmaṇas* in the neighborhood went out with sandal water and flowers and respectfully welcomed Them to the city. All the residents of Mathurā began to talk among themselves about the elevated and pious activities of the people of Vṛndāvana. The residents of Mathurā were surprised at the pious activities the cowherd men in Vṛndāvana must have performed in their previous lives to be able to see Kṛṣṇa and Balarāma daily as cowherd boys.

While Kṛṣṇa and Balarāma were passing in this way, They saw a washerman and dyer of clothing. Kṛṣṇa was pleased to ask him for some nice clothing. He also promised that if the washerman would deliver the nicest dyed cloth to Him, the washerman would become very happy, and all good fortune would be his. Kṛṣṇa was not a beggar, nor was He in need of clothing, but by this request He indicated that everyone should be ready to offer Kṛṣṇa whatever He wants. That is the meaning of Kṛṣṇa consciousness.

Unfortunately, this washerman was a servant of Kaṁsa and therefore could not appreciate the demand of Lord Kṛṣṇa, the Supreme Personality of Godhead. This is the effect of bad association. He could have immediately delivered the clothing to the Supreme Personality of Godhead, who promised him all good fortune, but being a servant of Kaṁsa, the sinful demon could not accept the offer. Instead of being pleased, he was very angry and refused the Lord's request, saying, "How is it that You are asking for clothing which is meant for the King?" The washerman then began to instruct Kṛṣṇa and Balarāma: "My dear boys, in the future don't be so impudent as to ask for things which belong to the King. Otherwise, You will be punished by the government men. They will arrest You and punish You, and You will be in difficulty. I have practical experience of this fact. Anyone who unlawfully wants to use the King's property is very severely punished."

On hearing this, Lord Kṛṣṇa, the son of Devakī, became very angry at the washerman, and striking him with the upper portion of His hand, He separated the man's head from his body. The washerman fell down dead on the ground. In this way Lord Kṛṣṇa confirmed the statement of the *Brahma-saṁhitā* that every limb of His body is capable of doing everything He likes. Without a sword, but simply with His hand, He cut off the head of the washerman. This is proof that the Supreme Lord is omnipotent. If He wants to do something, He can do it without extraneous help.

After this ghastly incident, the employees of the washerman immediately dispersed, leaving the clothing. Kṛṣṇa and Balarāma took possession of it and dressed according to Their choice; the rest of the clothes were offered to the cowherd boys, who also used them as they desired. What they did not use remained there. Kṛṣṇa, Balarāma and the boys then proceeded along the main road. In the meantime, a devotee-tailor took the opportunity of service and prepared some nice clothes from the cloth for Kṛṣṇa and Balarāma. Thus being very nicely attired, Kṛṣṇa and Balarāma looked like elephants dressed with colored clothing on the full-moon day or the dark-moon day. Kṛṣṇa was very pleased with the tailor and gave him the benediction of *sārūpya-mukti,* which means that after leaving his body he would be liberated and would attain a four-handed body exactly like that of Nārāyaṇa in the Vaikuṇṭha planets. Kṛṣṇa also granted him that as long as he would live he would earn sufficient opulence to be able to enjoy sense gratification. By this incident Kṛṣṇa proved that those who are Kṛṣṇa conscious devotees will not be lacking material enjoyment of sense gratification. They will have sufficient opportunity for such things, but after leaving this body they will be allowed to enter the spiritual planets of Vaikuṇṭhaloka or Kṛṣṇaloka, Goloka Vṛndāvana.

After dressing nicely, Kṛṣṇa and Balarāma went to a florist of the name Sudāmā. As soon as They reached the precinct of his house, the florist immediately came out and with great devotion fell down on his face to offer his respectful obeisances. He offered a nice seat to Kṛṣṇa and Balarāma and asked his assistant to bring out flowers, betel nuts and pulp of *candana.* The florist's welcome greatly satisfied the Lord.

The florist very humbly and submissively offered his prayers to the Lord, saying, "My dear Lord, because You have come to my place, I think all my forefathers and all my worshipable superiors are pleased and delivered. My dear Lord, You are the supreme cause of all causes of this cosmic manifestation, but for the benefit of the residents of this earthly planet, You have appeared with Your plenary portion to give protection to Your devotees and annihilate the demons. You are equally disposed as the friend of all living entities; You are the Supersoul, and You do not discriminate between friend and enemy. Yet You are pleased to give Your devotees the special result of their devotional activities. My Lord, I am praying that You please tell me whatever You wish me to do, because I am Your eternal servant. If You would order me to do something, it would be a great favor to me." The florist, Sudāmā, was greatly pleased within his heart by seeing Kṛṣṇa and Balarāma in his place, and thus, as his choicest desire, he made two exquisite garlands of various flowers and presented them to the Lord. Kṛṣṇa and Balarāma were very much pleased with his sincere service, and Kṛṣṇa offered the florist His salutation and benedictions, which He is always prepared to bestow upon the surrendered souls. When the florist was offered benedictions, he begged from the Lord that he might remain His eternal servant in devotional service and by such service do good to all living creatures. By this, it is clear that a devotee of the Lord in Kṛṣṇa consciousness should not be satisfied simply by his own advancement in devotional service; he must be willing to work for the welfare of all others. This example was followed by the six Gosvāmīs of Vṛndāvana. It is therefore stated in a prayer about them, *lokānāṁ hita-kāriṇau:* Vaiṣṇavas, or devotees of the Lord, are not selfish. Whatever benefits they derive from the Supreme Personality of Godhead as benedictions they want to distribute to all other persons. That is the greatest of all humanitarian activities. Being satisfied with the florist, Lord Kṛṣṇa not only gave him whatever benedictions he wanted, but over and above that He offered him all material opulences, family prosperity, a long duration of life and whatever else his heart desired within the material world.

Thus ends the Bhaktivedanta purport of the Forty-first Chapter of Kṛṣṇa, *"Kṛṣṇa Enters Mathurā."*

CHAPTER 42

The Breaking of the Bow in the Sacrificial Arena

AFTER LEAVING THE FLORIST'S PLACE, Kṛṣṇa and Balarāma saw a hunchbacked young woman carrying a dish of sandalwood pulp through the streets. Since Kṛṣṇa is the reservoir of all pleasure, He wanted to make all His companions joyous by cutting a joke with the hunchbacked woman. Kṛṣṇa addressed her, "O tall young woman, who are you? Tell Me, for whom are you carrying this sandalwood pulp in your hand? I think you should offer this sandalwood to Me, and if you do so I am sure you will be fortunate." Kṛṣṇa is the Supreme Personality of Godhead, and He knew everything about the hunchback. By His inquiry He indicated that there was no use in serving a demon; she would do better to serve Kṛṣṇa and Balarāma and get an immediate result of the service.

The woman replied to Kṛṣṇa, "My dear Śyāmasundara, dear beautiful dark boy, You may know that I am engaged as a maidservant of Kaṁsa. I am supplying him pulp of sandalwood daily. The King is very pleased with me for supplying this nice thing, but now I see that there is no one who can better be served by this pulp of sandalwood than You two brothers." Being captivated by the beautiful features of Kṛṣṇa and Balarāma, Their talking, Their smiling, Their glancing and Their other activities, the hunchbacked woman began to smear all the pulp of sandalwood over Their bodies with great satisfaction and devotion. The two transcendental brothers, Kṛṣṇa and Balarāma, were naturally beautiful and had beautiful complexions, and They were nicely dressed in colorful garments. The upper portions of Their bodies were already very attractive, and when the hunchbacked woman smeared Their bodies with sandalwood pulp, They looked even more beautiful. Kṛṣṇa was very pleased by this service, and He began to consider how to reward her. In other words, in order to draw the attention of the Lord, the Kṛṣṇa conscious devotee has to serve Him in great love and devotion. Kṛṣṇa cannot be pleased by any action other than transcendental loving service unto Him. Thinking like this, Lord Kṛṣṇa pressed the feet of the hunchbacked woman with His toes and, capturing her cheeks with His fingers, gave her a jerk in order to make her straight. At once the hunchbacked woman became a beautiful straight girl, with broad hips, thin waist and very nice, well-shaped breasts. Since Kṛṣṇa was pleased with the service of the hunchbacked woman, and since she was touched by Kṛṣṇa's hands, she became the most beautiful girl among women. This incident shows that by serving Kṛṣṇa the devotee immediately becomes elevated to the most exalted position in all respects. Devotional service is so potent that anyone who takes to it becomes qualified with all godly qualities. Kṛṣṇa was attracted to the hunchbacked woman not for her beauty but for her service; as soon as she rendered service, she immediately became the most beautiful woman. A Kṛṣṇa conscious person does not have to be qualified or beautiful; after becoming Kṛṣṇa conscious and rendering service unto Kṛṣṇa, he becomes very much qualified and beautiful.

When the woman was turned by Kṛṣṇa's favor into an exquisitely beautiful young girl, she naturally felt very much obliged to Kṛṣṇa, and she was also attracted by His beauty. Without hesitation, she caught the rear part of His cloth and began to pull it. She smiled flirtatiously and admitted that she was agitated by lusty desires. She forgot that she was on the street and before the elder brother of Kṛṣṇa and His friends.

She frankly proposed to Kṛṣṇa, "My dear hero, I cannot leave You in this way. You must come to my place. I am already very much attracted to Your beauty, so I must receive You well, and since You are the best among males, You must also be very kind upon me." In plain words she proposed that Kṛṣṇa come to her home and satisfy her lusty desires. Kṛṣṇa, of course, felt a little bit embarrassed in front of His elder brother, Balarāma, but He knew that the girl was simple and attracted; therefore He simply smiled at her words. Looking toward His cowherd boyfriends, He replied to the girl, "My dear beautiful girl, I am very much pleased by your invitation, and I must come to your home after finishing My other business here. Such a beautiful girl as you is the only means of solace for persons like Us, who are away from home and not married. Certainly, a suitable girlfriend like you can give Us relief from all kinds of mental agitation." Kṛṣṇa satisfied the girl in this way with sweet words. Leaving her there, He proceeded down the street of the marketplace, where the citizens were prepared to receive Him with various kinds of presentations, especially betel nuts, flowers and sandalwood pulp.

The mercantile men in the market worshiped Kṛṣṇa and Balarāma with great respect. When Kṛṣṇa was passing through the street, all the women in the surrounding houses came to see Him, and some of the younger ones almost fainted, being captivated by His beauty. Their hair and tight clothing loosened, and they forgot where they were standing.

Kṛṣṇa next inquired from the citizens as to the location of the place of sacrifice. Kaṁsa had arranged for the sacrifice called Dhanur-yajña, and to designate this particular sacrifice he had placed a big bow near the sacrificial altar. The bow was very big and wonderful and resembled a rainbow in the sky. Within the sacrificial arena, this bow was protected by many constables and watchmen engaged by King Kaṁsa. As Kṛṣṇa and Balarāma approached the bow, They were warned not to go nearer, but Kṛṣṇa ignored this warning. He forcibly went up and immediately took the big bow in His left hand. After stringing the bow in the presence of the crowd, He drew it and broke it at the middle into two parts, exactly as an elephant breaks sugarcane in the field. Everyone present appreciated Kṛṣṇa's power. The sound of the bow cracking filled both sky and land and was heard by Kaṁsa. When Kaṁsa heard what had happened, he began to fear for his life. The caretakers of the bow, who were standing by watching, became very angry, and with their respective weapons in hand they rushed toward Kṛṣṇa, shouting, "Arrest Him! Arrest Him! Kill Him! Kill Him!" Kṛṣṇa and Balarāma were surrounded. When They understood the sinister motives of the guards, They became angry, and taking up the two pieces of the broken bow, They began to beat down all of Kaṁsa's caretakers. While this turmoil was going on, Kaṁsa sent a small group of troops to assist the caretakers, but Kṛṣṇa and Balarāma fought with them also and killed them.

After this, Kṛṣṇa did not proceed further into the sacrificial arena but went out the gate and proceeded toward Their resting camp. Along the way, He visited various places in Mathurā City with great delight. Seeing the activities and wonderful prowess of Kṛṣṇa, all the citizens of Mathurā began to consider the two brothers to be demigods who had come down to Mathurā, and they all looked upon Them with great astonishment. The two brothers strolled carefree in the street, not caring for the law and order of Kaṁsa.

As sunset approached, Kṛṣṇa, Balarāma and Their cowherd boyfriends went to the outskirts of the city, where all their carts were assembled. Thus Kṛṣṇa and Balarāma gave some preliminary hints of Their arrival to Kaṁsa, and he could understand what severe type of danger was awaiting him the next day in the sacrificial arena.

When Kṛṣṇa and Balarāma had been going from Vṛndāvana to Mathurā, the inhabitants of Vṛndāvana had imagined the great fortune of the citizens of Mathurā in being able to see the wonderful beauty of Kṛṣṇa, who is worshiped by His pure devotees as well as the goddess of fortune. The fantasies of the residents of Vṛndāvana were now actually realized, for the citizens of Mathurā became fully satisfied by seeing Kṛṣṇa.

When Kṛṣṇa returned to His camp, He was taken care of by servants who washed His lotus feet, gave Him a nice seat and offered Him milk and palatable dishes. After taking supper and thinking of the next day's program, He very peacefully took rest. Thus He passed the night there.

On the other side, when Kaṁsa came to understand about the breaking of his wonderful bow and the killing of the caretakers and soldiers by Kṛṣṇa, he could partially realize the power of the Supreme Personality of Godhead. He could realize that the eighth son of Devakī had appeared and that now his death was imminent. Thinking of his imminent death, he was restless the entire night. He began to have many inauspicious visions, and he could understand that Kṛṣṇa and Balarāma, who had approached the precincts of the city, were his messengers of death. Kaṁsa saw various kinds of inauspicious signs while both awake and dreaming. When he looked in the mirror he could not see his head, although the head was actually present. He saw the luminaries in the sky in double, although there was only one set factually. He began to see holes in his shadow, and he heard a high buzzing sound within his ears. All the trees before him appeared to be made of gold, and he could not see his own footprints in dust or muddy clay. In dreams he saw various kinds of ghosts being carried in a carriage drawn by donkeys. He also dreamed that someone gave him poison and he was drinking it. He dreamed also that he was going naked with a garland of flowers and was smearing oil all over his body. Thus, as Kaṁsa saw various signs of death while both awake and sleeping, he could understand that death was certain, and thus in great anxiety he could not rest that night. Just after the night expired, he busily arranged for the wrestling match.

The wrestling arena was nicely cleansed and decorated with flags, festoons and flowers, and the match was announced by the beating of kettledrums. The platform appeared very beautiful due to streamers and flags. Different types of galleries were arranged for respectable persons—kings, *brāhmaṇas* and *kṣatriyas.* The various kings had reserved thrones, and others had arranged seats also. Kaṁsa finally arrived, accompanied by various ministers and secretaries, and he sat on the raised platform especially meant for him. Unfortunately, although he was sitting in the center of all his governing executive heads, his heart was palpitating in fear of death. Cruel death evidently does not care even for a person as powerful as Kaṁsa. When death comes, it does not care for anyone's exalted position.

When everything was complete, the wrestlers who were to exhibit their skills before the assembly walked into the arena. They were decorated with nice ornaments and dress. Some of the famous wrestlers were Cāṇūra, Muṣṭika, Śala, Kūṭa and Tośala.

Being enlivened by the musical concert, they passed through with great alacrity. All the respectable cowherd men who came from Vṛndāvana, headed by Nanda, were also welcomed by Kaṁsa. After presenting Kaṁsa with the milk products they had brought with them, the cowherd men also took their respective seats by the side of the King, on a platform especially meant for them.

Thus ends the Bhaktivedanta purport of the Forty-second Chapter of Kṛṣṇa, *"The Breaking of the Bow in the Sacrificial Arena."*

CHAPTER 43

The Killing of the Elephant Kuvalayāpīḍa

AFTER TAKING THEIR BATHS and finishing all other morning duties, Kṛṣṇa and Balarāma could hear the beating of the kettledrums in the wrestling arena. They immediately prepared Themselves to proceed to the spot to see the fun. When Kṛṣṇa and Balarāma reached the gate of the wrestling arena, They saw a big elephant of the name Kuvalayāpīḍa being tended by a caretaker riding on its head. The caretaker was deliberately blocking Their entrance by keeping the elephant in front of the gateway. Kṛṣṇa could understand the purpose of the caretaker, and He prepared Himself by tightening His clothes before combating the elephant. He addressed the caretaker in a very grave voice, as resounding as a cloud: "You miscreant caretaker, give way and let Me pass through the gate. If you block My way, I shall send you and your elephant to the house of death personified."

The caretaker, being thus insulted by Kṛṣṇa, became very angry, and in order to challenge Kṛṣṇa, as was previously planned, he provoked the elephant to attack. The elephant then moved before Kṛṣṇa like inevitable death. It rushed toward Him and tried to catch Him with its trunk, but Kṛṣṇa very dexterously moved behind the elephant. Being able to see only to the end of its trunk, the elephant could not see Kṛṣṇa hiding behind its legs, but it tried to capture Him with its trunk. Kṛṣṇa again very quickly escaped capture, and He again ran behind the elephant and caught its tail. Holding the elephant by its tail, Kṛṣṇa began to pull it, and with very great strength He dragged it for at least twenty-five yards, just as Garuḍa drags an insignificant snake. Kṛṣṇa pulled the elephant from this side to that, from right to left, just as He used to pull a calf by its tail in His childhood. After this, Kṛṣṇa went in front of the elephant and gave it a strong slap. He then slipped away from the elephant's view and ran to its back. Then, falling down on the ground, Kṛṣṇa placed Himself in front of the elephant's two legs and caused it to trip and fall. Kṛṣṇa immediately got up, but the elephant, thinking that He was still lying down, tried to push an ivory tusk through the body of Kṛṣṇa by forcibly stabbing it into the ground. Although the elephant was harassed and angry, the caretaker riding on its head tried to provoke it further. The elephant then rushed madly toward Kṛṣṇa. As soon as it came within reach, Kṛṣṇa caught hold of the trunk and pulled the elephant down. When the elephant and caretaker fell, Kṛṣṇa jumped up on the elephant, broke off one of its tusks, and with it killed the elephant and the caretaker also. After killing the elephant, Kṛṣṇa took the ivory tusk on His shoulder. Decorated with drops of perspiration and sprinkled with the blood of the elephant, He looked very beautiful, and thus He proceeded toward the wrestling arena. Lord Balarāma took the other tusk of the elephant on His shoulder. Accompanied by Their cowherd boyfriends, They entered the arena.

When Kṛṣṇa entered the wrestling arena with Balarāma and Their friends, He appeared differently to different people according to their different relationships (*rasas*) with Him. Kṛṣṇa is the reservoir of all pleasure and all kinds of *rasas,* both favorable and unfavorable. He appeared to the wrestlers exactly like a thunderbolt. To the people in general He appeared as the most beautiful personality. To the females He appeared to be the most attractive male, Cupid personified, and thus He increased their lust. The cowherd men who were present there looked upon Kṛṣṇa as their own kinsman, coming from the same village of Vṛndāvana. The impious *kṣatriya* kings who were present saw Him as the strongest ruler and their chastiser. To the parents of Kṛṣṇa, Nanda and Yaśodā, He appeared to be the most loving child. To Kaṁsa, the king of the Bhoja dynasty, He appeared to be death personified. To the unintelligent, He appeared to be an incapable personality. To the *yogīs* present, He appeared to be the Supersoul. To the members of the Vṛṣṇi dynasty He appeared to be the most celebrated descendant. Thus appreciated differently by different kinds of people present, Kṛṣṇa entered the wrestling arena with Balarāma and His cowherd boyfriends. Having heard that Kṛṣṇa had already killed the elephant Kuvalayāpīḍa, Kaṁsa knew beyond doubt that Kṛṣṇa was formidable. He thus became very much afraid of Him. Kṛṣṇa and Balarāma had long arms. They were beautifully dressed, and They were attractive to all the people assembled there. They were dressed as if They were going to act on a dramatic stage, and They drew the attention of all people.

The citizens of Mathurā City who saw Kṛṣṇa, the Supreme Personality of Godhead, became very pleased and began to look on His face with insatiable glances, as if they were drinking the nectar of heaven. Seeing Kṛṣṇa gave them so much pleasure that it appeared as if they were not only drinking the nectar of seeing His face but were also smelling the aroma and licking up the taste of His body and were embracing Him and Balarāma with their arms. They began to talk among themselves about the two transcendental brothers. For a long time they had heard of the beauty and activities of Kṛṣṇa and Balarāma, but now they were personally seeing Them face to face. They thought that Kṛṣṇa and Balarāma were two plenary incarnations of the Supreme Personality of Godhead, Nārāyaṇa, who had appeared in Vṛndāvana.

The citizens of Mathurā began to recite Kṛṣṇa's pastimes—His birth as the son of Vasudeva, His being taken into the care of Nanda Mahārāja and his wife in Gokula, and all those events leading to His coming to Mathurā to favor them. They spoke of the killing of the demon Pūtanā, as well as the killing of Tṛṇāvarta, who came as a whirlwind. They also recalled the deliverance of the twin brothers from within the *yamala-arjuna* trees. The citizens of Mathurā spoke among themselves: "Śaṅkhacūḍa, Keśī, Dhenukāsura and many other demons were killed by Kṛṣṇa and Balarāma in Vṛndāvana. Kṛṣṇa also saved all the cowherd men of Vṛndāvana from a devastating fire. He chastised the Kāliya snake in the water of the Yamunā, and He curbed the false pride of the heavenly King, Indra. Kṛṣṇa held up the great Govardhana Hill in one hand for seven continuous days and saved all the people of Gokula from incessant rain, hurricane and hailstorm." They also began to remember other enlivening activities: "The damsels of Vṛndāvana were so pleased by seeing Kṛṣṇa's beauty and participating in His activities that they forgot the troubles of material existence. By seeing Kṛṣṇa and thinking of Him, they forgot all sorts of fatigue." The Mathurā citizens discussed the dynasty of Yadu, saying that because of Kṛṣṇa's appearance in this dynasty the Yadus would remain the most celebrated family in the whole universe. The citizens of Mathurā then began to talk about Balarāma. They spoke of His very beautiful lotus-petal eyes, and they remarked of Him, "This boy has killed the Pralamba demon and many others also." While they were thus talking about the activities of Kṛṣṇa and Balarāma, they heard the vibrations of different bands announcing the wrestling match.

The famous wrestler Cāṇūra then began to talk with Kṛṣṇa and Balarāma. "My dear Kṛṣṇa and Balarāma," he said, "we have heard about Your past activities. You are great heroes, and therefore the King has called You. We have heard that Your arms are very strong. The King and all the people present here desire to see a display of Your wrestling abilities. A citizen should be obedient and please the mind of the ruling king; acting in that way, the citizen attains all kinds of good fortune. One who does not care to act obediently is made unhappy because of the king's anger. You are cowherd boys, and we have heard that while tending Your cows in the forest You enjoy wrestling with each other. We wish, therefore, for You to join with us in wrestling so that all the people present here, including the King, will be pleased."

Kṛṣṇa immediately understood the purpose of Cāṇūra's statements, and He prepared to wrestle with him. But according to the time and circumstances, He spoke as follows: "You are the subject of the King of the Bhojas, and you live in the jungle. We are also indirectly his subjects, and We try to please him as far as possible. This offer of wrestling is a great favor of his, but the fact is that We are simply boys. We sometimes play in the forest of Vṛndāvana with Our friends who are Our own age. We think that to combat persons of equal age and strength is good for Us, but to fight great wrestlers like you would not be good for the audience. It would contradict their religious principles." Kṛṣṇa thus indicated that the celebrated, strong wrestlers should not challenge Kṛṣṇa and Balarāma to fight.

In reply to this, Cāṇūra said, "My dear Kṛṣṇa, we can understand very well that You are neither a child nor a young man. You are transcendental to everyone, as is Your big brother, Balarāma. You have already killed the elephant Kuvalayāpīḍa, who was capable of fighting thousands of other elephants. You have killed him in a wonderful way. Because of Your strength, it behooves You to compete with the strongest wrestlers amongst us. I therefore wish to wrestle with You, and Your elder brother, Balarāma, will wrestle with Muṣṭika."

Thus ends the Bhaktivedanta purport of the Forty-third Chapter of Kṛṣṇa, *"The Killing of the Elephant Kuvalayāpīḍa."*

CHAPTER 44

The Killing of Kaṁsa

After Kaṁsa's wrestlers expressed their determination, the Supreme Personality of Godhead, the killer of Madhu, confronted Cāṇūra, and Lord Balarāma, the son of Rohiṇī, confronted Muṣṭika. Kṛṣṇa and Cāṇūra and then Balarāma and Muṣṭika locked themselves hand to hand, leg to leg, and each began to press against the other with a view to coming out victorious. They joined palm to palm, calf to calf, head to head, chest to chest and began to strike each other. The fighting increased as they pushed each other from one place to another. One captured the other and threw him down on the ground, and another rushed from the back to the front of another and tried to overcome him with a hold. The fighting increased step by step. There was picking up, dragging and pushing, and then the legs and hands were locked together. All the arts of wrestling were perfectly exhibited by the parties as each tried his best to defeat his opponent.

But the audience in the wrestling arena was not very much satisfied because the combatants did not appear to be equally matched. They considered Kṛṣṇa and Balarāma to be mere boys before Cāṇūra and Muṣṭika, who were the strongest wrestlers, as solid as stone. Being compassionate and favoring Kṛṣṇa and Balarāma, the many ladies in the audience began to talk as follows: "Dear friends, there is injustice here." Another said, "Even in front of the King this wrestling is going on between incompatible sides." The ladies had lost their sense of enjoyment. They could not encourage the fighting between the strong and the weak. "Muṣṭika and Cāṇūra are just like thunderbolts, as strong as great mountains, and Kṛṣṇa and Balarāma are two delicate boys of very tender age. The principle of justice has already left this assembly. Persons who are aware of the civilized principles of justice will not remain to watch this unfair match. Those taking part in watching this wrestling match are not very much enlightened; therefore whether they speak or remain silent, they are being subjected to the reactions of sinful activities."

"But my dear friends," another lady in the assembly spoke out, "just look at the face of Kṛṣṇa. There are drops of perspiration on His face from chasing His enemy, and His face appears like a lotus flower with drops of water."

Another lady said, "Don't you see how the face of Lord Balarāma has turned especially beautiful? There is a reddish hue on His white face because He is engaged in a strenuous wrestling match with Muṣṭika."

Another lady in the assembly addressed her friend, "Dear friend, just imagine how fortunate is the land of Vṛndāvana, where the Supreme Personality of Godhead Himself is present, always decorated with flower garlands and engaged in tending cows along with His brother, Lord Balarāma. He is always accompanied by His cowherd boyfriends, and He plays His transcendental flute. The residents of Vṛndāvana are fortunate to be able to constantly see the lotus feet of Kṛṣṇa and Balarāma, which are worshiped by great demigods like Lord Śiva and by the goddess of fortune. We cannot estimate how many pious activities were executed by the damsels of Vrajabhūmi so that they were able to enjoy the Supreme Personality of Godhead by looking upon the unparalleled beauty of His transcendental body. The beauty of the Lord is beyond compare. No one is higher than or equal to Him in beauty of complexion or bodily luster. Kṛṣṇa and Balarāma are the reservoir of all kinds of opulence—namely wealth, strength, beauty, fame, knowledge and renunciation. The *gopīs* are so fortunate that they can see and think of Kṛṣṇa twenty-four hours a day, beginning from their milking the cows or husking the paddy or churning the butter in the morning. While engaged in cleaning their houses and washing their floors, they are always absorbed in thought of Kṛṣṇa."

The *gopīs* give a perfect example of how one can execute Kṛṣṇa consciousness even while performing various types of material engagements. By constantly being absorbed in the thought of Kṛṣṇa, one cannot be affected by the contamination of material activities. The *gopīs,* therefore, are perfectly in trance, *samādhi,* the highest perfectional stage of mystic power. In the *Bhagavad-gītā,* it is confirmed that one who is constantly thinking of Kṛṣṇa is a first-class *yogī* among all kinds of *yogīs.* "My dear friends," one lady told another, "we must accept the activities of the *gopīs* to be the highest form of piety; otherwise, how could they have achieved the opportunity of seeing Kṛṣṇa both morning and evening—in the morning when He goes to the pasturing ground with His cows and cowherd boyfriends, and in the evening when He returns with them, playing on His flute and smiling very brilliantly?"

When Lord Kṛṣṇa, the Supersoul of every living being, understood that the ladies in the assembly were anxious for Him, He decided not to continue wrestling but to kill the wrestlers immediately. The parents of Kṛṣṇa and Balarāma, namely Nanda Mahārāja, Yaśodā, Vasudeva and Devakī, were also very anxious because they did not know the unlimited strength of their children. Lord Balarāma was fighting with the wrestler Muṣṭika in the same way that Kṛṣṇa, the Supreme Personality of Godhead, was fighting and wrestling with Cāṇūra. Lord Kṛṣṇa appeared to be cruel to Cāṇūra, and He immediately struck him thrice with His fist. The great wrestler was jolted, to the astonishment of the audience. Cāṇūra then took his last chance and attacked Kṛṣṇa, just as one hawk swoops upon another. Folding his two hands, he began to strike the chest of Kṛṣṇa, but Lord Kṛṣṇa was not even slightly disturbed, any more than an elephant is when hit by a flower garland. Kṛṣṇa quickly caught the two hands of Cāṇūra and began to wheel him around, and simply by this centrifugal action, Cāṇūra lost his life. Kṛṣṇa then threw him to the ground. Cāṇūra fell just like the flag of Indra, and all his nicely fashioned ornaments were scattered hither and thither.

Muṣṭika also struck Balarāma, and Balarāma returned the stroke with great force. Muṣṭika began to tremble and vomit blood. Distressed, he gave up his vital force and fell down just as a tree falls down in a hurricane.

After the two wrestlers were killed, a wrestler named Kūṭa came forward. Lord Balarāma immediately caught him in His left hand and killed him nonchalantly. A wrestler of the name Śala came forward, and Kṛṣṇa immediately cracked his head with a kick. A wrestler named Tośala came forward and was killed in the same way. Thus all the great wrestlers were killed by Kṛṣṇa and Balarāma, and the remaining wrestlers fled from the assembly out of fear for their lives. All the cowherd boyfriends of Kṛṣṇa and Balarāma approached Them and congratulated Them with great pleasure. While trumpets resounded and drums were beaten, the leg bells on the feet of Kṛṣṇa and Balarāma tinkled.

All the people gathered there began to clap in great ecstasy, and no one could estimate the bounds of their pleasure. The *brāhmaṇas* present began to praise Kṛṣṇa and Balarāma ecstatically. Only Kaṁsa was morose; he neither clapped nor offered benediction to Kṛṣṇa. Kaṁsa resented that the trumpets and drums should be played for Kṛṣṇa's victory, and he was very sorry that the wrestlers had been killed and had fled the assembly. He therefore immediately ordered the band to stop playing and addressed his men as follows: "I order that these two sons of Vasudeva be immediately driven out of Mathurā. The cowherd boys who have come with Them should be plundered and all their riches taken away. Nanda Mahārāja should immediately be arrested and killed for his cunning behavior, and that rascal Vasudeva should also be killed without delay. Also my father, Ugrasena, who has always supported my enemies against my will, should be killed."

When Kaṁsa spoke in this way, Lord Kṛṣṇa became very angry with him, and within a second He jumped onto the high dais of King Kaṁsa. Kaṁsa was prepared for Kṛṣṇa's attack, for he knew from the beginning that Kṛṣṇa was to be the supreme cause of his death. Kaṁsa immediately unsheathed his sword and prepared to answer the challenge of Kṛṣṇa with sword and shield. As Kaṁsa wielded his sword up and down, hither and thither, Lord Kṛṣṇa, the supreme powerful Lord, caught hold of him with great force. The Supreme Personality of Godhead, who is the shelter of the complete creation and from whose lotus navel the whole creation is manifested, immediately knocked the crown from the head of Kaṁsa and grabbed his long hair in His hand. He then dragged Kaṁsa from his seat to the wrestling dais and threw him down. Then Kṛṣṇa at once straddled his chest and began to strike him over and over again. Simply from the strokes of His fist, Kaṁsa lost his vital force.

To assure His parents that Kaṁsa was dead, Lord Kṛṣṇa dragged him just as a lion drags an elephant after killing it. When people saw this, there was a great roaring sound from all sides as some spectators expressed their jubilation and others cried in lamentation. From the day Kaṁsa had heard he would be killed by the eighth son of Devakī, he was always thinking of Kṛṣṇa with His wheel in hand, and because he was very much afraid of his death, he was thinking of Kṛṣṇa in that form twenty-four hours a day, without stopping—even while eating, while walking and while breathing—and naturally he got the blessing of liberation. In the *Bhagavad-gītā* it is stated, *sadā tad-bhāva-bhāvitaḥ:* a person gets his next life according to the thoughts in which he is always absorbed. Kaṁsa was thinking of Kṛṣṇa with His wheel, which means Nārāyaṇa, who holds a wheel, conchshell, lotus flower and club.

According to the opinion of authorities, Kaṁsa attained *sārūpya-mukti* after death; that is to say, he attained the same form as Nārāyaṇa (Viṣṇu). On the Vaikuṇṭha planets all the inhabitants have the same bodily features as Nārāyaṇa. After his death, Kaṁsa attained liberation and was promoted to Vaikuṇṭhaloka. From this instance we can understand that even a person who thinks of the Supreme Personality of Godhead as an enemy gets liberation or a place in a Vaikuṇṭha planet, so what to speak of the pure devotees, who are always absorbed in favorable thoughts of Kṛṣṇa? Even an enemy killed by Kṛṣṇa gets liberation and is placed in the impersonal *brahmajyoti*. Since the Supreme Personality of Godhead is all-good, anyone thinking of Him, either as an enemy or as a friend, gets liberation. But the liberation of the devotee and the liberation of the enemy are not the same. The enemy generally gets the liberation of *sāyujya*, and sometimes he gets *sārūpya* liberation.

Kaṁsa had eight brothers, headed by Kaṅka, all of them younger than he, and when they learned that their elder brother had been killed, they combined together and rushed toward Kṛṣṇa in great anger to kill Him. Kaṁsa and his brothers were all Kṛṣṇa's maternal uncles, brothers of Kṛṣṇa's mother, Devakī. When Kṛṣṇa killed Kaṁsa He killed His maternal uncle, which is against the regulations of Vedic injunctions. Although Kṛṣṇa is independent of all Vedic injunctions, He violates the Vedic injunctions only in inevitable cases. Kaṁsa could not be killed by anyone but Kṛṣṇa; therefore Kṛṣṇa was obliged to kill him. But as far as Kaṁsa's eight brothers were concerned, Balarāma took charge of killing them. Balarāma's mother, Rohiṇī, although the wife of Vasudeva, was not the sister of Kaṁsa; therefore Balarāma took charge of killing all of Kaṁsa's eight brothers. He immediately took up an available weapon (most probably the elephant's tusk which He carried) and killed the eight brothers one after another, just as a lion kills a flock of deer. Kṛṣṇa and Balarāma thus verified the statement that the Supreme Personality of Godhead appears in order to give protection to the pious and to kill the impious demons, who are always enemies of the demigods.

The demigods from the higher planetary systems showered flowers, congratulating Kṛṣṇa and Balarāma. Among the demigods were powerful personalities like Lord Brahmā and Lord Śiva, and all joined together in showing their jubilation over Kaṁsa's death. There were beating of drums and showering of flowers from the heavenly planets, and the wives of the demigods danced in ecstasy.

The wives of Kaṁsa and his eight brothers were aggrieved at the sudden death of their husbands, and all of them struck their foreheads and shed torrents of tears. Crying loudly and embracing the bodies of their husbands, which lay on the wrestling dais, the wives of Kaṁsa and his brothers lamented, addressing the dead bodies: "Our dear husbands, you are so kind and are the protectors of your dependents. Now, after your death, we are also dead, along with your homes and children. We no longer look auspicious. On account of your death, the auspicious functions to take place, such as the sacrifice of the bow, have all been spoiled. Our dear husbands, you treated persons ill who were faultless, and as a result you have been killed. This is inevitable because a person who torments an innocent person must be punished by the laws of nature. We know that Lord Kṛṣṇa is the Supreme Personality of Godhead. He is the supreme master and supreme enjoyer of everything; therefore, one who neglects His authority can never be happy, and ultimately, as you have, he meets death."

Since Kṛṣṇa was kind and affectionate to His aunts, He solaced them as far as possible. The ritualistic ceremonies performed after death were then conducted under the personal supervision of Kṛṣṇa because He happened to be the nephew of all the dead princes. After finishing this business, Kṛṣṇa and Balarāma immediately released Their father and mother, Vasudeva and Devakī, who had been imprisoned by Kaṁsa. Kṛṣṇa and Balarāma fell at Their parents' feet and offered them prayers. Vasudeva and Devakī had suffered so much trouble from Kaṁsa because Kṛṣṇa was their son. Devakī and Vasudeva were fully conscious of Kṛṣṇa's exalted position as the Supreme Personality of Godhead; therefore, although Kṛṣṇa touched their feet and offered them obeisances and prayers, they did not embrace Him but simply stood up to hear the Supreme Personality of Godhead. Although Kṛṣṇa was born as their son, Vasudeva and Devakī were always conscious of His position.

Thus ends the Bhaktivedanta purport of the Forty-fourth Chapter of Kṛṣṇa, *"The Killing of Kaṁsa."*

CHAPTER 45

Kṛṣṇa Recovers the Son of His Teacher

WHEN LORD KṚṢṆA SAW VASUDEVA and Devakī standing in a reverential attitude, He immediately expanded His influence of *yogamāyā* so that they could treat Him and Balarāma as children. As in the material world the relationship existing between father and mother and children can be established amongst different living entities by the influence of the illusory energy, so, by the influence of *yogamāyā,* the devotee can establish a relationship in which the Supreme Personality of Godhead is his child. After creating this situation by His *yogamāyā,* Kṛṣṇa, appearing with His elder brother, Balarāma, as the most illustrious son in the dynasty of the Sātvatas, very submissively and respectfully addressed Vasudeva and Devakī: "My dear father and mother, although you have always been anxious for the protection of Our lives, you could not enjoy the pleasure of having Us as your babies, as your growing boys and as your adolescent youths." Kṛṣṇa indirectly praised the fatherhood of Nanda Mahārāja and motherhood of Yaśodā as most glorious because although He and Balarāma were not their born sons, Nanda and Yaśodā actually enjoyed Their childhood pastimes. By nature's own arrangement, the childhood of the embodied living being is enjoyed by his parents. Even in the animal kingdom, parents are found to be affectionate to their cubs. Being captivated by the activities of their offspring, they take much care for their well-being. As for Vasudeva and Devakī, they were always anxious for the protection of their sons, Kṛṣṇa and Balarāma. That is why Kṛṣṇa, after His appearance, was immediately transferred to another's house. Balarāma was also transferred, from Devakī's womb to Rohiṇī's womb.

Vasudeva and Devakī were full of anxieties for Kṛṣṇa's and Balarāma's protection, but they could not enjoy Their childhood pastimes. Kṛṣṇa said, "Unfortunately, being ordered by Our fate, We could not be raised by Our own parents to enjoy childhood pleasures at home. My dear father and mother, a man cannot repay his debt to his parents, from whom he gets this body, which can bestow upon him all the benefits of material existence. According to the Vedic injunctions, this human form of life enables one to perform all kinds of religious activities, fulfill all kinds of desires and acquire all kinds of wealth. And only in this human form is there every possibility that one can get liberation from material existence. This body is produced by the combined efforts of the father and mother. Every human being should be obliged to his parents and understand that he cannot repay his debt to them. If, after growing up, a son does not try to satisfy his parents by his actions or by an endowment of riches, he is surely punished after death by the superintendent of death and made to eat his own flesh. If a person is able to care for or give protection to old parents, a chaste wife, children, the spiritual master, *brāhmaṇas* and other dependents but does not do so, he is considered already dead, although he is supposedly breathing. My dear father and mother, you have always been anxious for Our protection, but unfortunately We could not render any service to you. Until now We have simply wasted Our time; due to reasons beyond Our control, We could not serve you. Mother and father, please excuse Us for Our sinfulness."

When the Supreme Personality of Godhead was speaking as an innocent boy in very sweet words, Vasudeva and Devakī became captivated by parental affection and embraced Him with great pleasure. They were amazed and could not speak or answer the words of Kṛṣṇa, but simply embraced Him and Balarāma in great affection and remained silent, shedding incessant tears.

Thus having consoled His father and mother, the Supreme Personality of Godhead, appearing as the beloved son of Devakī, approached His grandfather Ugrasena and announced that Ugrasena would now be the King of the Yadu kingdom. Kaṁsa had been forcibly ruling the kingdom of Yadu, in spite of the presence of his father, whom he had arrested. But after the death of Kaṁsa, his father was released and announced to be the monarch of the Yadu kingdom. It appears that in those days in the western part of India there were many small kingdoms, ruled by the Yadu dynasty, Andhaka dynasty, Vṛṣṇi dynasty and Bhoja dynasty. Mahārāja Ugrasena belonged to the Bhoja dynasty; therefore Kṛṣṇa indirectly declared that the King of the Bhoja dynasty would be the emperor of the other small kingdoms. Kṛṣṇa willingly asked Mahārāja Ugrasena to rule over Himself and Balarāma because They were his subjects. The word *prajā* is used both for progeny and for citizens, so Kṛṣṇa belonged to the *prajā,* both as a grandson of Mahārāja Ugrasena's and as a member of the Yadu dynasty. Thus He voluntarily accepted the rule of Mahārāja Ugrasena. He informed Ugrasena, "Being cursed by Yayāti, the kings of the Yadu dynasty may not occupy the throne. It will be Our pleasure to act as your servants. My full cooperation with you will make your position more exalted and secure so that the kings of other dynasties will not hesitate to pay their respective revenues. Protected by Me, you will be honored even by the demigods from the heavenly planets. My dear grandfather, out of fear of My late uncle Kaṁsa, all the kings belonging to the Yadu, Vṛṣṇi, Andhaka, Madhu, Daśārha and Kukura dynasties were very anxious and disturbed. Now you can pacify them all and give them assurance of security. The whole kingdom will be peaceful."

All the kings in the neighboring area had left their homes in fear of Kaṁsa and were living in distant parts of the country. Now, after the death of Kaṁsa and the reinstallment of Ugrasena as king, the neighboring kings were given all kinds of presentations and comforts. Then they returned to their respective homes. After this nice political arrangement, the citizens of Mathurā were pleased to live in Mathurā, being protected by the strong arms of Kṛṣṇa and Balarāma. On account of good government in the presence of Kṛṣṇa and Balarāma, the inhabitants of Mathurā felt complete satisfaction in the fulfillment of all their material desires and necessities, and because they saw Kṛṣṇa and Balarāma daily, face to face, they soon forgot all material miseries completely. As soon as they saw Kṛṣṇa and Balarāma coming out on the street, very nicely dressed and smiling and looking at the citizens with grace, the citizens were immediately filled with loving ecstasies simply by seeing the personal presence of Mukunda. The name Mukunda refers to one who can award liberation and transcendental bliss. Kṛṣṇa's presence acted as such a vitalizing tonic that not only the younger generation but even the old men of Mathurā became fully invigorated with youthful energy and strength by regularly seeing Him.

Nanda Mahārāja and Yaśodā were also living in Mathurā because Kṛṣṇa and Balarāma were there, but after some time they wanted to go back to Vṛndāvana. Kṛṣṇa and Balarāma went before Nanda and Yaśodā and very affectionately embraced them, and then the two Lords spoke as follows: "Dear father and mother, although We were born of Vasudeva and Devakī, you have been Our real father and mother, because from Our very birth and childhood you raised Us with great affection and love. Your affectionate love for Us was more than anyone can offer one's own children. You are actually Our father and mother, because you raised Us as your own children when We were just like orphans. For certain reasons We were rejected by Our father and mother, and you protected Us. Dear father and mother, We know that you will feel separation upon returning to Vṛndāvana and leaving Us here, but please rest assured that We shall come back to Vṛndāvana just after giving some satisfaction to Our real father and mother, Vasudeva and Devakī, and Our grandfather and other family members." Kṛṣṇa and Balarāma thus satisfied Nanda and Yaśodā by sweet words and by presentations of various kinds of clothing, ornaments and copper utensils. They satisfied them, along with their friends and neighbors who had come with them from Vṛndāvana to Mathurā, as fully as possible. On account of excessive parental affection for Balarāma and Kṛṣṇa, Nanda Mahārāja felt tears in his eyes, and he embraced Them and started with the cowherd men for Vṛndāvana.

After this, Vasudeva had his sons initiated by sacred thread as the token of second birth, which is essential for the higher castes of human society. Vasudeva called for his family priest and learned *brāhmaṇas,* and the sacred thread ceremony of Kṛṣṇa and Balarāma was duly performed. During this ceremony, Vasudeva gave various ornaments in charity to the *brāhmaṇas* and endowed them with cows decorated with silken cloths and golden ornaments. Then Vasudeva remembered the cows he had wanted to give in charity to the *brāhmaṇas* after the birth of Kṛṣṇa and Balarāma. But being imprisoned by Kaṁsa at that time, Vasudeva had been able to do so only within his mind, for Kaṁsa had stolen all his cows. With the death of Kaṁsa his cows were released, and now Vasudeva gave the actual cows to the *brāhmaṇas.* Then Balarāma and Kṛṣṇa were duly initiated with the sacred thread ceremony, and They repeated the chanting of the Gāyatrī *mantra.* The Gāyatrī *mantra* is offered to disciples after the sacred thread ceremony, and Balarāma and Kṛṣṇa properly discharged the duties of chanting this *mantra.* Anyone who executes the chanting of this *mantra* has to abide by certain principles and vows. Although Balarāma and Kṛṣṇa are transcendental personalities, They strictly followed the regulative principles. They were initiated by Their family priest, Gargācārya, usually known as Garga Muni, the *ācārya* of the Yadu dynasty. According to Vedic culture, every respectable family has an *ācārya,* or spiritual master. One is not considered a perfectly cultured man without being initiated and trained by an *ācārya.* It is said, therefore, that one who has approached an *ācārya* is actually in perfect knowledge. Lord Kṛṣṇa and Lord Balarāma are the Supreme Personality of Godhead, the master of all education and knowledge. There was no need for Them to accept a spiritual master, or *ācārya,* yet for the instruction of ordinary men They also accepted a spiritual master for advancement in spiritual knowledge.

It is customary, after being initiated in the Gāyatrī *mantra,* for one to live away from home for some time under the care of the *ācārya,* to be trained in spiritual life. During this period, one has to work under the spiritual master as an ordinary menial servant. There are many rules and regulations for a *brahmacārī* living under the care of an *ācārya,* and Kṛṣṇa and Balarāma strictly followed those regulative principles while living under the instruction of their spiritual master, Sāndīpani Muni, who was a resident of Avantipura, in the northern Indian district of Ujjain. According to scriptural injunctions, a spiritual master should be respected and regarded on an equal level with the Supreme Personality of Godhead. Kṛṣṇa and Balarāma exactly followed those principles with great devotion and underwent the regulations of *brahmacarya.* Thus They satisfied Their spiritual master, who instructed Them in Vedic knowledge. Being very satisfied, Sāndīpani Muni instructed Them in all the intricacies of Vedic wisdom and in supplementary literatures such as the *Upaniṣads.* Because Kṛṣṇa and Balarāma happened to be *kṣatriyas,* They were specifically trained in military science, politics and ethics. Politics includes such departments of knowledge as how to make peace, how to fight, how to pacify, how to divide and rule and how to give shelter. All these items were fully explained and instructed to Kṛṣṇa and Balarāma.

The ocean is the source of water in a river. The cloud is created by the evaporation of ocean water, and the same water is distributed as rain all over the surface of the earth and then returns to the ocean in rivers. So Kṛṣṇa and Balarāma, the Supreme Personality of Godhead, are the source of all knowledge, but because They were playing like ordinary human boys, They set the example so that everyone would receive knowledge from the right source. Thus They agreed to take knowledge from a spiritual master.

After hearing only once from Their teacher, Kṛṣṇa and Balarāma learned all the arts and sciences. In sixty-four days and sixty-four nights, They learned all the necessary arts and sciences required in human society. During the daytime They took lessons on a subject from the teacher, and by nightfall They were expert in that department of knowledge.

First of all They learned how to sing, how to compose songs and how to recognize the different tunes; They learned the favorable and unfavorable accents and meters, how to sing different kinds of rhythms and melodies, and how to follow them by beating different kinds of drums. They learned how to dance to the rhythm of melody and different songs. They learned how to write dramas, and They learned the various types of paintings, beginning from simple village arts up to the highest perfectional stage. They also learned how to paint *tilaka* on the face by making different kinds of dots on the forehead and cheeks. Then They learned the art of making paintings on the floor with a liquid paste of rice and flour; such paintings are very popular at auspicious ceremonies performed at household affairs or in the temple. They learned how to make a resting place with flowers and how to decorate clothing and limbs with colorful paintings. They also learned how to set valuable jewels in ornaments. They learned the art of ringing waterpots. Waterpots are filled with water to a certain measurement so that as one beats on the pots, different tones are produced, and when the pots are beaten together they produce a melodious sound. They also learned how to splash water in the rivers or lakes while taking a bath among friends. They learned how to decorate with flowers. This art of decorating can still be seen in various temples of Vṛndāvana during the summer season. It is called *phulla-bāḍi.* The dais, the throne, the walls and the ceiling are all fully decorated, and a small, aromatic fountain of flowers is fixed in the center. Because of these floral decorations, the people, fatigued from the heat of the summer, become refreshed.

Kṛṣṇa and Balarāṃa learned the art of dressing hair in various styles and fixing a helmet in different positions on the head. They also learned how to set up a theatrical stage, how to decorate dramatic actors with clothes and with flower ornaments over the ear, and how to sprinkle sandalwood pulp and water to produce a nice fragrance. They also learned the art of performing magical feats. Within the magical field there is an art called *bahu-rūpī,* by which a person dresses himself in such a way that when he approaches a friend he cannot be recognized. Kṛṣṇa and Balarāma also learned how to make various syrups and beverages required at various times, having various tastes and intoxicating effects. They also learned different types of sewing and embroidery work, as well as how to manipulate thin threads for dancing puppets. This art includes how to string wires on musical instruments, such as the *vīṇā,* sitar, *esarāja* and tamboura, to produce melodious sounds. Then They learned how to make and solve riddles. They learned the art of how even a dull student can very quickly learn the alphabet and read books. Then They learned how to rehearse and act out a drama. They also studied the art of solving crossword puzzles, filling up the missing spaces and making complete words.

They also learned how to draw and read pictographic literature. In some countries in the world, pictographic literature is still current. A story is represented by pictures; for instance, a man and house are pictured to represent a man going home. Kṛṣṇa and Balarāma also learned the art of architecture—how to construct residential buildings. They learned to recognize valuable jewels by studying their luster and colors. Then They learned the art of placing jewels in a gold and silver setting so that they look very beautiful. They also learned how to study soil to find minerals. This study of soil is now a greatly specialized science, but formerly it was common knowledge even for the ordinary man. They learned to study herbs and plants to discover how they would act as medicine for different ailments. By studying the different species of plants, They learned how to crossbreed plants and trees and get different types of fruits. They learned how to train and engage rams and cocks in fighting for sport. They then learned how to teach parrots to speak and to answer the questions of human beings.

They learned practical psychology—how to influence another's mind and thus induce another to act according to one's own desire. Sometimes this is called hypnotism. They learned how to wash hair, dye it different colors and curl it in different ways. They learned the art of telling what is written in someone's book without actually seeing it. They learned to tell what is contained in another's fist. Sometimes children imitate this art, although not very accurately. One child keeps something within his fist and asks his friend, "Can you tell what is within?" and the friend gives some suggestion, although he actually cannot tell. But there is an art by which one can understand and actually tell what is held within the fist.

Kṛṣṇa and Balarāma learned how to speak and understand the languages of various countries. Not only did They learn the languages of human beings; Kṛṣṇa could also speak even with animals and birds. Evidence of this is found in the Vaiṣṇava literature compiled by the Gosvāmīs. Then They learned how to make carriages and airplanes from flowers. It is said in the *Rāmāyaṇa* that after defeating Rāvaṇa, Rāmacandra was carried from Laṅkā to Bhārata-varṣa on a plane of flowers, called a *puṣpa-ratha.* Kṛṣṇa and Balarāma then learned the art of foretelling events by seeing signs. In a book called *Khanara-vacana,* the various types of signs and omens are described. If when one is going out one sees someone with a bucket full of water, that is a very good sign. But if one sees someone with an empty bucket, it is not a good sign. Similarly, if one sees a cow being milked alongside its calf, it is a good sign. The result of understanding these signs is that one can foretell events, and Kṛṣṇa and Balarāma learned the science. They also learned the art of composing *mātṛkā.* A *mātṛkā* is like a crossword box, with three numbers in each row. If one adds any three from any side, it will come to nine. The *mātṛkās* are of different kinds and for different purposes.

Kṛṣṇa and Balarāma learned the art of cutting valuable stones such as diamonds, and They also learned the art of questioning and answering by immediately composing poetry within the mind. They learned the science of the action and reaction of physical combinations and permutations. They learned the art of a psychiatrist, who can understand the psychic movements of another person. They learned how to satisfy one's desires. Desires are very difficult to fulfill; but if one desires something which is unreasonable and can never be fulfilled, the desire can be subdued and satisfied, and that is an art. By this art one can also subdue sex impulses when they are aroused, as they are even in *brahmacārī* life. By this art one can make even an enemy one's friend or transfer the direct action of a physical element to other things.

Lord Kṛṣṇa and Balarāma, the reservoir of all knowledge, exhibited Their perfect understanding of all the arts and sciences mentioned above. Then They offered to serve Their teacher by awarding him anything he desired. This offering by the student to the teacher or spiritual master is called *guru-dakṣiṇā.* It is essential that a student satisfy the teacher in return for any learning received, either material or spiritual. When Kṛṣṇa and Balarāma offered Their service in this way, the teacher, Sāndīpani Muni, thought it wise to ask Them for something extraordinary, something no common student could offer. He therefore consulted with his wife about what to ask from Them. He and his wife had already seen the extraordinary potencies of Kṛṣṇa and Balarāma and could understand that the two boys were the Supreme Personality of

Godhead. They decided to ask for the return of their son, who had drowned in the ocean near the shore at Prabhāsa-kṣetra.

When Kṛṣṇa and Balarāma heard from Their teacher about the death of his son, They immediately started for Prabhāsa-kṣetra on Their chariot. Reaching the beach, They asked the controlling deity of the ocean to return the son of Their teacher. The ocean deity immediately appeared before the Lord and offered Him all respectful obeisances with great humility.

The Lord said, "Some time back you caused the drowning of the son of Our teacher. I order you to return him."

The ocean deity replied, "The boy was not actually taken by me but was captured by a demon named Pañcajana. This great demon generally remains deep in the water in the shape of a conchshell. The son of Your teacher might be within the belly of the demon, having been devoured by him."

On hearing this, Kṛṣṇa dove deep into the water and caught hold of the demon Pañcajana. He killed him on the spot but could not find the son of His teacher within his belly. Therefore He took the demon's dead body (in the shape of a conchshell) and returned to His chariot on the beach of Prabhāsa-kṣetra. From there He started for Saṁyamanī, the residence of Yamarāja, the superintendent of death. Accompanied by His elder brother, Balarāma, who is also known as Halāyudha, Kṛṣṇa arrived there and blew on His conchshell.

Hearing the vibration, Yamarāja appeared and received Śrī Kṛṣṇa with all respectful obeisances. Yamarāja could understand who Kṛṣṇa and Balarāma were, and therefore he immediately offered his humble service to the Lord. Kṛṣṇa had appeared on the surface of the earth like an ordinary human being, but actually Kṛṣṇa and Balarāma are the Supersoul living within the heart of every living entity. They are Viṣṇu Himself, but were playing just like ordinary human boys. When Yamarāja offered his services to the Lord, Śrī Kṛṣṇa asked him to return His teacher's son, who had come to him as a result of his work. "Considering My ruling supreme," said Kṛṣṇa, "you should immediately return the son of My teacher."

Yamarāja returned the boy to the Supreme Personality of Godhead, and Kṛṣṇa and Balarāma brought him to his father. The brothers asked if Their teacher had anything more to ask from Them, but he replied, "My dear sons, You have done enough for me. I am now completely satisfied. What further want can there be for a man who has disciples like You? My dear boys, You may now go home. These glorious acts of Yours will always be renowned all over the world. You are above all blessing, yet it is my duty to bless You. I therefore give You the benediction that whatever You speak will remain as eternally fresh as the instructions of the *Vedas*. Your teachings will be honored not only within this universe or in this millennium but in all places and ages and will remain increasingly new and important." Due to this benediction from His teacher,

Lord Kṛṣṇa's *Bhagavad-gītā* is ever increasingly fresh and is renowned not only within this universe but in other planets and other universes also.

Being ordered by Their teacher, Kṛṣṇa and Balarāma immediately returned home on Their chariot. They traveled at great speed, like the wind, and made sounds like the crashing of clouds. All the residents of Mathurā, who had not seen Kṛṣṇa and Balarāma for a long time, were very pleased to see Them again. They felt joyful, like a person who has regained his lost property.

Thus ends the Bhaktivedanta purport of the Forty-fifth Chapter of Kṛṣṇa, *"Kṛṣṇa Recovers the Son of His Teacher."*

CHAPTER 46

Uddhava Visits Vṛndāvana

NANDA MAHĀRĀJA RETURNED TO VṚNDĀVANA without Kṛṣṇa and Balarāma. He was accompanied only by the cowherd boys and men. It was certainly a very pathetic scene for the *gopīs,* mother Yaśodā, Śrīmatī Rādhārāṇī and all the residents of Vṛndāvana. Many devotees have tried to make adjustments to Kṛṣṇa's being away from Vṛndāvana because, according to expert opinion, Kṛṣṇa, the original Supreme Personality of Godhead, never goes even a step out of Vṛndāvana. He always remains there. The explanation of expert devotees is that Kṛṣṇa was actually not absent from Vṛndāvana; He came back with Nanda Mahārāja as promised.

When Kṛṣṇa was starting for Mathurā on the chariot driven by Akrūra and the *gopīs* were blocking the way, Kṛṣṇa assured them that He was coming back just after finishing His business in Mathurā. He told them not to be overwhelmed and in this way pacified them. But when He failed to come back with Nanda Mahārāja, it appeared that He either cheated them or could not keep His promise. Expert devotees, however, have decided that Kṛṣṇa was neither a cheater nor a breaker of promises. Kṛṣṇa, in His original identity, returned with Nanda Mahārāja and stayed with the *gopīs* and mother Yaśodā in His *bhāva* expansion. Kṛṣṇa and Balarāma remained in Mathurā, not in Their original forms but in Their expansions as Vāsudeva and Saṅkarṣaṇa. The real Kṛṣṇa and Balarāma were in Vṛndāvana in Their *bhāva* manifestation, whereas in

Mathurā They appeared in the *prabhava* and *vaibhava* expansions. This is the expert opinion of advanced devotees of Kṛṣṇa. Externally, however, They were absent from Vṛndāvana. Therefore, when Nanda Mahārāja was preparing to return to Vṛndāvana, there was some discussion between him and the boys concerning how they could live in separation. The conclusion to separate was reached by mutual agreement.

Vasudeva and Devakī, who happened to be the real parents of Kṛṣṇa and Balarāma, wanted to keep Them now because of the death of Kaṁsa. While Kaṁsa was alive, Kṛṣṇa and Balarāma were kept under the protection of Nanda Mahārāja in Vṛndāvana. Now, naturally, the father and mother of Kṛṣṇa and Balarāma wanted Them to remain, specifically for the reformatory function of purification, the sacred thread ceremony. They also wanted to give Them a proper education, for this is the duty of the father. Another consideration was that all the friends of Kaṁsa outside Mathurā were planning to attack Mathurā. For that reason also Kṛṣṇa's presence was required. Kṛṣṇa did not want Vṛndāvana disturbed by enemies like Dantavakra and Jarāsandha. If Kṛṣṇa were to go to Vṛndāvana, these enemies would not only attack Mathurā but would go on to Vṛndāvana, and the peaceful inhabitants of Vṛndāvana would be disturbed. Kṛṣṇa therefore decided to remain in Mathurā, and Nanda Mahārāja went back to Vṛndāvana. Although the inhabitants of Vṛndāvana felt separation from Kṛṣṇa, the resulting ecstasy (*bhāva*) caused them to perceive that Kṛṣṇa was always present with them by His *līlā*, or pastimes.

Since Kṛṣṇa had departed from Vṛndāvana and gone to Mathurā, the inhabitants of Vṛndāvana, especially mother Yaśodā, Nanda Mahārāja, Śrīmatī Rādhārāṇī, the *gopīs* and the cowherd boys, were simply thinking of Kṛṣṇa at every step. They were thinking, "Here Kṛṣṇa was playing in this way. Here Kṛṣṇa was blowing His flute. Kṛṣṇa was joking with us in this way, and Kṛṣṇa was embracing us like this." This is called *līlā-smaraṇa,* and it is the process of association with Kṛṣṇa most recommended by great devotees; even Lord Caitanya, when He was at Purī, enjoyed *līlā-smaraṇa* association with Kṛṣṇa. Those in the most exalted position of devotional service and ecstasy can live with Kṛṣṇa always by remembering His pastimes. Śrīla Viśvanātha Cakravartī Ṭhākura has given us a transcendental literature entitled *Kṛṣṇa-bhāvanāmṛta,* which is full with Kṛṣṇa's pastimes. Exalted devotees can remain absorbed in Kṛṣṇa-thought by reading such books. Any book of *kṛṣṇa-līlā,* even this book, *Kṛṣṇa,* or our *Teachings of Lord Caitanya,* is actually solace for devotees feeling separation from Kṛṣṇa.

That Kṛṣṇa and Balarāma did not return to Vṛndāvana can be adjusted as follows: They did not break Their promise to return to Vṛndāvana, nor were They absent, but Their presence was necessary in Mathurā.

In the meantime, Uddhava, a cousin-brother of Kṛṣṇa's, came to see Kṛṣṇa from Dvārakā. He was the son of Vasudeva's brother and was almost the same age as Kṛṣṇa. His bodily features resembled Kṛṣṇa's almost exactly. After Kṛṣṇa returned from His teacher's home, He was pleased to see Uddhava, who happened to be His dearmost friend. Kṛṣṇa wanted to send him to Vṛndāvana with a message to the residents to pacify their deep feelings of separation.

As stated in the *Bhagavad-gītā, ye yathā māṁ prapadyante tāṁs tathaiva bhajāmy aham:* Kṛṣṇa is very responsive. He responds in proportion to the devotee's advancement in devotional service. Thus, as the *gopīs* were thinking of Kṛṣṇa in separation twenty-four hours a day, so Kṛṣṇa was also always thinking of the *gopīs,* mother Yaśodā, Nanda Mahārāja and the other residents of Vṛndāvana. Although He appeared to be away from them, He could understand how they were transcendentally aggrieved, and so He immediately wanted to send Uddhava to give them a message of solace.

Uddhava is described as the most exalted personality in the Vṛṣṇi dynasty, being almost equal to Kṛṣṇa. He was a great friend of Kṛṣṇa's, and being the direct student of Bṛhaspati, the teacher and priest of the heavenly planets, he was very intelligent and sharp in decision. Intellectually, he was highly qualified. Kṛṣṇa, being his very loving friend, wanted to send Uddhava to Vṛndāvana just to study the highly elevated ecstatic devotional service practiced there. Even if one is highly elevated in material education and is even the disciple of Bṛhaspati, he still has to learn from the *gopīs* and the other residents of Vṛndāvana how to love Kṛṣṇa to the highest degree. It was Kṛṣṇa's special favor to Uddhava to send him to Vṛndāvana with a message for the residents there, which was meant to pacify them.

Lord Kṛṣṇa is also named Hari, which means "one who takes away all distress from the surrendered souls." Lord Caitanya states that there cannot be at any time a worship as exalted as that realized by the *gopīs.* Being very anxious about the *gopīs'* grief, Kṛṣṇa talked with Uddhava and politely requested him to go to Vṛndāvana. Shaking Uddhava's hand with His own hands, He said, "My dear gentle friend Uddhava, please go immediately to Vṛndāvana and try to pacify My father and mother, Nanda Mahārāja and Yaśodā-devī, and the *gopīs.* They are grief-stricken, as if suffering from great ailments. Go and give them a message. I hope their ailments will be partially relieved. The *gopīs* are always absorbed in thoughts of Me. They have dedicated body, desire, life and soul to Me. I am anxious not only for the *gopīs* but for anyone who sacrifices society, friendship, love and personal comforts for Me. It is My duty to protect such exalted devotees. The *gopīs* are the most dear. They always think of Me in such a way that they remain overwhelmed and almost dead in anxiety due to separation from Me. They are keeping alive simply by thinking that I am returning to them very soon."

Requested by Lord Kṛṣṇa, Uddhava immediately left on his chariot and carried the message to Gokula. He approached Vṛndāvana at sunset, when the cows were returning home from the pasturing ground. Uddhava and his chariot were covered by the dust raised by the hooves of the cows. He saw bulls running after cows for mating; other cows, with overladen milk bags, were running after their calves to feed them with milk. Uddhava saw that the entire land of Vṛndāvana was filled with white cows and their calves, running here and there all over Gokula, and he could hear the sound of milking. Every residential house in Vṛndāvana was decorated for the worship of the sun-god and the fire-god and for the reception of guests, cows, *brāhmaṇas* and demigods. Every home was sanctified by lights and incense. All over Vṛndāvana there were nice gardens filled with flowers and the sounds of humming bees and singing birds. The lakes were filled with lotus flowers and with ducks and swans.

Uddhava entered the house of Nanda Mahārāja and was received as a representative of Vāsudeva. Nanda Mahārāja offered him a sitting place and sat down with him to ask about messages from Kṛṣṇa, Balarāma and other family members in Mathurā. He could understand that Uddhava was a very confidential friend of Kṛṣṇa's and therefore must have come with good messages. "My dear Uddhava," he said, "how is my friend Vasudeva enjoying life? He is now released from the prison of Kaṁsa, and he is now with his friends and his children, Kṛṣṇa and Balarāma. So he must be very happy. Tell me about him and his welfare. We are also very happy that Kaṁsa, the most sinful demon, has been killed. He was always envious of the family of the Yadus, his relatives. Now, because of his sinful activities, he is dead and gone, along with all his brothers.

"Please let us know whether Kṛṣṇa now remembers His father and mother and His friends and companions in Vṛndāvana. Does He like to remember His cows, His *gopīs*, His Govardhana Hill, His pasturing grounds in Vṛndāvana? Or has He now forgotten all these? Is there any possibility of His coming back to His friends and relatives so we can again see His beautiful face, with its raised nose and lotuslike eyes? We remember how He saved us from the forest fire, how He saved us from the great snake Kāliya in the Yamunā, and how He saved us from so many other demons, and we simply think of how much we are obliged to Him for giving us protection in many dangerous situations. My dear Uddhava, when we think of Kṛṣṇa's beautiful face and eyes and His different activities here in Vṛndāvana, we become so overwhelmed that all our activities cease. We simply think of Kṛṣṇa—how He used to smile and how He looked upon us with grace. When we go to the banks of the Yamunā or the lakes of Vṛndāvana or near Govardhana Hill or the pasturing fields, we see that the impressions of Kṛṣṇa's footprints are still on the surface of the earth. We remember Him playing in those places, because He was constantly visiting them. When His appearance within our minds becomes manifest, we immediately become absorbed in thought of Him.

"We think, therefore, that Kṛṣṇa and Balarāma may be chief demigods in heaven who have appeared before us like ordinary boys to execute particular duties on earth. This was foretold by Garga Muni when making Kṛṣṇa's horoscope. If Kṛṣṇa were not a great personality, how could He have killed Kaṁsa, who possessed the strength of ten thousand elephants? Besides Kaṁsa, there were very strong wrestlers, as well as the giant elephant Kuvalayāpīḍa. Kṛṣṇa killed all these animals and demons just as a lion kills an ordinary animal. How wonderful it is that Kṛṣṇa took in one hand the big, heavy bow made of three joined palm trees and broke it very quickly. How wonderful it is that for seven days continuously He held up Govardhana Hill with one hand. How wonderful it is that He has killed all the demons like Pralambāsura, Dhenukāsura, Ariṣṭāsura, Tṛṇāvarta and Bakāsura. They were so strong that even the demigods in the heavenly planets were afraid of them, but Kṛṣṇa killed them as easily as anything."

While describing the uncommon activities of Kṛṣṇa before Uddhava, Nanda Mahārāja gradually became overwhelmed and could no longer speak. As for mother Yaśodā, she sat by the side of her husband and heard the pastimes of Kṛṣṇa without speaking. She simply cried incessantly, and milk poured from her breasts. When Uddhava saw Mahārāja Nanda and Yaśodā so extraordinarily overwhelmed with thoughts of Kṛṣṇa, the Supreme Personality of Godhead, and when he experienced their extraordinary affection for Him, he also became overwhelmed and spoke as follows: "My dear mother Yaśodā and Nanda Mahārāja, you are most respectable among human beings because no one but you can meditate in such transcendental ecstasy."

Uddhava continued, "Balarāma and Kṛṣṇa are the original Personalities of Godhead, from whom the cosmic manifestation emanates. They are chief among all personalities. Each of Them is both the material and the efficient cause of this material creation. Material nature is conducted by the *puruṣa* incarnations, who all act under Kṛṣṇa and Balarāma. By Their partial representation They enter the hearts of all living entities. They are the source of all knowledge and all forgetfulness also." This is confirmed by Kṛṣṇa in the *Bhagavad-gītā,* Fifteenth Chapter: "I am present in everyone's heart, and I cause one to remember and forget. I am the original compiler of the *Vedānta,* and I am the actual knower of the *Vedas.*" Uddhava continued, "If at the time of death a person can fix his pure mind upon Kṛṣṇa even for a moment, after giving up his material body he becomes eligible to appear in his original, spiritual body, just as the sun rises with all illumination. Passing from his life in this way, he immediately enters into the spiritual kingdom, Vaikuṇṭha."

This is the result of Kṛṣṇa conscious practice. If we practice Kṛṣṇa consciousness in this present body while in a healthy condition and in good mind, simply by chanting the holy *mahā-mantra,* Hare Kṛṣṇa, we will have every possibility of fixing the mind upon Kṛṣṇa at the time of death. If we do this, then our lives become successful without any doubt. But if we keep our minds always absorbed in fruitive activities for material enjoyment, then naturally at the time of death we shall think of such activities and again be forced to enter material, conditioned bodies to suffer the threefold miseries of material existence. Therefore, to remain always absorbed in Kṛṣṇa consciousness was the standard of the inhabitants of Vṛndāvana, as exhibited by Mahārāja Nanda,

Yaśodā and the *gopīs.* If we can simply follow in their footsteps, even to a minute proportion, our lives will surely become successful, and we shall enter the spiritual kingdom, Vaikuṇṭha.

"My dear mother Yaśodā and Nanda Mahārāja," Uddhava continued, "you have thus fixed your minds wholly and solely upon that Supreme Personality of Godhead, Nārāyaṇa, whose transcendental form is the cause of impersonal Brahman. The Brahman effulgence is only the bodily rays of Nārāyaṇa, and because you are always absorbed in ecstatic thought of Kṛṣṇa and Balarāma, what pious activity remains for you to perform? I have brought a message from Kṛṣṇa that He will very soon come back to Vṛndāvana and satisfy you by His personal presence. Kṛṣṇa promised that He would come back to Vṛndāvana after finishing His business in Mathurā. This promise He will surely fulfill. I therefore request the two of you, who are the best among all who are fortunate, not to be aggrieved on account of Kṛṣṇa's absence.

"You are already perceiving His presence twenty-four hours a day, yet He will come and see you very soon. Actually He is present everywhere and in everyone's heart, just as fire is present in wood. Since Kṛṣṇa is the Supersoul, He regards everyone equally: He sees no one as His enemy, no one as His friend, and no one as lower or higher than He. He actually has no father, mother, brother or relative, nor does He require society, friendship and love. He does not have a material body like us; He never appears or takes birth like an ordinary human being. He does not appear in higher or lower species of life like ordinary living entities, who are forced to take birth on account of their previous fruitive activities. He appears by His internal potency just to give protection to His devotees. He is never influenced by the modes of material nature, but when He appears within this material world He seems to act like an ordinary living entity under the spell of the modes of material nature. But in fact, He is the overseer of this material creation, and while remaining unaffected by the material modes of nature, He creates, maintains and dissolves the whole cosmic manifestation. We wrongly look upon Kṛṣṇa and Balarāma as ordinary human beings, just as whirling men see the whole world whirling around them. The Personality of Godhead is no one's son; He is actually everyone's father, mother and supreme controller. There is no doubt of this. Whatever is already being experienced, whatever is not being experienced, whatever already exists, does not exist or will exist in the future, whatever is the smallest and whatever is the biggest have no existence outside the Supreme Personality of Godhead. Everything rests in Him, but He is untouched by everything manifested."

Nanda and Uddhava thus passed the whole night discussing Kṛṣṇa. In the morning, the *gopīs* prepared for morning *ārati* by lighting their lamps and sprinkling butter mixed with yogurt. After finishing their *maṅgala-ārati,* they engaged themselves in churning butter from yogurt. While the *gopīs* were thus engaged, the lamps reflected on their ornaments made the ornaments still brighter. Their churning rods, their arms, their earrings, their bangles, their breasts—everything moved, and *kuṅkuma* powder gave their faces a saffron luster comparable to the rising sun. While making sounds by churning, they also sang the glories of Kṛṣṇa. The two sound vibrations mixed together, ascended to the sky and sanctified the whole atmosphere.

After sunrise the *gopīs* came as usual to offer their respects to Nanda Mahārāja and Yaśodā, but when they saw the golden chariot of Uddhava at the door, they began to inquire among themselves: What was that chariot, and to whom did it belong? Some of them inquired whether Akrūra, who had taken away Kṛṣṇa, had returned. They were not very pleased with Akrūra because, being engaged in the service of Kaṁsa, he had taken lotus-eyed Kṛṣṇa away to the city of Mathurā. All the *gopīs* conjectured that Akrūra might have come again to fulfill another cruel plan. But they thought, "We are now dead bodies without our supreme master, Kṛṣṇa. What further act can Akrūra perpetrate against these dead bodies?" While they were talking in this way, Uddhava finished his morning ablutions, prayers and chanting and came before them.

Thus ends the Bhaktivedanta purport of the Forty-sixth Chapter of Kṛṣṇa, *"Uddhava Visits Vṛndāvana."*

CHAPTER 47

Delivery of the Message of Kṛṣṇa to the Gopīs

WHEN THE *GOPĪS* SAW UDDHAVA, they observed that his features almost exactly resembled those of Kṛṣṇa, and they could understand that he was a great devotee of Kṛṣṇa's. His arms were very long and his eyes were just like the petals of the lotus flower. He was dressed in yellow garments and wore a garland of lotus flowers. His face was very beautiful. Having achieved the liberation of *sārūpya* and thus having the same bodily features as the Lord, Uddhava looked almost like Kṛṣṇa. In Kṛṣṇa's absence, the *gopīs* had been coming dutifully to visit mother Yaśodā's house early in the morning. They knew that Nanda Mahārāja and mother Yaśodā were always grief-stricken, and they had made it their first duty to come and pay their respects to the most exalted elderly personalities of Vṛndāvana. Seeing the friends of Kṛṣṇa, Nanda and Yaśodā would remember Kṛṣṇa Himself and be satisfied, and the *gopīs* also would be pleased by seeing Nanda and Yaśodā.

When the *gopīs* saw that Uddhava was representing Kṛṣṇa even in his bodily features, they thought he must be a soul completely surrendered unto the Supreme Personality of Godhead. They began to contemplate, "Who is this boy who looks just like Kṛṣṇa? He has the same eyes like lotus petals, the same raised nose and beautiful face, and he is smiling in the same way. In all respects he resembles Kṛṣṇa, Śyāmasundara, the beautiful blackish boy. He is even dressed exactly like Kṛṣṇa. Where has this boy come from? Who is the fortunate girl who has him for her husband?" Thus they talked among themselves. They were very anxious to know about him, and because they were simple, unsophisticated village girls, they surrounded Uddhava.

When the *gopīs* understood that Uddhava had a message from Kṛṣṇa, they became very happy and called him to a secluded place and offered him a nice sitting place. They wanted to talk with him very freely and did not want to be embarrassed before unknown persons. They welcomed him with polite words, in great submissiveness: "We know that you are a most confidential associate of Kṛṣṇa and that He has therefore sent you to Vṛndāvana to give solace to His father and mother. We can understand that family affection is very strong. Even great sages who have taken to the renounced order of life cannot give up family affection cent percent. Sometimes they think of their family members. Kṛṣṇa has therefore sent you to His father and mother; otherwise He has no further business in Vṛndāvana. He is now in town. What does He have to know about Vṛndāvana village or the cows' pasturing grounds? These are not at all useful for Kṛṣṇa because He is now a man of the city.

"Surely He has nothing to do with persons who do not happen to be His family members. Friendships with those outside the family continue as long as there is some selfish interest in them; otherwise, why should one bother about those outside the family? Specifically, a person attached to the wives of others is interested in them as long as there is a need of sense gratification, just as the bumblebees have interest in flowers as long as they want to take the honey out of them. It is psychologically very natural that a prostitute does not care for her paramour as soon as he loses his money. Similarly, when the citizens find that a government is incapable of giving them full protection, they leave the country. A student, after finishing his education, gives up his relationship with the teacher and the school. A priest, after taking his reward from the worshiper, gives him up. When the fruit season is over, birds are no longer interested in the tree. Just after eating in the house of a host, the guest gives up his relationship with him. After a forest fire, when there is a scarcity of green grass, deer and other animals give up the forest. And so a man, after enjoying his girlfriend, gives up his connection with her." In this way, all the *gopīs* indirectly accused Kṛṣṇa by citing many examples.

Uddhava understood that the *gopīs* of Vṛndāvana were all simply absorbed in the thought of Kṛṣṇa and His childhood activities. While talking about Kṛṣṇa with Uddhava, they forgot all about their household business. They even forgot about themselves as their interest in Kṛṣṇa increased more and more.

One of the *gopīs,* namely Śrīmatī Rādhārāṇī, was so much absorbed in thoughts of Kṛṣṇa by dint of Her personal touch with Him that She actually began to talk with a bumblebee which was flying there and trying to touch Her lotus feet. While the other *gopīs* were talking with Kṛṣṇa's messenger Uddhava, Śrīmatī Rādhārāṇī took that bumblebee to be a messenger from Kṛṣṇa and began to talk with it as follows: "Bumblebee, you are accustomed to drinking honey from flower to flower, and therefore you have preferred to be a messenger of Kṛṣṇa, who is of the same nature as you. I can see on your mustaches the red powder of *kuṅkuma* which was smeared on the flower garland of Kṛṣṇa while it was pressed against the breasts of some other girl who is My competitor. You feel very proud because of having touched that garland, and your mustaches have become reddish. You have come here carrying a message for Me, anxious to touch My feet. But My dear bumblebee, let Me warn you—don't touch Me! I don't want any messages from your unreliable master. You are the unreliable servant of an unreliable master."

It may be that Śrīmatī Rādhārāṇī purposely addressed the bumblebee sarcastically in order to indirectly criticize the messenger Uddhava. Like the other *gopīs*, Śrīmatī Rādhārāṇī saw that Uddhava's bodily features resembled Kṛṣṇa's, but She also saw Uddhava as being equal to Kṛṣṇa. Indirectly, therefore, She indicated that Uddhava was as unreliable as Kṛṣṇa Himself. Śrīmatī Rādhārāṇī wanted to give specific reasons why She was dissatisfied with Kṛṣṇa and His messenger.

She addressed the bumblebee, "Your master Kṛṣṇa is exactly of your quality. You sit down on a flower, and after tasting a little honey you immediately fly away and sit in another flower and taste. You're just like your master Kṛṣṇa. Similarly, only once did your master Kṛṣṇa give Me the chance to taste the touch of His lips, and then He left Me altogether. I know also that the goddess of fortune, Lakṣmī, who is always in the midst of the lotus flower, is constantly engaged in Kṛṣṇa's service. But I do not know how she has become so captivated by Kṛṣṇa and why she is so much attached to Kṛṣṇa, although she knows His actual character. Maybe she is so much captivated by Kṛṣṇa's sweet words that she cannot understand His real character. As far as We are concerned, We are more intelligent than the goddess of fortune. We are not going to be cheated anymore by Kṛṣṇa or His messengers."

According to expert opinion, Lakṣmī, the goddess of fortune, is a subordinate expansion of Śrīmatī Rādhārāṇī. As Kṛṣṇa has numerous expansions of *viṣṇu-mūrtis*, so His pleasure potency, Rādhārāṇī, also has innumerable expansions of goddesses of fortune. Therefore the goddess of fortune, Lakṣmījī, is always eager to be elevated to the position of the *gopīs*.

Śrīmatī Rādhārāṇī continued, "You foolish bumblebee, you are trying to satisfy Me and get a reward by singing the glories of Kṛṣṇa, but it is a useless attempt. We *gopīs* are bereft of all our possessions. We are away from our homes and families. We know very well about Kṛṣṇa. We know even more than you. So whatever you make up about Him will be old stories to us. Kṛṣṇa is now in the city and is better known as the friend of Arjuna. He now has many new girlfriends, who are no doubt very happy in His association. Because the lusty, burning sensation of their breasts has been satisfied by Kṛṣṇa, they are now happy. If you go there and glorify Kṛṣṇa, they may be pleased to reward you. You are just trying to pacify Me by your behavior as a flatterer, and therefore you have put your head under My feet. But I know the trick you are trying to play. I know that you are a messenger coming from an even greater trickster, Kṛṣṇa. Therefore, please leave Me.

"I can understand that you are expert in reuniting two opposing parties, but at the same time you must know that I cannot place My reliance upon you, nor upon your master, Kṛṣṇa. We left our husbands, children and relatives only for Kṛṣṇa, yet He did not feel any obligation in exchange. At last He left us forlorn. Do you think we can place our faith in Him again? We know that Kṛṣṇa cannot live for a moment without the association of young women. That is His nature. He is finding difficulty in Mathurā because He is no longer in the village among innocent cowherd girls. He is in aristocratic society and must be feeling difficulty in making friendships with other young girls. Perhaps you have come here to canvass again or to take us there. But why should Kṛṣṇa expect us to go there? He is greatly qualified to entice all other girls, not only in Vṛndāvana or Mathurā but all over the universe. His wonderfully enchanting smile is so attractive and the movements of His eyebrows are so beautiful that He can call for any woman from the heavenly, middle or plutonic planets. Even Mahā-Lakṣmī, the greatest of all goddesses of fortune, hankers to render Him some service. In comparison to all these women of the universe, what are we? We are very insignificant.

"Kṛṣṇa advertises Himself as magnanimous, and He is praised by great saints. His qualifications would be perfectly utilized if He would only show us some mercy, for we are so much downtrodden and neglected by Him. You poor messenger, you are only a less intelligent servant. You do not know much about Kṛṣṇa—how ungrateful and hardhearted He has been, not only in this life but in His previous lives also. We have all heard this from our grandmother Paurṇamāsī. She has informed us that Kṛṣṇa was born in a *kṣatriya* family previous to this birth and was known as Rāmacandra. In that birth, instead of killing Vāli, an enemy of His friend, in the manner of a *kṣatriya,* He killed him just like a hunter. A hunter takes a secure hiding place and then kills an animal without facing it. So Lord Rāmacandra, as a *kṣatriya,* should have fought with Vāli face to face, but, instigated by His friend, He killed him from behind a tree. Thus He deviated from the religious principles of a *kṣatriya.* Also, He was so attracted by the beauty of Sītā that He converted Śūrpaṇakhā, the sister of Rāvaṇa, into an ugly woman by cutting off her nose and ears. Śūrpaṇakhā proposed an intimate relationship with Him, and as a *kṣatriya* He should have satisfied her. But He was so henpecked that He could not forget Sītādevī and converted Śūrpaṇakhā into an ugly woman. Before that birth as a *kṣatriya,* He took His birth as a *brāhmaṇa* boy known as Vāmanadeva and asked charity from Bali Mahārāja. Bali Mahārāja was so magnanimous that he gave Him whatever he had, yet Kṛṣṇa as Vāmanadeva ungratefully arrested him just like a crow and pushed him down to the Pātāla kingdom. We know all about Kṛṣṇa and how ungrateful He is. But here is the difficulty: in spite of His being so cruel and hardhearted, it is very difficult for us to give up talking about Him. And it is not only we who are unable to give up this talk, but great sages and saintly persons also engage in talking about Him. We *gopīs* of Vṛndāvana do not want to make any more friendships with this blackish boy, but we do not know how we shall be able to give up remembering and talking about His activities."

Since Kṛṣṇa is absolute, His so-called unkind activities are as relishable as His kind activities. Therefore saintly persons and great devotees like the *gopīs* cannot give up Kṛṣṇa in any circumstances. Lord Caitanya therefore prayed, "Kṛṣṇa, You are free and independent in all respects. You can either embrace Me or crush Me under Your feet—whatever You like. You may make Me brokenhearted by not letting Me see You throughout My whole life, but You are My only object of love."

"In My opinion," Śrīmatī Rādhārāṇī continued, "one should not hear about Kṛṣṇa, because as soon as a drop of the nectar of His transcendental activities is poured into the ear, one immediately rises above the duality of attraction and rejection. Being completely freed from the contamination of material attachment, one gives up attachment for this material world, including family, home, wife, children and everything else materially dear to every person. Being deprived of all material acquisitions, one makes his relatives and himself unhappy. Then he wanders in search of Kṛṣṇa, either as a human being or in other species of life, even as a bird, and voluntarily accepts the profession of a mendicant. It is very difficult to actually understand Kṛṣṇa—His name, His qualities, His form, His pastimes, His paraphernalia and His entourage."

Śrīmatī Rādhārāṇī continued to speak to the black messenger of Kṛṣṇa: "Please do not talk anymore about Kṛṣṇa. It is better to talk about something else. We are already doomed, like the black-spotted she-deer in the forest who are enchanted by the sweet musical vibration of the hunter. In the same way, we have been enchanted by the sweet words of Kṛṣṇa, and by thinking of the rays of His toenails again and again, we are becoming more and more lusty for His association. Therefore, I request you not to talk of Kṛṣṇa anymore."

These talks of Rādhārāṇī with the bumblebee messenger, including Her accusing Kṛṣṇa in so many ways and at the same time expressing Her inability to give up talking about Him, are signs of the topmost transcendental ecstasy, called *mahā-bhāva*. The ecstatic *mahā-bhāva* manifestation is possible only in the persons of Rādhārāṇī and Her associates. Great *ācāryas* like Śrīla Rūpa Gosvāmī and Viśvanātha Cakravartī Ṭhākura have analyzed these *mahā-bhāva* speeches of Śrīmatī Rādhārāṇī and described their different varieties, such as *udghūrṇā*, or bewilderment, and *jalpa-pratijalpa*, or talking in different ways. These are the signs of *ujjvala-rasa,* or the brightest jewel of love of God.

While Rādhārāṇī was talking with the bee and the bee was flying hither and thither, it all of a sudden disappeared from Her sight. She was in full mourning due to separation from Kṛṣṇa and felt ecstasy by talking with the bee. But as soon as the bee disappeared, She became almost mad, thinking that the messenger-bee might have returned to Kṛṣṇa to inform Him all about Her talking against Him. "Kṛṣṇa must be very sorry to hear it," She thought. In this way She was overwhelmed by another type of ecstasy.

In the meantime, the bee, flying hither and thither, appeared before Her again. She thought, "Kṛṣṇa is still kind to Me. In spite of the messenger's carrying disruptive messages, He is so kind that He has again sent the bee to take Me to Him." Śrīmatī Rādhārāṇī was very careful this time not to say anything against Kṛṣṇa. "My dear friend, I welcome you," She said. "Kṛṣṇa is so kind that He has again sent you. Kṛṣṇa is so kind and affectionate to Me that He has fortunately sent you back, in spite of your carrying My message against Him. All good fortune to you, My dear friend. Now you may ask from Me whatever you want. I shall give you anything because you are so kind to Me. You have come to take Me to Kṛṣṇa because He is not able to come here, being surrounded by new girlfriends in Mathurā. But you are a tiny creature. How can you take Me there? How will you be able to help Me meet Kṛṣṇa while He is taking rest there with the goddess of fortune and embracing her to His chest? Never mind. Let us forget all these things about My going there or sending you. Please let Me know how Kṛṣṇa is faring in Mathurā. Tell Me if He still remembers His foster father, Nanda Mahārāja, His affectionate mother, Yaśodā, His cowherd friends and His poor friends like us, the *gopīs.* I am sure He must sometimes sing about us, who served Him just like maidservants, without any payment. Is there any possibility that Kṛṣṇa will come back and place His *aguru*-scented hand on our heads? Please put all these inquiries to Kṛṣṇa."

Uddhava was standing near, and he heard Rādhārāṇī talking in this way, as if She had become almost mad for Kṛṣṇa. He was exceedingly surprised at how the *gopīs* were accustomed to thinking of Kṛṣṇa constantly in that topmost ecstasy of *mahā-bhāva* love. He had brought a message in writing from Kṛṣṇa, and now he wanted to present it before the *gopīs,* just to pacify them. He said, "My dear *gopīs,* your mission of human life is now successful. You are all wonderful devotees of the Supreme Personality of Godhead; therefore you are eligible to be worshiped by all kinds of people. You are worshipable throughout the three worlds because your minds are wonderfully absorbed in the thought of Vāsudeva, Kṛṣṇa. He is the goal of all pious activities and ritualistic performances, such as giving charity, rigidly following the austerity of vows, undergoing severe penances and igniting the fire of sacrifice. He is the purpose behind chanting different *mantras,* reading the *Vedas,* controlling the senses and concentrating the mind in meditation. These are some of the many different processes for self-realization and attainment of perfection of life. But actually they are meant only for realizing Kṛṣṇa and dovetailing oneself in the transcendental loving service of the Supreme Personality of Godhead." This is the last instruction of the *Bhagavad-gītā* also; although there are descriptions of different processes of self-realization, at the end Kṛṣṇa recommends that one give up everything and simply surrender unto Him. All other processes are meant for teaching one how to surrender ultimately unto the lotus feet of Kṛṣṇa. The *Bhagavad-gītā* also says that this surrendering process is completed by a sincere person after executing the processes of self-realization in wisdom and austerity for many births.

Since the perfection of such austerity was completely manifested in the lives of the *gopīs,* Uddhava was fully satisfied upon seeing their transcendental position. He continued, "My dear *gopīs,* the mentality you have developed in relationship with Kṛṣṇa is very, very difficult to attain, even for great sages and saintly persons. You have attained the highest perfectional stage of life. It is a great boon for you that you have fixed your minds upon Kṛṣṇa and have decided to have Kṛṣṇa only, giving up your families, homes, relatives, husbands and children for the sake of the Supreme Personality. Because your minds are now fully absorbed in Kṛṣṇa, the Supreme Soul, universal love has automatically developed in you. I think myself very fortunate that I have been favored, by your grace, to see you in this situation."

When Uddhava said that he had a message from Kṛṣṇa, the *gopīs* were more interested in hearing the message than in hearing about their exalted position. They did not very much like being praised for their high position. They showed their anxiety to hear the message Uddhava had brought from Kṛṣṇa. Uddhava said, "My dear *gopīs,* I am especially deputed to carry this message to you, who are such great and gentle devotees. Kṛṣṇa has specifically sent me to you because I am His most confidential servitor."

Uddhava did not deliver to the *gopīs* the written message brought from Kṛṣṇa, but he personally read it to them. The message was very gravely written, so that not only the *gopīs* but all empiric philosophers might understand how pure love of God is intrinsically integrated with all the different energies of the Supreme Lord. From Vedic information it is understood that the Supreme Lord has multi-energies: *parāsya śaktir vividhaiva śrūyate.* Also, the *gopīs* were such intimate personal friends of Kṛṣṇa that while He was writing the message for them He was so moved that He could not write distinctly. Uddhava, as a student of Bṛhaspati, had very sharp intelligence, so instead of handing over the written message, he thought it wise to read it personally and explain it to them.

Uddhava continued, "These are the words of the Personality of Godhead: 'My dear *gopīs,* My dear friends, please know that separation between ourselves is impossible at any time, at any place or under any circumstances, because I am all-pervading.'"

This all-pervasiveness of Kṛṣṇa is explained in the *Bhagavad-gītā,* in both the Ninth and Seventh chapters. In the Ninth Chapter Kṛṣṇa is described as all-pervasive in His impersonal feature; everything rests in Him, but He is not personally present everywhere. And in the Seventh Chapter it is stated that the five gross elements (earth, water, fire, air and sky) and the three subtle elements (mind, intelligence and ego) are all His inferior energies. But there is another, superior energy, which is called the living entity. The living entities are also directly part and parcel of Kṛṣṇa. Therefore Kṛṣṇa is both the material and the efficient cause of everything. He is always intermingled with everything as cause and effect. Not only the *gopīs* but all living entities are always inseparably connected with Kṛṣṇa in all circumstances. The *gopīs,* however, are perfectly and thoroughly in cognition of this relationship with Kṛṣṇa, whereas the living entities under the spell of *māyā,* the illusory energy, are forgetful of Kṛṣṇa and think themselves separate identities having no connection with Him.

Love of Kṛṣṇa, or Kṛṣṇa consciousness, is therefore the perfection of real knowledge in understanding things as they are. Our minds can never be vacant. The mind is constantly occupied with some kind of thought, and the subject matter of such thought cannot be outside the eight elements of Kṛṣṇa's energy. One who knows this philosophical aspect of all thoughts is actually a wise man, and he surrenders unto Kṛṣṇa. The *gopīs* are the epitome of this perfectional stage of knowledge. They are not simple mental speculators. Their minds are always in Kṛṣṇa. The mind is nothing but the energy of Kṛṣṇa. Actually, any person who can think, feel and will cannot be separated from Kṛṣṇa. But the stage in which he can understand his eternal relationship with Kṛṣṇa is called Kṛṣṇa consciousness. The diseased condition in which he cannot understand his eternal relationship with Kṛṣṇa is the contaminated stage, or *māyā.* Since the *gopīs* are on the platform of pure transcendental knowledge, their minds are always filled with Kṛṣṇa consciousness. For example, as there is no separation between fire and air, there is no separation between Kṛṣṇa and the living entities. When the living entities forget Kṛṣṇa, they are not in their normal condition. As for the *gopīs,* because they are always thinking of Kṛṣṇa, they are on the absolute stage of perfection in knowledge. The so-called empiric philosophers sometimes think that the path of *bhakti* is meant for the less intelligent, but unless the so-called man of knowledge comes to the platform of *bhakti,* his knowledge is certainly impure and imperfect. Actually, the stage of forgetfulness of our eternal relationship with Kṛṣṇa is separation. But that is also illusory because there is no such separation. The *gopīs* were not situated in that illusory condition of life, so even from the philosophical point of view, for them there was no separation.

Uddhava continued reading Kṛṣṇa's message: "'Nothing is separate from Me; the whole cosmic manifestation is resting on Me and is not separate from Me. Before the creation, I was existing.'" This is confirmed in the Vedic literature: *eko nārāyaṇa āsīn na brahmā na īśānaḥ.* "Before creation, there was only Nārāyaṇa. There was no Brahmā and no Śiva." The whole cosmic manifestation is manipulated by the three modes of material nature. It is said that Brahmā, the incarnation of the quality of passion, created this universe. But Brahmā is the secondary creator: the original creator is Nārāyaṇa. This is confirmed by Śaṅkarācārya: *nārāyaṇaḥ paro 'vyaktāt.* "Nārāyaṇa is transcendental, beyond this cosmic creation." In this way, nothing within this cosmic manifestation is separate from Kṛṣṇa, although Kṛṣṇa's original form is not visible in everything.

Kṛṣṇa creates, maintains and annihilates the whole cosmic manifestation by expanding Himself in different incarnations. Everything is Kṛṣṇa, and everything depends on Kṛṣṇa, but He is not perceived in the material energy, and therefore it is called *māyā,* or illusion. In the spiritual energy, however, Kṛṣṇa is perceived at every step, in all circumstances. This perfectional stage of understanding is represented by the *gopīs.* As Kṛṣṇa is always aloof from the cosmic manifestation although it is completely dependent on Him, so a living entity is also completely aloof from his material, conditioned life although the material body has developed on the basis of spiritual existence. In the *Bhagavad-gītā* the whole cosmic manifestation is accepted as the mother of the living entities, and Kṛṣṇa is the father. As the father impregnates the mother by injecting the living entity within the womb, Kṛṣṇa injects all the living entities into the womb of the material nature. They come out in different bodies according to their different fruitive activities. But in all circumstances, the living entity is aloof from this material, conditioned life. If we simply study our own bodies, we can understand how a living entity is always aloof from this bodily encagement. Every action of the body takes place by the interactions of the three modes of material nature. We can see at every moment many changes taking place in our bodies, but the spirit soul is aloof from all changes. One can neither create nor annihilate nor interfere with the actions of material nature. The living entity is therefore entrapped by the material body and conditioned in three stages, namely while awake, asleep and unconscious. The mind acts throughout all three conditions of life; the living entity in his sleeping or dreaming condition sees something as real, and when awake he sees the same thing as unreal. It is concluded, therefore, that under certain circumstances he accepts something as real, and under other circumstances he accepts the very same thing as unreal. These matters are the subject of study for the empiric philosopher or the *sāṅkhya-yogī.* To come to the right conclusion, *sāṅkhya-yogīs* undergo severe austerities and penances, practicing control of the senses and renunciation.

All these different ways of determining the ultimate goal of life are compared to rivers, and Kṛṣṇa is compared to the ocean. As the rivers flow down toward the ocean, all attempts for knowledge flow toward Kṛṣṇa. After many, many births of endeavor, when one actually comes to Kṛṣṇa, he attains the perfectional stage. Kṛṣṇa says in the

Bhagavad-gītā, kleśo 'dhikataras teṣām avyaktāsakta-cetasām: "All are pursuing the path of realizing Me, but those who have adopted courses without any *bhakti* find their endeavor very troublesome." Kṛṣṇa cannot be understood unless one comes to the point of *bhakti.*

Three paths are enunciated in the *Bhagavad-gītā: karma-yoga, jñāna-yoga* and *bhakti-yoga.* Those who are too much addicted to fruitive activities are advised to perform actions which will bring them to *bhakti.* Those who are addicted to the pursuit of empiric philosophy are also advised to act in such a way that they will realize *bhakti. Karma-yoga* is therefore different from ordinary *karma,* and *jñāna-yoga* is different from ordinary *jñāna.* Ultimately, as stated by the Lord in the *Bhagavad-gītā, bhaktyā mām abhijānāti:* only through execution of devotional service can one understand Kṛṣṇa. The perfectional stage of devotional service was achieved by the *gopīs* because they did not care to know anything but Kṛṣṇa. It is confirmed in the *Vedas, kasmin bhagavo vijñāte sarvam idaṁ vijñātaṁ bhavati.* This means that simply by knowing Kṛṣṇa one automatically acquires all other knowledge.

Uddhava continued reading Kṛṣṇa's message: "'Transcendental knowledge of the Absolute is no longer necessary for you. You were accustomed to loving Me from the very beginning of your lives.'" Knowledge of the Absolute Truth is specifically required for persons who want liberation from material existence. But one who has attained love for Kṛṣṇa is already on the platform of liberation. As stated in the *Bhagavad-gītā,* anyone engaged in unalloyed devotional service is to be considered situated on the transcendental platform of liberation. The *gopīs* did not actually feel any pangs of material existence, but they felt the separation of Kṛṣṇa. Kṛṣṇa therefore said, "My dear *gopīs,* to increase your superexcellent love for Me, I have purposely separated Myself from you so that you may be in constant meditation on Me."

The *gopīs* are in the perfectional stage of meditation. *Yogīs* are generally more fond of meditating than of executing devotional service to the Lord, but they do not know that the perfection of the *yoga* system is the attainment of devotion. This constant meditation on Kṛṣṇa by the *gopīs* is confirmed in the *Bhagavad-gītā* to be the topmost *yoga.* Kṛṣṇa knew very well the psychology of women. When a woman's beloved is away, she thinks of him more in meditation than when he is present before her. Kṛṣṇa wanted to teach through the behavior of the *gopīs* that one who is constantly in trance like the *gopīs* surely attains His lotus feet.

Lord Caitanya taught people in general the method of *vipralambha-sevā,* which is the method of rendering service unto the Supreme Personality of Godhead in the feeling of separation. The six Gosvāmīs also taught worship of Kṛṣṇa in the feeling of the *gopīs* in separation. The prayers composed by Śrīnivāsācārya about the Gosvāmīs explain these matters very clearly. Śrīnivāsācārya said that the Gosvāmīs were always absorbed in the ocean of transcendental feelings in the mood of the *gopīs.* When they lived in Vṛndāvana they were searching for Kṛṣṇa, crying, "Where are You, Kṛṣṇa? O *gopīs,* where are you? Where are You, Śrīmatī Rādhārāṇī?" They never said, "We have now seen Rādhā and Kṛṣṇa, and therefore our mission is fulfilled." Their mission remained always unfulfilled: they never met Rādhā and Kṛṣṇa.

Kṛṣṇa reminded the *gopīs* that at the time of the *rāsa* dance those of them who could not join Him for the *rāsa-līlā* gave up their bodies simply by thinking of Him. Absorption in Kṛṣṇa consciousness by feeling separation is thus the quickest method for attainment of the lotus feet of Kṛṣṇa. By the personal statement of Kṛṣṇa, the *gopīs* were convinced about the strength of feelings of separation. They were actually experiencing the supernatural method of Kṛṣṇa worship and were much relieved by understanding that Kṛṣṇa was not away from them but always with them.

The *gopīs* therefore received Uddhava very happily and began to speak as follows: "We have heard that King Kaṁsa, who was always a source of trouble for the Yadu dynasty, has now been killed. This is good news for us. We hope, therefore, that the members of the Yadu dynasty are very happy in the association of Kṛṣṇa, who can fulfill all the desires of His devotees. My dear Uddhava, kindly let us know whether Kṛṣṇa sometimes thinks of us while in the midst of the highly enlightened society girls in Mathurā. We know that the women and girls in Mathurā are not village women. They are enlightened and beautiful. Their bashful smiling glances and other feminine features must be very pleasing to Kṛṣṇa. We know very well that Kṛṣṇa is always fond of the behavior of beautiful women. It seems, therefore, that He has been entrapped by the women of Mathurā. My dear Uddhava, will you kindly let us know if Kṛṣṇa sometimes remembers us while in the midst of other women?"

Another *gopī* inquired, "Does He remember that night in the midst of *kumuda* flowers and moonlight, when Vṛndāvana became exceedingly beautiful? Kṛṣṇa was dancing with us, and the atmosphere was surcharged with the sound of foot bells. We exchanged pleasing conversation then. Does He remember that particular night? We remember that night, and we feel separation. Separation from Kṛṣṇa makes us agitated, as if there were fire in our bodies. Does He propose to come back to Vṛndāvana to extinguish that fire, just as a cloud appears in the sky to extinguish a forest fire by its downpour?"

Another *gopī* said, "Kṛṣṇa has killed His enemy, and He has victoriously achieved the kingdom of Kaṁsa. Maybe He is married with a king's daughter by this time and living happily among His kinsmen and friends. Therefore, why should He come to this village of Vṛndāvana?"

Another *gopī* said, "Kṛṣṇa is the Supreme Personality of Godhead, the husband of the goddess of fortune, and He is self-sufficient. He has no business either with us, the girls in the Vṛndāvana forest, or with the city girls in Mathurā. He is the great Supersoul; He has nothing to do with any of us, either here or there."

Another *gopī* said, "It is an unreasonable hope for us to expect Kṛṣṇa to come back to Vṛndāvana. We should try instead to be happy in disappointment. Even Piṅgalā, the great prostitute, said that disappointment is the greatest pleasure. We all know these things, but it is very difficult for us to give up the expectation of Kṛṣṇa's coming back. Who can forget a solitary conversation with Kṛṣṇa, on whose chest the goddess of fortune always remains, in spite of Kṛṣṇa's not desiring her? My dear Uddhava, Vṛndāvana is the land of rivers, forests and cows. Here the vibration of the flute was heard, and Kṛṣṇa, along with His elder brother, Śrī Balarāma, enjoyed the atmosphere in our company. Thus the environment of Vṛndāvana constantly reminds us of Kṛṣṇa and Balarāma. On the land of Vṛndāvana are the impressions of His footprints, the residence of the goddess of fortune, and because of such signs we cannot forget Kṛṣṇa."

The *gopīs* further expressed that Vṛndāvana was still full of all opulence and good fortune; there was no scarcity or want in Vṛndāvana as far as material necessities were concerned. But in spite of such opulence they could not forget Kṛṣṇa and Balarāma.

"We constantly remember various attractive features of beautiful Kṛṣṇa—His walking, His smiling, His joking words. We have all become lost by the dealings of Kṛṣṇa, and it is impossible for us to forget Him. We always pray for Him, exclaiming, 'Dear Lord, dear husband of the goddess of fortune, dear Lord of Vṛndāvana and deliverer of the distressed devotees! We are now fallen and merged in an ocean of distress. Please, therefore, come back to Vṛndāvana and deliver us from this pitiable condition.'"

Uddhava minutely studied the transcendental abnormal condition of the *gopīs* in their separation from Kṛṣṇa, and he thought it wise to repeat again and again all the pastimes the *gopīs* had enjoyed with Him. Materialistic persons are always burning in a blazing fire of material miseries. The *gopīs* were burning in a transcendental blazing fire due to separation from Kṛṣṇa. The blazing fire exasperating the *gopīs,* however, is different from the fire of the material world. The *gopīs* constantly wanted the association of Kṛṣṇa, whereas materialistic persons constantly want the advantage of material comforts.

It is stated by Viśvanātha Cakravartī Ṭhākura that Kṛṣṇa saved the cowherd boys from the blazing forest fire within a second, while their eyes were closed. Similarly, Uddhava advised the *gopīs* that they could be saved from the fire of separation by closing their eyes and meditating on the activities of Kṛṣṇa from the very beginning of their association with Him.

From the outside, the *gopīs* could visualize all the pastimes of Kṛṣṇa by hearing the descriptions of Uddhava, and from within they could remember those pastimes. From the instructions of Uddhava, the *gopīs* could understand that Kṛṣṇa was not separate from them. As they were constantly thinking of Kṛṣṇa, Kṛṣṇa was also thinking of them constantly at Mathurā.

Uddhava's messages and instructions saved the *gopīs* from immediate death, and the *gopīs* acknowledged the benediction from Uddhava. Uddhava practically acted as the preceptor spiritual master of the *gopīs,* and in return they worshiped him as they would worship Kṛṣṇa. It is recommended in authoritative scriptures that the spiritual master be worshiped on the level of the Supreme Personality of Godhead because of being His very confidential servitor, and it is accepted by great authorities that the spiritual master is the external manifestation of Kṛṣṇa. The *gopīs* were relieved from their transcendental burning condition by realizing that Kṛṣṇa was with them. Internally, they remembered His association within their hearts, and externally Uddhava helped them associate with Kṛṣṇa by his conclusive instructions.

The Supreme Personality of Godhead is described in the scriptures as *adhokṣaja,* which indicates that He is beyond the perception of all material senses. Although beyond the material senses, He is present in everyone's heart. At the same time, He is present everywhere by His all-pervasive feature of Brahman. One can realize all three transcendental features of the Absolute Truth (Bhagavān, the Personality of Godhead; Paramātmā, the localized Supersoul; and the all-pervasive Brahman) simply by studying the condition of the *gopīs* in their meeting with Uddhava, as described in *Śrīmad-Bhāgavatam.*

It is said by Śrīnivāsācārya that the six Gosvāmīs were always merged in thoughts of the activities of the *gopīs.* Caitanya Mahāprabhu has also recommended the *gopīs'* method of worshiping the Supreme Personality of Godhead as superexcellent. Śrīla Śukadeva Gosvāmī has also recommended that anyone who hears from the right source about the dealings of the *gopīs* with Kṛṣṇa and who follows the instructions laid down by the previous *ācāryas* will be elevated to the topmost position of devotional service and be able to give up the lust of material enjoyment.

All the *gopīs* were solaced by the instructions of Uddhava, and they requested him to stay in Vṛndāvana for a few days more. Uddhava agreed to their proposal and stayed with them not only for a few days but for a few months. He always kept them engaged in thinking of the transcendental message of Kṛṣṇa and His pastimes, and the *gopīs* felt as if they were experiencing direct association with Kṛṣṇa. While Uddhava remained in Vṛndāvana, the inhabitants enjoyed his association. As they discussed the activities of Kṛṣṇa, the days passed just like moments. Vṛndāvana's natural atmosphere, with the presence of the river Yamunā, its nice orchards of trees decorated with various fruits, Govardhana Hill, caves, blooming flowers—all combined to inspire Uddhava to narrate Kṛṣṇa's pastimes. The inhabitants enjoyed Uddhava's association in the same way that they enjoyed the association of Kṛṣṇa.

Uddhava was attracted by the attitude of the *gopīs* because they were completely attached to Kṛṣṇa, and he was inspired by the *gopīs'* anxiety for Kṛṣṇa. He offered them his respectful obeisances and composed songs in praise of their transcendental qualities as follows: "Among all the living entities who have accepted the human form of life, the *gopīs* are superexcellently successful in their mission. Their thought is eternally absorbed in the lotus feet of Kṛṣṇa. Great sages and we ourselves also try to be absorbed in meditation on the lotus feet of Kṛṣṇa, but the *gopīs,* having lovingly accepted the Lord, are automatically accustomed to this and do not depend on any yogic practice. The conclusion is that one who has attained the *gopīs'* condition of life does not have to take birth as Lord Brahmā or be born in a *brāhmaṇa* family or be initiated as a *brāhmaṇa.*"

Śrī Uddhava confirmed Lord Kṛṣṇa's statement in the *Bhagavad-gītā* that one who takes shelter of Him for the right purpose, be that person a *śūdra,* a woman or a member of a low-grade family, will attain the highest goal of life. The *gopīs* have set the standard of devotion for the whole world. One who follows in the footsteps of the *gopīs* by constantly thinking of Kṛṣṇa can attain the highest perfectional stage of spiritual life. The *gopīs* were born not of any highly cultured family but of cowherd men, yet they developed the highest love of Kṛṣṇa, who is the Supersoul, the Supreme Personality of Godhead and the Supreme Brahman. For self-realization or God realization there is no need to take birth in a high family. The only thing needed is development of ecstatic love of God. For achieving perfection in Kṛṣṇa consciousness, no qualification is required other than to be constantly engaged in the loving service of Kṛṣṇa, the supreme nectar, the reservoir of all pleasure. The effect of taking up Kṛṣṇa consciousness is just like that of drinking nectar: with or without one's knowledge, it will act. The active principle of Kṛṣṇa consciousness will equally manifest itself everywhere; it does not matter how and where one has taken his birth. Kṛṣṇa will bestow His benediction upon anyone who takes to Kṛṣṇa consciousness, without any doubt.

Uddhava continued, "The supreme benediction attained by the *gopīs* in spite of their being born in the families of cowherd men was never attained even by the goddess of fortune herself, and certainly not by the denizens of heaven, though the bodily scent of the women there is exactly like the scent of the lotus. The *gopīs* are so fortunate that during the *rāsa-līlā* Kṛṣṇa personally embraced them with His arms and kissed them face to face. Certainly it is not possible for any women in the three worlds to achieve this except the *gopīs.*

"Therefore I wish to take birth as one of the plants or creepers in Vṛndāvana, who are so fortunate that the *gopīs* trample them. The *gopīs* have so lovingly served Kṛṣṇa, Mukunda Himself, the giver of liberation, who is searched after by great sages and saintly persons. For His sake they left everything—their families, their children, their friends, their homes and all worldly connections."

Uddhava appreciated the exalted position of the *gopīs* and wished to fall down and take the dust of their feet on his head. Yet he dared not ask the *gopīs* to offer the dust from their feet; perhaps they would not be agreeable. Therefore, to have his head smeared with the dust of the *gopīs'* feet without their knowledge, he desired to become only an insignificant clump of grass or herbs in the land of Vṛndāvana.

The *gopīs* were so much attracted to Kṛṣṇa that when they heard the vibration of His flute they instantly left their homes, families, children, honor and feminine bashfulness and ran toward the place where Kṛṣṇa was standing. They did not consider whether they were passing over the road or through the jungles. Imperceptibly, the dust of their feet was bestowed on small grasses and herbs of Vṛndāvana. Not daring to place the dust of the *gopīs'* feet on his own head in this life, Uddhava aspired to have a future birth in Vṛndāvana in the position of a clump of grass or herbs. He would then be able to have the dust of the *gopīs'* feet.

Uddhava appreciated the extraordinary fortune of the *gopīs*, who were relieved of all material pangs and anxieties by placing on their beautiful high breasts the lotus feet of Kṛṣṇa, which are worshiped not only by the goddess of fortune but by such exalted demigods as Brahmā and Lord Śiva, and which great *yogīs* meditate upon within their hearts. Thus Uddhava prayed to be constantly honored by the dust from the lotus feet of the *gopīs*, whose chanting of Lord Kṛṣṇa's transcendental pastimes has become celebrated all over the three worlds.

After living in Vṛndāvana for some time, Uddhava desired to go back to Kṛṣṇa, and he begged permission to leave from Nanda Mahārāja and Yaśodā. He had a farewell meeting with the *gopīs*, and, taking permission from them also, he mounted his chariot to start for Mathurā.

When Uddhava was about to leave, all the inhabitants of Vṛndāvana, headed by Mahārāja Nanda and Yaśodā, came to bid him good-bye and presented him with various kinds of valuable goods secured in Vṛndāvana. They expressed their feelings with tears in their eyes due to intense attachment for Kṛṣṇa. All of them desired a benediction from Uddhava. They desired to always remember the glorious activities of Kṛṣṇa and wanted their minds to be always fixed upon His lotus feet, their words to be always engaged in glorifying Him, and their bodies to be always engaged in bowing down as they constantly remembered Him. This prayer of the inhabitants of Vṛndāvana is the superexcellent type of self-realization. The method is very simple: to fix the mind always on the lotus feet of Kṛṣṇa, to talk always of Kṛṣṇa without passing on to any other subject matter, and to engage the body in Kṛṣṇa's service constantly. Especially in this human form of life, one should engage his life, resources, words and intelligence for the service of the Lord. Only such activities can elevate a human being to the highest level of perfection. This is the verdict of all authorities.

The inhabitants of Vṛndāvana said, "By the will of the supreme authority and according to the results of our own work, we may take our birth anywhere. It doesn't matter where we are born, but our only prayer is that we may simply be engaged in Kṛṣṇa consciousness." A pure devotee of Lord Kṛṣṇa never desires to be promoted to the heavenly planets, or even to Vaikuṇṭha or Goloka Vṛndāvana, because he has no desire for his own personal satisfaction. A pure devotee regards heaven and hell to be on an equal level. Without Kṛṣṇa, heaven is hell; and with Kṛṣṇa, hell is heaven.

When Uddhava had been sufficiently honored and worshiped by the pure devotees of Vṛndāvana, he returned to Mathurā and to his master, Kṛṣṇa. After offering respects by bowing down before Lord Kṛṣṇa and Balarāma, he described the wonderful devotional life of the inhabitants of Vṛndāvana. Then he presented to Vasudeva, Kṛṣṇa's father, and Ugrasena, Kṛṣṇa's grandfather, all the gifts given by the inhabitants of Vṛndāvana.

Thus ends the Bhaktivedanta purport of the Forty-seventh Chapter of Kṛṣṇa, *"Delivery of the Message of Kṛṣṇa to the* Gopīs."

CHAPTER 48

Kṛṣṇa Pleases His Devotees

FOR DAYS TOGETHER, Kṛṣṇa heard from Uddhava all the details of his visit to Vṛndāvana, especially the condition of His father and mother and of the *gopīs* and the cowherd boys. Lord Kṛṣṇa was fully satisfied that Uddhava was able to solace them by his instructions and by the message delivered to them.

Lord Kṛṣṇa then decided to go to the house of Kubjā, the hunchback woman who had pleased Him by offering Him sandalwood pulp when He was entering the city of Mathurā. As stated in the *Bhagavad-gītā*, Kṛṣṇa always tries to please His devotees as much as the devotees try to please Kṛṣṇa. As the devotees always think of Kṛṣṇa within their hearts, Kṛṣṇa also thinks of His devotees within Himself. When Kubjā was converted into a beautiful society girl, she wanted Kṛṣṇa to come to her place so that she could try to receive and worship Him in her own way. Society girls generally try to satisfy their clients by offering their bodies for the men to enjoy. But this society girl, Kubjā, was actually captivated by a lust to satisfy her senses with Kṛṣṇa. When Kṛṣṇa desired to go to the house of Kubjā, He certainly had no desire for sense gratification. By supplying the sandalwood pulp to Kṛṣṇa, Kubjā had already satisfied His senses. On the plea of her sense gratification, however, He decided to go to her house, not actually for sense gratification but to turn her into a pure devotee. Kṛṣṇa is always served by many thousands of goddesses of fortune; therefore He has no need to satisfy His senses by going to a society girl. But because He is kind to everyone, He decided to go there. It is said that the moon does not withhold its shining from the courtyard of a crooked person. Similarly, Kṛṣṇa's transcendental mercy is never denied to anyone who has rendered service unto Him, whether through lust, anger, fear or pure love. In the *Caitanya-caritāmṛta* it is stated that if one wants to serve Kṛṣṇa and at the same time wants to satisfy his own lusty desires, Kṛṣṇa will handle the situation so that the devotee forgets his lusty desires and becomes fully purified and constantly engaged in the service of the Lord.

To fulfill His promise, Kṛṣṇa, along with Uddhava, went to the house of Kubjā, who was very eager to get Kṛṣṇa for the satisfaction of her lusty desires. When Kṛṣṇa reached her house, He saw that it was completely decorated in a way to excite the lusty desires of a man. This suggests that there were many nude pictures, on top of which were canopies and flags embroidered with pearl necklaces, along with comfortable beds and cushioned chairs. The rooms were provided with flower garlands and were nicely scented with incense and sprinkled with scented water. And the rooms were illuminated by nice lamps.

When Kubjā saw that Lord Kṛṣṇa had come to her house to fulfill His promised visit, she immediately got up from her chair to receive Him cordially. Accompanied by her many girlfriends, she began to talk with Him with great respect and honor. After offering Him a nice place to sit, she worshiped Lord Kṛṣṇa in a manner just suitable to her position. Uddhava was similarly received by Kubjā and her girlfriends, but he did not want to sit on an equal level with Kṛṣṇa, and thus he simply sat down on the floor.

As one usually does in such situations, Kṛṣṇa entered the bedroom of Kubjā without wasting time. In the meantime, Kubjā took her bath and smeared her body with sandalwood pulp. She dressed herself with nice garments, valuable jewelry, ornaments and flower garlands. After chewing betel nut and other intoxicating eatables and spraying herself with scents, she appeared before Kṛṣṇa. Her smiling glance and moving eyebrows were full of feminine bashfulness as she stood gracefully before Lord Kṛṣṇa, who is known as Mādhava, the husband of the goddess of fortune. When Kṛṣṇa saw Kubjā hesitating to come before Him, He immediately caught hold of her hand, which was decorated with bangles. With great affection, He dragged her near Him and made her sit by His side. Simply by having previously supplied pulp of sandalwood to the Supreme Lord, Kṛṣṇa, Kubjā became free from all sinful reactions and eligible to enjoy with Him. She then took Kṛṣṇa's lotus feet and placed them on her breasts, which were burning with the blazing fire of lust. By smelling the fragrance of Kṛṣṇa's lotus feet, she was immediately relieved of all lusty desires. She was thus allowed to embrace Kṛṣṇa with her arms and mitigate her long-cherished desire to have Him as a visitor in her house.

It is stated in the *Bhagavad-gītā* that one must be freed of all material sinful reactions before one can engage in the transcendental loving service of the Lord. Simply by supplying sandalwood pulp to Kṛṣṇa, Kubjā was thus rewarded. She was not trained to worship Kṛṣṇa in any other way; therefore she wanted to satisfy Him by her profession. It is confirmed in the *Bhagavad-gītā* that the Lord can be worshiped even by one's profession, if it is sincerely offered for the pleasure of the Lord. Kubjā told Kṛṣṇa, "My dear friend, kindly remain with me at least for a few days and enjoy with me. My dear lotus-eyed friend, I cannot leave You immediately. Please grant my request."

As stated in the Vedic versions, the Supreme Personality of Godhead has multipotencies. According to expert opinion, Kubjā represents the *bhū-śakti* potency of Kṛṣṇa, just as Śrīmatī Rādhārāṇī represents His *cit-śakti* potency. Although Kubjā requested Kṛṣṇa to remain with her for some days, Kṛṣṇa politely impressed upon her that it was not possible for Him to stay. Kṛṣṇa visits this material world occasionally, whereas His connection with the spiritual world is eternal. Kṛṣṇa is always present either in the Vaikuṇṭha planets or in the Goloka Vṛndāvana planet. The technical term of His presence in the spiritual world is *aprakaṭa-līlā*.

After satisfying Kubjā with sweet words, Kṛṣṇa returned home with Uddhava. There is a warning in the *Śrīmad-Bhāgavatam* that Kṛṣṇa is not very easily worshiped, for He is the Supreme Personality of Godhead, the chief among the *viṣṇu-tattvas*. To worship Kṛṣṇa or have association with Him is not very easy. Specifically, there is a warning for devotees attracted to Kṛṣṇa through conjugal love: it is not good for them to desire sense gratification by direct association with Kṛṣṇa. Actually, the activities of sense gratification are material. In the spiritual world there are symptoms like kissing and embracing, but there is no sense-gratificatory process as it exists in the material world. This warning is specifically for those known as *sahajiyās*, who take it for granted that Kṛṣṇa is an ordinary human being. They desire to enjoy sex life with Him in a perverted way. In a spiritual relationship, sense gratification is most insignificant. Anyone who desires a relationship of perverted sense gratification with Kṛṣṇa must be considered less intelligent. His mentality requires to be reformed.

After a while, Kṛṣṇa fulfilled His promise to visit Akrūra at his house. Akrūra was in relationship with Kṛṣṇa as His servitor, and Kṛṣṇa wanted to get some service from him. He went there accompanied by Lord Balarāma and Uddhava. When Kṛṣṇa, Balarāma and Uddhava approached the house of Akrūra, Akrūra came forward, embraced Uddhava and offered respectful obeisances, bowing down before Lord Kṛṣṇa and Balarāma. Kṛṣṇa, Balarāma and Uddhava offered him obeisances in turn and were offered appropriate sitting places. When all were comfortably seated, Akrūra washed their feet and sprinkled the water on his head. Then he offered nice clothing, flowers and sandalwood pulp in regular worship. All three of them were very satisfied by Akrūra's behavior. Akrūra then bowed down before Kṛṣṇa, putting his head on the ground. Then, placing Kṛṣṇa's lotus feet on his lap, Akrūra gently began to massage them. When Akrūra was fully satisfied in the presence of Kṛṣṇa and Balarāma, his eyes filled with tears of love for Kṛṣṇa, and he began to offer his prayers as follows.

"My dear Lord Kṛṣṇa and Balarāma, it is very kind of You to have killed Kaṁsa and his associates. You have delivered the whole family of the Yadu dynasty from the greatest calamity. The Yadus will always remember Your saving of their great dynasty. My dear Lord Kṛṣṇa and Balarāma, both of You are the original personality from whom everything has emanated, the original cause of all causes. You have inconceivable energy, and You are all-pervasive. There is no cause and effect, gross or subtle, but You. You are the Supreme Brahman realized through the study of the *Vedas*. By Your inconceivable energy, You are actually visible before us. You create this cosmic manifestation by Your own potencies, and You enter into it Yourself. As the five material elements—earth, water, fire, air and sky—are distributed in everything manifested by different kinds of bodies, so You alone enter the various bodies created by Your own energy. You enter the body as the individual soul and, independently, as the Supersoul." It is confirmed in the *Bhagavad-gītā* that the material body is created by Kṛṣṇa's inferior energy, that the living entities—the individual souls—are His parts and parcels, and that the Supersoul is His localized representation. Thus while the material body, the living entity and the Supersoul constitute an individual living being, originally they are all different energies of the one Supreme Lord.

Akrūra continued, "In the material world, You create, maintain and dissolve the whole manifestation by the interactions of the three material qualities, namely goodness, passion and ignorance. But You are not implicated in the activities of those material qualities, for Your supreme knowledge is never overcome like the knowledge of the individual living entity."

The Supreme Lord enters the material cosmos and causes creation, maintenance and destruction in their due course, whereas the part-and-parcel living entity enters the material elements and has his material body created for him. The difference between the living entity and the Lord is that the living entity is part and parcel of the Supreme Lord and has the tendency to be overcome by the interactions of the material qualities. Kṛṣṇa, the Parabrahman, or the Supreme Brahman, being always situated in full knowledge, is never overcome by such activities. Therefore Kṛṣṇa is called Acyuta, meaning "He who never falls down." Kṛṣṇa's knowledge of His spiritual identity is never overcome by material action, whereas the minute part-and-parcel living entities are prone to forget their spiritual identity due to material action. The individual living entities are eternally part and parcel of God, minute sparks of the original fire, Kṛṣṇa. As sparks are prone to be extinguished, but not the blazing fire, so the living entities can be overcome by material activities, whereas Kṛṣṇa never can.

Akrūra continued, "Less intelligent men misunderstand Your transcendental form to be made of material energy. But that concept is not at all applicable to You. Actually, You are all-spiritual, and there is no difference between You and Your body. Therefore, there is no question of Your being conditioned or liberated. You are ever liberated in any condition of life. As stated in the *Bhagavad-gītā,* only fools and rascals consider You an ordinary man. To consider Your Lordship one of us, conditioned by the material nature, is a mistake due to our imperfect knowledge. When people deviate from the original knowledge of the *Vedas,* they try to identify the ordinary living entities with Your Lordship, who have appeared on this earth in Your original form to reestablish the real knowledge that the living entities are neither one with nor equal to the Supreme God. My dear Lord, You are always situated in uncontaminated goodness (*śuddha-sattva*). Your appearance is necessary to reestablish actual Vedic knowledge, as opposed to the atheistic philosophy which tries to establish that God and the living entities are one and the same. My dear Lord Kṛṣṇa, this time You have appeared in the home of Vasudeva as His son, with Your plenary expansion, Śrī Balarāma. Your mission is to kill all the atheistic royal families and destroy their huge military strength. You have advented Yourself to minimize the burden of the world, and to fulfill this mission You have glorified the dynasty of Yadu by appearing as one of its members.

"My dear Lord, today my home has been purified by Your presence. I have become the most fortunate person in the world. The Supreme Personality of Godhead, who is worshipable by all different kinds of demigods, Pitās, kings, emperors and other living entities and who is the Supersoul of everything, has come into my home. The water of His lotus feet purifies the three worlds, and now He has kindly come to my place. Who in the three worlds among factually learned men will not take shelter of Your lotus feet and surrender unto You? Who, knowing well that no one can be as affectionate as You are to Your devotees, is so foolish that he will decline to become Your devotee? Throughout the Vedic literature it is declared that You are the dearmost friend of every living entity. This is confirmed in the *Bhagavad-gītā: suhṛdaṁ sarva-bhūtānām.* You are the Supreme Personality of Godhead, completely capable of fulfilling the desires of Your devotees. You are the real friend of everyone. In spite of giving Yourself to Your devotees, You are never depleted of Your original potency. Your potency neither decreases nor increases in volume.

"My dear Lord, it is very difficult for even great mystic *yogīs* and demigods to ascertain Your movements or approach You, yet out of Your causeless mercy You have kindly consented to come to my home. This is the most auspicious moment in the journey of my material existence. By Your grace only, I can now understand that my home, my wife, my children and my worldly possessions are all bonds to material existence. Please cut the knot and save me from this entanglement of false society, friendship and love."

Lord Śrī Kṛṣṇa was very much pleased by Akrūra's offering of prayers. With His smile captivating Akrūra more and more, the Lord replied to his submissive devotional statements with the following sweet words: "My dear Akrūra, in spite of your submissiveness, I consider you My superior, on the level with My father and teacher and most well-wishing friend. You are therefore to be worshiped by Me, and since you are My uncle I am always to be protected by you. I desire you to maintain Me, for I am one of your own children. Apart from this filial relationship, an exalted devotee like you is always to be worshiped by everyone. Anyone who desires good fortune must offer his respectful obeisances unto personalities like you, who are greater than the demigods. People worship the demigods when in need of some sense gratification, and the demigods offer benedictions to their devotees after being worshiped. But a devotee like you, Akrūra, is always ready to offer people the greatest benediction. A saintly person or devotee is free to offer benedictions to everyone, whereas the demigods can offer benedictions only after being worshiped. One can take advantage of a place of pilgrimage only after going there, and worshiping a particular demigod involves waiting a long time for the fulfillment of one's desire, but saintly persons like you, My dear Akrūra, can immediately fulfill all the desires of a devotee. My dear Akrūra, you are always Our friend and well-wisher. You are always ready to act for Our welfare. Kindly, therefore, go to Hastināpura and see what arrangement has been made for the Pāṇḍavas."

Kṛṣṇa was anxious to know about the sons of Pāṇḍu because at a very young age they had lost their father. Being very friendly to His devotees, Kṛṣṇa was anxious to know about them, and therefore He deputed Akrūra to go to Hastināpura and get information of the real situation. Kṛṣṇa continued, "I have heard that after King Pāṇḍu's death, his young sons—Yudhiṣṭhira, Bhīma, Arjuna, Nakula and Sahadeva—along with their widowed mother, have come under the charge of Dhṛtarāṣṭra, who is to look after them as their guardian. But I have also heard that Dhṛtarāṣṭra is not only blind from birth but also blind in his affection for his cruel son Duryodhana. The five Pāṇḍavas are the sons of King Pāṇḍu, but Dhṛtarāṣṭra, due to Duryodhana's plans and designs, is not favorably disposed toward them. Kindly go there and study how Dhṛtarāṣṭra is dealing with the Pāṇḍavas. On receipt of your report, I shall consider how to favor them." In this way the Supreme Personality of Godhead, Kṛṣṇa, ordered Akrūra to go to Hastināpura, and then He returned home, accompanied by Balarāma and Uddhava.

Thus ends the Bhaktivedanta purport of the Forty-eighth Chapter of Kṛṣṇa, *"Kṛṣṇa Pleases His Devotees."*

CHAPTER 49

Ill-motivated Dhṛtarāṣṭra

THUS ORDERED by the Supreme Personality of Godhead, Śrī Kṛṣṇa, Akrūra visited Hastināpura, said to be the site of what is now New Delhi. The part of New Delhi still known as Indraprastha is accepted by people in general as the old capital of the Pāṇḍavas. The very name Hastināpura suggests that there were many *hastīs,* or elephants; because the Pāṇḍavas kept many elephants in the capital, it was called Hastināpura. Keeping elephants is very expensive; to keep many elephants, therefore, the kingdom must be very rich, and Hastināpura, as Akrūra saw when he reached it, was full of elephants, horses, chariots and other opulences. The kings of Hastināpura were taken to be the ruling kings of the whole world. Their fame was widely spread throughout the entire kingdom, and their administration was conducted under the good counsel of learned *brāhmaṇas.*

After seeing the very opulent capital city, Akrūra met King Dhṛtarāṣṭra. He also saw grandfather Bhīṣma sitting with him. After meeting them, he went to see Vidura and then Kuntī, Akrūra's cousin. One after another, he saw King Bāhlīka and his son Somadatta, Droṇācārya, Kṛpācārya, Karṇa and Suyodhana. (Suyodhana is another name of Duryodhana.) Then he saw the son of Droṇācārya, Aśvatthāmā, as well as the five Pāṇḍava brothers and other friends and relatives living in the city. All those who met Akrūra, known also as the son of Gāndinī, were very much pleased to receive him and inquire about the welfare of their respective relatives. He was offered a good seat at his receptions, and he in turn inquired all about the welfare and activities of his relatives.

Since he was deputed by Lord Kṛṣṇa to visit Hastināpura, it is understood that he was very intelligent in studying a diplomatic situation. Dhṛtarāṣṭra was unlawfully occupying the throne after the death of King Pāṇḍu, despite the presence of Pāṇḍu's sons. Akrūra could understand very well that ill-motivated Dhṛtarāṣṭra was much inclined in favor of his own sons. In fact, Dhṛtarāṣṭra had already usurped the kingdom and was now intriguing to dispose of the five Pāṇḍava brothers. Akrūra knew that all the sons of Dhṛtarāṣṭra, headed by Duryodhana, were very crooked politicians. Dhṛtarāṣṭra did not act in accordance with the good instructions given by Bhīṣma and Vidura; instead, he was being conducted by the ill instructions of such persons as Karṇa and Śakuni. Akrūra decided to stay in Hastināpura for a few months to study the whole political situation.

Gradually Akrūra learned from Kuntī and Vidura that the sons of Dhṛtarāṣṭra were intolerant and envious of the five Pāṇḍava brothers because of their extraordinary learning in military science and their greatly developed bodily strength. The Pāṇḍavas acted as truly chivalrous heroes, exhibited all the good qualities of *kṣatriyas* and were very responsible princes, always thinking of the welfare of the citizens. Akrūra also learned that the envious sons of Dhṛtarāṣṭra had tried to kill the Pāṇḍavas by poisoning them.

Akrūra happened to be one of the cousins of Kuntī; therefore, after meeting him, she began to inquire about her paternal relatives. Thinking of her birthplace and beginning to cry, she asked Akrūra whether her father, mother, brothers, sisters and other friends at home still remembered her. She especially inquired about Kṛṣṇa and Balarāma, her glorious nephews. She asked, "Does Kṛṣṇa, the Supreme Personality of Godhead, who is very affectionate to His devotees, remember my sons? Does Balarāma remember us?" Inside herself, Kuntī felt like a she-deer in the midst of tigers, and actually her position was like that. After the death of her husband, King Pāṇḍu, she was supposed to take care of the five Pāṇḍava children, but the sons of Dhṛtarāṣṭra were always planning to kill them. She was certainly living like a poor innocent animal in the midst of several tigers. Being a devotee of Lord Kṛṣṇa, she always thought of Him and expected that one day Kṛṣṇa would come and save them from their dangerous position. She inquired from Akrūra whether Kṛṣṇa proposed to come to advise the fatherless Pāṇḍavas how to get free of the intrigues of Dhṛtarāṣṭra and his sons. Talking with Akrūra about all these affairs, she felt herself helpless and exclaimed, "My dear Kṛṣṇa, my dear Kṛṣṇa! You are the supreme mystic, the Supersoul of the universe. You are the real well-wisher of the whole universe. My dear Govinda, at this time You are far away from me, yet I pray to surrender unto Your lotus feet. I am now grief-stricken with my five fatherless sons. I can fully understand that but for Your lotus feet there is no shelter or protection. Your lotus feet can deliver all aggrieved souls because You are the Supreme Personality of Godhead. One can be safe from the clutches of repeated birth and death by Your mercy only. My dear Kṛṣṇa, You are the supreme pure one, the Supersoul and the master of all *yogīs*. What can I say? I can simply offer my respectful obeisances unto You. Accept me as Your fully surrendered devotee."

Although Kṛṣṇa was not present before her, Kuntī offered her prayers to Him as if she were in His presence face to face. This is possible for anyone following in the footsteps of Kuntī. Kṛṣṇa does not have to be physically present everywhere. He is actually present everywhere by spiritual potency, and one simply has to surrender unto Him sincerely.

When Kuntī was offering her prayers very feelingly to Kṛṣṇa, she could not check herself and began to cry loudly before Akrūra. Vidura was also present, and both Akrūra and Vidura became very sympathetic to the mother of the Pāṇḍavas and began to solace her by glorifying her five sons, namely Yudhiṣṭhira, Arjuna, Bhīma, Nakula and Sahadeva. They pacified her, saying that her sons were extraordinarily powerful; she should not be perturbed about them, since they were born of great demigods like Yamarāja, Indra and Vāyu.

Akrūra decided to return home and report on the strained circumstances in which he found Kuntī and her five sons. He first wanted to give good advice to Dhṛtarāṣṭra, who was so favorably inclined toward his own sons and unfavorably inclined toward the Pāṇḍavas. When King Dhṛtarāṣṭra was sitting among friends and relatives, Akrūra began to address him, calling him Vaicitravīrya. Vaicitravīrya means "the son of Vicitravīrya." Vicitravīrya was the name of Dhṛtarāṣṭra's father, but Dhṛtarāṣṭra was actually the begotten son not of Vicitravīrya but of Vyāsadeva. Formerly it was the system that if a man were unable to beget a child, his brother could beget a child in the womb of his wife (*devareṇa sutotpattiḥ*). That system is now forbidden in this Age of Kali. Akrūra called Dhṛtarāṣṭra Vaicitravīrya sarcastically because he was not actually begotten by his father. He was the son of Vyāsadeva. When a child was begotten in the wife by the husband's brother, the child was claimed by the husband, but of course the child was not begotten by the husband. This sarcastic remark pointed out that Dhṛtarāṣṭra was falsely claiming the throne on hereditary grounds. Actually Pāṇḍu had been the rightful king, and in the presence of Pāṇḍu's sons, the Pāṇḍavas, Dhṛtarāṣṭra should not have occupied the throne.

Akrūra said, "My dear son of Vicitravīrya, you have unlawfully usurped the throne of the Pāṇḍavas. Anyway, somehow or other you are now on the throne. Therefore I beg to advise you to please rule the kingdom on moral and ethical principles. If you do so and try to please your subjects in that way, your name and fame will be perpetual." Akrūra hinted that although Dhṛtarāṣṭra was ill-treating his nephews, the Pāṇḍavas, they happened to be his subjects. "Even if you treat them not as the owners of the throne but as your subjects, you should impartially think of their welfare as though they were your own sons. But if you do not follow this principle and act in just the opposite way, you will be unpopular among your subjects, and in the next life you will have to live in a hellish condition. I therefore hope you will treat your sons and the sons of Pāṇḍu equally." Akrūra hinted that if Dhṛtarāṣṭra did not treat the Pāṇḍavas and his sons as equals, surely there would be a fight between the two camps of cousins. Since the cause of the Pāṇḍavas was just, they would come out victorious, and the sons of Dhṛtarāṣṭra would be killed. This was a prophecy told by Akrūra to Dhṛtarāṣṭra.

Akrūra further advised Dhṛtarāṣṭra, "In this material world, no one can remain an eternal companion to another. Only by chance do we assemble together in a family, society, community or nation, but at the end, because every one of us has to give up the body, we must be separated. One should not, therefore, be unnecessarily affectionate toward family members." Dhṛtarāṣṭra's affection was also unlawful and did not show much intelligence. In plain words, Akrūra hinted to Dhṛtarāṣṭra that his staunch family affection was due to his gross ignorance of fact or his blindness to moral principles. Although we appear combined together in a family, society or nation, each of us has an individual destiny. Everyone takes birth according to individual past work; therefore everyone must individually enjoy or suffer the result of his own *karma.* There is no possibility of improving one's destiny by cooperative living. Sometimes it happens that one's father accumulates wealth by illegal ways, and the son takes away the money, although it is hard-earned by the father, just as a small fish in the ocean eats the material body of a large, old fish. One ultimately cannot accumulate wealth illegally for the gratification of his family, society, community or nation. An illustration of this principle is that many great empires which developed in the past are no longer existing because their wealth was squandered away by later descendants. One who does not know this subtle law of fruitive activities and who thus gives up the moral and ethical principles carries with him only the reactions of his sinful activities. His ill-gotten wealth and possessions are taken by someone else, and he goes to the darkest region of hellish life. One should not, therefore, accumulate more wealth than allotted to him by destiny; otherwise he will be factually blind to his own interest. Instead of fulfilling his self-interest, he will act in just the opposite way, for his own downfall.

Akrūra continued, "My dear Dhṛtarāṣṭra, I beg to advise you not to be blind to the facts of material existence. Material, conditioned life, either in distress or in happiness, is to be accepted as a dream. One should try to bring his mind and senses under control and live peacefully for spiritual advancement in Kṛṣṇa consciousness." In the *Caitanya-caritāmṛta* it is said that except for persons in Kṛṣṇa consciousness, everyone is always disturbed in mind and full of anxiety. Even those trying for liberation, or merging into the Brahman effulgence, or the *yogīs* who try to achieve perfection in mystic power cannot have peace of mind. Pure devotees of Kṛṣṇa have no demands to make of Kṛṣṇa. They are simply satisfied with service to Him. Actual peace and mental tranquillity can be attained only in perfect Kṛṣṇa consciousness.

After hearing these moral instructions from Akrūra, Dhṛtarāṣṭra replied, "My dear Akrūra, you are very charitable in giving me good instructions, but unfortunately I cannot accept them. A person destined to die does not utilize the effects of nectar, although it may be administered to him. I can understand that your instructions are valuable. Unfortunately, they do not stay in my flickering mind, just as the glittering lightning in the sky does not stay fixed in a cloud. I can understand only that no one can stop the onward progress of the supreme will. I understand that the Supreme Personality of Godhead, Kṛṣṇa, has appeared in the family of the Yadus to decrease the burdensome load on this earth."

Dhṛtarāṣṭra hinted to Akrūra that he had complete faith in Kṛṣṇa, the Supreme Personality of Godhead. At the same time, he was very partial to his family members. In the very near future, Kṛṣṇa would vanquish all the members of his family, and in a helpless condition Dhṛtarāṣṭra would take shelter of Kṛṣṇa's lotus feet. To show His special favor to a devotee, Kṛṣṇa usually takes away all the objects of his material affection, thus forcing the devotee to be materially helpless, with no alternative but to accept the lotus feet of Kṛṣṇa. This actually happened to Dhṛtarāṣṭra after the end of the Battle of Kurukṣetra. Dhṛtarāṣṭra could realize two opposing factors acting before him. He could understand that Kṛṣṇa was there to remove all the unnecessary burdens of the world. His sons were an unnecessary burden, and so he expected that they would be killed. At the same time, he could not rid himself of his unlawful affection for his sons. Understanding these two contradictory factors, he offered his respectful obeisances to the Supreme Personality of Godhead. "The contradictory ways of material existence are very difficult to understand; they can be taken only as the inconceivable execution of the plan of the Supreme, who by His inconceivable energy creates this material world and enters into it and sets into motion the three modes of nature. When everything is created, He enters into each and every living entity and into the smallest atom. No one can understand the incalculable plans of the Supreme Lord."

After hearing this statement, Akrūra could clearly understand that Dhṛtarāṣṭra was not going to change his policy of discriminating against the Pāṇḍavas in favor of his sons. He at once took leave of his friends in Hastināpura and returned to his home in the kingdom of the Yadus. After returning home, he vividly informed Lord Kṛṣṇa and Balarāma of the actual situation in Hastināpura and the intentions of Dhṛtarāṣṭra. Akrūra was sent to Hastināpura by Kṛṣṇa to study these, and by the grace of the Lord he was successful.

Thus ends the Bhaktivedanta purport of the Forty-ninth Chapter of Kṛṣṇa, *"Ill-motivated Dhṛtarāṣṭra."*

CHAPTER 50

Kṛṣṇa Erects the Dvārakā Fort

UPON KAṀSA'S DEATH, his two wives became widows. According to Vedic civilization, a woman is never independent. She has three stages of life: in childhood a woman should live under the protection of her father, a youthful woman should live under the protection of her young husband, and in the event of the death of her husband she should live under the protection of her grown-up sons, or if she has no grown-up sons she must go back to her father and live as a widow under his protection. It appears that Kaṁsa had no grown-up sons. Therefore, after his wives became widows they returned to the shelter of their father. Kaṁsa had two queens, Asti and Prāpti, and both happened to be the daughters of King Jarāsandha, the lord of Bihar Province (known in those days as Magadha). After reaching home, the two queens explained their awkward position following Kaṁsa's death. The King of Magadha, Jarāsandha, was mortified on hearing of the pitiable condition of his daughters. When informed of the death of Kaṁsa, Jarāsandha decided on the spot that he would rid the world of all the members of the Yadu dynasty. He decided that since Kṛṣṇa had killed Kaṁsa, the whole dynasty of the Yadus should be killed.

He began to make extensive arrangements to attack the kingdom of Mathurā with his innumerable military phalanxes, consisting of many thousands of chariots, horses, elephants and infantry soldiers. Jarāsandha prepared thirteen such military phalanxes to retaliate the death of Kaṁsa. Taking with him all his military strength, he attacked the capital of the Yadu kings, Mathurā, surrounding it from all directions. Śrī Kṛṣṇa, who appeared like an ordinary human being, saw the immense strength of Jarāsandha, which appeared like an ocean about to cover a beach at any moment. He also perceived that the inhabitants of Mathurā were overwhelmed with fear. He began to think within Himself about His mission as an incarnation and how to tackle the present situation before Him. He thought that since He was not going to conquer the kingdom of Magadha, to kill the King of Magadha, namely Jarāsandha, was useless. His mission was to diminish the overburdening population of the whole world; therefore He took the opportunity to face so many men, chariots, elephants and horses. The military strength of Jarāsandha had appeared before Him, and He decided to kill the entire force of Jarāsandha so that he would go back and reorganize his military strength.

While Lord Kṛṣṇa was thinking in that way, two beautiful chariots, fully equipped with drivers, weapons, flags and other paraphernalia, arrived for Him from outer space. Kṛṣṇa saw the two chariots present before Him and immediately addressed His elder brother, Balarāma, who is also known as Saṅkarṣaṇa: "My dear elder brother, best among the Āryans, You are the Lord of the universe, and, specifically, You are the protector of the Yadu dynasty. The members of the Yadu dynasty sense great danger before the soldiers of Jarāsandha, and they are very much aggrieved. Just to give them protection, Your chariot is also here, filled with weapons. I request You to sit on Your chariot and kill all these soldiers, the entire military strength of the enemy. The two of Us have descended on this earth just to annihilate such unnecessary bellicose forces and give protection to the pious devotees. So we have the opportunity to fulfill Our mission. Please let Us execute it." Thus Kṛṣṇa and Balarāma, the descendants of Daśārha, decided to annihilate the thirteen military companies of Jarāsandha.

After equipping Themselves with military dress, Kṛṣṇa and Balarāma mounted Their chariots. Kṛṣṇa rode the chariot on which Dāruka was the driver. With a small army They came out of the city of Mathurā, blowing Their respective conchshells. Curiously enough, although the other party was equipped with greater military strength, when they heard the vibration of Kṛṣṇa's conchshell their hearts were shaken. When Jarāsandha saw Balarāma and Kṛṣṇa, he was a little bit compassionate because They happened to be related to him as grandsons. He specifically addressed Kṛṣṇa as *puruṣādhama,* meaning "the lowest among men." Actually Kṛṣṇa is known in all Vedic literatures as Puruṣottama, the highest among men. Jarāsandha had no intention of addressing Kṛṣṇa as Puruṣottama, but great scholars have determined the true meaning of the word *puruṣādhama* to be "one who makes all other personalities go downward." Actually no one can be equal to or greater than the Supreme Personality of Godhead.

Jarāsandha said, "It will be a great dishonor for me to fight with boys like Kṛṣṇa and Balarāma." Because Kṛṣṇa had killed Kaṁsa, Jarāsandha specifically addressed Him as the killer of His own relatives. Kaṁsa had killed many of his own nephews, yet Jarāsandha did not take notice; but because Kṛṣṇa had killed His maternal uncle, Kaṁsa, Jarāsandha tried to criticize Him. That is the way of demoniac dealings. Demons do not try to find their own faults or those of their friends, but try to find the faults of their enemies. Jarāsandha also criticized Kṛṣṇa for not even being a *kṣatriya.* Because He was raised by Mahārāja Nanda, Kṛṣṇa was not a *kṣatriya* but a *vaiśya. Vaiśyas* are generally called *guptas,* and the word *gupta* can also be used to mean "hidden." So Kṛṣṇa was both hidden and raised by Nanda Mahārāja. Jarāsandha accused Kṛṣṇa of three faults: that He killed His own maternal uncle, that He was not even a *kṣatriya* and that He was hidden in His childhood. And therefore Jarāsandha felt ashamed to fight with Him.

Next he turned toward Balarāma and addressed Him: "You, Balarāma! If You like You can fight along with Him, and if You have patience, then You can wait to be killed by my arrows. Thus You can be promoted to heaven." It is stated in the *Bhagavad-gītā* that a *kṣatriya* can benefit in either of two ways while fighting. If a *kṣatriya* gains victory in the fight, he enjoys the results of victory, but even if killed he is promoted to the heavenly kingdom.

After hearing Jarāsandha speak in that way, Kṛṣṇa answered, "My dear King Jarāsandha, heroes do not talk much. Rather, they show their prowess. Because you are talking a great deal, it appears that you are assured of your death in this battle. We do not care to hear you any longer, for it is useless to hear the words of a person who is going to die or of one who is very distressed." To fight with Kṛṣṇa, Jarāsandha surrounded Him from all sides with great military strength. As the sun appears covered by cloudy air and dust, Kṛṣṇa, the supreme sun, was covered by the military strength of Jarāsandha. Kṛṣṇa's and Balarāma's chariots were marked with pictures of Garuḍa and palm trees, respectively. The women of Mathurā all stood on the tops of the houses, palaces and gates to see the wonderful fight, but when Kṛṣṇa's chariot was surrounded by Jarāsandha's military force and was no longer visible to them, they were so frightened that some of them fainted. Kṛṣṇa saw Himself overwhelmed by the military strength of Jarāsandha. His small army of soldiers was being harassed, so He immediately took up His bow, named Śārṅga.

He took His arrows from their quiver, and one after another He set them on the bowstring and shot them toward the enemy. They were so accurate that the elephants, horses and infantry soldiers of Jarāsandha were quickly killed. The incessant arrows shot by Kṛṣṇa appeared like a whirlwind of blazing fire killing all the military strength of Jarāsandha. As Kṛṣṇa released His arrows, all the elephants gradually began to fall, their heads severed by the arrows. Similarly, all the horses fell, their necks severed, and the chariots fell also, along with their flags and the fighters and drivers on the chariots. Almost all the infantry soldiers fell on the field of battle, their heads, hands and legs cut off. In this way, many thousands of elephants, horses and men were killed, and their blood flowed just like the waves of a river. In that river, the severed arms of men appeared like snakes, and their heads like tortoises. The dead bodies of the elephants appeared like small islands, and the dead horses appeared like sharks. By the arrangement of the supreme will, there was a great river of blood filled with paraphernalia. The hands and legs of the infantry soldiers floated just like different kinds of fish, the hair of the soldiers floated like seaweed and moss, and the floating bows of the soldiers resembled waves of the river. And all the jewelry from the bodies of the soldiers and commanders seemed like many pebbles flowing down the river of blood.

Lord Balarāma, who is also known as Saṅkarṣaṇa, began to fight with His club in such a heroic way that the river of blood created by Kṛṣṇa overflooded. Cowards became very much afraid upon seeing the ghastly and horrible scene, and heroes began to talk delightedly among themselves about the heroism of the two brothers. Although Jarāsandha was equipped with a vast ocean of military strength, the fighting of Lord Kṛṣṇa and Balarāma converted the whole situation into a ghastly scene far beyond ordinary fighting. Persons of ordinary merit cannot estimate how it could be possible, but when such activities are accepted as pastimes of the Supreme Personality of Godhead, under whose will everything is possible, then this can be understood. The Supreme Personality of Godhead creates, maintains and dissolves the cosmic manifestation merely by His will. For Him to create such a vast scene of devastation while fighting with an enemy is not so wonderful. And yet, because Kṛṣṇa and Balarāma were fighting with Jarāsandha just like ordinary human beings, the affair appeared wonderful.

When all the soldiers of Jarāsandha had been killed and he was the only one left alive, certainly he was very much depressed. Śrī Balarāma immediately arrested him with great strength, just as one lion captures another. But while Lord Balarāma was binding Jarāsandha with the rope of Varuṇa and ordinary ropes also, Lord Kṛṣṇa, with a greater plan in mind for the future, asked Lord Balarāma not to arrest him. Kṛṣṇa then released Jarāsandha. As a great fighting hero, Jarāsandha was ashamed, and he decided that he would no longer live as a king but would resign from his position in the royal order and go to the forest to practice meditation under severe austerities and penances.

As he was returning home with his royal friends, however, they advised him not to retire but to regain strength to fight again with Kṛṣṇa in the near future. The princely friends of Jarāsandha instructed him that ordinarily it would not have been possible for him to be defeated by the strength of the Yadu kings; the defeat he had experienced was simply due to his ill luck. The princely order encouraged King Jarāsandha. His fighting, they said, was certainly heroic; therefore, he should not take his defeat very seriously, since it was due only to his past misdeeds. After all, there was no fault in his fighting.

In this way, Jarāsandha, the King of Magadha Province, having lost all his strength and having been insulted by his arrest and subsequent release, could do nothing but return to his kingdom. Thus Lord Kṛṣṇa conquered the soldiers of Jarāsandha. Although Kṛṣṇa's army was tiny in comparison to Jarāsandha's, not a pinch of His strength was lost, whereas all of Jarāsandha's men were killed.

The denizens of heaven were very pleased, and they offered their respects by chanting in glorification of the Lord and showering Him with flowers, accepting the victory with great appreciation. Jarāsandha returned to his kingdom, and Mathurā City was saved from the danger of imminent attack. The citizens of Mathurā organized the combined services of professional singers like *sūtas* and *māgadhas,* along with poets who could compose nice songs, and they began to chant the victory glorification of Lord Kṛṣṇa. When Lord Kṛṣṇa entered the city after the victory, many bugles, conches and kettledrums sounded, and the vibrations of various musical instruments like *bherīs, tūryas, vīṇās,* flutes and *mṛdaṅgas* all joined together to make a beautiful reception. While Kṛṣṇa was entering, the whole city was cleansed, all the different streets and roads were sprinkled with water, and the inhabitants, being joyous, decorated their respective houses and shops with flags and festoons. The *brāhmaṇas* chanted Vedic *mantras* at numerous places. The people constructed road crossings and gates at entrances to lanes and streets. When Lord Kṛṣṇa was entering the nicely decorated city of Mathurā in a festive attitude, the ladies and girls of Mathurā prepared different kinds of flower garlands to make the ceremony most auspicious. In accordance with the Vedic custom, they took yogurt mixed with fresh green grass and strewed it here and there to make the victory jubilation even more auspicious. As Kṛṣṇa passed through the street, all the ladies and women regarded Him with eyes bright with great affection. Kṛṣṇa and Balarāma carried various kinds of ornaments, jewels and other booty carefully collected from the battlefield and presented it all to King Ugrasena. Kṛṣṇa thus offered His respect to His grandfather because Ugrasena was at that time the crowned king of the Yadu dynasty.

Jarāsandha, the King of Magadha, besieged the city of Mathurā not only once but seventeen times in the same way, equipped with the same number of military phalanxes. Each and every time, he was defeated and all his soldiers were killed by Kṛṣṇa, and each time he had to return home disappointed. Each time, the princely order of the Yadu dynasty arrested Jarāsandha in the same way and again released him in an insulting manner, and each time Jarāsandha shamelessly returned home.

While Jarāsandha was attempting his eighteenth attack, a Yavana king somewhere to the south of Mathurā became attracted by the opulence of the Yadu dynasty and also attacked the city. It is said that the King of the Yavanas, known as Kālayavana, was induced to attack by Nārada. This story is narrated in the *Viṣṇu Purāṇa*. Once, Garga Muni, the priest of the Yadu dynasty, was taunted by his brother-in-law. When the kings of the Yadu dynasty heard the taunt they laughed at him, and Garga Muni became angry at the Yadu kings. He decided that he would produce someone who would be very fearful to the Yadu dynasty, so he pleased Lord Śiva and received from him the benediction of a son. He begot this son, Kālayavana, in the wife of a Yavana king. This Kālayavana inquired from Nārada, "Who are the most powerful kings in the world?" Nārada informed him that the Yadus were the most powerful. Thus informed, Kālayavana attacked the city of Mathurā at the same time that Jarāsandha tried to attack it for the eighteenth time. Kālayavana was very eager to declare war on a king of the world who would be a suitable combatant for him, but he had not found any. However, being informed about Mathurā by Nārada, he thought it wise to attack this city with thirty million Yavana soldiers.

When Mathurā was thus besieged, Lord Śrī Kṛṣṇa began to consider, in consultation with Baladeva, how much the Yadu dynasty was in distress, being threatened by the attacks of two formidable enemies, Jarāsandha and Kālayavana. Time was growing short. Kālayavana was already besieging Mathurā from all sides, and it was expected that the day after next, Jarāsandha would also come, equipped with the same number of divisions of soldiers as in his previous seventeen attempts. Kṛṣṇa was certain that Jarāsandha would take advantage of the opportunity to capture Mathurā when it was also being besieged by Kālayavana. He therefore thought it wise to take precautionary measures for defending against an attack upon Mathurā from two strategic points. If both Kṛṣṇa and Balarāma were engaged in fighting with Kālayavana at one place, Jarāsandha might come at another to attack the whole Yadu family and take his revenge. Jarāsandha was very powerful, and having been defeated seventeen times, he might vengefully kill the members of the Yadu family or arrest them and take them to his kingdom. Kṛṣṇa therefore decided to construct a formidable fort where no two-legged animal, either man or demon, could enter. He decided to keep His relatives there so that He would then be free to fight the enemy. It appears that formerly Dvārakā was also part of the kingdom of Mathurā. In *Śrīmad-Bhāgavatam* it is stated that Kṛṣṇa constructed the fort in the midst of the sea. Remnants of the fort Kṛṣṇa constructed still exist in the Bay of Dvārakā.

Kṛṣṇa first of all constructed a very strong wall covering ninety-six square miles, and the wall itself was within the sea. It was certainly wonderful and was planned and constructed by Viśvakarmā. No ordinary architect could construct such a fort within the sea, but an architect like Viśvakarmā, who is considered to be the engineer among the demigods, can execute such wonderful craftsmanship anywhere in the universe. If huge planets can float in weightlessness in outer space by the arrangement of the

Supreme Personality of Godhead, surely the architectural construction of a fort covering ninety-six square miles within the sea was not very wonderful.

It is stated in *Śrīmad-Bhāgavatam* that this new, well-constructed city, developed within the sea, had regular planned roads, streets and lanes. There were also well-planned parks and gardens filled with plants known as *kalpa-vṛkṣas,* or desire trees. These desire trees are not like the ordinary trees of the material world; the desire trees are found in the spiritual world. By Kṛṣṇa's supreme will, everything is possible, so such desire trees were planted in Dvārakā, the city constructed by Kṛṣṇa. The city was also filled with many palaces and *gopuras,* or big gates. These *gopuras* are still found in some of the larger temples. They are very high and constructed with fine artistic skill. Such palaces and gates held golden waterpots (*kalaśa*). These waterpots on the gates or on the palaces are considered auspicious signs.

Almost all the palaces were skyscrapers. In each and every house there were underground rooms containing big golden and silver pots for stocking grain. And there were many golden waterpots within the rooms. The bedrooms were all bedecked with jewels, and the floors were mosaic pavements of *marakata* jewels. The Viṣṇu Deity, worshiped by the descendants of Yadu, was installed in each house in the city. The residential quarters were so arranged that the different castes—*brāhmaṇas, kṣatriyas, vaiśyas* and *śūdras*—had their respective quarters. It appears from this that the caste system mentioned in the *Bhagavad-gītā* existed even at that time. In the center of the city was a residence made specifically for King Ugrasena. This was the most dazzling of all the houses.

When the demigod Indra saw that Kṛṣṇa was constructing a particular city of His own choice, he sent the celebrated *pārijāta* tree of the heavenly planets to be planted in the new city, and he also sent a parliamentary house, Sudharmā. The specific quality of this assembly house was that anyone participating in a meeting within it would overcome the influence of invalidity due to old age. The demigod Varuṇa presented a horse, which was all white except for black ears and which could run at the speed of the mind. Kuvera, the treasurer of the demigods, presented the art of attaining the eight perfectional stages of material opulence. In this way, all the demigods began to present their respective gifts according to their different capacities. There are thirty-three million demigods, each entrusted with a particular department of universal management. All the demigods took the opportunity of the Supreme Personality of Godhead's constructing a city of His own choice to present their respective gifts, making the city of Dvārakā unique within the universe. This proves that while there are undoubtedly innumerable demigods, none of them is independent of Kṛṣṇa. As stated in the *Caitanya-caritāmṛta,* Kṛṣṇa is the supreme master, and all others are His servants. So all the demigods took the opportunity to render service to Kṛṣṇa when He was personally present within this universe. This example should be followed by all, especially those who are Kṛṣṇa conscious, for they should serve Kṛṣṇa by their respective abilities.

When the new city was fully constructed according to plan, Kṛṣṇa transferred all the inhabitants of Mathurā and installed Śrī Balarāma as the city father. After this He consulted with Balarāma, and, being garlanded with lotus flowers but carrying no weapons, He came out of the city to meet Kālayavana, who had already surrounded Mathurā.

Thus ends the Bhaktivedanta purport of the Fiftieth Chapter of Kṛṣṇa, *"Kṛṣṇa Erects the Dvārakā Fort."*

CHAPTER 51

The Deliverance of Mucukunda

WHEN KṚṢṆA CAME OUT of the city, Kālayavana, who had never seen Kṛṣṇa before, saw Him to be extraordinarily beautiful, dressed in yellow garments. Passing through Kālayavana's assembly of soldiers, Kṛṣṇa appeared like the moon in the sky passing through the assembled clouds. Kālayavana was fortunate enough to see the lines of Śrīvatsa, a particular impression on the chest of Śrī Kṛṣṇa, and the Kaustubha jewel He was wearing. Kālayavana saw Him, however, in His Viṣṇu form, with a well-built body, four hands, and eyes like the petals of a newly blooming lotus. Kṛṣṇa appeared blissful, with a handsome forehead and beautiful smiling face, restless eyebrows and moving earrings. Before seeing Kṛṣṇa, Kālayavana had heard about Him from Nārada, and now the descriptions of Nārada were confirmed. Kālayavana noticed Kṛṣṇa's specific marks and the jewels on His chest, His beautiful garland of lotus flowers, His lotuslike eyes and similar beautiful bodily features. He concluded that this beautiful personality must be Vāsudeva, for every description he had previously heard from Nārada was substantiated by the presence of Kṛṣṇa. Kālayavana was astonished to see Kṛṣṇa passing through his army without any weapon in His hands and without any chariot. He was simply walking on foot. Kālayavana had come to fight with Kṛṣṇa, and yet he had sufficient principles not to take up any kind of weapon. He decided to fight with Him hand to hand. Thus he prepared to capture Kṛṣṇa and fight.

Kṛṣṇa, however, went ahead without looking at Kālayavana. Kālayavana followed Him with a desire to capture Him, but in spite of his swift running, he could not capture Kṛṣṇa. Kṛṣṇa cannot be captured even by great *yogīs* traveling at the speed of the mind. He can be captured only by those who follow the path of devotional service, and Kālayavana was not practiced in devotional service. He wanted to capture Kṛṣṇa, and since he could not do so he followed Him from behind.

Kālayavana began running very fast, thinking, "Now I am nearer; I will capture Him," but he could not. Kṛṣṇa led him far away and entered the cave of a hill. Kālayavana thought that Kṛṣṇa was trying to avoid fighting him and was therefore taking shelter of the cave. He rebuked Him with the following words: "O Kṛṣṇa! I heard that You are a great hero born in the dynasty of Yadu, but I see that You are running away from fighting, like a coward. It is not worthy of Your good name and family tradition." Kālayavana was following, running very fast, but still he could not catch Kṛṣṇa because he was not freed from all contaminations of sinful life.

According to Vedic culture, anyone who does not follow the regulative principles observed by the higher castes—the *brāhmaṇas, kṣatriyas* and *vaiśyas*—or even those observed by the laborer class—the *śūdras*—is called a *mleccha* or *yavana.* The Vedic social situation is so planned that persons accepted as *śūdras* can gradually be elevated to the position of *brāhmaṇas* by the cultural advancement known as *saṁskāra,* or the purificatory process. The verdict of the Vedic scriptures is that no one becomes a *brāhmaṇa* or a *mleccha* simply by birth; by birth everyone is accepted as a *śūdra.* One has to elevate himself by the purificatory process to the stage of brahminical life. If he doesn't, if he degrades himself further, he is then called a *mleccha* or *yavana.* Kālayavana belonged to the class of *mlecchas* and *yavanas.* Contaminated by sinful activities, he could not approach Kṛṣṇa. The principles from which higher-class men are restricted, namely illicit sexual indulgence, meat-eating, gambling and intoxication, are an integral part of the lives of the *mlecchas* and *yavanas.* Being bound by such sinful activities, one cannot make any advancement in God realization. The *Bhagavad-gītā* confirms that only one who is completely freed from all sinful reactions can engage in devotional service, or Kṛṣṇa consciousness.

When Kṛṣṇa entered the cave of the hill, Kālayavana followed, chastising Him with various harsh words. Kṛṣṇa suddenly disappeared from the demon's sight, but Kālayavana followed and also entered the cave. The first thing he saw was a man lying down asleep within the cave. Kālayavana was eager to fight with Kṛṣṇa, and when he could not see Kṛṣṇa but instead saw only a man lying down, he thought that Kṛṣṇa was sleeping within this cave. Kālayavana was very much puffed up and proud of his strength, and he thought Kṛṣṇa was avoiding the fight. Therefore, he strongly kicked the sleeping man, thinking him to be Kṛṣṇa. The sleeping man had been lying down for a very long time. When awakened by the kicking of Kālayavana, he immediately opened his eyes and began to look around in all directions. At last he saw Kālayavana standing nearby. The man had been untimely awakened and was therefore very angry, and when he looked upon Kālayavana in his angry mood, rays of fire emanated from his eyes, and Kālayavana burned to ashes within a moment.

When Mahārāja Parīkṣit heard this incident of Kālayavana's being burned to ashes, he inquired about the sleeping man from Śukadeva Gosvāmī: "Who was he? Why was he sleeping there? How had he achieved so much power that instantly, by his glance, Kālayavana was burned to ashes? How did he happen to be lying down in the cave of the hill?" He put many questions before Śukadeva Gosvāmī, and Śukadeva answered as follows.

"My dear King, this person was born in the very great family of King Ikṣvāku, in which Lord Rāmacandra was also born, and he happened to be the son of a great king known as Māndhātā. He himself was also a great soul and was known popularly as Mucukunda. King Mucukunda was a strict follower of the Vedic principles of brahminical culture, and he was truthful to his promise. He was so powerful that even demigods like Indra used to ask him to help in fighting the demons, and as such he often fought against the demons to protect the demigods."

The commander in chief of the demigods, known as Kārttikeya, was satisfied with the fighting of King Mucukunda, but once he asked that the King, having taken too much trouble in fighting the demons, retire from fighting and take rest. Kārttikeya addressed King Mucukunda, "My dear King, you have sacrificed everything for the sake of the demigods. You had a very nice kingdom, undisturbed by any kind of enemy. But you left that kingdom, neglected your opulence and possessions, and never cared for fulfillment of your personal ambitions. Due to your long absence from your kingdom while fighting the demons on behalf of the demigods, your queen, your children, your relatives and your ministers have all passed away in due course of time. Time and tide wait for no man. Now even if you return to your home, you will find no one living there. The influence of time is very strong. Time is so powerful because it is a representation of the Supreme Personality of Godhead; time is therefore stronger than the strongest. The influence of time can effect changes in subtle things without difficulty. No one can check the progress of time. As an animal tamer tames animals according to his will, time also adjusts things according to its own will. No one can supersede the arrangement made by supreme time."

Thus addressing Mucukunda, the demigod requested him to ask any benediction he might be pleased with, except the benediction of liberation. Liberation cannot be awarded by any living entity but the Supreme Personality of Godhead, Viṣṇu. Therefore another name of Lord Viṣṇu or Kṛṣṇa is Mukunda, "He who can award liberation."

King Mucukunda had not slept for many, many years. He was engaged in the duty of fighting, and therefore he was very tired. So when the demigod offered a benediction, Mucukunda simply thought of sleeping. He replied as follows: "My dear Kārttikeya, best of the demigods, I want to sleep now, and I want from you the following benediction. Grant me the power to burn to ashes, by my mere glance, anyone who disturbs my sleep and awakens me untimely. Please give me this benediction." The demigod agreed and also gave him the benediction that he would be able to take complete rest. Then King Mucukunda entered the cave of the mountain.

On the strength of the benediction of Kārttikeya, Mucukunda burned Kālayavana to ashes simply by glancing at him. When the incident was over, Kṛṣṇa came before King Mucukunda. Kṛṣṇa had actually entered the cave to deliver King Mucukunda because of his austerity, but Kṛṣṇa did not appear before him first. He arranged that first Kālayavana should come before him. That is the way of the activities of the Supreme Personality of Godhead: He does one thing in such a way that many other purposes are served. He wanted to deliver King Mucukunda, who was sleeping in the cave, and at the same time He wanted to kill Kālayavana, who had attacked Mathurā City. By this action He served all purposes.

When Lord Kṛṣṇa appeared before Mucukunda, the King saw Him dressed in a yellow garment, His chest marked with the symbol of Śrīvatsa, and the Kaustubha jewel hanging around His neck. Kṛṣṇa appeared before him with four hands, as *viṣṇu-mūrti*, with a garland called Vaijayantī hanging from His neck down to His knees. He looked lustrous, His face was beautifully smiling, and He wore nice jeweled earrings on His ears. Kṛṣṇa appeared more beautiful than a human can conceive. Not only did He appear in this feature, but He glanced over Mucukunda with great affection, attracting the King's mind. Although He was the Supreme Personality of Godhead, the oldest of all, He looked like a fresh young boy, and His movements were just like those of a free deer. Still, He appeared extremely powerful; His influence and vast power are so great that every human being should be afraid of Him.

When King Mucukunda saw Kṛṣṇa's magnificent features, he wondered about His identity, and with great humility he asked the Lord, "My dear Lord, may I inquire how it is that You happened to be in the cave of this mountain? Who are You? I can see that Your feet are just like soft lotus flowers. How could You walk in the forest full of thorns and pebbles? I am simply surprised to see this! Are You not, therefore, the Supreme Personality of Godhead, the most powerful amongst the powerful? Are You not the original source of all illumination and fire? Can I consider You one of the great demigods, like the sun-god, the moon-god or Indra, King of heaven? Or are You the predominating deity of some other planet?"

Mucukunda knew well that every higher planetary system has a predominating deity. He was not ignorant like modern men who think that this planet earth is full of living entities and all others are vacant. The inquiry from Mucukunda about Kṛṣṇa's being the predominating deity of a planet unknown to him is quite appropriate. Because he was a pure devotee of the Lord, King Mucukunda could immediately understand that Lord Kṛṣṇa, who had appeared before him in such an opulent feature, could not be one of the predominating deities of the material planets. He must be the Supreme Personality of Godhead, Kṛṣṇa, who has many Viṣṇu forms. Mucukunda therefore took Him to be Puruṣottama, Lord Viṣṇu. He could see also that the dense darkness within the mountain cave had been dissipated by the Lord's presence; therefore He could not be other than the Supreme Personality of Godhead. Mucukunda knew very well that wherever the Lord is personally present by His transcendental name, qualities, form and so on, there cannot be any darkness of ignorance. He is like a lamp placed in the darkness; He immediately illuminates a dark place.

King Mucukunda was eager to know the identity of Lord Kṛṣṇa, and therefore he said, "O best of human beings, if You think I am fit to know Your identity, kindly tell me who You are. What is Your parentage? What is Your occupational duty, and what is Your family tradition?" King Mucukunda thought it wise, however, to identify himself to the Lord first; otherwise he had no right to ask the Lord's identity. Etiquette is such that a person of less importance cannot ask the identity of a person of higher importance without first disclosing his own identity. King Mucukunda therefore told Lord Kṛṣṇa, "My dear Lord, let me first inform You of my identity. I belong to the most celebrated dynasty of King Ikṣvāku, but personally I am not as great as my forefather. My name is Mucukunda. My father's name was Māndhātā, and my grandfather was the great king Yuvanāśva. I was very much fatigued due to not resting for many thousands of years, and because of this all my bodily limbs were slack and almost incapable of acting. To revive my energy, I was taking rest in this solitary cave, but I have been awakened by some unknown man who has forced me to wake up although I was not willing to do so. For such an offensive act, I have burned this person to ashes simply by glancing over him. Fortunately, now I can see You in this grand and beautiful feature. I think, therefore, that You are the cause of my killing my enemy. My dear Lord, I must admit that due to Your bodily effulgence, unbearable to my eyes, I cannot see You properly. I can fully realize that the influence of Your effulgence has diminished my power. I can understand that You are quite fit for being worshiped by all living entities."

Seeing King Mucukunda eager to know about His identity, Lord Kṛṣṇa answered smilingly as follows: "My dear King, it is practically impossible to tell about My birth, appearance, disappearance and activities. Perhaps you know that My incarnation Anantadeva has unlimited mouths, and for an unlimited time He has been trying to narrate fully about My name, fame, qualities, activities, appearance, disappearance and incarnations, but still He has not been able to finish. Therefore, it is not possible to know exactly how many names and forms I possess. It may be possible for a material scientist to estimate the number of atomic particles which make up this earthly planet, but the scientist cannot enumerate My unlimited names, forms and activities. Many great sages and saintly persons have tried to list My different forms and activities, yet they have failed to make a complete list. But since you are so eager to know about Me, I may inform you that I have now appeared on this planet just to annihilate the demoniac principles of the people in general and reestablish the religious principles enjoined in the *Vedas*. I have been invited for this purpose by Brahmā, the superintending deity of this universe, and thus I have now appeared in the dynasty of the Yadus as one of their family members. I have specifically taken My birth as the son of Vasudeva in the Yadu dynasty, and people therefore know Me as Vāsudeva, the son of Vasudeva. You may also know that I have killed Kaṁsa, who in a previous life was known as Kālanemi, as well as Pralambāsura and many other demons. They have acted as My enemies, and I have killed them. The demon who was present before you also acted as My enemy, and you have very kindly burned him to ashes by glancing over him. My dear King Mucukunda, you are My great devotee, and just to show you My causeless mercy I have appeared in this cave. I am very affectionately inclined toward My devotees, and in your previous life, before your present condition, you acted as My great devotee and prayed for My causeless mercy. I have therefore come to see you to fulfill your desire. Now you can see Me to your heart's content. My dear King, now you may ask from Me any benediction you wish, and I am prepared to fulfill your desire. It is My eternal principle that anyone who comes under My shelter must have all his desires fulfilled by My grace."

When Lord Kṛṣṇa ordered King Mucukunda to ask a benediction from Him, the King was joyful, and he immediately remembered the prediction of Garga Muni, who had foretold long before that in the twenty-eighth millennium of Vaivasvata Manu, Lord Kṛṣṇa would appear on this planet. As soon as he remembered this prediction, he understood that the Supreme Person, Nārāyaṇa, was present before Him as Lord Kṛṣṇa. He immediately fell down at His lotus feet and began to pray as follows.

"My dear Lord, O Supreme Personality of Godhead, I can understand that all living entities on this planet are illusioned by Your external energy and enamored of the illusory satisfaction of sense gratification. Being fully engaged in illusory activities, they are reluctant to worship Your lotus feet, and because they are unaware of the benefits of surrendering unto Your lotus feet, they are subjected to various miserable conditions of material existence. They are foolishly attached to so-called society, friendship and love, which merely produce different kinds of miseries. Illusioned by Your external energy, everyone, whether man or woman, is attached to this material existence, and all are engaged in cheating one another in a great society of the cheaters and the cheated. These foolish persons, not knowing how fortunate they are to have obtained this human form of life, are reluctant to worship Your lotus feet. By the influence of Your external energy, they are attached to the glare of material activities, to so-called society, friendship and love, like dumb animals that have fallen into a dark well." The example of a dark well is given because in the fields there are many wells, unused for years and covered over by grass, and poor animals, not knowing of them, fall into them, and unless rescued they die. Being captivated by a few blades of grass, the animals fall into a dark well and meet death. Similarly, foolish persons, without knowing the importance of the human form of life, spoil it simply for sense gratification and die without any useful purpose.

"My dear Lord, I am not an exception to this universal law of material nature. I am also a foolish person who has wasted his time for nothing. And my position is especially difficult. On account of my being situated in the royal order, I was more puffed up than ordinary persons. An ordinary man thinks he is the proprietor of his body or his family, but I began to think in that way on a larger scale. I wanted to be the master of the whole world, and as I became puffed up with ideas of sense gratification, my bodily concept of life became stronger and stronger. My attachment for home, wife and children, for money and supremacy over the world, became more and more acute; in fact, it was limitless. So I remained always attached to thoughts of my material living conditions.

"Therefore, my dear Lord, I wasted so much of my valuable lifetime with no benefit. As my misconception of life intensified, I began to think of this material body, which is just a bag of flesh and bones, as the all in all, and in my vanity I believed I had become the king of human society. In this misconception of bodily life I traveled all over the world, accompanied by my military strength—soldiers, charioteers, elephants and horses. Assisted by many commanders and puffed up by power, I could not trace out Your Lordship, who always sit within my heart as the most intimate friend. I did not care for You, and this was the fault of my so-called exalted material condition. I think that, like me, all living creatures are careless about spiritual realization and are always full of anxieties, thinking, 'What is to be done? What is next?' But because we are strongly bound by material desires, we continue to remain in craziness.

"Yet in spite of our being so absorbed in material thought, inevitable time, which is only a form of Yourself, is always careful about its duty, and as soon as the allotted time is over, Your Lordship immediately ends all the activities of our material dreams. As the time factor, You end all our activities, as a hungry black snake swiftly swallows up a small rat without leniency. Due to the action of cruel time, the royal body which was always decorated with golden ornaments during life and which moved on a chariot drawn by beautiful horses or on the back of an elephant nicely decorated with golden ornaments, and which was advertised as the king of human society—that same royal body decomposes under the influence of inevitable time and becomes fit for being eaten by worms and insects or being turned into ashes or the stool of an animal. This beautiful body may be recognized as a royal body while in the living condition, but after death the body of even a king is eaten by an animal and therefore turned into stool or is cremated in a crematorium and turned into ashes or is put into an earthly grave, where different kinds of worms and insects are produced of it.

"My dear Lord, we come under the full control of this inevitable time not only after death but also, in a different way, while living. For example, I may be a powerful king, and yet when I come home after conquering the world I become subjected to many material conditions. When I come back victorious, all subordinate kings may come and offer their respects, but as soon as I enter the inner section of my palace, I myself become an instrument in the hands of the queens, and for sense gratification I have to fall down at the feet of women. The material way of life is so complicated that before taking the enjoyment of material life one has to work so hard that there is scarcely an opportunity for peacefully enjoying. And to attain all material facilities one has to undergo severe austerities and penances and be elevated to the heavenly planets. If one gets the opportunity to take birth in a very rich or royal family, even then he is always anxious to maintain the status quo and prepare for the next life by performing various sacrifices and distributing charity. Even in royal life one is full of anxieties, not only because of political administration but also in regard to being elevated to the heavenly planets.

"It is therefore very difficult to get out of material entanglement, but if one is somehow or other favored by You, by Your mercy alone he is given the opportunity to associate with a pure devotee. That is the beginning of liberation from the entanglement of material, conditioned life. My dear Lord, only by the association of pure devotees is one able to approach Your Lordship, who are the controller of both the material and spiritual existences. You are the supreme goal of all pure devotees, and by association with pure devotees one can develop his dormant love for You. Therefore, development of Kṛṣṇa consciousness in the association of pure devotees is the cause of liberation from this material entanglement.

"My dear Lord, You are so merciful that in spite of my being reluctant to associate with Your pure devotees, You have shown Your extreme mercy upon me as a result of my slight contact with such a pure devotee as Garga Muni. By Your causeless mercy only have I lost all my material opulences, my kingdom and my family. I do not think I could have gotten rid of all these entanglements without Your causeless mercy. Kings and emperors sometimes accept the life of an ascetic to forget their royal life, but by Your special causeless mercy I have already been bereft of royalty. I do not need to become a mendicant or practice renunciation.

"My dear Lord, I therefore pray that I may simply be engaged in rendering transcendental loving service unto Your lotus feet. This is the ambition of pure devotees, who are freed from all material contamination. You are the Supreme Personality of Godhead, and You can offer me anything I want, including liberation. But who is such a fool that after pleasing You he would ask from You something which might cause entanglement in this material world? I do not think any sane man would ask such a benediction from You. I therefore surrender unto You because You are the Supreme Personality of Godhead, You are the Supersoul living in everyone's heart, and You are the impersonal Brahman effulgence. Moreover, You are also this material world, because this material world is only the manifestation of Your external energy. Therefore, from any angle of vision, You are the supreme shelter for everyone. Whether on the material plane or the spiritual plane, everyone must take shelter under Your lotus feet. I therefore submit unto You, my Lord.

"For many, many births I have been suffering from the threefold miseries of this material existence, and I am now tired of it. I have been impelled only by my senses, and I was never satisfied. I therefore take shelter of Your lotus feet, which are the source of all peaceful life and which can eradicate all lamentation caused by material contamination. My dear Lord, You are the Supersoul of everyone, and You can understand everything. Now I am free from all contamination of material desire. I do not wish to enjoy this material world, nor do I wish to take advantage of merging into Your spiritual effulgence, nor do I wish to meditate upon Your localized aspect of Paramātmā, for I know that simply by taking shelter of You, I shall become completely peaceful and undisturbed."

On hearing this statement by King Mucukunda, Lord Kṛṣṇa replied, "My dear King, I am very pleased with your statement. You have been the king of all the lands on this planet, but I am surprised to find that your mind is now freed from all material contamination. You are now fit to execute devotional service. I am most pleased to see that although I offered you the opportunity to ask from Me any kind of benediction, you did not take advantage of asking for material benefits. I can understand that your mind is now fixed in Me, and it is not disturbed by any material quality."

The material qualities are three, namely goodness, passion and ignorance. When one is placed into the mixed material qualities of passion and ignorance, various kinds of greed and lusty desires impel one to try to find comfort in this material world. When situated in the material quality of goodness, one tries to purify himself by performing various penances and austerities. When one reaches the platform of a real *brāhmaṇa,* he aspires to merge into the existence of the Lord. But when one desires only to render service unto the lotus feet of the Lord, he is transcendental to all these three qualities. The pure Kṛṣṇa conscious person is therefore always free from all material qualities.

"My dear King," Lord Kṛṣṇa continued, "I offered to give you any kind of benediction just to test how much you have advanced in devotional service. Now I can see that you are on the platform of the pure devotees, for your mind is not disturbed by any greedy or lusty desires of this material world. The *yogīs* who try to elevate themselves by controlling the senses and who meditate upon Me by practicing the breathing exercise of *prāṇāyāma* are not so thoroughly freed from material desires. It has been seen in several cases that as soon as there is allurement, such *yogīs* again come down to the material platform."

The vivid example verifying this statement is Viśvāmitra Muni. Viśvāmitra Muni was a great *yogī* who practiced *prāṇāyāma,* a breathing exercise, but when he was visited by Menakā, a society woman of the heavenly planets, he lost all control and begot in her a daughter named Śakuntalā. But the pure devotee Haridāsa Ṭhākura was never disturbed, even when all such allurements were offered by a prostitute.

"My dear King," Lord Kṛṣṇa continued, "I therefore give you the special benediction that you will always think of Me. Thus you will be able to traverse this material world freely, without being contaminated by the material qualities." This statement by the Lord confirms that a person in true Kṛṣṇa consciousness, engaged in the transcendental loving service of the Lord under the direction of the spiritual master, is never subject to the contamination of material qualities.

"My dear King," the Lord said, "because you are a *kṣatriya,* you have committed the offense of slaughtering animals, both in hunting and in political engagements. To become purified, just engage yourself in the practice of *bhakti-yoga* and always keep your mind absorbed in Me. Very soon you will be freed from all reactions to such sordid activities." In this statement it appears that although *kṣatriyas* are allowed to kill animals in hunting, they are not freed from the resultant contamination of sinful reactions. Therefore whether one is a *kṣatriya, vaiśya* or *brāhmaṇa,* everyone is recommended to take *sannyāsa* at the end of life, to engage himself completely in the service of the Lord and thus become freed from all sinful reactions of his past life.

The Lord then assured King Mucukunda, "In your next life you will take your birth as a first-class Vaiṣṇava, the best of *brāhmaṇas,* and in that life your only business will be to engage yourself in My transcendental service." A Vaiṣṇava is a first-class *brāhmaṇa* because one who has not acquired the qualification of a bona fide *brāhmaṇa* cannot come to the platform of a Vaiṣṇava. When one becomes a Vaiṣṇava, he is completely engaged in welfare activities for all living entities. The highest welfare activity for living entities is the preaching of Kṛṣṇa consciousness. It is stated herein that those who are specifically favored by the Lord can become absolutely Kṛṣṇa conscious and be engaged in the work of preaching the Vaiṣṇava philosophy.

Thus ends the Bhaktivedanta purport of the Fifty-first Chapter of Kṛṣṇa, *"The Deliverance of Mucukunda."*

CHAPTER 52

Kṛṣṇa, the Raṇacora

WHEN MUCUKUNDA, THE CELEBRATED DESCENDANT of the Ikṣvāku dynasty, was favored by Lord Kṛṣṇa, he circumambulated the Lord within the cave and then came out. On coming out of the cave, Mucukunda saw that the human species had surprisingly been reduced in stature to pygmy size. Similarly, the trees had also been far reduced in size, and Mucukunda could immediately understand that the current age was Kali-yuga. Therefore, without diverting his attention, he began to travel north. Eventually he reached the mountain known as Gandhamādana, where there were many trees, such as sandalwood and other flowering trees, whose fragrance made anyone who reached them joyful. He decided to remain in that Gandhamādana Mountain region to execute austerities and penances for the rest of his life. It appears that this place is situated in the northernmost part of the Himalayan Mountains, where the abode of Nara-Nārāyaṇa is situated. This place is still existing and is called Badarikāśrama. In Badarikāśrama he engaged himself in the worship of Lord Kṛṣṇa, tolerating all kinds of pains and pleasures and the other dualities of this material world.

Lord Kṛṣṇa returned to the vicinity of Mathurā, where He fought with the soldiers of Kālayavana and killed them one after another. After this, He collected all the booty from the dead bodies, and under His direction it was loaded on bullock carts and brought back to Dvārakā.

Meanwhile, Jarāsandha again attacked Mathurā, this time with bigger divisions of soldiers, numbering twenty-three *akṣauhiṇīs.*

Lord Śrī Kṛṣṇa wanted to save Mathurā from the eighteenth attack of the great military divisions of King Jarāsandha. To prevent further killing of soldiers and to attend to other important business, Lord Kṛṣṇa left the battlefield without fighting. Actually He was not at all afraid, but He pretended to be an ordinary human being frightened by the immense quantity of soldiers and resources of Jarāsandha. Without any weapons Kṛṣṇa left the battlefield. Although His lotus feet were as soft as the petals of a lotus flower, He proceeded for a very long distance on foot.

This time, Jarāsandha thought that Kṛṣṇa and Balarāma were very much afraid of His military strength and were fleeing the battlefield. He followed Them with all his chariots, horses and infantry. He thought Kṛṣṇa and Balarāma to be ordinary human beings, and he was trying to measure the activities of the Lord. Due to this pastime Kṛṣṇa is known as Raṇacora, which means "one who has left the battlefield." In India, especially in Gujarat, there are many temples of Kṛṣṇa known as temples of Raṇacorajī. Ordinarily, if a king leaves the battlefield without fighting he is called a coward, but when Kṛṣṇa enacts this pastime, leaving the battlefield without fighting, He is worshiped by the devotees. A demon always tries to measure the opulence of Kṛṣṇa, whereas a devotee never tries to measure His strength and opulence but always surrenders unto Him and worships Him. By following in the footsteps of pure devotees, we can know that Kṛṣṇa, the Raṇacorajī, left the battlefield not because He was afraid but because He had some other purpose. The purpose, as it will be revealed, was to attend to a confidential letter sent by Rukmiṇī, His future first wife. Kṛṣṇa's leaving the battlefield is a display of one of His six opulences. Kṛṣṇa is the supreme powerful, the supreme wealthy, the supreme famous, the supreme wise and the supreme beautiful; similarly, He is the supreme renouncer. *Śrīmad-Bhāgavatam* clearly states that He left the battlefield in spite of having ample military strength. Even without His militia, He alone would have been sufficient to defeat the army of Jarāsandha, as He had done seventeen times before. Therefore, His leaving the battlefield is an example of His supermost opulence, renunciation.

After traversing a very long distance, the brothers pretended to become tired. To mitigate Their weariness, They climbed up a mountain many miles above sea level. This mountain was called Pravarṣaṇa due to constant rain, for the peak was always covered with clouds sent by Indra. Jarāsandha took it for granted that the two brothers were afraid of his military power and had hidden Themselves at the top of the mountain. First he tried to find Them, searching for a long time, but when he failed he decided to trap and kill Them by setting fires around the peak. He therefore surrounded the peak with firewood and set it ablaze. As the fire spread more and more, Kṛṣṇa and Balarāma jumped from the top of the mountain down to the ground—a distance of eighty-eight miles. Thus, while the peak was burning up, Kṛṣṇa and Balarāma escaped, unseen by Jarāsandha or his men. Jarāsandha concluded that the two brothers had burned to ashes and that there was no need of further fighting. Thinking himself successful in his efforts, he left the city of Mathurā and returned to his home in the kingdom of Magadha. Gradually Kṛṣṇa and Balarāma reached the city of Dvārakā, which was surrounded by the sea.

Following this, Śrī Balarāma married Revatī, daughter of King Raivata, ruler of Ānarta Province. This is explained in the Ninth Canto of *Śrīmad-Bhāgavatam.* After the marriage of Baladeva, Kṛṣṇa married Rukmiṇī. Rukmiṇī was the daughter of King Bhīṣmaka, ruler of the province known as Vidarbha. Just as Kṛṣṇa is the Supreme Personality of Godhead, Vāsudeva, Rukmiṇī is the supreme goddess of fortune, Mahā-Lakṣmī. According to the authority of the *Caitanya-caritāmṛta,* the expansion of Kṛṣṇa and that of Śrīmatī Rādhārāṇī are simultaneous: Kṛṣṇa expands Himself into various *viṣṇu-tattva* forms, and Śrīmatī Rādhārāṇī expands Herself into various *śakti-tattva* forms, by Her internal potency, as multiforms of the goddess of fortune.

According to Vedic convention, there are eight kinds of marriage. In the first-class marriage system, the parents of the bride and bridegroom arrange the marriage date. Then, in royal style, the bridegroom goes to the house of the bride, and in the presence of *brāhmaṇas,* priests and relatives, the bride is given in charity to the bridegroom. Besides this, there are other systems, such as the *gāndharva* and *rākṣasa* marriages. Kṛṣṇa married Rukmiṇī according to the *rākṣasa* system, since He kidnapped her in the presence of His many rivals, like Śiśupāla, Jarāsandha and Śālva. While Rukmiṇī was being given in charity to Śiśupāla, Kṛṣṇa snatched her from the marriage arena exactly as Garuḍa snatched a pot of nectar from the demigods. Rukmiṇī, the only daughter of King Bhīṣmaka, was exquisitely beautiful. She was known as Rucirānanā, which means "one who has a beautiful face expanded like a lotus flower."

Devotees of Kṛṣṇa are always eager to hear about the transcendental activities of the Lord. His activities of fighting, kidnapping and running away from the battlefield are all transcendental, being on the absolute platform, and devotees take a transcendental interest in hearing of them. The pure devotee does not make the distinction that some activities of the Lord should be heard and others avoided. There is, however, a class of so-called devotees known as *prākṛta-sahajiyās* who are very interested in hearing about Kṛṣṇa's *rāsa-līlā* with the *gopīs* but not about His fighting with His enemies. They do not know that His bellicose activities and His friendly activities with the *gopīs* are equally transcendental, being on the absolute platform. All the transcendental pastimes of Kṛṣṇa described in *Śrīmad-Bhāgavatam* are relished by pure devotees through submissive aural reception. They do not reject even a drop.

The story of Kṛṣṇa's marriage with Rukmiṇī is described as follows. The King of Vidarbha, Mahārāja Bhīṣmaka, was very qualified and devoted. He had five sons and only one daughter. The first son was known as Rukmī; the second, Rukmaratha; the third, Rukmabāhu; the fourth, Rukmakeśa; and the fifth, Rukmamālī. The brothers had one young sister, Rukmiṇī. She was beautiful and chaste and was meant to be married to Lord Kṛṣṇa. Many saintly persons and sages like Nārada Muni used to visit the palace of King Bhīṣmaka. Naturally Rukmiṇī had a chance to talk with them, and in this way she obtained information about Kṛṣṇa. She was informed about the six opulences of Kṛṣṇa, and simply by hearing about Him she desired to surrender herself to His lotus feet and become His wife. Kṛṣṇa had also heard of Rukmiṇī. She was the reservoir of all transcendental qualities: intelligence, auspicious physical features, liberal-mindedness, exquisite beauty and righteous behavior. Kṛṣṇa therefore decided that she was fit to be His wife. All of the relatives of King Bhīṣmaka decided that Rukmiṇī should be given in marriage to Kṛṣṇa. But her elder brother Rukmī, despite the desire of the others, arranged for her marriage with Śiśupāla, a determined enemy of Kṛṣṇa. When the black-eyed, beautiful Rukmiṇī heard of the settlement, she immediately became very morose. However, being a king's daughter, she understood political diplomacy and decided that there was no use in simply being morose. Some steps should be taken immediately. After some deliberation, she decided to send a message to Kṛṣṇa, and so that she might not be deceived, she selected a qualified *brāhmaṇa* as her messenger. Such a qualified *brāhmaṇa* is always truthful and is a devotee of Viṣṇu. Without delay, she sent the *brāhmaṇa* to Dvārakā.

Reaching the gate of Dvārakā, the *brāhmaṇa* informed the doorkeeper of his arrival, and the doorkeeper led him to the place where Kṛṣṇa was sitting on a golden throne. Since the *brāhmaṇa* had the opportunity to be Rukmiṇī's messenger, he was fortunate enough to see the Supreme Personality of Godhead Kṛṣṇa, the original cause of all causes. A *brāhmaṇa* is the spiritual teacher of all the social divisions. Lord Śrī Kṛṣṇa, in order to teach everyone the Vedic etiquette of how to respect a *brāhmaṇa,* immediately got up and offered him His throne. When the *brāhmaṇa* was seated on the golden throne, Lord Śrī Kṛṣṇa began to worship him exactly as the demigods worship Kṛṣṇa. In this way, He taught everyone that worshiping His devotee is more valuable than worshiping Him.

In due time, the *brāhmaṇa* took his bath, accepted his meals and lay down to rest on a bedstead completely bedecked with soft silk. As he was resting, Lord Śrī Kṛṣṇa silently approached and, with great respect, put the *brāhmaṇa's* legs on His lap and began to massage them. In this way, Kṛṣṇa appeared before the *brāhmaṇa* and said, "My dear *brāhmaṇa,* I hope that you are executing the religious principles without difficulty and that your mind is always peaceful." Different classes of people in the social system are engaged in various professions, and when one inquires as to the well-being of a particular person, he should do so on the basis of that person's occupation. Therefore, when one inquires as to the welfare of a *brāhmaṇa,* the questions should be worded according to his condition of life so as not to disturb him. A peaceful mind is the basis for becoming truthful, clean, equipoised, self-controlled and tolerant. Thus by attaining knowledge and knowing its practical application in life, one becomes convinced about the Absolute Truth. The *brāhmaṇa* knew Kṛṣṇa to be the Supreme Personality of Godhead, and still he accepted the respectful service of the Lord on the grounds of Vedic social convention. Lord Śrī Kṛṣṇa was playing just like a human being. Because He belonged to the *kṣatriya* division of the social system and was a young boy, it was His duty to show respect to such a *brāhmaṇa.*

Lord Kṛṣṇa continued, "O best of all the *brāhmaṇas,* you should always remain satisfied, for if a *brāhmaṇa* is always self-satisfied he will not deviate from his prescribed duties; and simply by sticking to one's prescribed duties, everyone, especially a *brāhmaṇa,* can attain the highest perfection of all desires. Even if a person is as opulent as the King of heaven, Indra, if he is not satisfied he inevitably has to transmigrate from one planet to another. Such a person can never be happy under any circumstances; but if one's mind is satisfied, even if he is bereft of all possessions, he can be happy living anywhere."

This instruction by Kṛṣṇa to the *brāhmaṇa* is very significant. The purport is that a true *brāhmaṇa* should not be disturbed in any situation. In this modern age, Kali-yuga, the so-called *brāhmaṇas* have accepted the abominable position of *śūdras* or less and still want to pass as qualified *brāhmaṇas.* Actually, a qualified *brāhmaṇa* always sticks to his own duties and never accepts those of a *śūdra* or of one less than a *śūdra.* It is advised in the authorized scriptures that a *brāhmaṇa* may, under awkward circumstances, accept the profession of a *kṣatriya* or even a *vaiśya,* but never is he to accept the profession of a *śūdra.* Lord Kṛṣṇa declared that a *brāhmaṇa* will never be disturbed by any adverse conditions if he scrupulously sticks to his religious principles. In conclusion, Lord Śrī Kṛṣṇa said, "I offer My respectful obeisances to the *brāhmaṇas* and Vaiṣṇavas, for the *brāhmaṇas* are always self-satisfied and the Vaiṣṇavas are always engaged in actual welfare activities for human society. They are the best friends of the people in general; they are free from false egoism and are always in a peaceful condition of mind."

Lord Kṛṣṇa then desired to know about the rulers (*kṣatriyas*) in the *brāhmaṇa's* kingdom, so He inquired whether the citizens of the kingdom were all happy. A king's qualification is judged by the temperament of the people in the kingdom. If they are happy in all respects, it is to be understood that the king is honest and is executing his duties rightly. Kṛṣṇa said that the king in whose kingdom the citizens are happy is very dear to Him. Of course, Kṛṣṇa could understand that the *brāhmaṇa* had come with a confidential message; therefore He said, "If you have no objection, I give you liberty to speak about your mission."

Thus, being very much satisfied by these transcendental pastimes with the Lord, the *brāhmaṇa* narrated the whole story of his mission in coming to see Kṛṣṇa. He got out the letter Rukmiṇī had written to Kṛṣṇa and said, "These are the words of Princess Rukmiṇī: 'My dear Kṛṣṇa, O infallible and most beautiful one, any human being who happens to hear about Your transcendental form and pastimes immediately absorbs through his ears Your name, fame and qualities; thus all his material pangs subside, and he fixes Your form in his heart. Through such transcendental love for You, he always sees You within himself; and by this process all his desires are fulfilled. Similarly, I have heard of Your transcendental qualities. I may be shameless in expressing myself directly, but You have captivated me and taken my heart. You may doubt my steadiness of character, since how could an unmarried young girl like me approach You without any shame? But my dear Mukunda, You are the supreme lion among human beings, the supreme person among persons. Any girl, though not yet having left her home, or even any woman of the highest chastity, would desire to marry You, being captivated by Your unprecedented character, knowledge, opulence and position. I know that You are the husband of the goddess of fortune and are very kind toward Your devotees; therefore I have decided to become Your eternal maidservant. My dear Lord, I dedicate my life and soul unto Your lotus feet. I have selected Your Lordship as my husband, and I therefore request You to accept me as Your wife. You are the supreme powerful, O lotus-eyed one. Now I belong to You. If that which is enjoyable for the lion to eat is taken away by the jackal, it will be a ludicrous affair; therefore I request You to immediately take care of me before I am taken away by Śiśupāla and other princes like him. My dear Lord, in my previous life I may have done public welfare work like digging wells and planting trees, or pious activities such as performing ritualistic ceremonies and sacrifices and serving superiors like the spiritual master, *brāhmaṇas* and Vaiṣṇavas. By these activities, perhaps I have pleased the Supreme Personality of Godhead, Nārāyaṇa. If this be so, then I wish that You, Lord Kṛṣṇa, the brother of Lord Balarāma, please come here and catch hold of my hand so that I shall not be touched by Śiśupāla and his company.'"

Rukmiṇī's marriage with Śiśupāla was already settled; therefore she suggested that Kṛṣṇa kidnap her so that this might be changed. This sort of marriage, in which the girl is kidnapped by force, is known as *rākṣasa* and is practiced among *kṣatriyas,* or men with an administrative, martial spirit. Because her marriage was already arranged to take place the next day, Rukmiṇī suggested that Kṛṣṇa come there incognito to kidnap her and then fight with Śiśupāla and his allies like the King of Magadha. Knowing that no one could conquer Kṛṣṇa, who would certainly emerge victorious, she addressed Him as Ajita, "the unconquerable Lord."

Rukmiṇī told Kṛṣṇa not to be concerned that the fighting would take place within the palace and that many of her family members, including other women, might thus be wounded or even killed. As the king of a country thinks of diplomatic ways to achieve his object, Rukmiṇī, being the daughter of a king, was diplomatic in suggesting how this unnecessary and undesirable killing could be avoided. She explained that it was the custom of her family to visit the temple of goddess Durgā, their family deity, before a marriage. (The *kṣatriya* kings were mostly staunch Vaiṣṇavas, worshiping Lord Viṣṇu in either the Rādhā-Kṛṣṇa or Lakṣmī-Nārāyaṇa form; still, for their material welfare they used to worship goddess Durgā. They never made the mistake, however, of accepting the demigods as the Supreme Lord on the level of *viṣṇu-tattva,* as do some less intelligent men.) To avoid the unnecessary killing of her relatives, Rukmiṇī suggested that it would be easiest for Him to kidnap her while she was either going from the palace to the temple or else returning home.

She also explained to Kṛṣṇa why she was anxious to marry Him, even though her marriage was to take place with Śiśupāla, who was also qualified, being the son of a great king. Rukmiṇī said that she did not think anyone was greater than Kṛṣṇa, not even Lord Śiva, who is known as Mahādeva, the greatest of all demigods. Lord Śiva also seeks the pleasure of Lord Kṛṣṇa in order to be delivered from his entanglement in the quality of ignorance within the material world. Although Lord Śiva is the greatest of all great souls, *mahātmās,* he keeps on his head the purifying water of the Ganges, which emanates from a hole in this material universe made by the toe of Lord Viṣṇu. Lord Śiva is in charge of the material quality of ignorance, and to keep himself in a transcendental position he always meditates on Lord Viṣṇu, or Kṛṣṇa, and always tries to purify himself with the water of the Ganges. Therefore Rukmiṇī knew very well that obtaining the favor of Kṛṣṇa was not easy. Since even Lord Śiva must purify himself for this purpose, surely it would be difficult for Rukmiṇī, who was only the daughter of a *kṣatriya* king. Thus she desired to dedicate her life to observing severe austerities and penances, such as fasting and going without bodily comforts. If it were not possible in this lifetime to gain Kṛṣṇa's favor by these activities, she was prepared to die from such austerities and to undergo similar difficulties lifetime after lifetime. In the *Bhagavad-gītā* it is said that pure devotees of the Lord execute devotional service with great determination. Such determination, as exhibited by Rukmiṇīdevī, is the only price for purchasing Kṛṣṇa's favor. One should be strongly determined in Kṛṣṇa consciousness, and that is the way to ultimate success.

After relaying Rukmiṇīdevī's statement to Kṛṣṇa, the *brāhmaṇa* said, "My dear Kṛṣṇa, chief of the Yadu dynasty, I have brought this confidential message for You from Rukmiṇī; now it is placed before You for Your consideration. After due deliberation, You may act as You please, but if You want to do something, You must do it immediately. There is not much time left for action."

Thus ends the Bhaktivedanta purport of the Fifty-second Chapter of Kṛṣṇa, *"Kṛṣṇa, the Raṇacora."*

CHAPTER 53

Kṛṣṇa Kidnaps Rukmiṇī

AFTER HEARING RUKMIṆĪ'S STATMENT, Lord Kṛṣṇa was very pleased. He immediately shook hands with the *brāhmaṇa* and said, "My dear *brāhmaṇa,* I am very glad to hear that Rukmiṇī is eager to marry Me, since I am also eager to get her hand. My mind is always absorbed in thoughts of the daughter of Bhīṣmaka, and sometimes I cannot sleep at night because I am thinking of her. I can understand that the marriage of Rukmiṇī with Śiśupāla has been arranged by her elder brother in a spirit of animosity toward Me; so I am determined to give a good lesson to all of these princes. Just as one extracts and uses fire after manipulating ordinary wood, after dealing with these demoniac princes I shall bring forth Rukmiṇī, like fire, from their midst."

Kṛṣṇa, upon being informed of the specific date of Rukmiṇī's marriage, was anxious to leave immediately. He asked His driver, Dāruka, to harness the horses for His chariot and prepare to go to the kingdom of Vidarbha. After hearing this order, the driver brought Kṛṣṇa's four special horses. The names and descriptions of these horses are mentioned in the *Padma Purāṇa.* The first one, Śaibya, was greenish; the second, Sugrīva, was grayish like ice; the third, Meghapuṣpa, was the color of a new cloud; and the last, Balāhaka, was of ashen color. When the horses were yoked and the chariot was ready to go, Kṛṣṇa helped the *brāhmaṇa* up and gave him a seat by His side. Immediately they started from Dvārakā and within one night arrived at the province of Vidarbha. The kingdom of Dvārakā is situated in the western part of India, and Vidarbha is situated in the northern part. They are separated by a distance of not less than one thousand miles, but the horses were so fast that they reached their destination, a town called Kuṇḍina, within one night or, at most, twelve hours.

King Bhīṣmaka was not enthusiastic about handing his daughter over to Śiśupāla, but he was obliged to accept the marriage settlement due to his affectionate attachment for his eldest son, who had negotiated it. As a matter of duty, the King was decorating the city for the marriage ceremony and acting in great earnestness to make it very successful. Water was sprinkled all over the streets, and the city was cleansed very nicely. Since India is situated in the tropical zone, the atmosphere is always dry. Dust always accumulates on the streets and roads, so they must be sprinkled with water at least once a day, and in big cities like Calcutta twice a day. The roads of Kuṇḍina were arrayed with colored flags and festoons, and gates were constructed at particular crossings. The whole city was decorated very nicely. The beauty of the city was enhanced by the inhabitants, both men and women, who were dressed in fresh, washed clothes and decorated with sandalwood pulp, pearl necklaces and flower garlands. Incense burned everywhere, and fragrances like *aguru* scented the air. Priests and *brāhmaṇas* were sumptuously fed and, according to ritualistic ceremony, were given sufficient wealth and cows in charity. In this way, they were engaged in chanting Vedic hymns. The King's daughter, Rukmiṇī, was exquisitely beautiful. She was very clean and had beautiful teeth. The auspicious sacred thread was tied on her wrist. She was given various types of jewelry to wear and long silken cloth to cover the upper and lower parts of her body. Learned priests gave her protection by chanting *mantras* from the *Sāma Veda, Ṛg Veda* and *Yajur Veda.* Then they chanted *mantras* from the *Atharva Veda* and offered oblations in the fire to pacify the influence of different stars.

King Bhīṣmaka was experienced in dealing with *brāhmaṇas* and priests when such ceremonies were held. He specifically honored the *brāhmaṇas* by giving them large quantities of gold and silver, grain mixed with molasses, and cows decorated with cloth and ornaments. Damaghoṣa, Śiśupāla's father, executed all kinds of ritualistic performances to invoke good fortune for his son. Śiśupāla's father was known as Damaghoṣa due to his superior ability to cut down unregulated citizens. *Dama* means curbing down, and *ghoṣa* means famous; so he was famous for controlling the citizens. Damaghoṣa thought that if Kṛṣṇa came to disturb the marriage ceremony, he would certainly cut Him down with his military power. Therefore, after performing the various auspicious ceremonies, Damaghoṣa gathered his military divisions. He took many elephants garlanded with golden necklaces, and many similarly decorated chariots and horses. It appeared that Damaghoṣa, along with his son and other companions, was going to Kuṇḍina not exactly to get Śiśupāla married but mainly to fight.

When King Bhīṣmaka learned that Damaghoṣa and his party were arriving, he left the city to receive them. Outside the city gate were many gardens where guests were welcome to stay. In the Vedic system of marriage, the bride's father receives the large party of the bridegroom and accommodates them in a suitable place for two or three days until the marriage ceremony is performed. The party led by Damaghoṣa contained thousands of men, among whom the prominent kings and personalities were Jarāsandha, Dantavakra, Vidūratha and Pauṇḍraka. It was an open secret that Rukmiṇī was meant to be married to Kṛṣṇa but that her elder brother Rukmī had arranged her marriage to Śiśupāla. There was also some whispering about a rumor that Rukmiṇī had sent a messenger to Kṛṣṇa; therefore the soldiers suspected that Kṛṣṇa might cause a disturbance by attempting to kidnap Rukmiṇī. Even though they were not without fear, they were all prepared to give Kṛṣṇa a good fight to prevent the girl from being taken away. Śrī Balarāma received the news that Kṛṣṇa had left for Kuṇḍina accompanied only by a *brāhmaṇa* and that Śiśupāla was there with a large number of soldiers. Balarāma suspected that they would attack Kṛṣṇa, and thus out of great affection for His brother He took strong military divisions of chariots, infantry, horses and elephants and went to the precincts of Kuṇḍina.

Meanwhile, inside the palace, Rukmiṇī was expecting Kṛṣṇa to arrive, but when neither He nor the *brāhmaṇa* who took her message appeared, she was full of anxiety and began to think how unfortunate she was. "There is only one night between today and my marriage day, and still neither the *brāhmaṇa* nor Śyāmasundara has returned. I cannot ascertain any reason for this." Having little hope, she thought that perhaps Kṛṣṇa had found reason to become dissatisfied and had rejected her fair proposal. As a result, the *brāhmaṇa* might have become disappointed and not come back. Although she was thinking of various causes for the delay, she expected them both at any moment.

Rukmiṇī further thought that demigods such as Lord Brahmā, Lord Śiva and goddess Durgā might have been displeased. It is generally said that the demigods become angry when not properly worshiped. For instance, when Indra found that the inhabitants of Vṛndāvana were not worshiping him (Kṛṣṇa having stopped the Indra-yajña), he became angry and wanted to chastise them. Thus Rukmiṇī thought that since she did not worship Lord Śiva or Lord Brahmā very much, they might have become angry and tried to frustrate her plan. Similarly she thought that goddess Durgā, the wife of Lord Śiva, might have taken the side of her husband. Lord Śiva is known as Rudra, and his wife is known as Rudrāṇī. Rudrāṇī and Rudra refer to those who are accustomed to putting others in distress to cry forever. Rukmiṇī was thinking of goddess Durgā as Girijā, the daughter of the Himalayan Mountains. The Himalayan Mountains are very cold and hard, and she thought of goddess Durgā as hardhearted and cold. In her anxiety to see Kṛṣṇa, Rukmiṇī, who was after all still a child, thought this way about the different demigods. The *gopīs* worshiped goddess Kātyāyanī to get Kṛṣṇa as their husband; similarly Rukmiṇī was thinking of the various types of demigods not for material benefit but in respect to Kṛṣṇa. Praying to the demigods to achieve the favor of Kṛṣṇa is not irregular, and Rukmiṇī was fully absorbed in thoughts of Kṛṣṇa.

Even though she pacified herself by thinking that the time for Govinda to arrive had not yet expired, Rukmiṇī felt that she was hoping against hope. Not expressing her mind to anyone, she simply shed tears, unobserved by others, and when her tears became more forceful, she closed her eyes in helplessness. While Rukmiṇī was in such deep thought, auspicious symptoms appeared in different parts of her body. Trembling began to occur in her left eyelid, arm and thigh. When trembling occurs in these parts of the body, it is an auspicious sign indicating that something lucrative can be expected.

Just then, Rukmiṇī, full of anxiety, saw the *brāhmaṇa* messenger. Kṛṣṇa, being the Supersoul of all living beings, could understand Rukmiṇī's anxiety; therefore He sent the *brāhmaṇa* inside the palace to let her know that He had arrived. When Rukmiṇī saw the *brāhmaṇa,* she could understand the auspicious trembling of her body and immediately became elated. She smiled and inquired whether Kṛṣṇa had already come. The *brāhmaṇa* replied that the son of the Yadu dynasty, Śrī Kṛṣṇa, had arrived; he further encouraged her by saying that Kṛṣṇa had promised to carry her away without fail. Rukmiṇī was so elated by the *brāhmaṇa's* message that she wanted to give him in charity everything she possessed. However, finding nothing suitable for presentation, she simply offered him her respectful obeisances. The significance of offering respectful obeisances to a superior is that the one offering obeisances is obliged to the respected person. In other words, Rukmiṇī implied that she would remain ever grateful to the *brāhmaṇa.* Anyone who gets the favor of the goddess of fortune, as did this *brāhmaṇa,* is without a doubt always happy in material opulence.

When King Bhīṣmaka heard that Kṛṣṇa and Balarāma had come, he invited Them to see the marriage ceremony of his daughter. Immediately he arranged to receive Them, along with Their soldiers, in a suitable garden house. As was the Vedic custom, the King offered Kṛṣṇa and Balarāma honey and fresh, washed clothes. He was hospitable not only to Kṛṣṇa, Balarāma and kings such as Jarāsandha but also to many other kings and princes according to their personal strength, age and material possessions. Out of curiosity and eagerness, the people of Kuṇḍina assembled before Kṛṣṇa and Balarāma to drink the nectar of Their beauty. With tearful eyes, they offered Kṛṣṇa and Balarāma their silent respects. They were very pleased, considering Lord Kṛṣṇa the suitable match for Rukmiṇī. They were so eager to unite Kṛṣṇa and Rukmiṇī that they prayed to the Personality of Godhead, "Our dear Lord, if we have performed any pious activities with which You are satisfied, kindly be merciful upon us and accept the hand of Rukmiṇī." It appears that Rukmiṇī was a very popular princess, and all the citizens, out of intense love for her, prayed for her best fortune. In the meantime, Rukmiṇī, being very nicely dressed and protected by bodyguards, came out of the palace to visit the temple of Ambikā, goddess Durgā.

Deity worship in the temple has been in existence since the beginning of Vedic culture. There is a class of men described in the *Bhagavad-gītā* as *veda-vāda-rata:* they believe only in the Vedic ritualistic ceremonies but not in temple worship. Such foolish people may here take note that although this marriage of Kṛṣṇa and Rukmiṇī took place more than five thousand years ago, there were arrangements for temple worship. In the *Bhagavad-gītā* the Lord says, *yānti deva-vratā devān:* "The worshipers of the demigods attain the abodes of the demigods." There were many people who worshiped the demigods and many who directly worshiped the Supreme Personality of Godhead. The system of demigod worship was directed mainly to Lord Brahmā, Lord Śiva, Lord Gaṇeśa, the sun-god and goddess Durgā. Lord Śiva and goddess Durgā were worshiped even by the royal families; other, minor demigods were worshiped by silly, lower-class people. As far as the *brāhmaṇas* and Vaiṣṇavas are concerned, they simply worship Lord Viṣṇu, the Supreme Personality of Godhead. In the *Bhagavad-gītā* the worship of demigods is condemned but not forbidden; there it is clearly stated that less intelligent men worship the demigods for material benefit. On the other hand, even though Rukmiṇī was the goddess of fortune, she went to the temple of goddess Durgā because the family deity was worshiped there. In *Śrīmad-Bhāgavatam* it is stated that as Rukmiṇī proceeded toward the temple of goddess Durgā, within her heart she always thought of the lotus feet of Kṛṣṇa. Therefore when Rukmiṇī went to the temple it was not with the intention of an ordinary person, who goes to beg for material benefits; her only goal was Kṛṣṇa.

As Rukmiṇī proceeded toward the temple, she was silent and grave. Her mother and her girlfriends were by her side, and the wife of a *brāhmaṇa* was in the center; surrounding her were royal bodyguards. (This custom of a would-be bride's going to the temple of a demigod is still practiced in India.) As the procession continued, various musical sounds were heard. *Paṇavas* and other drums, conchshells, and bugles of different sizes, such as *tūryas* and *bherīs,* combined to make a sound which was not only auspicious but very sweet to hear. Thousands of wives of respectable *brāhmaṇas* were present, all dressed very nicely with suitable ornaments. They presented Rukmiṇī with flower garlands, sandalwood pulp and a variety of colorful garments to assist her in worshiping Lord Śiva and goddess Durgā. Some of these ladies were very old and knew perfectly well how to chant prayers to goddess Durgā and Lord Śiva; so, followed by Rukmiṇī and others, they led these prayers before the deity.

Rukmiṇī offered her prayers to the deity by saying, "My dear goddess Durgā, I offer my respectful obeisances unto you as well as to your children." Goddess Durgā has four famous children: two daughters—the goddess of fortune, Lakṣmī, and the goddess of learning, Sarasvatī—and two sons, Lord Gaṇeśa and Lord Kārttikeya. They are all considered to be demigods and goddesses. Since goddess Durgā is always worshiped with her famous children, Rukmiṇī specifically offered her respectful obeisances to the deity in that way; however, her prayers were special. Ordinary people pray to goddess Durgā for material wealth, fame, profit, strength and so on; Rukmiṇī, however, desired to have Kṛṣṇa for her husband and therefore prayed that the deity be pleased with her and bless her with that benediction. Since she desired only Kṛṣṇa, her worship of the demigods is not condemned. While Rukmiṇī was praying, she presented a variety of items before the deity, chief of which were water, different kinds of flames, incense, garments, garlands and various foods prepared with ghee, such as *purīs* and *kachaurīs.* She also offered fruits, sugarcane, betel nuts and spices. With great devotion, Rukmiṇī offered them to the deity according to the regulative principles, directed by the old *brāhmaṇa* ladies. After this ritualistic ceremony, the ladies offered the remnants of the food to Rukmiṇī as *prasādam,* which she accepted with great respect. Then Rukmiṇī offered her obeisances to the ladies and to goddess Durgā. After the business of deity worship was finished, Rukmiṇī caught hold of the hand of one of her girlfriends in her own hand, which was decorated with a jeweled ring, and left the temple in the company of the others.

All the princes and visitors who came to Kuṇḍina for the marriage had assembled outside the temple to see Rukmiṇī. The princes were especially eager to see her because they all actually thought that they would have Rukmiṇī as their wife. Struck with wonder upon seeing Rukmiṇī, they thought she was especially manufactured by the Creator to bewilder all the great chivalrous princes. Her body was well constructed, the middle portion being thin. Her high hips were adorned with a jeweled locket, she had pink lips, and the beauty of her face was enhanced by her slightly scattered hair and by different kinds of earrings. The bodily luster and beauty of Rukmiṇī appeared as if painted by an artist perfectly presenting beauty following the descriptions of great poets. Rukmiṇī's breasts are described as being somewhat high, indicating that she was just a youth not more than thirteen or fourteen years old. Her beauty was specifically intended to attract the attention of Kṛṣṇa. Although the princes gazed upon her beautiful features, she was not at all proud. Her eyes moved restlessly, and when she smiled very simply, like an innocent girl, her teeth appeared just like jasmine buds. Expecting Kṛṣṇa to take her away at any moment, she proceeded slowly toward her home. Her legs moved just like a full-grown swan, and her ankle bells tinkled mildly.

The chivalrous princes assembled there were so overwhelmed by Rukmiṇī's beauty that they became almost unconscious and fell from their horses and elephants. Full of lust, they hopelessly desired Rukmiṇī's hand, comparing their own beauty to hers. Śrīmatī Rukmiṇī, however, was not interested in any of them; in her heart she was simply expecting Kṛṣṇa to come and carry her away. As she was adjusting the ornaments on a finger of her left hand, she happened to look upon the princes and suddenly saw that Kṛṣṇa was present amongst them. Although Rukmiṇī had never before seen Kṛṣṇa, she was always thinking of Him; thus she had no difficulty recognizing Him amongst the princely order. Kṛṣṇa, unconcerned with the other princes, immediately took the opportunity to place Rukmiṇī on His chariot, marked by a flag bearing an image of Garuḍa. He then proceeded slowly, without fear, taking Rukmiṇī away exactly as a lion takes a deer from the midst of jackals. Meanwhile, Balarāma appeared on the scene with the soldiers of the Yadu dynasty.

Jarāsandha, who had many times experienced defeat by Kṛṣṇa, roared, "How is this? Kṛṣṇa is taking Rukmiṇī away from us without opposition! What is the use of our being chivalrous fighters with arrows? My dear princes, just look! We are losing our reputation. He is just like a jackal taking booty from a lion."

Thus ends the Bhaktivedanta purport of the Fifty-third Chapter of Kṛṣṇa, *"Kṛṣṇa Kidnaps Rukmiṇī."*

CHAPTER 54

Kṛṣṇa Defeats All the Princes and Takes Rukmiṇī Home to Dvārakā

JARĀSANDHA AND ALL THE OTHER PRINCES were very angry at Kṛṣṇa for having kidnapped Rukmiṇī. Struck by Rukmiṇī's beauty, they had fallen from the backs of their horses and elephants, but now they began to stand up and properly arm themselves. Picking up their bows and arrows, they began to chase Kṛṣṇa on their chariots, horses and elephants. To check their progress, the soldiers of the Yadu dynasty turned and faced them. Thus terrible fighting began between the two belligerent groups. The princes opposing Kṛṣṇa, who were led by Jarāsandha and were all expert in fighting, shot their arrows at the Yadu soldiers just as a cloud splashes the face of a mountain with torrents of rain. Gathered on the face of a mountain, a cloud does not move very much, and therefore the force of rain is much more severe on a mountain than anywhere else.

The opposing princes were determined to defeat Kṛṣṇa and recapture Rukmiṇī from His custody, and they fought with Him as severely as possible. Rukmiṇī, seated by the side of Kṛṣṇa, saw arrows raining from the opposing party onto the faces of the

Yadu soldiers. In a fearful attitude, she looked upon Kṛṣṇa's face, expressing her gratefulness that He had taken such a great risk for her sake only. Her eyes moving, she appeared sorry, and Kṛṣṇa, who could immediately understand her mind, encouraged her with these words: "My dear Rukmiṇī, don't worry. Please rest assured that the soldiers of the Yadu dynasty will kill all the opposing soldiers without delay."

As Kṛṣṇa was speaking with Rukmiṇī, the commanders of the Yadu dynasty's soldiers, headed by Lord Balarāma, who is also known as Saṅkarṣaṇa, as well as by Gada, not tolerating the defiant attitude of the opposing soldiers, began to strike their horses, elephants and chariots with arrows. As the fighting progressed, the princes and soldiers of the enemy began to fall from their horses, elephants and chariots. Within a short time, millions of severed heads, decorated with helmets and earrings, had fallen on the battlefield. The soldiers' hands were severed along with their bows and arrows and clubs; arms were piled upon arms, thighs upon thighs, and horses upon horses. Similarly, other animals, such as camels, elephants and asses, as well as infantry soldiers, all fell with severed heads.

When the enemy, headed by Jarāsandha, found that they were gradually being defeated by the soldiers of Kṛṣṇa, they thought it unwise to risk losing their armies in the battle for the sake of Śiśupāla. Śiśupāla himself should have fought to rescue Rukmiṇī from the hands of Kṛṣṇa, but when the soldiers saw that Śiśupāla was not competent to fight with Kṛṣṇa, they decided not to lose their armies unnecessarily; therefore they ceased fighting and dispersed.

Some of the princes, as a matter of etiquette, appeared before Śiśupāla. They saw that Śiśupāla was discouraged, like one who has lost his wife. His face appeared dried up, he had lost all his energy, and all the luster of his body had disappeared. They addressed Śiśupāla thus: "Our dear Śiśupāla, don't be discouraged in this way. You belong to the royal order and are the chief amongst the fighters. There is no question of distress or happiness for a person like you because neither of these conditions is everlasting. Take courage. Don't be disappointed by this temporary reversal. After all, we are not the final actors; as puppets dance in the hands of a magician, we are all dancing by the will of the Supreme, and according to His plan alone we suffer distress or enjoy happiness. We should therefore be equipoised in all circumstances."

Although in the beginning the princes had been full of hope for success in their heroic action, after their defeat they could only try to encourage Śiśupāla with flattering words. Thus Śiśupāla, instead of marrying Rukmiṇī, had to be satisfied with the flattering words of his friends, and he returned home in disappointment. The kings who had come to assist him, also disappointed, then returned to their respective kingdoms.

The whole catastrophe of the defeat was due to the envious nature of Rukmiṇī's elder brother Rukmī. Having seen his sister forcibly taken away by Kṛṣṇa after he had planned to marry her to Śiśupāla, Rukmī was frustrated. So after Śiśupāla, his friend and intended brother-in-law, returned home, Rukmī, very much agitated, was determined to teach Kṛṣṇa a lesson personally. He called for his own soldiers—a military phalanx consisting of several thousand elephants, horses, chariots and infantry—and equipped with this military strength, he began to follow Kṛṣṇa to Dvārakā. To show his prestige, Rukmī promised all the returning kings, "You could not help Śiśupāla marry my sister, Rukmiṇī, but I cannot allow Rukmiṇī to be taken away by Kṛṣṇa. I shall teach Him a lesson. Now I am going to follow Him." He presented himself as a big commander and vowed before all the princes, "Unless I kill Kṛṣṇa in the fight and bring back my sister from His clutches, I shall not return to my capital city, Kuṇḍina. I make this vow before you all, and you will see that I shall fulfill it." After thus vibrating all these boasting words, Rukmī immediately got on his chariot and told his chariot driver to pursue Kṛṣṇa. He said, "I want to fight with Him immediately. This cowherd boy has become proud of His tricky way of fighting with *kṣatriyas,* but today I shall teach Him a good lesson. Because He had the impudence to kidnap my sister, I, with my sharp arrows, shall teach Him very good lessons indeed." Thus this unintelligent man, Rukmī, ignorant of the extent of the strength and activities of the Supreme Personality of Godhead, voiced his impudent threats.

In great stupidity, he soon stood before Kṛṣṇa, telling Him repeatedly, "Stop for a minute and fight with me!" After saying this he drew his bow and directly shot three forceful arrows against Kṛṣṇa's body. Then he condemned Kṛṣṇa as the most abominable descendant of the Yadu dynasty and asked Him to stand before him for a minute so that he could teach Him a good lesson. "You are carrying away my sister just like a crow stealing clarified butter meant for use in a sacrifice. You are proud of Your military strength, but You cannot fight according to regulative principles. You have stolen my sister; now I shall relieve You of Your false prestige. You can keep my sister in Your possession only until I beat You to the ground for good with my arrows."

Lord Kṛṣṇa, after hearing all these crazy words from Rukmī, immediately shot an arrow and severed the string of Rukmī's bow, making him unable to use another arrow. Rukmī immediately took another bow and shot another five arrows at Kṛṣṇa. Being attacked for the second time, Kṛṣṇa again severed Rukmī's bowstring. Rukmī took a third bow, and Kṛṣṇa again cut its string. This time, to teach Rukmī a lesson, Kṛṣṇa shot six arrows at him and then shot another eight arrows, killing four horses with four arrows, killing the chariot driver with another arrow, and chopping off the upper portion of Rukmī's chariot, including the flag, with the remaining three arrows.

Rukmī, having run out of arrows, took assistance from swords, shields, tridents, lances and similar weapons used for fighting hand to hand, but Kṛṣṇa immediately broke them all in the same way. Being repeatedly baffled in his attempts, Rukmī took his sword and ran swiftly toward Kṛṣṇa, just as a fly proceeds toward a fire. But as soon as Rukmī reached Kṛṣṇa, Kṛṣṇa cut his weapon to pieces. This time Kṛṣṇa took out His sharp sword and was about to kill him immediately, but Rukmī's sister, Rukmiṇī, understanding that this time Kṛṣṇa would not excuse her brother, fell down at Kṛṣṇa's lotus feet and in a very grievous tone, trembling with great fear, began to plead with her husband.

Rukmiṇī first addressed Kṛṣṇa as Yogeśvara. Yogeśvara means "one who is possessed of inconceivable opulence and energy." Kṛṣṇa possesses inconceivable opulence and energy, whereas Rukmiṇī's brother had only limited military potency. Kṛṣṇa is immeasurable, whereas her brother was measured in every step of his life. Therefore, Rukmī was not comparable even to an insignificant insect before the unlimited power of Kṛṣṇa. She also addressed Kṛṣṇa as the God of the gods. There are many powerful demigods, such as Lord Brahmā, Lord Śiva, Indra, Candra and Varuṇa, but Kṛṣṇa is the Lord of all these gods, whereas Rukmiṇī's brother was not only an ordinary human being but in fact the lowest of all because he had no understanding of Kṛṣṇa. In other words, a human being who has no conception of the actual position of Kṛṣṇa is the lowest in human society. Then Rukmiṇī addressed Kṛṣṇa as Mahābhuja, which means "one with unlimited strength." She also addressed Kṛṣṇa as Jagatpati, the master of the whole cosmic manifestation. In comparison, her brother was only an ordinary prince.

In this way, Rukmiṇī compared the position of Rukmī with that of Kṛṣṇa and very feelingly pleaded with her husband not to kill her brother just at the auspicious time of her being united with Kṛṣṇa, but to excuse him. In other words, she displayed her real position as a woman. She was happy to get Kṛṣṇa as her husband at the moment when her marriage to another was to be performed, but she did not want it to be at the loss of her elder brother, who, after all, loved his young sister and wanted to hand her over to one who, according to his own calculations, was a better man. While Rukmiṇī was praying to Kṛṣṇa for the life of her brother, her whole body trembled, and because of her anxiety, her face appeared to dry up and her throat became choked, and due to her trembling, the ornaments on her body loosened and fell scattered on the ground. In this manner, when Rukmiṇī was very much perturbed, she fell down on the ground, and Lord Kṛṣṇa immediately became compassionate and agreed not to kill the foolish Rukmī. But, at the same time, He wanted to give him some light punishment, so He tied him up with a piece of cloth and snipped at his mustache, beard and hair, keeping some spots here and there.

While Kṛṣṇa was dealing with Rukmī in this way, the soldiers of the Yadu dynasty, commanded by Balarāma Himself, broke the whole strength of Rukmī's army just as an elephant in a tank discards the feeble stem of a lotus flower. In other words, as an elephant breaks the whole construction of a lotus flower while bathing in a reservoir of water, the military strength of the Yadus broke up Rukmī's forces.

When the commanders of the Yadu dynasty came back to see Kṛṣṇa, they were all surprised to see the condition of Rukmī. Lord Balarāma became especially compassionate toward His sister-in-law, who was newly married to His brother. To please Rukmiṇī, Balarāma personally untied Rukmī, and to further please her, Balarāma, as the elder brother of Kṛṣṇa, spoke some words of chastisement. "Kṛṣṇa, Your action is not at all satisfactory," He said. "This is an abomination very much contrary to Our family tradition! To cut someone's hair and shave his mustache and beard is almost comparable to killing him. Whatever Rukmī might have been, he is now Our brother-in-law, a relative of Our family, and You should not have put him in such a condition."

After this, to pacify Rukmiṇī, Lord Balarāma said to her, "You should not be sorry that your brother has been made odd-looking. Everyone suffers or enjoys the results of his own actions." Lord Balarāma wanted to impress upon Rukmiṇī that she should not be sorry for the consequences her brother suffered due to his actions. There was no need of being too affectionate toward such a brother.

Lord Balarāma again turned toward Kṛṣṇa and said, "My dear Kṛṣṇa, a relative, even though he commits such a blunder and deserves to be killed, should be excused. For when such a relative is conscious of his own fault, that consciousness itself is like death. Therefore, there is no need to kill him."

Balarāma again turned toward Rukmiṇī and informed her that the current duty of the *kṣatriya* in human society is so fixed that, according to the principles of fighting, one's own brother may become an enemy. Then a *kṣatriya* does not hesitate to kill his own brother. In other words, Lord Balarāma wanted to instruct Rukmiṇī that Rukmī and Kṛṣṇa were right in not showing mercy to each other in the fighting, despite the family consideration that they happened to be brothers-in-law. Śrī Balarāma informed Rukmiṇī that *kṣatriyas* are typical emblems of the materialistic way of life; they become puffed up whenever there is a question of material acquisition. Therefore, when there is a fight between two belligerent *kṣatriyas* for kingdom, land, wealth, women, prestige or power, they try to put one another into the most abominable condition. Balarāma instructed Rukmiṇī that her affection toward her brother Rukmī, who had created enmity with so many persons, was a perverse consideration befitting an ordinary materialist. Her brother's character was not at all admirable, considering his treatment toward his friends, and yet Rukmiṇī, as an ordinary woman, was affectionate toward him. He was not fit to be her brother, and still Rukmiṇī was lenient toward him.

"Besides that," Balarāma continued, "the consideration that a person is neutral or is one's friend or enemy is generally made by persons in the bodily concept of life. Such foolish persons are bewildered by the illusory energy of the Supreme Lord. The spirit soul is of the same pure quality in any embodiment of matter, but those who are not sufficiently intelligent see only the bodily differences between animals and men, literates and illiterates, rich and poor, which cover the pure spirit soul. Such differences, observed merely on the basis of the body, are exactly like the differences between fires in terms of the various types of fuel they consume. Whatever the size and shape of the fuel, there is no such variety of size and shape in the fire which comes out. Similarly, in the sky there are no differences in size or shape."

In this way Balarāma reconciled the situation by His moral and ethical instructions to Rukmiṇī and Kṛṣṇa. To Rukmiṇī He stated further, "This body is part of the material manifestation, consisting of the material elements, living conditions and interactions of the modes of material nature. The living entity, or spirit soul, being in contact with these, is transmigrating from one body to another due to illusory enjoyment, and that transmigration is known as material existence. This contact of the living entity with the material manifestation has neither integration nor disintegration. My dear chaste sister-in-law, the spirit soul is, of course, the cause of this material body, just as the sun is the cause of sunlight, eyesight and the forms of material manifestation."

The example of the sunshine and the material manifestation is very appropriate in understanding the living entity's contact with the material world. In the morning the sun rises, and the heat and light gradually expand throughout the whole day. The sun is the cause of all material shapes and forms, for it is due to the sun that integration and disintegration of material elements take place. But as soon as the sun sets, the whole manifestation is no longer connected to the sun, which has passed from one place to another. When the sun passes from the eastern to the western hemisphere, the results of the interactions due to the sunshine in the eastern hemisphere remain, but the sunshine itself is visible in the western hemisphere. Similarly, the living entity accepts or produces different bodies and different bodily relationships in a particular circumstance, but as soon as he gives up the present body and accepts another, he has nothing to do with the former body. Similarly, the living entity has nothing to do with the next body he accepts. He is always free from the contact of this bodily contamination. "Therefore," continued Balarāma, "the appearance and disappearance of the body have nothing to do with the living entity, just as the waxing and waning of the moon have nothing to do with the moon." When the moon waxes we falsely think that the moon is developing, and when it wanes we think the moon is decreasing. Factually, the moon, as it is, is always the same; it has nothing to do with such visible activities of waxing and waning.

Lord Balarāma continued, "One's consciousness in material existence can be compared to sleeping and dreaming. When a man sleeps, he dreams of many nonfactual happenings, and as a result of dreaming he becomes subject to different kinds of distress and happiness. Similarly, when a person is in the dream of material consciousness, he suffers the effects of accepting a body and giving it up again in material existence. Opposite to this material consciousness is Kṛṣṇa consciousness. In other words, when a man is elevated to the platform of Kṛṣṇa consciousness, he becomes free from this false conception of life."

In this way, Śrī Balarāma instructed Rukmiṇī in spiritual knowledge. He further addressed His sister-in-law thus: "Sweet, smiling Rukmiṇī, do not be aggrieved by false notions caused by ignorance. Only because of false notions does one become unhappy, but one can immediately remove this unhappiness by discussing the philosophy of actual life. Be happy on that platform only."

After hearing such enlightening instructions from Śrī Balarāma, Rukmiṇī immediately became pacified and happy and adjusted her mind, which was very much afflicted by the degraded position of her brother Rukmī. As far as Rukmī was concerned, his promise was not fulfilled, nor was his mission successful. He had come from home with his soldiers and military phalanx to defeat Kṛṣṇa and release his sister, but on the contrary he lost all his soldiers and military strength. He was personally degraded and very sorry, but by the grace of the Lord he could continue his life to its fixed destination. Because he was a *kṣatriya,* he could remember his promise that he would not return to his capital city, Kuṇḍina, without killing Kṛṣṇa and releasing his sister, which he had failed to do; therefore, he decided in anger not to return to his capital city, and he constructed a small cottage in the village known as Bhojakaṭa, where he resided for the rest of his life.

After defeating all the opposing elements and forcibly carrying away Rukmiṇī, Kṛṣṇa brought her to His capital city, Dvārakā, and then married her according to the Vedic ritualistic principle. After this marriage, Kṛṣṇa became the King of the Yadus at Dvārakā. On the occasion of His marriage with Rukmiṇī, all the inhabitants were happy, and in every house there were great ceremonies. The inhabitants of Dvārakā City were so pleased that they dressed themselves with the nicest possible ornaments and garments and went to present gifts, according to their means, to the newly married couple, Kṛṣṇa and Rukmiṇī. All the houses of Yadupurī (Dvārakā) were decorated with flags, festoons and flowers. Each and every house had an extra gate specifically prepared for this occasion, and on both sides of the gate were big water jugs filled with water. The whole city was made fragrant by the burning of fine incense, and at night there was illumination from thousands of lamps, which decorated every building.

The entire city appeared jubilant on the occasion of Lord Kṛṣṇa's marriage with Rukmiṇī. Everywhere in the city there were profuse decorations of banana trees and betel-nut trees. These two trees are considered very auspicious in happy ceremonies. At the same time there was an assembly of many elephants, who carried the respective kings of different friendly kingdoms. It is the habit of the elephant that whenever he sees some small plants and trees, out of his sportive and frivolous nature he uproots the trees and throws them hither and thither. The elephants assembled on this occasion also scattered the banana and betel nut trees, but in spite of such intoxicated action, the whole city, with the trees thrown here and there, looked very nice.

The friendly kings of the Kurus and the Pāṇḍavas were represented by Bhīṣma, Dhṛtarāṣṭra, the five Pāṇḍava brothers, King Drupada, King Santardana and Rukmiṇī's father, Bhīṣmaka. Because of Kṛṣṇa's kidnapping Rukmiṇī, there was initially some misunderstanding between the two families, but Bhīṣmaka, King of Vidarbha, being approached by Śrī Balarāma and persuaded by many saintly persons, was induced to participate in the marriage ceremony of Kṛṣṇa and Rukmiṇī. Although the incident of the kidnapping was not a very happy occurrence in the kingdom of Vidarbha, kidnapping was not an unusual affair among *kṣatriyas*. Kidnapping was, in fact, current in almost all their marriages. Anyway, King Bhīṣmaka was from the very beginning inclined to hand over his beautiful daughter to Kṛṣṇa. In one way or another his purpose had been served, and so he was pleased to join the marriage ceremony, even though his eldest son was degraded in the fight. It is mentioned in the *Padma Purāṇa* that Mahārāja Nanda and the cowherd boys of Vṛndāvana joined the marriage ceremony. Kings from the kingdoms of Kuru, Sṛñjaya, Kekaya, Vidarbha and Kunti all came to Dvārakā on this occasion and met with one another very joyfully.

The story of Rukmiṇī's being kidnapped by Kṛṣṇa was poeticized, and professional readers recited it everywhere. All the assembled kings and their daughters especially were struck with wonder and very pleased upon hearing the chivalrous activities of Kṛṣṇa. In this way, all the visitors as well as the inhabitants of Dvārakā City were joyful to see Kṛṣṇa and Rukmiṇī together. In other words, the goddess of fortune was now united with the Supreme Lord, the maintainer of everyone, and thus all the people felt extremely jubilant.

Thus ends the Bhaktivedanta purport of the Fifty-fourth Chapter of Kṛṣṇa, *"Kṛṣṇa Defeats All the Princes and Takes Rukmiṇī Home to Dvārakā."*

CHAPTER 55

Pradyumna Born to Kṛṣṇa and Rukmiṇī

IT IS SAID THAT CUPID, who is directly part and parcel of Lord Vāsudeva and who was formerly burned to ashes by the anger of Lord Śiva, took birth from the womb of Rukmiṇī, begotten by Kṛṣṇa. This is Kāmadeva, a demigod of the heavenly planets especially capable of inducing lusty desires. The Supreme Personality of Godhead, Kṛṣṇa, has many grades of parts and parcels, but the quadruple expansions of Kṛṣṇa—Vāsudeva, Saṅkarṣaṇa, Pradyumna and Aniruddha—are directly in the Viṣṇu category. Kāma, or the Cupid demigod, who later took his birth from the womb of Rukmiṇī, was also named Pradyumna, but he cannot be the Pradyumna of the Viṣṇu category. He belongs to the category of *jīva-tattva,* but for exhibiting special power in the category of demigods he was a part and parcel of the superprowess of Pradyumna. That is the verdict of the Gosvāmīs. Therefore, when Cupid was burned to ashes by the anger of Lord Śiva, he merged into the body of Vāsudeva, and to get his body again he was begotten in the womb of Rukmiṇī by Lord Kṛṣṇa Himself. Thus he was born as the son of Kṛṣṇa and celebrated by the name Pradyumna. Because he was begotten by Lord Kṛṣṇa directly, his qualities were most similar to those of Kṛṣṇa.

There was a demon of the name Śambara who was destined to be killed by Pradyumna. The Śambara demon knew of his destiny, and as soon as he learned that

Pradyumna had been born, he took the shape of a woman and kidnapped the baby from the maternity home less than ten days after his birth. The demon took him and threw him directly into the sea. But, as it is said, "Whoever is protected by Kṛṣṇa, no one can kill, and whoever is destined to be killed by Kṛṣṇa, no one can protect." When Pradyumna was thrown into the sea, a big fish immediately swallowed him. Later this fish was caught in the net of a fisherman, and the fish was later sold to the Śambara demon. In the kitchen of the demon was a maidservant whose name was Māyāvatī. This woman had formerly been the wife of Cupid, called Rati. When the fish was presented to the demon Śambara, it was taken charge of by his cook, who was to make it into a palatable fish preparation. Demons and Rākṣasas are accustomed to eating meat, fish and similar nonvegetarian foods. Demons like Rāvaṇa, Kaṁsa and Hiraṇyakaśipu, although born of *brāhmaṇa* and *kṣatriya* fathers, used to take meat and flesh without discrimination. This practice is still prevalent in India, and those who eat meat and fish are generally called demons and Rākṣasas.

When the cook was cutting the fish, he found within its stomach a nice baby, which he immediately presented to the charge of Māyāvatī, who was an assistant in the kitchen affairs. This woman was surprised to see how such a nice baby could remain within the belly of a fish, and the situation perplexed her. The great sage Nārada then appeared and explained to her about the birth of Pradyumna and how the baby had been taken away by Śambara and later thrown into the sea. In this way the whole story was disclosed to Māyāvatī. Māyāvatī knew that she had previously been Rati, the wife of Cupid; after her husband was burned to ashes by the wrath of Lord Śiva, she was always expecting him to come back in a material form. This woman was engaged for cooking rice and dhal in the kitchen, but when she got this nice baby and understood that he was Cupid, her own husband, she naturally took charge of him and with great affection began to bathe him regularly. Miraculously, the baby swiftly grew up, and within a very short period he became a beautiful young man. His eyes were just like the petals of lotus flowers, and his arms were long, down to his knees; any woman who happened to see him was captivated by his bodily beauty.

Māyāvatī could understand that her former husband, Cupid, born as Pradyumna, had grown into such a nice young man, and she also gradually became captivated and lusty. Smiling before him with a feminine attractiveness, she expressed her desire for sexual union. He therefore inquired from her, "How is it possible that first you were affectionate like a mother and now you are expressing the symptoms of a lusty woman? What is the reason for such a change?" On hearing this statement from Pradyumna, the woman, Rati, replied, "My dear sir, you are the son of Lord Kṛṣṇa. Before you were ten days old, you were stolen by the Śambara demon and later thrown into the water and swallowed by a fish. In this way you have come under my care, but actually, in your former life as Cupid, I was your wife; therefore, my manifestation of conjugal symptoms is not at all incompatible. Śambara wanted to kill you, and he is endowed with various mystic powers. Therefore, before he again attempts to kill you, please kill him as soon as possible with your divine power. Since you were stolen by Śambara, your mother, Rukmiṇīdevī, has been in a very grievous condition, like a *kurarī* bird who has lost her babies. She is very affectionate toward you, and since you have been taken away from her, she has been living like a cow aggrieved over the loss of its calf."

Māyāvatī had mystic knowledge of supernatural powers. Supernatural powers are generally known as *māyā,* and to surpass all such powers there is another supernatural power, called *mahā-māyā.* Māyāvatī had the knowledge of the mystic power of *mahā-māyā,* and she delivered to Pradyumna this specific energetic power in order to defeat the mystic powers of the Śambara demon. Thus being empowered by his wife, Pradyumna immediately went before Śambara and challenged him to fight. Pradyumna addressed him in very strong language, so that his temper would be agitated and he would be moved to fight. At Pradyumna's words, the demon Śambara, being insulted, felt just as a snake feels after being struck by someone's foot. A serpent cannot tolerate being kicked by another animal or by a man, and it immediately bites its opponent.

Śambara felt the words of Pradyumna as if they were a kick. He immediately took his club in his hand and appeared before Pradyumna to fight. Roaring like a thundering cloud, in great anger the demon began to beat Pradyumna with his club, just as a thunderbolt beats a mountain. Pradyumna protected himself with his own club and eventually struck the demon very severely. In this way, the fighting between Śambarāsura and Pradyumna began in earnest.

But Śambarāsura knew the art of mystic powers and could raise himself into the sky and fight from outer space. There is a demon of the name Maya, and Śambarāsura had learned many mystic powers from him. He thus raised himself high into the sky and threw various types of nuclear weapons at the body of Pradyumna. To combat the mystic powers of Śambarāsura, Pradyumna invoked another mystic power, known as *mahāvidyā,* which was different from the black mystic power. The *mahāvidyā* mystic power is based on the quality of goodness. Śambara, understanding that his enemy was formidable, took assistance from various kinds of demoniac mystic powers belonging to the Guhyakas, the Gandharvas, the Piśācas, the snakes and the Rākṣasas. But although the demon exhibited his mystic powers and took shelter of supernatural strength, Pradyumna was able to counteract his strength and powers by the superior power of *mahāvidyā.* When Śambarāsura was defeated in every respect, Pradyumna took his sharp sword and immediately cut off the demon's head, which was decorated with a helmet and valuable jewels. When Pradyumna thus killed the demon, all the demigods in the higher planetary systems showered flowers on him.

Pradyumna's wife, Māyāvatī, could travel in outer space, and therefore they directly reached Dvārakā, his father's capital, by the airways. They passed above the palace of Lord Kṛṣṇa and came down as a cloud comes down with lightning. The inner section of a palace is known as the *antaḥ-pura* (private apartments). Pradyumna and Māyāvatī could see many women there, and they set down among them. When the women saw Pradyumna, dressed in yellowish garments, with very long arms, curling hair, beautiful reddish eyes, a smiling face, jewelry and ornaments, they at first could not recognize him as a personality different from Kṛṣṇa. They all felt very bashful at the sudden presence of Kṛṣṇa and wanted to hide in a different corner of the palace.

When the women saw, however, that not all the characteristics of Lord Kṛṣṇa were present in the personality of Pradyumna, out of curiosity they came back to see him and his wife, Māyāvatī. All of them were conjecturing as to who he was, for he was so beautiful. Among the women was Rukmiṇīdevī, who was equally beautiful, with her lotuslike eyes. Seeing Pradyumna, she naturally remembered her own son, and milk began to flow from her breasts out of motherly affection. She then began to wonder, "Who is this beautiful young boy? He appears to be the most beautiful person. Who is the fortunate young woman able to conceive this nice boy in her womb and become his mother? And who is that young woman who has accompanied him? How have they met? Remembering my own son, who was stolen from the maternity home, I can only guess that if he is living somewhere, he might have grown by this time to be like this boy." Simply by intuition, Rukmiṇī could understand that Pradyumna was her own lost son. She could also observe that Pradyumna resembled Lord Kṛṣṇa in every respect. She was struck with wonder as to how he had acquired all the characteristics of Lord Kṛṣṇa. She therefore began to think more confidently that the boy must be her own grown-up son because she felt so much affection for him, and, as an auspicious sign, her left arm was trembling.

At that very moment, Lord Kṛṣṇa, along with His father and mother, Devakī and Vasudeva, appeared on the scene. Kṛṣṇa, the Supreme Personality of Godhead, could understand everything, yet in that situation He remained silent. However, by the desire of Lord Śrī Kṛṣṇa, the great sage Nārada also appeared, and he disclosed all the incidents—how Pradyumna had been stolen from the maternity home and how he had grown up and had come there with his wife, Māyāvatī, who had formerly been Rati, the wife of Cupid. When everyone was informed of the mysterious disappearance of Pradyumna and how he had grown up, they were all struck with wonder because they had gotten back their dead son after they were almost hopeless of his return. When they understood that it was Pradyumna who was present, they received him with great delight. One after another, all the members of the family—Devakī, Vasudeva, Lord Śrī Kṛṣṇa, Lord Balarāma, Rukmiṇī and all the women of the family—embraced Pradyumna and his wife, Māyāvatī. When the news of Pradyumna's return spread all over the city of Dvārakā, all the astonished citizens came with great eagerness to see the lost Pradyumna. "The dead son has come back," they said. "What can be more pleasing than this?"

Śrīla Śukadeva Gosvāmī has explained that in the beginning all the ladies of the palace, who were all mothers and stepmothers of Pradyumna, mistook him to be Kṛṣṇa and were all bashful, infected by the desire for conjugal love. The explanation is that Pradyumna's personal appearance was exactly like Kṛṣṇa's, and he was factually Cupid himself. There was no cause for astonishment, therefore, when the mothers of Pradyumna and the other women mistook him in that way. It is clear from this statement that Pradyumna's bodily characteristics were so similar to Kṛṣṇa's that he was mistaken for Kṛṣṇa even by his mother.

Thus ends the Bhaktivedanta purport of the Fifty-fifth Chapter of Kṛṣṇa, *"Pradyumna Born to Kṛṣṇa and Rukmiṇī."*

Appendixes

A NOTE ABOUT THIS EDITION

Śrīla Prabhupāda completed *Kṛṣṇa, the Supreme Personality of Godhead* (popularly known as *Kṛṣṇa Book*) in 1970, and his Bhaktivedanta Book Trust published it that year in two volumes and soon again in three. In 1986, the BBT published a one-volume edition with minor revisions.

For the present edition, the editors have gone back to the original tapes of Śrīla Prabhupāda's dictation of the text and compared them word-for-word with the previous edition. In the course of their work they found that the original transcribers and editors had for the most part done an excellent job. Occasionally, however, they erred, perhaps owing to Śrīla Prabhupāda's heavily accented English, the uneven quality of the recordings, or the difficult philosophical concepts in some passages of the Tenth Canto. These errors, constituting less than one percent of the total text, have now been corrected, so that an already perfect book has become even more perfect for its increased fidelity to Śrīla Prabhupāda's original words.

THE AUTHOR

His Divine Grace A.C. Bhaktivedanta Swami Prabhupāda appeared in this world in 1896 in Calcutta, India. He first met his spiritual master, Śrīla Bhaktisiddhānta Sarasvatī Gosvāmī, in Calcutta in 1922. Bhaktisiddhānta Sarasvatī, a prominent religious scholar and the founder of the Gauḍīya Maṭhas (Vedic institutes), liked this educated young man and convinced him to dedicate his life to teaching Vedic knowledge. Śrīla Prabhupāda became his student and, in 1933, his formally initiated disciple.

At their first meeting, in 1922, Śrīla Bhaktisiddhānta Sarasvatī requested Śrīla Prabhupāda to broadcast Vedic knowledge in English. In the years that followed, Śrīla Prabhupāda wrote a commentary on the *Bhagavad-gītā,* assisted the Gauḍīya Maṭha in its work and, in 1944, started *Back to Godhead,* an English fortnightly magazine. Singlehandedly, Śrīla Prabhupāda edited it, typed the manuscripts, checked the galley proofs and even distributed the individual copies. The magazine is now being continued by his disciples in the West.

In 1950 Śrīla Prabhupāda retired from married life, adopting the *vānaprastha* (retired) order to devote more time to his studies and writing. He traveled to the holy city of Vṛndāvana, where he lived in humble circumstances in the historic temple of Rādhā-Dāmodara. There he engaged for several years in deep study and writing. He accepted the renounced order of life (*sannyāsa*) in 1959. At Rādhā-Dāmodara, Śrīla Prabhupāda began work on his life's masterpiece: a multivolume commentated translation of the eighteen-thousand verse *Śrīmad-Bhāgavatam* (*Bhāgavata Purāṇa*). He also wrote *Easy Journey to Other Planets.*

After publishing three volumes of the *Bhāgavatam,* Śrīla Prabhupāda came to the United States, in September 1965, to fulfill the mission of his spiritual master. Subsequently, His Divine Grace wrote more than fifty volumes of authoritative commentated translations and summary studies of the philosophical and religious classics of India.

When he first arrived by freighter in New York City, Śrīla Prabhupāda was practically penniless. Only after almost a year of great difficulty did he establish the International Society for Krishna Consciousness, in July of 1966. Before he passed away on November 14, 1977, he had guided the Society and seen it grow to a worldwide confederation of more than one hundred *āśramas,* schools, temples, institutes and farm communities.

Śrīla Prabhupāda also inspired the construction of several large international cultural centers in India. The center at Śrīdhāma Māyāpur is the site for a planned spiritual city, an ambitious project for which construction will extend over many years to come. In Vṛndāvana are the magnificent Kṛṣṇa-Balarāma temple and International Guesthouse, *gurukula* school, and the Śrīla Prabhupāda Memorial and Museum. There is also a major cultural and educational center in Mumbai. Other centers are planned in a dozen important locations on the Indian subcontinent.

Śrīla Prabhupāda's most significant contribution, however, is his books. Highly respected by scholars for their authority, depth and clarity, they are used as textbooks in numerous college courses. His writings have been translated into over eighty languages. The Bhaktivedanta Book Trust, established in 1972 to publish the works of His Divine Grace, has thus become the world's largest publisher of books in the field of Indian religion and philosophy.

In just twelve years, from his arrival in America in 1965 till his passing away in Vṛndāvana in 1977, despite his advanced age Śrīla Prabhupāda circled the globe fourteen times on lecture tours that took him to six continents. Notwithstanding such a vigorous schedule, Śrīla Prabhupāda continued to write prolifically. His writings constitute a veritable library of Vedic philosophy, religion, literature and culture.

GLOSSARY

Ācārya—one who knows and explains the import of all the Vedic literatures, abides by their rules and regulations, and teaches his disciples to act in the same way.

Aguru—the fragrant Aloe wood and tree.

Akṣauhiṇī—a large military division consisting of 21,870 chariots, 21,870 elephants, 109,350 infantry soldiers and 65,610 horses.

Āmalaka—the Emblic Myrobalan tree, a kind of wild almond tree with round or pear-shaped fruits.

Ambikā—a name of Durgā meaning "mother."

Ārati—a ceremony for greeting the Lord with offerings of food, lamps, fans, flowers and incense, accompanied by chanting.

Āryan—a civilized follower of Vedic culture; one whose goal is spiritual advancement.

Aśoka—a tree of moderate size with magnificent red flowers.

Āśrama—a place of spiritual practice; one of the four spiritual orders according to the Vedic social system: *brahmacarya* (student life), *gṛhastha* (householder life), *vānaprastha* (retirement) and *sannyāsa* (renunciation).

Asura—a demon or nondevotee.

Āśutoṣa—a name of Śiva meaning "one who is easily pleased."

Ātmārāma—a self-satisfied sage.

Avabhṛta—a ceremonial bath at the end of a sacrifice.

Avatāra—an incarnation of Godhead who descends from the spiritual world.

Bael fruit—the fruit of the wood-apple tree, a thorny shrub. The actual Sanskrit name of this tree is *bilva,* and the fruits are sometimes called Bengal quince.

Bhagavad-gītā—the book that records the spiritual instructions given by Kṛṣṇa to His friend Arjuna on the Battlefield of Kurukṣetra.

Bhakta—a devotee.

Bhakti-yoga—the *yoga* of devotional service to the Lord.

Bherī—a kettle-drum.

Bhūr—earth, the first of the three worlds spoken of in the Vedic literature.

Bhūtas—malignant spirits that haunt cemeteries, animate dead bodies, and delude and devour human beings. The Bhūtas are attendants of Lord Śiva, and he is said to be their king.

Bhuvar—the second of the three worlds (the world between the earth planet and the sun).

Brahmā—the first created being and secondary creator of this material universe.

Brahmacārī—a celibate student under the guidance of a spiritual master.

Brahmajyoti—the impersonal effulgence that emanates from the body of Kṛṣṇa.

Brāhma-muhūrta—the period of the day just before dawn. It is especially favorable for spiritual practices.

Brahman—the impersonal feature of the Absolute Truth.

Brāhmaṇas—the spiritual order of society whose occupation is the cultivation of Vedic knowledge.

Brahma-rākṣasa—a man-eating demon who was a fallen *brāhmaṇa* in his last life.

Brahma-saṁhitā—a very ancient Sanskrit scripture recording the prayers of Brahmā to the Supreme Lord, Govinda.

Caitanya Mahāprabhu (1486–1534)—the Supreme Lord appearing as His own greatest devotee to teach love of God, especially through the process of congregational chanting of His holy names.

Cāmara—a yak-tail whisk.

Campaka—a species of magnolia with highly fragrant, yellowish or orange flowers.

Candra—the demigod in charge of the moon.

Capātī—an unleavened, pancake-sized whole-wheat bread.

Cāraṇas—the panegyrists of the demigods.

Cāturmāsya—the four months of the rainy season in India, during which devotees of Viṣṇu observe special austerities.

Daityas—the (demoniac) offspring of Diti and Kaśyapa.

Ḍākinīs—female demonic attendants of Kālī who feed on human flesh and drink blood.

Darśa-pūrṇamāsa—a twice-monthly Vedic sacrifice meant to elevate one to the heavenly planets.
Deva—a demigod or devotee.

Ekādaśī—a special day for increased remembrance of Kṛṣṇa that comes on the eleventh day after both the full and new moon. Abstinence from grains and beans is prescribed.
Esarāj—a stringed instrument played with a bow and nowadays found mainly in Bengal.

Gandharvas—denizens of the heavenly planets who sing very beautifully.
Gāndharva marriage—marriage by mutual agreement between husband and wife.
Garuḍa—the giant bird-carrier of Viṣṇu.
Gautama—the sage who established the Nyāya system of philosophy.
Gavaya—a wild species of oxen.
Gāyatrī mantra—the Vedic prayer chanted silently by *brāhmaṇas* at sunrise, noon and sunset.
Gopīs—cowherd girls, specifically the transcendental girlfriends of Lord Kṛṣṇa.
Gopura—a big gate, usually an entrance to a town or a temple.
Gṛhastha—one who is in the householder order of life.
Guhyakas—("hidden beings") inferior celestials who serve Kuvera by guarding his hidden treasures.
Guru—a spiritual master.

Halavā—a dessert made from toasted grains, butter and sugar.
Halāyudha—a name of Balarāma that means "one armed with a plough."
Hṛṣīkeśa—a name of God meaning "the controller of the senses."

Indra—the chief of the administrative demigods, king of the heavenly planets and presiding deity of rain.
Īśopaniṣad—one of the principal *Upaniṣads.*

Jaimini—the sage who established the Karma-mīmāṁsā school of philosophy, which teaches methods of interpreting Vedic texts; author of the *Mimāṁsa-sūtra.*
Janoloka—a heavenly planetary system situated between Maharloka and Tapoloka populated by celibate sages.
Jñāna-yoga—the path of spiritual realization through a speculative philosophical search for truth.
Jñānī—one adhering to the path of *jñāna-yoga.*

Jyotiṣṭoma—a Vedic sacrifice meant to elevate one to the heavenly planets.

Kachaurī—a crispy fried pastry filled with spiced lentils or vegetables.
Kadamba—a tree with orange-colored fragrant blossoms; said to grow only in the Vṛndāvana area.
Kahlāra—the lotus known as the white lily, also called white Egyptian lotus.
Kalaśa—a waterpot.
Kaṇāda—the sage who established the Vaiśeṣika system of philosophy, a materialistic theory of atomism, and wrote the *Vaiśeṣika-sūtra*. The name "Kanāḍa" means " atom-eater."
Kañja—a word for the lotus flower meaning "born from the water."
Kapila—the sage who established the atheistic Sāṅkhya system of philosophy (different from Kapila, the son of Devahūti, mentioned in *Śrīmad-Bhāgavatam.*)
Kāraṇa Ocean—the Causal Ocean, wherein Kāraṇodakaśāyī Viṣṇu (Mahā-Viṣṇu) lies.
Karma—fruitive activities or their reactions.
Karma-kāṇḍa—the part of the *Vedas* that prescribes means for obtaining material benedictions.
Karmī—a fruitive worker.
Kaumudī—an especially fragrant water-lily found on the bank of the Yamunā River.
Kaustubha—a transcendental jewel worn around the neck of the Supreme Personality of Godhead.
Kṛṣṇa-kathā—narrations spoken by or about Lord Kṛṣṇa.
Kṣatriyas—members of the Vedic social order whose occupation is governmental administration and military protection of the citizens.
Kunda—a kind of jasmine.
Kuṅkuma—a sweetly flavored reddish powder used to decorate the body.
Kurarī—an osprey.
Kuśa—the sacred grass used at religious ceremonies.
Kūṣmāṇḍa—a kind of evil spirit said to harass children.

Līlā—pastimes.

Māgadhas—professional singers for sacrifices.
Mahā-bhāgavata—a highly advanced devotee of Kṛṣṇa.
Mahā-mantra—the Hare Kṛṣṇa *mantra:* Hare Kṛṣṇa, Hare Kṛṣṇa, Kṛṣṇa Kṛṣṇa, Hare Hare/ Hare Rāma, Hare Rāma, Rāma Rāma, Hare Hare.
Mahātmā—a "great soul"; a liberated person who is fully Kṛṣṇa conscious.
Mālatī—a kind of jasmine with fragrant white flowers.

Mallikā—a kind of jasmine.

Mantra—a transcendental sound or Vedic hymn that can deliver the mind from illusion.

Marakata—an emerald.

Māyā (Mahāmāyā)—the external, material energy of the Supreme Lord, which covers the conditioned soul and does not allow him to understand the Supreme Personality of Godhead.

Māyāvādī—one who adheres to impersonalist or voidist philosophy and does not accept the eternal existence of the transcendental form of the Lord.

Mṛdaṅga—a clay drum with two heads.

Mukti—liberation from material bondage.

Mukunda—Lord Kṛṣṇa, who awards liberation and whose smiling face is like a *kunda* flower.

Nāga—a tree (*Mesua Roxburghii*) with fragrant flowers.

Nirguṇa—literally "without qualities" (used to describe the Supreme Lord, who has no material qualities).

Oṁkāra—the sacred syllable that represents the Absolute Truth.

Paṇava—a kind of drum.

Pañca-śūna—the five *mahā-yajñas,* or great sacrifices. They include reciting the *Vedas,* offering oblations into the sacrificial fire, waiting on guests, making offerings to the forefathers, and offering a share of one's food to living entities in general.

Pāṇḍavas—the five sons of King Pāṇḍu, namely Yudhiṣṭhira, Bhīma, Arjuna, Nakula and Sahadeva.

Pannagas—semicelestial demoniac beings belonging to the Nāga race.

Paramahaṁsa—a topmost, swanlike devotee of the Supreme Lord.

Paramātmā—an expansion of the Supreme Lord who lives in the heart of all living entities.

Pārijāta—a type of flower found on the heavenly planets.

Paṭaha—a small drum.

Patañjali—the sage who systemized the philosophy of Yoga and wrote the *Patañjali-yoga-sūtras.*

Patnī-saṁyāja—the ritual in which the sponsor of a sacrifice offers oblations together with his wife.

Piśācas—evil spirits placed by the *Vedas* lower than Rākṣasas; the most vile and malignant order of demoniac beings.

Pitās—forefathers.

Prākṛta-sahajiyā—a pseudo devotee of Lord Kṛṣṇa who fails to understand His absolute, transcendental position and imitates His pastimes.

Pramathas—a class of Bhūtas. *See also:* Bhūtas.

Prāṇāyāma—the yogic breathing exercises.

Prasādam—food first offered to the Supreme Lord and then distributed.

Pretas—evil spirits animating corpses and haunting cemeteries and other places.

Purī—puffed white bread fried in ghee.

Rabrī—cooked-down, sweetened milk.

Rajas—the material mode of passion.

Rākṣasa marriage—marriage in which the bride is forcibly stolen from one's rival suitors.

Rasas—the loving moods or mellows relished in the exchange of love with the Supreme Lord.

Rāsa-līlā—Lord Kṛṣṇa's transcendental pastime of dancing with the *gopīs.*

Rūpa Gosvāmī—a great Vaiṣṇava author and the leader of the six Gosvāmīs of Vṛndāvana, the principal followers of Lord Caitanya.

Śāla—a tall, strong tree whose wood is used for building houses.

Sālokya-mukti—the liberation of being elevated to live on the same planet as the Lord.

Samādhi—trance; deep absorption in meditation upon the Supreme.

Sāmīpya-mukti—the liberation of attaining the association of the Lord.

Samosā—a fried pastry stuffed with spiced vegetables or fruits.

Sanātana-dhāma—the eternal abode of the Supreme Lord (Vaikuṇṭha).

Saṅkīrtana-yajña—the chanting of the holy names of God, which is the recommended sacrifice for this age.

Sannyāsī—one who is in the renounced order of life.

Sarasvatī—a holy river in ancient India, approximately parallel to the present Indus river. The Sarasvatī dried up thousands of years ago.

Śarat—autumn.

Sārṣṭi-mukti—the liberation of enjoying the same opulence as the Lord.

Sārūpya-mukti—the liberation of attaining the same bodily features as the Lord.

Śāstras—revealed scriptures.

Śataghnī—the *śakti* spear of Bhaumāsura.

Sattva—the material mode of goodness.

Sāyujya-mukti—the liberation of merging into the existence of the Supreme Lord.

Siddhas—a class of semi-divine beings of great purity and holiness who dwell in the regions of the sky between the earth and the sun.

Siddhi—a mystic yogic perfection.

Śikṣāṣṭaka—eight verses by Lord Caitanya Mahāprabhu glorifying the chanting of the Lord's holy name.

Sindhī—born in the province Sindh (now in Pakistan).

Sitar—a stringed musical instrument.

Śiva—the demigod in charge of annihilation and the mode of ignorance.

Śrīdhara Svāmī—an important commentator on *Śrīmad-Bhāgavatam.*

Śrīmad-Bhāgavatam—the *Purāṇā,* or history, written by Śrīla Vyāsadeva specifically to give a deep understanding of Lord Kṛṣṇa, His devotees and devotional service.

Śrīvatsa—three lines of white hair on the chest of Lord Viṣṇu, representing the goddess of fortune.

Sudarśana—the wheel that is the personal weapon of Lord Viṣṇu or Kṛṣṇa.

Śūdra—a laborer; the fourth of the Vedic social orders.

Sūta—a mixed class who are originally the offspring of *kṣatriya* fathers and *brāhmaṇa* mothers. Their occupations are reciting *Purāṇas* and epic histories, and driving chariots.

Svar—the third of the three worlds (the heavenly kingdom).

Svayaṁvara—a ceremony where a princess selects her husband from a group of princes.

Śyāmasundara—a name of Kṛṣṇa meaning "blackish (*śyāma*) and very beautiful (*sundara*)."

Tamas—the material mode of ignorance.

Tamboura—a musical instrument with four strings.

Tantras—traditional supplementary post-Vedic texts. *Tantras* in the mode of goodness describe knowledge of God and are aimed at liberation; those in the lower modes describe different kinds of magic, rituals and worship.

Tapasyā—austerity.

Tapoloka—a heavenly planetary system situated between Janoloka and Satyaloka populated by great ascetics.

Tilaka—auspicious clay markings placed by devotees on the forehead and other parts of the body.

Tulasī—a great devotee in the form of a plant; she is very dear to Lord Kṛṣṇa.

Tūrya—musical instrument.

Udumbara—a kind of fig (*Ficus glomerata*).

Upaniṣads—108 philosophical treatises that appear within the *Vedas*.
Utpala—the blue lotus flower.

Vaiṣṇava—a devotee of the Supreme Lord Viṣṇu or Kṛṣṇa.
Vaiśya—a farmer or merchant; the third Vedic social order.
Vandī—a bard who sings the praises of royalty or accompanies an army and sings martial songs.
Vedānta-sūtra—the philosophical treatise written by Vyāsadeva. It consists of succinct aphorisms that embody the essential meaning of the *Upaniṣads*.
Vetālas—a class of evil spirits, largely followers of Lord Śiva. They dance and feast on flesh and blood on the battlefield.
Vidyādharas—a race of celestial beings who are attendants of Lord Śiva and who possess material mystic knowledge.
Vīṇā—a musical instrument with five, seven or more strings.
Vināyakas—a variety of evil spirits who are followers of Lord Śiva.
Viṣṇu—an all-pervasive, fully empowered expansion of Lord Kṛṣṇa qualified by full truth, full knowledge and full bliss.
Viṣṇu-sahasra-nāma—a section of the *Mahābharata* consisting of one thousand names of Lord Viṣṇu.
Vyāsadeva—the compiler of the *Vedas* and author of the *Purāṇas, Mahābharata* and *Vedānta-sūtra*.
Vyāsāsana—the elevated seat of the representatives of Vyāsadeva (those speaking on the subject of transcendental knowledge).

Yajña—sacrifice.
Yakṣas—a class of supernatural beings (sometimes considered evil) attendant on Kuvera, the god of wealth.
Yoga—the process of linking with the Supreme.
Yogamāyā—the principal internal (spiritual) potency of the Supreme Lord.
Yogī—one who practices *yoga*.

SANSKRIT PRONUNCIATION GUIDE

The system of transliteration used in this book conforms to a system which scholars have accepted to indicate the pronunciation of each sound in the Sanskrit language.

The short vowel **a** is pronounced like the **u** in b**u**t, long **ā** like the **a** in f**a**r. Short **i** is pronounced as **i** in p**i**n, long **ī** as in p**i**que, short **u** as in p**u**ll and long **ū** as in r**u**le. The vowel **ṛ** is pronounced like **ri** in **ri**m, **e** like the **ey** in th**ey**, **o** like the **o** in g**o**, **ai** like the **ai** in **ai**sle and **au** like the **ow** in h**ow**. The *anusvāra* (**ṁ**) is pronounced like the **n** in the French word *bo***n**, and *visarga* (**ḥ**) is pronounced as a final **h** sound. At the end of a couplet, **aḥ** is pronounced **aha** and **iḥ** is pronounced **ihi**.

The guttural consonants—**k, kh, g, gh** and **ṅ**—are pronounced from the throat in much the same manner as in English. **K** is pronounced as in **k**ite, **kh** as in E**ckh**art, **g** as in **g**ive, **gh** as in di**g-h**ard and **ṅ** as in si**ng**.

The palatal consonants—**c, ch, j, jh** and **ñ**—are pronounced with the tongue touching the firm ridge behind the teeth. **C** is pronounced as in **ch**air, **ch** as in staun**ch-h**eart, **j** as in **j**oy, **jh** as in he**dgeh**og and **ñ** as in ca**n**yon.

The cerebral consonants—**ṭ, ṭh, ḍ, ḍh** and **ṇ**—are pronounced with the tip of the tongue turned up and drawn back against the dome of the palate. **Ṭ** is pronounced as in **t**ub, **ṭh** as in ligh**t-h**eart, **ḍ** as in **d**ove, **ḍh** as in re**d-h**ot and **ṇ** as in **n**ut.

The dental consonants—**t, th, d, dh** and **n**—are pronounced in the same manner as the cerebrals, but with the forepart of the tongue against the teeth.

The labial consonants—**p, ph, b, bh** and **m**—are pronounced with the lips. **P** is pronounced as in **p**ine, **ph** as in u**ph**ill, **b** as in **b**ird, **bh** as in ru**b-h**ard and **m** as in **m**other.

The semivowels—**y, r, l** and **v**—are pronounced as in **y**es, **r**un, **l**ight and **v**ine respectively. The sibilants—**ś, ṣ** and **s**—are pronounced, respectively, as in the German word **s**_prechen_ and the English words **sh**ine and **s**un. The letter **h** is pronounced as in **h**ome.

London Temple

Situated in London's West End, amidst the commotion of the modern city, the Radha-Krishna Temple is an oasis of spiritual culture. From Monday to Saturday at 1 pm and 6 pm, we hold open classes on the philosophy of Krishna consciousness. On Sundays, our famous Hare Krishna love feast entertains and inspires many guests with spiritual music, philosophy, and sumptuous vegetarian food.

To experience a revitalising taste of Krishna consciousness, please feel more than welcome to come and pay us a visit. Our temple is located at 10 Soho Street, two minutes' walk from Tottenham Court Road tube station.

For further information regarding our programmes, please visit our website www.iskcon-london.com or phone us on 020 7437 3662.

Bhaktivedanta Manor

Set in 70 acres of countryside, Bhaktivedanta Manor, a farm and spiritual community of around fifty residents, is open to all visitors. There is a full curriculum of classes and workshops, with courses in subjects from Vedic medicine (Ayurveda) and mantra meditation to vegetarian cooking; we'll even give you hands-on training in ploughing with a team of oxen! And if you're looking to deepen your spiritual experience, you can also come on a retreat, joining in the life of the community for a weekend or more. Special introductory talks on the philosophy of *Bhagavad-gītā* are included.

The Manor is only 13 miles from London, just a short distance from junction 5 of the M1, and close to tube and rail stations.

Please write or phone for further information: Bhaktivedanta Manor, Hillfield Lane, Aldenham, Watford, Herts, WD25 8EZ / Tel: 01923 857244/ 854270

Swansea Temple (Wales)

Come and experience Krishna consciousness at our Swansea temple. You will find a haven of spiritual culture and sumptuous vegetarian cuisine, just two minutes walk from the city centre. Our famous *Govinda's* restaurant and gift shop is open Monday to Wednesday 12–3 pm; Thursday to Saturday 12–8.30 pm. Every Sunday we hold an introductory programme, including chanting, philosophy and vegetarian feast, between 4 pm and 6 pm. For more information contact: Govinda's Vegetarian Restaurant & Gift Shop, 8 Craddock St, Swansea SA1 3EN / Tel: 01792 468469
E-mail: govin_das@hotmail.com

Karuna Bhavan (ISKCON Scotland)

Situated 22 miles south of Glasgow off the M74 motorway, the small community sits neatly on the hill overlooking the old Scottish village of Lesmahagow, and the atmosphere is tranquil, set in peaceful countryside. If you would like to visit the Temple please telephone us first, so that we can make proper arrangements to receive you nicely.

For further information regarding visits, programmes, festivals, etc., please telephone 01555 894790 or 01555 894559 and ask for Prabhupada Vani (Graham). Fax 01555 894526, Mobile 07957 647168 before 7 pm weekdays, 07977 297532 after 7 pm and at weekends.
E-mail: karuna.bhavan@virgin.net

Visit our websites: www.iskcon.org and www.iskcon.org.uk

Centers of the International Society for Krishna Consciousness

Founder-*Ācārya:* His Divine Grace A. C. Bhaktivedanta Swami Prabhupāda

For further information on classes, programs, festivals, residential courses and local meetings, please contact the center nearest you.

UNITED KINGDOM

Belfast — Sri Sri Radha-Madhava Mandir, Brooklands, 140 Upper Dunmurray Lane, Belfast, BT17 0HE
Tel: +44 (0)28 9062 0530

Birmingham — 84 Stanmore Rd, Edgbaston, Birmingham, B16 9TB / Tel: +44 (0)121 420 4999

Coventry — Kingfield Rd, Coventry (mail: 19 Gloucester St, Coventry CV1 3BZ) / Tel: +44 (0)24 7655 2822 or 5420
e-mail: haridas.kds@pamho.net

Dublin — Chaitanya Centre, 24 Thorncastle St., Dublin 2, Irish Republic / Tel: +353 (0)1 668 3767
e-mail: uddhava@eircom.net

Leicester — 21 Thoresby St, North Evington, Leicester, LE5 4GU / Tel & fax: +44 (0)116 236 7723 or 276 2587
mobile: +44 (0)7887 560260
e-mail: gauranga.sundara@pamho.net

London (central) — Sri Sri Radha-Krishna Temple, 10 Soho St, London, W1D 3DL / Tel: +44 (0)20 7437 3662
Fax: +44 (0)20 7439 1127 / e-mail: london@pamho.net.
web: www.iskcon-london.com

London (south) — 42 Enmore Rd, South Norwood, London, SE25 5NG / Tel: +44 (0)20 8656 4296

Manchester — 20 Mayfield Rd, Whalley Range, Manchester, M16 8FT / Tel: +44 (0)161 226 4416

Newcastle-upon-Tyne — 304 Westgate Rd, Newcastle-upon-Tyne, NE4 6AR / Tel: +44 (0)191 272 1911
e-mail: bhakti.rasa@pamho.net

Scotland — Karuna Bhavan, Bankhouse Rd, Lesmahagow, Lanarkshire, ML11 0ES / Tel: +44 (0)1555 894790 / Fax: +44 (0)1555 894526 / e-mail: karuna.bhavan@virgin.net

Rural Communities

Upper Lough Erne (Northern Ireland) — Govindadwipa Dharma, Inisrath Island, Derrylin, Co. Fermanagh, BT92 9GN / Tel: +44 (0)28 6772 1512
e-mail: govindadwipa@pamho.net

Watford — Bhaktivedanta Manor, Hillfield Lane, Watford, WD25 8EZ / Tel: +44 (0)1923 857244
Fax: +44 (0)1923 852896

Restaurants

Dublin — Govinda's, 4 Aungier St, Dublin 2, Irish Republic
Tel: +353 (0)1 475 0309 / e-mail pragosa@connect.ie

London — Govinda's, 10 Soho St, London, W1D 3DL
Tel: +44 (0)20 7437 4928

Swansea — Govinda's, 8 Craddock St, Swansea, SA1 3EN
Tel: +44 (0)1792 468469 / e-mail: govin_das@hotmail.com

Hare Krishna meetings are held regularly in more than 40 towns in the UK. For more information, contact: ISKCON Reader Services, P.O. Box 730, Watford, WD25 8ZE

Website: www.iskcon.org.uk

OTHER COUNTRIES

Abentheuer, Germany — Böckingstr. 8, 55767
Tel: +49 (0)6782 980436 / Fax: 980437
e-mail: goloka.dhama.temple@pamho.net

Amsterdam, The Netherlands — Van Hilligaertstraat 17, 1072 JX / Tel: +31 (0)20 675-1404 / Fax: +31 (0)20 675-1405 / e-mail: amsterdam@pamho.net

Durban, South Africa — 50 Bhaktivedanta Swami Circle (mail: P.O. Box 56003), Chatsworth, 4030
Tel: +27 (0)31 403-3328 / Fax: +27 (0)31 403-4429
E-mail: iskcon.durban@pamho.net

Florence, Italy (Villa Vrindavan) — Via Comunale Scopeti 108, 50026 San Casciano in Val di Pesa (FI)
Tel: +39 055 820054 / Fax: +39 055 828470

Grödinge, Sweden (New Radhakunda) — Korsnäs Gård, 14792 Grödinge / Tel: +46 (0)8 530-29800
Fax: +46 (0)8 530-25062 / e-mail: info@pamho.net

Guadalajara, Spain (New Vraja Mandala) — (Santa Clara) Brihuega / Tel: +34 949 280436
e-mail: new.vrajamandala@pamho.net

Los Angeles, USA — 3764 Watseka Ave., 90034
Tel: +1 310 836-2676 / Fax: +1 310 839-2715
e-mail: nirantara@juno.com

Mumbai, India (Bombay) — Hare Krishna Land, Juhu 400 049 / Tel: +91 (0)22 620-6860 / Fax: (0)22 620-5214
e-mail: iskcon.juhu@pamho.net

New Delhi, India — Sant Nagar Main Rd. (Garhi), behind Nehru Place Complex (mail: P. O. Box 7061), 110 065
Tel: (011) 623-5133 / Fax: (011) 6221-5421 or 628-0067
e-mail: kratu.acbsp@pamho.net

New York, USA — 305 Schermerhorn St., Brooklyn, 11217
Tel: +1 718 855-6714 / Fax: +1 718 875-6127
e-mail: ramabhadra@aol.com

Paris, France — 31 rue du docteur Jean Vaquier, 93160 Noisy le Grand / Tel. & fax: +33 (0)1 4303-0951
e-mail: nitai.gaurasundara.tkg@pamho.net

Radhadesh, Belgium — Chateau de Petite Somme, 6940 Septon-Durbuy / Tel: +32 (0)86 322926
Fax: +32 (0)86 322929 / e-mail: radhadesh@pamho.net

Stockholm, Sweden — Fridhemsgatan 22, 11240
Tel: +46 (0)8 654-9002 / Fax: +46 (0)8 650-8813
e-mail: tapas.rns@pamho.net

Sydney, Australia — 180 Falcon St., North Sydney, NSW 2060 (mail: P.O. Box 459, Cammeray, NSW 2062)
Tel: +61 (0)29 9959-4558 / Fax: +61 (0)29 99957-1893
e-mail: sydney@pamho.net

Zürich, Switzerland — Bergstrasse 54, 8030
Tel: +41 (0)1 262-3388 / Fax: +41 (0)1 262-3114
e-mail: kgs@pamho.net

This is a partial list of centers. For a full list, please contact one of the above addresses or visit us on the web at www.iskcon.com or www.krishna.com.